THE DOCKER WORKSHOP

Learn how to use Docker containers effectively to speed up the development process

Vincent Sesto, Onur Yılmaz, Sathsara Sarathchandra, Aric Renzo, and Engy Fouda

THE DOCKER WORKSHOP

Authors: Vincent Sesto, Onur Yılmaz, Sathsara Sarathchandra, Aric Renzo, and Engy Fouda

Reviewers: Ankit Mishra, Fiodar Sazanavets, Craig Newton, and Earl Waud

Managing Editors: Prachi Jain and Clara Joseph

Acquisitions Editors: Royluis Rodrigues, Sneha Shinde, Archie Vankar, Karan Wadekar, and Alicia Wooding

Production Editor: Shantanu Zagade

Editorial Board: Megan Carlisle, Samuel Christa, Mahesh Dhyani, Heather Gopsill, Manasa Kumar, Alex Mazonowicz, Monesh Mirpuri, Bridget Neale, Dominic Pereira, Shiny Poojary, Abhishek Rane, Brendan Rodrigues, Erol Staveley, Ankita Thakur, Nitesh Thakur, and Jonathan Wray

First published: October 2020

Production reference: 2250221

ISBN: 978-1-83898-344-4

Published by Packt Publishing Ltd.

Livery Place, 35 Livery Street

Birmingham B3 2PB, UK

WHY LEARN WITH A PACKT WORKSHOP?

LEARN BY DOING

Packt Workshops are built around the idea that the best way to learn something new is by getting hands-on experience. We know that learning a language or technology isn't just an academic pursuit. It's a journey towards the effective use of a new tool—whether that's to kickstart your career, automate repetitive tasks, or just build some cool stuff.

That's why Workshops are designed to get you writing code from the very beginning. You'll start fairly small—learning how to implement some basic functionality—but once you've completed that, you'll have the confidence and understanding to move onto something slightly more advanced.

As you work through each chapter, you'll build your understanding in a coherent, logical way, adding new skills to your toolkit and working on increasingly complex and challenging problems.

CONTEXT IS KEY

All new concepts are introduced in the context of realistic use-cases, and then demonstrated practically with guided exercises. At the end of each chapter, you'll find an activity that challenges you to draw together what you've learned and apply your new skills to solve a problem or build something new.

We believe this is the most effective way of building your understanding and confidence. Experiencing real applications of the code will help you get used to the syntax and see how the tools and techniques are applied in real projects.

BUILD REAL-WORLD UNDERSTANDING

Of course, you do need some theory. But unlike many tutorials, which force you to wade through pages and pages of dry technical explanations and assume too much prior knowledge, Workshops only tell you what you actually need to know to be able to get started making things. Explanations are clear, simple, and to-the-point. So you don't need to worry about how everything works under the hood; you can just get on and use it.

Written by industry professionals, you'll see how concepts are relevant to real-world work, helping to get you beyond "Hello, world!" and build relevant, productive skills. Whether you're studying web development, data science, or a core programming language, you'll start to think like a problem solver and build your understanding and confidence through contextual, targeted practice.

ENJOY THE JOURNEY

Learning something new is a journey from where you are now to where you want to be, and this Workshop is just a vehicle to get you there. We hope that you find it to be a productive and enjoyable learning experience.

Packt has a wide range of different Workshops available, covering the following topic areas:

- Programming languages

- Web development

- Data science, machine learning, and artificial intelligence

- Containers

Once you've worked your way through this Workshop, why not continue your journey with another? You can find the full range online at http://packt.live/2MNkuyl.

If you could leave us a review while you're there, that would be great. We value all feedback. It helps us to continually improve and make better books for our readers, and also helps prospective customers make an informed decision about their purchase.

Thank you,
The Packt Workshop Team

Table of Contents

Chapter 3: Managing Your Docker Images   87

Chapter 6: Introduction to Docker Networking   195

Chapter 7: Docker Storage   263

Chapter 9: Docker Swarm 345

Chapter 12: Best Practices   477

PREFACE

ABOUT THE BOOK

Docker containers are the future of highly scalable software systems and make it easy to create, run, and deploy apps.

If you're looking to leverage them without getting overwhelmed by the technicalities, add *The Docker Workshop* to your reading list!

With this book, you'll be able to jumpstart your knowledge and work with containers and Docker using interactive activities.

The workshop starts with an overview of Docker containers, enabling you to understand how they work. You'll run third-party Docker images and also create your own images using Dockerfiles and multi-stage Dockerfiles. Next, you'll create environments for Docker images, and expedite your deployment process with continuous integration. Moving ahead, you'll tap into interesting topics and learn how to implement production-ready environments using Docker Swarm. To further secure Docker images and ensure that production environments are running at maximum capacity, you'll apply best practices. Later, you'll gain the skills to successfully move Docker containers from development to testing, and then into production. While doing so, you'll learn how to troubleshoot issues, clear up resource bottlenecks and optimize the performance of services.

By the end of this Docker book, you'll be well-versed with Docker fundamentals and be able to use Docker containers in real-world use cases.

AUDIENCE

If you're a developer or a Docker beginner who wants to gain a practical understanding of Docker containers, this book is the ideal guide. Experience in running command shells and knowledge of either the IntelliJ, Atom, or VSCode editor are required before you get started with this Docker containers book.

ABOUT THE CHAPTERS

Chapter 1, Running My First Docker Container, begins with a basic introduction to Docker, providing a discussion of the background architecture, ecosystem, and basic Docker commands.

Chapter 2, Getting Started with Dockerfiles, introduces you to the Dockerfile, its background, and how to use the Dockerfile to create and run your first Docker containers.

Chapter 3, Managing Your Docker Images, provides more details on Docker images, image repositories, and publishing your own images.

Chapter 4, Multi-Stage Dockerfiles, shows you how to extend your Dockerfile further, using a multi-stage Dockerfile in your project.

Chapter 5, Composing Environments with Docker Compose, introduces Docker Compose and how you can use docker-compose files to generate entire working environments.

Chapter 6, Introduction to Docker Networking, explains why networking needs to be approached differently in Docker and how you can implement communication between services and host systems.

Chapter 7, Docker Storage, details the utilization of storage in your Docker containers and environments.

Chapter 8, CI/CD Pipeline, describes the creation of a continuous integration/ continuous deployment pipeline using Jenkins.

Chapter 9, Docker Swarm, covers the orchestration of your Docker services using Swarm.

Chapter 10, Kubernetes, takes your orchestration to the next level, introducing you to Kubernetes and how to deploy your container images across a basic cluster.

Chapter 11, Docker Security, walks you through ways to make your Docker images and containers as secure as possible, providing ways in which you can reduce risk while using containers.

Chapter 12, Best Practices, provides information on how you can ensure that your containers are running as efficiently as possible.

Chapter 13, Monitoring Docker Metrics, covers metrics collection for your running Docker containers and how to implement Prometheus to help monitor these metrics.

Chapter 14, Collecting Container Logs, teaches you how to use Splunk to collect logs from your running Docker containers, which will allow you to aggregate, search, and display your logging details.

Chapter 15, Extending Docker with Plugins, covers the ways in which you can extend Docker further by creating your own plugins to use with your Docker application.

> **NOTE**
>
> There is also a bonus chapter, *What's Next for Docker* available at: http://packt.live/3tR0iMY.

CONVENTIONS

Code words in text, database table names, folder names, filenames, file extensions, pathnames, dummy URLs, and user input are shown as follows:

"Create a file named **docker-compose.yml** in your current working directory."

A block of code, a terminal command, or text to create a YAML file is set as follows:

```
docker build -t test .
```

New important words are shown like this: "Docker provides an online repository to store your images called **Docker Hub**."

Words that you see on the screen (for example, in menus or dialog boxes) appear in the text like this: "On the left sidebar, click on **Settings** and then on **Users**."

Key parts of code snippets are highlighted as follows:

```
1 FROM alpine
2
3 RUN apk update
4 RUN apk add wget curl
5
6 RUN wget -O test.txt https://github.com/PacktWorkshops/
    The-Docker-Workshop/raw/master/Chapter3/Exercise3.02/
      100MB.bin
7
8 CMD mkdir /var/www/
9 CMD mkdir /var/www/html/
```

Long code snippets are truncated, and the corresponding names of the code files on GitHub are placed at the top of the truncated code. The permalinks to the entire code are placed below the code snippet. It should look as follows:

Dockerfile

```
7 # create root directory for our project in the container
7 RUN mkdir /service
9 RUN mkdir /service/static
10
11# Set the working directory to /service
12 WORKDIR /service
```

The complete code for this example can be found at https://packt.live/2E9OErr.

SETTING UP YOUR ENVIRONMENT

Before we explore the book in detail, we need to set up specific software and tools. In the following section, we shall see how to do that.

HARDWARE REQUIREMENTS

You need at least a dual-core CPU with virtualization support, 4 GB of memory, and 20 GB of free disk space.

OPERATING SYSTEM REQUIREMENTS

The recommended operating system is Ubuntu 20.04 LTS. If you are using Mac or Windows, you should be able to run the commands in this book, but it is not guaranteed that they will all work as expected. We suggest you install a virtualized environment on your system using an application such as VirtualBox or VMware. We have also provided the instructions at the end of this section on how you can set up dual boot on your Windows system to use Ubuntu.

INSTALLATION AND SETUP

This section lists installation instructions for Docker and Git as they are the main requirements for this workshop. Installation instructions for any other software that's used will be provided in the specific chapter that covers it. Since we are recommending Ubuntu, we will use the APT package manager to install most of the required software in Ubuntu.

UPDATING YOUR PACKAGE LISTS

Before you use APT to install any packages in Ubuntu, make sure that your packages are up to date. Use the following command:

```
sudo apt update
```

Furthermore, you may choose to upgrade any upgradable packages on your machine by using the following command:

```
sudo apt upgrade
```

INSTALLING GIT

The code bundle for this workshop is available on our GitHub repository. You can use Git to clone the repository to get all the code files.

Use the following command to install Git on Ubuntu:

```
sudo apt install git-all
```

DOCKER

Docker is the default containerization engine used by this workshop. You will learn more about the application as you move through the chapters.

Use the following command to install Docker on Ubuntu:

```
sudo apt install docker.io -y
```

When the installation is complete, you will need to make sure that the Docker daemon is started and running on your system. Do this with the following command, making sure that you are running this as an elevated user with the **sudo** command:

```
sudo systemctl start docker
```

Ensure that the Docker daemon starts the next time you start your system. Run the following command to make sure that Docker starts each time you stop or restart the system you are installing it on:

```
sudo systemctl enable docker
```

Verify the version of Docker you have installed by using the **docker** command with the **--version** option. Run the following command:

```
docker -version
```

You should see a similar output to the following:

```
Docker version 19.03.8, build afacb8b7f0
```

There is a good chance that if you are not performing commands as the root user, you will not be able to run the majority of the commands needed. If you run the example following command, you may experience an access issue connecting to the Docker daemon:

```
docker ps
```

If you are running the command as a user that does not have elevated privileges, you may see the following error:

```
Got permission denied while trying to connect to the
Docker daemon socket at unix:///var/run/docker.sock: Get
http://%2Fvar%2Frun%2Fdocker.sock/v1.40/containers/json:
dial unix /var/run/docker.sock: connect: permission denied
```

To resolve this issue, add the current user to the Docker group that was created when you installed the application. Use the following command to perform this on your system:

```
sudo usermod -aG docker ${USER}
```

To activate these changes, you will need to either log out of your system and then log back in, or perform the following command to create a new session for your current user:

```
sudo su ${USER}
```

Run the **docker ps** command again to ensure that your changes were successful:

```
docker ps
```

If everything has worked correctly, you should see an output similar to the following, showing that you have no Docker containers running on your system:

```
CONTAINER ID   IMAGE   COMMAND   CREATED   STATUS   PORTS   NAMES
```

DUAL-BOOTING UBUNTU FOR WINDOWS USERS

In this section, you will find instructions on how to dual-boot Ubuntu if you are running Windows.

> **NOTE**
>
> Before installing any operating systems, it is highly recommended that you back up your system state and all of your data.

RESIZING PARTITIONS

If you have Windows set up on your machine, it is most likely that your hard disk is completely utilized—that is, all of the available space is partitioned and formatted. You will need to have some unallocated space on the hard disk, so resize a partition with plenty of free space to make space for your Ubuntu partitions:

1. Open the **Computer Management** utility. Press *Win + R* and type `compmgmt.msc`:

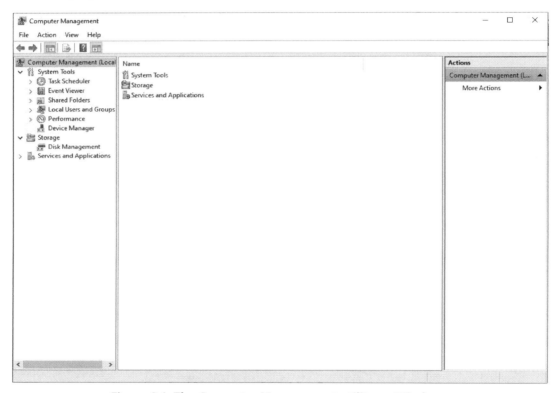

Figure 0.1: The Computer Management utility on Windows

2. On the left-hand pane, go to the **Storage > Disk Management** option, as shown in the following screenshot:

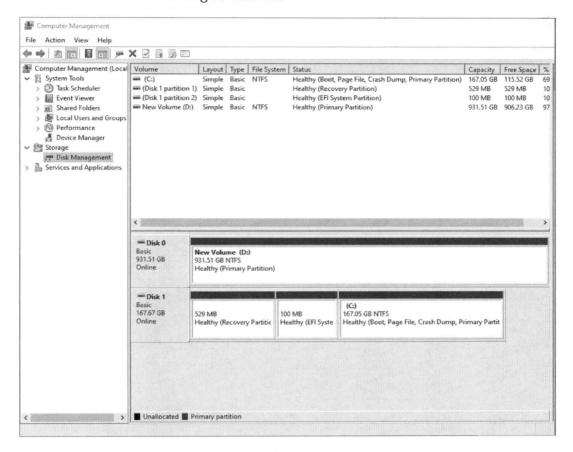

Figure 0.2: Disk Management

You will see a summary of all your partitions in the lower half of the screen. You can also see the drive letters associated with all the partitions and information about the Windows boot drive. If you have a partition that has plenty of free space (20 GB +) and is neither the boot drive (**C:**), nor the recovery partition, nor the **Extensible Firmware Interface (EFI)** system partition, this will be the ideal option to choose. If there is no such partition, then you can resize the **C:** drive.

3. In this example, you will choose the **D:** drive. Right-click on any partition and open **Properties** to check the free space available:

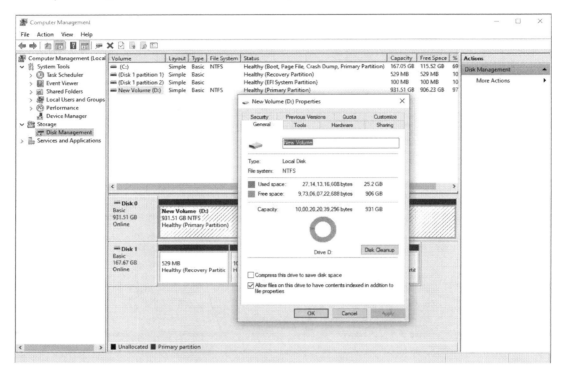

Figure 0.3: Checking the properties of the D: drive

Now, before you resize the partition, you need to ensure that there are no errors on the filesystem or any hardware faults. Do this using the **chkdsk** utility on Windows.

4. Open Command Prompt by pressing *Win + R* and typing **cmd.exe**. Now, run the following command:

```
chkdsk D: /f
```

Replace the drive letter with the one that you want to use. You should see a response similar to the following:

```
The type of the file system is NTFS.
Volume label is New Volume.

Stage 1: Examining basic file system structure ...
  768 file records processed.
File verification completed.
  0 large file records processed.
  0 bad file records processed.

Stage 2: Examining file name linkage ...
  279 reparse records processed.
  864 index entries processed.
Index verification completed.
  0 unindexed files scanned.
  0 unindexed files recovered to lost and found.
  279 reparse records processed.

Stage 3: Examining security descriptors ...
Security descriptor verification completed.
  48 data files processed.

Windows has scanned the file system and found no problems.
No further action is required.

 976759807 KB total disk space.
  26404304 KB in 464 files.
       260 KB in 50 indexes.
         0 KB in bad sectors.
     96531 KB in use by the system.
     65536 KB occupied by the log file.
 950258712 KB available on disk.

      4096 bytes in each allocation unit.
 244189951 total allocation units on disk.
 237564678 allocation units available on disk.
```

Figure 0.4: Scanning a drive for any filesystem errors

Note that in *Figure 0.4*, Windows reported that it had scanned the filesystem and found no problems. If any problems are encountered for your case, you should get them fixed first to prevent the loss of data.

5. Now, return to the **Computer Management** window, right-click on the desired drive, and then click on **Shrink Volume**, as shown in the following screenshot:

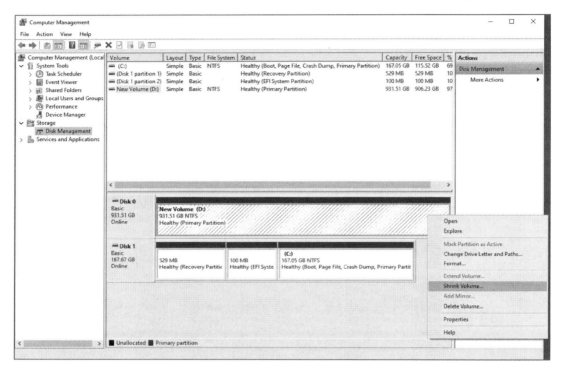

Figure 0.5: Opening the Shrink Volume dialog box

6. In the prompt window, enter the amount of space that you want to shrink. In this example, you are clearing approximately 25 GB of disk space by shrinking your **D :** drive:

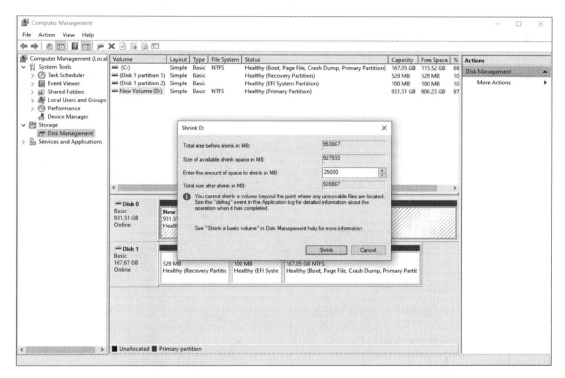

Figure 0.6: Clearing 25 GB by shrinking the existing volume

After you shrink your drive, you should be able to see unallocated space on your drive:

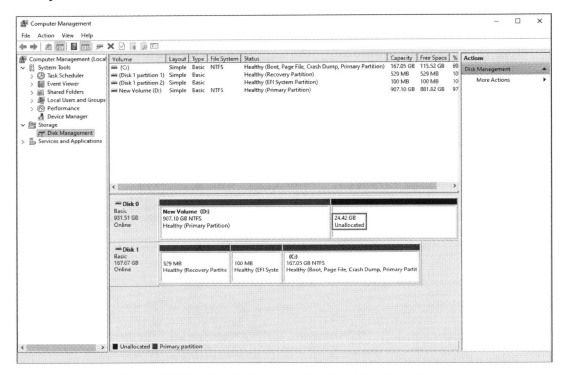

Figure 0.7: Unallocated space after shrinking the volume

Now you are ready to install Ubuntu. But first, you need to download it and create a bootable USB, which is one of the most convenient installation mediums.

CREATING A BOOTABLE USB DRIVE TO INSTALL UBUNTU

You will need a flash drive with a minimum capacity of 4 GB to create a bootable USB drive. Note that all the data on this will be erased:

1. Download the ISO image for Ubuntu Desktop from https://releases.ubuntu.com/20.04/.

2. Next, burn the ISO image to a USB flash disk and create a bootable USB drive. There are many tools available for this, and you can use any of them. In this example, you will use Rufus, which is free and open source. You can get it from https://www.fosshub.com/Rufus.html.

3. Once you have installed Rufus, plug in your USB flash disk and open Rufus. Ensure that the proper **Device** option is selected, as shown in *Figure 0.8*.

4. Press the **SELECT** button under **Boot selection** and then open the Ubuntu 20.04 image that you have downloaded.

5. The choice for **Partition scheme** will depend on how your BIOS and your disk drive are configured. **GPT** will be the best option for most modern systems, while **MBR** will be compatible with older systems:

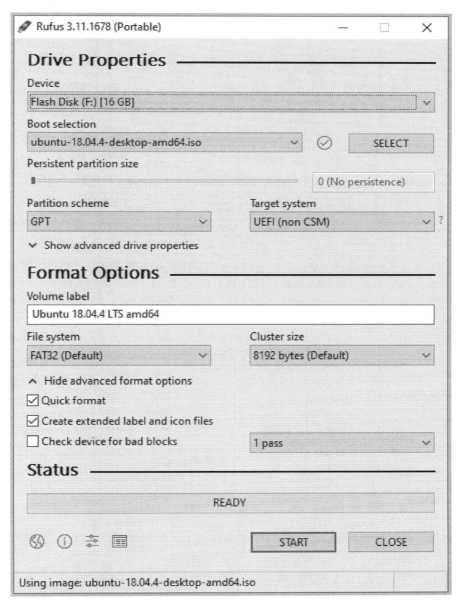

Figure 0.8: Configurations for Rufus

6. You may leave all other options on their defaults, and then press **START**. After completion, close Rufus. You now have a bootable USB drive ready to install Ubuntu.

INSTALLING UBUNTU

Now, use the bootable USB drive to install Ubuntu:

1. To install Ubuntu, boot using the bootable installation media that you just created. In most cases, you should be able to do that by simply having the USB drive plugged in while starting up your machine. If you don't automatically boot into the Ubuntu setup, go into your BIOS settings and ensure that your USB device is at the highest boot priority and that Secure Boot is turned off. The instructions for entering the BIOS setup are usually displayed on the splash screen (the screen with your PC manufacturer logo when you start up your computer) during POST checks. You may also have the option to enter a boot menu while starting up. Usually, you have to hold down *Delete*, *F1*, *F2*, *F12*, or some other key while your PC boots up. It depends on your motherboard's BIOS.

    You should see a screen with a **Try Ubuntu** or **Install Ubuntu** option. If you don't see this screen, and instead you see a shell with a message that begins with **Minimal BASH Like Line Editing is Supported...**, then it is likely that there may have been some data corruption while downloading the ISO file or creating your bootable USB drive. Check the integrity of the downloaded ISO file by calculating the **MD5**, **SHA1**, or **SHA256** hash of your downloaded file and comparing it to the ones you can find in the files named **MD5SUMS**, **SHA1SUMS**, or **SHA256SUMS** on the Ubuntu download page mentioned earlier. Then, repeat the steps in the previous section to reformat and recreate the bootable USB drive.

    If you have set the highest boot priority to the correct USB device in the BIOS and you are still unable to boot using your USB device (your system may just ignore it and boot into Windows instead), then you are most likely dealing with one or both of the following issues:

    - The USB drive was not properly configured to be recognized as a bootable device or the GRUB bootloader was not properly set up. Verifying the integrity of your downloaded image and recreating the bootable USB drive should fix this in most cases.

    - You have chosen the wrong **Partition scheme** option for your system configuration. Try the other one and recreate the USB drive.

2. Once you boot your machine using the USB drive, select **Install Ubuntu**.

3. Choose the language that you want and then press **Continue**.

4. On the next screen, choose the appropriate keyboard layout and continue to the next screen.

5. On the next screen, select the **Normal installation** option.

    Check the **Download updates while installing Ubuntu** and **Install third-party software for graphics and Wi-Fi hardware and additional media formats** options.

    Then, continue to the next screen.

6. On the next screen, select **Install Ubuntu alongside Windows Boot Manager**, and then click **Install now**. You will see a prompt describing the changes that Ubuntu will make to your system, such as the new partitions that will be created. Confirm the changes and proceed to the next screen.

7. On the next screen, choose your region and press **Continue**.

8. On the next screen, set your name (optional), username, computer name, and password, and then press **Continue**.

    The installation should now begin. It will take a while, depending on your system configurations. Once the installation is complete, you will be prompted to restart your computer. Unplug your USB drive, and then click **Restart Now**.

    If you forget to remove your USB drive, you may boot back into the Ubuntu installation. In that case, just exit the setup. If a live instance of Ubuntu has been started up, restart your machine. Remember to remove the USB drive this time.

    If, after restarting, you boot directly into Windows with no option to choose the operating system, the likely issue is that the GRUB bootloader installed by Ubuntu has not taken precedence over the Windows bootloader. In some systems, the precedence/priority for bootloaders on your hard disk is set in the BIOS. You will need to explore your BIOS settings menu to find the appropriate setting. It may be named something similar to **UEFI Hard Disk Drive Priorities**. Ensure that **GRUB/Ubuntu** is set to the highest priority.

    After installing any operating system, it is a good idea to ensure that all of your hardware components are working as expected.

OTHER REQUIREMENTS

Docker Hub account: You can create a free Docker account at https://hub.docker.com/.

ACCESSING THE CODE FILES

You can find the complete code files in our GitHub repository for this workshop, at https://packt.live/2RC99QI.

After installing Git, you can clone the repository using the following command:

```
git clone https://github.com/PacktWorkshops/The-Docker-Workshop

cd The-Docker-Workshop
```

If you have any issues with or questions about installation, please email us at **workshops@packt.com**.

1

RUNNING MY FIRST DOCKER CONTAINER

OVERVIEW

In this chapter, you will learn the basics of Docker and containerization, and explore the benefits of migrating traditional multi-tier applications to a fast and reliable containerized infrastructure. By the end of this chapter, you will have a firm understanding of the benefits of running containerized applications as well as the basics of running containers using the `docker run` command. This chapter will not only introduce you to the fundamentals of Docker but also provide a solid understanding of the Docker concepts that will be built upon throughout this workshop.

INTRODUCTION

In recent years, technological innovations across all industries are rapidly increasing the rate at which software products are delivered. Due to trends in technology, such as agile development (a methodology for quickly writing software) and continuous integration pipelines, which enable the rapid delivery of software, operations' staff have recently struggled to build infrastructure quickly enough to quell the increasing demand. In order to keep up, many organizations have opted to migrate to cloud infrastructure.

Cloud infrastructure provides hosted virtualization, network, and storage solutions that can be leveraged on a pay-as-you-go model. These providers allow any organization or individual to sign up and receive access to infrastructure that would traditionally require large amounts of space and expensive hardware to implement on-site or in a data center. Cloud providers such as Amazon Web Services and Google Cloud Platform provide easy-to-use APIs that allow for the creation of large fleets of **virtual machines** (or **VMs**) almost instantly.

Deploying infrastructure to the cloud provided a solution to many of the dilemmas that organizations were facing with traditional infrastructure solutions, but also created additional problems related to managing costs in running these services at scale. How do companies manage the on-going monthly and yearly expenditures of running expensive servers 24 hours a day, 7 days a week?

VMs revolutionized infrastructure by leveraging hypervisors to create smaller servers on top of larger hardware. The downside of virtualization was how resource-intensive it was to run a VM. VMs themselves look, act, and feel like real bare metal hardware since hypervisors such as Zen, KVM, and VMWare allocate resources to boot and manage an entire operating system image. The dedicated resources associated with VMs make them large and somewhat difficult to manage. Moving VMs between an on-premises hypervisor and the cloud could potentially mean moving hundreds of gigabytes worth of data per VM.

To provide a greater degree of automation, make better use of compute density, and optimize their cloud presence, companies find themselves moving toward containerization and microservices architectures as a solution. Containers provide process-level isolation or running software services within isolated sections of the kernel of the host operating system. Instead of running an entire operating system kernel to provide isolation, containers can share the kernel of the host operating system to run multiple software applications. This is accomplished in the Linux kernel through features known as **control groups** (or **cgroups**) and **namespace isolation**. On a single VM or bare metal machine, a user could potentially run hundreds of containers that run individual software application instances on a single host operating system.

This is in stark contrast to a traditional VM architecture. Generally, when we deploy a VM, we purpose that machine to run a single server or a minor subset of services. This creates a waste of valuable CPU cycles that could be allocated to other tasks and serve other requests. We could, in theory, resolve this dilemma by installing multiple services on a single VM. However, this can create a tremendous amount of confusion regarding which machine is running which service. It also places the ownership of hosting multiple software installations and backend dependencies in a single operating system.

A containerized microservices approach solves this by allowing the container runtime to schedule and run containers on the host operating system. The container runtime does not care what application is running inside the container, but rather that a container exists and can be downloaded and executed on the host operating system. It doesn't matter if the application running inside the container is a Go web API, a simple Python script, or a legacy Cobol application. Since the container is in a standard format, the container runtime will download the container image and execute the software within it. Throughout this book, we will study the Docker container runtime and learn the basics of running containers both locally and at scale.

Docker is a container runtime that was developed in 2013 and designed to take advantage of the process isolation features of the Linux kernel. What separated Docker from other container runtime implementations is that Docker developed a system to not only run containers but also to build and push containers to container repositories. This innovation led to the concept of container immutability—only changing containers by building and pushing new versions of the containers when software changes occur.

As seen in the following diagram (*Figure 1.1*), we have a series of containerized applications deployed across two Docker servers. Between two server instances, seven containerized applications have been deployed. Each container hosts its own set of binaries, libraries, and self-contained dependencies. When Docker runs a container, the container itself hosts everything that it requires to function properly. It is even possible to deploy different versions of the same application framework since each container exists in its own kernel space:

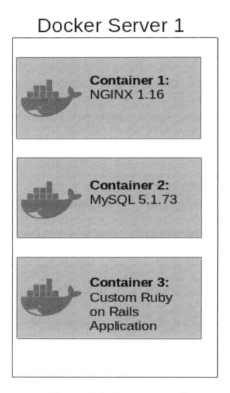
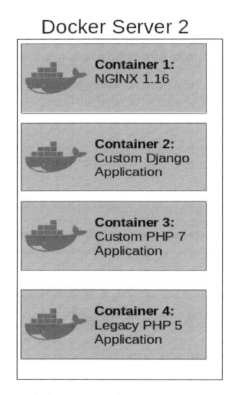

Figure 1.1: Seven containers running across two different container servers

In this chapter, you will get to know various advantages provided by Docker with the help of containerization. You will also learn the basics of running containers using the **docker run** command.

ADVANTAGES OF USING DOCKER

In a traditional VM approach, code changes would require operations folk or a configuration management tool to access that machine and install a new version of the software. The principle of immutable containers means that when a code change occurs, a new version of that container image will be built and created as a new artifact. If this change needed to be rolled back, it would be as easy as downloading and restarting the older version of the container image.

Leveraging a containerized approach also enables software development teams to predictably and reliably test applications in various scenarios and multiple environments locally. Since the Docker runtime environment provides a standard execution environment, software developers can quickly recreate issues and debug problems easily. Because of container immutability, developers can be assured that the same code is running across all environments because the same Docker images can be deployed in any environment. This means that configuration variables such as invalid database connection strings, API credentials, or other environment-specific variance are the primary source of failures. This eases the operational burden and provides an unparalleled degree of efficiency and reusability.

Another advantage of using Docker is that containerized applications are traditionally quite small and flexible compared to their traditional infrastructure counterparts. Instead of providing a full operating system kernel and execution environment, containers generally only provide the necessary libraries and packages that are required to run an application.

When building Docker containers, developers are no longer at the mercy of packages and tools installed on the host operating system, which may differ between environments. They can pack inside a container image only the exact versions of libraries and utilities that the application requires to run. When deployed onto a production machine, developers and operations teams are no longer concerned about what hardware or operating system version the container is running on, as long as their container is running.

For example, as of January 1, 2020, Python 2 is no longer supported. As a result, many software repositories are phasing out Python 2 packages and runtimes. Leveraging a containerized approach, you can continue to run legacy Python 2 applications in a controlled, secure, and reliable fashion until the legacy applications can be rewritten. This removes the fear of worrying about installing operating-system-level patches, which may remove Python 2 support and break legacy application stacks. These Python 2 containers can even run in parallel on Docker servers with Python 3 applications to provide precise testing as these applications are migrated to the new modernized stacks.

Now that we have taken a look at what Docker is and how it works, we can start to work with Docker to get an idea of how process isolation differs from virtualization and other similar technologies.

> **NOTE**
>
> Before we can begin to run containers, you must first have a working installation of Docker on your local development workstation. For details, please review the *Preface* section of this book.

DOCKER ENGINE

Docker Engine is the interface that provides access to the process isolation features of the Linux kernel. Since only Linux exposes the features that allow containers to run, Windows and macOS hosts leverage a Linux VM in the background to make container execution possible. For Windows and macOS users, Docker provides the **"Docker Desktop"** suite of packages that deploy and run this VM in the background for you. This allows Docker commands to be executed natively from the terminal or PowerShell console of the macOS or Windows host. Linux hosts have the privilege of directly executing the Docker Engine natively because modern versions of the Linux kernel support `cgroups` and namespace isolation.

NOTE

Since Windows, macOS, and Linux have fundamentally different operating system architectures in terms of networking and process management, a few of the examples in this book (specifically in regard to networking) are sometimes called out as having different behaviors depending on the operating system that is running on your development workstation. These differences are called out as they occur.

Docker Engine supports not only the execution of container images but also provides built-in mechanisms to build and test container images from source code files known as **Dockerfiles**. When container images are built, they can be pushed to container **image registries**. An **image registry** is a repository of container images from which other Docker hosts can download and execute container images. The Docker engine supports running container images, building container images, and even hosting container image registries when configured to run as such.

When a container is started, Docker will, by default, download the container image, store it in its local container image cache, and finally execute the container's **entrypoint** directive. The **entrypoint** directive is the command that will start the primary process of the application. When this process stops or goes down, the container will also cease to run.

Depending on the application running inside the container, the **entrypoint** directive might be a long-running server daemon that is available all the time, or it could be a short-lived script that will naturally stop when the execution is completed. Alternatively, many containers execute **entrypoint** scripts that complete a series of setup steps before starting the primary process, which could be long- or short-lived.

Before running any container, it is a best practice to first understand the type of application that will be running inside the container and whether it will be a short-lived execution or a long-running server daemon.

RUNNING DOCKER CONTAINERS

Best practices for building containers and microservices architecture dictate that a container should only run a single process. Keeping this principle in mind, we can design containers that are easy to build, troubleshoot, scale, and deploy.

The life cycle of a container is defined by the state of the container and the running processes within it. A container can be in a running or stopped state based on actions taken by the operator, the container orchestrator, or the state of the application running inside the container itself. For example, an operator can manually stop or start a container using the **docker stop** or **docker start command-line interface** (**CLI**) interface commands. Docker itself may automatically stop or restart a container if it detects that the container has entered an unhealthy state. Furthermore, if the primary application running inside the container fails or stops, the running container instance should also stop. Many container runtime platforms such as Docker even provide automated mechanisms to restart containers that enter a stopped state automatically. Many container platforms use this principle to build job and task execution functionality.

Since containers terminate when the primary process within the container finishes, containers are excellent platforms to execute scripts and other types of jobs that have an indefinite lifespan. The following *Figure 1.2* illustrates the life cycle of a typical container:

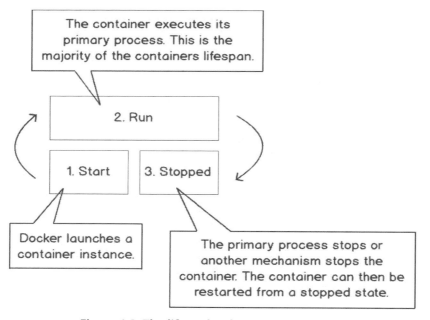

Figure 1.2: The life cycle of a typical container

Once you have Docker downloaded and installed on your targeted operating system, you can start running containers. The Docker CLI has an aptly named **docker run** command specifically for starting and running Docker containers. As we learned previously, containers provide isolation from the rest of the applications and processes running on the system. Due to this fact, the life cycle of a Docker container is determined by the primary process running inside that container. When a container stops, Docker may attempt to restart the container to ensure continuity of the application.

To see the running containers on our host system, we will also be leveraging the **docker ps** command. The **docker ps** command is similar to the Unix-style **ps** command that is used to show the running processes on a Linux or Unix-based operating system.

Remember that when Docker first runs a container, if it does not have the container image stored in its local cache, it will download the container image from a container image registry. To view the container images that are stored locally, use the **docker images** command.

The following exercise will demonstrate how to use the **docker run**, **docker ps**, and **docker images** commands to start and view the status of a simple **hello-world** container.

EXERCISE 1.01: RUNNING THE HELLO-WORLD CONTAINER

A simple "Hello World" application is generally the first line of code a developer writes when learning software development or starting a new programming language, and containerization is no different. Docker has published a **hello-world** container that is extremely small in size and simple to execute. This container demonstrates the nature of containers running a single process with an indefinite lifespan.

In this exercise, you will use the **docker run** command to start the **hello-world** container and the **docker ps** command to view the status of the container after it has finished execution. This will provide a basic overview of running containers in your local development environment:

1. Enter the **docker run** command in a Bash terminal or PowerShell window. This instructs Docker to run a container called **hello-world**:

```
$ docker run hello-world
```

Your shell should return output similar to the following:

```
Unable to find image 'hello-world: latest' locally
latest: Pulling from library/hello-world
0e03bdcc26d7: Pull complete
Digest: sha256:
8e3114318a995a1ee497790535e7b88365222a21771ae7e53687ad76563e8e76
Status: Downloaded newer image for hello-world:latest


Hello from Docker!
This message shows that your installation appears to be working
correctly.


To generate this message, Docker took the following steps:
 1. The Docker client contacted the Docker daemon.
 2. The Docker daemon pulled the "hello-world" image from the
Docker Hub.
    (amd64)
 3. The Docker daemon created a new container from that image
which runs the executable that produces the output you are
currently reading.
 4. The Docker daemon streamed that output to the Docker
client, which sent it to your terminal.
To try something more ambitious, you can run an Ubuntu
container with:
 $ docker run -it ubuntu bash
Share images, automate workflows, and more with a free Docker ID:
 https://hub.docker.com/
For more examples and ideas, visit:
 https://docs.docker.com/get-started/
```

What just happened? You told Docker to run the container, **hello-world**. So, first, Docker will look in its local container cache for a container by that same name. If it doesn't find one, it will look to a container registry on the internet in an attempt to satisfy the command. By simply specifying the name of the container, Docker will, by default, query Docker Hub for a published container image by that name.

As you can see, it was able to find a container called the **library/hello-world** and began the process of pulling in the container image layer by layer. You will get a closer look into container images and layers in *Chapter 2, Getting Started with Dockerfiles*. Once the image has fully downloaded, Docker runs the image, which displays the **Hello from Docker** output. Since the primary process of this image is simply to display that output, the container then stops itself and ceases to run after the output displays.

2. Use the **docker ps** command to see what containers are running on your system. In your Bash or PowerShell terminal, type the following command:

```
$ docker ps
```

This will return output similar to the following:

```
CONTAINER ID       IMAGE       COMMAND       CREATED
    STATUS                 PORTS                 NAMES
```

The output of the **docker ps** command is empty because it only shows currently running containers by default. This is similar to the Linux/Unix **ps** command, which only shows the running processes.

3. Use the **docker ps -a** command to display all the containers, even the stopped ones:

```
$ docker ps -a
```

In the output returned, you should see the **hello-world** container instance:

```
CONTAINER ID       IMAGE           COMMAND       CREATED
    STATUS                         PORTS         NAMES
24c4ce56c904       hello-world     "/hello"      About a minute ago
    Exited (0)  About a minute ago                inspiring_moser
```

As you can see, Docker gave the container a unique container ID. It also displays the **IMAGE** that was run, the **COMMAND** within that image that was executed, the **TIME** it was created, and the **STATUS** of the process running that container, as well as a unique human-readable name. This particular container was created approximately one minute ago, executed the program **/hello**, and ran successfully. You can tell that the program ran and executed successfully since it resulted in an **Exited (0)** code.

4. You can query your system to see what container images Docker cached locally. Execute the **docker images** command to view the local cache:

```
$ docker images
```

The returned output should display the locally cached container images:

```
REPOSITORY       TAG         IMAGE ID        CREATED         SIZE
hello-world      latest      bf756fb1ae65    3 months ago    13.3kB
```

The only image cached so far is the **hello-world** container image. This image is running the **latest** version, which was created 3 months ago, and has a size of 13.3 kilobytes. From the preceding output, you know that this Docker image is incredibly slim and that developers haven't published a code change for this image in 3 months. This output can be very helpful for troubleshooting differences between software versions in the real world.

Since you simply told Docker to run the **hello-world** container without specifying a version, Docker will pull the latest version by default. You can specify different versions by specifying a tag in your **docker run** command. For example, if the **hello-world** container image had a version **2.0**, you could run that version using the **docker run hello-world:2.0** command.

Imagine for a minute that the container was a bit more complex than a simple **hello-world** application. Imagine your colleague wrote software with the requirement to download very specific versions of many third-party libraries. If you run this application traditionally, you would have to download the runtime environment for the language they develop in, plus all of the third-party libraries, as well as detailed instructions on how to build and execute their code.

However, if they publish a Docker image of their code to an internal Docker registry, all they have to provide to you is the **docker run** syntax for running the container. Since you have Docker, the container image will run the same no matter what your underlying platform is. The container image itself already has the libraries and runtime details baked in.

5. If you execute the same **docker run** command over again, then, for each **docker run** command a user inputs, a new container instance will be created. It should be noted that one of the benefits of containerization is the ability to easily run multiple instances of a software application. To see how Docker handles multiple container instances, run the same **docker run** command again to create another instance of the **hello-world** container:

```
$ docker run hello-world
```

You should see the following output:

```
Hello from Docker!
This message shows that your installation appears to be
working correctly.
To generate this message, Docker took the following steps:
 1. The Docker client contacted the Docker daemon.
 2. The Docker daemon pulled the "hello-world" image from
    the Docker Hub.
    (amd64)
 3. The Docker daemon created a new container from that image
    which runs the executable that produces the output you
    are currently reading.
 4. The Docker daemon streamed that output to the Docker client,
    which sent it to your terminal.

To try something more ambitious, you can run an Ubuntu container
with:
 $ docker run -it ubuntu bash

Share images, automate workflows, and more with a free Docker ID:
 https://hub.docker.com/

For more examples and ideas, visit:
 https://docs.docker.com/get-started/
```

Notice that, this time, Docker did not have to download the container image from Docker Hub again. This is because you now have that container image cached locally. Instead, Docker was able to directly run the container and display the output to the screen. Let's see what your **docker ps -a** output looks like now.

6. In your terminal, run the **docker ps -a** command again:

```
docker ps -a
```

In the output, you should see that the second instance of this container image has completed its execution and entered a stopped state, as indicated by **Exit (0)** in the **STATUS** column of the output:

```
CONTAINER ID      IMAGE          COMMAND        CREATED
    STATUS                       PORTS          NAMES
e86277ca07f1      hello-world    "/hello"       2 minutes ago
    Exited (0) 2 minutes ago                    awesome_euclid
24c4ce56c904      hello-world    "/hello"       20 minutes ago
    Exited (0) 20 minutes ago                   inspiring_moser
```

You now have a second instance of this container showing in your output. Each time you execute the **docker run** command, Docker will create a new instance of that container with its attributes and data. You can run as many instances of a container as your system resources will allow. You created one instance in this example 20 minutes ago. The second instance you created 2 minutes ago.

7. Check the base image again by executing the **docker images** command once more:

```
$ docker images
```

The returned output will show the single base image that Docker created two running instances from:

```
REPOSITORY      TAG        IMAGE ID        CREATED        SIZE
hello-world     latest     bf756fb1ae65    3 months ago   13.3kB
```

In this exercise, you used **docker run** to start the **hello-world** container. To accomplish this, Docker downloaded the image from the Docker Hub registry and executed it in the Docker Engine. Once the base image was downloaded, you could create as many instances of that container as you wanted using subsequent **docker run** commands.

Docker container management is more complex than simply starting and viewing the status of containers running in your development environment. Docker also supports many other actions that help provide insight into the status of applications running on Docker hosts. In the next section, we will learn how to manage Docker containers using different commands.

MANAGING DOCKER CONTAINERS

Throughout our container journey, we will be pulling, starting, stopping, and removing containers from our local environment quite frequently. Prior to deploying a container in a production environment, it is critical that we first run the container locally to understand how it functions and what normal behavior looks like. This includes starting containers, stopping containers, getting verbose details about how the container is running, and, of course, accessing the container logs to view critical details about the applications running inside the containers. These basic commands are outlined as follows:

- **docker pull**: This command downloads a container image to the local cache

- **docker stop**: This command stops a running container instance

- **docker start**: This command starts a container instance that is no longer in a running state

- **docker restart**: This command restarts a running container

- **docker attach**: This command allows users to gain access (or attach) to the primary process of a running Docker container instance

- **docker exec**: This command executes a command inside a running container

- **docker rm**: This command deletes a stopped container

- **docker rmi**: This command deletes a container image

- **docker inspect**: This command shows verbose details about the state of a container

Container life cycle management is a critical component of effective container management in production environments. Knowing how to investigate running containers is critical when looking to evaluate the health of your containerized infrastructure.

In the following exercise, we are going to work with these commands individually to get an in-depth understanding of how they work and how they can be leveraged to provide visibility into the health of your containerized infrastructure.

EXERCISE 1.02: MANAGING CONTAINER LIFE CYCLES

When managing containers in both development and production environments, it is critical to understand the status of container instances. Many developers use base container images that contain a specific baseline configuration on top of which their applications can be deployed. Ubuntu is a commonly used base image that users use to package their applications.

Unlike the full operating system image, the Ubuntu base container image is quite slim and intentionally leaves out a lot of packages the full operating system installation has. Most base images do have package systems that will allow you to install any missing packages.

Keep in mind that when building container images, you want to keep the base images as slim as possible, only installing the most necessary packages. This ensures that container images can quickly be pulled and started by Docker hosts.

In this exercise, you will work with the official Ubuntu base container image. This image will be used to start container instances that will be used to test the various container life cycle management commands, such as **docker pull**, **docker start**, and **docker stop**. This container image is useful because the default base image allows us to run container instances in long-running sessions to understand how the container life cycle management commands function. In this exercise, you will also pull the **Ubuntu 18.04** container image and compare it with the **Ubuntu 19.04** container image:

1. In a new terminal or PowerShell window, execute the **docker pull** command to download the **Ubuntu 18.04** container image:

```
$ docker pull ubuntu:18.04
```

You should see the following output indicating that Docker is downloading all the layers of the base image:

```
5bed26d33875: Pull complete
f11b29a9c730: Pull complete
930bda195c84: Pull complete
78bf9a5ad49e: Pull complete
Digest: sha256:bec5a2727be7fff3d308193cfde3491f8fba1a2ba392
        b7546b43a051853a341d
Status: Downloaded newer image for ubuntu:18.04
docker.io/library/ubuntu:18.04
```

2. Use the **docker pull** command to download the **Ubuntu 19.04** base image:

```
$ docker pull ubuntu:19.04
```

You will see similar output as Docker downloads the **Ubuntu 19.04** base image:

```
19.04: Pulling from library/ubuntu
4dc9c2fff018: Pull complete
0a4ccbb24215: Pull complete
c0f243bc6706: Pull complete
5ff1eaecba77: Pull complete
Digest: sha256:2adeae829bf27a3399a0e7db8ae38d5adb89bcaf1bbef
        378240bc0e6724e8344
Status: Downloaded newer image for ubuntu:19.04
docker.io/library/ubuntu:19.04
```

3. Use the **docker images** command to confirm that the container images are downloaded to the local container cache:

```
$ docker images
```

The contents of the local container cache will display the **Ubuntu 18.04** and **Ubuntu 19.04** base images, as well as our **hello-world** image from the earlier exercise:

```
REPOSITORY      TAG       IMAGE ID        CREATED         SIZE
ubuntu          18.04     4e5021d210f6    4 weeks ago     64.2MB
ubuntu          19.04     c88ac1f841b7    3 months ago    70MB
hello-world     latest    bf756fb1ae65    3 months ago    13.3kB
```

4. Before running these images, use the **docker inspect** command to get verbose output about what makes up the container images and how they differ. In your terminal, run the **docker inspect** command and use the image ID of the **Ubuntu 18.04** container image as the main argument:

```
$ docker inspect 4e5021d210f6
```

The **inspect** output will contain a large list of all the attributes that define that container. For example, you can see what environment variables are configured within the container, whether the container has a hostname set when the image was last updated, and a breakdown of all the layers that define that container. This output contains critical debugging details that can prove valuable when planning an upgrade. The following is the truncated output of the **inspect** command. In the **Ubuntu 18.04** image, the **"Created"** parameter should provide the date and time the container image was built:

```
"Id": "4e5021d210f6d4a0717f4b643409eff23a4dc01c4140fa378b1b
       f0a4f8f4",
"Created": "2020-03-20T19:20:22.835345724Z",
"Path": "/bin/bash",
"Args": [],
```

5. Inspecting the **Ubuntu 19.04** container, you can see that this parameter is different. Run the **docker inspect** command in the **Ubuntu 19.04** container image ID:

```
$ docker inspect c88ac1f841b7
```

In the displayed output, you will see that this container image was created on a different date to the **18.04** container image:

```
"Id": "c88ac1f841b74e5021d210f6d4a0717f4b643409eff23a4dc0
       1c4140fa"
"Created": "2020-01-16T01:20:46.938732934Z",
"Path": "/bin/bash",
"Args": []
```

This could be critical if you knew that a security vulnerability might be present in an Ubuntu base image. This information can also prove vital to helping you determine which version of the container you want to run.

6. After inspecting both the container images, it will be clear that your best choice is to stick with the Ubuntu Long Term Support 18.04 release. As you saw from the preceding outputs, the 18.04 release is more up to date than the 19.04 release. This is to be expected as Ubuntu will generally provide more stable updates to the long-term support releases.

7. Use the **docker run** command to start an instance of the Ubuntu 18.04 container:

```
$ docker run -d ubuntu:18.04
```

Notice that this time we are using the **docker run** command with the **-d** flag. This tells Docker to run the container in daemon mode (or in the background). If we omit the **-d** flag, the container will take over our current terminal until the primary process inside the container terminates.

> **NOTE**
>
> A successful invocation of the **docker run** command will usually only return the container ID as output. Some versions of Docker will not return any output.

8. Check the status of the container using the **docker ps -a** command:

```
$ docker ps -a
```

This will reveal a similar output to the following:

```
CONTAINER ID      IMAGE           COMMAND        CREATED
   STATUS                         PORTS          NAMES
c139e44193de      ubuntu:18.04    "/bin/bash"    6 seconds ago
   Exited (0) 4 seconds ago                      xenodochial_banzai
```

As you can see, your container is stopped and exited. This is because the primary process inside the container is **/bin/bash**, which is a shell. The Bash shell cannot run without being executed in an interactive mode since it expects text input and output from a user.

9. Run the **docker run** command again, passing in the **-i** flag to make the session interactive (expecting user input), and the **-t** flag to allocate a **pseudo-tty** handler to the container. **pseudo-tty** handler will essentially link the user's terminal to the interactive Bash shell running inside the container. This will allow Bash to run properly since it will instruct the container to run in an interactive mode, expecting user input. You can also give the container a human-readable name by passing in the **--name** flag. Type the following command in your Bash terminal:

```
$ docker run -i -t -d --name ubuntu1 ubuntu:18.04
```

10. Execute the **docker ps -a** command again to check the status of the container instance:

```
$ docker ps -a
```

You should now see the new instance running, as well as the instance that failed to start moments ago:

```
CONTAINER ID     IMAGE          COMMAND          CREATED
   STATUS               PORTS                 NAMES
f087d0d92110     ubuntu:18.04   "/bin/bash"       4 seconds ago
   Up 2 seconds                              ubuntu1
c139e44193de     ubuntu:18.04   "/bin/bash"       5 minutes ago
   Exited (0) 5 minutes ago                  xenodochial_banzai
```

11. You now have an Ubuntu container up and running. You can run commands inside this container using the **docker exec** command. Run the **exec** command to access a Bash shell, which will allow us to run commands inside the container. Similar to **docker run**, pass in the **-i** and **-t** flags to make it an interactive session. Also pass in the name or ID of the container, so that Docker knows which container you are targeting. The final argument of **docker exec** is always the command you wish to execute. In this case, it will be **/bin/bash** to start a Bash shell inside the container instance:

```
docker exec -it ubuntu1 /bin/bash
```

You should immediately see your prompt change to a root shell. This indicates that you have successfully launched a shell inside your Ubuntu container. The hostname of the container, **cfaa37795a7b**, is taken from the first twelve characters of the container ID. This allows the user to know for certain which container are they accessing, as seen in the following example:

```
root@cfaa37795a7b:/#
```

12. From inside the container, you are very limited in terms of what tools you have available. Unlike a VM image, container images are extremely minimal in terms of the packages that come preinstalled. The **echo** command should be available, however. Use **echo** to write a simple message to a text file:

```
root@cfaa37795a7b:/# echo "Hello world from ubuntu1" > hello-world.
txt
```

13. Run the **exit** command to exit from the Bash shell of the **ubuntu1** container. You should return to your normal terminal shell:

```
root@cfaa37795a7b:/# exit
```

The command will return output like the following. Please note that the output may vary for every user running the command:

```
user@developmentMachine:~/
```

14. Now create a second container called **ubuntu2** that will also run in your Docker environment using the **Ubuntu 19.04** image:

```
$ docker run -i -t -d --name ubuntu2 ubuntu:19.04
```

15. Run **docker exec** to access a shell of this second container. Remember to use the name or container ID of the new container you created. Likewise, access a Bash shell inside this container, so the final argument will be **/bin/bash**:

```
$ docker exec -it ubuntu2 /bin/bash
```

You should observe your prompt change to a Bash root shell, similar to how it did for the **Ubuntu 18.04** container image:

```
root@875cad5c4dd8:/#
```

16. Run the **echo** command inside the **ubuntu2** container instance to write a similar **hello-world**-type greeting:

```
root@875cad5c4dd8:/# echo "Hello-world from ubuntu2!" > hello-world.txt
```

17. Currently, you have two Ubuntu container instances running in your Docker environment with two separate **hello-world** greeting messages in the home directory of the root account. Use **docker ps** to see the two running container images:

```
$ docker ps
```

The list of running containers should reflect the two Ubuntu containers, as well as the time elapsed since they have been created:

```
CONTAINER ID      IMAGE           COMMAND         CREATED
   STATUS               PORTS                 NAMES
875cad5c4dd8      ubuntu:19.04    "/bin/bash"     3 minutes ago
   Up 3 minutes                               ubuntu2
cfaa37795a7b      ubuntu:18.04    "/bin/bash"     15 minutes ago
   Up 15 minutes                              ubuntu1
```

18. Instead of using **docker exec** to access a shell inside our containers, use it to display the output of the **hello-world.txt** files you wrote by executing the **cat** command inside the containers:

```
$ docker exec -it ubuntu1 cat hello-world.txt
```

The output will display the **hello-world** message you passed into the container in the previous steps. Notice that as soon as the **cat** command was completed and the output displayed, the user was moved back to the context of your main terminal. This is because the **docker exec** session will only exist for as long as the command the user is executing will run.

In the earlier example of the Bash shell, Bash will only exit if the user terminates it by using the **exit** command. In this example, only the **Hello world** output is displayed because the **cat** command displayed the output and exited, ending the **docker exec** session:

```
Hello world from ubuntu1
```

You will observe the contents of the **hello-world** file displayed, followed by a return to your main terminal session.

19. Run the same **cat** command in the **ubuntu2** container instance:

```
$ docker exec -it ubuntu2 cat hello-world.txt
```

Similar to the first example, the **ubuntu2** container instance will display the contents of the **hello-world.txt** file provided previously:

```
Hello-world from ubuntu2!
```

As you can see, Docker was able to allocate an interactive session on both the containers, execute the command, and return the output directly in our running container instances.

20. In a similar manner to that you used to execute commands inside our running containers, you can also stop, start, and restart them. Stop one of your container instances using the **docker stop** command. In your terminal session, execute the **docker stop** command, followed by the name or container ID of the **ubuntu2** container:

```
$ docker stop ubuntu2
```

This command should return no output.

21. Use the **docker ps** command to view all running container instances:

```
$ docker ps
```

The output will display the **ubuntu1** container up and running:

```
CONTAINER ID      IMAGE           COMMAND           CREATED
  STATUS                 PORTS                 NAMES
cfaa37795a7b      ubuntu:18.04    "/bin/bash"       26 minutes ago
  Up 26 minutes                                ubuntu1
```

22. Execute the **docker ps -a** command to view all container instances, regardless of whether they are running, to see your container in a stopped state:

```
$ docker ps -a
```

The command will return the following output:

```
CONTAINER ID      IMAGE           COMMAND           CREATED
  STATUS                 PORTS                 NAMES
875cad5c4dd8      ubuntu:19.04     "/bin/bash"       14 minutes ago
  Exited (0) 6 seconds ago                    ubuntu2
```

23. Use the **docker start** or **docker restart** command to restart the container instance:

```
$ docker start ubuntu2
```

This command will return no output, although some versions of Docker may display the container ID.

24. Verify that the container is running again by using the **docker ps** command:

```
$ docker ps
```

Notice that **STATUS** shows that this container has only been up for a short period (**1 second**), although the container instance was created 29 minutes ago:

```
CONTAINER ID      IMAGE           COMMAND           CREATED
  STATUS                 PORTS                 NAMES
875cad5c4dd8      ubuntu:19.04    "/bin/bash"       17 minutes ago
  Up 1 second                                  ubuntu2
cfaa37795a7b      ubuntu:18.04    "/bin/bash"       29 minutes ago
  Up 29 minutes                                ubuntu1
```

From this state, you can experiment with starting, stopping, or executing commands inside these containers.

25. The final stage of the container management life cycle is cleaning up the container instances you created. Use the **docker stop** command to stop the **ubuntu1** container instance:

```
$ docker stop ubuntu1
```

This command will return no output, although some versions of Docker may return the container ID.

26. Perform the same **docker stop** command to stop the **ubuntu2** container instance:

```
$ docker stop ubuntu2
```

27. When container instances are in a stopped state, use the **docker rm** command to delete the container instances altogether. Use **docker rm** followed by the name or container ID to delete the **ubuntu1** container instance:

```
$ docker rm ubuntu1
```

This command will return no output, although some versions of Docker may return the container ID.

Perform this same step on the **ubuntu2** container instance:

```
$ docker rm ubuntu2
```

28. Execute **docker ps -a** to see all containers, even the ones in a stopped state. You will find that the stopped containers no longer exist due to the fact they have been deleted by our previous command. You may also delete the **hello-world** container instances, as well. Delete the **hello-world** container using the container ID captured from the **docker ps -a** output:

```
$ docker rm b291785f066c
```

29. To completely reset the state of our Docker environment, delete the base images you downloaded during this exercise as well. Use the **docker images** command to view the cached base images:

```
$ docker images
```

The list of Docker images and all associated metadata in your local cache will display:

```
REPOSITORY       TAG        IMAGE ID        CREATED         SIZE
ubuntu           18.04      4e5021d210f6    4 weeks ago     64.2MB
ubuntu           19.04      c88ac1f841b7    3 months ago    70MB
hello-world      latest     bf756fb1ae65    3 months ago    13.3kB
```

30. Execute the **docker rmi** command followed by the image ID to delete the first image ID:

```
$ docker rmi 4e5021d210f6
```

Similar to **docker pull**, the **rmi** command will delete each image and all associated layers:

```
Untagged: ubuntu:18.04
Untagged: ubuntu@sha256:bec5a2727be7fff3d308193cfde3491f8fba1a2b
a392b7546b43a051853a341d
Deleted: sha256:4e5021d210f65ebe915670c7089120120bc0a303b9020859
2851708c1b8c04bd
Deleted: sha256:1d9112746e9d86157c23e426ce87cc2d7bced0ba2ec8ddbd
fbcc3093e0769472
Deleted: sha256:efcf4a93c18b5d01aa8e10a2e3b7e2b2eef0378336456d86
53e2d123d6232c1e
Deleted: sha256:1e1aa31289fdca521c403edd6b37317bf0a349a941c7f19b
6d9d311f59347502
Deleted: sha256:c8be1b8f4d60d99c281fc2db75e0f56df42a83ad2f0b0916
21ce19357e19d853
```

Perform this step for each image you wish to delete, substituting in the various image IDs. For each base image you delete, you will see all of the image layers get untagged and deleted along with it.

It is important to periodically clean up your Docker environment as frequently building and running containers can cause large amounts of hard disk usage over time. Now that you know how to run and manage Docker containers in your local development environment, you can use more advanced Docker commands to understand how a container's primary process functions and how to troubleshoot issues. In the next section, we will look at the **docker attach** command to directly access the primary process of a container.

> **NOTE**
>
> To streamline the process of cleaning up your environment, Docker provides a **prune** command that will automatically remove old containers and base images:
>
> ```
> $ docker system prune -fa
> ```
>
> Executing this command will remove any container images that are not tied to an existing running container, along with any other resources in your Docker environment.

ATTACHING TO CONTAINERS USING THE ATTACH COMMAND

In the previous exercise, you saw how to use the **docker exec** command to spin up a new shell session in a running container instance in which to execute commands. The **docker exec** command is very good for quickly gaining access to a containerized instance for debugging, troubleshooting, and understanding the context the container is running in.

However, as covered earlier in the chapter, Docker containers run as per the life of the primary process running inside the container. When this process exits, the container will stop. If you wanted to access the primary process inside the container directly (as opposed to a secondary shell session), then Docker provides the **docker attach** command to attach to the primary running process inside the container.

When using **docker attach**, you are gaining access to the primary process running in the container. If this process is interactive, such as a Bash or Bourne shell session, you will be able to execute commands directly through a **docker attach** session (similar to **docker exec**). However, if the primary process in your container terminates, so will the entire container instance, since the Docker container life cycle is dependent on the running state of the primary process.

In the following exercise, you will use the **docker attach** command to directly access the primary process of an Ubuntu container. By default, the primary process of this container is **/bin/bash**.

EXERCISE 1.03: ATTACHING TO AN UBUNTU CONTAINER

The **docker attach** command is used to attach to a running container in the context of the primary process. In this exercise, you will use the **docker attach** command to attach to running containers and investigate the main container **entrypoint** process directly:

1. Use the **docker run** command to start a new Ubuntu container instance. Run this container in interactive mode (**-i**), allocate a TTY session (**-t**), and run it in the background (**-d**). Call this container **attach-example1**:

```
docker run -itd --name attach-example1 ubuntu:latest
```

   This will start a new Ubuntu container instance named **attach-example1** using the latest version of the Ubuntu container image.

2. Use the **docker ps** command to check that this container is running in our environment:

```
docker ps
```

   The details of the running container instance will be displayed. Take note that the primary process of this container is a Bash shell (**/bin/bash**):

```
CONTAINER ID    IMAGE           COMMAND        CREATED
  STATUS                PORTS              NAMES
90722712ae93    ubuntu:latest   "/bin/bash"    18 seconds ago
  Up 16 seconds                       attach-example1
```

3. Run the **docker attach** command to attach to the primary process inside this container, (**/bin/bash**). Use **docker attach** followed by the name or ID of the container instance:

```
$ docker attach attach-example1
```

   This should drop you into the primary Bash shell session of this container instance. Note that your terminal session should change to a root shell session, indicating you have successfully accessed the container instance:

```
root@90722712ae93:/#
```

It should be noted here that using commands such as **exit** to terminate a shell session will result in stopping the container instance because you are now attached to the primary process of the container instance. By default, Docker provides the shortcut key sequence of *Ctrl + P* and then *Ctrl + Q* to gracefully detach from an **attach** session.

4. Use the keyboard combinations *Ctrl + P* and then *Ctrl + Q* to detach from this session gracefully:

```
root@90722712ae93:/# CTRL-p CTRL-q
```

> **NOTE**
>
> You will not type the words **CTRL-p CTRL-q**; rather, you will press and hold the *Ctrl* key, press the *P* key, and then release both keys. Then, press and hold the *Ctrl* key again, press the *Q* key, and then again release both keys.

Upon successful detachment of the container, the words **read escape sequence** will be displayed before returning you to your main terminal or PowerShell session:

```
root@90722712ae93:/# read escape sequence
```

5. Use **docker ps** to verify that the Ubuntu container is still running as expected:

```
$ docker ps
```

The **attach-example1** container will be displayed, still running as expected:

```
CONTAINER ID    IMAGE             COMMAND         CREATED
  STATUS                 PORTS               NAMES
90722712ae93    ubuntu:latest     "/bin/bash"     13 minutes ago
  Up 13 minutes                              attach-example1
```

6. Use the **docker attach** command to attach once more to the **attach-example1** container instance:

```
$ docker attach attach-example1
```

You should be put back into the Bash session of the primary process:

```
root@90722712ae93:/#
```

7. Now, terminate the primary process of this container using the **exit** command. In the Bash shell session, type the **exit** command:

```
root@90722712ae93:/# exit
```

The terminal session should have exited, returning you once more to your primary terminal.

8. Use the **docker ps** command to observe that the **attach-example1** container should no longer be running:

```
$ docker ps
```

This should return no running container instances:

```
CONTAINER ID    IMAGE          COMMAND          CREATED
    STATUS              PORTS            NAMES
```

9. Use the **docker ps -a** command to view all the containers, even ones that have been stopped or have exited:

```
$ docker ps -a
```

This should display the **attach-example1** container in a stopped state:

```
CONTAINER ID    IMAGE                COMMAND
    CREATED         STATUS    PORTS          NAMES
90722712ae93    ubuntu:latest        "/bin/bash"
    20 minutes ago    Exited (0) 3 minutes ago   attach-example1
```

As you can see, the container has gracefully terminated (**Exited (0)**) approximately 3 minutes ago. The **exit** command gracefully terminates a Bash shell session.

10. Use the **docker system prune -fa** command to clean up the stopped container instances:

```
docker system prune -fa
```

This should remove all stopped container instances, including the **attach-example1** container instance, as seen in the following output:

```
Deleted Containers:
ry6v87v9a545hjn7535jk2kv9x8cv09wnkjnscas98v7a762nvnw7938798vnand
Deleted Images:
untagged: attach-example1
```

In this exercise, we used the **docker attach** command to gain direct access to the primary process of a running container. This differs from the **docker exec** command we explored earlier in the chapter because **docker exec** executes a new process inside a running container, whereas **docker attach** attaches to the main process of a container directly. Careful attention must be paid, however, when attaching to a container not to stop the container by terminating the main process.

In the next activity, we will put together the Docker management commands we covered in this chapter to start putting together the building block containers that will become the Panoramic Trekking microservices application stack.

ACTIVITY 1.01: PULLING AND RUNNING THE POSTGRESQL CONTAINER IMAGE FROM DOCKER HUB

Panoramic Trekking is the multi-tier web application that we will be building throughout this book. Similar to any web application, it will consist of a web server container (NGINX), a Python Django backend application, and a PostgreSQL database. Before you can start deploying the web application or the frontend web server, you must first deploy the backend database.

In this activity, you are asked to start a PostgreSQL version 12 database container with default credentials.

> **NOTE**
>
> The official Postgres container image provides many environment variable overrides you can leverage to configure the PostgreSQL instance. Review the documentation for the container on Docker Hub at https://hub.docker.com/_/postgres.

Perform the following steps:

1. Create a Postgres database container instance that will serve as the data tier of our application stack.

2. Use environment variables to configure the container at runtime to use the following database credentials:

```
username: panoramic
password: trekking
```

3. Verify whether the container is running and healthy.

Expected Output:

The following output should be returned on running **docker ps** command:

```
CONTAINER ID    IMAGE          COMMAND                 CREATED
   STATUS                 PORTS              NAMES
29f115af8cdd    postgres:12    "docker-entrypoint.s…"  4 seconds ago
   Up 2 seconds           5432/tcp           blissful_kapitsa
```

> **NOTE**
>
> The solution for this activity can be found on page 650.

In the next activity, you will access the database that has just been set up in this activity inside the container instance. You will also interact with the container to fetch the list of databases running in the container.

ACTIVITY 1.02: ACCESSING THE PANORAMIC TREKKING APP DATABASE

This activity will involve accessing the database running inside the container instance using the **PSQL** CLI utility. Once you have logged in using the credentials (**panoramic/trekking**), you will query for the list of databases running in the container.

Perform the following steps:

1. Log in to the Postgres database container using the PSQL command-line utility.

2. Once logged in to the database, return a list of databases in Postgres by default.

> **NOTE**
>
> If you are not familiar with the PSQL CLI, the following is a list of reference commands to assist you with this activity:
>
> Logging in: **psql --username username --password**
>
> Listing the database: **\l**
>
> Quitting the PSQL shell: **\q**

Expected Output:

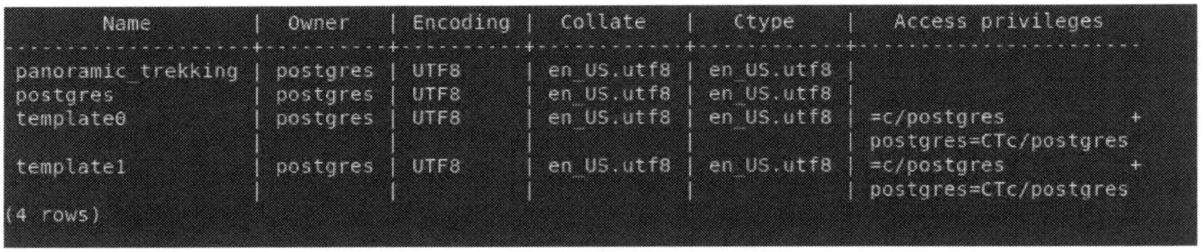

```
        Name         |  Owner   | Encoding |  Collate    |   Ctype     |   Access privileges
---------------------+----------+----------+-------------+-------------+------------------------
 panoramic_trekking  | postgres | UTF8     | en_US.utf8  | en_US.utf8  |
 postgres            | postgres | UTF8     | en_US.utf8  | en_US.utf8  |
 template0           | postgres | UTF8     | en_US.utf8  | en_US.utf8  | =c/postgres           +
                     |          |          |             |             | postgres=CTc/postgres
 template1           | postgres | UTF8     | en_US.utf8  | en_US.utf8  | =c/postgres           +
                     |          |          |             |             | postgres=CTc/postgres
(4 rows)
```

Figure 1.3: Expected output of Activity 1.02

> **NOTE**
>
> The solution for this activity can be found on page 651.

SUMMARY

In this chapter, you learned the fundamentals of containerization, the benefits of running applications in containers, and the basic Docker life cycle commands to manage containerized instances. You learned that containers serve as a universal software deployment package that truly can be built once and run anywhere. Because we are running Docker locally, we can know for certain that the same container images running in our local environment can be deployed in production and run with confidence.

Using commands such as **docker run**, **docker start**, **docker exec**, **docker ps**, and **docker stop**, we have explored the basics of container life cycle management through the Docker CLI. Through the various exercises, we launched container instances from the same base image, configured them using **docker exec**, and cleaned up the deployments using other basic container life cycle commands such as **docker rm** and **docker rmi**.

In the final portion of this chapter, we jumped in head-first, taking the first steps toward running our Panoramic Trekking application by launching a PostgreSQL database container instance. Using environment variables that we placed within the **docker run** command, we created an instance configured with a default username and password. We tested the configuration by executing the PSQL command-line tool from inside the container and querying the database to see the schema.

Although this is only scratching the surface of what Docker is capable of, we hope it was able to whet your appetite for the material that will be covered in the upcoming chapters. In the next chapter, we will discuss building truly immutable containers using **Dockerfiles** and the **docker build** command. Writing custom **Dockerfiles** to build and deploy unique container images will demonstrate the power of running containerized applications at scale.

2

GETTING STARTED WITH DOCKERFILES

OVERVIEW

In this chapter, you will study the form and function of a **Dockerfile** and its directives, including **FROM**, **LABEL**, and **CMD**, with which you will dockerize an application. The chapter will provide you with knowledge of the layered filesystem of Docker images and the use of caching during the Docker build process. By the end of this chapter, you will be able to write a **Dockerfile** using the common directives and build custom Docker images with the **Dockerfile**.

INTRODUCTION

In the previous chapter, we learned how to run our first Docker container by pulling a pre-built Docker image from the Docker Hub. While it is useful to get pre-built Docker images from Docker Hub, we must know how to create custom Docker images. This is important for running our applications on Docker by installing new packages and customizing the settings of the pre-built Docker images. In this chapter, we are going to learn how to create our custom Docker image and run a Docker container based on it.

This will be done using a text file called a **Dockerfile**. This file consists of commands that can be executed by Docker to create a Docker image. Docker images are created from a **Dockerfile** using the **docker build** (or **docker image build**) command.

> **NOTE**
>
> Beginning with Docker 1.13, the **Docker CLI** syntax has been restructured to the form of Docker **COMMAND SUBCOMMAND**. For example, the **docker build** command was replaced by the **docker image build** command. This restructuring was carried out to clean up the Docker CLI syntax and gain a more consistent grouping of commands. Currently, both syntaxes are supported, but the old syntax is expected to be deprecated in the future.

A Docker image consists of multiple layers, each layer representing the commands provided in the **Dockerfile**. These read-only layers are stacked on top of one another to create the final Docker image. Docker images can be stored in a Docker **registry**, such as **Docker Hub**, which is a place where you can store and distribute Docker images.

A Docker **container** is a running instance of the Docker image. One or more Docker containers can be created from a single Docker image using the **docker run** (or **docker container run**) command. Once a Docker container is created from the Docker image, a new writeable layer will be added on top of the read-only layers from the Docker image. Docker containers can then be listed with the docker ps (or docker container list) command:

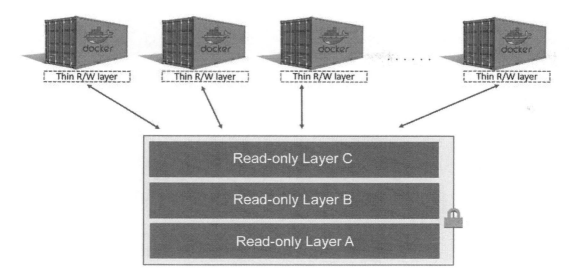

Figure 2.1: Image layers and a container layer

As illustrated in the preceding diagram, there can be one or more read-only layers that make up the Docker image. These read-only layers are generated for each command in the **Dockerfile** during the Docker image build process. Once a Docker container is created from the image, a new read-write layer (known as the **Container layer**) will be added on top of the image layers and will host all the changes made on the running container.

In this chapter, we will write our first **Dockerfile**, build the Docker image from the **Dockerfile**, and run a Docker container from our custom Docker image. Before we can perform any of these tasks, however, we must first define a **Dockerfile**.

WHAT IS A DOCKERFILE?

A **Dockerfile** is a text file that contains instructions on how to create a Docker image. These commands are known as **directives**. A **Dockerfile** is a mechanism that we use to create a custom Docker image as per our requirements.

The format of a **Dockerfile** is as follows:

```
# This is a comment
DIRECTIVE argument
```

A **Dockerfile** can contain multiple lines of comments and directives. These lines will be executed in order by the **Docker Engine** while building the Docker image. Like programming languages, a **Dockerfile** can also contain comments.

All statements starting with the # symbol will be treated as a comment. Currently, **Dockerfiles** only support single-line comments. If you wish you write a multi-line comment, you need to add the # symbol at the beginning of each line.

However, unlike most programming languages, instructions within the **Dockerfile** are not case-sensitive. Even though the **DIRECTIVE** is case-insensitive, it is a best practice to write all directives in uppercase to distinguish them from arguments.

In the next section, we will discuss the common directives that we can use in **Dockerfiles** to create a custom Docker image.

> **NOTE**
>
> If you are using ubuntu versions later than 18.04, there will be a prompt to enter time zone. Please suppress the prompt with `ARG DEBIAN_FRONTEND=non_interactive`

COMMON DIRECTIVES IN DOCKERFILES

As discussed in the previous section, a directive is a command that is used to create a Docker image. In this section, we will be discussing the following five **Dockerfile** directives:

1. The **FROM** directive
2. The **LABEL** directive
3. The **RUN** directive
4. The **CMD** directive
5. The **ENTRYPOINT** directive

THE FROM DIRECTIVE

A **Dockerfile** usually starts with the **FROM** directive. This is used to specify the parent image of our custom Docker image. The parent image is the starting point of our custom Docker image. All the customization that we do will be applied on top of the parent image. The parent image can be an image from Docker Hub, such as Ubuntu, CentOS, Nginx, and MySQL. The **FROM** directive takes a valid image name and a tag as arguments. If the tag is not specified, the **latest** tag will be used.

A FROM directive has the following format:

```
FROM <image>:<tag>
```

In the following **FROM** directive, we are using the **ubuntu** parent image with the **20.04** tag:

```
FROM ubuntu:20.04
```

Additionally, we can use the base image if we need to build a Docker image from scratch. The base image, known as the scratch image, is an empty image mostly used to build other parent images.

In the following **FROM** directive, we are using the **scratch** image to build our custom Docker image from scratch:

```
FROM scratch
```

Now, let's understand what a **LABEL** directive is in the next section.

THE LABEL DIRECTIVE

A **LABEL** is a key-value pair that can be used to add metadata to a Docker image. These labels can be used to organize the Docker images properly. An example would be to add the name of the author of the **Dockerfile** or the version of the **Dockerfile**.

A **LABEL** directive has the following format:

```
LABEL <key>=<value>
```

A **Dockerfile** can have multiple labels, adhering to the preceding key-value format:

```
LABEL maintainer=sathsara@mydomain.com
LABEL version=1.0
LABEL environment=dev
```

Or these labels can be included on a single line separated by spaces:

```
LABEL maintainer=sathsara@mydomain.com version=1.0 environment=dev
```

Labels on an existing Docker image can be viewed with the **docker image inspect** command.

The output should be like the following on running the **docker image inspect**
<image>:<tag> command:

```
...
...
"Labels": {
    "environment": "dev",
    "maintainer": "sathsara@mydomain.com",
    "version": "1.0"
}
...
...
```

As shown here, the docker image inspect command will output the key-value pairs
configured in the **Dockerfile** using the **LABEL** directive.

In the next section, we will learn how to execute commands during the image build
time using the **RUN** directive.

THE RUN DIRECTIVE

The **RUN** directive is used to execute commands during the image build time. This will
create a new layer on top of the existing layer, execute the specified command, and
commit the results to the newly created layer. The **RUN** directive can be used to install
the required packages, update the packages, create users and groups, and so on.

The **RUN** directive takes the following format:

```
RUN <command>
```

<command> specifies the shell command you want to execute as part of the image
build process. A **Dockerfile** can have multiple **RUN** directives adhering to the
preceding format.

In the following example, we are running two commands on top of the parent image.
The **apt-get update** is used to update the package repositories, and **apt-get**
install nginx -y is used to install the Nginx package:

```
RUN apt-get update
RUN apt-get install nginx -y
```

Alternatively, you can add multiple shell commands to a single **RUN** directive by separating them with the **&&** symbol. In the following example, we have used the same two commands, but this time in a single **RUN** directive, separated by an **&&** symbol:

```
RUN apt-get update && apt-get install nginx -y
```

Now, let's move on to the next section where we will learn about the **CMD** directive.

THE CMD DIRECTIVE

A Docker container is normally expected to run one process. A **CMD** directive is used to provide this default initialization command that will be executed when a container is created from the Docker image. A **Dockerfile** can execute only one **CMD** directive. If there is more than one **CMD** directive in the **Dockerfile**, Docker will execute only the last one.

The **CMD** directive has the following format:

```
CMD ["executable","param1","param2","param3", ...]
```

For example, use the following command to echo "**Hello World**" as the output of a Docker container:

```
CMD ["echo","Hello World"]
```

The preceding **CMD** directive will produce the following output when we run the Docker container with the **docker container run <image>** command (replace **<image>** with the name of the Docker image):

```
$ docker container run <image>
Hello World
```

However, if we send any command-line arguments with **docker container run <image>**, these arguments will take precedence over the **CMD** command that we defined. For example, if we execute the following command (replace **<image>** with the name of the Docker image), the default "**Hello World**" output defined with the **CMD** directive will be ignored. Instead, the container will output "**Hello Docker !!!**":

```
$ docker container run <image> echo "Hello Docker !!!"
```

As we discussed, both the **RUN** and **CMD** directives can be used to execute a shell command. The main difference between these two directives is that the command provided with the **RUN** directive will be executed during the image build process, while the command provided with the **CMD** directive will be executed once a container is launched from the built image.

Another notable difference between the **RUN** and **CMD** directives is that there can be multiple **RUN** directives in a **Dockerfile**, but there can be only one **CMD** directive (if there are multiple **CMD** directives, all others except the last one will be ignored).

As an example, we can use the **RUN** directive to install a software package during the Docker image build process and the **CMD** directive to start the software package once a container is launched from the built image.

In the next section, we will learn about the **ENTRYPOINT** directive, which provides the same functionality as the **CMD** directive, except for overriding.

THE ENTRYPOINT DIRECTIVE

Similar to the **CMD** directive, the **ENTRYPOINT** directive is also used to provide this default initialization command that will be executed when a container is created from the Docker image. The difference between the **CMD** directive and the **ENTRYPOINT** directive is that, unlike the **CMD** directive, we cannot override the **ENTRYPOINT** command using the command-line parameters sent with the **docker container run** command.

> **NOTE**
>
> The `--entrypoint` flag can be sent with the **docker container run** command to override the default **ENTRYPOINT** of the image.

The **ENTRYPOINT** directive has the following format:

```
ENTRYPOINT ["executable","param1","param2","param3", ...]
```

Similar to the **CMD** directive, the **ENTRYPOINT** directive also allows us to provide the default executable and the parameters. We can use the **CMD** directive with the **ENTRYPOINT** directive to provide additional arguments to the executable.

In the following example, we have used **"echo"** as the default command and **"Hello"** as the default parameter using the **ENTRYPOINT** directive. We have also provided **"World"** as the additional parameter using the **CMD** directive:

```
ENTRYPOINT ["echo","Hello"]
CMD ["World"]
```

The output of the **echo** command will differ based on how we execute the **docker container run** command.

If we launch the Docker image without any command-line parameters, it will output the message as **Hello World**:

```
$ docker container run <image>
Hello World
```

But if we launch the Docker image with additional command-line parameters (for example, **Docker**), the output message will be **Hello Docker**:

```
$ docker container run <image> "Docker"
Hello Docker
```

Before discussing the **Dockerfile** directives any further, let's start by creating our first **Dockerfile** in the next exercise.

EXERCISE 2.01: CREATING OUR FIRST DOCKERFILE

In this exercise, you will create a Docker image that can print the arguments you pass to the Docker image, preceded by the text **You are reading**. For example, if you pass **hello world**, it will output **You are reading hello world** as the output. If no argument is provided, **The Docker Workshop** will be used as the standard value:

1. Create a new directory named **custom-docker-image** using the **mkdir** command. This directory will be the **context** for your Docker image. **Context** is the directory that contains all the files needed to successfully build an image:

```
$ mkdir custom-docker-image
```

2. Navigate to the newly created **custom-docker-image** directory using the **cd** command as we will be creating all the files required during the build process (including the **Dockerfile**) within this directory:

```
$ cd custom-docker-image
```

3. Within the **custom-docker-image** directory, create a file named
    Dockerfile using the **touch** command:

```
$ touch Dockerfile
```

4. Now, open the **Dockerfile** using your favorite text editor:

```
$ vim Dockerfile
```

5. Add the following content to the **Dockerfile**, save it, and exit from
    the **Dockerfile**:

```
# This is my first Docker image
FROM ubuntu
LABEL maintainer=sathsara@mydomain.com
RUN apt-get update
CMD ["The Docker Workshop"]
ENTRYPOINT ["echo", "You are reading"]
```

The Docker image will be based on the Ubuntu parent image. You then
use the **LABEL** directive to provide the email address of the author of the
Dockerfile. The next line executes the **apt-get update** command to
update the package list of Debian to the latest available version. Finally, you will
use the **ENTRYPOINT** and **CMD** directives to define the default executable and
parameters of the container.

We have provided **echo** as the default executable and **You are reading**
as the default parameter that cannot be overridden with command-line
parameters. Also, we have provided **The Docker Workshop** as an additional
parameter that can be overridden with command-line parameters with a
docker container run command.

In this exercise, we created our first **Dockerfile** using the common directives
that we learned in the previous sections. The next step of the process is to build the
Docker image from the **Dockerfile**. You can only run a Docker container after
building the Docker image from the **Dockerfile**. In the next section, we are going
to look at how to build a Docker image from the **Dockerfile**.

BUILDING DOCKER IMAGES

In the last section, we learned how to create a **Dockerfile**. The next step of the process is to build a **Docker image** using the **Dockerfile**.

A **Docker image** is the template used to build Docker containers. This is analogous to how a house plan can be used to create multiple houses from the same design. If you are familiar with **object-oriented programming** concepts, a Docker image and a Docker container have the same relationship as a **class** and an **object**. A class in object-oriented programming can be used to create multiple objects.

A Docker image is a binary file consisting of multiple layers based on the instructions provided in the **Dockerfile**. These layers are stacked on top of one another, and each layer is dependent on the previous layer. Each of the layers is a result of the changes from the layer below it. All the layers of the Docker image are read-only. Once we create a Docker container from a Docker image, a new writable layer will be created on top of other read-only layers, which will contain all the modifications made to the container filesystem:

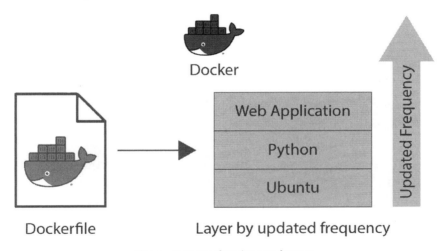

Figure 2.2: Docker image layers

As illustrated in the preceding image, the docker image build command will create a Docker image from the **Dockerfile**. The layers of the Docker image will be mapped to the directives provided in the **Dockerfile**.

This image build process is initiated by the Docker CLI and executed by the Docker daemon. To generate a Docker image, the Docker daemon needs access to the **Dockerfile**, source code (for example, **index.html**), and other files (for example, properties files) that are referenced in the **Dockerfile**. These files are typically stored in a directory that is known as the build context. This context will be specified while executing the docker image build command. The entire context will be sent to the Docker daemon during the image build process.

The **docker image build** command takes the following format:

```
$ docker image build <context>
```

We can execute the docker image build command from the folder that contains the **Dockerfile** and the other files, as shown in the following example. Note that the dot (.) at the end of the command is used to denote the current directory:

```
$ docker image build.
```

Let's see the Docker image build process for the following sample **Dockerfile**:

```
FROM ubuntu:latest
LABEL maintainer=sathsara@mydomain.com
CMD ["echo","Hello World"]
```

This **Dockerfile** uses the latest **ubuntu** images as the parent image. Then, the **LABEL** directive is used to specify **sathsara@mydomain.com** as the maintainer. Finally, the **CMD** directive is used to echo **"Hello World"** as the output of the image.

Once we execute the docker image build command for the preceding **Dockerfile**, we can see an output similar to the following on the console during the build process:

```
Sending build context to Docker daemon 2.048kB
Step 1/3 : FROM ubuntu:latest
latest: Pulling from library/ubuntu
2746a4a261c9: Pull complete
4c1d20cdee96: Pull complete
0d3160e1d0de: Pull complete
c8e37668deea: Pull complete
Digest: sha256:250cc6f3f3ffc5cdaa9d8f4946ac79821aafb4d3afc93928
        f0de9336eba21aa4
```

```
Status: Downloaded newer image for ubuntu:latest
 ---> 549b9b86cb8d
Step 2/3 : LABEL maintainer=sathsara@mydomain.com
 ---> Running in a4a11e5e7c27
Removing intermediate container a4a11e5e7c27
 ---> e3add5272e35
Step 3/3 : CMD ["echo","Hello World"]
 ---> Running in aad8a56fcdc5
Removing intermediate container aad8a56fcdc5
 ---> dc3d4fd77861
Successfully built dc3d4fd77861
```

The first line of the output is **Sending build context to Docker daemon**, which indicates that the building starts by sending the build context to the Docker daemon. All the files available in the context will be sent recursively to the Docker daemon (unless specifically asked to ignore certain files).

Next, there are steps mentioned as **Step 1/3** and **Step 2/3**, which correspond to the instructions in the **Dockerfile**. As the first step, the Docker daemon will download the parent image. In the preceding output shown, Pulling from library/ ubuntu indicates this. For each line of the **Dockerfile**, a new intermediate container will be created to execute the directive, and once this step is completed, this intermediate container will be removed. The lines **Running in a4a11e5e7c27** and **Removing intermediate container a4a11e5e7c27** are used to indicate this. Finally, the **Successfully built dc3d4fd77861** line is printed when the build is completed without any errors. This line prints the ID of the newly built Docker image.

Now, we can list the available Docker images using the **docker image list** command:

```
$ docker image list
```

This list contains the locally built Docker images and Docker images pulled from remote Docker repositories:

```
REPOSITORY     TAG        IMAGE ID        CREATED          SIZE
<none>         <none>     dc3d4fd77861    3 minutes ago    64.2MB
ubuntu         latest     549b9b86cb8d    5 days ago       64.2MB
```

As shown in the preceding output, we can see two Docker images. The first Docker image with the IMAGE ID of **dc3d4fd77861** is the locally built Docker image during the build process. We can see that this **IMAGE ID** is identical to the ID in the last line of the **docker image build** command. The next image is the ubuntu image that we used as the parent image of our custom image.

Now, let's build the Docker image again using the **docker image build** command:

```
$ docker image build
Sending build context to Docker daemon  2.048kB
Step 1/3 : FROM ubuntu:latest
 ---> 549b9b86cb8d
Step 2/3 : LABEL maintainer=sathsara@mydomain.com
 ---> Using cache
 ---> e3add5272e35
Step 3/3 : CMD ["echo","Hello World"]
 ---> Using cache
 ---> dc3d4fd77861
Successfully built dc3d4fd77861
```

This time, the image build process was instantaneous. The reason for this is the cache. Since we did not change any content of the **Dockerfile**, the Docker daemon took advantage of the cache and reused the existing layers from the local image cache to accelerate the build process. We can see that the cache was used this time with the **Using cache** lines available in the preceding output.

The Docker daemon will perform a validation step before starting the build process to make sure that the **Dockerfile** provided is syntactically correct. In the case of an invalid syntax, the build process will fail with an error message from the Docker daemon:

```
$ docker image build
Sending build context to Docker daemon  2.048kB
Error response from daemon: Dockerfile parse error line 5:
unknown instruction: INVALID
```

Now, let's revisit the locally available Docker images with the **docker image list** command:

```
$ docker image list
```

The command should return the following output:

```
REPOSITORY      TAG         IMAGE ID        CREATED         SIZE
<none>          <none>      dc3d4fd77861    3 minutes ago   64.2MB
ubuntu          latest      549b9b86cb8d    5 days ago      64.2MB
```

Note that there was no name for our custom Docker image. This was because we did not specify any repository or tag during the build process. We can tag an existing image with the docker image tag command.

Let's tag our image with **IMAGE ID dc3d4fd77861** as **my-tagged-image:v1.0**:

```
$ docker image tag dc3d4fd77861 my-tagged-image:v1.0
```

Now, if we list our images again, we can see the Docker image name and the tag under the **REPOSITORY** and **TAG** columns:

```
REPOSITORY          TAG         IMAGE ID        CREATED          SIZE
my-tagged-image     v1.0        dc3d4fd77861    20 minutes ago   64.2MB
ubuntu              latest      549b9b86cb8d    5 days ago       64.2MB
```

We can also tag an image during the build process by specifying the **-t** flag:

```
$ docker image build -t my-tagged-image:v2.0 .
```

The preceding command will print the following output:

```
Sending build context to Docker daemon   2.048kB
Step 1/3 : FROM ubuntu:latest
 ---> 549b9b86cb8d
Step 2/3 : LABEL maintainer=sathsara@mydomain.com
 ---> Using cache
 ---> e3add5272e35
Step 3/3 : CMD ["echo","Hello World"]
 ---> Using cache
 ---> dc3d4fd77861
Successfully built dc3d4fd77861
Successfully tagged my-tagged-image:v2.0
```

This time, in addition to the **Successfully built dc3d4fd77861** line, we can see a **Successfully tagged my-tagged-image:v2.0** line, which indicates the tagging on our Docker image.

In this section, we learned how to build a Docker image from a **Dockerfile**. We discussed the difference between a **Dockerfile** and a Docker image. Then, we discussed how a Docker image is made up of multiple layers. We also experienced how caching can accelerate the build process. Finally, we tagged the Docker images.

In the next exercise, we are going to build a Docker image from the **Dockerfile** that we created in *Exercise 2.01: Creating Our First Dockerfile*.

EXERCISE 2.02: CREATING OUR FIRST DOCKER IMAGE

In this exercise, you will build the Docker image from the **Dockerfile** that you created in *Exercise 2.01: Creating Our First Dockerfile* and run a Docker container from the newly built image. First, you will run the Docker image without passing any arguments, expecting You are reading The Docker Workshop as the output. Next, you will run the Docker image with **Docker Beginner's Guide** as the argument and expect You are reading Docker Beginner's Guide as the output:

1. First, make sure you are in the **custom-docker-image** directory created in *Exercise 2.01: Creating Our First Dockerfile*. Confirm that the directory contains the following **Dockerfile** created in *Exercise 2.01: Creating Our First Dockerfile*:

```
# This is my first Docker image
FROM ubuntu
LABEL maintainer=sathsara@mydomain.com
RUN apt-get update
CMD ["The Docker Workshop"]
ENTRYPOINT ["echo", "You are reading"]
```

2. Build the Docker image with the **docker image build** command. This command has the optional **-t** flag to specify the tag of the image. Tag your image as **welcome:1.0**:

```
$ docker image build -t welcome:1.0 .
```

> **NOTE**
>
> Do not forget the dot (.) at the end of the preceding command, which is used to denote the current directory as the build context.

It can be seen from the following output that all five steps mentioned in the **Dockerfile** are executed during the build process. The last two lines of the output suggest that the image is successfully built and tagged:

```
Removing intermediate container a0bffecb3f19
 ---> e3f8d93f029b
Step 3/5 : RUN apt-get update
 ---> Running in 39b2a2132f68
Get:1 http://security.ubuntu.com/ubuntu focal-security InRelease [107 kB]
Get:2 http://archive.ubuntu.com/ubuntu focal InRelease [265 kB]
Get:3 http://security.ubuntu.com/ubuntu focal-security/restricted amd64 Packages [39.1 kB]
Get:4 http://archive.ubuntu.com/ubuntu focal-updates InRelease [111 kB]
Get:5 http://security.ubuntu.com/ubuntu focal-security/universe amd64 Packages [66.4 kB]
Get:6 http://security.ubuntu.com/ubuntu focal-security/main amd64 Packages [207 kB]
Get:7 http://archive.ubuntu.com/ubuntu focal-backports InRelease [98.3 kB]
Get:8 http://security.ubuntu.com/ubuntu focal-security/multiverse amd64 Packages [1078 B]
Get:9 http://archive.ubuntu.com/ubuntu focal/multiverse amd64 Packages [177 kB]
Get:10 http://archive.ubuntu.com/ubuntu focal/main amd64 Packages [1275 kB]
Get:11 http://archive.ubuntu.com/ubuntu focal/universe amd64 Packages [11.3 MB]
Get:12 http://archive.ubuntu.com/ubuntu focal/restricted amd64 Packages [33.4 kB]
Get:13 http://archive.ubuntu.com/ubuntu focal-updates/main amd64 Packages [430 kB]
Get:14 http://archive.ubuntu.com/ubuntu focal-updates/universe amd64 Packages [205 kB]
Get:15 http://archive.ubuntu.com/ubuntu focal-updates/multiverse amd64 Packages [17.3 kB]
Get:16 http://archive.ubuntu.com/ubuntu focal-updates/restricted amd64 Packages [39.3 kB]
Get:17 http://archive.ubuntu.com/ubuntu focal-backports/universe amd64 Packages [3216 B]
Fetched 14.4 MB in 25s (566 kB/s)
Reading package lists...
Removing intermediate container 39b2a2132f68
 ---> 45dbce98c626
Step 4/5 : CMD ["The Docker Workshop"]
 ---> Running in 05978b1c9bbd
Removing intermediate container 05978b1c9bbd
 ---> a319741666e3
Step 5/5 : ENTRYPOINT ["echo", "You are reading"]
 ---> Running in 5498f64b1640
Removing intermediate container 5498f64b1640
 ---> 59f2cel1ea31
Successfully built 59f2cel1ea31
Successfully tagged welcome:1.0
/docker $ █
```

Figure 2.3: Building the welcome:1.0 Docker image

3. Build this image again without changing the **Dockerfile** content:

```
$ docker image build -t welcome:2.0 .
```

Note that this build process completed much quicker than the previous process due to the cache being used:

```
Sending build context to Docker daemon  423.4MB
Step 1/5 : FROM ubuntu
 ---> 4e2eef94cd6b
Step 2/5 : LABEL maintainer=sathsara@mydomain.com
 ---> Using cache
 ---> e3f8d93f029b
Step 3/5 : RUN apt-get update
 ---> Using cache
 ---> 45dbce98c626
Step 4/5 : CMD ["The Docker Workshop"]
 ---> Using cache
 ---> a319741666e3
Step 5/5 : ENTRYPOINT ["echo", "You are reading"]
 ---> Using cache
 ---> 59f2ce11ea31
Successfully built 59f2ce11ea31
Successfully tagged welcome:2.0
/docker $ ▮
```

Figure 2.4: Building the welcome:1.0 Docker image using the cache

4. Use the **docker image list** command to list all the Docker images available on your computer:

```
$ docker image list
```

These images are available on your computer, either when you pull them from a Docker registry, or when you build on your computer:

```
REPOSITORY    TAG      IMAGE ID       CREATED          SIZE
welcome       1.0      98f571a42e5c   23 minutes ago   91.9MB
welcome       2.0      98f571a42e5c   23 minutes ago   91.9MB
ubuntu        latest   549b9b86cb8d   2 weeks ago      64.2MB
```

As you can see from the preceding output, there are three Docker images available. The **ubuntu** image is pulled from the Docker Hub, and version (**tag**) **1.0** and **2.0** of the **welcome** images are built on your computer.

5. Execute the **docker container run** command to start a new container from the Docker image that you built in **step 1** (**welcome:1.0**):

```
$ docker container run welcome:1.0
```

The output should be as follows:

```
You are reading The Docker Workshop
```

You receive the expected output of **You are reading The Docker Workshop**. **You are reading** is due to the parameter provided with the **ENTRYPOINT** directive, and **The Docker Workshop** comes from the parameter provided with the **CMD** directive.

6. Finally, execute the **docker container run** command again, this time with command-line arguments:

```
$ docker container run welcome:1.0 "Docker Beginner's Guide"
```

You will get the output **You are reading Docker Beginner's Guide** because of the command-line argument, **Docker Beginner's Guide**, and the **You are reading** argument provided in the **ENTRYPOINT** directive:

```
You are reading Docker Beginner's Guide
```

In this exercise, we learned how to build a custom Docker image using the **Dockerfile** and run a Docker container from the image. In the next section, we are going to learn other Docker directives that we can use in the **Dockerfile**.

OTHER DOCKERFILE DIRECTIVES

In the section Common Directives in Dockerfile, we discussed the common directives available for a **Dockerfile**. In that section, we discussed **FROM, LABEL, RUN, CMD**, and **ENTRYPOINT** directives and how to use them to create a simple **Dockerfile**.

In this section, we will be discussing more advanced **Dockerfile** directives. These directives can be used to create more advanced Docker images. For example, we can use the **VOLUME** directive to bind the filesystem of the host machine to a Docker container. This will allow us to persist the data generated and used by the Docker container. Another example is the **HEALTHCHECK** directive, which allows us to define health checks to evaluate the health status of Docker containers. We will look into the following directives in this section:

1. The **ENV** directive

2. The **ARG** directive

3. The **WORKDIR** directive

4. The **COPY** directive

5. The **ADD** directive

6. The **USER** directive

7. The **VOLUME** directive

8. The **EXPOSE** directive

9. The **HEALTHCHECK** directive

10. The **ONBUILD** directive

THE ENV DIRECTIVE

The ENV directive in **Dockerfile** is used to set environment variables.
Environment variables are used by applications and processes to get information
about the environment in which a process runs. One example would be the **PATH**
environment variable, which lists the directories to search for executable files.

Environment variables are defined as key-value pairs as per the following format:

```
ENV <key> <value>
```

The PATH environment variable is set with the following value:

```
$PATH:/usr/local/myapp/bin/
```

Hence, it can be set using the **ENV** directive as follows:

```
ENV PATH $PATH:/usr/local/myapp/bin/
```

We can set multiple environment variables in the same line separated by spaces.
However, in this form, the **key** and **value** should be separated by the equal to
(=) symbol:

```
ENV <key>=<value> <key>=<value> ...
```

In the following example, there are two environment variables configured. The **PATH**
environment variable is configured with the value of **$PATH:/usr/local/myapp/
bin/**, and the **VERSION** environment variable is configured with the value of **1.0.0**:

```
ENV PATH=$PATH:/usr/local/myapp/bin/ VERSION=1.0.0
```

Once an environment variable is set with the **ENV** directive in the **Dockerfile**,
this variable is available in all subsequent Docker image layers. This variable is
even available in the Docker containers launched from this Docker image.

In the next section, we will look into the **ARG** directive.

THE ARG DIRECTIVE

The **ARG** directive is used to define variables that the user can pass at build time. **ARG** is the only directive that can precede the **FROM** directive in the **Dockerfile**.

Users can pass values using **--build-arg <varname>=<value>**, as shown here, while building the Docker image:

```
$ docker image build -t <image>:<tag> --build-arg <varname>=<value> .
```

The **ARG** directive has the following format:

```
ARG <varname>
```

There can be multiple **ARG** directives in a **Dockerfile**, as follows:

```
ARG USER
ARG VERSION
```

The **ARG** directive can also have an optional default value defined. This default value will be used if no value is passed at build time:

```
ARG USER=TestUser
ARG VERSION=1.0.0
```

Unlike the **ENV** variables, **ARG** variables are not accessible from the running container. They are only available during the build process.

In the next exercise, we will use the knowledge gained so far to use **ENV** and **ARG** directives in a **Dockerfile**.

EXERCISE 2.03: USING ENV AND ARG DIRECTIVES IN A DOCKERFILE

Your manager has asked you to create a **Dockerfile** that will use ubuntu as the parent image, but you should be able to change the ubuntu version at build time. You will also need to specify the publisher's name and application directory as the environment variables of the Docker image. You will use the **ENV** and **ARG** directives in the **Dockerfile** to perform this exercise:

1. Create a new directory named **env-arg-exercise** using the **mkdir** command:

    ```
    mkdir env-arg-exercise
    ```

2. Navigate to the newly created **env-arg-exercise** directory using the **cd** command:

    ```
    cd env-arg-exercise
    ```

3. Within the **env-arg-exercise** directory, create a file named **Dockerfile**:

```
touch Dockerfile
```

4. Now, open the **Dockerfile** using your favorite text editor:

```
vim Dockerfile
```

5. Add the following content to the **Dockerfile**. Then, save and exit from the **Dockerfile**:

```
# ENV and ARG example
ARG TAG=latest
FROM ubuntu:$TAG
LABEL maintainer=sathsara@mydomain.com
ENV PUBLISHER=packt APP_DIR=/usr/local/app/bin
CMD ["env"]
```

This **Dockerfile** first defined an argument named **TAG** with the default value of the latest. The next line is the **FROM** directive, which will use the ubuntu parent image with the **TAG** variable value sent with the **build** command (or the default value if no value is sent with the build command). Then, the **LABEL** directive sets the value for the maintainer. Next is the **ENV** directive, which defines the environment variable of **PUBLISHER** with the value **packt**, and **APP_DIR** with the value of **/usr/local/app/bin**. Finally, use the **CMD** directive to execute the **env** command, which will print all the environment variables.

6. Now, build the Docker image:

```
$ docker image build -t env-arg --build-arg TAG=19.04 .
```

Note the **env-arg --build-arg TAG=19.04** flag used to send the **TAG** argument to the build process. The output should be as follows:

```
Sending build context to Docker daemon  3.072kB
Step 1/5 : ARG TAG=latest
Step 2/5 : FROM ubuntu:$TAG
19.04: Pulling from library/ubuntu
4dc9c2fff018: Pull complete
0a4ccbb24215: Pull complete
c0f243bc6706: Pull complete
5ff1eaecba77: Pull complete
Digest: sha256:2adeae829bf27a3399a0e7db8ae38d5adb89bcaf1bbef378240bc0e6724e8344
Status: Downloaded newer image for ubuntu:19.04
 ---> c88ac1f841b7
Step 3/5 : LABEL maintainer=sathsara@mydomain.com
 ---> Running in 07f8ec89c8e8
Removing intermediate container 07f8ec89c8e8
 ---> 6d3ef4f6a516
Step 4/5 : ENV PUBLISHER=packt APP_DIR=/usr/local/app/bin
 ---> Running in 7be9dd3c7e84
Removing intermediate container 7be9dd3c7e84
 ---> 54402dbad487
Step 5/5 : CMD ["env"]
 ---> Running in 96ca64f2768d
Removing intermediate container 96ca64f2768d
 ---> bdfcfc9f722f
Successfully built bdfcfc9f722f
Successfully tagged env-arg:latest
 /docker $ 
```

Figure 2.5: Building the env-arg Docker image

Note that the **19.04** tag of the ubuntu image was used as the parent image. This is because you sent the **--build-arg flag** with the value of **TAG=19.04** during the build process.

7. Now, execute the **docker container run** command to start a new container from the Docker image that you built in the last step:

```
$ docker container run env-arg
```

As we can see from the output, the **PUBLISHER** environment variable is available with the value of **packt**, and the **APP_DIR** environment variable is available with the value of **/usr/local/app/bin**:

```
 /docker $ docker container run env-arg
PATH=/usr/local/sbin:/usr/local/bin:/usr/sbin:/usr/bin:/sbin:/bin
HOSTNAME=d0b5046097c7
PUBLISHER=packt
APP_DIR=/usr/local/app/bin
HOME=/root
 /docker $ █
```

Figure 2.6: Running the env-arg Docker container

In this exercise, we defined environment variables for a Docker image using the **ENV** directive. We also experienced how to use **ARG** directives to pass values during the Docker image build time. In the next section, we will be covering the **WORKDIR** directive, which can be used to define the current working directory of the Docker container.

THE WORKDIR DIRECTIVE

The **WORKDIR** directive is used to specify the current working directory of the Docker container. Any subsequent **ADD**, **CMD**, **COPY**, **ENTRYPOINT**, and **RUN** directives will be executed in this directory. The **WORKDIR** directive has the following format:

```
WORKDIR /path/to/workdir
```

If the specified directory does not exist, Docker will create this directory and make it the current working directory, which means this directive executes both **mkdir** and **cd** commands implicitly.

There can be multiple **WORKDIR** directives in the **Dockerfile**. If a relative path is provided in a subsequent **WORKDIR** directive, that will be relative to the working directory set by the previous **WORKDIR** directive:

```
WORKDIR /one
WORKDIR two
WORKDIR three
RUN pwd
```

In the preceding example, we are using the **pwd** command at the end of the **Dockerfile** to print the current working directory. The output of the **pwd** command will be **/one/two/three**.

In the next section, we will discuss the **COPY** directive that is used to copy files from the local filesystem to the Docker image filesystem.

THE COPY DIRECTIVE

During the Docker image build process, we may need to copy files from our local filesystem to the Docker image filesystem. These files can be source code files (for example, JavaScript files), configuration files (for example, properties files), or artifacts (for example, JAR files). The **COPY** directive can be used to copy files and folders from the local filesystem to the Docker image during the build process. This directive takes two arguments. The first one is the source path from the local filesystem, and the second one is the destination path on the image filesystem:

```
COPY <source> <destination>
```

In the following example, we are using the **COPY** directive to copy the **index.html** file from the local filesystem to the **/var/www/html/** directory of the Docker image:

```
COPY index.html /var/www/html/index.html
```

Wildcards can also be specified to copy all files that match the given pattern. The following example will copy all files with the **.html** extension from the current directory to the **/var/www/html/** directory of the Docker image:

```
COPY *.html /var/www/html/
```

In addition to copying files, the **--chown** flag can be used with the **COPY** directive to specify the user and group ownership of the files:

```
COPY --chown=myuser:mygroup *.html /var/www/html/
```

In the preceding example, in addition to copying all the HTML files from the current directory to the **/var/www/html/** directory, the **--chown** flag is used to set file ownership, with the user as **myuser** and group as **mygroup**:

> **NOTE**
>
> The **--chown** flag is only supported from Docker version 17.09 and above. For Docker versions below 17.09, you need to run the **chown** command after the **COPY** command to change file ownership.

In the next section, we will look at the **ADD** directive.

THE ADD DIRECTIVE

The **ADD** directive is also similar to the **COPY** directive, and has the following format:

```
ADD <source> <destination>
```

However, in addition to the functionality provided by the **COPY** directive, the **ADD** directive also allows us to use a URL as the **<source>** parameter:

```
ADD http://sample.com/test.txt /tmp/test.txt
```

In the preceding example, the **ADD** directive will download the **test.txt** file from **http://sample.com** and copy the file to the **/tmp** directory of the Docker image filesystem.

Another feature of the **ADD** directive is automatically extracting the compressed files. If we add a compressed file (gzip, bzip2, tar, and so on) to the **<source>** parameter, the **ADD** directive will extract the archive and copy the content to the image filesystem.

Imagine we have a compressed file named **html.tar.gz** that contains **index. html** and **contact.html** files. The following command will extract the **html. tar.gz** file and copy the **index.html** and **contact.html** files to the **/var/ www/html** directory:

```
ADD html.tar.gz /var/www/html
```

Since the **COPY** and **ADD** directives provide almost the same functionality, it is recommended to always use the **COPY** directive unless you need the additional functionality (add from a URL or extract a compressed file) provided by the **ADD** directive. This is because the **ADD** directive provides additional functionality that can behave unpredictably if used incorrectly (for example, copying files when you want to extract, or extracting files when you want to copy).

In the next exercise, we are going to use the **WORKDIR, COPY**, and **ADD** directives to copy files into the Docker image.

EXERCISE 2.04: USING THE WORKDIR, COPY, AND ADD DIRECTIVES IN THE DOCKERFILE

In this exercise, you will deploy your custom HTML file to the Apache web server. You will use Ubuntu as the base image and install Apache on top of it. Then, you will copy your custom index.html file to the Docker image and download the Docker logo (from the https://www.docker.com website) to be used with the custom index.html file:

1. Create a new directory named **workdir-copy-add-exercise** using the **mkdir** command:

```
mkdir workdir-copy-add-exercise
```

2. Navigate to the newly created **workdir-copy-add-exercise** directory:

```
cd workdir-copy-add-exercise
```

3. Within the **workdir-copy-add-exercise** directory, create a file named **index.html**. This file will be copied to the Docker image during build time:

```
touch index.html
```

4. Now, open **index.html** using your favorite text editor:

```
vim index.html
```

5. Add the following content to the **index.html** file, save it, and exit from **index.html**:

```
<html>
  <body>
    <h1>Welcome to The Docker Workshop</h1>
    <img src="logo.png" height="350" width="500"/>
  </body>
</html>
```

This HTML file will output **Welcome to The Docker Workshop** as the header of the page and **logo.png** (which we will download during the Docker image build process) as an image. You have defined the size of the **logo.png** image as a height of **350** and a width of **500**.

6. Within the **workdir-copy-add-exercise** directory, create a file named **Dockerfile**:

```
touch Dockerfile
```

7. Now, open the **Dockerfile** using your favorite text editor:

```
vim Dockerfile
```

8. Add the following content to the **Dockerfile**, save it, and exit from the **Dockerfile**:

```
# WORKDIR, COPY and ADD example
FROM ubuntu:latest
RUN apt-get update && apt-get install apache2 -y
WORKDIR /var/www/html/
COPY index.html .
ADD https://www.docker.com/sites/default/files/d8/2019-07/
  Moby-logo.png ./logo.png
CMD ["ls"]
```

This **Dockerfile** first defines the ubuntu image as the parent image. The next line is the **RUN** directive, which will execute **apt-get update** to update the package list, and **apt-get install apache2 -y** to install the Apache HTTP server. Then, you will set **/var/www/html/** as the working directory. Next, copy the **index.html** file that we created in *step 3* to the Docker image. Then, use the **ADD** directive to download the Docker logo from https://www.docker.com/sites/default/files/d8/2019-07/Moby-logo.png to the Docker image. The final step is to use the **ls** command to print the content of the **/var/www/html/** directory.

9. Now, build the Docker image with the tag of **workdir-copy-add**:

```
$ docker image build -t workdir-copy-add .
```

You will observe that the image is successfully built and tagged as **latest** since we did not explicitly tag our image:

```
Enabling module env.
Enabling module mime.
Enabling module negotiation.
Enabling module setenvif.
Enabling module filter.
Enabling module deflate.
Enabling module status.
Enabling module reqtimeout.
Enabling conf charset.
Enabling conf localized-error-pages.
Enabling conf other-vhosts-access-log.
Enabling conf security.
Enabling conf serve-cgi-bin.
Enabling site 000-default.
invoke-rc.d: could not determine current runlevel
invoke-rc.d: policy-rc.d denied execution of start.
Processing triggers for libc-bin (2.27-3ubuntu1.2) ...
Removing intermediate container cfd61968bf3a
 ---> 180c2fdf5fbe
Step 3/6 : WORKDIR /var/www/html/
 ---> Running in 6f15d517d3c9
Removing intermediate container 6f15d517d3c9
 ---> 43e449aeccd5
Step 4/6 : COPY index.html .
 ---> 67b170e5f319
Step 5/6 : ADD https://www.docker.com/sites/default/files/d8/2019-07/Moby-logo.png ./logo.png
Downloading [==================================================>]  22.77kB/22.77kB


 ---> 923d013113e6
Step 6/6 : CMD ["ls"]
 ---> Running in 6bcbdbcd0ca2
Removing intermediate container 6bcbdbcd0ca2
 ---> 8ffe19a249bc
Successfully built 8ffe19a249bc
Successfully tagged workdir-copy-add:latest
 /docker $ ▮
```

Figure 2.7: Building the Docker image using WORKDIR, COPY, and ADD directives

10. Execute the **docker container run** command to start a new container from the Docker image that you built in the previous step:

```
$ docker container run workdir-copy-add
```

As we can see from the output, both the **index.html** and **logo.png** files are available in the **/var/www/html/** directory:

```
index.html
logo.png
```

In this exercise, we observed how the **WORKDIR**, **ADD**, and **COPY** directives work with Docker. In the next section, we are going to discuss the **USER** directive.

THE USER DIRECTIVE

Docker will use the root user as the default user of a Docker container. We can use the **USER** directive to change this default behavior and specify a non-root user as the default user of a Docker container. This is a great way to improve security by running the Docker container as a non-privileged user. The username specified with the **USER** directive will be used to run all subsequent **RUN**, **CMD**, and **ENTRYPOINT** directives in the **Dockerfile**.

The **USER** directive takes the following format:

```
USER <user>
```

In addition to the username, we can also specify the optional group name to run the Docker container:

```
USER <user>:<group>
```

We need to make sure that the **<user>** and **<group>** values are valid user and group names. Otherwise, the Docker daemon will throw an error while trying to run the container:

```
docker: Error response from daemon: unable to find user my_user:
        no matching entries in passwd file.
```

Now, let's try our hands at using the **USER** directive in the next exercise.

EXERCISE 2.05: USING USER DIRECTIVE IN THE DOCKERFILE

Your manager has asked you to create a Docker image to run the Apache web server. He has specifically requested that you use a non-root user while running the Docker container due to security reasons. In this exercise, you will use the **USER** directive in the **Dockerfile** to set the default user. You will be installing the Apache web server and changing the user to **www-data**. Finally, you will execute the **whoami** command to verify the current user by printing the username:

> **NOTE**
>
> The **www-data** user is the default user for the Apache web server on Ubuntu.

1. Create a new directory named **user-exercise** for this exercise:

```
mkdir user-exercise
```

2. Navigate to the newly created **user-exercise** directory:

```
cd user-exercise
```

3. Within the **user-exercise** directory, create a file named **Dockerfile**:

```
touch Dockerfile
```

4. Now, open the **Dockerfile** using your favorite text editor:

```
vim Dockerfile
```

5. Add the following content to the **Dockerfile**, save it, and exit from the **Dockerfile**:

```
# USER example
FROM ubuntu
RUN apt-get update && apt-get install apache2 -y
USER www-data
CMD ["whoami"]
```

This **Dockerfile** first defines the Ubuntu image as the parent image. The next line is the **RUN** directive, which will execute **apt-get update** to update the package list, and **apt-get install apache2 -y** to install the Apache HTTP server. Next, you use the **USER** directive to change the current user to the **www-data** user. Finally, you have the **CMD** directive, which executes the **whoami** command, which will print the username of the current user.

6. Build the Docker image:

```
$ docker image build -t user .
```

The output should be as follows:

```
Sending build context to Docker daemon  3.072kB
Step 1/4 : FROM ubuntu:18.04
 ---> 6526a1858e5d
Step 2/4 : RUN apt-get update && apt-get install apache2 -y
 ---> Using cache
 ---> 180c2fdf5fbe
Step 3/4 : USER www-data
 ---> Running in 54158293b27b
Removing intermediate container 54158293b27b
 ---> 9224f5597ea6
Step 4/4 : CMD ["whoami"]
 ---> Running in 8419e37d38cd
Removing intermediate container 8419e37d38cd
 ---> 1139e23a1178
Successfully built 1139e23a1178
Successfully tagged user:latest
 /docker $ █
```

Figure 2.8: Building the user Docker image

7. Now, execute the **docker container** run command to start a new container from the Docker image that we built in the previous step:

```
$ docker container run user
```

As you can see from the following output, **www-data** is the current user associated with the Docker container:

```
www-data
```

In this exercise, we implemented the **USER** directive in the **Dockerfile** to set the **www-data** user as the default user of the Docker image.

In the next section, we will discuss the **VOLUME** directive.

THE VOLUME DIRECTIVE

In Docker, the data (for example, files, executables) generated and used by Docker containers will be stored within the container filesystem. When we delete the container, all the data will be lost. To overcome this issue, Docker came up with the concept of volumes. Volumes are used to persist the data and share the data between containers. We can use the **VOLUME** directive within the `Dockerfile` to create Docker volumes. Once a **VOLUME** is created in the Docker container, a mapping directory will be created in the underlying host machine. All file changes to the volume mount of the Docker container will be copied to the mapped directory of the host machine.

The **VOLUME** directive generally takes a JSON array as the parameter:

```
VOLUME ["/path/to/volume"]
```

Or, we can specify a plain string with multiple paths:

```
VOLUME /path/to/volume1 /path/to/volume2
```

We can use the `docker container inspect <container>` command to view the volumes available in a container. The output JSON of the docker container inspect command will print the volume information similar to the following:

```
"Mounts": [
    {
        "Type": "volume",
        "Name": "77db32d66407a554bd0dbdf3950671b658b6233c509ea
ed9f5c2a589fea268fe",
        "Source": "/var/lib/docker/volumes/77db32d66407a554bd0
dbdf3950671b658b6233c509eaed9f5c2a589fea268fe/_data",
        "Destination": "/path/to/volume",
        "Driver": "local",
        "Mode": "",
        "RW": true,
        "Propagation": ""
    }
],
```

As per the preceding output, there is a unique name given to the volume by Docker. Also, the source and destination paths of the volume are mentioned in the output.

Additionally, we can execute the **docker volume inspect <volume>** command to display detailed information pertaining to a volume:

```
[
    {
        "CreatedAt": "2019-12-28T12:52:52+05:30",
        "Driver": "local",
        "Labels": null,
        "Mountpoint": "/var/lib/docker/volumes/77db32d66407a554
bd0dbdf3950671b658b6233c509eaed9f5c2a589fea268fe/_data",
        "Name": "77db32d66407a554bd0dbdf3950671b658b6233c509eae
d9f5c2a589fea268fe",
        "Options": null,
        "Scope": "local"
    }
]
```

This is also similar to the previous output, with the same unique name and the mount path of the volume.

In the next exercise, we will learn how to use the **VOLUME** directive in a **Dockerfile**.

EXERCISE 2.06: USING VOLUME DIRECTIVE IN THE DOCKERFILE

In this exercise, you will be setting a Docker container to run the Apache web server. However, you do not want to lose the Apache log files in case of a Docker container failure. As a solution, you have decided to persist in the log files by mounting the Apache log path to the underlying Docker host:

1. Create a new directory named **volume-exercise**:

```
mkdir volume-exercise
```

2. Navigate to the newly created **volume-exercise** directory:

```
cd volume-exercise
```

3. Within the **volume-exercise** directory, create a file named **Dockerfile**:

```
touch Dockerfile
```

4. Now, open the **Dockerfile** using your favorite text editor:

```
vim Dockerfile
```

5. Add the following content to the **Dockerfile**, save it, and exit from the **Dockerfile**:

```
# VOLUME example
FROM ubuntu
RUN apt-get update && apt-get install apache2 -y
VOLUME ["/var/log/apache2"]
```

This **Dockerfile** started by defining the Ubuntu image as the parent image. Next, you will execute the **apt-get update** command to update the package list, and the **apt-get install apache2 -y** command to install the Apache web server. Finally, use the **VOLUME** directive to set up a mount point to the **/var/log/apache2** directory.

6. Now, build the Docker image:

```
$ docker image build -t volume .
```

The output should be as follows:

```
Sending build context to Docker daemon  3.072kB
Step 1/3 : FROM ubuntu:18.04
 ---> 6526a1858e5d
Step 2/3 : RUN apt-get update && apt-get install apache2 -y
 ---> Using cache
 ---> 180c2fdf5fbe
Step 3/3 : VOLUME ["/var/log/apache2"]
 ---> Running in bc4cd3233b65
Removing intermediate container bc4cd3233b65
 ---> 48d59c0de988
Successfully built 48d59c0de988
Successfully tagged volume:latest
 /docker $ █
```

Figure 2.9: Building the volume Docker image

7. Execute the docker container run command to start a new container from the Docker image that you built in the previous step. Note that you are using the **--interactive** and **--tty** flags to open an interactive bash session so that you can execute commands from the bash shell of the Docker container. You have also used the **--name** flag to define the container name as **volume-container**:

```
$ docker container run --interactive --tty --name volume-container
volume /bin/bash
```

Your bash shell will be opened as follows:

```
root@bc61d46de960: /#
```

8. From the Docker container command line, change directory to the **/var/log/apache2/** directory:

```
# cd /var/log/apache2/
```

This will produce the following output:

```
root@bc61d46de960: /var/log/apache2#
```

9. Now, list the available files in the directory:

```
# ls -l
```

The output should be as follows:

```
root@f30f5dbf8183:/var/log/apache2# ls -l
total 0
-rw-r----- 1 root adm 0 Aug 30 04:19 access.log
-rw-r----- 1 root adm 0 Aug 30 04:19 error.log
-rw-r----- 1 root adm 0 Aug 30 04:19 other_vhosts_access.log
root@f30f5dbf8183:/var/log/apache2#
```

Figure 2.10: Listing files of the /var/log/apache2 directory

These are the log files created by Apache while running the process. The same files should be available once you check the host mount of this volume.

10. Now, exit the container to check the host filesystem:

```
# exit
```

11. Inspect **volume-container** to view the mount information:

```
$ docker container inspect volume-container
```

Under the "**Mounts**" key, you can see the information relating to the mount:

```
"Mounts": [
    {
        "Type": "volume",
        "Name": "354d188e0761d82e1e7d9f3d5c6ee644782b7150f51cead8f140556e5d334bd5",
        "Source": "/var/lib/docker/volumes/354d188e0761d82e1e7d9f3d5c6ee644782b7150f51cead8f140556e5d334bd5/_data",
        "Destination": "/var/log/apache2",
        "Driver": "local",
        "Mode": "",
        "RW": true,
        "Propagation": ""
    }
],
```

Figure 2.11: Inspecting the Docker container

12. Inspect the volume with the **docker volume inspect <volume_name>** command. **<volume_name>** can be identified by the **Name** field of the preceding output:

```
$ docker volume inspect
354d188e0761d82e1e7d9f3d5c6ee644782b7150f51cead8f140556e5d334bd5
```

You should get the output similar to the following:

```
[
    {
        "CreatedAt": "2020-08-30T09:54:29+05:30",
        "Driver": "local",
        "Labels": null,
        "Mountpoint": "/var/lib/docker/volumes/354d188e0761d82e1e7d9f3d5c6ee644782b7150f51cead8f140556e5d334bd5/_data",
        "Name": "354d188e0761d82e1e7d9f3d5c6ee644782b7150f51cead8f140556e5d334bd5",
        "Options": null,
        "Scope": "local"
    }
]
```

Figure 2.12: Inspecting the Docker volume

We can see that the container is mounted to the host path of **"/var/lib/ docker/volumes/354d188e0761d82e1e7d9f3d5c6ee644782b 7150f51cead8f140556e5d334bd5/_data"**, which is defined as the **Mountpoint** field in the preceding output.

13. List the files available in the host file path. The host file path can be identified with the **"Mountpoint"** field of the preceding output:

```
$ sudo ls -l /var/lib/docker/
volumes/354d188e0761d82e1e7d9f3d5c6ee644782b7150f51cead8f14
0556e5d334bd5/_data
```

In the following output, you can see that the log files in the **/var/log/ apache2** directory of the container are mounted to the host:

```
/docker $ sudo ls -l /var/lib/docker/volumes/354d188e0761d82e1e7d9f3d5c6ee644782b7150f51cead8f140556e5d334bd5/_data
total 0
-rw-r----- 1 root adm 0 Aug 30 09:49 access.log
-rw-r----- 1 root adm 0 Aug 30 09:49 error.log
-rw-r----- 1 root adm 0 Aug 30 09:49 other_vhosts_access.log
/docker $ 
```

Figure 2.13: Listing files in the mount point directory

In this exercise, we observed how to mount the log path of the Apache web server to the host filesystem using the **VOLUME** directive. In the next section, we will learn about the **EXPOSE** directive.

THE EXPOSE DIRECTIVE

The **EXPOSE** directive is used to inform Docker that the container is listening on the specified ports at runtime. We can use the **EXPOSE** directive to expose ports through either TCP or UDP protocols. The **EXPOSE** directive has the following format:

```
EXPOSE <port>
```

However, the ports exposed with the **EXPOSE** directive will only be accessible from within the other Docker containers. To expose these ports outside the Docker container, we can publish the ports with the **-p** flag with the **docker container run** command:

```
docker container run -p <host_port>:<container_port> <image>
```

As an example, imagine that we have two containers. One is a NodeJS web app container that should be accessed from outside via port **80**. The second one is the MySQL container, which should be accessed from the node app container via port **3306**. In this scenario, we have to expose port **80** of the NodeJS app with the **EXPOSE** directive and use the **-p** flag with the **docker container run** command to expose it externally. However, for the MySQL container, we can only use the **EXPOSE** directive without the **-p** flag when running the container, as **3306** should only be accessible from the node app container.

So, in summary, the following statements define this directive:

- If we specify both the **EXPOSE** directive and **-p** flag, exposed ports will be accessible from other containers as well as externally.

- If we specify **EXPOSE** without the **-p** flag, exposed ports will only be accessible from other containers, but not externally.

You will learn about the **HEALTHCHECK** directive in the next section.

THE HEALTHCHECK DIRECTIVE

Health checks are used in Docker to check whether the containers are running healthily. For example, we can use health checks to make sure the application is running within the Docker container. Unless there is a health check specified, there is no way for Docker to say whether a container is healthy. This is very important if you are running Docker containers in production environments. The **HEALTHCHECK** directive has the following format:

```
HEALTHCHECK [OPTIONS] CMD command
```

There can be only one **HEALTHCHECK** directive in a **Dockerfile**. If there is more than one **HEALTHCHECK** directive, only the last one will take effect.

As an example, we can use the following directive to ensure that the container can receive traffic on the **http://localhost/** endpoint:

```
HEALTHCHECK CMD curl -f http://localhost/ || exit 1
```

The exit code at the end of the preceding command is used to specify the health status of the container. **0** and **1** are valid values for this field. 0 is used to denote a healthy container, and **1** is used to denote an unhealthy container.

In addition to the command, we can specify a few other parameters with the **HEALTHCHECK** directive, as follows:

- **--interval**: This specifies the period between each health check (the default is 30s).

- **--timeout**: If no success response is received within this period, the health check is considered failed (the default is 30s).

- **--start-period**: The duration to wait before running the first health check. This is used to give a startup time for the container (the default is 0s).

- **--retries**: The container will be considered unhealthy if the health check failed consecutively for the given number of retries (the default is 3).

In the following example, we have overridden the default values by providing our custom values with the **HEALTHCHECK** directive:

```
HEALTHCHECK --interval=1m --timeout=2s --start-period=2m --retries=3 \
    CMD curl -f http://localhost/ || exit 1
```

We can check the health status of a container with the **docker container list** command. This will list the health status under the **STATUS** column:

```
CONTAINER ID   IMAGE     COMMAND             CREATED
  STATUS                      PORTS           NAMES
d4e627acf6ec   sample    "apache2ctl -D FOREG..."   About a minute ago
  Up About a minute (healthy)   0.0.0.0:80->80/tcp   upbeat_banach
```

As soon as we start the container, the health status will be health: starting. Following the successful execution of the **HEALTHCHECK** command, the status will change to **healthy**.

In the next exercise, we are going to use the **EXPOSE** and **HEALTHCHECK** directives to create a Docker container with the Apache web server and define health checks for it.

EXERCISE 2.07: USING EXPOSE AND HEALTHCHECK DIRECTIVES IN THE DOCKERFILE

Your manager has asked you to dockerize the Apache web server to access the Apache home page from the web browser. Additionally, he has asked you to configure health checks to determine the health status of the Apache web server. In this exercise, you will use the **EXPOSE** and **HEALTHCHECK** directives to achieve this goal:

1. Create a new directory named **expose-healthcheck**:

```
mkdir expose-healthcheck
```

2. Navigate to the newly created **expose-healthcheck** directory:

```
cd expose-healthcheck
```

3. Within the **expose-healthcheck** directory, create a file named **Dockerfile**:

```
touch Dockerfile
```

4. Now, open the **Dockerfile** using your favorite text editor:

```
vim Dockerfile
```

5. Add the following content to the **Dockerfile**, save it, and exit from the **Dockerfile**:

```
# EXPOSE & HEALTHCHECK example
FROM ubuntu
RUN apt-get update && apt-get install apache2 curl -y
HEALTHCHECK CMD curl -f http://localhost/ || exit 1
EXPOSE 80
ENTRYPOINT ["apache2ctl", "-D", "FOREGROUND"]
```

This **Dockerfile** first defines the ubuntu image as the parent image. Next, we execute the **apt-get update** command to update the package list, and the **apt-get install apache2 curl -y** command to install the Apache web server and curl tool. **Curl** is required to execute the **HEALTHCHECK** command. Next, we define the **HEALTHCHECK** directive with curl to the **http://localhost/** endpoint. Then, we exposed port **80** of the Apache web server so that we can access the home page from our web browser. Finally, we start the Apache web server with the **ENTRYPOINT** directive.

6. Now, build the Docker image:

```
$ docker image build -t expose-healthcheck.
```

You should get the following output:

```
Enabling module filter.
Enabling module deflate.
Enabling module status.
Enabling module reqtimeout.
Enabling conf charset.
Enabling conf localized-error-pages.
Enabling conf other-vhosts-access-log.
Enabling conf security.
Enabling conf serve-cgi-bin.
Enabling site 000-default.
invoke-rc.d: could not determine current runlevel
invoke-rc.d: policy-rc.d denied execution of start.
Setting up curl (7.58.0-2ubuntu3.10) ...
Processing triggers for libc-bin (2.27-3ubuntu1.2) ...
Processing triggers for ca-certificates (20190110~18.04.1) ...
Updating certificates in /etc/ssl/certs...
0 added, 0 removed; done.
Running hooks in /etc/ca-certificates/update.d...
done.
Removing intermediate container 4309af357960
 ---> 55f7843eda20
Step 3/5 : HEALTHCHECK CMD curl -f http://localhost/ || exit 1
 ---> Running in f84e210e50dc
Removing intermediate container f84e210e50dc
 ---> 795a187362f3
Step 4/5 : EXPOSE 80
 ---> Running in ffa2e1fcda80
Removing intermediate container ffa2e1fcda80
 ---> a6717637a6c5
Step 5/5 : ENTRYPOINT ["apache2ctl", "-D", "FOREGROUND"]
 ---> Running in 998bc8a9e983
Removing intermediate container 998bc8a9e983
 ---> 17e5694e7e9e
Successfully built 17e5694e7e9e
Successfully tagged expose-healthcheck:latest
 /docker $ ▮
```

Figure 2.14: Building the expose-healthcheck Docker image

7. Execute the docker container run command to start a new container from the Docker image that you built in the previous step. Note that you are using the **-p** flag to redirect port **80** of the host to port **80** of the container. Additionally, you have used the **--name** flag to specify the container name as **expose-healthcheck-container**, and the **-d** flag to run the container in detached mode (this runs the container in the background):

```
$ docker container run -p 80:80 --name expose-healthcheck-container
-d expose-healthcheck
```

8. List the running containers with the **docker container list** command:

```
$ docker container list
```

In the following output, you can see that the **STATUS** of the **expose-healthcheck-container** is healthy:

```
/docker $ docker container list
CONTAINER ID        IMAGE             COMMAND            CREATED         STATUS                       PORTS
  NAMES
3ade927441b7        expose-healthcheck "apache2ctl -D FOREG..." 10 seconds ago  Up 9 seconds (health: starting)  0.0.0.0:80->80/
tcp    expose-healthcheck-container
/docker $ ▇
```

Figure 2.15: List of running containers

9. Now, you should be able to view the Apache home page. Go to the **http://127.0.0.1** endpoint from your favorite web browser:

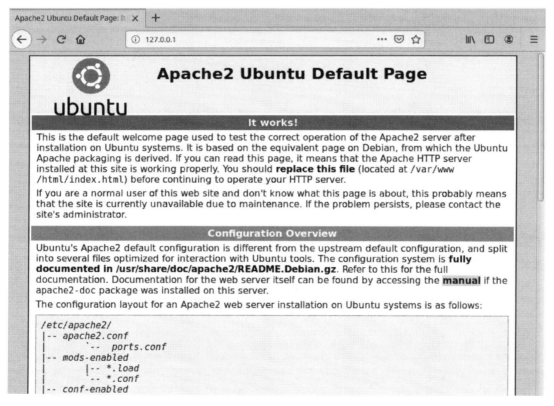

Figure 2.16: Apache home page

10. Now, clean up the container. First, stop the Docker container by using the **docker container stop** command:

```
$ docker container stop expose-healthcheck-container
```

11. Finally, remove the Docker container with the **docker container rm** command:

```
$ docker container rm expose-healthcheck-container
```

In this exercise, you utilized the **EXPOSE** directive to expose an Apache web server as a Docker container and used the **HEALTHCHECK** directive to define a health check to verify the healthy status of the Docker container.

In the next section, we will learn about the **ONBUILD** directive.

THE ONBUILD DIRECTIVE

The **ONBUILD** directive is used in the **Dockerfile** to create a reusable Docker image that will be used as the base for another Docker image. As an example, we can create a Docker image that contains all the prerequisites, such as dependencies and configurations, in order to run an application. Then, we can use this 'prerequisite' image as the parent image to run the application.

While creating the prerequisite image, we can use the **ONBUILD** directive, which will include the instructions that should only be executed when this image is used as the parent image in another **Dockerfile**. **ONBUILD** instructions will not be executed while building the **Dockerfile** that contains the **ONBUILD** directive, but only when building the child image.

The **ONBUILD** directive takes the following format:

```
ONBUILD <instruction>
```

As an example, consider that we have the following **ONBUILD** instruction in the **Dockerfile** of our custom base image:

```
ONBUILD ENTRYPOINT ["echo","Running ONBUILD directive"]
```

The **"Running ONBUILD directive"** value will not be printed if we create a Docker container from our custom base image. However, the **"Running ONBUILD directive"** value will be printed if we use our custom base image as the base for our new child Docker image.

We can use the **docker image inspect** command for the parent image to list the OnBuild triggers listed for the image:

```
$ docker image inspect <parent-image>
```

The command will return output similar to the following:

```
...
"OnBuild": [
    "CMD [\"echo\",\"Running ONBUILD directive\"]"
]
...
```

In the next exercise, we will be using the **ONBUILD** directive to define a Docker image to deploy the HTML files.

EXERCISE 2.08: USING ONBUILD DIRECTIVE IN THE DOCKERFILE

You have been asked by your manager to create a Docker image that is capable of running any HTML files provided by the software development team. In this exercise, you will build a parent image with the Apache web server and use the **ONBUILD** directive to copy the HTML files. The software development team can use this Docker image as the parent image to deploy and test any HTML files created by them:

1. Create a new directory named **onbuild-parent**:

   ```
   mkdir onbuild-parent
   ```

2. Navigate to the newly created **onbuild-parent** directory:

   ```
   cd onbuild-parent
   ```

3. Within the **onbuild-parent** directory, create a file named **Dockerfile**:

   ```
   touch Dockerfile
   ```

4. Now, open the **Dockerfile** using your favorite text editor:

   ```
   vim Dockerfile
   ```

5. Add the following content to the **Dockerfile**, save it, and exit from the **Dockerfile**:

   ```
   # ONBUILD example
   FROM ubuntu
   RUN apt-get update && apt-get install apache2 -y
   ONBUILD COPY *.html /var/www/html
   EXPOSE 80
   ENTRYPOINT ["apache2ctl", "-D", "FOREGROUND"]
   ```

This **Dockerfile** first defines the ubuntu image as the parent image. It then executes the **apt-get update** command to update the package list, and the **apt-get install apache2 -y** command to install the Apache web server. The **ONBUILD** directive is used to provide a trigger to copy all HTML files to the **/var/www/html** directory. The **EXPOSE** directive is used to expose port **80** of the container and **ENTRYPOINT** to start the Apache web server using the **apache2ctl** command.

6. Now, build the Docker image:

```
$ docker image build -t onbuild-parent .
```

The output should be as follows:

```
Sending build context to Docker daemon  3.072kB
Step 1/5 : FROM ubuntu:18.04
 ---> 6526a1858e5d
Step 2/5 : RUN apt-get update && apt-get install apache2 -y
 ---> Using cache
 ---> 180c2fdf5fbe
Step 3/5 : ONBUILD COPY *.html /var/www/html
 ---> Running in d1fef12fcfd6
Removing intermediate container d1fef12fcfd6
 ---> 64e1564a16d9
Step 4/5 : EXPOSE 80
 ---> Running in d670d0aabbb9
Removing intermediate container d670d0aabbb9
 ---> f3d8920e6c66
Step 5/5 : ENTRYPOINT ["apache2ctl", "-D", "FOREGROUND"]
 ---> Running in fe9d8fb513c3
Removing intermediate container fe9d8fb513c3
 ---> a3e6f2a2c363
Successfully built a3e6f2a2c363
Successfully tagged onbuild-parent:latest
 /docker $ █
```

Figure 2.17: Building the onbuild-parent Docker image

7. Execute the **docker container run** command to start a new container from the Docker image built in the previous step:

```
$ docker container run -p 80:80 --name onbuild-parent-container -d
onbuild-parent
```

In the preceding command, you have started the Docker container in detached mode while exposing port **80** of the container.

8. Now, you should be able to view the Apache home page. Go to the **http://127.0.0.1** endpoint from your favorite web browser. Note that the default Apache home page is visible:

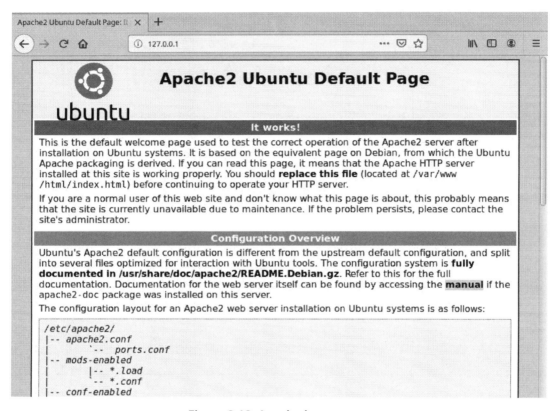

Figure 2.18: Apache home page

9. Now, clean up the container. Stop the Docker container by using the **docker container stop** command:

```
$ docker container stop onbuild-parent-container
```

10. Remove the Docker container with the **docker container rm** command:

```
$ docker container rm onbuild-parent-container
```

11. Now, create another Docker image using **onbuild-parent-container** as the parent image to deploy a custom HTML home page. First, change the directory back to the previous directory:

```
cd ..
```

12. Create a new directory named **onbuild-child** for this exercise:

```
mkdir onbuild-child
```

13. Navigate to the newly created **onbuild-child** directory:

```
cd onbuild-child
```

14. Within the **onbuild-child** directory, create a file named **index.html**. This file will be copied to the Docker image by the **ONBUILD** command during build time:

```
touch index.html
```

15. Now, open the **index.html** file using your favorite text editor:

```
vim index.html
```

16. Add the following content to the **index.html** file, save it, and exit from the **index.html** file:

```
<html>
  <body>
    <h1>Learning Docker ONBUILD directive</h1>
  </body>
</html>
```

This is a simple HTML file that will output the **Learning Docker ONBUILD** directive as the header of the page.

17. Within the **onbuild-child** directory, create a file named **Dockerfile**:

```
touch Dockerfile
```

18. Now, open the **Dockerfile** using your favorite text editor:

```
vim Dockerfile
```

19. Add the following content to the **Dockerfile**, save it, and exit from the **Dockerfile**:

```
# ONBUILD example
FROM onbuild-parent
```

This **Dockerfile** has only one directive. This will use the **FROM** directive to utilize the **onbuild-parent** Docker image that you created previously as the parent image.

20. Now, build the Docker image:

```
$ docker image build -t onbuild-child .

        Sending build context to Docker daemon  4.096kB
        Step 1/1 : FROM onbuild-parent
        # Executing 1 build trigger
         ---> 5e737cae6aa9
        Successfully built 5e737cae6aa9
        Successfully tagged onbuild-child:latest
         /docker $
```

Figure 2.19: Building the onbuild-child Docker image

21. Execute the **docker container run** command to start a new container from the Docker image that you built in the previous step:

```
$ docker container run -p 80:80 --name onbuild-child-container -d
onbuild-child
```

In this command, you have started the Docker container from the **onbuild-child** Docker image while exposing port **80** of the container.

22. You should be able to view the Apache home page. Go to the **http://127.0.0.1** endpoint from your favorite web browser:

Figure 2.20: Customized home page of the Apache web server

23. Now, clean up the container. First, stop the Docker container by using the **docker container stop** command:

```
$ docker container stop onbuild-child-container
```

24. Finally, remove the Docker container with the **docker container rm** command:

```
$ docker container rm onbuild-child-container
```

In this exercise, we observed how we can use the **ONBUILD** directive to create a reusable Docker image that is capable of running any HTML file provided to it. We created the reusable Docker image named **onbuild-parent** with the Apache web server, with port **80** exposed. This **Dockerfile** contains the **ONBUILD** directive to copy the HTML files in the context of the Docker image. Then, we created the second Docker image named **onbuild-child**, using **onbuild-parent** as the base image, that provided a simple HTML file to be deployed to the Apache web server.

Now, let's test our knowledge that we have acquired in this chapter by dockerizing the given PHP application using the Apache web server in the following activity.

ACTIVITY 2.01: RUNNING A PHP APPLICATION ON A DOCKER CONTAINER

Imagine that you want to deploy a PHP welcome page that will greet visitors based on the date and time using the following logic. Your task is to dockerize the PHP application given here, using the Apache web server installed on an Ubuntu base image:

```php
<?php

$hourOfDay = date('H');

if($hourOfDay < 12) {
    $message = "Good Morning";
} elseif($hourOfDay > 11 && $hourOfDay < 18) {
    $message = "Good Afternoon";
} elseif($hourOfDay > 17){
    $message = "Good Evening";
}

echo $message;

?>
```

This is a simple PHP file that will greet the user based on the following logic:

Time Between (Hour)	Message
0 to 11	Good Morning
12 to 17	Good Afternoon
18 to 23	Good Evening

Figure 2.21: Logic of PHP application

Execute the following steps to complete this activity:

1. Create a folder to store the activity files.

2. Create a **welcome.php** file with the code provided previously.

3. Create a **Dockerfile** and set up the application with PHP and Apache2 on an Ubuntu base image.

4. Build and run the Docker image.

5. Once completed, stop and remove the Docker container.

> **NOTE**
>
> The solution for this activity can be found on page 652.

SUMMARY

In this chapter, we discussed how we can use a **Dockerfile** to create our own custom Docker images. First, we discussed what is a **Dockerfile** and the syntax of a **Dockerfile**. We then discussed some common Docker directives, including the **FROM, LABEL, RUN, CMD,** and **ENTRYPOINT** directives. Then, we created our first **Dockerfile** with the common directives that we learned.

In the next section, we focused on building Docker images. We discussed multiple areas in depth regarding Docker images, including the layered filesystem of Docker images, the context in Docker builds, and the use of the cache during the Docker build process. Then, we discussed more advanced **Dockerfile** directives, including the **ENV, ARG, WORKDIR, COPY, ADD, USER, VOLUME, EXPOSE, HEALTHCHECK,** and **ONBUILD** directives.

In the next chapter, we will discuss what a Docker registry is, look at private and public Docker registries, and learn how we can publish Docker images to Docker registries.

3

MANAGING YOUR DOCKER IMAGES

OVERVIEW

In this chapter, we will look into Docker layers and analyze how caching can help to speed up an image build. We will also deep dive into Docker images and set up Docker registries to increase the reusability of the images.

By the end of this chapter, you will be able to demonstrate how Docker uses layers to build images and how image building can be sped up with caching. You will work with image tags and set up a tagging policy for Docker images. The chapter will enable you to utilize Docker Hub for your projects and differentiate between public and private registries. It will also help you to set up your own Docker Registry when working on your projects.

INTRODUCTION

Our previous chapters have done a lot of work already with Docker images. As you've seen, we've been able to take existing images, provided to the general public in Docker Hub, and have then been able to run them or reuse them after building on top of them for our purposes. The image itself helps us streamline our processes and reduce the work we need to do.

In this chapter, we are going to take a more in-depth look at images and how to work with them on your system. We'll learn how images can be better organized and tagged, understand how different layers of images work, and set up registries that are both public and private to further reuse the images we have created.

Docker images are perfect for application development as well. The image itself is a self-contained version of the application, which includes everything it needs in order to be run. This empowers developers to build an image on their local machine and deploy it on a development or test environment to ensure it works well with the rest of the application. If all goes well, they can then push the same image as a release to the production environment for users to then consume. We need to also be consistent when using our images, especially when we start to work within a larger group of developers.

This chapter will also help you set up policies to have consistent tagging for your services to help limit issues and make sure you can track down or roll back when issues arise. Understanding how to distribute images for consumption and collaboration is also something we will discuss further in the chapter. So, without further delay, let's get started with the chapter and understand what layers and caching in Docker are.

DOCKER LAYERS AND CACHING

A registry is a way to store and distribute your Docker images. When you pull a Docker image from a registry, you might have noticed that the image is pulled in pieces and not as a single image. The same thing happens when you build an image on your system.

This is because Docker images consist of layers. When you create a new image using a **Dockerfile**, it will create more layers on top of the existing image you've built from. Each command you specify in the **Dockerfile** will create a new layer, with each containing all of the filesystem changes that occur before the command was performed and then after. When you run the image as a container from a **Dockerfile**, you're creating readable and writable layers on top of an existing group of read-only layers. This writable layer is known as the **container layer**.

As you'll see in the following exercises, when you build a container from a **Dockerfile**, the output presented shows each command run in the **Dockerfile**. It also shows the layers that are created by running each command, which is represented by a randomly generated ID. Once the image has completed building, you can then view the layers created during the build process using the **docker history** command, including the image name or ID.

> **NOTE**
>
> When setting up your build environment and as you move further along in the development process, remember that the more layers you have, the larger your image will be. So, this extra storage and space can be expensive in both build times and the amount of disk space used in your development and production environments.

When building an image from a **Dockerfile**, layers are created when the **RUN**, **ADD**, and **COPY** commands are used. All other commands in the **Dockerfile** create intermediate layers. These intermediate layers are 0 B in size; therefore, they don't increase the size of the Docker image.

When building our Docker images, we can use the **docker history** command and the image name or ID to see the layers used to create the image. The output will provide details on commands used to generate the layer as well as the size of the layer:

```
docker history <image_name|image_id>
```

The **docker image inspect** command is useful in providing further details on where the layers of our images are located:

```
docker image inspect <image_id>
```

Later in this part of the chapter, when we look at creating our base images, we will use the **docker image** command, which is used in conjunction with a TAR file version of the image we are creating. If we are able to access a running container or virtual machine, we will be able to take a copy of the running system and place it in a TAR archive. The output of the archive is then piped out to the **docker import** command as demonstrated here:

```
cat <image_tar_file_name> | docker import - <new_image_name>
```

The next exercise will give you some hands-on experience of what we have learned so far and how to work with Docker image layers.

> **NOTE**
>
> Please use **touch** command to create files and **vim** command to work on the file using vim editor.

EXERCISE 3.01: WORKING WITH DOCKER IMAGE LAYERS

In this exercise, you will work with some basic **Dockerfiles** to see how Docker uses layers to build images. You will start by creating a **Dockerfile** and building a new image. You will then rebuild the image to see the advantage of using caching and how the build time is reduced due to its use:

1. Create a new file called **Dockerfile** with your favorite text editor and add in the following details:

```
FROM alpine

RUN apk update
RUN apk add wget
```

2. Save the **Dockerfile** and then, from the command line, make sure you are in the same directory as the **Dockerfile** you have created. Use the **docker build** command to create the new image using the **-t** option to name it **basic-app**:

```
docker build -t basic-app .
```

If the image has built successfully, you should see an output similar to the following. We've highlighted each of the build steps in bold. Each step is built as an intermediate layer and if it completes successfully, it is then transferred to a read-only layer:

```
Sending build context to Docker daemon 4.096kB
Step 1/3 : FROM alpine
latest: Pulling from library/alpine
9d48c3bd43c5: Pull complete
Digest: sha256:72c42ed48c3a2db31b7dafe17d275b634664a
        708d901ec9fd57b1529280f01fb
```

```
Status: Downloaded newer image for alpine:latest
  ---> 961769676411
Step 2/3 : RUN apk update
  ---> Running in 4bf85f0c3676
fetch http://dl-cdn.alpinelinux.org/alpine/v3.10/main/
  x86_64/APKINDEX.tar.gz
fetch http://dl-cdn.alpinelinux.org/alpine/v3.10/community/
  x86_64/APKINDEX.tar.gz
v3.10.2-64-g631934be3a [http://dl-cdn.alpinelinux.org/alpine
  /v3.10/main]
v3.10.2-65-ge877e766a2 [http://dl-cdn.alpinelinux.org/alpine
  /v3.10/community]
OK: 10336 distinct packages available
Removing intermediate container 4bf85f0c3676
  ---> bcecd2429ac0
Step 3/3 : RUN apk add wget
  ---> Running in ce2a61d90f77
(1/1) Installing wget (1.20.3-r0)
Executing busybox-1.30.1-r2.trigger
OK: 6 MiB in 15 packages
Removing intermediate container ce2a61d90f77
  ---> a6d7e99283d9
Successfully built 0e86ae52098d
Successfully tagged basic-app:latest
```

3. Use the **docker history** command along with the image name of
    basic-app to see the different layers of the image:

```
docker history basic-app
```

The history gives you creation details, including the size of each layer:

```
IMAGE          CREATED             CREATED BY
                        SIZE
a6d7e99283d9   About a minute ago  /bin/sh -c apk add wget
                        476kB
bcecd2429ac0   About a minute ago  /bin/sh -c apk update
                        1.4MB
961769676411   5 weeks ago         /bin/sh -c #(nop)
CMD ["/bin/sh"]         0B
<missing>      5 weeks ago         /bin/sh -c #(nop)
ADD file:fe6407fb…      5.6MB
```

> **NOTE**
>
> The **docker history** command shows the layer of the original image used as part of the **Dockerfile FROM** command as **<missing>**. It is showing as **missing** in our output as it was created on a different system and then pulled onto your system.

4. Run the build again without making any changes:

```
docker build -t basic-app .
```

This will show you the build is done using the layers stored in the Docker image cache, thereby speeding up our build. Although this is only a small image, a much larger image would show a significant increase:

```
Sending build context to Docker daemon   4.096kB
Step 1/3 : FROM alpine
 ---> 961769676411
Step 2/3 : RUN apk update
 ---> Using cache
 ---> bcecd2429ac0
Step 3/3 : RUN apk add wget
 ---> Using cache
 ---> a6d7e99283d9
Successfully built a6d7e99283d9
Successfully tagged basic-app:latest
```

5. Say you forgot to install the **curl** package as part of your image creation. Add the following line to the **Dockerfile** from *Step 1*:

```
FROM alpine

RUN apk update
RUN apk add wget curl
```

6. Build the image again, and you'll now see the image created with a mix of cached layers and new layers that need to be created:

```
docker build -t basic-app .
```

Step three of the output has been highlighted to show the change made in our **Dockerfile** now being built:

```
Sending build context to Docker daemon 4.096kB
Step 1/3 : FROM alpine
 ---> 961769676411
Step 2/3 : RUN apk update
 ---> Using cache
 ---> cb8098d0c33d
Step 3/3 : RUN apk add wget curl
 ---> Running in b041735ff408
(1/5) Installing ca-certificates (20190108-r0)
(2/5) Installing nghttp2-libs (1.39.2-r0)
(3/5) Installing libcurl (7.66.0-r0)
(4/5) Installing curl (7.66.0-r0)
(5/5) Installing wget (1.20.3-r0)
Executing busybox-1.30.1-r2.trigger
Executing ca-certificates-20190108-r0.trigger
OK: 8 MiB in 19 packages
Removing intermediate container b041735ff408
 ---> c7918f4f95b9
Successfully built c7918f4f95b9
Successfully tagged basic-app:latest
```

7. Run the **docker images** command again:

```
docker images
```

You will now notice the image named and tagged as **<none>** to show we have now created a dangling image:

```
REPOSITORY     TAG       IMAGE ID       CREATED          SIZE
basic-app      latest    c7918f4f95b9   25 seconds ago   8.8MB
<none>         <none>    0e86ae52098d   2 minutes ago    7.48MB
Alpine         latest    961769676411   5 weeks ago      5.58MB
```

> **NOTE**
>
> Dangling images, represented by **<none>** in our image list, are caused when a layer has no relationship to any image on our system. These dangling images no longer serve a purpose and will consume disk space on your system. Our example dangling image is only 7.48 MB, which is small, but this could add up over time.

8. Run the **docker image inspect** command using the image ID to see the location of where the dangling images are located on our system:

```
docker image inspect 0e86ae52098d
```

The following output has been reduced from the actual output to only show the directories of the image:

```
...
  "Data": {
    "LowerDir": "/var/lib/docker/overlay2/
      41230f31bb6e89b6c3d619cafc309ff3d4ca169f9576fb003cd60fd4ff
      4c2f1f/diff:/var/lib/docker/overlay2/
      b8b90262d0a039db8d63c003d96347efcfcf57117081730b17585e163f
      04518a/diff",
    "MergedDir": "/var/lib/docker/overlay2/
      c7ea9cb56c5bf515a1b329ca9fcb2614f4b7f1caff30624e9f6a219049
      32f585/
      merged",
    "UpperDir": "/var/lib/docker/overlay2/
      c7ea9cb56c5bf515a1b329ca9fcb2614f4b7f1caff30624e9f6a21904
      932f585/diff",
    "WorkDir": "/var/lib/docker/overlay2/
      c7ea9cb56c5bf515a1b329ca9fcb2614f4b7f1caff30624e9f6a21904
      932f585/work"
  },
...
```

All of our images are located in the same location as the dangling image. As they are sharing the same directory, any dangling images would waste space on our system.

9. Run the **du** command from the command line to see the total disk space being used by our images:

```
du -sh /var/lib/docker/overlay2/
```

The command will return the total disk space used by your images

```
11M     /var/lib/docker/overlay2/
```

> **NOTE**
>
> If you're using Docker Desktop, maybe on a Mac, you'll notice that you won't be able to see the images as Docker is run on a virtual image on your system, even though the **docker image inspect** command will show the same location as we have above.

10. Run the **docker images** command again using the **-a** option:

```
docker images -a
```

It will also show the intermediate layers used when our image is being built:

REPOSITORY	TAG	IMAGE ID	CREATED	SIZE
basic-app	latest	c7918f4f95b9	25 seconds ago	8.8MB
<none>	<none>	0e86ae52098d	2 minutes ago	7.48MB
<none>	<none>	112a4b041305	11 minutes ago	7MB
Alpine	latest	961769676411	5 weeks ago	5.58MB

11. Run the **docker image prune** command to remove all the dangling images. You could remove all the dangling images one at a time using the **docker rmi** command using the image ID, but the **docker image prune** command is an easier way to do that:

```
docker image prune
```

You should get output like the following:

```
WARNING! This will remove all dangling images.
Are you sure you want to continue? [y/N] y
Deleted Images:
deleted: sha256:0dae3460f751d16f41954e0672b0c41295d46ee99d71
         d63e7c0c8521bd9e6493
deleted: sha256:d74fa92b37b74820ccccea601de61d45ccb3770255b9
         c7dd22edf16caabafc1c


Total reclaimed space: 476.4kB
```

12. Run the **docker images** command again:

```
docker images
```

You will see we no longer have the dangling image in our list of images:

```
REPOSITORY    TAG       IMAGE ID        CREATED           SIZE
basic-app     latest    c7918f4f95b9    25 seconds ago    8.8MB
Alpine        latest    961769676411    5 weeks ago       5.58MB
```

13. Run the **du** command again over the image's directory:

```
du -sh /var/lib/docker/overlay2/
```

You should also observe a small decrease in size:

```
10M    /var/lib/docker/overlay2/
```

This exercise has shown only smaller image sizes, but this is definitely something to keep in mind when running production and development environments. This part of the chapter has provided you with the foundations of how Docker uses layers and caching as part of its build process.

For our next exercise, we will look further at our layers and caching to see how they can be used to speed up the image build process.

EXERCISE 3.02: INCREASING BUILD SPEED AND REDUCING LAYERS

You have been working with smaller builds so far. However, as your applications increase in size and functionality, you'll start to consider both the size and number of layers of the Docker images you're creating and the speed at which you're creating them. The goal of this exercise is to speed up the build times and reduce the size of your images, as well as use the **--cache-from** option when building your Docker images:

1. Create a new **Dockerfile** to demonstrate the change you are going to make, but first, clear up all the images on your system. Run the **docker rmi** command with the **-f** option to force any removals needed, and the command in brackets will provide a list of all image IDs on your system. Use the **-a** option to show all running and stopped containers and the **-q** option to only show the container image hash value and nothing else:

```
docker rmi -f $(docker images -a -q)
```

The command should return output like the following:

```
Untagged: hello-world:latest
...
deleted: sha256:d74fa92b37b74820ccccea601de61d45ccb3770255
         b9c7dd22edf16caabafc1c
```

It can be observed that the **hello-world: latest** image is untagged and the image with ID **sha256:d74fa92b37b74820ccccea601 de61d45ccb3770255b9c7dd22edf16caabafc1c** is removed.

> **NOTE**
>
> Please note that we can remove the images using both the **rmi** and **prune** commands. Here, we have used the **rmi** command because **prune** was not always available until recently.

2. Add the following code to your **Dockerfile** (which you created in *Exercise 3.01*). It will simulate a simple web server, as well as print the output of our **Dockerfile** during the build process:

```
1 FROM alpine
2
3 RUN apk update
4 RUN apk add wget curl
5
6 RUN wget -O test.txt https://github.com/PacktWorkshops/
    The-Docker-Workshop/blob/master/Chapter03/Exercise3.02/100MB.bin
7
8 CMD mkdir /var/www/
9 CMD mkdir /var/www/html/
10
11 WORKDIR /var/www/html/
12
13 COPY Dockerfile.tar.gz /tmp/
14 RUN tar -zxvf /tmp/Dockerfile.tar.gz -C /var/www/html/
15 RUN rm /tmp/Dockerfile.tar.gz
16
17 RUN cat Dockerfile
```

You'll notice *line 6* of the **Dockerfile** is doing a fairly menial task (downloading a 100 MB file, named **100MB.bin**), which would not normally be performed in a **Dockerfile**. We have added it in to represent a build task or something similar that may be added during your build process, for example, downloading content or building software from a file.

3. Download your base image using the **docker pull** command so that you can start with the same image for each test we do:

```
docker pull alpine
```

4. Create a TAR file to be added to our image as we have instructed in *line 13* of our **Dockerfile**:

```
tar zcvf Dockerfile.tar.gz Dockerfile
```

5. Build a new image using the same name as **basic-app**. You will use the **time** command at the start of the code to allow us to gauge the time it takes to build our image:

```
time docker build -t basic-app .
```

The output will return the time taken to build the image:

```
...
real  4m36.810s
user  0m0.354s
sys   0m0.286s
```

6. Run the **docker history** command over the new **basic-app** image:

```
docker history basic-app
```

We have a few extra commands in our **Dockerfile** compared to the previous exercise. So, there should be no surprise that we will see 12 layers in our new image:

```
IMAGE          CREATED        CREATED BY                            SIZE
5b2e3b253899   2 minutes ago  /bin/sh -c cat Dockerfile             0B
c4895671a177   2 minutes ago  /bin/sh -c rm /tmp/Dockerfile.tar.gz  0B
aaf18a11ba25   2 minutes ago  /bin/sh -c tar -zxvf /tmp/Dockfil...  283B
507161de132c   2 minutes ago  /bin/sh -c #(nop) COPY file:e39f2a0...  283B
856689ad2bb6   2 minutes ago  /bin/sh -c #(nop) WORKDIR /var/...    0B
206675d145d4   2 minutes ago  /bin/sh -c #(nop)  CMD ["/bin/sh"...  0B
c947946a36b2   2 minutes ago  /bin/sh -c #(nop)  CMD ["/bin/sh"...  0B
32b0abdaa0a9   2 minutes ago  /bin/sh -c curl https://github.com...  105MB
e261358addb2   2 minutes ago  /bin/sh -c apk add wget curl          1.8MB
b6f77a768f90   2 minutes ago  /bin/sh -c apk update                 1.4MB
961769676411   6 weeks ago    /bin/sh -c #(nop)  CMD ["/bin/sh"]    0B
<missing>      6 weeks ago    /bin/sh -c #(nop) ADD file:fe3dc...   5.6MB
```

We can see that the **RUN**, **COPY**, and **ADD** commands in our **Dockerfile** are creating layers of a particular size relevant to the commands being run or files being added, and all the other commands in the **Dockerfile** are of size 0 B.

7. Reduce the number of layers in the image by combining the **RUN** commands in *lines 3 and 4* and combining the **CMD** commands in *lines 8 and 9* of the **Dockerfile** created in *step 1* of this exercise. With these changes, our **Dockerfile** should now look like the following:

```
1 FROM alpine
2
3 RUN apk update && apk add wget curl
4
5 RUN wget -O test.txt https://github.com/PacktWorkshops/
    The-Docker-Workshop/blob/master/Chapter03/Exercise3.02/100MB.bin
6
7 CMD mkdir -p /var/www/html/
8
9 WORKDIR /var/www/html/
10
11 COPY Dockerfile.tar.gz /tmp/
12 RUN tar -zxvf /tmp/Dockerfile.tar.gz -C /var/www/html/
13 RUN rm /tmp/Dockerfile.tar.gz
14
15 RUN cat Dockerfile
```

Running **docker build** again will reduce the number of layers for our new image from 12 to 9 layers, as even though there is the same number of commands being run, they are chained together in *lines 3* and *7*.

8. *Lines 11*, *12*, and *13* of our **Dockerfile** are using the **COPY** and **RUN** commands to **copy** and **unzip** our archived file, and then remove the original unzipped file. Replace these lines with the **ADD** command without needing to run the lines that unzip and remove the **.tar** file:

```
1 FROM alpine
2
3 RUN apk update && apk add wget curl
4
5 RUN wget -O test.txt https://github.com/PacktWorkshops/
    The-Docker-Workshop/blob/master/Chapter03/Exercise3.02/100MB.bin
6
7 CMD mkdir -p /var/www/html/
8
```

```
9 WORKDIR /var/www/html/
10
11 ADD Dockerfile.tar.gz /var/www/html/
12 RUN cat Dockerfile
```

9. Build the image again to reduce the number of layers in your new image from 9 to 8. If you have been watching the builds run, you will probably notice a lot of the time the build run as part of *lines 3* and *5* of our **Dockerfile**, where we run **apk update**, then install **wget** and **curl**, and then grab content from a website. Doing this once or twice will not be an issue, but if we create our base image, which the **Dockerfile** can then run on, you will be able to remove these lines completely from your **Dockerfile**.

10. Move into a new directory and create a new **Dockerfile** that will only pull the base image and run the **apk** commands, as listed here:

```
1 FROM alpine
2
3 RUN apk update && apk add wget curl
4
5 RUN wget -O test.txt https://github.com/PacktWorkshops/
    The-Docker-Workshop/blob/master/Chapter03/Exercise3.02/100MB.bin
```

11. Build the new base image from the preceding **Dockerfile** and name it **basic-base**:

```
docker build -t basic-base .
```

12. Remove *line 3* from the original **Dockerfile** as it will no longer be needed. Move into the project directory and update the image that is being used in the **FROM** command to **basic-base** and remove the **apk** commands in *line 3*. Our **Dockerfile** should now look like the following code:

```
1 FROM basic-base
2
3 CMD mkdir -p /var/www/html/
4
5 WORKDIR /var/www/html/
6
7 ADD Dockerfile.tar.gz /var/www/html/
8 RUN cat Dockerfile
```

13. Run the build again for our new **Dockerfile**. Using the **time** command again with our build, we now see the build complete in just over 1 second:

```
time docker build -t basic-app .
```

If you've been watching the build, you'll notice that compared to our previous builds, it runs a lot quicker:

```
...
real  0m1.810s
user  0m0.117s
sys   0m0.070s
```

> **NOTE**
>
> You will observe that the layers of the image will remain the same as we are building the base image on our system, which performs the **apk** commands. It's a great result still to speed up the build even though we are not reducing the number of layers.

14. There is a different way we can use the **basic-base** image we used earlier. Use the **docker build** command with the **--cache-from** option to specify the cache layers that will be used when the image is built. Set out the **FROM** command to still use the **alpine** image and use the **--cache-from** option that follows to make sure the layers used to build **basic-base** are being used for our current image:

```
docker build --cache-from basic-base -t basic-app .
```

We still have some more tasks before we complete this exercise. In the following steps, we will look at committing changes to our image to see how it affects our layers. This is not something we would use often but there are times when we need to copy production data over to a development or test environment, and one way to do this is by using a Docker image with the **commit** command, which will make changes to the top writable layer of our running container.

15. Run **basic-app** in interactive shell mode to create some production data. To do this, run the following **docker run** command with the **-it** option to run in interactive mode and use the **sh** shell to access the running container:

```
docker run -it basic-app sh
/var/www/html #
```

16. Use the vi text editor to create a new text file called **prod_test_data.txt**:

```
vi prod_test_data.txt
```

17. Add the following line of text as some test data. The data in the text is not important; it is just a sample to show we can then copy these changes to another image:

18. This is a sample production piece of data. Exit out of the running container and then check the container ID using the **docker ps** command with the **-a** option:

```
docker ps -a
```

You will get output like the following:

```
CONTAINER ID     IMAGE         COMMAND      CREATED
ede3d51bba9e     basic-app     "sh"         4 minutes ago
```

19. Run the **docker commit** command with the container ID to create a new image that will include all those changes. Make sure to add the name of the new image. In this example, use **basic-app-test**:

```
docker commit ede3d51bba9e basic-app-test
```

You will get output like the following:

```
sha256:0717c29d29f877a7dafd6cb0555ff6131179b457
        e8b8c25d9d13c2a08aa1e3f4
```

20. Run the **docker history** command on the newly created image:

```
docker history basic-app-test
```

This should now show us an extra layer where we added the sample production data, showing in our output as 72B in size:

```
IMAGE           CREATED         CREATED BY                        SIZE
0717c29d29f8    2 minutes ago   sh                                72B
302e01f9ba6a    2 minutes ago   /bin/sh -c cat Dockerfile         0B
10b405ceda34    2 minutes ago   /bin/sh -c #(nop) ADD file:e39f…   283B
397f533f4019    2 minutes ago   /bin/sh -c #(nop) WORKDIR /var/…   0B
c8782986b276    2 minutes ago   /bin/sh -c #(nop)  CMD ["/bin/sh"… 0B
6dee05f36f95    2 minutes ago   /bin/sh -c apk update && apk ad    3.2MB
961769676411    6 weeks ago     /bin/sh -c #(nop)  CMD ["/bin/sh"] 0B
<missing>       6 weeks ago     /bin/sh -c #(nop) ADD file:fe3dc…  5.6MB
```

21. Now, run the newly created **basic-app-test** image and **cat**, the new file we added:

```
docker run basic-app-test cat prod_test_data.txt
```

This should show us the output we added, showing we can reuse existing images if needed:

```
This is a sample production piece of data
```

> **NOTE**
>
> As of the time of writing, the **docker build** command also allows a new experimental feature using the **-squash** option. The option attempts to merge all the layers into one layer during build time. We haven't covered this feature as it is still in an experimental phase.

This exercise demonstrated how the build cache and image layers work to improve the build time. We have started all our builds so far using an image we have pulled down from Docker Hub, but there are options to start with an image you have created yourself if you wish to control things even further. The next section will help you to create your base Docker images.

CREATING BASE DOCKER IMAGES

Creating your base Docker image is actually straightforward. Just as we used the **docker commit** command previously to create an image from a running container, we can also create an image from a system or server we have originally been running our applications on. We need to remember that creating a base image still needs to remain small and lightweight. It is not simply a matter of moving existing applications running on existing servers over to Docker.

We could use the system we are specifically working on, but if you are using a production server, the image could actually be pretty big. If you have a small virtual machine you would think is perfect for a base image, you could use the following steps to create a base image from it. Similar to the **docker commit** command, this can be used for any system you can access.

EXERCISE 3.03: CREATING YOUR BASE DOCKER IMAGES

The following exercise will use the **basic-app** image we are currently running and show how easy it is to create a base image. These same steps would be used for larger, more complex environments as well:

1. Execute the **docker run** command to run the container and log in at the same time:

```
docker run -it basic-app sh
```

2. Run the **tar** command on the running container to create a backup of the system. To limit the information you have in the new image, exclude the **.proc**, **.tmp**, **.mnt**, **.dev**, and **.sys** directories, and create everything under the **basebackup.tar.gz** file:

```
tar -czf basebackup.tar.gz --exclude=backup.tar.gz --exclude=proc
--exclude=tmp --exclude=mnt --exclude=dev --exclude=sys /
```

3. To ensure that you have data in your **basebackup.tar.gz** file, run the **du** command to make sure it is of substantial size:

```
du -sh basebackup.tar.gz
```

The output returns the size of the **basebackup.tar.gz** file:

```
4.8M      basebackup.tar.gz
```

4. Run the **docker ps** command to find the container ID that is currently holding your new backup file, the **.tar** file:

```
docker ps
```

The command will return the container ID of the image:

```
CONTAINER ID        IMAGE         COMMAND        CREATED
6da7a8c1371a        basic-app     "sh"           About a minute ago
```

5. Copy the **.tar** file onto your development system with the **docker cp** command, using the container ID of our running container and the location and file you want to copy. The following command will do this with your container ID and move it into your **/tmp** directory:

```
docker cp 6da7a8c1371a:/var/www/html/basebackup.tar.gz /tmp/
```

6. Create a new image using the **docker import** command. Simply pipe the output of the **basebackup.tar.gz** file into the **docker import** command, naming the new image in the process. In our example, call it **mynew-base**:

```
cat /tmp/basebackup.tar.gz | docker import - mynew-base
```

7. Use the **docker images** command with the name of your new image to verify that it has been created in the previous step:

```
docker images mynew-base
```

You should get output like the following:

```
REPOSITORY     TAG      IMAGE ID        CREATED          SIZE
mynew-base     latest   487e14fca064    11 seconds ago   8.79MB
```

8. Run the **docker history** command:

```
docker history mynew-base
```

You will see that we only have one layer in our new image:

```
IMAGE           CREATED            CREATED BY   SIZE     COMMENT
487e14fca064    37 seconds ago                  .79MB    Imported from -
```

9. To test your new image, run the **docker run** command on the new image, and list the files in your **/var/www/html/** directory:

```
docker run mynew-base ls -l /var/www/html/
```

The command should return the similar output:

```
total 4
-rw-r--r--    1 501        dialout        283 Oct  3 04:07 Dockerfile
```

It can be seen that the image has been successfully created and there are 24 files in the **/var/www/html/** directory.

This exercise has shown you how to create a base image from a running system or environment, but if you're wanting to create a small base image, then the next section will show you how to use the **scratch** image.

THE SCRATCH IMAGE

The scratch image is an image created by Docker specifically available for building minimal images. If you have a binary application, written in Java, C++, and so on, as well as compiled, that can be run by itself without any supporting applications, then scratch will help you run that image with one of the smallest images you can create.

When we use the **FROM scratch** command in our **Dockerfile**, we are specifying that we will be using Docker's reserved minimal image, which is named **scratch** for building our new container image.

EXERCISE 3.04: USING THE SCRATCH IMAGE

In this exercise, you will create a small C application to run on the image. You don't really need to know anything about the C language to complete this exercise. The application will be installed on your scratch base image to ensure the image is as small as possible. The application you create will show you how to create one of the most minimal base images available:

1. Pull the scratch image using the **docker pull** command:

```
docker pull scratch
```

You'll notice you won't be able to pull the image and will receive an error:

```
Using default tag: latest
Error response from daemon: 'scratch' is a reserved name
```

2. Create a C program that you will build into the image to use in our **Dockerfile**. Create a program file called **test.c**:

```
touch test.c
```

3. Open the file and add in the following code, which will simply count from 1 to 10 on the console:

```
#include <stdio.h>
int main()
{
    int i;
    for (i=1; i<=10; i++)
    {
        printf("%d\n", i);
    }
    return 0;
}
```

4. Build the image from the command line by running the following command to build the C program:

```
g++ -o test -static test.c
```

> **NOTE**
>
> If you want to test it before you build it in your image, you can do so by running `./test` on the command line.

5. Create the **Dockerfile**. The **Dockerfile** will be pretty minimal but needs to start with **FROM scratch**. The rest of the file will add the C program to your image and then run it in *line 4*:

```
1 FROM scratch
2
3 ADD test /
4 CMD ["/test"]
```

6. Build a new image. In this instance, call the image **scratchtest** using the following command:

```
docker build -t scratchtest .
```

7. Run the image from the command line:

```
docker run scratchtest
```

You will see the output of the test C file you created and compiled earlier in this exercise:

```
1
2
3
4
5
6
7
8
9
10
```

8. Run the **docker images** command for your new image:

```
docker images scratchtest
```

This will show you some pretty impressive results as your image is only **913 kB** in size:

```
REPOSITORY     TAG       IMAGE ID       CREATED          SIZE
scratch        latest    221adbe23c26   20 minutes ago   913kB
```

9. View the layers of the image using the **docker history** command:

```
docker history scratchtest
```

You will see a similar output to the following one and it has only two layers, the original layer from scratch and the layer where we **ADD** the test C program:

```
IMAGE          CREATED          CREATED BY                               SIZE
221adbe23c26   23 minutes ago   /bin/sh -c #(nop)  CMD ["/test"]         0B
09b61a3a1043   23 minutes ago   /bin/sh -c #(nop) ADD file:80933...      913kB
```

The scratch image we've created in this exercise goes part of the way to creating an image that is both functional and minimal, and also demonstrates that if you think a little about what you are trying to achieve, it will be easy to speed up your builds and reduce the size of your images.

We will now take a break from working with building images and take a closer look at naming and tagging our Docker images.

DOCKER IMAGE NAMING AND TAGGING

We've touched on tags, but as we work more closely with Docker images, it's probably a good time to look at image tags in more depth. In simple terms, a tag is a label on the Docker image and should provide the user of the image with some useful information about the image or version of the image they are using.

Until now, we've been working with our images as if we're solo developers, but when we start to work with a larger development team, a need arises to think a little harder about how we'll be naming and tagging our images. The following section of the chapter will add to your previous work and allow you to start putting together a naming and tagging strategy for your projects and work.

There are two main methods for naming and tagging your Docker images. You can use the **docker tag** command, or you can use the **-t** option when you build your image from a **Dockerfile**. To use the **docker tag** command, you specify the source repository name you will be using as the base and the target name and tag you will be creating:

```
docker tag <source_repository_name>:<tag> <target_repository_name>:tag
```

When you name your image using the **docker build** command, the **Dockerfile** used will create your source, and then use the **-t** option to name and tag your images as follows:

```
docker build -t <target_repository_name>:tag Dockerfile
```

The repository name can sometimes be prefixed with a hostname, but this is optional and will be used to let Docker know where the repository is located. We'll demonstrate this later in this chapter when we create our own Docker Registry. If you're pushing your images to Docker Hub, you also need to prefix your repository name with your Docker Hub username, like this:

```
docker build -t <dockerhub_user>/<target_repository_name>:tag Dockerfile
```

Using more than two prefixes in your image name is only supported in local image registries and is generally not used. The next exercise will guide you through the process of tagging Docker images.

EXERCISE 3.05: TAGGING DOCKER IMAGES

In the following exercise, you will work with a different image, using the lightweight **busybox** image to demonstrate the process of tagging and start to implement tags in your project. BusyBox is used to combine tiny versions of many common UNIX utilities into a single small executable:

1. Run the **docker rmi** command to clear up the images you currently have on your system, so you don't get confused with a large number of images around:

```
docker rmi -f $(docker images -a -q)
```

2. On the command line, run the **docker pull** command to download the latest **busybox** container:

```
docker pull busybox
```

3. Run the **docker images** command:

```
docker images
```

This will give us the information we need to start putting some tag commands together:

```
REPOSITORY      TAG        IMAGE ID        CREATED         SIZE
Busybox         latest     19485c79a9bb    2 weeks ago     1.22MB
```

4. Name and tag the image using the **tag** command. You can either use the image ID or repository name to tag the images. Start by using the image ID, but note that on your system you'll have a different image ID. Name the repository **new_busybox** and include the tag **ver_1**:

```
docker tag 19485c79a9bb new_busybox:ver_1
```

5. Use the repository name and image tag. Create a new repository using your name and tag with a new version of **ver_1.1** as follows:

```
docker tag new_busybox:ver_1 vince/busybox:ver_1.1
```

> **NOTE**
>
> We have used the author's name (**vince**) in this example.

6. Run the **docker images** command:

```
docker images
```

You should see a similar output to the one that follows. Of course, your image IDs will be different, but the repository names and tags should be similar:

```
REPOSITORY        TAG        ID             CREATED        SIZE
Busybox           latest     19485c79a9bb   2 weeks ago    1.22MB
new_busybox       ver_1      19485c79a9bb   2 weeks ago    1.22MB
vince/busybox     ver_1.1    19485c79a9bb   2 weeks ago    1.22MB
```

7. Create a basic image using a **Dockerfile** and the **-t** option of the **docker build** command to name and tag the image. You've done this a few times already in this chapter, so from the command line, run the following command to create a basic **Dockerfile**, using the **new_busybox** image you named earlier. Also include the tag for the image name, as Docker will try to use the **latest** tag and, as this does not exist, it will fail:

```
echo "FROM new_busybox:ver_1" > Dockerfile
```

8. Run the **docker build** command to create the image while naming and tagging it at the same time:

```
docker build -t built_image:ver_1.1.1 .
```

9. Run the **docker images** command:

```
docker images
```

You should now have four images available on your system. All have the same container ID but will have different repository names and tagged versions:

```
REPOSITORY        TAG        ID             CREATED        SIZE
built_image       ver_1.1.1  19485c79a9bb   2 weeks ago    1.22MB
Busybox           latest     19485c79a9bb   2 weeks ago    1.22MB
new_busybox       ver_1      19485c79a9bb   2 weeks ago    1.22MB
vince/busybox     ver_1.1    19485c79a9bb   2 weeks ago    1.22MB
```

Tagging images with a proper version that is relevant to your organization or team does not take too much time, especially with a little practice. This section of the chapter has shown you how to tag your images so they are no longer tagged with the default tag of the **latest**. You will see in the next section that using the **latest** tag and hoping it will work correctly could actually cause you some extra issues.

USING THE LATEST TAG IN DOCKER

As we've been working with our tags, we've mentioned a few times not to use the **latest** tag, which is provided by Docker as a default tag. As you will see shortly, using the **latest** tag can cause a lot of issues, especially if you're deploying images into production environments.

The first thing we need to realize is that **latest** is simply a tag, just as we were using **ver_1** in our previous example. It definitely does not mean the latest version of our code either. It simply means the most recent build of our image, which did not include a tag.

Using the **latest** will also cause a lot of issues in large teams, deploying to environments multiple times a day. It also means you will have no history, which makes rolling back bad changes difficult. So, remember that every time you build or pull an image if you don't specify a tag, Docker will use the **latest** tag and will not do anything to ensure the image is the most up-to-date version. In the next exercise, we will check what issues can be caused when using the **latest** tag.

EXERCISE 3.06: ISSUES WHEN USING LATEST

You may still be new to both using Docker and using tags, so you may not have experienced any issues using the **latest** tag as yet. This exercise will give you some clear ideas on how using the **latest** tag could cause problems with your development process and provide you with reasons as to why you should avoid it. You created a simple **Dockerfile** in the previous exercise using the **new_busybox:ver_1** image. In this exercise, you will extend this file further:

1. Open the **Dockerfile** and amend the file to now look like the following file. It is a simple script that will create the **version.sh** script with simple code to output the latest version of our service. The new file will be called **Dockerfile_ver1**.

```
1 FROM new_busybox:ver_1
2
3 RUN echo "#!/bin/sh\n" > /version.sh
4 RUN echo "echo \"This is Version 1 of our service\""
  >> /version.sh
5
6 ENTRYPOINT ["sh", "/version.sh"]
```

2. Build the image and name it with your name and show the image is just a test:

```
docker build -t vince/test .
```

> **NOTE**
>
> We have used **vince** as the name here, but you can use any desirable name.

3. Run the image using the **docker run** command:

```
docker run vince/test
```

You should now see the output of the **versions.sh** script:

```
This is Version 1 of our service
```

4. Use the **docker tag** command to tag this image as **version1**:

```
docker tag vince/test vince/test:version1
```

5. Open the **Dockerfile** and make the following change to *line 4*:

```
1 FROM new_busybox:ver_1
2
3 RUN echo "#!/bin/sh\n" > /version.sh
4 RUN echo "echo \"This is Version 2 of our service\""
  >> /version.sh
5
6 ENTRYPOINT ["sh", "/version.sh"]
```

6. Build your amended **Dockerfile** and tag it with **version2**:

```
docker build -t vince/test:version2 .
```

7. Run the amended image using the **docker run** command:

```
docker run vince/test
```

You should see your latest code changes as well:

```
This is Version 1 of our service
```

This isn't the version we were looking for, was it? Without using the correct tag, Docker will run what is the most recent version of the image that was tagged with the **latest**. This image was created in *step 3*.

8. Now, run both images with the **latest** and **version2** tags:

```
docker run vince/test:latest
This is Version 1 of our service
```

We can now see the difference in the output:

```
docker run vince/test:version2
This is Version 2 of our service
```

As you may have already thought, you need to specify the **version2** tag to run the amended version of the code. You may have seen this coming but remember this is going to make things more difficult to keep track of if you have multiple developers pushing images to a shared registry. If your team is using orchestration and using the **latest** version, you may end up with mixed versions of your services running across your production environment.

These exercises have given you examples on how to use tags as well as showing you what the consequences could be if you decide to only use the **latest** tag. The following section will introduce tagging policies and how to implement automated processes.

DOCKER IMAGE TAGGING POLICIES

As development teams increase in size and the projects they work on increase in complexity, a standardized tagging policy for your team becomes even more important. If your team is not getting its tagging correct, as we've demonstrated in our previous sections, this can cause a lot of confusion and actually cause more issues. It's a good habit to decide on a tagging policy early to make sure you don't run into any of these issues.

In this section of the chapter, we are going to cover some of the different tagging policies you could use within your team with some examples on how they can also be implemented. There are rarely any right or wrong answers when it comes to setting up your tagging policy, but it is necessary to make a decision early and ensure everyone in the team is in agreement.

Semantic versioning is a versioning system that can also be used as part of your tagging policy. If you're not familiar with semantic versioning, it is a trusted version system that uses a three-component number in the format of `major_version.minor_version.patch`. For example, if you saw the semantic version of an application as 2.1.0, it would show version 2 as the major release version, 1 as the minor release version, and 0 as there are no patches. Semantic versioning can be easily automated, especially in an automated build environment. Another option is to use a hash value, like the `git commit` hash for your code. This means you can match the tag back to your repository, so anyone can see specifically the code changes that have been made since the code was implemented. You could also use a date value, which can once again be easily automated.

The common theme here is that our tagging policy should be automated to ensure it is used, understood, and adhered to. In the following exercise, we are going to look at using hash values as part of your tagging policy and we will then create a script to build our Docker images and add semantic versioning to our tags.

EXERCISE 3.07: AUTOMATING YOUR IMAGE TAGGING

In this exercise, you are going to look at automating your image tagging to limit the amount of individual intervention needed in tagging your Docker images. This exercise uses the **basic-base** image again:

1. Create the **basic-base** image again by creating the following **Dockerfile**:

```
1 FROM alpine
2
3 RUN apk update && apk add wget curl
```

2. Build the new base image from the preceding **Dockerfile** and name it **basic-base**:

```
docker build -t basic-base .
```

3. With the **basic-base** image created, set up the **Dockerfile** named **Dockerfile_ver1** to build a **basic-app** again. In this instance, return to the previous **Dockerfile** as listed here:

```
1 FROM basic-base
2
3 CMD mkdir -p /var/www/html/
4
5 WORKDIR /var/www/html/
6
```

```
7 ADD Dockerfile.tar.gz /var/www/html/
8 RUN cat Dockerfile
```

4. If you've been using Git to track and commit the changes in your code, you can tag your images with the commit hash from Git using the **git log** command. So, build your new image, as you normally would, with the **docker build** command, but in this instance, add the tag to provide the short commit hash from **git**:

```
docker build -t basic-app:$(git log -1 --format=%h) .
...
Successfully tagged basic-app:503a2eb
```

> **NOTE**
>
> If you are new to using Git, it is a source control application that allows you to track your changes and collaborate with other users on different coding projects. If you have never used Git before, the following commands will initialize your repository, add the **Dockerfile** to the repository, and commit these changes, so we have a Git log present:
>
> **git init; git add Dockerfile; git commit -m "initial commit"**

5. Use your **Dockerfile** to add arguments when your image is being built. Open the **Dockerfile** you've been using for your **basic-app** and add in the following two lines to set variables as unknown, and then set **LABEL** as the value offered at build time, using the **git-commit** build argument. Your **Dockerfile** should now appear as follows:

```
1 FROM basic-base
2
3 ARG GIT_COMMIT=unknown
4 LABEL git-commit=$GIT_COMMIT
5
6 CMD mkdir -p /var/www/html/
7
8 WORKDIR /var/www/html/
9
10 ADD Dockerfile.tar.gz /var/www/html/
11 RUN cat Dockerfile
```

6. Build the image again using the **--build-arg** option with the **GIT_COMMIT** argument, which is now equal to your **git commit** hash value:

```
docker build -t basic-app --build-arg GIT_COMMIT=$(git log -1
--format=%h) .
```

7. Run the **docker inspect** command searching for the **"git-commit"** label:

```
docker inspect -f '{{index .ContainerConfig.Labels "git-commit"}}'
basic-app
```

You can see the Git hash label you added at build time:

```
503a2eb
```

This is starting to move in the direction you need, but what if you need to use semantic versioning as your team has decided this is the best option for your development? The rest of this exercise will set up a build script to both build and set the tag as the semantic version number.

8. Alongside your **Dockerfile**, create a version file simply named **VERSION**. Set the new version as **1.0.0** for this build of **basic-app**:

```
echo "1.0.0" > VERSION
```

9. Make changes to the **Dockerfile** to remove the **GIT_COMMIT** details added previously and add the **VERSION** file as part of your build. Adding it into the image itself means users can always refer to the **VERSION** file if ever they need to verify the image version number:

```
1 FROM basic-base
2
3 CMD mkdir -p /var/www/html/
4
5 WORKDIR /var/www/html/
6
7 ADD VERSION /var/www/html/
8 ADD Dockerfile.tar.gz /var/www/html/
9 RUN cat Dockerfile
```

10. Create a build script to both build and tag your image. Call this **build.sh** and it will reside in the same directory as your **Dockerfile** and **VERSION** file:

```
touch build.sh
```

11. Add the following details to **build.sh**. *Line 3* will be your Docker Hub username, and *line 4* is the name of the image or service you are building (in the following example, **basic-app**). The script then grabs the version number from your **VERSION** file and brings all your variables together to build your image with a nice name and tag relevant to your new semantic version:

```
1 set -ex
2
3 USER=<your_user_name>
4 SERVICENAME=basic-app
5
6 version=`cat VERSION`
7 echo "version: $version"
8
9 docker build -t $USER/$SERVICENAME:$version .
```

12. Make sure the build script is set to run as an executable script using the **chmod** command on the command line:

```
chmod +x build.sh
```

13. Run the build script from the command line. **set -xe** in *line 1* of the script will make sure all commands are output to the console and ensure that if any of the commands cause an error, the script will stop. Run the build script now, as follows:

```
./build.sh
```

Only the output of the build script is shown here as the rest of the build process happens as normal:

```
++ USERNAME=vincesestodocker
++ IMAGE=basic-app
+++ cat VERSION
++ version=1.0.0
++ echo 'version: 1.0.0'
version: 1.0.0
++ docker build -t vincesestodocker/basic-app:1.0.0 .
```

14. View the image using the **docker images** command:

```
docker images vincesestodocker/basic-app
```

It should reflect the name and tags created as part of the build script:

```
REPOSITORY                    TAG     IMAGE ID
   CREATED              SIZE
vincesestodocker/basic-app    1.0.0   94d0d337a28c
   29 minutes ago       8.8MB
```

This exercise goes a long way in automating our tagging process, and it allows the **build** script to be added to source control and run easily as part of a build pipeline. It is just a start though, and you will see in the activities at the end of the chapter that we will extend this build script further. For now, we have completed this section on the tagging and naming of our images, and it fits in nicely with the next section, which covers storing and publishing your Docker images.

STORING AND PUBLISHING YOUR DOCKER IMAGES

Since the early days of Docker's history, one of its main attractions has been a central website where users can download images, reuse and improve these images for their purposes, and reupload them to grant access to other users. Docker Hub has grown and although it has had some security issues, it is still usually the first place people will look when they need new images or resources for their projects.

As a public repository, Docker Hub is still one of the first places people go to research and use images needed to streamline or improve their new development project. It is also an important place for companies and developers to host their open-source images, available for the public to utilize. However, Docker Hub is not the only solution for you to store and distribute your Docker images.

For development teams, a public repository on Docker Hub, although accessible and highly available, may not be the best option. These days, your team may look to store production images in a cloud-based registry solution such as Amazon Elastic Container Registry, Google Container Registry, or, as you'll see later in this chapter, another option would be to set up a local registry.

In this part of the chapter, we'll start by seeing how you can actually move images from machine to machine and then take a closer look at using Docker Hub. We'll see how to start moving our images across to Docker Hub as a publicly stored image. We will then look at setting up a locally hosted Docker registry on your development system.

The **docker save** command will be used to save the images from the command line. Here, we use the **-o** option to specify the output file and directory we are going to save our image to:

```
docker save -o <output_file_and_Directory> <image_repo_name/image_
name:tag>
```

We will then be able to use the **load** command similar to the **import** command when we created a new base image earlier in the chapter, specifying the file we created previously:

```
docker load -i <output_file_and_Directory>
```

Keep in mind that not all images on Docker Hub should be treated the same way, as it comes with a mixture of both official images that have been created by Docker Inc. and community images created by Docker users. Official images are still open source images and solutions available for you to add to your projects. Community images are offered usually by companies or individuals wanting you to leverage their technology.

> **NOTE**
>
> Use caution when sourcing images, even from Docker Hub. Try to limit pulling images from sources that are not reputable and have not been reviewed or downloaded by a large number of users as they could pose a potential security risk.

EXERCISE 3.08: TRANSPORTING DOCKER IMAGES MANUALLY

Sometimes, whether there are issues with firewalls or other security measures on your network, you may need to copy an image directly from one system to another. Fortunately, Docker has a way of achieving this and, in this exercise, you will move an image from one system to another without using a registry:

1. Run the **docker save** command with the **-o** option to save the image you created in the last part of this chapter. The command needs the user to specify both the filename and the directory. In the following example,
   - it is **/tmp/basic-app.tar**. Also specify the user, image name, and tag of the image:

```
docker save -o /tmp/basic-app.tar vincesestodocker/basic-app:1.0.0
```

You should now see the packaged-up image in the **/tmp** directory. You are using **.tar** as the extension of your filename as the **save** command creates a TAR file of the image. You could actually use any name for the extension of the file.

2. Use the **du** command to verify that the **basic-app.tar** file has data in it:

```
du -sh /tmp/basic-app.tar

8.9M    /tmp/basic-app.tar
```

3. You can now move the image as you need to, whether it be via **rsync**, **scp**, or **cp**. As it is a TAR file, you could also compress the file as a ZIP file if you need to save some space during the transfer. In this example, you will simply delete the image from your current system. Run the **docker rmi** command with the ID of the image you have just saved:

```
docker rmi -f 94d0d337a28c
```

4. Load the new image back as a Docker image using the **docker load** command with the **-i** option, pointing to where the packaged image is located. In this case, it is the **/tmp** directory:

```
docker load -i /tmp/basic-app.tar
```

You should get output like the following:

```
Loaded image: vincesestodocker/basic-app:1.0.0
```

5. Use the **docker image** command to bring up the image you have just loaded into your local environment:

```
docker images vincesestodocker/basic-app
```

You should get output like the following:

```
REPOSITORY                    TAG      IMAGE ID
   CREATED            SIZE
vincesestodocker/basic-app    1.0.0    2056b6e48b1a
   29 minutes ago     8.8MB
```

This was just a simple exercise, but it hopefully served to show you that if there is ever a situation where you are unable to connect to a registry, you are still able to transport your Docker images. The next exercises are more focused on the usual methods of storing, publishing, and distributing your Docker images.

STORING AND DELETING DOCKER IMAGES IN DOCKER HUB

Although you can work with Docker Hub without paying any money, you need to know you will only get one private repository free of charge on your account. If you want more, you'll need to pay for a monthly plan on Docker. If Docker Hub is the solution your team has chosen to use, you will rarely need only one private repository. If you decide a free account is for you, then you get an unlimited number of free repositories.

EXERCISE 3.09: STORING DOCKER IMAGES IN DOCKER HUB AND DELETING THE REPOSITORY

In this exercise, you will create a new repository for the **basic-app** that you've been working on and store the images in Docker Hub. Once you have pushed the images in Docker Hub, you will also look at how you can delete the repository:

> **NOTE**
>
> The following exercise will need you to have your account on Docker Hub. We will only be using free repositories, so you will not need to be on a paid monthly plan, but if you haven't signed up for a free account on Docker Hub, go to https://hub.docker.com/signup.

1. Log in to your Docker Hub account and, under the **Repositories** section, you'll have the option **Create Repository** as a blue button on the right of the screen. Click this button so that you can set up a repository for the **basic-app** you have been working on:

Figure 3.1: Creating a repository in Docker Hub

2. When creating a new repository, you'll be presented with a page like the one that follows. Fill in the **Name** of the repository, which is usually the name of the image or service you are storing (in this case, `basic-app`). You also have the option to set the repository as **Public** or **Private**, and in this instance, select **Public**:

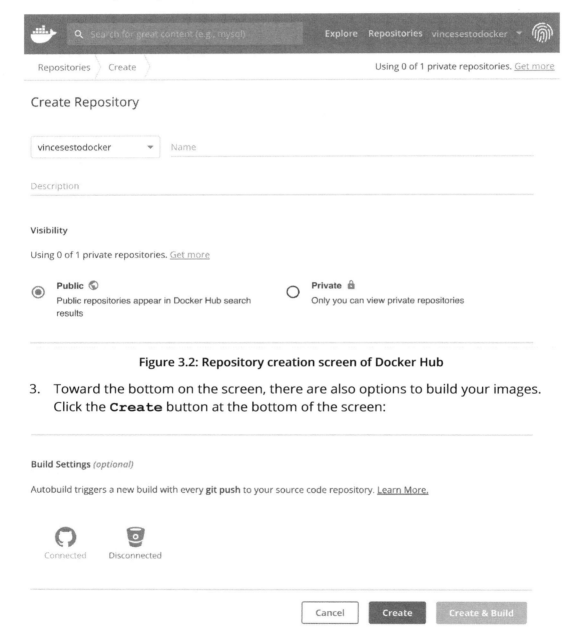

Figure 3.2: Repository creation screen of Docker Hub

3. Toward the bottom on the screen, there are also options to build your images. Click the **Create** button at the bottom of the screen:

Build Settings *(optional)*

Autobuild triggers a new build with every **git push** to your source code repository. Learn More.

Connected   Disconnected

Cancel   Create   Create & Build

Figure 3.3: Repository creation screen of Docker Hub

4. Once your new repository is created, it will provide details on how to start pushing your images to your new repository. Tag your image with **<account_name>/<image_name>:tag** to let Docker know where it will be pushing the image and which repository Docker will be pushing it to:

```
docker tag basic-app vincesestodocker/basic-app:ver1
```

5. Now, Docker on your system knows where to push the image. Push the image using the **docker push <account_name>/<image_name>:tag** command:

```
docker push vincesestodocker/basic-app:ver1
denied: requested access to the resource is denied
```

You need to make sure you are logged in to Docker Hub from the command line as well as the web interface.

6. Use the **docker login** command and enter the same credentials you were using when you logged in to create the new repository:

```
docker login

Login with your Docker ID to push and pull images from Docker Hub. If
you don't have a Docker ID, head over to https://hub.docker.com to
create one.
Username: vincesestodocker
Password:
Login Succeeded
```

7. Now, push your image to your new repository, as you did in *step 5* of this exercise, which previously failed. It should give you a successful result:

```
docker push basic-app vincesestodocker/basic-app:ver1
```

8. Move back to the Docker Hub web interface and you should now see the image version you have pushed, sitting in your newly created repository:

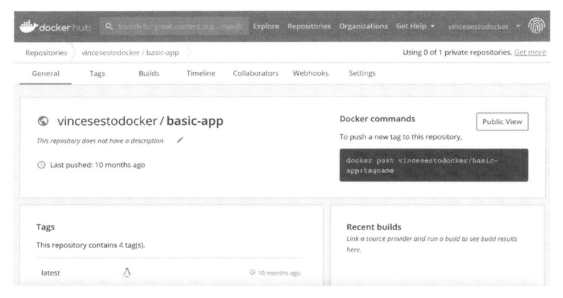

Figure 3.4: Your newly created Docker Hub repository with image

You now have a public repository available for anyone wanting to pull your image down and reuse it for their purposes. If someone needed to use your image, they would simply use the full name of the image, including tags with the **docker pull** command or **FROM** command in a **Dockerfile**.

9. You'll notice in the preceding image that, on the right-hand side of the screen, there is the **Public View** button. This gives you an option to see specifically what the public will see when they search for your image. Click the button and you should see a similar screen to the following:

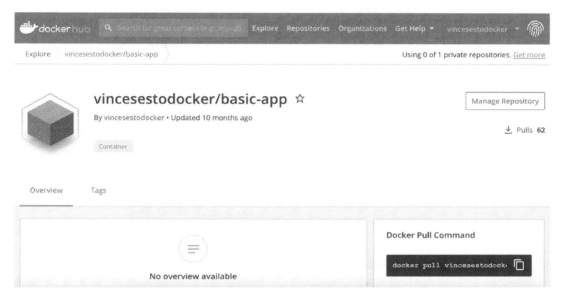

Figure 3.5: The public view of your Docker Hub repository

This is exactly what the public will see of your repository. It's now up to you to make sure you have the overview up to date and ensure your image is supported to make sure there are no problems with anyone wanting to use your image.

10. Lastly, for this exercise, clean up the repository you've just created. If you are not still in the web interface of your repository, move back onto the Docker Hub web page and click the **Settings** tab at the top of the screen:

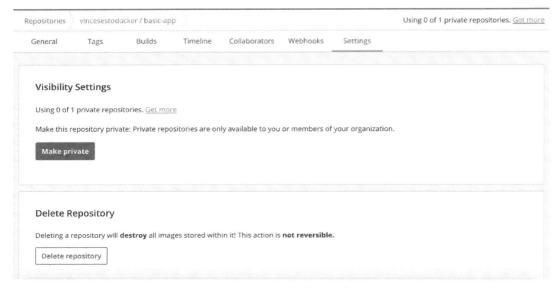

Figure 3.6: The Settings screen of the Docker Hub repository

11. Here you will have the option to make your repository private, but in this exercise, you will delete the repository. Click the **Delete Repository** option and confirm you now want to delete it.

As demonstrated in this exercise, Docker Hub provides you with an easy way to distribute images to allow other users to collaborate or utilize the work you've already done. A public repository is not always the best option for an enterprise, but just as GitHub has allowed developers to distribute their code and collaborate with other developers, Docker Hub can do the same for your Docker Images.

THE DOCKER REGISTRY

The Docker Registry is a service that hosts your images. Most of the time, registries are private and only available for the team that has access to them. There are a lot of great options available and one of those options is the registry image made available and maintained by Docker.

There are a few different reasons why you would want to be running your own Docker registry. It could be due to security issues, or you don't want your latest work publicly available. It could even be the simple convenience of having your registry running on the system you're working on. In this part of the chapter, we'll set up a registry on your working environment and start storing your images on the registry.

> **NOTE**
>
> Docker simplifies things for us as they have a registry image available on Docker Hub to download and use for your projects. For more information on the image we will be using, you can find it at the following location:
>
> https://hub.docker.com/_/registry.

EXERCISE 3.10: CREATING A LOCAL DOCKER REGISTRY

In this exercise, you will set up a Docker registry for your images and run them on your system. You are not going to set up a registry available to your team, or the outside world. You will set up a nice domain to use on your systems that reflect the work you are doing. This will help you decide whether to then have this registry available to your team or other users:

1. To set up your domain, add a domain for your local registry to your system hosts file. On a Windows system, you will need to access the hosts file at **C:\Windows\System32\drivers\etc\hosts**, while on a Linux or Max, it will be **/etc/hosts**. Open the **hosts** file and add the following line to the file:

    ```
    127.0.0.1          dev.docker.local
    ```

    This will allow you to use the **dev.docker.local** domain instead of using localhost for your local registry.

2. Pull the latest **registry** image down from Docker Hub:

    ```
    docker pull registry
    ```

3. Use the following command to run the registry container. Provide the ports you can access the registry with; in this case, use port **5000**. You also need to use the **--restart=always** option, which will make sure the container restarts if Docker or your system needs to restart:

```
docker run -d -p 5000:5000 --restart=always --name registry registry
```

> **NOTE**
>
> In the following chapters, you will learn how to extend the file capacity of your Docker container by mounting a directory from your host system that will then run as part of your running container. To do this, you will use the **-v** or **--volume** option as part of your **docker run** command, providing the file and the mount point on the container. For example, you could run the preceding command to mount a directory on your host system as follows:
>
> ```
> docker run -d -p 5000:5000 --restart=always
> --volume <directory_name>:/var/lib/registry:rw
> --name registry
> ```

4. Run the **docker ps** command to show the **registry** container running on your system, which is ready to accept and store new images:

```
docker ps
```

The command will return the output like the following:

```
CONTAINER ID   IMAGE      COMMAND              CREATED
41664c379bec   registry   "/entrypoint.sh /etc…"  58 seconds ago
```

5. Run the **docker tag** command to tag your existing images with the registry hostname and port **dev.docker.local:5000**.

```
docker tag vincesestodocker/basic-app:ver1 dev.docker.local:5000/
basic-app:ver1
```

This will ensure that your **basic-app** image will be automatically pushed to the local registry:

```
docker push dev.docker.local:5000/basic-app:ver1
```

6. Delete the original images from the system you are currently working on using the **docker image remove** command:

```
docker image remove dev.docker.local:5000/basic-app:ver1
```

7. Now, pull down the image from your local registry by including the registry hostname and port **dev.docker.local:5000** as part of the **pull** command:

```
docker pull dev.docker.local:5000/basic-app:ver1
```

This brings us to the end of this section where we have created our registry to store our Docker images on our local system. The registry itself is simple and is not really supported but does go a long way to help you understand how a registry will work and how it can work with your team. If you are looking for a more robust and supported image, Docker also provides Docker Trusted Registry, which is a commercial offering by Docker.

It's time to test the knowledge acquired so far. In the next activity, we will modify the build script for the **PostgreSQL** container image to use the Git commit hash instead of semantic versioning.

ACTIVITY 3.01: BUILD SCRIPTS USING GIT HASH VERSIONING

Earlier in the chapter, you created a build script that automated the tagging and versioning process of your images being built. In this activity, you will work further with the Panoramic Trekking app and will be tasked with setting up a build script for the **PostgreSQL** container image. You can use the previous build script you created earlier, but you will need to modify the script to no longer use semantic versioning and instead use the current Git commit hash. Also, make sure that your build script pushed the built image onto your Docker registry.

The steps required for completion are as follows:

1. Ensure you have a running **Dockerfile** created for your **PostgreSQL** container image.

2. Create your build script, which performs the following actions:

    a) Sets the variables for your Docker registry, the service name being built, and the Git hash version

    b) Prints the Git hash version to the screen

    c) Builds your PostgreSQL Docker images

    d) Pushes your Docker image to your registry

3. Ensure that the build script runs and completes successfully.

Expected Output:

```
./BuildScript.sh
++ REGISTRY=dev.docker.local:5000
++ SERVICENAME=basic-app
+++ git log -1 --format=%h
++ GIT_VERSION=49d3a10
++ echo 'version: 49d3a10 '
version: 49d3a10
++ docker build -t dev.docker.local:5000/basic-app:49d3a10 .
Sending build context to Docker daemon  3.072kB
Step 1/1 : FROM postgres
 ---> 873ed24f782e
Successfully built 873ed24f782e
Successfully tagged dev.docker.local:5000/basic-app:49d3a10
++ docker push dev.docker.local:5000/basic-app:49d3a10
The push refers to repository [dev.docker.local:5000/basic-app]
```

> **NOTE**
>
> The solution for this activity can be found on page 656.

In the next activity, you will configure your local Docker registry storage by changing the **docker run** command to store it in a directory on your home directory.

ACTIVITY 3.02: CONFIGURING YOUR LOCAL DOCKER REGISTRY STORAGE

During this chapter, you set up your registry and began using basic options to get it running. The registry itself is storing images on the host filesystem. In this activity, you want to change the **docker run** command to store it in a directory on your home directory. You will create a directory called **test_registry** and run the Docker command to store images in this **test_registry** directory in your home directory.

The steps required for completion are as follows:

1. Create a directory within your home directory to mount your local registry.

2. Run the local registry. This time mount the newly created volume as part of the registry.

3. Test your changes by pushing a new image to the local registry.

> **HINT**
>
> Use the **-v** or **--volume** option when you run your registry container.

Expected Output:

While listing all the files in the local directory, you will be able to see the pushed images:

```
ls   ~/test_registry/registry/docker/registry/v2/repositories/

basic-app
```

> **NOTE**
>
> The solution for this activity can be found on page 658.

SUMMARY

This chapter demonstrated how Docker allows users to work with images to package their applications together with a working environment to be moved across different working environments. You've seen how Docker uses layers and caching to improve build speed and ensure you can also work with these layers to reserve resources or disk space.

We also spent some time creating a base image with only one layer of our image. We've explored tagging and tagging practices you can adopt in order to counter issues associated with deploying and publishing your images. We also took a look at different ways we can publish our images and share them with other users and developers. We are only just getting started and still have a long way to go.

In the next chapter, we'll be working further with our **Dockerfiles** to learn how multistage **Dockerfiles** work. We'll also find more ways in which we can optimize our Docker images for better performance when they're released into a production environment.

MULTI-STAGE DOCKERFILES

OVERVIEW

In this chapter, we will discuss a normal Docker build. You will review and practice `Dockerfile` best practices and learn to create and optimize the size of the Docker images using a builder pattern and multi-stage `Dockerfile`.

INTRODUCTION

In the previous chapter, we learned about Docker registries, including private and public registries. We created our own private Docker registry to store the Docker images. We also learned how to set up access and store our Docker images in the Docker Hub. In this chapter, we will be discussing the concept of multi-stage **Dockerfiles**.

Multi-stage **Dockerfiles** are a feature introduced in Docker version 17.05. This feature is preferable when we want to optimize Docker image size while running Docker images in production environments. To achieve this, a multi-stage **Dockerfile** will create multiple intermediate Docker images during the build process and selectively copy only essential artifacts from one stage to the other.

Before multi-stage Docker builds were introduced, the builder pattern was used to optimize the Docker image size. Unlike multi-stage builds, the builder pattern needs two **Dockerfiles** and a shell script to create efficient Docker images.

In this chapter, we will first examine normal Docker builds and the problems associated with them. Next, we will learn how to use the builder pattern to optimize the Docker image size and discuss the problems associated with the builder pattern. Finally, we will learn to use multi-stage **Dockerfiles** to overcome the problems of the builder pattern.

NORMAL DOCKER BUILDS

With Docker, we can use **Dockerfiles** to create custom Docker images. As we discussed in *Chapter 2, Getting Started with Dockerfiles*, a **Dockerfile** is a text file that contains instructions on how to create a Docker image. However, it is critical to have minimal-sized Docker images when running them in production environments. This allows developers to speed up their Docker containers' build and deployment times. In this section, we will build a custom Docker image to observe the problems associated with the normal Docker build process.

Consider an example where we build a simple Golang application. We are going to deploy a **hello world** application written in Golang using the following **Dockerfile**:

```
# Start from latest golang parent image
FROM golang:latest

# Set the working directory
WORKDIR /myapp
```

```
# Copy source file from current directory to container
COPY helloworld.go .

# Build the application
RUN go build -o helloworld .

# Run the application
ENTRYPOINT ["./helloworld"]
```

This **Dockerfile** starts with the latest Golang image as the parent image. This parent image contains all the build tools required to build our Golang application. Next, we will set the **/myapp** directory as the current working directory and copy the **helloworld.go** source file from the host filesystem to the container filesystem. Then, we will use the **RUN** directive to execute the **go build** command to build the application. Finally, the **ENTRYPOINT** directive is used to run the **helloworld** executable created in the previous step.

The following is the content of the **helloworld.go** file. This is a simple file that will print the text **"Hello World"** when executed:

```go
package main

import "fmt"

func main() {
    fmt.Println("Hello World")
}
```

Once the **Dockerfile** is ready, we can build the Docker image using the **docker image build** command. This image will be tagged as **helloworld:v1**:

```
$ docker image build -t helloworld:v1 .
```

Now, observe the built image with the **docker image ls** command. You will get an output similar to the following:

```
REPOSITORY    TAG    IMAGE ID      CREATED          SIZE
helloworld    v1     23874f841e3e  10 seconds ago   805MB
```

Notice the image size. This build has resulted in a huge Docker image of 805 MB in size. It is not efficient to have these large Docker images in production environments as they will take a lot of time and bandwidth to be pushed and pulled over networks. Small Docker images are much more efficient and can be pushed and pulled quickly and deployed faster.

In addition to the size of the image, these Docker images can be vulnerable to attacks since they contain build tools that can have potential security vulnerabilities.

> **NOTE**
>
> Potential security vulnerabilities may vary depending on what packages are in the given Docker image. As an example, Java JDK has a number of vulnerabilities. You can have a detailed look at the vulnerabilities related to Java JDK at the following link:
>
> https://www.cvedetails.com/vulnerability-list/vendor_id-93/product_id-19116/Oracle-JDK.html.

To reduce the attack surface, it is recommended to have only the essential artifacts (for example, compiled code) and runtimes when running Docker images in production environments. As an example, with Golang, the Go compiler is required to build the application, but not to run the application.

Ideally, you want a minimal-sized Docker image that only contains the runtime tools and excludes all the build tools that we used to build the application.

We will now build such a Docker image using the normal build process in the following exercise.

EXERCISE 4.01: BUILDING A DOCKER IMAGE WITH THE NORMAL BUILD PROCESS

Your manager has asked you to dockerize a simple Golang application. You are provided with the Golang source code file, and your task is to compile and run this file. In this exercise, you will build a Docker image using the normal build process. You will then observe the image size of the final Docker image:

1. Create a new directory named **normal-build** for this exercise:

```
$ mkdir normal-build
```

2. Navigate to the newly created **normal-build** directory:

```
$ cd normal-build
```

3. Within the **normal-build** directory, create a file named **welcome.go**. This file will be copied to the Docker image during the build time:

```
$ touch welcome.go
```

4. Now, open the **welcome.go** file using your favorite text editor:

```
$ vim welcome.go
```

5. Add the following content to the **welcome.go** file, save it, and exit from the **welcome.go** file:

```
package main

import "fmt"

func main() {
    fmt.Println("Welcome to multi-stage Docker builds")
}
```

This is a simple **hello world** application written in Golang. This will output **"Welcome to multi-stage Docker builds"** on execution.

6. Within the **normal-build** directory, create a file named **Dockerfile**:

```
$ touch Dockerfile
```

7. Now, open the **Dockerfile** using your favorite text editor:

```
$ vim Dockerfile
```

8. Add the following content to the **Dockerfile** and save the file:

```
FROM golang:latest
WORKDIR /myapp
COPY welcome.go .
RUN go build -o welcome .
ENTRYPOINT ["./welcome"]
```

The **Dockerfile** starts with the **FROM** directive that specifies the latest Golang image as the parent image. This will set the **/myapp** directory as the current working directory of the Docker image. Then, the **COPY** directive will copy the **welcome.go** source file that you created in *step 3* to the Docker filesystem. Next is the **go build** command, which will build the Golang code that you created. Finally, the welcome code will be executed.

9. Now, build the Docker image:

```
$ docker build -t welcome:v1 .
```

You will see that the image is successfully built with the image ID as **b938bc11abf1** and tagged as **welcome:v1**:

```
Sending build context to Docker daemon  4.096kB
Step 1/5 : FROM golang:latest
latest: Pulling from library/golang
d6ff36c9ec48: Pull complete
c958d65b3090: Pull complete
edaf0a6b092f: Pull complete
80931cf68816: Pull complete
813643441356: Pull complete
d2d74a4aa2e6: Pull complete
568efbaeb143: Pull complete
Digest: sha256:4c3279e05a0131c0565466ac538755f104d8d936efbc4c30ba7d717c73f3e2c2
Status: Downloaded newer image for golang:latest
 ---> 75605a415539
Step 2/5 : WORKDIR /myapp
 ---> Running in 6d03d0adbb8d
Removing intermediate container 6d03d0adbb8d
 ---> 808fee03696f
Step 3/5 : COPY welcome.go .
 ---> 1af1f63c6f65
Step 4/5 : RUN go build -o welcome .
 ---> Running in 22fc4a276303
Removing intermediate container 22fc4a276303
 ---> 6dfecd457c96
Step 5/5 : ENTRYPOINT ["./welcome"]
 ---> Running in 8a7938601015
Removing intermediate container 8a7938601015
 ---> cc0804e7c390
Successfully built cc0804e7c390
Successfully tagged welcome:v1
 /docker $ ▮
```

Figure 4.1: Building the Docker image

10. Use the **docker image ls** command to list all the Docker images available on your computer:

```
$ docker image ls
```

The command should return the following output:

```
/docker $ docker image ls
REPOSITORY          TAG          IMAGE ID          CREATED          SIZE
welcome             v1           cc0804e7c390      4 minutes ago    841MB
golang              latest       75605a415539      2 weeks ago      839MB
 /docker $ ▮
```

Figure 4.2: Listing all Docker images

It can be observed in the preceding output that the image size of the **welcome:v1** image is **805MB**.

In this section, we discussed how to use the normal Docker build process to build a Docker image and observed its size. The result was a huge Docker image, over 800 MB in size. The main disadvantage of these large Docker images is that they will take significant time to build, deploy, push, and pull over the networks. So, it is recommended to create minimal-sized Docker images whenever possible. In the next section, we will discuss how we can use the builder pattern to optimize the image size.

WHAT IS THE BUILDER PATTERN?

The **builder pattern** is a method used to create optimally sized Docker images. It uses two Docker images and selectively copies essential artifacts from one to the other. The first Docker image is known as the **build image** and is used as the build environment to build the executables from the source code. This Docker image contains compilers, build tools, and development dependencies required during the build process.

The second Docker image is known as the **runtime image** and is used as the runtime environment to run the executables created by the first Docker container. This Docker image contains only the executables, the dependencies, and the runtime tools. A shell script is used to copy the artifacts using the **docker container cp** command.

The entire process of building the image using the builder pattern consists of the following steps:

1. Create the **Build** Docker image.

2. Create a container from the **Build** Docker image.

3. Copy the artifacts from the **Build** Docker image to the local filesystem.

4. Build the **Runtime** Docker image using copied artifacts:

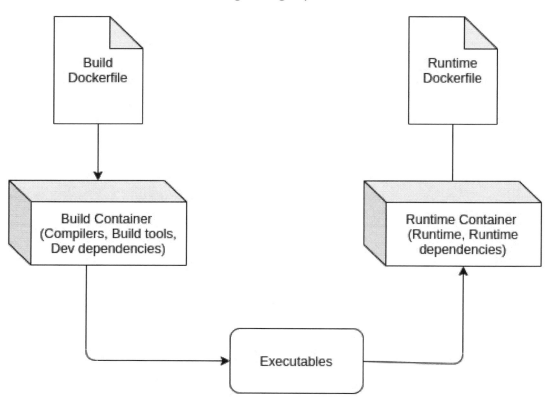

Figure 4.3: Building images using the builder pattern

As illustrated in the preceding image, the **Build Dockerfile** is used to create the build container that will contain all the tools required to build the source code, including compilers and build tools such as Maven, Gradle, and development dependencies. Once the build container is created, the shell script will copy the executables from the build container to the Docker host. Finally, the **Runtime** container will be created with the executables copied from the **Build** container.

Now, observe how the builder pattern can be used to create minimal Docker images. The following is the first **Dockerfile** used to create the **Build** Docker container. This **Dockerfile** is named Dockerfile.build to distinguish it from the **Runtime Dockerfile**:

```
# Start from latest golang parent image
FROM golang:latest

# Set the working directory
WORKDIR /myapp

# Copy source file from current directory to container
COPY helloworld.go .

# Build the application
RUN go build -o helloworld .

# Run the application
ENTRYPOINT ["./helloworld"]
```

This is the same **Dockerfile** that we observed with the normal Docker builds. This was used to create the **helloworld** executable from the **helloworld.go** source file.

The following is the second **Dockerfile** used to build the **Runtime** Docker container:

```
# Start from latest alpine parent image
FROM alpine:latest

# Set the working directory
WORKDIR /myapp

# Copy helloworld app from current directory to container
COPY helloworld .

# Run the application
ENTRYPOINT ["./helloworld"]
```

As opposed to the first **Dockerfile**, created from the **golang** parent image, this second **Dockerfile** uses the **alpine** image as its parent image because it is a minimal-sized Docker image, at only 5 MB. This image uses Alpine Linux, a lightweight Linux distribution. Next, the **/myapp** directory is configured as the working directory. Finally, the **helloworld** artifact is copied to the Docker image, and the **ENTRYPOINT** directive is used to run the application.

This **helloworld** artifact is the result of the **go build -o helloworld .** command executed in the first **Dockerfile**. We will be using a shell script to copy this artifact from the **build** Docker container to the local filesystem, from where this artifact will be copied to the runtime Docker image.

Consider the following shell script used to copy the build artifacts between Docker containers:

```
#!/bin/sh

# Build the builder Docker image
docker image build -t helloworld-build -f Dockerfile.build .

# Create container from the build Docker image
docker container create --name helloworld-build-container
  helloworld-build

# Copy build artifacts from build container to the local filesystem
docker container cp helloworld-build-container:/myapp/helloworld .

# Build the runtime Docker image
docker image build -t helloworld .

# Remove the build Docker container
docker container rm -f helloworld-build-container

# Remove the copied artifact
rm helloworld
```

This shell script will first build the **helloworld-build** Docker image using the **Dockerfile.build** file. The next step is to create a Docker container from the **helloworld-build** image so that we can copy the **helloworld** artifact to the Docker host. Once the container is created, we need to execute the command to copy the **helloworld** artifact from the **helloworld-build-container** to the current directory of the Docker host. Now, we can build the runtime container with the **docker image build** command. Finally, we will execute the necessary cleanup tasks by removing the intermediate artifacts, such as the **helloworld-build-container** container and the **helloworld** executable.

Once we execute the shell script, we should be able to see two Docker images:

```
REPOSITORY          TAG        IMAGE ID        CREATED        SIZE
helloworld          latest     faff247e2b35    3 hours ago    7.6MB
helloworld-build    latest     f8c10c5bd28d    3 hours ago    805MB
```

Note the size difference between the two Docker images. The **helloworld** Docker image is only 7.6 MB in size, which is a huge reduction from the **helloworld-build** image at 805 MB.

As we can see, the builder pattern can drastically reduce the size of the Docker images by copying only the essential artifacts to the final image. However, the disadvantage with the builder pattern is that we need to maintain two **Dockerfiles** and a shell script.

In the next exercise, we will gain hands-on experience in creating an optimized Docker image using the builder pattern.

EXERCISE 4.02: BUILDING A DOCKER IMAGE WITH THE BUILDER PATTERN

In *Exercise 4.01*, *Building a Docker Image with the Normal Build Process*, you created a Docker image to compile and run the Golang application. Now the application is ready to go live, but the manager is not happy with the size of the Docker image. You have been asked to create a minimal-sized Docker image to run the application. In this exercise, you will optimize the Docker image using the builder pattern:

1. Create a new directory named **builder-pattern** for this exercise:

```
$ mkdir builder-pattern
```

2. Navigate to the newly created **builder-pattern** directory:

```
$ cd builder-pattern
```

3. Within the **builder-pattern** directory, create a file named **welcome.go**. This file will be copied to the Docker image at build time:

```
$ touch welcome.go
```

4. Now, open the **welcome.go** file using your favorite text editor:

```
$ vim welcome.go
```

5. Add the following content to the **welcome.go** file, and then save and exit this file:

```
package main

import "fmt"

func main() {
    fmt.Println("Welcome to multi-stage Docker builds")
}
```

This is a simple **hello world** application written in Golang. This will output **"Welcome to multi-stage Docker builds"** once executed.

6. Within the **builder-pattern** directory, create a file named **Dockerfile.build**. This file will contain all the instructions that you are going to use to create the **build** Docker image:

```
$ touch Dockerfile.build
```

7. Now, open the **Dockerfile.build** using your favorite text editor:

```
$ vim Dockerfile.build
```

8. Add the following content to the **Dockerfile.build** file and save the file:

```
FROM golang:latest
WORKDIR /myapp
COPY welcome.go .
RUN go build -o welcome .
ENTRYPOINT ["./welcome"]
```

This has the same content that you created for the **Dockerfile** in *Exercise 4.01, Building a Docker Image with the Normal Build Process*.

9. Next, create the **Dockerfile** for the runtime container. Within the **builder-pattern** directory, create a file named **Dockerfile**. This file will contain all the instructions that you are going to use to create the runtime Docker image:

```
$ touch Dockerfile
```

10. Now, open the **Dockerfile** using your favorite text editor:

```
$ vim Dockerfile
```

11. Add the following content to the **Dockerfile** and save the file:

```
FROM scratch
WORKDIR /myapp
COPY welcome .
ENTRYPOINT ["./welcome"]
```

This **Dockerfile** uses the scratch image, which is the most minimal image in Docker, as the parent. Then, it will configure the **/myapp** directory as the working directory. Next, the welcome executable is copied from the Docker host to the runtime Docker image. Finally, the **ENTRYPOINT** directive is used to execute the welcome executable.

12. Create the shell script to copy the executables between Docker containers. Within the **builder-pattern** directory, create a file named **build.sh**. This file will contain the steps to coordinate the build process between the two Docker containers:

```
$ touch build.sh
```

13. Now, open the **build.sh** file using your favorite text editor:

```
$ vim build.sh
```

14. Add the following content to the shell script and save the file:

```
#!/bin/sh

echo "Creating welcome builder image"

docker image build -t welcome-builder:v1 -f Dockerfile.build .

docker container create --name welcome-builder-container
  welcome-builder:v1
```

```
docker container cp welcome-builder-container:/myapp/welcome .

docker container rm -f welcome-builder-container

echo "Creating welcome runtime image"

docker image build -t welcome-runtime:v1 .

rm welcome
```

This shell script will first build the **welcome-builder** Docker image and create a container from it. Then it will copy the compiled Golang executable from the container to the local filesystem. Next, the **welcome-builder-container** container is removed as it is an intermediate container. Finally, the **welcome-runtime** image is built.

15. Add execution permissions to the **build.sh** shell script:

```
$ chmod +x build.sh
```

16. Now that you have the two **Dockerfiles** and the shell script, build the Docker image by executing the **build.sh** shell script:

```
$ ./build.sh
```

The image will be successfully built and tagged as **welcome-runtime:v1**:

```
Sending build context to Docker daemon  2.042MB
Step 1/4 : FROM scratch
 --->
Step 2/4 : WORKDIR /myapp
 ---> Using cache
 ---> 78f84b9685c1
Step 3/4 : COPY welcome .
 ---> Using cache
 ---> fff4a492c4d3
Step 4/4 : ENTRYPOINT ["./welcome"]
 ---> Using cache
 ---> be3b3f630159
Successfully built be3b3f630159
Successfully tagged welcome-runtime:v1
 /docker $ █
```

Figure 4.4: Building the Docker image

17. Use the **docker image** ls command to list all the Docker images available on your computer:

```
docker image ls
```

You should get the list of all the available Docker images as shown in the following figure:

```
/docker $ docker image ls
REPOSITORY          TAG       IMAGE ID        CREATED          SIZE
welcome-runtime     v1        be3b3f630159    2 minutes ago    2.03MB
welcome-builder     v1        cc0804e7c390    7 minutes ago    841MB
welcome             v1        cc0804e7c390    7 minutes ago    841MB
golang              latest    75605a415539    2 weeks ago      839MB
 /docker $ ▊
```

Figure 4.5: Listing all Docker images

As you can see from the preceding output, there are two Docker images available. welcome-builder has all the builds tools and is 805 MB, while welcome-runtime has a significantly lower image size of 2.01 MB. **golang:latest** is the Docker image we used as the parent image of **welcome-builder**.

In this exercise, you learned how to use the builder pattern to reduce the size of the Docker image. However, using the builder pattern to optimize the size of the Docker image means that we have to maintain two **Dockerfiles** and one shell script. In the next section, let's observe how we can eliminate them by using a multi-stage **Dockerfile**.

INTRODUCTION TO MULTI-STAGE DOCKERFILES

Multi-stage Dockerfiles are a feature that allows for a single **Dockerfile** to contain multiple stages that can produce optimized Docker images. As we observed with the builder pattern in the previous section, the stages will usually include a builder state to build the executables from source code, and a runtime stage to run the executables. Multi-stage **Dockerfiles** will use multiple **FROM** directives within the **Dockerfile** for each stage, and each stage will start with a different base image. Only the essential files will be copied selectively from one stage to the other. Before multi-stage **Dockerfiles**, this was achieved with the builder pattern, as we discussed in the previous section.

Multi-stage Docker builds allow us to create minimal-sized Docker images that are similar to the builder pattern but eliminate the problems associated with it. As we have seen in the previous example, the builder pattern needs to maintain two **Dockerfiles** and a shell script. In contrast, multi-stage Docker builds will need only one **Dockerfile** and do not require any shell script to copy the executables between Docker containers. Also, the builder pattern requires that you copy the executables to the Docker host before copying them to the final Docker image. This is not required with the multi-stage Docker builds as we can use the **--from** flag to copy the executables between Docker images without copying them to the Docker host.

Now, let's observe the structure of a multi-stage **Dockerfile**:

```
# Start from latest golang parent image
FROM golang:latest

# Set the working directory
WORKDIR /myapp

# Copy source file from current directory to container
COPY helloworld.go .

# Build the application
RUN go build -o helloworld .


# Start from latest alpine parent image
FROM alpine:latest

# Set the working directory
WORKDIR /myapp

# Copy helloworld app from current directory to container
COPY --from=0 /myapp/helloworld .

# Run the application
ENTRYPOINT ["./helloworld"]
```

The main difference between a normal **Dockerfile** and a multi-stage **Dockerfile** is that a multi-stage **Dockerfile** will use multiple **FROM** directives to build each phase. Each new phase will start with a new parent image and does not contain anything from the previous image other than the selectively copied executables. **COPY --from=0** is used to copy the executable from the first stage to the second stage.

Build the Docker image and tag the image as **multi-stage:v1**:

```
docker image build -t multi-stage:v1 .
```

Now, you can list the available Docker images:

```
REPOSITORY      TAG        IMAGE ID       CREATED        SIZE
multi-stage     latest     75e1f4bcabd0   7 seconds ago  7.6MB
```

You can see that this has resulted in a Docker image of the same size that we observed with the builder pattern.

> **NOTE**
>
> Multi-stage **Dockerfiles** reduce the number of **Dockerfiles** required and eliminate the shell script without making any difference to the size of the image.

By default, the stages in the multi-stage **Dockerfile** are referred to by an integer number, starting with **0** from the first stage. These stages can be named to increase readability and maintainability by adding **AS <NAME>** to the **FROM** directive. The following is the improved version of the multi-stage **Dockerfile** that you observed in the preceding code block:

```
# Start from latest golang parent image
FROM golang:latest AS builder

# Set the working directory
WORKDIR /myapp

# Copy source file from current directory to container
COPY helloworld.go .
```

```
# Build the application
RUN go build -o helloworld .


# Start from latest alpine parent image
FROM alpine:latest AS runtime

# Set the working directory
WORKDIR /myapp

# Copy helloworld app from current directory to container
COPY --from=builder /myapp/helloworld .

# Run the application
ENTRYPOINT ["./helloworld"]
```

In the preceding example, we named the first stage **builder** and second stage **runtime**, as shown here:

```
FROM golang:latest AS builder
FROM alpine:latest AS runtime
```

Then, while copying the artifacts in the second stage, you used the name **builder** for the **--from** flag:

```
COPY --from=builder /myapp/helloworld .
```

While building a multi-stage **Dockerfile**, there might be instances where you want to build only up to a specific build stage. Consider that your **Dockerfile** has two stages. The first one is to build the development stage and contains all the build and debug tools, and the second is to build the production image that will contain only the runtime tools. During the code development phase of the project, you might only need to build up to the development stage to test and debug your code whenever necessary. In this scenario, you can use the **--target** flag with the **docker build** command to specify an intermediate stage as the final stage for the resulting image:

```
docker image build --target builder -t multi-stage-dev:v1 .
```

In the preceding example, you used **--target builder** to stop the build at the builder stage.

In the next exercise, you will learn to use a multi-stage **Dockerfile** to create a size-optimized Docker image.

EXERCISE 4.03: BUILDING A DOCKER IMAGE WITH A MULTI-STAGE DOCKER BUILD

In *Exercise 4.02, Building a Docker Image with the Builder Pattern*, you used the builder pattern to optimize the size of the Docker image. However, there is an operational burden, as you need to manage two **Dockerfiles** and a shell script during the Docker image build process. In this exercise, you are going to use a multi-stage **Dockerfile** to eliminate this operational burden.

1. Create a new directory named **multi-stage** for this exercise:

```
mkdir multi-stage
```

2. Navigate to the newly created **multi-stage** directory:

```
cd multi-stage
```

3. Within the **multi-stage** directory, create a file named **welcome.go**. This file will be copied to the Docker image during the build time:

```
$ touch welcome.go
```

4. Now, open the **welcome.go** file using your favorite text editor:

```
$ vim welcome.go
```

5. Add the following content to the **welcome.go** file, and then save and exit this file:

```
package main

import "fmt"

func main() {
    fmt.Println("Welcome to multi-stage Docker builds")
}
```

This is a simple **hello world** application written in Golang. This will output **"Welcome to multi-stage Docker builds"** once executed.

Within the multi-stage directory, create a file named **Dockerfile**. This file will be the multi-stage **Dockerfile**:

```
touch Dockerfile
```

6. Now, open the **Dockerfile** using your favorite text editor:

```
vim Dockerfile
```

7. Add the following content to the **Dockerfile** and save the file:

```
FROM golang:latest AS builder
WORKDIR /myapp
COPY welcome.go .
RUN go build -o welcome .


FROM scratch
WORKDIR /myapp
COPY --from=builder /myapp/welcome .
ENTRYPOINT ["./welcome"]
```

This multi-stage **Dockerfile** uses the latest **golang** image as the parent image and this stage is named **builder**. Next, the **/myapp** directory is specified as the current working directory. Then, the **COPY** directive is used to copy the **welcome.go** source file and the **RUN** directive is used to build the Golang file.

The next stage of the **Dockerfile** uses the **scratch** image as the parent image. This will set the **/myapp** directory as the current working directory of the Docker image. Then, the **COPY** directive is used to copy the **welcome** executable from the builder stage to this stage. Finally, **ENTRYPOINT** is used to run the **welcome** executable.

8. Build the Docker image using the following command:

```
docker build -t welcome-optimized:v1 .
```

The image will be successfully built and tagged as **welcome-optimized:v1**:

```
Sending build context to Docker daemon  4.096kB
Step 1/8 : FROM golang:latest AS builder
 ---> 75605a415539
Step 2/8 : WORKDIR /myapp
 ---> Using cache
 ---> 808fee03696f
Step 3/8 : COPY welcome.go .
 ---> Using cache
 ---> 1af1f63c6f65
Step 4/8 : RUN go build -o welcome .
 ---> Using cache
 ---> 6dfecd457c96
Step 5/8 : FROM scratch
 --->
Step 6/8 : WORKDIR /myapp
 ---> Using cache
 ---> 78f84b9685c1
Step 7/8 : COPY --from=builder /myapp/welcome .
 ---> 402eba14a6c1
Step 8/8 : ENTRYPOINT ["./welcome"]
 ---> Running in 4c81f247e514
Removing intermediate container 4c81f247e514
 ---> 04cf352dfc37
Successfully built 04cf352dfc37
Successfully tagged welcome-optimized:v1
 /docker $ █
```

Figure 4.6: Building the Docker image

9. Use the **docker image ls** command to list all the Docker images available on your computer. These images are available on your computer, either when you pull them from Docker Registry or when you build them on your computer:

```
docker images
```

As you can see from the following output, the **welcome-optimized** image has the same size as the **welcome-runtime** image that you built in *Exercise 4.02, Building a Docker Image with the Builder Pattern*:

```
/docker $ docker images
REPOSITORY          TAG       IMAGE ID        CREATED           SIZE
welcome-optimized   v1        04cf352dfc37    25 seconds ago    2.03MB
welcome-runtime     v1        be3b3f630159    3 minutes ago     2.03MB
welcome-builder     v1        cc0804e7c390    8 minutes ago     841MB
welcome             v1        cc0804e7c390    8 minutes ago     841MB
golang              latest    75605a415539    2 weeks ago       839MB
 /docker $ █
```

Figure 4.7: Listing all Docker images

In this exercise, you learned how to use multi-stage **Dockerfiles** to build optimized Docker images. The following table presents a summary of the key differences between the builder pattern and multi-stage **Docker Builds**:

Builder Pattern	Multi-Stage Docker Builds
Need to maintain two `Dockerfiles` and a shell script	Needs only one `Dockerfile`
Need to copy the executables to the Docker host before copying them to the final Docker image	Can use the `--from` flag to copy the executables between stages without copying them to the Docker host

Figure 4.8: Differences between the builder pattern and multi-stage Docker Builds

In the next section, we will review the best practices to follow when writing a **Dockerfile**.

DOCKERFILE BEST PRACTICES

In the previous section, we discussed how we can build an efficient Docker image with multi-stage **Dockerfiles**. In this section, we will cover other recommended best practices for writing **Dockerfiles**. These best practices will ensure reduced build time, reduced image size, increased security, and increased maintainability of the Docker images produced.

USING AN APPROPRIATE PARENT IMAGE

Using the appropriate base image is one of the key recommendations when building efficient Docker images.

It is always encouraged to use official images from the **Docker Hub** as the parent image when you are building custom Docker images. These official images will ensure that all best practices are followed, documentation is available, and security patches are applied. For example, if you need the **JDK (Java Development Kit)** for your application, you can use the **openjdk** official Docker image instead of using the generic **ubuntu** image and installing the JDK on top of the **ubuntu** image:

Inefficient Dockerfile	Efficient Dockerfile

`FROM ubuntu`
`RUN apt-get update && \`
`    apt-get install -y openjdk-8-jdk`
	`FROM openjdk`

Figure 4.9: Using appropriate parent images

Secondly, avoid using the **latest** tag for the parent image when building Docker images for production environments. The **latest** tag might get pointed to a newer version of the image as the new versions are released to the Docker Hub, and the newer version might not be backward compatible with your applications, leading to failures in your production environments. Instead, the best practice is to always use a specific versioned tag as the parent image:

Inefficient Dockerfile	Efficient Dockerfile
FROM openjdk:latest	FROM openjdk:8

Figure 4.10: Avoiding the use of the latest tag of the parent image

Finally, using the minimal version of the parent image is critical to getting a minimal-sized Docker image. Most of the official Docker images in Docker Hub have a minimal-sized image built around the Alpine Linux image. Also, in our example, we can use the **JRE (Java Runtime Environment)** to run the application instead of the JDK, which contains the build tools:

Inefficient Dockerfile	Efficient Dockerfile
FROM openjdk:8	FROM openjdk:8-jre-alpine

Figure 4.11: Using minimal-sized images

The **openjdk:8-jre-alpine** image will be only 84.9 MB in size, whereas **openjdk:8** will be 488 MB in size.

USING A NON-ROOT USER FOR BETTER SECURITY

By default, Docker containers run with the root (**id = 0**) user. This allows the user to perform all the necessary administrative activities, such as changing system configurations, installing packages, and binding to privileged ports. However, this is high risk and is considered a bad security practice when running Docker containers in production environments since hackers can gain root access to the Docker host by hacking the applications running inside the Docker container.

Running containers as a non-root user is a recommended best practice to improve the security of the Docker container. This will adhere to the principle of least privilege, which ensures that the application has only the bare minimum privileges to perform its tasks. There are two methods that we can use to run a container as a non-root user: with the **--user** (or **-u**) flag, and with the **USER** directive.

Using the **--user** (or **-u**) flag with the **docker run** command is one method for changing the default user while running a Docker container. Either the username or the user ID can be specified with the **--user** (or **-u**) flag:

```
$ docker run --user=9999 ubuntu:focal
```

In the preceding command, we have specified the user ID as **9999**. If we are specifying the user as an ID, the corresponding user does not have to be available in the Docker container.

Additionally, we can use the **USER** directive within the **Dockerfile** to define the default user. However, this value can be overridden with the **--user** flag while starting the Docker container:

```
FROM ubuntu:focal
RUN apt-get update
RUN useradd demo-user
USER demo-user
CMD whoami
```

In the preceding example, we have used the **USER** directive to set the default user to **demo-user**. This means that any command after the **USER** directive will be executed as a **demo-user**.

USING DOCKERIGNORE

The **.dockerignore** file is a special text file within the Docker context that is used to specify a list of files to be excluded from the Docker context while building the Docker image. Once we execute the **docker build** command, the Docker client will package the entire build context as a TAR archive and upload it to the Docker daemon. When we execute the **docker build** command, the first line of the output is **Sending build context to Docker daemon**, which indicates that the Docker client is uploading the build context to the Docker daemon:

```
Sending build context to Docker daemon   18.6MB
Step 1/5 : FROM ubuntu:focal
```

Each time we build the Docker image, the build context will be sent to the Docker daemon. As this will take time and bandwidth during the Docker image build process, it is recommended to exclude all the files that are not needed in the final Docker image. The **.dockerignore** file can be used to achieve this purpose. In addition to saving time and bandwidth, the **.dockerignore** file is used to exclude the confidential files, such as password files and key files from the build context.

The `.dockerignore` file should be created in the root directory of the build context. Before sending the build context to the Docker daemon, the Docker client will look for the `.dockerignore` file in the root of the build context. If the `.dockerignore` file exists, the Docker client will exclude all the files mentioned in the `.dockerignore` file from the build context.

The following is the content of a sample `.dockerignore` file:

```
PASSWORDS.txt
tmp/
*.md
!README.md
```

In the preceding example, we have specifically excluded the **PASSWORDS.txt** file and **tmp** directory from the build context, as well as all files with the `.md` extension except for the **README.md** file.

MINIMIZING LAYERS

Each line in the **Dockerfile** will create a new layer that will take up space in the Docker image. So, it is recommended to create as few layers as possible when building the Docker image. To achieve this, combine the **RUN** directives whenever possible.

As an example, consider the following **Dockerfile**, which will update the package repository first and then install the **redis-server** and **nginx** packages:

```
FROM ubuntu:focal
RUN apt-get update
RUN apt-get install -y nginx
RUN apt-get install -y redis-server
```

This **Dockerfile** can be optimized by combining the three **RUN** directives:

```
FROM ubuntu:focal
RUN apt-get update \
   && apt-get install -y nginx redis-server
```

DON'T INSTALL UNNECESSARY TOOLS

Not installing unnecessary debugging tools (such as **vim**, **curl**, and **telnet**) and removing unnecessary dependencies can help to create efficient Docker images that are small in size. Some package managers such as **apt** will install recommended and suggested packages automatically alongside required packages. We can avoid this by specifying the **no-install-recommends** flag with the **apt-get install** command:

```
FROM ubuntu:focal
RUN apt-get update \
  && apt-get install --no-install-recommends -y nginx
```

In the preceding example, we are installing the **nginx** package with the **no-install-recommends** flag, which will help to reduce the final image size by around 10 MB.

In addition to using the **no-install-recommends** flag, we can also remove the cache of the **apt** package manager to further reduce the final Docker image size. This can be achieved by running **rm -rf /var/lib/apt/lists/*** at the end of the **apt-get install** command:

```
FROM ubuntu:focal
RUN apt-get update \
    && apt-get install --no-install-recommends -y nginx \
    && rm -rf /var/lib/apt/lists/*
```

In this section, we discussed the best practices when writing a **Dockerfile**. Following these best practices will help to reduce build time, reduce the image size, increase security, and increase the maintainability of the Docker image.

Now, let's test our knowledge by deploying a Golang HTTP server with a multi-stage Docker build in the next activity.

ACTIVITY 4.01: DEPLOYING A GOLANG HTTP SERVER WITH A MULTI-STAGE DOCKER BUILD

Imagine that you have been tasked with deploying a Golang HTTP server to a Docker container. Your manager has asked you to build a minimal-sized Docker image and observe best practices while building the **Dockerfile**.

This Golang HTTP server will return different responses based on the invoke URL:

Invoke URL	Message
`http://127.0.0.1:<port>/`	`Home Page`
`http://127.0.0.1:<port>/contact`	`Contact Us`
`http://127.0.0.1:<port>/login`	`Login Page`

Figure 4.12: Responses based on the invoke URL

Your task is to dockerize the Golang application given in the following code block using a multi-stage **Dockerfile**:

```
package main

import (
    "net/http"
    "fmt"
    "log"
    "os"
)

func main() {

    http.HandleFunc("/", defaultHandler)
    http.HandleFunc("/contact", contactHandler)
    http.HandleFunc("/login", loginHandler)

    port := os.Getenv("PORT")
    if port == "" {
        port = "8080"
    }

    log.Println("Service started on port " + port)
```

```go
    err := http.ListenAndServe(":"+port, nil)
    if err != nil {
        log.Fatal("ListenAndServe: ", err)
        return
    }
}


func defaultHandler(w http.ResponseWriter, r *http.Request) {
    fmt.Fprintf(w, "<h1>Home Page</h1>")
}

func contactHandler(w http.ResponseWriter, r *http.Request) {
    fmt.Fprintf(w, "<h1>Contact Us</h1>")
}

func loginHandler(w http.ResponseWriter, r *http.Request) {
    fmt.Fprintf(w, "<h1>Login Page</h1>")
}
```

Execute the following steps to complete this activity:

1. Create a folder to store the activity files.

2. Create a **main.go** file with the code provided in the preceding code block.

3. Create a multi-stage **Dockerfile** with two stages. The first stage will use the **golang** image. This stage will build the Golang application using the **go build** command. The second stage will use an **alpine** image. This stage will copy the executable from the first stage and execute it.

4. Build and run the Docker image.

5. Once completed, stop and remove the Docker container.

You should get the following output when you navigate to the URL
`http://127.0.0.1:8080/`:

Figure 4.13: Expected output of Activity 4.01

> NOTE
>
> The solution for this activity can be found on page 659.

SUMMARY

We started this chapter by defining a normal Docker build and creating a simple
Golang Docker image using the normal Docker build process. Then we observed the
size of the resulting Docker image and discussed how a minimal-sized Docker image
can speed up the build and deployment times for Docker containers and enhance
security by reducing the attack surface.

We then used the builder pattern to create minimal-sized Docker images, utilizing
two **Dockerfiles** and a shell script in this process to create the image. We
explored multi-stage Docker builds—a new feature introduced to Docker in version
17.05 that can help to eliminate the operational burden of having to maintain
two **Dockerfiles** and a shell script. Finally, we discussed the best practices for
writing **Dockerfiles** and how these best practices can ensure reduced build time,
reduced image size, and increased security, while increasing the maintainability of the
Docker image.

In the next chapter, we will cover **docker-compose** and how it can be used to
define and run multi-container Docker applications.

5

COMPOSING ENVIRONMENTS WITH DOCKER COMPOSE

OVERVIEW

This chapter covers the creation and management of multi-container applications using Docker Compose. You will learn how to create Docker Compose files to define complex containerized applications and how to run the Docker Compose CLI to manage the life cycle of multi-container applications. This chapter will enable you to configure Docker Compose applications with different methods and design applications with dependencies on other applications.

INTRODUCTION

In the previous chapters, we discussed how to use Docker containers and `Dockerfiles` to create containerized applications. As apps get more complicated, the management of the containers and their configurations becomes more involved.

For example, imagine you are developing an online shop with frontend, backend, payment, and ordering microservices. Each microservice is implemented with the most appropriate programming language before being built, packaged, and configured. Thus, complex applications are designed to run in separate containers in the Docker ecosystem. Different containers require multiple `Dockerfiles` to define Docker images.

They also need complex commands to configure, run, and troubleshoot applications. All this can be achieved using **Docker Compose**, a tool for defining and managing applications in multiple containers. Complex applications such as YAML files can be configured and run with a single command in Docker Compose. It is suitable for various environments, including development, testing, **Continuous Integration (CI)** pipelines, and production.

The essential features of Docker Compose can be grouped into three categories:

- **Isolation**: Docker Compose allows you to run multiple instances of your complex application in complete isolation. Although it seems like a trivial feature, it makes it possible to run multiple copies of the same application stack on developer machines, CI servers, or shared hosts. Therefore, sharing resources increases utilization while decreasing operational complexity.

- **Stateful data management**: Docker Compose manages the volumes of your containers so that they do not lose their data from previous runs. This feature makes it easier to create and operate applications that store their state on disks, such as databases.

- **Iterative design**: Docker Compose works with an explicitly defined configuration that consists of multiple containers. The containers in the configuration can be extended with new containers. For instance, imagine you have two containers in your application. If you add a third container and run Docker Compose commands, the first two containers will not be restarted or recreated. Docker Compose will only create and join the newly added third container.

These features make Compose an essential tool for creating and managing applications as multiple containers in various platforms. In this chapter, you will see how Docker Compose helps you to manage the complete life cycle of complicated applications.

You will start by diving deep into Compose CLI and file anatomy. Following this, you will learn how to configure applications with multiple techniques and how to define service dependencies. Since Docker Compose is an essential tool for the Docker environment, both technical and hands-on experience are vital to have in your toolbox.

DOCKER COMPOSE CLI

Docker Compose works with **Docker Engine** to create and manage multi-container applications. To interact with Docker Engine, Compose uses a CLI tool named **docker-compose**. On Mac and Windows systems, **docker-compose** is already a part of Docker Desktop. However, on Linux systems, you need to install the **docker-compose** CLI tool after installing Docker Engine. It is packaged into a single executable, and you can install it with the following commands on Linux systems.

INSTALLING DOCKER COMPOSE CLI IN LINUX

1. Download the binary to **/usr/local/bin** with the following command in your Terminal:

```
sudo curl -L "https://github.com/docker/compose/releases/
download/1.25.0/docker-compose-$(uname -s)-$(uname -m)" -o /usr/
local/bin/docker-compose
```

2. Make the downloaded binary executable with the following command:

```
sudo chmod +x /usr/local/bin/docker-compose
```

3. Test the CLI and installation with the following command in the Terminal on all operating systems:

```
docker-compose version
```

If it is installed correctly, you will see the versions of the CLI and its dependencies as follows. For instance, in the following output, the **docker-compose** CLI has version **1.25.1-rc1** and its dependencies, **docker-py**, **CPython**, and **OpenSSL**, are also listed with their versions:

```
[ /docker-ws $ docker-compose version
docker-compose version 1.25.1-rc1, build d92e9bee
docker-py version: 4.1.0
CPython version: 3.7.4
OpenSSL version: OpenSSL 1.1.1c  28 May 2019
 /docker-ws $ 
```

Figure 5.1: docker-compose version output

Up until now, we have learned how to install the Docker Compose CLI in Linux. Now we will look into the commands and subcommands that manage the complete life cycle of multi-container applications.

DOCKER COMPOSE CLI COMMANDS

The **docker-compose** command is capable of managing the complete life cycle of multi-containers applications. With the subcommands, it is possible to start, stop, and recreate services. Also, it is possible to check the status of the running stacks and get the logs. You will get hands-on experience with the essential commands throughout this chapter. Likewise, a preview of all capabilities can be listed with the following command:

```
docker-compose --help
```

The output of the command should look like the following:

```
/docker-ws $ docker-compose --help
Define and run multi-container applications with Docker.

Usage:
  docker-compose [-f <arg>...] [options] [COMMAND] [ARGS...]
  docker-compose -h|--help

Options:
  -f, --file FILE             Specify an alternate compose file
                              (default: docker-compose.yml)
  -p, --project-name NAME     Specify an alternate project name
                              (default: directory name)
  ...
  ...
Commands:
  build         Build or rebuild services
  bundle        Generate a Docker bundle from the Compose file
  config        Validate and view the Compose file
  create        Create services
  down          Stop and remove containers, networks, images, and volumes
  events        Receive real time events from containers
  exec          Execute a command in a running container
  help          Get help on a command
  images        List images
  kill          Kill containers
  logs          View output from containers
  pause         Pause services
  port          Print the public port for a port binding
  ps            List containers
  pull          Pull service images
  push          Push service images
  restart       Restart services
  rm            Remove stopped containers
  run           Run a one-off command
  scale         Set number of containers for a service
  start         Start services
  stop          Stop services
  top           Display the running processes
  unpause       Unpause services
  up            Create and start containers
  version       Show the Docker-Compose version information
/docker-ws $
```

Figure 5.2: docker-compose commands

There are three essential **docker-compose** commands that are used to manage the life cycle of applications. The life cycle and commands can be illustrated as follows:

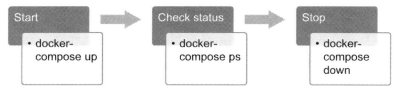

Figure 5.3: docker-compose life cycle

- **docker-compose up**: This command creates and starts the containers defined in the configuration. It is possible to build container images or use pre-built images from the registry. In addition, it is possible to run the containers in the background in **detached** mode with the **-d** or **--detach** flags. It is convenient to use **detached** mode for long-running containers, such as web servers, that we do not expect to stop in the short term. Additional options and flags can be checked with the **docker-compose up --help** command.

- **docker-compose ps**: This command lists the containers and their status information. It is helpful for troubleshooting and container health checks. For instance, if you create a two-container application with a backend and a frontend, you can check the status of each container with the **docker-compose ps** command. It helps to find out whether your backend or frontend is down, is not responding to their health checks, or has failed to start due to misconfiguration.

- **docker-compose down**: This command stops and removes all the resources, including containers, networks, images, and volumes.

DOCKER COMPOSE FILE

Multi-container applications are run and defined using the **docker-compose** CLI. By convention, the default name of these files is **docker-compose.yaml**. Docker Compose is a powerful tool; however, its power depends on the configuration. Therefore, knowing how to create **docker-compose.yaml** files is essential and requires great attention.

> **NOTE**
>
> Docker Compose works with the **docker-compose.yaml** and **docker-compose.yml** file extensions by default.

docker-compose.yaml files consist of four main sections, as illustrated
in *Figure 5.4*:

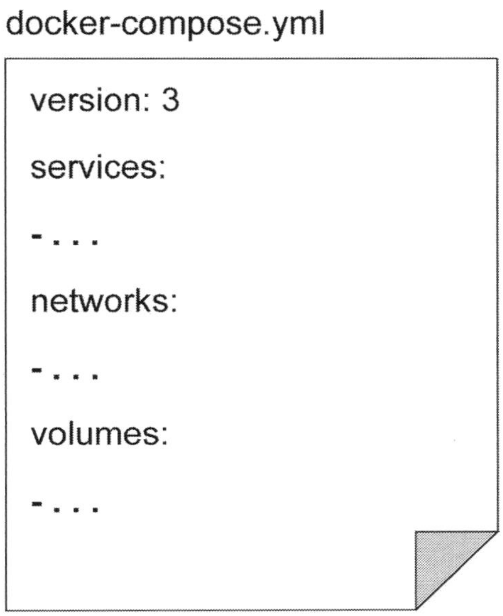

docker-compose.yml

```
version: 3

services:

- . . .

networks:

- . . .

volumes:

- . . .
```

Figure 5.4: The docker-compose file structure

- **version**: This section defines the syntax version for the **docker-compose**
  file, and currently, the latest syntax version is **3**.

- **services**: This section describes the Docker containers that will be built if
  needed and will be started by **docker-compose**.

- **networks**: This section describes the networks that will be used by the services.

- **volumes**: This section describes the data volumes that will be mounted to the
  containers in services.

For the **services** section, there are two essential options to create containers. The
first option is to build the container, and the second is to use Docker images from the
registry. When you are creating and testing containers locally, it is advisable to build
the images. On the other hand, it is faster and easier to use Docker images from the
registry for production and CI/CD systems.

Imagine you want to build your server container by using a **Dockerfile** named **Dockerfile-server**. Then, you need to put the file in the **server** folder with the following folder structure:

```
[ /docker-ws $ tree
.
├── docker-compose.yml
└── server
        └── Dockerfile-server

1 directory, 2 files
 /docker-ws $ 
```

Figure 5.5: Folder structure

The output of the **tree** command shows that there is a **server** folder containing **Dockerfile-server**.

When the following content is defined in the **docker-compose.yaml** file in the root directory, the **server** container will be built before running the service:

```
version: "3"
services:
  server:
    build:
      context: ./server
      dockerfile: Dockerfile-server
```

Similarly, if you want to use an image from the Docker registry, you can define a service with only the **image** field:

```
version: "3"
services:
  server:
    image: nginx
```

Docker Compose creates a single network by default, and each container connects to this network. In addition, containers can connect to other containers using hostnames. For instance, let's assume you have the following **docker-compose.yaml** file in the **webapp** folder:

```
version: "3"
services:
  server:
```

```
    image: nginx
  db:
    image: postgres
    ports:
      - "8032:5432"
```

When you start **docker-compose** with this configuration, it first creates the network with the name **webapp_default**. Following that, **docker-compose** creates the **server** and **db** containers and joins the **webapp_default** network with the names **server** and **db**, respectively.

In addition, the **server** container can connect to the database using its **container** port and hostname as follows: **postgres://db:5432**. Similarly, the database is reachable from the host machine by host port **8032** as follows: **postgres://localhost:8032**. The network structure is presented in the following diagram:

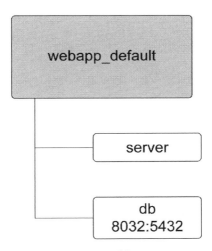

Figure 5.6: Networking structure

Within the **docker-compose.yaml** file, you can define custom networks instead of using the default network. The **network** configuration enables you to create sophisticated network technologies based on your custom network drivers. Networking for Docker containers is comprehensively covered in *Chapter 6, Introduction to Docker Networking*. Extending Docker Engine with custom network drivers will be covered in the following chapters.

Docker Compose also creates and manages volumes as a part of the **docker-compose.yaml** file. Volumes provide persistency among containers and are managed by Docker Engine. All service containers can reuse volumes. In other words, data can be shared between the containers for synchronization, data preparation, and backup operations. In *Chapter 7, Docker Storage*, volumes for Docker will be presented in full detail.

With the following **docker-compose.yaml** file, **docker-compose** will create a volume named **data** using the default volume plugin in Docker Engine. This volume will be mounted to the **/database** path of the **database** container and the **/backup** path of the **backup** container. This YAML file and its content create a service stack that runs a database and continuously backs up without downtime:

```
version: "3"
services:
  database:
    image: my-db-service
    volumes:
      - data:/database
  backup:
    image: my-backup-service
    volumes:
      - data:/backup
volumes:
  data:
```

> **NOTE**
>
> The official reference documentation for Docker Compose files is available at https://docs.docker.com/compose/compose-file/.

In the following exercise, a multi-container application with networking and volume usage will be created with Docker Compose.

> **NOTE**
>
> Please use **touch** command to create files and **vim** command to work on the file using vim editor.

EXERCISE 5.01: GETTING STARTED WITH DOCKER COMPOSE

Web servers in containers require operational tasks before starting, such as configuration, file downloads, or dependency installations. With **docker-compose**, it is possible to define those operations as multi-container applications and run them with a single command. In this exercise, you will create a preparation container to generate static files, such as **index.html** files. Then, the server container will serve the static files, and it will be reachable from the host machine by the network configuration. You will also manage the life cycle of the application using various **docker-compose** commands.

To complete the exercise, execute the following steps:

1. Create a folder named **server-with-compose** and navigate into it using the **cd** command:

```
mkdir server-with-compose
cd server-with-compose
```

2. Create a folder with the name **init** and navigate into it using the **cd** command:

```
mkdir init
cd init
```

3. Create a Bash script file with the following content and save it as **prepare.sh**:

```
#!/usr/bin/env sh


rm /data/index.html
echo "<h1>Welcome from Docker Compose!</h1>" >> /data/index.html
echo "<img src='http://bit.ly/moby-logo' />" >> /data/index.html
```

This script generates a sample HTML page with the **echo** commands.

4. Create a **Dockerfile** with the name **Dockerfile** and the following content:

```
FROM busybox

ADD prepare.sh /usr/bin/prepare.sh
RUN chmod +x /usr/bin/prepare.sh

ENTRYPOINT ["sh", "/usr/bin/prepare.sh"]
```

This **Dockerfile** is based on **busybox**, which is a tiny operating system for space-efficient containers, and it adds the **prepare.sh** script into the filesystem. In addition, it makes the file executable and set it as the **ENTRYPOINT** command. The **ENTRYPOINT** command, in our case, the **prepare.sh** script is initialized with the start of the Docker container.

5. Change the directory to the parent folder with the **cd ..** command and create a **docker-compose.yaml** file with the following content:

```
version: "3"

services:

  init:
    build:
      context: ./init
    volumes:
      - static:/data

  server:
    image: nginx
    volumes:
      - static:/usr/share/nginx/html
    ports:
      - "8080:80"
volumes:
  static:
```

This **docker-compose** file creates one volume named **static**, and two services with the names **init** and **server**. The volume is mounted to both containers. In addition, the server has published port **8080**, connecting to container port **80**.

6. Start the application with the following command in **detach** mode to continue using the Terminal:

```
docker-compose up --detach
```

The following image shows what happens when the preceding command is executed:

```
[ /docker-ws $ docker-compose up --detach
WARNING: The Docker Engine you're using is running in swarm mode.

Compose does not use swarm mode to deploy services to multiple nodes in a swarm. All containe
rs will be scheduled on the current node.

To deploy your application across the swarm, use `docker stack deploy`.

Creating network "server-with-compose_default" with the default driver
Building init
Step 1/4 : FROM busybox
 ---> af2f74c517aa
Step 2/4 : ADD prepare.sh /usr/bin/prepare.sh
 ---> 1e33b4433804
Step 3/4 : RUN chmod +x /usr/bin/prepare.sh
 ---> Running in 8a9a79bf6356
Removing intermediate container 8a9a79bf6356
 ---> 635fb9f247ce
Step 4/4 : ENTRYPOINT ["sh", "/usr/bin/prepare.sh"]
 ---> Running in 9f94417a56f1
Removing intermediate container 9f94417a56f1
 ---> ab167de1cd89
Successfully built ab167de1cd89
Successfully tagged server-with-compose_init:latest
WARNING: Image for service init was built because it did not already exist. To rebuild this i
mage you must use `docker-compose build` or `docker-compose up --build`.
Pulling server (nginx:)...
latest: Pulling from library/nginx
Digest: sha256:b2d89d0a210398b4d1120b3e3a7672c16a4ba09c2c4a0395f18b9f7999b768f2
Status: Downloaded newer image for nginx:latest
Creating server-with-compose_init_1    ... done
Creating server-with-compose_server_1 ... done
 /docker-ws $ ▒
```

Figure 5.7: Starting the application

The preceding command creates and starts the containers in **detached** mode. It starts by creating the **server-with-compose_default** network and the **server-with-compose_static** volume. Then, it builds the **init** container using the **Dockerfile** from *step 4*, downloads the **nginx** Docker image for the server, and starts the containers. Finally, it prints the names of the containers and makes them run in the background.

> **NOTE**
>
> You can disregard the warning about Swarm mode since we want to deploy all containers to the same node.

7. Check the status of the application with the **docker-compose ps** command:

```
/docker-ws $ docker-compose ps
            Name                    Command          State              Ports
-----------------------------------------------------------------------------------
server-with-compose_init_1      sh /usr/bin/prepare.sh   Exit 0
server-with-compose_server_1    nginx -g daemon off;     Up        0.0.0.0:8080->80/tcp
/docker-ws $ ▊
```

Figure 5.8: Application status

This output lists two containers. The **init** container exited successfully with code **0**, while the **server** container is **Up** and its port is available. This is the expected output since the **init** container is designed to prepare the **index. html** file and complete its operations, whereas the **server** container should always be up and running.

8. Open **http://localhost:8080** in the browser. The following figure shows the output:

Welcome from Docker Compose!

Figure 5.9: Server output

Figure 5.9 shows the **index.html** page created by the **init** container. In other words, it shows that **docker-compose** created the volume, mounted it to the containers, and started them successfully.

9. Stop and remove all the resources with the following command if you do not need the application up and running:

```
docker-compose down
```

The command will return output like the following:

```
| /docker-ws $ docker-compose down
Stopping server-with-compose_server_1 ... done
Removing server-with-compose_server_1 ... done
Removing server-with-compose_init_1   ... done
Removing network server-with-compose_default
 /docker-ws $
```

Figure 5.10: Stopping the application

In this exercise, a multi-container application was created and configured by **docker-compose**. Networking and volume options were stored in the **docker-compose.yaml** file. In addition, CLI commands were shown in action for creating applications, checking the status, and removing the applications.

In the following section, configuration options for applications in the Docker Compose environment will be presented.

CONFIGURATION OF SERVICES

Cloud-native applications are expected to store their configuration in environment variables. Environment variables are easy to change between different platforms without source code changes. Environment variables are dynamic values that are stored in Linux-based systems and used by applications. In other words, the variables can be used to configure applications by changing their values.

For instance, assume your application uses a **LOG_LEVEL** environment variable to configure what is logged. If you change the **LOG_LEVEL** environment variable from **INFO** to **DEBUG** and restart your application, you would see more logs and be able to troubleshoot problems more easily. In addition, you can deploy the same application with different sets of environment variables to staging, testing, and production. Likewise, the method of configuring services in Docker Compose is to set environment variables for the containers.

There are three methods of defining environment variables in Docker Compose, with the following priority:

1. Using the Compose file

2. Using shell environment variables

3. Using the environment file

If the environment variables do not change very often but are required by the containers, it is better to store them in **docker-compose.yaml** files. If there are sensitive environment variables, such as passwords, it is recommended to pass them via shell environment variables before calling the **docker-compose** CLI. However, if the number of the variables is high and varies between the testing, staging, or production systems, it is easier to collect them in **.env** files and pass them into **docker-compose.yaml** files.

In the **services** part of the **docker-compose.yaml** file, environment variables can be defined for each service. For example, the **LOG_LEVEL** and **METRICS_PORT** environment variables are set in the Docker Compose file as follows for the **server** service:

```
server:
  environment:
    - LOG_LEVEL=DEBUG
    - METRICS_PORT=8444
```

When the values are not set for the environment variables in the **docker-compose.yaml** file, it is possible to get the values from the shell by running a **docker-compose** command. For instance, the **HOSTNAME** environment variable for the **server** service will be set straight from the shell:

```
server:
  environment:
    - HOSTNAME
```

When the shell running the **docker-compose** command has no value for the **HOSTNAME** environment variable, the container will start with an empty environment variable.

In addition, it is possible to store the environment variables in **.env** files and configure them in **docker-compose.yaml** files. An example **database.env** file can be structured with key-value lists as follows:

```
DATABASE_ADDRESS=mysql://mysql:3535
DATABASE_NAME=db
```

In the **docker-compose.yaml** file, the environment variable file field is configured under the corresponding service as follows:

```
server:
  env_file:
    - database.env
```

When Docker Compose creates the **server** service, it will set all the environment variables listed in the **database.env** file to the container.

In the following exercise, you will configure an application using all three configuration methods in Docker Compose.

EXERCISE 5.02: CONFIGURING SERVICES WITH DOCKER COMPOSE

Services in Docker Compose are configured by environment variables. In this exercise, you will create a Docker Compose application that is configured by different methods of setting variables. In a file called **print.env**, you will define two environment variables. In addition, you will create and configure one environment variable in the **docker-compose.yaml** file and pass one environment variable from the Terminal on the fly. You will see how four environment variables from different sources come together in your container.

To complete the exercise, execute the following steps:

1. Create a folder named **server-with-configuration** and navigate into it using the **cd** command:

```
mkdir server-with-configuration
cd server-with-configuration
```

2. Create an **.env** file with the name **print.env** and the following content:

```
ENV_FROM_ENV_FILE_1=HELLO
ENV_FROM_ENV_FILE_2=WORLD
```

In this file, two environment variables, **ENV_FROM_ENV_FILE_1** and **ENV_FROM_ENV_FILE_2**, are defined with their values.

3. Create a file with the name **docker-compose.yaml** and the following content:

```
version: "3"

services:

  print:
    image: busybox
    command: sh -c 'sleep 5 && env'
    env_file:
    - print.env
    environment:
    - ENV_FROM_COMPOSE_FILE=HELLO
    - ENV_FROM_SHELL
```

In this file, a single-container application is defined, and the container runs the **env** command to print the environment variables. It also uses the environment file named **print.env**, and two additional environment variables, **ENV_FROM_COMPOSE_FILE** and **ENV_FROM_SHELL**.

4. Export **ENV_FROM_SHELL** to the shell with the following command:

```
export ENV_FROM_SHELL=WORLD
```

5. Start the application with the **docker-compose up** command. The output should look like the following:

```
[ /docker-ws $ docker-compose up
WARNING: The Docker Engine you're using is running in swarm mode.

Compose does not use swarm mode to deploy services to multiple nodes in a swarm. All containe
rs will be scheduled on the current node.

To deploy your application across the swarm, use `docker stack deploy`.

Creating network "server-with-configuration_default" with the default driver
Creating server-with-configuration_print_1 ... done
Attaching to server-with-configuration_print_1
print_1  | PATH=/usr/local/sbin:/usr/local/bin:/usr/sbin:/usr/bin:/sbin:/bin
print_1  | HOSTNAME=bd9029ae5476
print_1  | ENV_FROM_ENV_FILE_1=HELLO
print_1  | ENV_FROM_ENV_FILE_2=WORLD
print_1  | ENV_FROM_COMPOSE_FILE=HELLO
print_1  | ENV_FROM_SHELL=WORLD
print_1  | HOME=/root
server-with-configuration_print_1 exited with code 0
 /docker-ws $ 
```

Figure 5.11: Starting the application

The output is the result of the **print** container defined in the **docker-compose** file. The container has one command to run, **env**, and it prints the available environment variables. As expected, there are two environment variables, **ENV_FROM_ENV_FILE_1** and **ENV_FROM_ENV_FILE_2**, with the corresponding values of **HELLO** and **WORLD**. In addition, the environment variable defined in the **docker-compose.yaml** file in *step 3* is available with the name **ENV_FROM_COMPOSE_FILE** and the value **HELLO**. Finally, the environment variable exported in *step 4* is available with the name **ENV_FROM_SHELL** and the value **WORLD**.

In this exercise, a Docker Compose application was created and configured with different methods. Using Docker Compose files, environment definition files and exported values can be used to deploy the same application to different platforms.

Since Docker Compose manages multi-container applications, there is a need to define the interdependencies between them. The interdependencies of the containers in the Docker Compose applications will be presented in the following section.

SERVICE DEPENDENCY

Docker Compose runs and manages multi-container applications defined in **docker-compose.yaml** files. Although the containers are designed as independent microservices, creating services that depend on each other is highly expected. For instance, let's assume you have a two-tier application with database and backend components, such as a PostgreSQL database and a Java backend. The Java backend component requires PostgreSQL to be up and running since it should connect to the database to run the business logic. Therefore, you could need to define the dependency between the services of the multi-container applications. With Docker Compose, it is possible to control the order of the startup and shutdown of the services.

Say you have a three-container application with the following **docker-compose.yaml** file:

```
version: "3"
services:
  init:
    image: busybox
  pre:
    image: busybox
    depends_on:
```

```
    - "init"
  main:
    image: busybox
    depends_on:
    - "pre"
```

In this file, the **main** container depends on the **pre** container, whereas the **pre** container depends on the **init** container. Docker Compose starts the containers in the order of **init**, **pre**, and **main**, as illustrated in *Figure 5.12*. In addition, the containers will be stopped in reverse order: **main**, **pre**, and then **init**:

Figure 5.12: Service startup order

In the following exercise, the order of containers will be used to fill the contents of a file and then serve it with a web server.

EXERCISE 5.03: SERVICE DEPENDENCY WITH DOCKER COMPOSE

Services in Docker Compose can be configured to depend on other services. In this exercise, you will create an application with four containers. The first three containers will run consecutively to create a static file that will be served by the fourth container.

To complete the exercise, execute the following steps:

1. Create a folder named **server-with-dependency** and navigate into it using the **cd** command:

```
mkdir server-with-dependency
cd server-with-dependency
```

2. Create a file with the name **docker-compose.yaml** and the following content:

```
version: "3"

services:

  clean:
    image: busybox
    command: "rm -rf /static/index.html"
    volumes:
```

```yaml
        - static:/static

  init:
    image: busybox
    command: "sh -c 'echo This is from init container >>
      /static/index.html'"
    volumes:
      - static:/static
    depends_on:
    - "clean"

  pre:
    image: busybox
    command: "sh -c 'echo This is from pre container >>
      /static/index.html'"
    volumes:
      - static:/static
    depends_on:
    - "init"

  server:
    image: nginx
    volumes:
      - static:/usr/share/nginx/html
    ports:
      - "8080:80"
    depends_on:
    - "pre"

volumes:
  static:
```

This file consists of four services and one volume. The volume is named **static**, and it is mounted to all services. The first three services take individual actions on the static volume. The **clean** container removes the **index.html** file, and then the **init** container starts filling **index.html**. Following that, the **pre** container writes an additional line to the **index.html** file. Finally, the **server** container serves the content in the **static** folder.

3. Start the application with the **docker-compose up** command. The output should look like the following:

```
/docker-ws $ docker-compose up
WARNING: The Docker Engine you're using is running in swarm mode.

Compose does not use swarm mode to deploy services to multiple nodes in a swarm. All containe
rs will be scheduled on the current node.

To deploy your application across the swarm, use `docker stack deploy`.

Creating server-with-dependency_clean_1 ... done
Creating server-with-dependency_init_1  ... done
Creating server-with-dependency_pre_1   ... done
Creating server-with-dependency_server_1 ... done
Attaching to server-with-dependency_clean_1, server-with-dependency_init_1, server-with-depen
dency_pre_1, server-with-dependency_server_1
server-with-dependency_clean_1 exited with code 0
server-with-dependency_init_1 exited with code 0
server-with-dependency_pre_1 exited with code 0
```

Figure 5.13: Starting the application

The output shows that Docker Compose creates the containers in the order of **clean**, **init**, and then **pre**.

4. Open **http://localhost:8080** in the browser:

```
This is from init container
This is from pre container
```

Figure 5.14: Server output

The output from the server shows that the **clean**, **init**, and **pre** containers work in the expected order.

5. Return to the Terminal in *step 3* and use *Ctrl + C* to close the application gracefully. You will see some HTTP request logs and, in the end, the **Stopping server-with-dependency_server_1** line:

```
/docker-ws $ docker-compose up
WARNING: The Docker Engine you're using is running in swarm mode.

Compose does not use swarm mode to deploy services to multiple nodes in a swarm. All containe
rs will be scheduled on the current node.

To deploy your application across the swarm, use `docker stack deploy`.

Creating server-with-dependency_clean_1 ... done
Creating server-with-dependency_init_1  ... done
Creating server-with-dependency_pre_1   ... done
Creating server-with-dependency_server_1 ... done
Attaching to server-with-dependency_clean_1, server-with-dependency_init_1, server-with-depen
dency_pre_1, server-with-dependency_server_1
server-with-dependency_clean_1 exited with code 0
server-with-dependency_init_1 exited with code 0
server-with-dependency_pre_1 exited with code 0
server_1    | 192.168.32.1 - - [06/Jan/2020:11:04:44 +0000] "GET / HTTP/1.1" 200 55 "-" "Mozill
a/5.0 (Macintosh; Intel Mac OS X 10_15_2) AppleWebKit/537.36 (KHTML, like Gecko) Chrome/79.0.
3945.88 Safari/537.36" "-"
server_1    | 2020/01/06 11:04:45 [error] 6#6: *1 open() "/usr/share/nginx/html/favicon.ico" fa
iled (2: No such file or directory), client: 192.168.32.1, server: localhost, request: "GET /
favicon.ico HTTP/1.1", host: "localhost:8080", referrer: "http://localhost:8080/"
server_1    | 192.168.32.1 - - [06/Jan/2020:11:04:45 +0000] "GET /favicon.ico HTTP/1.1" 404 555
 "http://localhost:8080/" "Mozilla/5.0 (Macintosh; Intel Mac OS X 10_15_2) AppleWebKit/537.36
 (KHTML, like Gecko) Chrome/79.0.3945.88 Safari/537.36" "-"
^CGracefully stopping... (press Ctrl+C again to force)
Stopping server-with-dependency_server_1 ... done
/docker-ws $
```

Figure 5.15: Stopping the application

In this exercise, a Docker Compose application was created with interdependent services. How Docker Compose starts and manages containers in a defined order was shown. This is an essential feature of Docker Compose with which you can create complex multi-container applications.

Now, let's test the knowledge we have gained so far in this chapter by implementing the following activity. In the next activity, you will learn how to install WordPress using Docker Compose.

ACTIVITY 5.01: INSTALLING WORDPRESS USING DOCKER COMPOSE

You are assigned to design and deploy a blog with its database as microservices in Docker. You will be using **WordPress** since it is the most popular **Content Management System** (**CMS**), used by more than one-third of all the websites on the internet. Also, the development and testing teams require the installation of both WordPress and the database multiple times on different platforms with isolation. Therefore, you are required to design it as a Docker Compose application and manage it with the **docker-compose** CLI.

Perform the following steps to complete this activity:

1. Start by creating a directory for your **docker-compose.yaml** file.

2. Create a service for the database using MySQL and a volume defined in the **docker-compose.yaml** file. Ensure that the **MYSQL_ROOT_PASSWORD**, **MYSQL_DATABASE**, **MYSQL_USER**, and **MYSQL_PASSWORD** environment variables are set.

3. Create a service for WordPress defined in the **docker-compose.yaml** file. Ensure that the WordPress containers start after the database. For the configuration of WordPress, do not forget to set the **WORDPRESS_DB_HOST**, **WORDPRESS_DB_USER**, **WORDPRESS_DB_PASSWORD**, and **WORDPRESS_DB_NAME** environment variables in accordance with *step 2*. In addition, you need to publish its port to be able to reach it from the browser.

4. Start the Docker Compose application in **detached** mode. Upon successful deployment, you will have two containers running:

```
/docker-ws $ docker-compose ps
        Name                    Command              State           Ports
--------------------------------------------------------------------------------
wordpress_database_1    docker-entrypoint.sh mysqld     Up      3306/tcp, 33060/tcp
wordpress_wordpress_1   docker-entrypoint.sh apach ...  Up      0.0.0.0:8080->80/tcp
/docker-ws $
```

Figure 5.16: WordPress and database containers

You will then be able to reach the setup screen of WordPress in the browser:

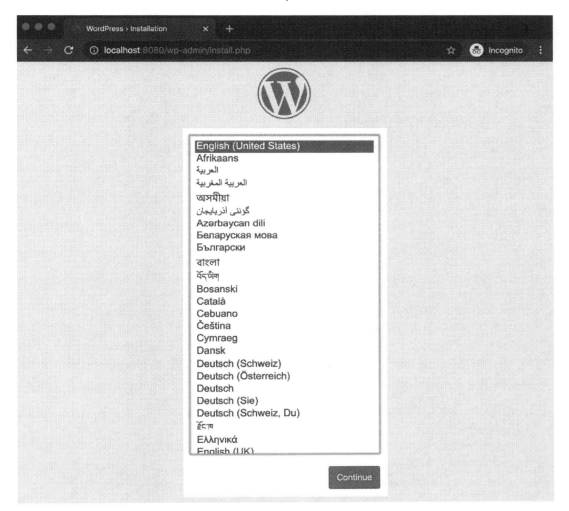

Figure 5.17: WordPress setup screen

NOTE

The solution for this activity can be found on page 664

In the next activity, you will get hands-on experience installing the Panoramic Trekking App using Docker Compose by creating a three-container Docker application and managing it with the `docker-compose` CLI.

ACTIVITY 5.02: INSTALLING THE PANORAMIC TREKKING APP USING DOCKER COMPOSE

You are tasked with creating a deployment of the Panoramic Trekking App using Docker Compose. You will take advantage of the three-tier architecture of the Panoramic Trekking App and create a three-container Docker application, with containers for the database, the web backend, and **nginx**. Therefore, you will design it as a Docker Compose application and manage it with the **docker-compose** CLI.

Perform the following steps to complete this activity:

1. Create a directory for your **docker-compose.yaml** file.

2. Create a service for the database using PostgreSQL and a volume defined in the **docker-compose.yaml** file. Ensure that the **POSTGRES_PASSWORD** environment variable is set to **docker**. In addition, you need to create a **db_data** volume in **docker-compose.yaml** and mount it to the **/var/lib/postgresql/data/** to store the database files.

3. Create a service for the Panoramic Trekking App defined in the **docker-compose.yaml** file. Ensure that you are using the **packtworkshops/the-docker-workshop:chapter5-pta-web** Docker image, which is prebuilt and ready to use from the registry. In addition, since the application is dependent on the database, you should configure the container to start after the database. To store the static files, create a **static_data** volume in **docker-compose.yaml** and mount it to **/service/static/**.

    Finally, create a service for **nginx** and ensure that you are using the **packtworkshops/the-docker-workshop:chapter5-pta-nginx** Docker image from the registry. Ensure that the **nginx** container starts after the Panoramic Trekking App container. You also need to mount the same **static_data** volume to the **/service/static/** location. Do not forget to publish **nginx** port **80** to **8000** to reach from the browser.

4. Start the Docker Compose application in **detached** mode. Upon successful deployment, you will have three containers running:

```
/docker-ws $ docker-compose ps
        Name                      Command            State         Ports
----------------------------------------------------------------------------------
pta-compose_db_1       docker-entrypoint.sh postgres    Up      5432/tcp
pta-compose_nginx_1    nginx -g daemon off;             Up      0.0.0.0:8000->80/tcp
pta-compose_web_1      ./entrypoint.sh gunicorn p ...   Up
 /docker-ws $
```

Figure 5.18: The application, database, and nginx containers

5. Go to the administration section of the Panoramic Trekking App in the browser with the address `http://0.0.0.0:8000/admin`:

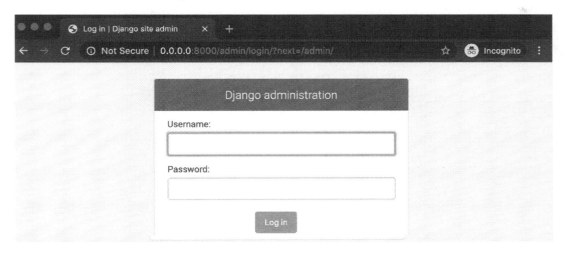

Figure 5.19: Admin setup logon

You can log in with the username **admin** and password **changeme** and add new photos and countries:

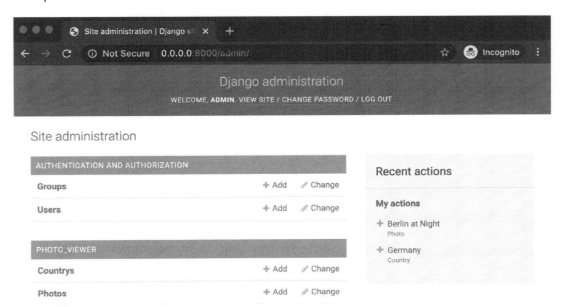

Figure 5.20: Admin setup view

6. Access the Panoramic Trekking App at the address
   `http://0.0.0.0:8000/photo_viewer` in the browser:

Berlin at Night

Oberbaum Bridge...

May 11, 2020 | Country: Germany

Read More

Figure 5.21: Application view

NOTE

The solution for this activity can be found on page 667.

SUMMARY

This chapter focused on using Docker Compose to design, create, and manage multi-container applications. The complexity of containerized applications has increased with the rise of the microservice architecture. Thus, it has become difficult to create, manage, and troubleshoot multi-container applications without the appropriate tooling. Docker Compose is the official tool in the Docker toolbox for this purpose.

In this chapter, the main focus was to learn **docker-compose** comprehensively. With this aim, the chapter started with the capabilities of the **docker-compose** CLI with its commands and flags. Then, the anatomy of **docker-compose.yaml** files was presented. The power of Docker Compose actually comes from the configuration capabilities defined in the **docker-compose.yaml** files. Therefore, it is essential to learn how to use these files to manage multi-container applications.

Following that, the configuration of services in Docker Compose was illustrated. You have learned how to configure services for different environments and adapt to changes in the future. We then moved on to service dependencies to learn how to create more complex containerized applications.

Every exercise in this chapter aimed to show the capabilities of Docker, including different CLI commands and YAML file sections. It is essential to get hands-on experience of the CLI and the files needed to create multi-container applications for use in testing and production environments.

In the next chapter, you will learn about networking in Docker. Networking in containerized and scalable applications is one of the critical parts of the infrastructure, as it glues together the distributed parts. That's why networking in Docker consists of pluggable drivers and options to enhance the containerized application development and management experience.

6

INTRODUCTION TO DOCKER NETWORKING

OVERVIEW

The goal of this chapter is to provide you with a concise overview of how container networking works, how it differs from networking at the level of the Docker host, and how containers can leverage Docker networking to provide direct network connectivity to other containerized services. By the end of this chapter, you will know how to deploy containers using networking configurations such as `bridge`, `overlay`, `macvlan`, and `host`. You will learn the benefits of different networking drivers and under which circumstances you should choose certain network drivers. Finally, we will look at containerized networking between hosts deployed in a Docker swarm cluster.

INTRODUCTION

Throughout this workshop, we have looked at many aspects of containerization and microservices architecture in relation to Docker. We have learned about how encapsulating applications into microservices that perform discrete functions creates an incredibly flexible architecture that enables rapid deployments and powerful horizontal scaling. Perhaps one of the more interesting and complex topics as it relates to containerization is networking. After all, in order to develop a flexible and agile microservices architecture, proper networking considerations need to be made to ensure reliable connectivity between container instances.

When referring to **container networking**, always try to keep in mind the difference between networking on the container host (underlay networking) and networking between containers on the same host or within different clusters (`overlay` networking). Docker supports many different types of network configurations out of the box that can be customized to suit the needs of your infrastructure and deployment strategy.

For example, a container may have an IP address, unique to that container instance, that exists on a virtual subnet between the container hosts. This type of networking is typical of a Docker swarm clustered configuration in which network traffic gets encrypted and passed over the host machine's network interfaces, only to be decrypted on a different host and then passed to the receiving microservice. This type of network configuration usually involves Docker maintaining a mapping of container and service names to container IP addresses. This provides powerful service discovery mechanisms that allow container networking even when containers terminate and restart on different cluster hosts.

Alternatively, containers may run in a more simplistic host networking mode. In this scenario, containers running in a cluster or a standalone host expose ports on the host machine's network interfaces to send and receive network traffic. The containers themselves may still have their IP addresses, which get mapped to physical network interfaces on the hosts by Docker. This type of network configuration is useful when your microservices need to communicate primarily with services that exist outside your containerized infrastructure.

By default, Docker operates in a **bridge network mode**. A `bridge` network creates a single network interface on the host that acts as a bridge to another subnet configured on the host. All incoming (ingress) and outgoing (egress) network traffic travel between the container subnet and the host using the `bridge` network interface.

After installing Docker Engine in a Linux environment, if you run the `ifconfig` command, Docker will create a new virtual bridged network interface called **docker0**. This interface bridges a Docker private subnet that gets created by default (usually **172.16.0.0/16**) to the host machine's networking stack. If a container is running in the default Docker network with an IP address of **172.17.8.1** and you attempt to contact that IP address, the internal route tables will direct that traffic through the **docker0 bridge** interface and pass the traffic to the IP address of the container on the private subnet. Unless ports are published through Docker, this container's IP address cannot be accessed by the outside world. Throughout this chapter, we will dive deep into various network drivers and configuration options provided by Docker.

In the next exercise, we will look at creating Docker containers in the default Docker **bridge** network and how to expose container ports to the outside world.

EXERCISE 6.01: HANDS-ON WITH DOCKER NETWORKING

By default, when you run a container in Docker, the container instance you create will exist in a Docker network. Docker networks are collections of subnets, rules, and metadata that Docker uses to allocate network resources to containers running in the immediate Docker server or across servers in a Docker swarm cluster. The network will provide the container with access to other containers in the same subnet, and even outbound (egress) access to other external networks, including the internet. Each Docker network is associated with a network driver that determines how the network will function within the context of the system the containers are running on.

In this exercise, you will run Docker containers and use basic networking to run two simple web servers (Apache2 and NGINX) that will expose ports in a few different basic networking scenarios. You will then access the exposed ports of the container to learn more about how Docker networking works at the most basic level. Launching containers and exposing the service ports to make them available is one of the most common networking scenarios when first starting with containerized infrastructure:

1. List the networks that are currently configured in your Docker environment using the **docker network ls** command:

```
$ docker network ls
```

The output displayed will show all the configured Docker networks available on your system. It should resemble the following:

```
NETWORK ID        NAME       DRIVER      SCOPE
0774bdf6228d      bridge     bridge      local
f52b4a5440ad      host       host        local
9bed60b88784      none       null        local
```

2. When creating a container using Docker without specifying a network or networking driver, Docker will create the container using a **bridge** network. This network exists behind a **bridge** network interface configured in your host OS. Use **ifconfig** in a Linux or macOS Bash shell, or **ipconfig** in Windows PowerShell, to see which interface the Docker bridge is configured as. It is generally called **docker0**:

```
$ ifconfig
```

The output of this command will list all the network interfaces available in your environment, as shown in the following figure:

```
docker0: flags=4099<UP,BROADCAST,MULTICAST>  mtu 1500
        inet 172.17.0.1  netmask 255.255.0.0  broadcast 172.17.255.255
        ether 02:42:c5:b0:7a:34  txqueuelen 0  (Ethernet)
        RX packets 0  bytes 0 (0.0 B)
        RX errors 0  dropped 0  overruns 0  frame 0
        TX packets 0  bytes 0 (0.0 B)
        TX errors 0  dropped 0 overruns 0  carrier 0  collisions 0

enp1s0: flags=4163<UP,BROADCAST,RUNNING,MULTICAST>  mtu 1500
        inet 192.168.122.185  netmask 255.255.255.0  broadcast 192.168.122.255
        inet6 fe80::fcc1:6453:cb2f:37da  prefixlen 64  scopeid 0x20<link>
        ether 52:54:00:0a:6a:c1  txqueuelen 1000  (Ethernet)
        RX packets 11735  bytes 140578983 (140.5 MB)
        RX errors 0  dropped 0  overruns 0  frame 0
        TX packets 5826  bytes 428029 (428.0 KB)
        TX errors 0  dropped 0 overruns 0  carrier 0  collisions 0

lo: flags=73<UP,LOOPBACK,RUNNING>  mtu 65536
        inet 127.0.0.1  netmask 255.0.0.0
        inet6 ::1  prefixlen 128  scopeid 0x10<host>
        loop  txqueuelen 1000  (Local Loopback)
        RX packets 221  bytes 17799 (17.7 KB)
        RX errors 0  dropped 0  overruns 0  frame 0
        TX packets 221  bytes 17799 (17.7 KB)
        TX errors 0  dropped 0 overruns 0  carrier 0  collisions 0
```

Figure 6.1: Listing the available network interfaces

It can be observed in the preceding figure that the Docker **bridge** interface is called **docker0** and has an IP address of **172.17.0.1**.

3. Use the **docker run** command to create a simple NGINX web server container, using the **latest** image tag. Set the container to start in the background using the **-d** flag and give it a human-readable name of **webserver1** using the **--name** flag:

```
$ docker run -d --name webserver1 nginx:latest
```

If the command is successful, no output will be returned in the terminal session.

4. Execute the **docker ps** command to check whether the container is up and running:

```
$ docker ps
```

As you can see, the **webserver1** container is up and running as expected:

```
CONTAINER ID    IMAGE          COMMAND                 CREATED
   STATUS                      PORTS           NAMES
0774bdf6228d    nginx:latest   "nginx -g 'daemon of…"  4 seconds ago
   Up 3 seconds                80/tcp          webserver1
```

5. Execute the **docker inspect** command to check what networking configuration this container has by default:

```
$ docker inspect webserver1
```

Docker will return the verbose details about the running container in JSON format. For this exercise, focus on the **NetworkSettings** block. Pay special attention to the **Gateway**, **IPAddress**, **Ports**, and **NetworkID** parameters underneath the **networks** sub-block:

```
"NetworkSettings": {
    "Bridge": "",
    "SandboxID": "d8f43327a8b73a502a1fd0b3e33ac0136d324ea75b4ec73cf453c033ead7c9ba",
    "HairpinMode": false,
    "LinkLocalIPv6Address": "",
    "LinkLocalIPv6PrefixLen": 0,
    "Ports": {
        "80/tcp": null
    },
    "SandboxKey": "/var/run/docker/netns/d8f43327a8b7",
    "SecondaryIPAddresses": null,
    "SecondaryIPv6Addresses": null,
    "EndpointID": "cf88feaa92e4213034102159a4876b99d36ca707b9497aba8468678248bc4a40",
    "Gateway": "172.17.0.1",
    "GlobalIPv6Address": "",
    "GlobalIPv6PrefixLen": 0,
    "IPAddress": "172.17.0.2",
    "IPPrefixLen": 16,
    "IPv6Gateway": "",
    "MacAddress": "02:42:ac:11:00:02",
    "Networks": {
        "bridge": {
            "IPAMConfig": null,
            "Links": null,
            "Aliases": null,
            "NetworkID": "0774bdf6228d30a4758bc972566ac05b80627096d4694ebe96a3010dd18141aa",
            "EndpointID": "cf88feaa92e4213034102159a4876b99d36ca707b9497aba8468678248bc4a40",
            "Gateway": "172.17.0.1",
            "IPAddress": "172.17.0.2",
            "IPPrefixLen": 16,
            "IPv6Gateway": "",
            "GlobalIPv6Address": "",
            "GlobalIPv6PrefixLen": 0,
            "MacAddress": "02:42:ac:11:00:02",
            "DriverOpts": null
        }
    }
}
```

Figure 6.2: Output of the docker inspect command

From this output, it can be concluded that this container lives in the default Docker **bridge** network. Looking at the first 12 characters of **NetworkID**, you will observe that it is the same identifier used in the output of the **docker network ls** command, which was executed in *step 1*. It should also be noted that the **Gateway** this container is configured to use is the IP address of the **docker0 bridge** interface. Docker will use this interface as an egress point to access networks in other subnets outside itself, as well as forwarding traffic from our environment to the containers in the subnet. It can also be observed that this container has a unique IP address within the Docker bridge network, **172.17.0.2** in this example. Our local machine has the ability to route to this subnet since we have the **docker0 bridge** interface available to forward traffic. Finally, it can be observed that the NGINX container is by default exposing TCP port **80** for incoming traffic.

6. In a web browser, access the **webserver1** container by IP address over port **80**. Enter the IP address of the **webserver1** container in your favorite web browser:

Welcome to nginx!

If you see this page, the nginx web server is successfully installed and working. Further configuration is required.

For online documentation and support please refer to nginx.org. Commercial support is available at nginx.com.

Thank you for using nginx.

Figure 6.3: Accessing an NGINX web server container by IP address through the default Docker bridge network

7. Alternatively, use the **curl** command to see similar output, albeit in text format:

```
$ curl 172.17.0.2:80
```

The following HTML response indicates that you have received a response from the running NGINX container:

```
<!DOCTYPE html>
<html>
<head>
<title>Welcome to nginx!</title>
<style>
    body {
        width: 35em;
        margin: 0 auto;
        font-family: Tahoma, Verdana, Arial, sans-serif;
    }
</style>
</head>
<body>
<h1>Welcome to nginx!</h1>
<p>If you see this page, the nginx web server is successfully
installed and working. Further configuration is required.</p>

<p>For online documentation and support please refer to
<a href="http://nginx.org/">nginx.org</a>.<br/>
Commercial support is available at
<a href="http://nginx.com/">nginx.com</a>.</p>

<p><em>Thank you for using nginx.</em></p>
</body>
</html>
```

8. Accessing the IP address of a container in the local **bridge** subnet works well for testing containers locally. To expose your service on the network to other users or servers, use the **-p** flag in the **docker run** command. This will allow you to map a port on the host to an exposed port on the container. This is similar to port forwarding on a router or other network device. To expose a container by the port to the outside world, use the **docker run** command followed by the **-d** flag to start the container in the background. The **-p** flag will enable you to specify a port on the host, separated by a colon and the port on the container that you wish to expose. Also, give this container a unique name, **webserver2**:

```
$ docker run -d -p 8080:80 --name webserver2 nginx:latest
```

Upon successful container startup, your shell will not return anything. However, certain versions of Docker may show the full container ID.

9. Run the **docker ps** command to check whether you have two NGINX containers up and running:

```
$ docker ps
```

The two running containers, **webserver1** and **webserver2**, will be displayed:

```
CONTAINER ID IMAGE          COMMAND                 CREATED
  STATUS               PORTS                NAMES
b945fa75b59a nginx:latest  "nginx -g 'daemon of…"  1 minute ago
  Up About a minute    0.0.0.0:8080->80/tcp  webserver2
3267bf4322ed nginx:latest  "nginx -g 'daemon of…"  2 minutes ago
  Up 2 minutes         80/tcp               webserver1
```

In the **PORTS** column, you will see that Docker is now forwarding port **80** on the **webserver** container to port **8080** on the host machine. That is deduced from the **0.0.0.0:8080->80/tcp** part of the output.

> **NOTE**
>
> It is important to remember that the host machine port is always to the left of the colon, while the container port is to the right when specifying ports with the **-p** flag.

10. In your web browser, navigate to **http://localhost:8080** to see the running container instance you just spawned:

Figure 6.4: NGINX default page indicating that you have successfully forwarded a port to your web server container

11. Now, you have two NGINX instances running in the same Docker environment with slightly different networking configurations. The **webserver1** instance is running solely on the Docker network without any ports exposed. Inspect the configuration of the **webserver2** instance using the **docker inspect** command followed by the container name or ID:

```
$ docker inspect webserver2
```

The **NetworkSettings** section at the bottom of the JSON output will resemble the following. Pay close attention to the parameters (**Gateway**, **IPAddress**, **Ports**, and **NetworkID**) underneath the **networks** sub-block:

```
"NetworkSettings": {
    "Bridge": "",
    "SandboxID": "e271e27f8ea8855a574ed4481dfb0bad9de1da8924ee36cbce17ebabe03773ed",
    "HairpinMode": false,
    "LinkLocalIPv6Address": "",
    "LinkLocalIPv6PrefixLen": 0,
    "Ports": {
        "80/tcp": [
            {
                "HostIp": "0.0.0.0",
                "HostPort": "8080"
            }
        ]
    },
    "SandboxKey": "/var/run/docker/netns/e271e27f8ea8",
    "SecondaryIPAddresses": null,
    "SecondaryIPv6Addresses": null,
    "EndpointID": "55dd352f2dd5c1f096edb2c4c65fb7906c8201a5e89b32668904b08f51a2c4b4",
    "Gateway": "172.17.0.1",
    "GlobalIPv6Address": "",
    "GlobalIPv6PrefixLen": 0,
    "IPAddress": "172.17.0.3",
    "IPPrefixLen": 16,
    "IPv6Gateway": "",
    "MacAddress": "02:42:ac:11:00:03",
    "Networks": {
        "bridge": {
            "IPAMConfig": null,
            "Links": null,
            "Aliases": null,
            "NetworkID": "b1d6e724b189ee7fb6bd66d0152d9cd1f50787b82e423f4ff1da17472861e420",
            "EndpointID": "55dd352f2dd5c1f096edb2c4c65fb7906c8201a5e89b32668904b08f51a2c4b4",
            "Gateway": "172.17.0.1",
            "IPAddress": "172.17.0.3",
            "IPPrefixLen": 16,
            "IPv6Gateway": "",
            "GlobalIPv6Address": "",
            "GlobalIPv6PrefixLen": 0,
            "MacAddress": "02:42:ac:11:00:03",
            "DriverOpts": null
```

Figure 6.5: Output from the docker inspect command

As the **docker inspect** output displays, the **webserver2** container has an IP address of **172.17.0.3**, whereas your **webserver1** container has an IP address of **172.17.0.1**. The IP addresses in your local environment may be slightly different depending on how Docker assigns the IP addresses to the containers. Both the containers live on the same Docker network (**bridge**) and have the same default gateway, which is the **docker0 bridge** interface on the host machine.

12. Since both of these containers live on the same subnet, you can test communication between the containers within the Docker **bridge** network. Run the **docker exec** command to gain access to a shell on the **webserver1** container:

```
docker exec -it webserver1 /bin/bash
```

The prompt should noticeably change to a root prompt, indicating you are now in a Bash shell on the **webserver1** container:

```
root@3267bf4322ed:/#
```

13. At the root shell prompt, use the **apt** package manager to install the **ping** utility in this container:

```
root@3267bf4322ed:/# apt-get update && apt-get install -y inetutils-ping
```

The aptitude package manager will then install the **ping** utility in the **webserver1** container. Please note that the **apt** package manager will install **ping** as well as other dependencies that are required to run the **ping** command:

```
root@3267bf4322ed:/# apt-get update && apt-get install -y inetutils-ping
Hit:1 http://deb.debian.org/debian buster InRelease
Hit:2 http://security.debian.org/debian-security buster/updates InRelease
Hit:3 http://deb.debian.org/debian buster-updates InRelease
Reading package lists... Done
Reading package lists... Done
Building dependency tree
Reading state information... Done
The following additional packages will be installed:
  libidn11 netbase
The following NEW packages will be installed:
  inetutils-ping libidn11 netbase
0 upgraded, 3 newly installed, 0 to remove and 0 not upgraded.
Need to get 362 kB of archives.
After this operation, 718 kB of additional disk space will be used.
Get:1 http://deb.debian.org/debian buster/main amd64 netbase all 5.6 [19.4 kB]
Get:2 http://deb.debian.org/debian buster/main amd64 libidn11 amd64 1.33-2.2 [116 kB]
Get:3 http://deb.debian.org/debian buster/main amd64 inetutils-ping amd64 2:1.9.4-7 [226 kB]
Fetched 362 kB in 0s (3133 kB/s)
debconf: delaying package configuration, since apt-utils is not installed
Selecting previously unselected package netbase.
(Reading database ... 7203 files and directories currently installed.)
Preparing to unpack .../archives/netbase_5.6_all.deb ...
Unpacking netbase (5.6) ...
Selecting previously unselected package libidn11:amd64.
Preparing to unpack .../libidn11_1.33-2.2_amd64.deb ...
Unpacking libidn11:amd64 (1.33-2.2) ...
Selecting previously unselected package inetutils-ping.
Preparing to unpack .../inetutils-ping_2%3a1.9.4-7_amd64.deb ...
Unpacking inetutils-ping (2:1.9.4-7) ...
Setting up libidn11:amd64 (1.33-2.2) ...
Setting up netbase (5.6) ...
Setting up inetutils-ping (2:1.9.4-7) ...
Processing triggers for libc-bin (2.28-10) ...
```

Figure 6.6: Installing the ping command inside a Docker container

14. Once the **ping** utility has successfully installed, use it to ping the IP address of the other container:

```
root@3267bf4322ed:/# ping 172.17.0.3
```

The output should display ICMP response packets, indicating that the containers can successfully ping each other through the Docker **bridge** network:

```
PING 172.17.0.1 (172.17.0.3): 56 data bytes
64 bytes from 172.17.0.3: icmp_seq=0 ttl=64 time=0.221 ms
64 bytes from 172.17.0.3: icmp_seq=1 ttl=64 time=0.207 ms
```

15. You can also access the NGINX default web interface using the **curl** command. Install **curl** using the **apt** package manager:

```
root@3267bf4322ed:/# apt-get install -y curl
```

The following output should display, indicating that the **curl** utility and all required dependencies are being installed:

```
Building dependency tree
Reading state information... Done
Need to get 3471 kB of archives.
After this operation, 7725 kB of additional disk space will be used.
Get:1 http://deb.debian.org/debian buster/main amd64 krb5-locales all 1.17-3 [95.4 kB]
Get:2 http://security.debian.org/debian-security buster/updates/main amd64 libldap-common all 2.4.47+dfsg-3+deb10u2 [89.7 kB]
Get:3 http://deb.debian.org/debian buster/main amd64 libsasl2-modules-db amd64 2.1.27+dfsg-1+deb10u1 [69.1 kB]
Get:4 http://deb.debian.org/debian buster/main amd64 libsasl2-2 amd64 2.1.27+dfsg-1+deb10u1 [106 kB]
Get:5 http://deb.debian.org/debian buster/main amd64 ca-certificates all 20190110 [157 kB]
Get:6 http://deb.debian.org/debian buster/main amd64 libkeyutils1 amd64 1.6-6 [15.0 kB]
Get:7 http://deb.debian.org/debian buster/main amd64 libkrb5support0 amd64 1.17-3 [65.6 kB]
Get:8 http://deb.debian.org/debian buster/main amd64 libk5crypto3 amd64 1.17-3 [121 kB]
Get:9 http://deb.debian.org/debian buster/main amd64 libkrb5-3 amd64 1.17-3 [370 kB]
Setting up libsasl2-modules:amd64 (2.1.27+dfsg-1+deb10u1) ...
Setting up libnghttp2-14:amd64 (1.36.0-2+deb10u1) ...
Setting up krb5-locales (1.17-3) ...
Setting up libldap-common (2.4.47+dfsg-3+deb10u2) ...
Setting up libkrb5support0:amd64 (1.17-3) ...
Setting up libsasl2-modules-db:amd64 (2.1.27+dfsg-1+deb10u1) ...
Setting up librtmp1:amd64 (2.4+20151223.gitfa8646d.1-2) ...
Setting up libk5crypto3:amd64 (1.17-3) ...
Setting up libsasl2-2:amd64 (2.1.27+dfsg-1+deb10u1) ...
Setting up libssh2-1:amd64 (1.8.0-2.1) ...
Setting up libkrb5-3:amd64 (1.17-3) ...
Setting up openssl (1.1.1d-0+deb10u3) ...
Setting up publicsuffix (20190415.1030-1) ...
Setting up libldap-2.4-2:amd64 (2.4.47+dfsg-3+deb10u2) ...
Setting up ca-certificates (20190110) ...
debconf: unable to initialize frontend: Dialog
Updating certificates in /etc/ssl/certs...
128 added, 0 removed; done.
Setting up libgssapi-krb5-2:amd64 (1.17-3) ...
Setting up libcurl4:amd64 (7.64.0-4+deb10u1) ...
Setting up curl (7.64.0-4+deb10u1) ...
Processing triggers for libc-bin (2.28-10) ...
Processing triggers for ca-certificates (20190110) ...
Updating certificates in /etc/ssl/certs...
0 added, 0 removed; done.
Running hooks in /etc/ca-certificates/update.d...
done
```

Figure 6.7: Installing the curl utility

16. After installing **curl**, use it to curl the IP address of **webserver2**:

```
root@3267bf4322ed:/# curl 172.17.0.3
```

You should see the **Welcome to nginx!** page displayed in HTML format, indicating that you were able to successfully contact the IP address of the **webserver2** container through the Docker **bridge** network:

```
<!DOCTYPE html>
<html>
<head>
<title>Welcome to nginx!</title>
```

```
<style>
    body {
        width: 35em;
        margin: 0 auto;
        font-family: Tahoma, Verdana, Arial, sans-serif;
    }
</style>
</head>
<body>
<h1>Welcome to nginx!</h1>
<p>If you see this page, the nginx web server is successfully
installed and working. Further configuration is required.</p>

<p>For online documentation and support please refer to
<a href="http://nginx.org/">nginx.org</a>.<br/>
Commercial support is available at
<a href="http://nginx.com/">nginx.com</a>.</p>

<p><em>Thank you for using nginx.</em></p>
</body>
</html>
```

Since you are using **curl** to navigate to the NGINX welcome page, it will render on your terminal display in raw HTML format.

In this section, we have successfully spawned two NGINX web server instances in the same Docker environment. We configured one instance to not expose any ports outside the default Docker network, while we configured the second NGINX instance to run on the same network but to expose port **80** to the host system on port **8080**. We saw how these containers could be accessed using a standard internet web browser as well as by the **curl** utility in Linux.

During this exercise, we also saw how containers can use Docker networks to talk to other containers directly. We used the **webserver1** container to call the IP address of the **webserver2** container and display the output of the web page the container was hosting.

In this exercise, we were also able to demonstrate network connectivity between container instances using the native Docker **bridge** network. However, when we deploy containers at scale, there is no easy way to know which IP address in the Docker network belongs to which container.

In the next section, we will look at native Docker DNS and learn how to use human-readable DNS names to reliably send network traffic to other container instances.

NATIVE DOCKER DNS

One of the biggest benefits of running a containerized infrastructure is the ability to quickly and effortlessly scale your workloads horizontally. Having more than one machine in a cluster with a shared **overlay** network between them means that you can have many containers running across fleets of servers.

As we saw in the previous exercise, Docker gives us the power to allow containers to directly talk to other containers in a cluster through the various network drivers that Docker provides, such as **bridge**, **macvlan**, and **overlay** drivers. In the previous example, we leveraged Docker **bridge** networking to allow containers to talk to each other by their respective IP addresses. However, when your containers are deployed on real servers, you can't normally rely on containers having consistent IP addresses that they can use to talk to each other. Every time a new container instance terminates or respawns, Docker will give that container a new IP address.

Similar to a traditional infrastructure scenario, we can leverage DNS within container networks to give containers a reliable way to communicate with each other. By assigning human-readable names to containers within Docker networks, users no longer have to look up the IP address each time they want to initiate communication between containers on a Docker network. Docker itself will keep track of the IP addresses of the containers as they spawn and respawn.

In older legacy versions of Docker, simple DNS resolution was possible by establishing links between containers using the **--link** flag in the **docker run** command. Using linking, Docker would create an entry in the linked container's **hosts** file, which would enable simple name resolution. However, as you will see in the upcoming exercise, using links between containers can be slow, not scalable, and prone to errors. Recent versions of Docker support a native DNS service between containers running on the same Docker network. This allows containers to look up the names of other containers running in the same Docker network. The only caveat with this approach is that native Docker DNS doesn't work on the default Docker **bridge** network; thus, other networks must first be created to build your containers in.

For native Docker DNS to work, we must first create a new network using the **docker network create** command. We can then create new containers in that network using **docker run** with the **--network-alias** flag. In the following exercise, we are going to use these commands to learn how native Docker DNS works to enable scalable communication between container instances.

EXERCISE 6.02: WORKING WITH DOCKER DNS

In the following exercise, you will learn about name resolution between Docker containers running on the same network. You will first enable simple name resolution using the legacy link method. You will contrast this approach by using the newer and more reliable native Docker DNS service:

1. First, create two Alpine Linux containers on the default Docker **bridge** network that will communicate with each other using the **--link** flag. Alpine is a very good base image for this exercise because it contains the **ping** utility by default. This will enable you to quickly test the connectivity between containers in the various scenarios. To get started, create a container called **containerlink1** to indicate that you have created this container using the legacy link method:

```
$ docker run -itd --name containerlink1 alpine:latest
```

    This will start a container in the default Docker network called **containerlink1**.

2. Start another container in the default Docker bridge network, called **containerlink2**, which will create a link to **containerlink1** to enable rudimentary DNS:

```
$ docker run -itd --name containerlink2 --link containerlink1
alpine:latest
```

    This will start a container in the default Docker network called **containerlink2**.

3. Run the **docker exec** command to access a shell inside the **containerlink2** container. This will allow you to investigate how the link functionality is working. Since this container is running Alpine Linux, you do not have access to the Bash shell by default. Instead, access it using an **sh** shell:

```
$ docker exec -it containerlink2 /bin/sh
```

    This should drop you into a root **sh** shell in the **containerlink2** container.

4. From the shell of the **containerlink2** container, ping **containerlink1**:

```
/ # ping containerlink1
```

You will get a reply to the **ping** request:

```
PING container1 (172.17.0.2): 56 data bytes
64 bytes from 172.17.0.2: seq=0 ttl=64 time=0.307 ms
64 bytes from 172.17.0.2: seq=1 ttl=64 time=0.162 ms
64 bytes from 172.17.0.2: seq=2 ttl=64 time=0.177 ms
```

5. Use the **cat** utility to have a look at the **/etc/hosts** file of the **containerlink2** container. The **hosts** file is a list of routable names to IP addresses that Docker can maintain and override:

```
/ # cat /etc/hosts
```

The output of the **hosts** file should display and resemble the following:

```
127.0.0.1  localhost
::1    localhost ip6-localhost ip6-loopback
fe00::0    ip6-localnet
ff00::0    ip6-mcastprefix
ff02::1    ip6-allnodes
ff02::2    ip6-allrouters
172.17.0.2    containerlink1 032f038abfba
172.17.0.3    9b62c4a57ce3
```

From the output of the **hosts** file of the **containerlink2** container, observe that Docker is adding an entry for the **containerlink1** container name as well as its container ID. This enables the **containerlink2** container to know the name, and the container ID is mapped to the IP address **172.17.0.2**. Typing the **exit** command will terminate the **sh** shell session and bring you back to your environment's main terminal.

6. Run **docker exec** to access an **sh** shell inside the **containerlink1** container:

```
$ docker exec -it containerlink1 /bin/sh
```

This should drop you into the shell of the **containerlink1** container.

7. Ping the **containerlink2** container using the **ping** utility:

```
/ # ping containerlink2
```

You should see the following output:

```
ping: bad address 'containerlink2'
```

It is not possible to ping the **containerlink2** container since linking containers only works unidirectionally. The **containerlink1** container has no idea that the **containerlink2** container exists since no **hosts** file entry has been created in the **containerlink1** container instance.

> **NOTE**
>
> You can only link to running containers using the legacy link method between containers. This means that the first container cannot link to containers that get started later. This is one of the many reasons why using links between containers is no longer a recommended approach. We are covering the concept in this chapter to show you how the functionality works.

8. Due to the limitations using the legacy link method, Docker also supports native DNS using user-created Docker networks. To leverage this functionality, create a Docker network called **dnsnet** and deploy two Alpine containers within that network. First, use the **docker network create** command to create a new Docker network using a **192.168.56.0/24** subnet and using the IP address **192.168.54.1** as the default gateway:

```
$ docker network create dnsnet --subnet 192.168.54.0/24 --gateway
192.168.54.1
```

Depending on the version of Docker you are using, the successful execution of this command may return the ID of the network you have created.

> **NOTE**
>
> Simply using the **docker network create dnsnet** command will create a network with a Docker-allocated subnet and gateway. This exercise demonstrates how to specify the subnet and gateway for your Docker network. It should also be noted that if your computer is attached to a subnet in the **192.168.54.0/24** subnet or a subnet that overlaps that space, it may cause network connectivity issues. Please use a different subnet for this exercise.

9. Use the **docker network ls** command to list the Docker networks available in this environment:

```
$ docker network ls
```

The list of Docker networks should be returned, including the **dnsnet** network you just created:

```
NETWORK ID      NAME      DRIVER     SCOPE
ec5b91e88a6f    bridge    bridge     local
c804e768413d    dnsnet    bridge     local
f52b4a5440ad    host      host       local
9bed60b88784    none      null       local
```

10. Run the **docker network inspect** command to view the configuration for this network:

```
$ docker network inspect dnsnet
```

The details of the **dnsnet** network should be displayed. Pay close attention to the **Subnet** and **Gateway** parameters. These are the same parameters that you used to create a Docker network in *Step 8*:

```
[
    {
        "Name": "dnsnet",
        "Id": "c804e768413d14686d570451c8ef34b18a8bb975a1e4994a29cd9964ae8cd6ca",
        "Created": "2020-05-12T19:31:39.300406513-04:00",
        "Scope": "local",
        "Driver": "bridge",
        "EnableIPv6": false,
        "IPAM": {
            "Driver": "default",
            "Options": {},
            "Config": [
                {
                    "Subnet": "192.168.54.0/24",
                    "Gateway": "192.168.54.1"
                }
            ]
        },
        "Internal": false,
        "Attachable": false,
        "Ingress": false,
        "ConfigFrom": {
            "Network": ""
        },
        "ConfigOnly": false,
        "Containers": {},
        "Options": {},
        "Labels": {}
    }
]
```

Figure 6.8: Output from the docker network inspect command

11. Since this is a Docker **bridge** network, Docker will also create a corresponding bridge network interface for this network. The IP address of the **bridge** network interface will be the same IP address as the default gateway address you specified when creating this network. Use the **ifconfig** command to view the configured network interfaces on Linux or macOS. If you are using Windows, use the **ipconfig** command:

```
$ ifconfig
```

This should display the output of all available network interfaces, including the newly created **bridge** interface:

```
br-c804e768413d: flags=4099<UP,BROADCAST,MULTICAST>  mtu 1500
        inet 192.168.54.1  netmask 255.255.255.0  broadcast 192.168.54.255
        ether 02:42:d4:82:df:36  txqueuelen 0  (Ethernet)
        RX packets 0  bytes 0 (0.0 B)
        RX errors 0  dropped 0  overruns 0  frame 0
        TX packets 0  bytes 0 (0.0 B)
        TX errors 0  dropped 0 overruns 0  carrier 0  collisions 0

docker0: flags=4099<UP,BROADCAST,MULTICAST>  mtu 1500
        inet 172.17.0.1  netmask 255.255.0.0  broadcast 172.17.255.255
        ether 02:42:c2:01:cc:86  txqueuelen 0  (Ethernet)
        RX packets 0  bytes 0 (0.0 B)
        RX errors 0  dropped 0  overruns 0  frame 0
        TX packets 0  bytes 0 (0.0 B)
        TX errors 0  dropped 0 overruns 0  carrier 0  collisions 0

enp1s0: flags=4163<UP,BROADCAST,RUNNING,MULTICAST>  mtu 1500
        inet 192.168.122.185  netmask 255.255.255.0  broadcast 192.168.122.255
        inet6 fe80::fcc1:6453:cb2f:37da  prefixlen 64  scopeid 0x20<link>
        ether 52:54:00:0a:6a:c1  txqueuelen 1000  (Ethernet)
        RX packets 4356  bytes 63651269 (63.6 MB)
        RX errors 0  dropped 5  overruns 0  frame 0
        TX packets 2922  bytes 227533 (227.5 KB)
        TX errors 0  dropped 0 overruns 0  carrier 0  collisions 0
```

Figure 6.9: Analyzing the bridge network interface for the newly created Docker network

12. Now that a new Docker network has been created, use the **docker run** command to start a new container (**alpinedns1**) within this network. Use the **docker run** command with the **--network** flag to specify the **dnsnet** network that was just created, and the **--network-alias** flag to give your container a custom DNS name:

```
$ docker run -itd --network dnsnet --network-alias alpinedns1 --name
alpinedns1 alpine:latest
```

Upon successful execution of the command, the full container ID should be displayed before returning to a normal terminal prompt.

13. Start a second container (**alpinedns2**) using the same **--network** and **--network-alias** settings:

```
$ docker run -itd --network dnsnet --network-alias alpinedns2 --name
alpinedns2 alpine:latest
```

> **NOTE**
>
> It is important to understand the difference between the **−network-alias** flag and the **--name** flag. The **--name** flag is used to give the container a human-readable name within the Docker API. This makes it easy to start, stop, restart, and manage containers by name. The **--network-alias** flag, however, is used to create a custom DNS entry for the container.

14. Use the **docker ps** command to verify that the containers are running as expected:

```
$ docker ps
```

The output will display the running container instances:

```
CONTAINER ID    IMAGE           COMMAND        CREATED
  STATUS                PORTS                NAMES
69ecb9ad45e1    alpine:latest   "/bin/sh"      4 seconds ago
  Up 2 seconds                               alpinedns2
9b57038fb9c8    alpine:latest   "/bin/sh"      6 minutes ago
  Up 6 minutes                               alpinedns1
```

15. Use the **docker inspect** command to verify that the IP addresses of the container instances are from within the subnet (**192.168.54.0/24**) that was specified:

```
$ docker inspect alpinedns1
```

The following output is truncated to show the relevant details:

```
"Networks": {
    "dnsnet": {
        "IPAMConfig": null,
        "Links": null,
        "Aliases": [
            "alpinedns1",
            "69ecb9ad45e1"
        ],
        "NetworkID": "c804e768413d14686d570451c8ef34b18a8bb975a1e4994a29cd9964ae8cd6ca",
        "EndpointID": "c7f9b4f3a6aaabd7118eeeafcdd8f11db1af6f10d1c90c0b9eac6a098cda071a",
        "Gateway": "192.168.54.2",
        "IPAddress": "192.168.54.1",
        "IPPrefixLen": 24,
        "IPv6Gateway": "",
        "GlobalIPv6Address": "",
        "GlobalIPv6PrefixLen": 0,
        "MacAddress": "02:42:c0:a8:36:03",
        "DriverOpts": null
    }
}
```

Figure: 6.10: Output from the Networks section of the alpinedns1 container instance

It can be observed from the output that the **alpinedns1** container was deployed with an IP address of **192.168.54.2**, which is a part of the subnet that was defined during the creation of the Docker network.

16. Execute the **docker network inspect** command in a similar fashion for the **alpinedns2** container:

```
$ docker inspect alpinedns2
```

The output is again truncated to display the relevant networking details:

```
"Networks": {
    "dnsnet": {
        "IPAMConfig": null,
        "Links": null,
        "Aliases": [
            "alpinedns2",
            "69ecb9ad45e1"
        ],
        "NetworkID": "c804e768413d14686d570451c8ef34b18a8bb975a1e4994a29cd9964ae8cd6ca",
        "EndpointID": "c7f9b4f3a6aaabd7118eeeafcdd8f11db1af6f10d1c90c0b9eac6a098cda071a",
        "Gateway": "192.168.54.1",
        "IPAddress": "192.168.54.3",
        "IPPrefixLen": 24,
        "IPv6Gateway": "",
        "GlobalIPv6Address": "",
        "GlobalIPv6PrefixLen": 0,
        "MacAddress": "02:42:c0:a8:36:03",
        "DriverOpts": null
    }
}
```

Figure 6.11: Output of the Networks section of the alpinedns2 container instance

It can be observed in the preceding output that the **alpinedns2** container has an IP address of **192.168.54.3**, which is a different IP address within the **dnsnet** subnet.

17. Run the **docker exec** command to access a shell in the **alpinedns1** container:

```
$ docker exec -it alpinedns1 /bin/sh
```

This should drop you into a root shell inside of the containers.

18. Once inside the **alpinedns1** container, use the **ping** utility to ping the **alpinedns2** container:

```
/ # ping alpinedns2
```

The **ping** output should display successful network connectivity to the **alpinedns2** container instance:

```
PING alpinedns2 (192.168.54.3): 56 data bytes
64 bytes from 192.168.54.3: seq=0 ttl=64 time=0.278 ms
64 bytes from 192.168.54.3: seq=1 ttl=64 time=0.233 ms
```

19. Use the **exit** command to return to your primary terminal. Use the **docker exec** command to gain access to a shell inside the **alpinedns2** container:

```
$ docker exec -it alpinedns2 /bin/sh
```

This should drop you to a shell within the **alpinedns2** container.

20. Use the **ping** utility to ping the **alpinedns1** container by name:

```
$ ping alpinedns1
```

The output should display successful responses from the **alpinedns1** container:

```
PING alpinedns1 (192.168.54.2): 56 data bytes
64 bytes from 192.168.54.2: seq=0 ttl=64 time=0.115 ms
64 bytes from 192.168.54.2: seq=1 ttl=64 time=0.231 ms
```

> **NOTE**
>
> Docker DNS, as opposed to the legacy link method, allows bidirectional communication between containers in the same Docker network.

21. Use the **cat** utility inside any of the **alpinedns** containers to reveal that Docker is using true DNS as opposed to **/etc/hosts** file entries inside the container:

```
# cat /etc/hosts
```

This will reveal the contents of the **/etc/hosts** file inside the respective container:

```
127.0.0.1   localhost
::1   localhost ip6-localhost ip6-loopback
fe00::0     ip6-localnet
ff00::0     ip6-mcastprefix
ff02::1     ip6-allnodes
ff02::2     ip6-allrouters
192.168.54.2     9b57038fb9c8
```

Use the **exit** command to terminate the shell session inside of the **alpinedns2** container.

22. Clean up your environment by stopping all running containers using the **docker stop** command:

```
$ docker stop   containerlink1
$ docker stop   containerlink2
$ docker stop   alpinedns1
$ docker stop   alpinedns2
```

23. Use the **docker system prune -fa** command to clean the remaining stopped containers and networks:

```
$ docker system prune -fa
```

Successfully executing this command should clean up the **dnsnet** network as well as the container instances and images:

```
Deleted Containers:
69ecb9ad45e16ef158539761edc95fc83b54bd2c0d2ef55abfba1a300f141c7c
9b57038fb9c8cf30aaebe6485e9d223041a9db4e94eb1be9392132bdef632067
Deleted Networks:
dnsnet
```

```
Deleted Images:
untagged: alpine:latest
untagged: alpine@sha256:9a839e63dad54c3a6d1834e29692c8492d93f90c
    59c978c1ed79109ea4fb9a54
deleted:  sha256:f70734b6a266dcb5f44c383274821207885b549b75c8e119
    404917a61335981a
deleted:  sha256:3e207b409db364b595ba862cdc12be96dcdad8e36c59a03b
    b3b61c946a5741a


Total reclaimed space: 42.12M
```

Each section of the system prune output will identify and remove Docker resources that are no longer in use. In this case, it will remove the **dnsnet** network since no container instances are currently deployed in this network.

In this exercise, you looked at the benefits of using name resolution to enable communication between the containers over Docker networks. Using name resolution is efficient since applications don't have to worry about the IP addresses of the other running containers. Instead, communication can be initiated by simply calling the other containers by name.

We first explored the legacy link method of name resolution, by which running containers can establish a relationship, leveraging a unidirectional relationship using entries in the container's **hosts** file. The second and more modern way to use DNS between containers is by creating user-defined Docker networks that allow DNS resolution bidirectionally. This will enable all containers on the network to resolve all other containers by name or container ID without any additional configuration.

As we have seen in this section, Docker provides many unique ways to provide reliable networking resources to container instances, such as enabling routing between containers on the same Docker network and native DNS services between containers. This is only scratching the surface of the network options that are provided by Docker.

In the next section, we will learn about deploying containers using other types of networking drivers to truly provide maximum flexibility when deploying containerized infrastructure.

NATIVE DOCKER NETWORK DRIVERS

Since Docker is one of the most broadly supported container platforms in recent times, the Docker platform has been vetted across numerous production-level networking scenarios. To support various types of applications, Docker provides various network drivers that enable flexibility in how containers are created and deployed. These network drivers allow containerized applications to run in almost any networking configuration that is supported directly on bare metal or virtualized servers.

For example, containers can be deployed that share the host server's networking stack, or in a configuration that allows them to be assigned unique IP addresses from the underlay network infrastructure. In this section, we are going to learn about the basic Docker network drivers and how to leverage them to provide the maximum compatibility for various types of network infrastructures:

- **bridge**: A **bridge** is the default network that Docker will run containers in. If nothing is defined when launching a container instance, Docker will use the subnet behind the **docker0** interface, in which containers will be assigned an IP address in the **172.17.0.0/16** subnet. In a **bridge** network, containers have network connectivity to other containers in the **bridge** subnet as well as outbound connectivity to the internet. So far, all containers we have created in this chapter have been in **bridge** networks. Docker **bridge** networks are generally used for simple TCP services that only expose simple ports or require communication with other containers that exist on the same host.

- **host**: Containers running in the **host** networking mode have direct access to the host machine's network stack. This means that any ports that are exposed to the container are also exposed to the same ports on the host machine running the containers. The container also has visibility of all physical and virtual network interfaces running on the host. **host** networking is generally preferred when running container instances that consume lots of bandwidth or leverage multiple protocols.

- **none**: The **none** network provides no network connectivity to containers deployed in this network. Container instances that are deployed in the **none** network only have a loopback interface and no access to other network resources at all. No driver operates this network. Containers deployed using the **none** networking mode are usually applications that operate on storage or disk workloads and don't require network connectivity. Containers that are segregated from network connectivity for security purposes may also be deployed using this network driver.

- **macvlan**: **macvlan** networks created in Docker are used in scenarios in which your containerized application requires a MAC address and direct network connectivity to the underlay network. Using a **macvlan** network, Docker will allocate a MAC address to your container instance via a physical interface on the host machine. This makes your container appear as a physical host on the deployed network segment. It should be noted that many cloud environments, such as AWS, Azure, and many virtualization hypervisors, do not allow **macvlan** networking to be configured on container instances. **macvlan** networks allow Docker to assign containers IP addresses and MAC addresses from the underlay networks based on a physical network interface attached to the host machine. Using **macvlan** networking can easily lead to IP address exhaustion or IP address conflicts if not configured correctly. **macvlan** container networks are generally used in very specific network use cases, such as applications that monitor network traffic modes or other network-intensive workloads.

No conversation on Docker networking would be complete without a brief overview of **Docker overlay networking**. **Overlay** networking is how Docker handles networking with a swarm cluster. When a Docker cluster is defined between nodes, Docker will use the physical network linking the nodes together to define a logical network between containers running on the nodes. This allows containers to talk directly to each other between cluster nodes. In *Exercise 6.03, Exploring Docker Networks*, we will look at the various types of Docker network drivers that are supported in Docker by default, such as **host**, **none**, and **macvlan**. In *Exercise 6.04, Defining Overlay Networks*, we will then define a simple Docker swarm cluster to discover how **overlay** networking works between Docker hosts configured in a cluster mode.

EXERCISE 6.03: EXPLORING DOCKER NETWORKS

In this exercise, we will look into the various types of Docker network drivers that are supported in Docker by default, such as **host**, **none**, and **macvlan**. We will start with the **bridge** network and then look into the **none**, **host**, and **macvlan** networks:

1. First, you need to get an idea of how networking is set up in your Docker environment. From a Bash or PowerShell terminal, use the **ifconfig** or **ipconfig** command on Windows. This will display all the network interfaces in your Docker environment:

```
$ ifconfig
```

This will display all the network interfaces you have available. You should see a **bridge** interface called **docker0**. This is the Docker **bridge** interface that serves as the entrance (or ingress point) into the default Docker network:

```
docker0: flags=4099<UP,BROADCAST,MULTICAST>  mtu 1500
        inet 172.17.0.1  netmask 255.255.0.0  broadcast 172.17.255.255
        ether 02:42:06:ec:7e:9b  txqueuelen 0  (Ethernet)
        RX packets 0  bytes 0 (0.0 B)
        RX errors 0  dropped 0  overruns 0  frame 0
        TX packets 0  bytes 0 (0.0 B)
        TX errors 0  dropped 0 overruns 0  carrier 0  collisions 0

enp1s0: flags=4163<UP,BROADCAST,RUNNING,MULTICAST>  mtu 1500
        inet 192.168.122.185  netmask 255.255.255.0  broadcast 192.168.122.255
        inet6 fe80::fcc1:6453:cb2f:37da  prefixlen 64  scopeid 0x20<link>
        ether 52:54:00:0a:6a:c1  txqueuelen 1000  (Ethernet)
        RX packets 28682  bytes 111943401 (111.9 MB)
        RX errors 0  dropped 0  overruns 0  frame 0
        TX packets 11270  bytes 787399 (787.3 KB)
        TX errors 0  dropped 0 overruns 0  carrier 0  collisions 0
```

Figure 6.12: Example ifconfig output from your Docker development environment

2. Use the **docker network ls** command to view the networks available in your Docker environment:

```
$ docker network ls
```

This should list the three basic network types defined previously, displaying the network ID, the name of the Docker network, and the driver associated with the network type:

```
NETWORK ID      NAME      DRIVER    SCOPE
50de4997649a    bridge    bridge    local
f52b4a5440ad    host      host      local
9bed60b88784    none      null      local
```

3. View the verbose details of these networks using the **docker network inspect** command, followed by the ID or the name of the network you want to inspect. In this step, you will view the verbose details of the **bridge** network:

```
$ docker network inspect bridge
```

Docker will display the verbose output of the `bridge` network in JSON format:

```
[
    {
        "Name": "bridge",
        "Id": "50de4997649a36b77ac540f549d9931a64a7009ee2be8489b63a4a220b918b4e",
        "Created": "2020-05-01T20:56:38.522661526-04:00",
        "Scope": "local",
        "Driver": "bridge",
        "EnableIPv6": false,
        "IPAM": {
            "Driver": "default",
            "Options": null,
            "Config": [
                {
                    "Subnet": "172.17.0.0/16",
                    "Gateway": "172.17.0.1"
                }
            ]
        },
        "Internal": false,
        "Attachable": false,
        "Ingress": false,
        "ConfigFrom": {
            "Network": ""
        },
        "ConfigOnly": false,
        "Containers": {},
        "Options": {
            "com.docker.network.bridge.default_bridge": "true",
            "com.docker.network.bridge.enable_icc": "true",
            "com.docker.network.bridge.enable_ip_masquerade": "true",
            "com.docker.network.bridge.host_binding_ipv4": "0.0.0.0",
            "com.docker.network.bridge.name": "docker0",
            "com.docker.network.driver.mtu": "1500"
        },
        "Labels": {}
    }
]
```

Figure 6.13: Inspecting the default bridge network

Some key parameters to note in this output are the **Scope, Subnet**, and **Gateway** keywords. Based on this output, it can be observed that the scope of this network is only the local host machine (**Scope: Local**). This indicates the network is not shared between hosts in a Docker swarm cluster. The **Subnet** value of this network under the **Config** section is **172.17.0.0/16**, and the **Gateway** address for the subnet is an IP address within the defined subnet (**172.17.0.1**). It is critical that the **Gateway** value of a subnet is an IP address within that subnet to enable containers deployed in that subnet to access other networks outside the scope of that network. Finally, this network is tied to the host interface, **docker0**, which will serve as the **bridge** interface for the network. The output of the **docker network inspect** command can be very helpful in getting a full understanding of how containers deployed in that network are expected to behave.

4. View the verbose details of the **host** network using the **docker network inspect** command:

```
$ docker network inspect host
```

This will display the details of the **host** network in JSON format:

```
[
    {
        "Name": "host",
        "Id": "f52b4a5440ad41e44adb3e14f4892fb57e95479f99d5b67e39739f6bc0a8f13f",
        "Created": "2020-04-11T11:41:59.811741058-04:00",
        "Scope": "local",
        "Driver": "host",
        "EnableIPv6": false,
        "IPAM": {
            "Driver": "default",
            "Options": null,
            "Config": []
        },
        "Internal": false,
        "Attachable": false,
        "Ingress": false,
        "ConfigFrom": {
            "Network": ""
        },
        "ConfigOnly": false,
        "Containers": {},
        "Options": {},
        "Labels": {}
    }
]
```

Figure 6.14: docker network inspect output for the host network

As you can see, there is not very much configuration present in the **host** network. Since it uses the **host** networking driver, all the container's networking will be shared with the host. Hence, this network configuration does not need to define specific subnets, interfaces, or other metadata, as we have seen in the default **bridge** network from before.

5. Investigate the **none** network next. Use the **docker network inspect** command to view the details of the **none** network:

```
docker network inspect none
```

The details will be displayed in JSON format:

```
[
    {
        "Name": "none",
        "Id": "9bed60b88784312abcae6d6026dec4445abf34964f563e6f1552675a8fd03ab6",
        "Created": "2020-04-11T11:41:59.732455407-04:00",
        "Scope": "local",
        "Driver": "null",
        "EnableIPv6": false,
        "IPAM": {
            "Driver": "default",
            "Options": null,
            "Config": []
        },
        "Internal": false,
        "Attachable": false,
        "Ingress": false,
        "ConfigFrom": {
            "Network": ""
        },
        "ConfigOnly": false,
        "Containers": {},
        "Options": {},
        "Labels": {}
    }
]
```

Figure 6.15: docker network inspect output for the none network

Similar to the **host** network, the **none** network is mostly empty. Since containers deployed in this network will have no network connectivity by leveraging the **null** driver, there isn't much need for configuration.

> **NOTE**
>
> Be aware that the difference between the **none** and **host** networks lies in the driver they use, despite the fact that the configurations are almost identical. Containers launched in the **none** network have no network connectivity at all, and no network interfaces are assigned to the container instance. However, containers launched in the **host** network will share the networking stack with the host system.

6. Now create a container in the **none** network to observe its operation. In your terminal or PowerShell session, use the **docker run** command to start an Alpine Linux container in the **none** network using the **--network** flag. Name this container **nonenet** so we know that it is deployed in the **none** network:

```
$ docker run -itd --network none --name nonenet alpine:latest
```

This will pull and start an Alpine Linux Docker container in the **none** network.

7. Use the **docker ps** command to verify whether the container is up and running as expected:

```
$ docker ps
```

The output should display the **nonenet** container as up and running:

```
CONTAINER ID     IMAGE            COMMAND        CREATED
  STATUS                 PORTS              NAMES
972a80984703     alpine:latest    "/bin/sh"      9 seconds ago
  Up 7 seconds                              nonenet
```

8. Execute the **docker inspect** command, along with the container name, **nonenet**, to get a deeper understanding of how this container is configured:

```
$ docker inspect nonenet
```

The output of **docker inspect** will display the full container configuration in JSON format. A truncated version highlighting the **NetworkSettings** section is provided here. Pay close attention to the **IPAddress** and **Gateway** settings:

```
"NetworkSettings": {
    "Bridge": "",
    "SandboxID": "a1f59b07894b3903f11c0c145ed4e650f5cca1003c5fbbac5741552cf87078d3",
    "HairpinMode": false,
    "LinkLocalIPv6Address": "",
    "LinkLocalIPv6PrefixLen": 0,
    "Ports": {},
    "SandboxKey": "/var/run/docker/netns/a1f59b07894b",
    "SecondaryIPAddresses": null,
    "SecondaryIPv6Addresses": null,
    "EndpointID": "",
    "Gateway": "",
    "GlobalIPv6Address": "",
    "GlobalIPv6PrefixLen": 0,
    "IPAddress": "",
    "IPPrefixLen": 0,
    "IPv6Gateway": "",
    "MacAddress": "",
    "Networks": {
        "none": {
            "IPAMConfig": null,
            "Links": null,
            "Aliases": null,
            "NetworkID": "9bed60b88784312abcae6d6026dec4445abf34964f563e6f1552675a8fd03ab6",
            "EndpointID": "032b2f248b2f4122222129e4597561c7b4b29b11a16a9e65efc906e71437fe14",
            "Gateway": "",
            "IPAddress": "",
            "IPPrefixLen": 0,
            "IPv6Gateway": "",
            "GlobalIPv6Address": "",
            "GlobalIPv6PrefixLen": 0,
            "MacAddress": "",
            "DriverOpts": null
```

Figure 6.16: docker inspect output for the nonenet container

The **docker inspect** output will reveal that this container does not have an IP address, nor does it have a gateway or any other networking settings.

9. Use the **docker exec** command to access an **sh** shell inside this container:

```
$ docker exec -it nonenet /bin/sh
```

Upon successful execution of this command, you will be dropped into a root shell in the container instance:

```
/ #
```

10. Execute the **ip a** command to view the network interfaces available in the container:

```
/ $ ip a
```

This will display all network interfaces configured in this container:

```
1: lo: <LOOPBACK,UP,LOWER_UP> mtu 65536 qdisc noqueue state
UNKNOWN qlen 1000
    link/loopback 00:00:00:00:00:00 brd 00:00:00:00:00:00
    inet 127.0.0.1/8 scope host lo
    valid_lft forever preferred_lft forever
```

The only network interface available to this container is its **LOOPBACK** interface. As this container is not configured with an IP address or default gateway, common networking commands will not work.

11. Test the lack of network connectivity using the **ping** utility provided by default in the Alpine Linux Docker image. Try to ping the Google DNS servers located at IP address **8.8.8.8**:

```
/ # ping 8.8.8.8
```

The output of the **ping** command should reveal that it has no network connectivity:

```
PING 8.8.8.8 (8.8.8.8): 56 data bytes
ping: sendto: Network unreachable
```

Use the **exit** command to return to your main terminal session.

Now that you have taken a closer look at the **none** network, consider the **host** networking driver. The **host** networking driver in Docker is unique since it doesn't have any intermediate interfaces or create any extra subnets. Instead, the **host** networking driver shares the networking stack with the host operating system such that any network interfaces that are available to the host are also available to containers running in **host** mode.

12. To get started with running a container in **host** mode, execute **ifconfig** if you are running macOS or Linux, or use **ipconfig** if you are running on Windows, to take inventory of the network interfaces that are available on the host machine:

```
$ ifconfig
```

This should output a list of network interfaces available on your host machine:

```
docker0: flags=4099<UP,BROADCAST,MULTICAST>  mtu 1500
        inet 172.17.0.1   netmask 255.255.0.0   broadcast 172.17.255.255
        ether 02:42:06:ec:7e:9b   txqueuelen 0   (Ethernet)
        RX packets 0   bytes 0 (0.0 B)
        RX errors 0   dropped 0   overruns 0   frame 0
        TX packets 0   bytes 0 (0.0 B)
        TX errors 0   dropped 0 overruns 0   carrier 0   collisions 0

enp1s0: flags=4163<UP,BROADCAST,RUNNING,MULTICAST>  mtu 1500
        inet 192.168.122.185   netmask 255.255.255.0   broadcast 192.168.122.255
        inet6 fe80::fcc1:6453:cb2f:37da   prefixlen 64   scopeid 0x20<link>
        ether 52:54:00:0a:6a:c1   txqueuelen 1000   (Ethernet)
        RX packets 28682   bytes 111943401 (111.9 MB)
        RX errors 0   dropped 0   overruns 0   frame 0
        TX packets 11270   bytes 787399 (787.3 KB)
        TX errors 0   dropped 0 overruns 0   carrier 0   collisions 0
```

Figure 6.17: List of network interfaces configured on the host machine

In this example, the primary network interface of your host machine is **enp1s0** with an IP address of **192.168.122.185**.

> **NOTE**
>
> Some versions of Docker Desktop on macOS or Windows may not properly be able to start and run containers in **host** network mode or using **macvlan** network drivers, due to the dependencies on the Linux kernel to provide many of these functionalities. When running these examples on macOS or Windows, you may see the network details of the underlying Linux virtual machine running Docker, as opposed to the network interfaces available on your macOS or Windows host machine.

13. Use the **docker run** command to start an Alpine Linux container in the **host** network. Name it **hostnet1** to tell it apart from the other containers:

```
docker run -itd --network host --name hostnet1 alpine:latest
```

Docker will start this container in the background using the **host** network.

14. Use the **docker inspect** command to look at the network configuration of the **hostnet1** container you just created:

```
$ docker inspect hostnet1
```

This will reveal the verbose configuration of the running container, including the networking details, in JSON format:

```
"NetworkSettings": {
    "Bridge": "",
    "SandboxID": "67b54051821d44ffd55c7042e51444777fe53ed7b4e5e6a222c485d43321449d",
    "HairpinMode": false,
    "LinkLocalIPv6Address": "",
    "LinkLocalIPv6PrefixLen": 0,
    "Ports": {},
    "SandboxKey": "/var/run/docker/netns/default",
    "SecondaryIPAddresses": null,
    "SecondaryIPv6Addresses": null,
    "EndpointID": "",
    "Gateway": "",
    "GlobalIPv6Address": "",
    "GlobalIPv6PrefixLen": 0,
    "IPAddress": "",
    "IPPrefixLen": 0,
    "IPv6Gateway": "",
    "MacAddress": "",
    "Networks": {
        "host": {
            "IPAMConfig": null,
            "Links": null,
            "Aliases": null,
            "NetworkID": "f52b4a5440ad41e44adb3e14f4892fb57e95479f99d5b67e39739f6bc0a8f13f",
            "EndpointID": "7e7557baccc2cf640f7a8c59e685542f02a442f2531dd0aa7bf02a98735f972b",
            "Gateway": "",
            "IPAddress": "",
            "IPPrefixLen": 0,
            "IPv6Gateway": "",
            "GlobalIPv6Address": "",
            "GlobalIPv6PrefixLen": 0,
            "MacAddress": "",
            "DriverOpts": null
        }
    }
}
```

Figure 6.18: docker inspect output for the hostnet1 container

It should be noted that the output of the **NetworkSettings** block will look a lot like the containers you deployed in the **none** network. In the **host** networking mode, Docker will not assign an IP address or gateway to the container instance since it shares all network interfaces with the host machine directly.

15. Use **docker exec** to access an **sh** shell inside this container, providing the name **hostnet1**:

```
$ docker exec -it hostnet1 /bin/sh
```

This should drop you into a root shell inside the **hostnet1** container.

16. Inside the **hostnet1** container, execute the **ifconfig** command to list which network interfaces are available to it:

```
/ # ifconfig
```

The full list of network interfaces available inside of this container should be displayed:

```
docker0   Link encap:Ethernet  HWaddr 02:42:80:07:84:96
          inet addr:172.17.0.1  Bcast:172.17.255.255  Mask:255.255.0.0
          UP BROADCAST MULTICAST  MTU:1500  Metric:1
          RX packets:0 errors:0 dropped:0 overruns:0 frame:0
          TX packets:0 errors:0 dropped:0 overruns:0 carrier:0
          collisions:0 txqueuelen:0
          RX bytes:0 (0.0 B)  TX bytes:0 (0.0 B)

enp1s0    Link encap:Ethernet  HWaddr 52:54:00:0A:6A:C1
          inet addr:192.168.122.185  Bcast:192.168.122.255  Mask:255.255.255.0
          inet6 addr: fe80::fcc1:6453:cb2f:37da/64 Scope:Link
          UP BROADCAST RUNNING MULTICAST  MTU:1500  Metric:1
          RX packets:39516 errors:0 dropped:4 overruns:0 frame:0
          TX packets:6201 errors:0 dropped:0 overruns:0 carrier:0
          collisions:0 txqueuelen:1000
          RX bytes:66258728 (63.1 MiB)  TX bytes:542932 (530.2 KiB)

lo        Link encap:Local Loopback
          inet addr:127.0.0.1  Mask:255.0.0.0
          inet6 addr: ::1/128 Scope:Host
          UP LOOPBACK RUNNING  MTU:65536  Metric:1
          RX packets:611 errors:0 dropped:0 overruns:0 frame:0
          TX packets:611 errors:0 dropped:0 overruns:0 carrier:0
          collisions:0 txqueuelen:1000
          RX bytes:66073 (64.5 KiB)  TX bytes:66073 (64.5 KiB)
```

Figure 6.19: Displaying the available network interfaces inside the hostnet1 container

Note that this list of network interfaces is identical to that which you encountered when querying the host machine directly. This is because this container and the host machine are sharing the network directly. Anything available to the host machine will also be available to containers running in **host** network mode.

17. Use the **exit** command to end the shell session and return to the terminal of the host machine.

18. To understand more fully how the shared networking model works in Docker, start an NGINX container in **host** network mode. The NGINX container automatically exposes port **80**, which we previously had to forward to a port on the host machine. Use the **docker run** command to start an NGINX container on the host machine:

```
$ docker run -itd --network host --name hostnet2 nginx:latest
```

This command will start an NGINX container in the **host** networking mode.

19. Navigate to **http://localhost:80** using a web browser on the host machine:

Welcome to nginx!

If you see this page, the nginx web server is successfully installed and working. Further configuration is required.

For online documentation and support please refer to nginx.org. Commercial support is available at nginx.com.

Thank you for using nginx.

Figure 6.20: Accessing the NGINX default web page of a container running in host networking mode

You should be able to see the NGINX default web page displayed in your web browser. It should be noted that the **docker run** command did not explicitly forward or expose any ports to the host machine. Since the container is running in **host** networking mode, any ports that containers expose by default will be available directly on the host machine.

20. Use the **docker run** command to create another NGINX instance in the **host** network mode. Call this container **hostnet3** to differentiate it from the other two container instances:

```
$ docker run -itd --network host --name hostnet3 nginx:latest
```

21. Now use the **docker ps -a** command to list all the containers, both in running and stopped status:

```
$ docker ps -a
```

The list of running containers will be displayed:

```
CONTAINER ID  IMAGE         COMMAND                 CREATED
  STATUS                    PORTS           NAMES
da56fcf81d02  nginx:latest  "nginx -g 'daemon of…"  4 minutes ago
  Exited (1)  4 minutes ago                 hostnet3
5786dac6fd27  nginx:latest  "nginx -g 'daemon of…"  37 minutes ago
  Up 37 minutes                             hostnet2
648b291846e7  alpine:latest "/bin/sh"               38 minutes ago
  Up 38 minutes                             hostnet
```

22. Based on the preceding output, you can see that the **hostnet3** container exited and is currently in a stopped state. To understand more fully why this is the case, use the **docker logs** command to view the container logs:

```
$ docker logs hostnet3
```

The log output should be displayed as follows:

```
[200~2020/05/15 00:50:04 [emerg] 1#1: bind() to 0.0.0.0:80 failed (98: Address already in use)
nginx: [emerg] bind() to 0.0.0.0:80 failed (98: Address already in use)
2020/05/15 00:50:04 [emerg] 1#1: bind() to 0.0.0.0:80 failed (98: Address already in use)
nginx: [emerg] bind() to 0.0.0.0:80 failed (98: Address already in use)
2020/05/15 00:50:04 [emerg] 1#1: bind() to 0.0.0.0:80 failed (98: Address already in use)
nginx: [emerg] bind() to 0.0.0.0:80 failed (98: Address already in use)
2020/05/15 00:50:04 [emerg] 1#1: bind() to 0.0.0.0:80 failed (98: Address already in use)
nginx: [emerg] bind() to 0.0.0.0:80 failed (98: Address already in use)
2020/05/15 00:50:04 [emerg] 1#1: bind() to 0.0.0.0:80 failed (98: Address already in use)
nginx: [emerg] bind() to 0.0.0.0:80 failed (98: Address already in use)
2020/05/15 00:50:04 [emerg] 1#1: still could not bind()
nginx: [emerg] still could not bind()
```

Figure 6.21: NGINX errors in the hostnet3 container

Essentially, this second instance of an NGINX container was unable to start properly because it was unable to bind to port **80** on the host machine. The reason for this is that the **hostnet2** container is already listening on that port.

> **NOTE**
>
> Note that containers running in **host** networking mode need to be deployed with care and consideration. Without proper planning and architecture, container sprawl can lead to a variety of port conflicts across container instances that are running on the same machine.

23. The next type of native Docker network you will investigate is **macvlan**. In a **macvlan** network, Docker will allocate a MAC address to a container instance to make it appear as a physical host on a particular network segment. It can run either in **bridge** mode, which uses a parent **host** network interface to gain physical access to the underlay network, or in **802.1Q trunk** mode, which leverages a sub-interface that Docker creates on the fly.

24. To begin, create a new network utilizing the **macvlan** Docker network driver by specifying a physical interface on your host machine as the parent interface using the **docker network create** command.

25. Earlier in the **ifconfig** or **ipconfig** output, you saw that the **enp1s0** interface is the primary network interface on the machine. Substitute the name of the primary network interface of your machine. Since you are using the primary network interface of the host machine as the parent, specify the same subnet (or a smaller subnet within that space) for the network connectivity of our containers. Use a **192.168.122.0/24** subnet here, since it is the same subnet of the primary network interface. Likewise, you want to specify the same default gateway as the parent interface. Use the same subnet and gateway of your host machine:

```
$ docker network create -d macvlan --subnet=192.168.122.0/24
--gateway=192.168.122.1 -o parent=enp1s0 macvlan-net1
```

This command should create a network called **macvlan-net1**.

26. Use the **docker network ls** command to confirm that the network has been created and is using the **macvlan** network driver:

```
$ docker network ls
```

This command will output all the currently configured networks that are defined in your environment. You should see the **macvlan-net1** network:

```
NETWORK ID       NAME             DRIVER      SCOPE
f4c9408f22e2     bridge           bridge      local
f52b4a5440ad     host             host        local
b895c821b35f     macvlan-net1     macvlan     local
9bed60b88784     none             null        local
```

27. Now that the **macvlan** network has been defined in Docker, create a container in this network and investigate the network connectivity from the host's perspective. Use the **docker run** command to create another Alpine Linux container named **macvlan1** using the **macvlan** network **macvlan-net1**:

```
$ docker run -itd --name macvlan1 --network macvlan-net1
alpine:latest
```

This should start an Alpine Linux container instance called **macvlan1** in the background.

28. Use the **docker ps -a** command to check and make sure this container instance is running:

```
$ docker ps -a
```

This should reveal that the container named **macvlan1** is up and running as expected:

```
CONTAINER ID    IMAGE                    COMMAND      CREATED
   STATUS                   PORTS                NAMES
cd3c61276759    alpine:latest    "/bin/sh"     3 seconds ago
   Up 1 second                                  macvlan1
```

29. Use the **docker inspect** command to investigate the networking configuration of this container instance:

```
$ docker inspect macvlan1
```

The verbose output of the container configuration should be displayed. The following output has been truncated to show only the network settings section in JSON format:

```
"NetworkSettings": {
    "Bridge": "",
    "SandboxID": "bb6d07592adc5e5cf0dcc688b6ec0ea913c897aa8510429d79cc06238d02e4f1",
    "HairpinMode": false,
    "LinkLocalIPv6Address": "",
    "LinkLocalIPv6PrefixLen": 0,
    "Ports": {},
    "SandboxKey": "/var/run/docker/netns/bb6d07592adc",
    "SecondaryIPAddresses": null,
    "SecondaryIPv6Addresses": null,
    "EndpointID": "",
    "Gateway": "",
    "GlobalIPv6Address": "",
    "GlobalIPv6PrefixLen": 0,
    "IPAddress": "",
    "IPPrefixLen": 0,
    "IPv6Gateway": "",
    "MacAddress": "",
    "Networks": {
        "macvlan-net1": {
            "IPAMConfig": null,
            "Links": null,
            "Aliases": [
                "29ddcc291fd2"
            ],
            "NetworkID": "ed262b190ffd490e0c1b8d18a1adddf5829216a46aa9ce374f0321ced6cec3df",
            "EndpointID": "29a0222a16d7b410edffe693fa6a896cc1554fa88d93da0ff389506323b5a03e",
            "Gateway": "192.168.122.1",
            "IPAddress": "192.168.122.2",
            "IPPrefixLen": 24,
            "IPv6Gateway": "",
            "GlobalIPv6Address": "",
            "GlobalIPv6PrefixLen": 0,
            "MacAddress": "02:42:c0:a8:7a:02",
            "DriverOpts": null
        }
    }
}
```

Figure 6.22: The docker network inspect output of the macvlan1 network

From this output, you can see that this container instance (similar to containers in other networking modes) has both an IP address and a default gateway. It can also be concluded that this container also has an OSI Model Layer 2 MAC address within the **192.168.122.0/24** network, based on the **MacAddress** parameter under the **Networks** subsection. Other hosts within this network segment would believe this machine is another physical node living in this subnet, not a container hosted inside a node on the subnet.

30. Use **docker run** to create a second container instance named **macvlan2** inside the **macvlan-net1** network:

```
$ docker run -itd --name macvlan2 --network macvlan-net1
alpine:latest
```

This should start another container instance within the **macvlan-net1** network.

31. Run the **docker inspect** command to see the MAC address of the **macvlan-net2** container instance:

```
$ docker inspect macvlan2
```

This will output the verbose configuration of the **macvlan2** container instance in JSON format, truncated here to only show the relevant networking settings:

```
"NetworkSettings": {
    "Bridge": "",
    "SandboxID": "755e09e6e3e585b83f0e8432a39b2a0df0517864e90ee12c22b37ef3c4cc1096",
    "HairpinMode": false,
    "LinkLocalIPv6Address": "",
    "LinkLocalIPv6PrefixLen": 0,
    "Ports": {},
    "SandboxKey": "/var/run/docker/netns/755e09e6e3e5",
    "SecondaryIPAddresses": null,
    "SecondaryIPv6Addresses": null,
    "EndpointID": "",
    "Gateway": "",
    "GlobalIPv6Address": "",
    "GlobalIPv6PrefixLen": 0,
    "IPAddress": "",
    "IPPrefixLen": 0,
    "IPv6Gateway": "",
    "MacAddress": "",
    "Networks": {
        "macvlan-net1": {
            "IPAMConfig": null,
            "Links": null,
            "Aliases": [
                "07c0012644f1"
            ],
            "NetworkID": "ed262b190ffd490e0c1b8d18a1adddf5829216a46aa9ce374f0321ced6cec3df",
            "EndpointID": "42d9b81e0de6a0db9b398626d93547552c1575d6bffb2a10525d62b62d39499d",
            "Gateway": "192.168.122.1",
            "IPAddress": "192.168.122.3",
            "IPPrefixLen": 24,
            "IPv6Gateway": "",
            "GlobalIPv6Address": "",
            "GlobalIPv6PrefixLen": 0,
            "MacAddress": "02:42:c0:a8:7a:03",
            "DriverOpts": null
        }
    }
}
```

Figure 6.23: docker inspect output for the macvlan2 container

It can be seen in this output that the **macvlan2** container has both a different IP address and MAC address from the **macvlan1** container instance. Docker assigns different MAC addresses to ensure that Layer 2 conflicts do not arise when many containers are using **macvlan** networks.

32. Run the **docker exec** command to access an **sh** shell inside this container:

```
$ docker exec -it macvlan1 /bin/sh
```

This should drop you into a root session inside the container.

33. Use the **ifconfig** command inside the container to observe that the MAC address you saw in the **docker inspect** output on the **macvlan1** container is present as the MAC address of the container's primary network interface:

```
/ # ifconfig
```

In the details for the **eth0** interface, look at the **HWaddr** parameter. You may also note the IP address listed under the **inet addr** parameter, as well as the number of bytes transmitted and received by this network interface – **RX bytes** (bytes received) and **TX bytes** (bytes transmitted):

```
eth0        Link encap:Ethernet   HWaddr 02:42:C0:A8:7A:02
            inet addr:192.168.122.2   Bcast:192.168.122.255
                             Mask:255.255.255.0
            UP BROADCAST RUNNING MULTICAST  MTU:1500  Metric:1
            RX packets:353 errors:0 dropped:0 overruns:0 frame:0
            TX packets:188 errors:0 dropped:0 overruns:0 carrier:0
            collisions:0 txqueuelen:0
            RX bytes:1789983 (1.7 MiB)   TX bytes:12688 (12.3 KiB)
```

34. Install the **arping** utility using the **apk** package manager available in the Alpine Linux container. This is a tool used to send **arp** messages to a MAC address to check Layer 2 connectivity:

```
/ # apk add arping
```

The **arping** utility should install inside the **macvlan1** container:

```
fetch http://dl-cdn.alpinelinux.org/alpine/v3.11/main
/x86_64/APKINDEX.tar.gz
fetch http://dl-cdn.alpinelinux.org/alpine/v3.11/community
/x86_64/APKINDEX.tar.gz
(1/3) Installing libnet (1.1.6-r3)
(2/3) Installing libpcap (1.9.1-r0)
```

```
(3/3) Installing arping (2.20-r0)
Executing busybox-1.31.1-r9.trigger
OK: 6 MiB in 17 packages
```

35. Specify the Layer 3 IP address of the **macvlan2** container instance as the primary argument to **arping**. Now, **arping** will automatically look up the MAC address and check the Layer 2 connectivity to it:

```
/ # arping 192.168.122.3
```

The **arping** utility should report back the correct MAC address for the **macvlan2** container instance, indicating successful Layer 2 network connectivity:

```
ARPING 192.168.122.3
42 bytes from 02:42:c0:a8:7a:03 (192.168.122.3): index=0
time=8.563 usec
42 bytes from 02:42:c0:a8:7a:03 (192.168.122.3): index=1
time=18.889 usec
42 bytes from 02:42:c0:a8:7a:03 (192.168.122.3): index=2
time=15.917 use
type exit to return to the shell of your primary terminal.
```

36. Check the status of the containers using the **docker ps -a** command:

```
$ docker ps -a
```

The output of this command should show all the running and stopped container instances in your environment.

37. Next, stop all running containers using **docker stop**, followed by the container name or ID:

```
$ docker stop hostnet1
```

Repeat this step for all running containers in your environment.

38. Clean up the container images and unused networks using the **docker system prune** command:

```
$ docker system prune -fa
```

This command will clean up all unused container images, networks, and volumes remaining on your machine.

In this exercise, we looked at the four default networking drivers available by default in Docker: **bridge**, **host**, **macvlan**, and **none**. For each example, we explored how the network functions, how containers deployed using these network drivers function with the host machine, and how they function with other containers on the network.

The networking capability that Docker exposes by default can be leveraged to deploy containers in very advanced networking configurations, as we have seen so far. Docker also offers the ability to manage and coordinate container networking between hosts in a clustered swarm configuration.

In the next section, we will look at creating networks that will create overlay networks between Docker hosts to ensure direct connectivity between container instances.

DOCKER OVERLAY NETWORKING

Overlay networks are logical networks that are created on top of a physical (underlay) network for specific purposes. A **Virtual Private Network (VPN)**, for example, is a common type of **overlay** network that uses the internet to create a link to another private network. Docker can create and manage **overlay** networks between containers, which can be used for containerized applications to directly talk to one another. When containers are deployed into an **overlay** network, it does not matter which host in the cluster they are deployed on; they will have direct connectivity to other containerized services that exist in the same **overlay** network in the same way that they would if they existed on the same physical host.

EXERCISE 6.04: DEFINING OVERLAY NETWORKS

Docker **overlay** networking is used to create mesh networks between machines in a Docker swarm cluster. In this exercise, you will use two machines to create a basic Docker swarm cluster. Ideally, these machines will exist on the same networking segment to ensure direct network connectivity and fast network connectivity between them. Furthermore, they should be running the same version of Docker in a supported distribution of Linux, such as RedHat, CentOS, or Ubuntu.

You will define **overlay** networks that will span hosts in a Docker swarm cluster. You will then ensure that containers deployed on separate hosts can talk to one another via the **overlay** network:

> **NOTE**
>
> This exercise requires access to a secondary machine with Docker installed on it. Usually, cloud-based virtual machines or machines deployed in another hypervisor work best. Deploying a Docker swarm cluster on your system using Docker Desktop could lead to networking issues or serious performance degradation.

1. On the first machine, **Machine1**, run **docker --version** to find out which version of Docker is currently running on it.

```
Machine1 ~$ docker --version
```

The version details of the Docker installation of Machine1 will be displayed:

```
Docker version 19.03.6, build 369ce74a3c
```

Then, you can do the same for **Machine2**:

```
Machine2 ~$ docker --version
```

The version details of the Docker installation of Machine2 will be displayed:

```
Docker version 19.03.6, build 369ce74a3c
```

Verify that the installed version of Docker is the same before moving forward.

> **NOTE**
>
> The Docker version may vary depending on your system.

2. On **Machine1**, run the **docker swarm init** command to initialize a Docker swarm cluster:

```
Machine1 ~$ docker swarm init
```

This should print the command you can use on other nodes to join the Docker swarm cluster, including the IP address and **join** token:

```
docker swarm join --token SWMTKN-1-57n212qtvfnpu0ab28tewiorf3j9fxzo9v
aa7drpare0ic6ohg-5epus8clyzd9xq7e7ze1y0p0n
192.168.122.185:2377
```

3. On **Machine2**, run the **docker swarm join** command, which was provided by **Machine1**, to join the Docker swarm cluster:

```
Machine2 ~$ docker swarm join --token SWMTKN-1-57n212qtvfnpu0
ab28tewiorf3j9fxzo9vaa7drpare0ic6ohg-5epus8clyzd9xq7e7ze1y0p0n
192.168.122.185:2377
```

Machine2 should successfully join the Docker swarm cluster:

```
This node joined a swarm as a worker.
```

4. Execute the **docker info** command on both nodes to ensure they have successfully joined the swarm cluster:

Machine1:

```
Machine1 ~$ docker info
```

Machine2:

```
Machine2 ~$ docker info
```

The following output is a truncation of the **swarm** portion of the **docker info** output. From these details, you will see that these Docker nodes are configured in a swarm cluster and there are two nodes in the cluster with a single manager node (**Machine1**). These parameters should be identical on both nodes, except for the **Is Manager** parameter, for which **Machine1** will be the manager. By default, Docker will allocate a default subnet of **10.0.0.0/8** for the default Docker swarm **overlay** network:

```
swarm: active
 NodeID: oub9g5383ifyg7i52yq4zsu5a
 Is Manager: true
 ClusterID: x7chp0w3two04ltmkqjm32g1f
 Managers: 1
 Nodes: 2
 Default Address Pool: 10.0.0.0/8
 SubnetSize: 24
 Data Path Port: 4789
 Orchestration:
   Task History Retention Limit: 5
```

5. From the **Machine1** box, create an **overlay** network using the **docker network create** command. Since this is a network that will span more than one node in a simple swarm cluster, specify the **overlay** driver as the network driver. Call this network **overlaynet1**. Use a subnet and gateway that are not yet in use by any networks on your Docker hosts to avoid subnet collisions. Use **172.45.0.0/16** and **172.45.0.1** as the gateway:

```
Machine1 ~$ docker network create overlaynet1 --driver overlay
--subnet 172.45.0.0/16 --gateway 172.45.0.1
```

The **overlay** network will be created.

6. Use the **docker network ls** command to verify whether the network was created successfully and is using the correct **overlay** driver:

```
Machine1 ~$ docker network ls
```

A list of networks available on your Docker host will be displayed:

```
NETWORK ID      NAME                DRIVER      SCOPE
54f2af38e6a8    bridge              bridge      local
df5ebd75303e    docker_gwbridge     bridge      local
f52b4a5440ad    host                host        local
8hm1ouvt4z7t    ingress             overlay     swarm
9bed60b88784    none                null        local
60wqq8ewt8zq    overlaynet1         overlay     swarm
```

7. Use the **docker service create** command to create a service that will span multiple nodes in the swarm cluster. Deploying containers as services allow you to specify more than one replica of a container instance for horizontal scaling or scaling container instances across nodes in a cluster for high availability. To keep this example simple, create a single container service of Alpine Linux. Name this service **alpine-overlay1**:

```
Machine1 ~$ docker service create -t --replicas 1 --network
overlaynet1 --name alpine-overlay1 alpine:latest
```

A text-based progress bar will display the progress of the **alpine-overlay1** service deployment:

```
overall progress: 1 out of 1 tasks
1/1: running   [==========================================>]
verify: Service converged
```

8. Repeat the same **docker service create** command, but now specify **alpine-overlay2** as the service name:

```
Machine1 ~$ docker service create -t --replicas 1 --network
overlaynet1 --name alpine-overlay2 alpine:latest
```

A text-based progress bar will again display the progress of the service deployment:

```
overall progress: 1 out of 1 tasks
1/1: running   [=============================================>]
verify: Service converged
```

> **NOTE**
>
> More details on creating services in Docker swarm can be found in *Chapter 9, Docker Swarm*. As the scope of this exercise is networking, we will focus for now on the networking component.

9. From the **Machine1** node, execute the **docker ps** command to see which service is running on this node:

```
Machine1 ~$ docker ps
```

The running containers will be displayed. Docker will intelligently scale containers between nodes in a Docker swarm cluster. In this example, the container from the **alpine-overlay1** service landed on **Machine1**. Your environment may vary depending on how Docker deploys the services:

```
CONTAINER ID    IMAGE          COMMAND       CREATED
  STATUS              PORTS              NAMES
4d0f5fa82add    alpine:latest  "/bin/sh"     59 seconds ago
  Up 57 seconds                          alpine-overlay1.1.
r0tlm8w0dtdfbjaqyhobza94p
```

10. Run the **docker inspect** command to view the verbose details of the running container:

```
Machine1 ~$ docker inspect alpine-overlay1.1.r0tlm8w0dtdfbjaqyhobza
94p
```

The verbose details of the running container instance will be displayed. The following output has been truncated to display the **NetworkSettings** portion of the **docker inspect** output:

```
"NetworkSettings": {
        "Bridge": "",
        "SandboxID": "d0c102a81bc5f1833eab716f2c6641dba356f9d9482558e9eb7ef4e06d51e60e",
        "HairpinMode": false,
        "LinkLocalIPv6Address": "",
        "LinkLocalIPv6PrefixLen": 0,
        "Ports": {},
        "SandboxKey": "/var/run/docker/netns/d0c102a81bc5",
        "SecondaryIPAddresses": null,
        "SecondaryIPv6Addresses": null,
        "EndpointID": "",
        "Gateway": "",
        "GlobalIPv6Address": "",
        "GlobalIPv6PrefixLen": 0,
        "IPAddress": "",
        "IPPrefixLen": 0,
        "IPv6Gateway": "",
        "MacAddress": "",
        "Networks": {
            "overlaynet1": {
                "IPAMConfig": {
                    "IPv4Address": "172.45.0.11"
                },
                "Links": null,
                "Aliases": [
                    "4d0f5fa82add"
                ],
                "NetworkID": "60wqq8ewt8zqm9g5yyn1zbda9",
                "EndpointID": "de71dafbbec7f997494d0858e300db362f6b364b46fe2d4ec30bbf3fdfa99ec1",
                "Gateway": "",
                "IPAddress": "172.45.0.11",
                "IPPrefixLen": 16,
                "IPv6Gateway": "",
                "GlobalIPv6Address": "",
                "GlobalIPv6PrefixLen": 0,
                "MacAddress": "02:42:ac:2d:00:0b",
                "DriverOpts": null
```

Figure 6.24: Inspecting the alpine-overlay1 container instance

Notice that the IP address of this container is as expected within the subnet you have specified on **Machine1**.

11. On the **Machine2** instance, execute the **docker network ls** command to view the Docker networks available on the host:

```
Machine2 ~$ docker network ls
```

A list of all available Docker networks will be displayed on the Docker host:

```
NETWORK ID        NAME                DRIVER      SCOPE
8c7755be162f      bridge              bridge      local
28055e8c63a0      docker_gwbridge     bridge      local
c62fb7ac090f      host                host        local
8hm1ouvt4z7t      ingress             overlay     swarm
6182d77a8f62      none                null        local
60wqq8ewt8zq      overlaynet1         overlay     swarm
```

Notice the **overlaynet1** network defined on **Machine1** is also available on **Machine2**. This is because networks created using the **overlay** driver are available to all hosts in the Docker swarm cluster. This enables containers to be deployed using this network to run across all hosts in the cluster.

12. Use the **docker ps** command to list the running containers on this Docker instance:

```
Machine2 ~$ docker ps
```

A list of all running containers will be displayed. In this example, the container in the **alpine-overlay2** service landed on the **Machine2** cluster node:

```
CONTAINER ID      IMAGE           COMMAND       CREATED
  STATUS                  PORTS         NAMES
53747ca9af09      alpine:latest   "/bin/sh"      33 minutes ago
  Up 33 minutes                         alpine-overlay2.1.ui9vh6zn1
8i48sxjbr8k23t71
```

> **NOTE**
>
> Which node the services land on in your example may differ from what is displayed here. Docker makes decisions on how to deploy containers based on various criteria, such as available CPU bandwidth, memory, and scheduling restrictions placed on the deployed containers.

13. Use **docker inspect** to investigate the network configuration of this container as well:

```
Machine2 ~$ docker inspect alpine-overlay2.1.ui9vh6zn18i48sxjbr8k
23t71
```

The verbose container configuration will be displayed. This output has been truncated to display the **NetworkSettings** portion of the output in JSON format:

```
"NetworkSettings": {
        "Bridge": "",
        "SandboxID": "93b0ce48c1eedaf3d5dbbbb5b32031c64e4bc8ade230aefc20925c062e496752",
        "HairpinMode": false,
        "LinkLocalIPv6Address": "",
        "LinkLocalIPv6PrefixLen": 0,
        "Ports": {},
        "SandboxKey": "/var/run/docker/netns/93b0ce48c1ee",
        "SecondaryIPAddresses": null,
        "SecondaryIPv6Addresses": null,
        "EndpointID": "",
        "Gateway": "",
        "GlobalIPv6Address": "",
        "GlobalIPv6PrefixLen": 0,
        "IPAddress": "",
        "IPPrefixLen": 0,
        "IPv6Gateway": "",
        "MacAddress": "",
        "Networks": {
            "overlaynet1": {
                "IPAMConfig": {
                    "IPv4Address": "172.45.0.14"
                },
                "Links": null,
                "Aliases": [
                    "53747ca9af09"
                ],
                "NetworkID": "60wqq8ewt8zqm9g5yyn1zbda9",
                "EndpointID": "61d4dddf56329520bc17285f9c764a39246d1d7701446b0955e37aa468e0ea2c",
                "Gateway": "",
                "IPAddress": "172.45.0.14",
                "IPPrefixLen": 16,
                "IPv6Gateway": "",
                "GlobalIPv6Address": "",
                "GlobalIPv6PrefixLen": 0,
                "MacAddress": "02:42:ac:2d:00:0e",
                "DriverOpts": null
            }
        }
}
```

Figure 6.25: docker inspect output of the alpine-overlay2 container instance

Note that this container also has an IP address within the **overlaynet1 overlay** network.

14. Since both services are deployed within the same **overlay** network but exist in two separate hosts, you can see that Docker is using the **underlay** network to proxy the traffic for the **overlay** network. Check the network connectivity between the services by attempting a ping from one service to the other. It should be noted here that, similar to static containers deployed in the same network, services deployed on the same network can resolve each other by name using Docker DNS. Use the **docker exec** command on the **Machine2** host to access an **sh** shell inside the **alpine-overlay2** container:

```
Machine2 ~$ docker exec -it alpine-overlay2.1.ui9vh6zn18i48sxjbr8k
23t71 /bin/sh
```

This should drop you into a root shell on the **alpine-overlay2** container instance. Use the **ping** command to initiate network communication to the **alpine-overlay1** container:

```
/ # ping alpine-overlay1
PING alpine-overlay1 (172.45.0.10): 56 data bytes
64 bytes from 172.45.0.10: seq=0 ttl=64 time=0.314 ms
64 bytes from 172.45.0.10: seq=1 ttl=64 time=0.274 ms
64 bytes from 172.45.0.10: seq=2 ttl=64 time=0.138 ms
```

Notice that even though these containers are deployed across two separate hosts, the containers can communicate with each other by name, using the shared **overlay** network.

15. From the **Machine1** box, you can attempt the same communication to the **alpine-overlay2** service container. Use the **docker exec** command to access an **sh** shell on the **Machine1** box:

```
Machine1 ~$ docker exec -it alpine-overlay1.1.r0tlm8w0dtdfbjaqyhobza
94p /bin/sh
```

This should drop you into a root shell inside the container. Use the **ping** command to initiate communication to the **alpine-overlay2** container instance:

```
/ # ping alpine-overlay2
PING alpine-overlay2 (172.45.0.13): 56 data bytes
64 bytes from 172.45.0.13: seq=0 ttl=64 time=0.441 ms
64 bytes from 172.45.0.13: seq=1 ttl=64 time=0.227 ms
64 bytes from 172.45.0.13: seq=2 ttl=64 time=0.282 ms
```

Notice again that, by using Docker DNS, the IP address of the **alpine-overlay2** container can be resolved between hosts using the **overlay** networking driver.

16. Use the **docker service rm** command to delete both services from the **Machine1** node:

```
Machine1 ~$ docker service rm alpine-overlay1
Machine1 ~$ docker service rm alpine-overlay2
```

For each of these commands, the service name will appear briefly indicating the command execution was successful. On both nodes, **docker ps** will display that no containers are currently running.

17. Delete the **overlaynet1** Docker network by using the **docker rm** command and specifying the name **overlaynet1**:

```
Machine1 ~$ docker network rm overlaynet1
```

The **overlaynet1** network will be deleted.

In this exercise, we looked at Docker **overlay** networking between two hosts in a Docker swarm cluster. **Overlay** networking is enormously beneficial in a Docker container cluster because it allows the horizontal scaling of containers between nodes in a cluster. From a network perspective, these containers can directly talk to one another by using a service mesh proxied over the physical network interfaces of the host machines. This not only reduces latency but simplifies deployments by taking advantage of many of Docker's features, such as DNS.

Now that we have looked at all the native Docker network types and examples of how they function, we can look at another aspect of Docker networking that has recently been gaining popularity. Since Docker networking is very modular, as we have seen, Docker supports a plugin system that allows users to deploy and manage custom network drivers.

In the next section, we will learn about how non-native Docker networks work by installing a third-party network driver from Docker Hub.

NON-NATIVE DOCKER NETWORKS

In the final section of this chapter, we will discuss non-native Docker networks. Aside from the native Docker network drivers that are available, Docker also supports custom networking drivers that can be written by users or downloaded from third parties via Docker Hub. Custom third-party network drivers are useful in circumstances that require very particular network configurations, or where container networking is expected to behave in a certain way. For example, some network drivers provide the ability for users to set custom policies regarding access to internet resources, or other defining whitelists for communication between containerized applications. This can be helpful from a security, policy, and auditing perspective.

In the following exercise, we will download and install the Weave Net driver and create a network on a Docker host. Weave Net is a highly supported third-party network driver that provides excellent visibility into container mesh networks, allowing users to create complex service mesh infrastructures that can span multi-cloud scenarios. We will install the Weave Net driver from Docker Hub and configure a basic network in the simple swarm cluster we defined in the previous exercise.

EXERCISE 6.05: INSTALLING AND CONFIGURING THE WEAVE NET DOCKER NETWORK DRIVER

In this exercise, you will download and install the Weave Net Docker network driver and deploy it within the Docker swarm cluster you created in the previous exercise. Weave Net is one of the most common and flexible third-party Docker network drivers available. Using Weave Net, very complex networking configurations can be defined to enable maximum flexibility in your infrastructure:

1. Install the Weave Net driver from Docker Hub using the **docker plugin install** command on the **Machine1** node:

```
Machine1 ~$ docker plugin install store/weaveworks/net-plugin:2.5.2
```

This will prompt you to grant Weave Net permissions on the machine you are installing it on. It is safe to grant the requested permissions as Weave Net requires them to set up the network driver on the host operating system properly:

```
Plugin "store/weaveworks/net-plugin:2.5.2" is requesting
the following privileges:
 - network: [host]
 - mount: [/proc/]
 - mount: [/var/run/docker.sock]
```

```
- mount: [/var/lib/]
- mount: [/etc/]
- mount: [/lib/modules/]
- capabilities: [CAP_SYS_ADMIN CAP_NET_ADMIN CAP_SYS_MODULE]
Do you grant the above permissions? [y/N]
```

Answer the prompt by pressing the *y* key. The Weave Net plugin should be installed successfully.

2. On the **Machine2** node, run the same **docker plugin install** command. All nodes in the Docker swarm cluster should have the plugin installed since all nodes will be participating in the swarm mesh networking:

```
Machine2 ~$ docker plugin install store/weaveworks/net-plugin:2.5.2
```

The permissions prompt will be displayed. Respond with *y* when prompted to continue the installation:

```
Plugin "store/weaveworks/net-plugin:2.5.2" is requesting
the following privileges:
- network: [host]
- mount: [/proc/]
- mount: [/var/run/docker.sock]
- mount: [/var/lib/]
- mount: [/etc/]
- mount: [/lib/modules/]
- capabilities: [CAP_SYS_ADMIN CAP_NET_ADMIN CAP_SYS_MODULE]
Do you grant the above permissions? [y/N]
```

3. Create a network using the **docker network create** command on the **Machine1** node. Specify the Weave Net driver as the primary driver and the network name as **weavenet1**. For the subnet and gateway parameters, use a unique subnet that has not yet been used in the previous exercises:

```
Machine1 ~$  docker network create --driver=store/weaveworks/
net-plugin:2.5.2 --subnet 10.1.1.0/24 --gateway 10.1.1.1 weavenet1
```

This should create a network called **weavenet1** in the Docker swarm cluster.

4. List the available networks in the Docker swarm cluster using the **docker network ls** command:

```
Machine1 ~$ docker network ls
```

The **weavenet1** network should be displayed in the list:

```
NETWORK ID      NAME            DRIVER
  SCOPE
b3f000eb4699    bridge          bridge
  local
df5ebd75303e    docker_gwbridge bridge
  local
f52b4a5440ad    host            host
  local
8hm1ouvt4z7t    ingress         overlay
  swarm
9bed60b88784    none            null
  local
q354wyn6yvh4    weavenet1       store/weaveworks/net-plugin:2.5.2
  swarm
```

5. Execute the **docker network ls** command on the **Machine2** node to ensure that the **weavenet1** network is present on that machine as well:

```
Machine2 ~$ docker network ls
```

The **weavenet1** network should be listed:

```
NETWORK ID      NAME            DRIVER
  SCOPE
b3f000eb4699    bridge          bridge
  local
df5ebd75303e    docker_gwbridge bridge
  local
f52b4a5440ad    host            host
  local
8hm1ouvt4z7t    ingress         overlay
  swarm
9bed60b88784    none            null
  local
q354wyn6yvh4    weavenet1       store/weaveworks/net-plugin:2.5.2
  swarm
```

6. On the **Machine1** node, create a service called **alpine-weavenet1** that uses the **weavenet1** network using the **docker service create** command:

```
Machine1 ~$ docker service create -t --replicas 1 --network weavenet1
--name alpine-weavenet1 alpine:latest
```

A text-based progress bar will display the deployment status of the service. It should complete without any issues:

```
overall progress: 1 out of 1 tasks
1/1: running    [==============================================>]
verify: Service converged
```

7. Use the **docker service create** command again to create another service in the **weavenet1** network called **alpine-weavenet2**:

```
Machine1 ~$ docker service create -t --replicas 1 --network weavenet1
--name alpine-weavenet2 alpine:latest
```

A text-based progress bar will again display indicating the status of the service creation:

```
overall progress: 1 out of 1 tasks
1/1: running    [==============================================>]
verify: Service converged
```

8. Run the **docker ps** command to validate that an Alpine container is successfully running on each node in the cluster:

Machine1:

```
Machine1 ~$ docker ps
```

Machine2:

```
Machine2 ~$ docker ps
```

One of the service containers should be up and running on both machines:

Machine1:

```
CONTAINER ID      IMAGE          COMMAND       CREATED
   STATUS                PORTS           NAMES
acc47f58d8b1      alpine:latest    "/bin/sh"      7 minutes ago
   Up 7 minutes                    alpine-weavenet1.1.zo5folr5
yvu6v7cwqn23d2h97
```

Machine2:

```
CONTAINER ID       IMAGE              COMMAND        CREATED
   STATUS                      PORTS          NAMES
da2a45d8c895       alpine:latest      "/bin/sh"      4 minutes ago
   Up 4 minutes                            alpine-weavenet2.1.z8jpiup8yetj
rqca62ub0yz9k
```

9. Use the **docker exec** command to access an **sh** shell inside the **weavenet1.1** container instance. Make sure to run this command on the node in the swarm cluster that is running this container:

```
Machine1 ~$ docker exec -it alpine-weavenet1.1.zo5folr5yvu6v7cwqn23
d2h97 /bin/sh
```

This should drop you into a root shell inside the container:

```
/ #
```

10. Use the **ifconfig** command to view the network interfaces present inside this container:

```
/ # ifconfig
```

This will display a newly named network interface called **ethwe0**. A core part of Weave Net's core networking policy is to create custom-named interfaces within the container for easy identification and troubleshooting. It should be noted this interface is assigned an IP address from the subnet that we provided as a configuration parameter:

```
ethwe0    Link encap:Ethernet   HWaddr AA:11:F2:2B:6D:BA
          inet addr:10.1.1.3   Bcast:10.1.1.255   Mask:255.255.255.0
          UP BROADCAST RUNNING MULTICAST   MTU:1376   Metric:1
          RX packets:37 errors:0 dropped:0 overruns:0 frame:0
          TX packets:0 errors:0 dropped:0 overruns:0 carrier:0
          collisions:0 txqueuelen:0
          RX bytes:4067 (3.9 KiB)   TX bytes:0 (0.0 B)
```

11. From inside this container, ping the **alpine-weavenet2** service by name, using the **ping** utility:

```
ping alpine-weavenet2
```

You should see responses coming from the resolved IP address of the **alpine-weavenet2** service:

```
64 bytes from 10.1.1.4: seq=0 ttl=64 time=3.430 ms
64 bytes from 10.1.1.4: seq=1 ttl=64 time=1.541 ms
64 bytes from 10.1.1.4: seq=2 ttl=64 time=1.363 ms
64 bytes from 10.1.1.4: seq=3 ttl=64 time=1.850 ms
```

> **NOTE**
>
> Due to recent updates in the Docker libnetwork stack in recent versions of Docker and Docker Swarm, pinging the service by name: **alpine-weavenet2** may not work. To demonstrate the network is working as intended, try pinging the name of the container directly instead: **alpine-weavenet2.1.z8jpiup8yetjrqca62ub0yz9k** – Keep in mind, the name of this container will be different in your lab environment.

12. Try pinging Google DNS servers (**8.8.8.8**) on the open internet from these containers as well to ensure that these containers have internet access:

```
ping 8.8.8.8
```

You should see responses returning, indicating these containers have internet access:

```
/ # ping 8.8.8.8
PING 8.8.8.8 (8.8.8.8): 56 data bytes
64 bytes from 8.8.8.8: seq=0 ttl=51 time=13.224 ms
64 bytes from 8.8.8.8: seq=1 ttl=51 time=11.840 ms
type exit to quit the shell session in this container.
```

13. Use the **docker service rm** command to remove both services from the **Machine1** node:

```
Machine1 ~$ docker service rm alpine-weavenet1
Machine1 ~$ docker service rm alpine-weavenet2
```

This will delete both the services, stopping and removing the container instances.

14. Delete the Weave Net network that was created by running the following command:

```
Machine1 ~$ docker network rm weavenet1
```

The Weave Net network should be deleted and removed.

In the robust system of containerized networking concepts, Docker has a vast array of networking drivers to cover almost any circumstance that your workloads demand. However, for all the use cases that lie outside the default Docker networking drivers, Docker supports third-party custom drivers for almost any networking conditions that may arise. Third-party network drivers allow Docker to have flexible integrations with various platforms and even across multiple cloud providers. In this exercise, we looked at installing and configuring the Weave Net networking plugin and creating simple services in a Docker swarm cluster to leverage this network.

In the following activity, you will apply what you have learned in this chapter, using the various Docker network drivers, to deploy a multi-container infrastructure solution. These containers will communicate using different Docker networking drivers on the same hosts and even across multiple hosts in a Docker swarm configuration.

ACTIVITY 6.01: LEVERAGING DOCKER NETWORK DRIVERS

Earlier in the chapter, we looked at the various types of Docker network drivers and how they all function in different ways to bring various degrees of networking capability to deliver functionality in your container environment. In this activity, you are going to deploy an example container from the Panoramic Trekking application in a Docker **bridge** network. You will then deploy a secondary container in **host** networking mode that will serve as a monitoring server and will be able to use **curl** to verify that the application is running as expected.

Perform the following steps to complete this activity:

1. Create a custom Docker **bridge** network with a custom subnet and gateway IP.

2. Deploy an NGINX web server called **webserver1** in that **bridge** network, exposing forwarding port **80** on the container to port **8080** on the host.

3. Deploy an Alpine Linux container in **host** networking mode, which will serve as a monitoring container.

4. Use the Alpine Linux container to **curl** the NGINX web server and get a response.

Expected output:

When you connect to both the forwarded port **8080** and the IP address of the **webserver1** container directly on port **80** upon completion of the activity, you should get the following output:

```
Press ENTER or type command to continue
*   Trying 192.168.1.2:80...
* TCP_NODELAY set
* Connected to 192.168.1.2 (192.168.1.2) port 80 (#0)
> GET / HTTP/1.1
> Host: 192.168.1.2
> User-Agent: curl/7.67.0
> Accept: */*
>
* Mark bundle as not supporting multiuse
< HTTP/1.1 200 OK
< Server: nginx/1.19.0
< Date: Fri, 03 Jul 2020 13:41:31 GMT
< Content-Type: text/html
< Content-Length: 612
< Last-Modified: Tue, 26 May 2020 15:00:20 GMT
< Connection: keep-alive
< ETag: "5ecd2f04-264"
< Accept-Ranges: bytes
<
<!DOCTYPE html>
<html>
<head>
<title>Welcome to nginx!</title>
```

Figure 6.26: Accessing the NGINX web server from the IP address of the container instance

> **NOTE**
>
> The solution for this activity can be found on page 671.

In the next activity, we will look at how Docker **overlay** networking can be leveraged to provide horizontal scalability for our Panoramic Trekking application. By deploying Panoramic Trekking across multiple hosts, we can ensure reliability and durability, and make use of system resources from more than one node in our environment.

ACTIVITY 6.02: OVERLAY NETWORKING IN ACTION

In this chapter, you have seen how powerful **overlay** networking is when deploying multiple containers between cluster hosts with direct network connectivity between them. In this activity, you will revisit the two-node Docker swarm cluster and create services from the Panoramic Trekking application that will connect using Docker DNS between two hosts. In this scenario, different microservices will be running on different Docker swarm hosts but will still be able to leverage the Docker **overlay** network to directly communicate with each other.

To complete this activity successfully, perform the following steps:

1. A Docker **overlay** network using a custom subnet and gateway

2. One application Docker swarm service called **trekking-app** using an Alpine Linux container

3. One database Docker swarm service called **database-app** using a PostgreSQL 12 container (extra credit to supply default credentials)

4. Prove that the **trekking-app** service can communicate with the **database-app** service using **overlay** networking

Expected Output:

The **trekking-app** service should be able to communicate with the **database-app** service, which can be verified by ICMP replies such as the following:

```
PING database-app (10.2.0.5): 56 data bytes
64 bytes from 10.2.0.5: seq=0 ttl=64 time=0.261 ms
64 bytes from 10.2.0.5: seq=1 ttl=64 time=0.352 ms
64 bytes from 10.2.0.5: seq=2 ttl=64 time=0.198 ms
```

> **NOTE**
>
> The solution for this activity can be found on page 675.

SUMMARY

In this chapter, we looked at the many facets of networking in relation to microservices and Docker containers. Docker comes equipped with numerous drivers and configuration options that users can use to tune the way their container networking works in almost any environment. By deploying the correct networks and the correct drivers, powerful service mesh networks can quickly be spun up to enable container-to-container access without egressing any physical Docker hosts. Containers can even be created that will bind to the host networking fabric to take advantage of the underlying network infrastructure.

Quite arguably the most powerful network feature that can be enabled in Docker is the ability to create networks across clusters of Docker hosts. This can allow us to quickly create and deploy horizontal scaling applications between hosts for high availability and redundancy. By leveraging the underlay network, **overlay** networks within swarm clusters allow containers to directly contact containers running on other cluster hosts by taking advantage of the powerful Docker DNS system.

In the next chapter, we will look at the next pillar of a powerful containerized infrastructure: storage. By understanding how container storage can be utilized for stateful applications, extremely powerful solutions can be architected that involve not only containerized stateless applications, but containerized database services that can be deployed, scaled, and optimized as easily as other containers across your infrastructure.

7

DOCKER STORAGE

OVERVIEW

In this chapter, you will learn how Docker manages data. It is crucial to know where to store your data and how your services will access it. This chapter will explore running stateless versus stateful Docker containers, and will delve into the configuration setup options for storage for different applications. By the end of the chapter, you will be able to distinguish between the different storage types in Docker and identify the container's life cycle and its various states. You will also learn how to create and manage Docker volumes.

INTRODUCTION

In previous chapters, you learned how to run a container from an image and how to configure its networking. You also learned that you can pass various Docker commands while crafting containers from the images. In this chapter, you will learn how to control these containers after you have created them.

Assume that you have been assigned to build a web application for an e-store. You will need a database to store the products catalog, clients' information, and purchase transactions. To store these details, you need to configure the application's storage settings.

There are two types of data storage in Docker. The first one is storage that is tightly coupled to the container life cycle. If the container is removed, the files on that storage type are also removed and cannot be retrieved. These files are stored in the thin read/write layer inside the container itself. This type of storage is also known by other terms, such as the local storage, the **graphdriver** storage, and the storage driver. The first section of this chapter focuses on this type of storage. These files could be of any type—for example, the files Docker created after installing a new layer on top of the base image.

The second section of the chapter explores stateless and stateful services. Stateful applications are the ones that need persistent storage, such as databases that persist and outlive the container. In stateful services, the data can still be accessed even when the container is removed.

The container stores the data on the host in two ways: through volumes and bind mounts. Using a bind mount is not recommended because the bind mount binds an existing file or directory on the host to a path inside the container. This bind adds a burden in referencing by using the full or relative path on the host machine. However, a new directory is created within Docker's storage directory on the host machine when you use a volume, and Docker manages the directory's contents. We will focus on using volumes in the third section of this chapter.

Before exploring different types of storage in Docker, let's first explore the container life cycle.

THE CONTAINER LIFE CYCLE

Containers are crafted from their base images. The container inherits the filesystem of the image by creating a thin read/write layer on top of the image layers' stack. The base images stay intact, and no changes are made to them. All your changes happen in that top layer of the container. For example, say you create a container of **ubuntu: 14.08**. This image does not have the **wget** package in it. When you install the **wget** package, you actually install it on the top layer. So, you have a layer for the base image, and on top of it, another layer for **wget**.

If you install the **Apache** server as well, it will be the third layer on top of both of the previous layers. To save all your changes, you need to commit all these changes to a new image because you cannot write over the base image. If you do not commit the changes to a new image, these changes will be deleted with the container's removal.

The container undergoes many other states during its life cycle, so it is important to look into all the states that a container can have during its life cycle. So, let's dive into understanding the different container states:

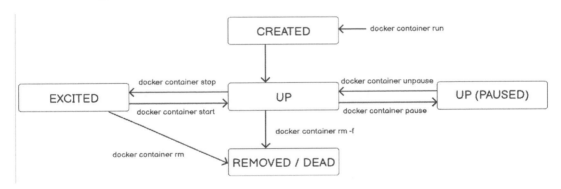

Figure 7.1: Container life cycle

The different stages that a container undergoes are as follows:

- The container enters the **CREATED** status using the **docker container run** subcommand, as shown in *Figure 7.1*.

- Inside every container, there is a main process running. When this process begins running, the container's status changes to the **UP** status.

- The container's status changes to **UP (PAUSED)** by using the **docker container pause** subcommand. The container freezes or suspends but is still in the **UP** state and is not stopped or removed.

- To resume running the container, use the **docker container unpause** subcommand. Here, the container's status will change to the **UP** status again.

- Use the **docker container stop** subcommand to stop the container without removing it. The container's status changes to the **EXITED** status.

- The container will exit if you execute the **docker container kill** or **docker container stop** subcommands. To kill the container, use the **docker container kill** subcommand. The container status changes to **EXITED**. However, to make the container exit, you should use **docker container stop** subcommand and not **docker container kill** subcommand. Do not kill your containers; always remove them because removing the container triggers a grace shutdown to the container, giving time, for example, to save the data to a database, which is a slower process. However, killing does not do that and might cause data inconsistency.

- After stopping or killing the container, you can also resume running the container. To start the container and return it to the **UP** status, use the **docker container start** or **docker container start -a** subcommands. **docker container start -a** is equal to running **docker container start** and then **docker container attach**. You cannot attach local standard input, output, and error streams to an exited container; the container must be in the **UP** state first to attach local standard input, output, and error streams.

- To restart a container, use the **docker container restart** subcommand. The restart subcommand acts like executing **docker container stop** followed by **docker container start**.

- Stopping or killing the container does not remove the container from the system. To remove the container entirely, use the **docker container rm** subcommand.

> **NOTE**
>
> You can concatenate several Docker commands to each other – for example, `docker container rm -f $(docker container ls -aq)`. The one that you want to execute first should be included in the brackets.
>
> In this case, `docker container ls -aq` tells Docker to list all the containers, even the exited one, in quiet mode. The `-a` option denotes displaying all the containers, whatever their states are. The `-q` option is used for quiet mode, which means displaying the numeric IDs only and not all the containers' details. The output of this command, `docker container ls -aq`, will be the input of the `docker container rm -f` command.

Understanding the Docker container life cycle events provides a good background as to why some applications may or may not need persistent storage. Before moving on to the different storage types present in Docker, let's execute the aforementioned commands and explore the different container states in the following exercise.

> **NOTE**
>
> Please use **touch** command to create files and **vim** command to work on the file using vim editor.

EXERCISE 7.01: TRANSITIONING THROUGH THE COMMON STATES FOR A DOCKER CONTAINER

Pinging www.google.com is a common practice to verify that the server or your cluster's node is connected to the internet. In this exercise, you will transit through all the states for a Docker container while checking whether the server or your cluster's node is connected to the internet.

You will use two terminals in this exercise. One terminal will be used to run a container to ping www.google.com, and the other one will be used to control this running container by executing the previously mentioned commands.

To ping www.google.com, you will craft a container called **testevents** from the **ubuntu:14.04** image:

1. Open the first terminal and execute the **docker container run** command to run a container. Use the **--name** option to give the container a specific nickname—for example, **testevents**. Don't let the Docker host generate a random name for your container. Use the **ubuntu:14.04** image and the **ping google.com** command to verify that the server is running on the container:

    ```
    $docker container run --name testevents ubuntu:14.04 ping google.com
    ```

    The output will be as follows:

    ```
    PING google.com (172.217.165.142) 56(84) bytes of data.
    64 bytes from lax30s03-in-f14.1e100.net (172.217.165.142):
    icmp_seq=1 ttl=115 time=68.9 ms
    64 bytes from lax30s03-in-f14.1e100.net (172.217.165.142):
    icmp_seq=2 ttl=115 time=349 ms
    64 bytes from lax30s03-in-f14.1e100.net (172.217.165.142):
    icmp_seq=3 ttl=115 time=170 ms
    ```

    As you can see in the preceding output, the pinging has started. You will find the packets being transmitted to **google.com**.

2. Dedicate the first terminal to the pinging output. Now, control this container by executing the commands in another terminal. In the second terminal, execute **docker container ls** to list all the running containers:

    ```
    $docker container ls
    ```

    Look for the container with the name **testevents**. The status should be **Up**:

    ```
    CONTAINER ID     IMAGE          COMMAND            CREATED
        STATUS            PORTS          NAMES
    10e235033813     ubuntu:14.04   "ping google.com"  10 seconds ago
        Up 5 seconds                     testevents
    ```

3. Now, run the **docker container pause** command in the second terminal to pause the running container in the first terminal:

    ```
    $docker container pause testevents
    ```

    You will see that the pinging has stopped, and no packets are being transmitted anymore.

4. List the running containers again by using **docker container ls** in the second terminal:

```
$docker container ls
```

As you can see in the following output, the status of **testevents** is **Up (Paused)**. This is because you ran the **docker container pause** command previously:

```
CONTAINER ID    IMAGE          COMMAND            CREATED
    STATUS            PORTS          NAMES
10e235033813    ubuntu:14.04   "ping google.com"  26 seconds ago
    Up 20 seconds (Paused)           testevents
```

5. Use **docker container unpause** in the second terminal to start the paused container and make it resume sending packets:

```
$docker container unpause testevents
```

You will find that the pinging resumes and new packets are transmitted in the first terminal.

6. In the second terminal, run the **docker container ls** command again to see the container's current status:

```
$docker container ls
```

You will see that the status of the **testevents** container is **Up**:

```
CONTAINER ID    IMAGE          COMMAND            CREATED
    STATUS            PORTS          NAMES
10e235033813    ubuntu:14.04   "ping google.com"  43 seconds ago
    Up 37 seconds                    testevents
```

7. Now, run the **docker container stop** command to stop the container:

```
$docker container stop testevents
```

You will observe that the container exits and the shell prompt returns in the first terminal:

```
64 bytes from lax30s03-in-f14.1e100.net (142.250.64.110):
icmp_seq = 42 ttl=115 time=19.8 ms
64 bytes from lax30s03-in-f14.1e100.net (142.250.64.110):
icmp_seq = 43 ttl=115 time=18.7 ms
```

8. Now, run the **docker container ls** command in any terminal:

```
$docker container ls
```

You will see that the **testevents** container is not in the list anymore because the **docker container ls** subcommand displays the up-and-running containers only:

```
CONTAINER ID      IMAGE        COMMAND        CREATED
     STATUS              PORTS                NAMES
```

9. Run the **docker container ls -a** command to display all the containers:

```
$docker container ls -a
```

You can see that the status of the **testevents** container is now **Exited**:

```
CONTAINER ID     IMAGE           COMMAND          CREATED
    STATUS              PORTS              NAMES
10e235033813     ubuntu:14.04    "ping google.com"  1 minute ago
    Exited (137)  13 seconds ago       testevents
```

10. Use the **docker container start** command to start the container. Also, add the **-a** option to attach local standard input, output, and error streams to the container and see its output:

```
$docker container start -a testevents
```

As you can see in the following snippet, the pinging resumes and is executed in the first terminal:

```
64 bytes from lax30s03-in-f14.1e100.net (142.250.64.110):
icmp_seq = 55 ttl=115 time=63.5 ms
64 bytes from lax30s03-in-f14.1e100.net (142.250.64.110):
icmp_seq = 56 ttl=115 time=22.2 ms
```

11. Run the **docker ls** command again in the second terminal:

```
$docker container ls
```

You will observe that **testevents** returns back to the list, its status is **Up**, and it is running:

```
CONTAINER ID     IMAGE          COMMAND           CREATED
    STATUS             PORTS              NAMES
10e235033813     ubuntu:14.04   "ping google.com"  43 seconds ago
    Up 37 seconds                       testevents
```

12. Now, remove the **testevents** container using the **rm** command with the **-f** option. The **-f** option is used to force-remove the container:

```
$docker container rm -f testevents
```

The first terminal stops executing the **ping** command and the second terminal will return the name of the container:

```
testevents
```

13. Run the **ls -a** command to check whether the container is running or not:

```
$docker container ls -a
```

You will not find the **testevents** container in the list because we just removed it from our system.

Now, you have seen all the various statuses of the container except **CREATED**. This is typical, as you usually will not see the **CREATED** status. Inside every container, there is a main process with a **Process ID (PID)** of 0 and **Parent Process ID (PPID)** of 1. This process has a different ID outside the container. When this process is killed or removed, the container is killed or removed as well. Normally, when the main process runs, the state of the container changes from **CREATED** to **UP**, and this indicates that the container has been created successfully. If the main process fails, the container state does not change from **CREATED**, and this is what you are going to set up:

14. Run the following command to see the **CREATED** status. Craft a container named **testcreate** from the **ubuntu:14.04** image using the **docker container run** command:

```
$docker container run --name testcreate ubuntu:14.04 time
```

The **time** command will generate an error because there is no such command inside **ubuntu:14.04**.

15. Now, list the running containers:

```
$docker container ls
```

You will see that the list is empty:

CONTAINER ID	IMAGE	COMMAND	CREATED
STATUS	PORTS	NAMES	

16. Now, list all the containers by adding the **-a** option:

```
$docker container ls -a
```

Look in the list for the container named **testcreate**; you will observe that its status is **Created**:

```
CONTAINER ID    IMAGE           COMMAND         CREATED
   STATUS              PORTS           NAMES
C262e6718724    ubuntu:14.04    "time"          30 seconds ago
   Created                         testcreate
```

If a container is stuck in the **CREATED** state, this is an indication that an error has been generated, and Docker was unable to get the container up and running.

In this exercise, you explored the container life cycle and its different states. You also learned how to start with attachment by using the **docker container start -a <container name or ID>** command and how to stop the container using **docker container rm <container name or ID>**. In the end, we discussed how to force-remove running containers by using **docker container rm -f <container name or ID>**. Then, we saw the rare case of **CREATED**, which is shown only when the command generates an error and the container fails to start.

So far, we have focused on the container's statuses and not its size. In the next exercise, we will learn how to determine the size of the memory occupied by the container.

EXERCISE 7.02: CHECKING THE CONTAINER SIZE ON DISK

When you first craft a container, it has the same size as the base image with a top read/write layer. With every layer that is added to the container, its size increases. In this exercise, you will create a container that has **ubuntu:14.04** as its base image. Update and install **wget** on top of it to highlight the effect of state transition on data retention:

1. Run the **docker container run** command with the **-it** option to create a container named **testsize**. The **-it** option is used to have an interactive terminal to run commands inside the running container:

```
$docker container run -it --name testsize ubuntu:14.04
```

The prompt will now look like **root@<container ID>:/#**, where the container ID is a number that the Docker Engine generates. Therefore, you will have a different number when you run this command on your machine. As mentioned before, being inside a container means that the container will be in the **UP** state.

2. Dedicate the first terminal to the running container and execute the commands in the second terminal. Having two terminals saves us from detaching the container to run a command and then reattaching to the container to run another command inside it.

   Now, verify that the container initially has the size of the base image, which is **ubuntu:14.04**. List the images using the **docker image ls** command in the second terminal. Check the size of the **ubuntu:14.04** image:

   ```
   $docker image ls
   ```

   As you can see in the following output, the size of the image is **188MB**:

   ```
   REPOSITORY       TAG       IMAGE ID       CREATED
       SIZE
   ubuntu           14.04     971bb3841501   23 months ago
       188MB
   ```

3. Now, check the size of the container by running the **docker container ls -s** command to get the container's size:

   ```
   $docker container ls -s
   ```

   Look for the **testsize** container. You will observe that the size is **0B (virtual 188MB)**:

   ```
   CONTAINER ID    IMAGE        COMMAND        CREATED
       STATUS       PORTS    NAMES     SIZE
   9f2d2d1ee3e0    ubuntu:14.04 "/bin/bash"    6 seconds ago
       Up 6 minutes          testsize  0B (virtual 188MB)
   ```

   The **SIZE** column indicates the size of the thin read/write layer of the container only, while the virtual size indicates the size of the thin read/write layer and all the previous layers encapsulated in the container. Thus, in this case, the thin layer equals **0B**, and the virtual size equals the image size.

4. Now, install the **wget** package. Run the **apt-get update** command in the first terminal. A general recommendation, in Linux, is to run **apt-get update** before installing any packages to update the latest versions of the packages that are currently on your system:

   ```
   root@9f2d2d1ee3e0: apt-get update
   ```

5. Run the following command when the container finishes updating to install the **wget** package on top of the base image. The **-y** option is used to answer yes automatically to all the installation questions:

```
root@9f2d2d1ee3e: apt-get install -y wget
```

6. When it finishes installing **wget** on top of **ubuntu:14.04**, recheck the container's size by running the **ls -s** command in the second terminal:

```
$docker container ls -s
```

As you can see from the following snippet, the size of the **testsize** container is **27.8 MB (virtual 216 MB)**:

```
CONTAINER ID      IMAGE            COMMAND        CREATED
   STATUS       PORTS     NAMES       SIZE
9f2d2d1ee3e0       ubuntu:14.04     "/bin/bash"   9 seconds ago
   Up 9 minutes          testsize    27.8MB (virtual 216MB)
```

Now, the thin layer equals **27.8MB**, and the virtual size equals the size of all the layers. In this exercise, the layers are the base image, with a size of 188 MB; the update; and the **wget** layer, which has a size of 27.8 MB. Therefore, the total size will be 216 MB after approximation.

In this exercise, you learned about the function of the **-s** option used with the **docker container ls** subcommand. This option is used to display the size of the base image and the size of the top writable layer. Knowing the size that every container consumes is useful to avoid an out-of-disk-space exception. Moreover, it can help us in troubleshooting and setting a maximum size for every container.

> **NOTE**
>
> Docker uses storage drivers to write in the writable layer. The storage drivers differ depending on the operating system that you are using. To find the updated list of storage drivers, check out https://docs.docker.com/storage/storagedriver/select-storage-driver/.
>
> To find out what driver your operating system is using, run the **$docker info** command.

An understanding of Docker container life cycle events provides a good background when studying why some applications may or may not need persistent storage and outlines the default host storage area (filesystem location) for Docker before a container is explicitly removed.

Now, let's delve into the stateful and stateless modes to decide which container needs persistent storage.

STATEFUL VERSUS STATELESS CONTAINERS/SERVICES

Containers and services can run in two modes: **stateful** and **stateless**. A stateless service is the one that does not retain persistent data. This type is much easier to scale and update than the stateful one. A stateful service requires persistent storage (as in databases). Therefore, it is harder to dockerize because stateful services need synchronization with the other components of the application.

Say you're dealing with an application that needs a certain file in order to work correctly. If this file is saved inside a container, as in the stateful mode, when this container is removed for whatever reason, the whole application crashes. However, if this file is saved in a volume or an external database, any container will be able to access it, and the application will work fine. Say business is booming and we need to scale up the number of containers running to fulfill the clients' needs. All the containers will be able to access the file, and scaling will be easy and smooth.

Apache and NGINX are examples of stateless services, while databases are examples of stateful containers. The *Docker Volumes and Stateful Persistence* section will focus on volumes that are needed for database images to operate properly.

In the following exercises, you will first create a stateless service and then a stateful one. Both will use the Docker playground, which is a website that offers Docker Engine in a matter of seconds. It is a free virtual machine in a browser, where you can execute Docker commands and create clusters in swarm mode.

EXERCISE 7.03: CREATING AND SCALING A STATELESS SERVICE, NGINX

Usually, in web-based applications, there is a frontend and a backend. For example, in the Panoramic Trekking application, you use NGINX in the frontend because it can handle a high volume of connections and distribute the loads to the slower database in the backend. Therefore, NGINX is used as the reverse proxy server and load balancer.

In this exercise, you will focus on creating a stateless service, NGINX, solely, and see how easy it is to scale it. You will initialize a swarm to create a cluster and scale NGINX on it. You will use the Docker playground to work in swarm mode:

1. Connect to the Docker playground at https://labs.play-with-docker.com/, as in *Figure 7.2*:

Figure 7.2: The Docker playground

2. Click on **ADD NEW INSTANCE** in the left menu to create a new node. Get the node IP from the top node information section. Now, create a swarm using the **docker swarm init** command with the **--advertise-addr** option to specify the node IP. As in *Figure 7.2*, the Docker Engine generates a long token to allow other nodes, whether managers or workers, to join the cluster:

```
$docker swarm init --advertise-addr <IP>
```

3. Use the **docker service create** command to create a service and specify port **80** using the **-p** option. Set the number of replicas as **2** for the **--replicas** option of the **nginx:1.14.2** image:

```
$ docker service create -p 80 --replicas 2 nginx:1.14.2
```

The **docker service create** command creates two replica services from the **nginx:1.14.2** image at port **80** inside the container. The Docker daemon chooses any available host port. In this case, it chooses port **30000**, as shown at the top of *Figure 7.2*.

4. To verify that the service has been created, list all of the available services using the **docker service ls** command:

```
$docker service ls
```

As shown in the following output, the Docker daemon auto-generated a service ID and assigned a name, **amazing_hellman**, to the service because you did not specify one using the **--name** option:

```
ID               NAME            MODE          REPLICAS  IMAGE
     PORTS
xmnp23wc0m6c   amazing_hellman   replicated    2/2       nginx:1.14.2
     *:30000->80/tcp
```

> **NOTE**
>
> In a container, the Docker daemon assigns a random **adjective_noun** name to the container.

5. Use the **curl <IP:Port Number>** Linux command to see the output of the service and connect to it without using a browser:

```
$curl 192.168.0.223:3000
```

The output is an HTML version of the welcome page of **NGINX**. This indicates it has been installed correctly:

```
<!DOCTYPE html>
<html>
<head>
<title>Welcome to nginx!</title>
<style>
    body {
        width: 35em;
        margin: 0 auto;
        font-family: Tahoma, Verdana, Arial, sans-serif;
    }
</style>
```

```
</head>
</body>
<h1>Welcome to nginx!<h1>
<p>If you see this page, the nginx web server is successfully
installed and working. Further configuration is required. </p>

<p>For online documentation and support please refer to
<a href="http://nginx.org/">nginx.org</a>.<br/>
Commercial support is available at
<a href="http://nginx.com/">nginx.com</a>.</p>

<p><em>Thank you for using nginx.</em></p>
</body>
<html>
```

6. Assume that business is booming even more, and two replicas are not enough. You need to scale it to five replicas instead of two. Use the **docker service scale <service name>=<number of replicas>** subcommand:

```
$docker service scale amazing_hellman=5
```

You will get an output like the following:

```
amazing_hellman scaled to 5
overall progress: 5 out of 5 tasks
1/5: running
2/5: running
3/5: running
4/5: running
5/5: running
verify: Service converged
```

7. To verify that the Docker swarm replicated the service, use the **docker service ls** subcommand one more time:

```
$docker service ls
```

The output shows that the number of replicas increased from **2** to **5** replicas:

```
ID              NAME            MODE        REPLICAS  IMAGE
      PORTS
xmnp23wc0m6c  amazing_hellman  replicated  5/5          nginx:1.14.2
      *:30000->80/tcp
```

8. Delete the service using the **docker service rm** subcommand:

```
$docker service rm amazing_hellman
```

The command will return the name of the service:

```
amazing_hellman
```

9. To verify that the service has been deleted, list the service one more time using the **docker service ls** subcommand:

```
$docker service ls
```

The output will be an empty list:

```
ID          NAME        MODE        REPLICAS        IMAGE        PORTS
```

In this exercise, you deployed a stateless service, NGINX, and scaled it using the **docker service scale** command. You then used the Docker playground (a free solution that you can use to create a cluster, and Swarm to initialize a swarm).

> **NOTE**
>
> This exercise uses Docker Swarm. To do the same using Kubernetes, you can follow the steps at https://kubernetes.io/docs/tasks/run-application/run-stateless-application-deployment/.

Now, we are done with the frontend example of NGINX. In the next exercise, you will see how to create a stateful service that requires persistent data. We will use a database service, MySQL, to complete the following exercise.

EXERCISE 7.04: DEPLOYING A STATEFUL SERVICE, MYSQL

As mentioned previously, web-based applications have a frontend and a backend. You have already seen an example of the frontend component in the previous exercise. In this exercise, you will deploy a single stateful MySQL container to be the database as a backend component.

To install MySQL, follow the steps at https://hub.docker.com/_/mysql in the **via stack deploy** section. Select and copy the **stack.yml** file to memory:

1. Use an editor to paste the **stack.yml** file. You can use the **vi** or **nano** Linux commands to open a text editor in Linux and paste the YAML file:

```
$vi stack.yml
```

Paste the following code:

```
# Use root/example as user/password credentials
version: '3.1'

services:

  db:
    image: mysql
    command: --default-authentication-plugin=
      mysql_native_password
    restart: always
    environment:
      MYSQL_ROOT_PASSWORD: example

  adminer:
    image: adminer
    restart: always
    ports:
      - 8080:8080
```

In this YAML file, you have two services: **db** and **adminer**. The **db** service is based on the **mysql** image, while the **adminer** image is the base image of the **adminer** service. The **adminer** image is a database management tool. In the **db** service, you enter the command and set the environment variable, which has the database password with a policy to always restart if it fails for any reason. Also, in the **adminer** service, the policy is set to always restart if it fails for any reason.

2. Press the *Esc* key on the keyboard. Then, run the following command to quit and save the code:

```
:wq
```

3. To verify that the file has saved correctly, use the **cat** Linux command to display the **stack.yml** contents:

```
$cat stack.yml
```

The file will be displayed. If there is an error, repeat the previous steps.

4. If the code is correct, deploy the **YML** file by using the **docker stack deploy** subcommand:

```
$docker stack deploy -c stack.yml mysql
```

You should see an output like the following:

```
Ignoring unsupported options: restart

Creating network mysql_default
Creating service mysql_db
Creating service mysql_adminer
```

To connect to the service, right-click on port **8080** at the top beside the node IP in the Docker playground window and open it in a new window:

Figure 7.3: Connecting to the service

5. Use the **docker stack ls** subcommand to list the stacks:

```
$docker stack ls
```

You should see an output like the following:

```
NAME     SERVICES   ORCHESTRATOR
mysql    2          Swarm
```

6. Use the **docker stack rm** subcommand to remove the stack:

```
$docker stack rm mysql
```

When removing the stack, Docker will remove the two services: **db** and **adminer**. It will also remove the network that it created by default to connect all the services:

```
Removing service mysql_adminer
Removing service mysql_db
Removing network mysql_default
```

In this exercise, you deployed a stateful service, MySQL, and were able to access the database service from the browser. Again, we used the Docker playground as our platform to execute the exercise.

> **NOTE**
>
> Replicating MySQL is not an easy task. You cannot run multiple replicas on one data folder as we did in *Exercise 7.03*, *Creating and Scaling a Stateless Service, NGINX*. This way does not work because data consistency and database locking and caching must be applied to ensure your data is correct. Hence, MySQL uses a master and subordinate replication, where you write to the master, and the data gets synchronized to the subordinates. To find out more about MySQL replication, please visit https://dev.mysql.com/doc/refman/8.0/en/replication.html.

We have learned that containers need persistent storage that outlives the container life cycle but have not yet covered how to do that. In the next section, we will learn about volumes to save persistent data.

DOCKER VOLUMES AND STATEFUL PERSISTENCE

We can use volumes to save persistent data without relying on the containers. You can think of a volume as a shared folder. In any instance, if you mount the volume to any number of containers, the containers will be able to access the data in the volume. There are two ways to create a volume:

- Create a volume as an independent entity outside any container by using the **docker volume create** subcommand.

Creating a volume as an independent object from the container adds flexibility to data management. These types of volumes are also called **named volumes** because you specify a name for it, rather than leaving the Docker Engine to generate an anonymous numeric one. Named volumes outlive all the containers that are in the system and preserve its data.

Despite these volumes being mounted to containers, the volumes will not be deleted even when all the containers in the system are deleted.

- Create a volume by using the `--mount` or `-v` or `--volume` options in the `docker container run` subcommand. Docker creates an anonymous volume for you. When the container is removed, the volume will not be removed as well unless indicated explicitly by using the `-v` option to the `docker container rm` subcommand or using a `docker volume rm` subcommand.

The following exercise will provide an example of each method.

EXERCISE 7.05: MANAGING A VOLUME OUTSIDE THE CONTAINER'S SCOPE AND MOUNTING IT TO THE CONTAINER

In this exercise, you will create a volume that is not confined to a container. You will start by creating a volume, mounting it to a container, and saving some data on it. You will then delete the container and list the volume to check whether the volume persists even when you do not have a container on your system:

1. Create a volume named **vol1** using the **docker volume create** command:

```
$docker volume create vol1
```

The command will return the name of the volume, as shown:

```
vol1
```

2. List all the volumes using the **docker volume ls** command:

```
$docker volume ls
```

This will result in the following output:

```
DRIVER              VOLUME NAME
Local               vol1
```

3. Inspect the volume to get its mount point using the following command:

```
$docker volume inspect vol1
```

You should get an output like the following:

```
[
    {
        "CreatedAt": "2020-06-16T16:44:13-04:00",
        "Driver": "local",
        "Labels": {},
        "Mountpoint: "/var/lib/docker/volumes/vol1/_data",
        "Name": "vol1",
        "Options": {},
        "Scope": "local"
    }
]
```

The volume inspection shows the date and time of its creation, its mount path, its name, and its scope.

4. Mount the volume to a container and modify its contents. Any data that is added to **vol1** will be copied to the volume inside the container:

```
$ docker container run -it -v vol1:/container_vol --name container1
ubuntu:14.04 bash
```

In the preceding command, you have crafted a container from the **ubuntu:14.04** image with the **bash** command. The **bash** command allows you to enter the commands inside the container. The **-it** option is used to have an interactive terminal. The **-v** option is for synchronizing the data between **vol1** at the host and **container_vol** inside the container. Use the **--name** option to name the container **container1**.

5. The prompt changes, indicating that you are now inside the container. Write the word **hello** in a file called **new_file.txt** onto the volume. The volume inside the container is called **container_vol**. In this case, this volume is shared between the host and the container. From the host, the volume is called **vol1**:

```
root@acc8900e4cf1:/# echo hello > /container_vol/new_file.txt
```

6. List the contents of the volume to verify that the file is saved:

```
root@acc8900e4cf1:/# ls /container_vol
```

7. Exit the container using the **exit** command:

```
root@acc8900e4cf1:/# exit
```

8. Check the contents of the new file from the host by running the following command:

```
$ sudo ls /var/lib/docker/volumes/vol1/_data
```

The command will return the name of the new file:

```
new_file.txt
```

9. Verify that the word **hello**, as the content of the file, is saved as well by running the following command:

```
$ sudo cat /var/lib/docker/volumes/vol1/_data/new_file.txt
```

10. Remove the container with the **-v** option to remove any volumes that are created within the container's scope:

```
$docker container rm -v container1
```

The command will return the name of the container:

```
container1
```

11. Verify that the volume still exists by listing all the volumes:

```
$docker volume ls
```

The volume, **vol1**, is listed, indicating that the volume was created outside the container, and even by using the **-v** option, it will not be removed when the container is removed:

```
DRIVER          VOLUME NAME
Local           vol1
```

12. Now, remove the volume using the **rm** command:

```
$docker volume rm vol1
```

The command should return the name of the volume:

```
vol1
```

13. Verify that the volume is removed by listing the current list of volumes:

```
$docker volume ls
```

An empty list will be displayed, indicating that the volume has been removed:

```
DRIVER          VOLUME NAME
```

In this exercise, you learned how to create volumes as independent objects in Docker without being within the container's scope, and how to mount this volume to a container. The volume was not removed when you removed the container because the volume was created outside the container's scope. In the end, you learned how to remove these types of volumes.

In the next exercise, we will create, manage, and remove an unnamed or anonymous volume that is within the container's scope.

EXERCISE 7.06: MANAGING A VOLUME WITHIN THE CONTAINER'S SCOPE

You do not need to create the volume before running the container as in the previous example. Docker will create an unnamed volume for you automatically. Again, the volume will not be removed when the container is removed, unless you specify the **-v** option in the **docker container rm** subcommand. In this exercise, you will create an anonymous volume within the container's scope and then learn how to remove it:

1. Create a container with an anonymous volume using the following command:

```
$docker container run -itd -v /newvol --name container2 ubuntu:14.04
bash
```

The command should return a long hex digit number, which is the volume ID.

2. List all the volumes:

```
$ docker volume ls
```

Observe that this time, **VOLUME NAME** is a long hex digit number and not a name. This type of volume is called an anonymous volume and can be removed by adding the **-v** option to the **docker container rm** subcommand:

```
DRIVER          VOLUME NAME
Local           8f4087212f6537aafde7eaca4d9e4a446fe99933c3af3884d
0645b66b16fbfa4
```

3. Remove the container with the volume, this time. Use the **-f** option to force remove the container since it is in detached mode and running in the background. Add the **v** option (making this **-fv**) to remove the volume as well. If this volume is not anonymous, and you named it, it will not be removed by this option and you must use **docker volume rm <volume name>** to remove it:

```
$docker container rm -fv container2
```

The command will return the name of the container.

4. Verify that the volume has been removed. Use the **docker volume ls** subcommand, and you will observe that the list is empty:

```
$ docker volume ls
```

Compared to the previous exercise, the volume was removed when the container was removed by using the **-v** option in the **rm** subcommand. Docker removed the volume this time because the volume was initially created within the container's scope.

> **NOTE**
>
> 1. If you are mounting a volume to a service and not to a container, you cannot use the **-v** or **--volume** options. You must use the **--mount** option.
>
> 2. To delete all the anonymous volumes that were not removed when their containers were removed, you can use the **docker volume prune** subcommand.
>
> For further details, visit https://docs.docker.com/storage/volumes/.

Now, we are going to see some more examples of volumes being used with stateful containers. Remember that using volumes with stateful containers as databases is the best practice. Containers are ephemeral, while data on databases should be saved as a persistent volume, where any new container can pick up and use the saved data. Therefore, the volume must be named, and you should not leave Docker to automatically generate an anonymous volume with a hex digit number as its name.

In the next exercise, you will run a PostgreSQL database container with a volume.

EXERCISE 7.07: RUNNING A POSTGRESQL CONTAINER WITH A VOLUME

Say you work in an organization where a PostgreSQL container with a database volume is used and the container gets deleted due to some mishap. However, the data persisted and outlived the container. In this exercise, you will run a PostgreSQL container with a database volume:

1. Run a PostgreSQL container with a volume. Name the container **db1**. If you do not have the image locally, Docker will pull the image for you. Create a container called **db1** from the **postgress** image. Use the **-v** option to share the **db** volume at the host with **/var/lib/postgresql/data** inside the container and the **-e** option to echo SQL to the standard output stream as well. Use the **POSTGRES_PASSWORD** option to set the database password and the **-d** option to run this container in detached mode:

```
$docker container run --name db1 -v db:/var/lib/postgresql/data -e
POSTGRES_PASSWORD=password -d postgres
```

2. Use the **exec** command to interact with the container from **bash**. The **exec** command does not create a new process but rather replaces **bash** with the command to be executed. Here, the prompt will change to **posgres=#** to indicate that you are inside the **db1** container:

```
$ docker container exec -it db1 psql -U postgres
```

The **psql** command allows you to interactively enter, edit, and execute SQL commands. The **-U** option is used to enter the database's username, which is **postgres**.

3. Create a table, **PEOPLE**, with two columns – **Name** and **age**:

```
CREATE TABLE PEOPLE(NAME TEXT, AGE int);
```

4. Insert some values into the **PEOPLE** table:

```
INSERT INTO PEOPLE VALUES('ENGY','41');
INSERT INTO PEOPLE VALUES('AREEJ','12');
```

5. Verify that the values are inserted correctly in the table:

```
SELECT * FROM PEOPLE;
```

The command will return two rows, which verifies that the data has been inserted correctly:

```
postgres=# SELECT * FROM PEOPLE;
 name  | age
-------+-----
 ENGY  |  41
 AREEJ |  12
(2 rows)
```

Figure 7.4: Output of the SELECT statement

6. Exit the container to quit the database. The shell prompt will return:

```
\q
```

7. Verify that your volume is a named one and not anonymous using the **volume ls** command:

```
$ docker volume ls
```

You should get an output like the following:

```
DRIVER          VOLUME NAME
Local           db
```

8. Remove the **db1** container with the **-v** option:

```
$ docker container rm -fv db1
```

The command will return the name of the container:

```
db1
```

9. List the volumes:

```
$ docker volume ls
```

The list shows that the volume is still there and is not removed with the container:

```
DRIVER          VOLUME NAME
Local           db
```

10. As in *step 1*, create a new container called **db2** and mount the volume, **db**:

```
$docker container run --name db2 -v db:/var/lib/postgresql/data -e
POSTGRES_PASSWORD=password -d postgres
```

11. Run the **exec** command to execute the commands from **bash** and verify that the data persists even when **db1** is removed:

```
$ docker container exec -it db2 psql -U postgres


postgres=# SELECT * FROM PEOPLE;
```

The preceding commands will result in an output like the following:

```
postgres=# SELECT * FROM PEOPLE;
 name  | age
-------+-----
 ENGY  |  41
 AREEJ |  12
(2 rows)
```

Figure 7.5: Output of the SELECT statement

12. Exit the container to quit the database:

```
\q
```

13. Now, remove the **db2** container using the following command:

```
$ docker container rm -f db2
```

The command will return the name of the container:

```
db2
```

14. Remove the **db** volume using the following command:

```
$ docker volume rm db
```

The command will return the name of the volume:

```
db
```

In this exercise, you used a named volume to save your database to keep the data persistent. You saw that the data persisted even after you removed the container. The new container was able to catch up and access the data that you saved in your database.

In the next exercise, you will run a PostgreSQL database without a volume to compare its effect with that of the previous exercise.

EXERCISE 7.08: RUNNING A POSTGRESQL CONTAINER WITHOUT A VOLUME

In this exercise, you will run a default PostgreSQL container without a database volume. You will then remove the container and its anonymous volume to check whether the data persisted after the removal of the container:

1. Run a PostgreSQL container without a volume. Name the container **db1**:

```
$ docker container run --name db1 -e POSTGRES_PASSWORD=password -d
postgres
```

2. Run the **exec** command to execute the commands from **bash**. The prompt will change to **posgres=#** to indicate that you are inside the **db1** container:

```
$ docker container exec -it db1 psql -U postgres
```

3. Create a table, **PEOPLE**, with two columns – **NAME** and **AGE**:

```
CREATE TABLE PEOPlE(NAME TEXT, AGE int);
```

4. Insert some values in the **PEOPLE** table:

```
INSERT INTO PEOPLE VALUES('ENGY','41');
INSERT INTO PEOPLE VALUES('AREEJ','12');
```

5. Verify that the values are inserted correctly in the table:

```
SELECT * FROM PEOPLE;
```

The command will return two rows, which verifies that the data is inserted correctly:

```
postgres=# SELECT * FROM PEOPLE;
 name  | age
-------+-----
 ENGY  |  41
 AREEJ |  12
(2 rows)
```

Figure 7.6: Output of the SELECT statement

6. Exit the container to quit the database. The shell prompt will return:

```
\q
```

7. List the volumes using the following command:

```
$ docker volume ls
```

Docker has created an anonymous volume for the **db1** container, as evident from the following output:

```
DRIVER        VOLUME NAME
Local         6fd85fbb83aa8e2169979c99d580daf2888477c654c
62284cea15f2fc62a42c32
```

8. Remove the container with its anonymous volume using the following command:

```
$ docker container rm -fv db1
```

The command will return the name of the container:

```
db1
```

9. List the volumes using the **docker volume ls** command to verify that the volume is removed:

```
$docker volume ls
```

You will observe that the list is empty:

```
DRIVER        VOLUME NAME
```

As opposed to the previous exercise, this exercise used an anonymous volume rather than a named one. Thus, the volume was within the container's scope and was removed from the container.

We can therefore conclude that the best practice is to share the database on a named volume to ensure that the data saved in the database will persist and outlive the container's life.

Up to now, you have learned how to list the volumes and inspect them. But there are other more powerful commands to get the information about your system and Docker objects, including the volumes. These will be the subject of the next section.

MISCELLANEOUS USEFUL DOCKER COMMANDS

A lot of commands can be used to troubleshoot and inspect your system, some of which are described as follows:

- Use the **docker system df** command to find out the size of all the Docker objects in your system:

```
$docker system df
```

As shown in the following output, the number of images, containers, and volumes are listed with their sizes:

TYPE	TOTAL	ACTIVE	SIZE	RECLAIMABLE
Images	6	2	1.261GB	47.9MB (75%)
Containers	11	2	27.78MB	27.78MB (99%)
Local Volumes	2	2	83.26MB	0B (0%)
Build Cache			0B	0B

- You can get more detailed information about the Docker objects by adding the **-v** option to the **docker system df** command:

```
$docker system df -v
```

It should return an output like the following:

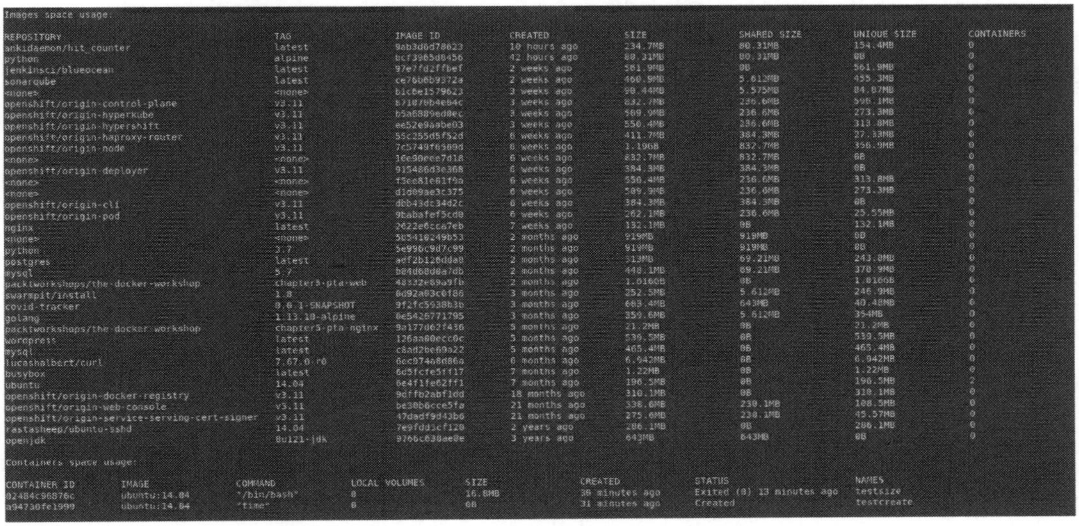

Figure 7.7: Output of the docker system df -v command

- Run the **docker volume ls** subcommand to list all the volumes that you have on your system:

```
$docker volume ls
```

Copy the name of the volume so that it can be used to get the name of the container that uses it:

```
DRIVER    VOLUME NAME
local     a7675380798d169d4d969e133f9c3c8ac17e733239330397ed
ba9e0bc05e509fc
local     db
```

Then, run the **docker ps -a --filter volume=<Volume Name>** command to get the name of the container that is using the volume:

```
$docker ps -a --filter volume=db
```

You will get the details of the container, like the following:

```
CONTAINER ID    IMAGE      COMMAND            CREATED
   STATUS       PORTS        NAMES
55c60ad38164    postgres   "docker-entrypoint.s…"  2 hours ago
   Up 2 hours   5432/tcp     db_with
```

So far, we have been sharing volumes between containers and the Docker host. This sharing type is not the only type available in Docker. You can also share volumes between containers. Let's see how to do that in the next section.

PERSISTENT AND EPHEMERAL VOLUMES

There are two types of volumes: persistent and ephemeral ones. What we have seen so far is persistent volumes, which are between the host and the container. To share the volume between containers, we use the **--volumes-from** option. This volume exists only as long as it is being used by a container. When the last container using the volume exits, the volume disappears. This type of volume can be passed from one container to the next but is not saved. These volumes are called ephemeral volumes.

Volumes can be used to share log files between the host and the container or between containers. It is much easier to share them on a volume with the host so that even if the container was removed for an error, we can still track the error by checking the log file on the host after the container's removal.

Another common use of volumes in practical microservices applications is sharing the code on a volume. The advantage of this practice is that you can achieve zero downtime. The developer team can edit the code on the fly. The team can work on adding new features or changing the interface. Docker monitors the update in the code so that it executes the new code.

In the following exercise, we will explore the data container and learn some new options to share volumes between containers.

EXERCISE 7.09: SHARING VOLUMES BETWEEN CONTAINERS

Sometimes, you need a data container to share data between various containers, each running a different operating system. It is useful to test the same data across different platforms before sending the data to production. In this exercise, you will use the data container, which will share volumes between containers using **--volume-from**:

1. Create a container, **c1**, with a volume, **newvol**, that is not shared with the host:

   ```
   $docker container run -v /newvol --name c1 -it ubuntu:14.04 bash
   ```

2. Move to the **newvol** volume:

   ```
   cd newvol/
   ```

3. Save a file inside this volume:

   ```
   echo hello > /newvol/file1.txt
   ```

4. Press the escape sequences, *CTRL + P* and then *CTRL + Q*, so that the container runs in a detached mode in the background.

5. Create a second container, **c2**, that mounts the **c1** container's volume using the **--volumes-from** option:

   ```
   $docker container run --name c2 --volumes-from c1 -it ubuntu:14.04 bash
   ```

6. Verify that **c2** can access **file1.txt**, which you saved from **c1**, using the **ls** command:

   ```
   cd newvol/
   ls
   ```

7. Add another file, **file2.txt**, inside **c2**:

```
echo hello2 > /newvol/file2.txt
```

8. Verify that **c2** can access **file1.txt** and **file2.txt**, which you saved from **c1**, using the **ls** command:

```
ls
```

You will see that both the files are listed:

```
file1.txt file2.txt
```

9. Attach the local standard input, output, and error streams to **c1**:

```
docker attach c1
```

10. Check that **c1** can access the two files using the **ls** command:

```
ls
```

You will see that both the files are listed:

```
file1.txt file2.txt
```

11. Exit **c1** using the following command:

```
exit
```

12. List the volumes using the following command:

```
$ docker volume ls
```

You will observe that the volume still exists even when you have exited **c1**:

```
DRIVER      VOLUME NAME
local       2d438bd751d5b7ec078e9ff84a11dbc1f11d05ed0f82257c
4e8004ecc5d93350
```

13. Remove **c1** with the **-v** option:

```
$ docker container rm -v c1
```

14. List the volumes again:

```
$ docker volume ls
```

You will find that the volume has not been removed with **c1** because **c2** is still using it:

```
DRIVER      VOLUME NAME
local       2d438bd751d5b7ec078e9ff84a11dbc1f11d05ed0f82257c
4e8004ecc5d93350
```

15. Now, remove **c2** with the **-v** option to remove its volumes as well. You must use the **-f** option as well to force-remove the container because it is up and running:

```
$ docker container rm -fv c2
```

16. List the volumes again:

```
$ docker volume ls
```

You will find that the volume list is empty now:

```
DRIVER              VOLUME NAME
```

This verifies that the ephemeral volumes are removed when all the containers using the volumes are removed.

In this exercise, you used the **--volumes-from** option to share volumes between containers. Also, this exercise demonstrated that the best practice is to always remove the container with the **-v** option. Docker will not remove the volume as long as there is at least one container that is using that volume.

If we committed any of these two containers, **c1** or **c2**, to a new image, the data saved on the shared volume still will not be uploaded to that new image. The data on any volume, even if the volume is shared between a container and host, will not be uploaded to the new image.

In the next section, we will see how to engrave this data into the newly committed image using the filesystem, rather than volumes.

VOLUMES VERSUS FILESYSTEM AND IMAGES

Note that volumes are not part of images, so the data saved on volumes won't be uploaded or downloaded with images. The volumes will be engraved in the image, but not its data. Therefore, if you want to save certain data in an image, save it as a file, not as a volume.

The next exercise will demonstrate and clarify the different outputs between saving data on volumes and when saving it on files.

EXERCISE 7.10: SAVING A FILE ON A VOLUME AND COMMITTING IT TO A NEW IMAGE

In this exercise, you will run a container with a volume, save some data on the volume, commit the container to a new image, and craft a new container based on this new image. When you check the data from inside the container, you will not find it. The data will be lost. This exercise will demonstrate how the data will be lost when committing the container to a new image. Remember that the data on the volumes will not be engraved in the new image:

1. Create a new container with a volume:

```
$docker container run --name c1 -v /newvol -it ubuntu:14.04 bash
```

2. Save a file inside this volume:

```
echo hello > /newvol/file.txt
cd newvol
```

3. Navigate to the **newvol** volume:

```
cd newvol
```

4. Verify that **c1** can access **file.txt** using the **ls** command:

```
ls
```

You will see that the file is listed:

```
file.txt
```

5. View the content of the file using the **cat** command:

```
cat file.txt
```

This will result in the following output:

```
hello
```

6. Exit from the container using the following command:

```
exit
```

7. Commit this container to a new image called **newimage**:

```
$ docker container commit c1 newimage
```

8. Inspect the image to verify that the volume is engraved inside it:

```
$ docker image inspect newimage --format={{.ContainerConfig.Volumes}}
```

This will result in the following output:

```
map[/newvol:{}]
```

9. Craft a container based on the **newimage** image that you just created:

```
$ docker container run -it newimage
```

10. Navigate to **newvol** and list the files in the volume and its data. You will find that the file and the word **hello** were not saved in the image:

```
cd newvol
ls
```

11. Exit the container using the following command:

```
exit
```

From this exercise, you learned that the data on a volume is not uploaded to the image. To solve this issue, use the filesystem instead of a volume.

Assume that the word **hello** is important data we want to be saved in **file.txt** inside the image so that we can access it when we craft a container from this image. You will see how to do that in the next exercise.

EXERCISE 7.11: SAVING A FILE IN THE NEW IMAGE FILESYSTEM

In this exercise, you will use the filesystem instead of a volume. You will create a directory instead of a volume and save the data in this new directory. Then, you will commit the container to a new image. When you craft a new container using this image as its base image, you will find the directory in the container and the data saved in it:

1. Remove any container that you might have from previous labs. You can concatenate several Docker commands to each other:

```
$ docker container rm -f $(docker container ls -aq)
```

The command will return the IDs of the containers that will be removed.

2. Create a new container without a volume:

```
$ docker container run --name c1 -it ubuntu:14.04 bash
```

3. Create a folder named **new** using the **mkdir** command and open it using the **cd** command:

```
mkdir new
cd new
```

4. Navigate to the **new** directory and save the word **hello** in a new file called **file.txt**:

```
echo hello > file.txt
```

5. View the content of the file using the following command:

```
cat file.txt
```

The command should return **hello**:

```
hello
```

6. Exit **c1** using the following command:

```
exit
```

7. Commit this container to a new image called **newimage**:

```
$ docker container commit c1 newimage
```

8. Craft a container based on the **newimage** image that you just created:

```
$ docker container run -it newimage
```

9. List the files using the **ls** command:

```
ls
```

You will find **file.txt** is saved this time:

```
bin   boot  dev   etc   home  lib   lib64  media  mnt   new   opt
proc  root  run   sbin  srv   sys   tmp    usr    var
```

10. Navigate to the **new** directory and verify that the container can access **file.txt** using the **ls** command:

```
cd new/
ls
```

You will see that the file is listed:

```
file.txt
```

11. Use the **cat** command to display the contents of **file.txt**:

```
cat file.txt
```

It will show that the word **hello** is saved:

```
hello
```

12. Exit from the container using the following command:

```
exit
```

In this exercise, you saw that data is uploaded to the image when the filesystem is used, compared to the situation we saw when data was saved on volumes.

In the following activity, we will see how to save a container's statuses in a PostgreSQL database. So, if the container crashes, we will be able to retrace what happened. It will act as a black box. Moreover, you will query these events using SQL statements in the following activity.

ACTIVITY 7.01: STORING CONTAINER EVENT (STATE) DATA ON A POSTGRESQL DATABASE

Logging and monitoring can be done in several ways in Docker. One of these methods is to use the **docker logs** command, which fetches what happens inside the individual container. Another is to use the **docker events** subcommand, which fetches everything that happens inside the Docker daemon in real-time. This feature is very powerful as it monitors all the objects' events that are sent to the Docker server—not just the containers. The objects include containers, images, volumes, networks, nodes, and so on. Storing these events in a database is useful because they can be queried and analyzed to debug and troubleshoot any errors if generated.

In this activity, you will be required to store a sample of a container's events' output to a PostgreSQL database in **JSON** format by using the **docker events --format '{{json .}}'** command.

Perform the following steps to complete this activity:

1. Clean your host by removing any Docker objects.

2. Open two terminals: one to see **docker events --format '{{json .}}'** in effect and the other to control the running container.

3. Click *Ctrl* + *C* in the **docker events** terminal to terminate it.

4. Understand the JSON output structure.

5. Run the PostgreSQL container.

6. Create a table.

7. Copy the **docker events** subcommand output from the first terminal.

8. Insert this JSON output into the PostgreSQL database.

9. Query the JSON data using the SQL **SELECT** statement with the following SQL queries.

    Query 1:

    ```
    SELECT * FROM events WHERE info ->> 'status' = 'pull';
    ```

    You should get the following output:

    ```
    postgres=# SELECT * FROM events WHERE info ->> 'status' = 'pull';
     id |
                                     info
    ----+-------------------------------------------------------------------
        |
        |
        |
      2 |  {"status":"pull","id":"ubuntu:14.04","Type":"image","Action":
    "pull","Actor":{"ID":"ubuntu:14.04","Attributes":{"name":"ubuntu"}},
    "scope":"local","time":1592516701,"timeNano":1592516701777557396}
    (1 row)
    ```

    Figure 7.8: Output of Query 1

Query 2:

```
SELECT * FROM events WHERE info ->> 'status' = 'destroy';
```

You will get an output like the following:

```
postgres=# SELECT * FROM events WHERE info ->> 'status' = 'destroy';
 id |
                                                              info

----+--------------------------------------------------------------------------------
------------------------------------------------------------------------------------
------------------------------------------------------------------------------------
------------------------------------------------------------------------------------
----------------------------------------
 10 | {"status":"destroy","id":"43903b966123a7c491b50116b40827daa03d
a5d350f8fef2a690fc4024547ce2","from":"ubuntu:14.04","Type":"containe
r","Action":"destroy","Actor":{"ID":"43903b966123a7c491b50116b40827d
aa03da5d350f8fef2a690fc4024547ce2","Attributes":{"image":"ubuntu:14.
04","name":"upbeat_johnson"}},"scope":"local","time":1592517215,"tim
eNano":1592517215322584221}
(1 row)
```

Figure 7.9: Output of Query 2

Query 3:

```
SELECT info ->> 'id' as id FROM events WHERE info ->> status'
    = 'destroy';
```

The final output should be similar to the following:

```
postgres=# SELECT info ->> 'id' as id FROM events WHERE info ->> 'st
atus' = 'destroy';
                                   id
------------------------------------------------------------------------
 43903b966123a7c491b50116b40827daa03da5d350f8fef2a690fc4024547ce2
(1 row)
```

Figure 7.10: Output of Query 3

> **NOTE**
>
> The solution for this activity can be found on page 677.

In the next activity, we will look at another example of sharing the container's NGINX log files, not just its events. You will also learn how to share log files between the container and the host.

ACTIVITY 7.02: SHARING NGINX LOG FILES WITH THE HOST

As we mentioned before, it is useful to share the log files of an application to the host. That way, if the container crashes, you can easily check its log files from outside the container since you will not be able to extract them from the container. This practice is useful with stateless and stateful containers.

In this activity, you will share the log files of a stateless container crafted from the NGINX image with the host. Then, verify these files by accessing the NGINX log files from the host.

Steps:

1. Verify that you do not have the **/var/mylogs** folder on your host.

2. Run a container based on the NGINX image. Specify the path of the shared volumes on the host and inside the container in the **run** command. Inside the container, NGINX uses the **/var/log/nginx** path for the log files. Specify the path on the host as **/var/mylogs**.

3. Go to the path of **/var/mylogs**. List all the files in that directory. You should find two files there:

```
access.log      error.log
```

> **NOTE**
>
> The solution for this activity can be found on page 684.

SUMMARY

This chapter covered the life cycle of Docker containers and various events. It compared stateful and stateless applications and how each one saves its data. If we need the data to be persistent, we should use volumes. The chapter covered the creation and management of a volume. It further discussed the different types of volumes, as well as the difference between the usage of volumes and the filesystem, and how the data in both is affected when the container is committed to a new image.

In the next chapter, you will learn about the concepts of continuous integration and continuous delivery. You will learn how to integrate GitHub, Jenkins, Docker Hub, and SonarQube to publish your images automatically to the registry to be ready for production.

8

CI/CD PIPELINE

OVERVIEW

This chapter introduces **Continuous Integration and Continuous Delivery** (**CI/CD**), the most crucial step before going to production. This is the intermediate stage between development and production. This chapter will demonstrate how Docker is a robust technology for CI and CD, and how easily it integrates with other widely used platforms. By the end of the chapter, you will be able to configure GitHub, Jenkins, and SonarQube and incorporate them to publish your images for production automatically.

INTRODUCTION

In previous chapters, you learned how to write `docker-compose` files and explored the networking and storage of the Services. In this chapter, you will learn how to integrate the various microservices of an application and test it as a whole.

CI/CD stands for **Continuous Integration and Continuous Delivery**. Sometimes, **CD** is used for **Continuous Deployment** as well. Deployment here means making an application publicly accessible from a specific URL through an automated pipeline workflow, while delivery means making the application ready to be deployed. In this chapter, we will focus on the concept of CI/CD.

This chapter discusses how Docker integrates into the CI/CD pipeline in step-by-step exercises. You will also learn how to install and run Jenkins as a Docker container. Jenkins is an open-source automation server. You can use it to build, test, deploy, and facilitate CI/CD by automating parts of software development. The installation of Jenkins is merely one Docker command. Installing Jenkins on Docker is more robust than installing it as an application, and it won't be tightly coupled to a specific operating system.

> **NOTE**
>
> If you do not have accounts on GitHub and Docker Hub, please create them. You can do so for free at the following links: www.github.com and http://hub.docker.com.

WHAT IS CI/CD?

CI/CD is a method that helps application development teams to provide code changes to users more frequently and reliably. CI/CD introduces automation into the stages of code deployment.

When several developers collaborate and contribute to the same application (each of them responsible for a certain microservice or fixing a specific bug), they use a code version control provider to aggregate the application using the latest code versions that the developers have uploaded and pushed. GitHub, Bitbucket, and Assembla are examples of version control systems. The developers and testers push the application code and Docker files to automation software to build, test, and deploy the CI/CD pipeline. Jenkins, Circle CI, and GitLab CI/CD are examples of such automation platforms.

After passing the testing, a Docker image is built and published to your repository. These repositories can be either Docker Hub, your company's **Docker Trusted Register (DTR)**, or Amazon **Elastic Container Registry (ECR)**.

In this chapter, as in *Figure 8.1*, we will use a GitHub repository for the code version control. Then, we will use Jenkins to build and publish the framework and Docker Hub as a registry.

Figure 8.1: CI/CD pipeline

You must build the Docker image before the production stage since there is no **build** keyword in the **docker-stack.yml** file that is used in production. The image will then be deployed to production in an integrated and automated target environment. In production, the operations (or DevOps) people configure the orchestrators to pull the images from the registry. Kubernetes, Docker Swarm, and Google Kubernetes Engine are examples of production orchestrators and management services that can be used to pull images from the registry.

To summarize, we have three main steps:

1. Upload the code to GitHub.

2. Create a project in Jenkins and enter the GitHub and Docker Hub credentials. Jenkins will automatically build the image and push it for you to the Docker Hub account. When you push the code to GitHub, Jenkins automatically detects, tests, and builds the image. If no errors are generated, Jenkins pushes the image to the registry.

3. Verify that the image is on your Docker Hub account.

In the next exercise, you will install Jenkins as a container that will be used to build the image. Jenkins is one of the most popular platforms for testing and is in great demand in the market. Jenkins has several project types. In this chapter, we will use the Freestyle project type.

> **NOTE**
>
> Please use **touch** command to create files and **vim** command to work on the file using vim editor.

EXERCISE 8.01: INSTALLING JENKINS AS A CONTAINER

In this exercise, you will install Jenkins, finish its setup, and install the preliminary plugins. You will install the Git and GitHub plugins that will be used throughout this chapter. Perform the following steps to successfully install Jenkins as a container:

1. Run the following command to pull the Jenkins image:

```
$docker run -d -p 8080:8080 -v /var/run/docker.sock:/var/run/docker.
sock jenkinsci/blueocean
```

This results in an output similar to the following:

```
e7c96db7181b: Pull complete
f910a506b6cb: Pull complete
c2274a1a0e27: Pull complete
32d53281836a: Pull complete
d19882e06da9: Pull complete
bb5ae2dd7604: Pull complete
da600481a343: Pull complete
b2eee6194b25: Pull complete
7e6c909f6612: Pull complete
bfd4a2f697a1: Pull complete
26ef4ee2d217: Pull complete
613d0d828036: Pull complete
be508f36e226: Pull complete
6fea20b6c414: Pull complete
cb5f343890a8: Pull complete
Digest: sha256:abb5f3dc9f68a8159a3f2cb0f3b043e2ca0a7d129511aff6962e21c2f86c1655
Status: Downloaded newer image for jenkinsci/blueocean:latest
d14eaaeac339d545f641c7253b4b7585a4968182ab380a19514ad6ce530d4da7
```

Figure 8.2: Output of the docker run command

> **NOTE**
>
> There are many Jenkins images on Docker Hub. Feel free to pull any of them and play with the ports and shared volume, but pay attention to the deprecated images as the Jenkins official image is now deprecated for the **Jenkins/Jenkins:lts** image. So, read the documentation of the images carefully. However, do not worry if one does not work. It might not be your mistake. Look for another and follow the instructions of the documentation carefully.

2. Open the browser and connect to the Jenkins service at **http://localhost:8080**.

   If it gives you an error message stating it cannot reach the Docker daemon, add Jenkins to the **docker** group using the following commands:

```
$ sudo groupadd docker
$ sudo usermod -aG docker jenkins
```

> **NOTE**
>
> If your machine's operating system is Windows, the localhost might not be resolved. Run the **ipconfig** command in Windows PowerShell. In the second section of the output, **ipconfig** displays the information of the **switch** network. Copy the IPv4 address, and use it instead of the localhost throughout the exercises.
>
> You can also get the IP address from **Control Panel** > **Network and Sharing Center** and then clicking on **Details** for your Ethernet or Wi-Fi connection.

After installation, Jenkins will ask for an **Administrator password** to unlock it:

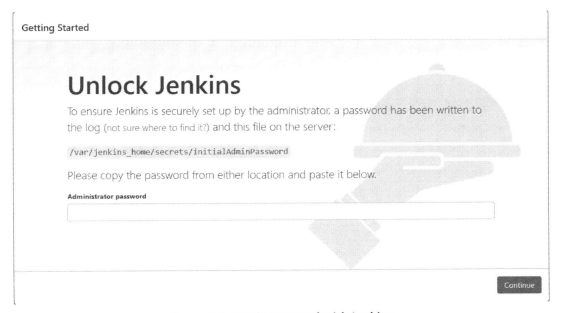

Figure 8.3: Getting started with Jenkins

Jenkins autogenerates a password for you to use to unlock the application. In the next step, you will see how to get this password.

3. Run the **docker container ls** command to get the list of the currently running containers:

```
$ docker container ls
```

You will get the details of the container that is crafted from the **jekinsci/blueocean** image:

```
CONTAINER ID IMAGE              COMMAND                CREATED
   STATUS            PORTS
9ed51541b036 jekinsci/blueocean "/sbin/tini../usr/.." 5 minutes ago
   Up 5 minutes        0.0.0.0:8080->8080/tcp, 5000/tcp
```

4. Copy the container ID and run the **docker logs** command:

```
$ docker logs 9ed51541b036
```

At the end of the log file, you will find six lines of asterisks. The password will be in between them. Copy it and paste it in the browser:

```
************************************************************
************************************************************
************************************************************

Jenkins initial setup is required. An admin user has been created and a password generated.
Please use the following password to proceed to installation:

a8315d1744844f5baab8ba6cb10c06ca

This may also be found at: /var/jenkins_home/secrets/initialAdminPassword

************************************************************
************************************************************
************************************************************
```

Figure 8.4: Output of the docker logs command

5. Select **Install suggested plugins**. Then, click **Skip and continue as admin**. Click **Save and Finish**:

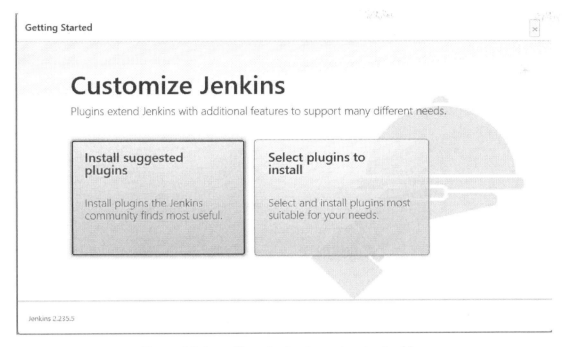

Figure 8.5: Installing plugins to customize Jenkins

In the suggested plugins, there are Git and GitHub plugins that Jenkins will install automatically for you. You will need these plugins for all the coming exercises.

> **NOTE**
>
> In *Exercise 8.04, Integrating Jenkins and Docker Hub,* you will need to install more plugins so Jenkins can push the image to the Docker Hub registry. This will be discussed in detail later, as well as how to manage Jenkins plugins in a step-by-step lab.

6. After installation, it will display **Jenkins is ready!**. Click **Start using Jenkins**:

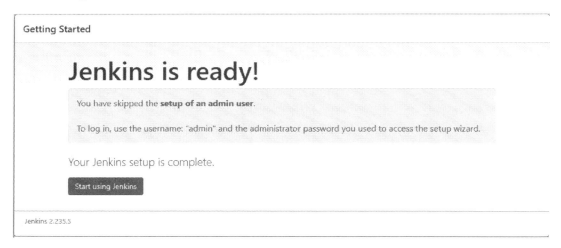

Figure 8.6: Setting up Jenkins

7. Click on **Create a job** to build the software project:

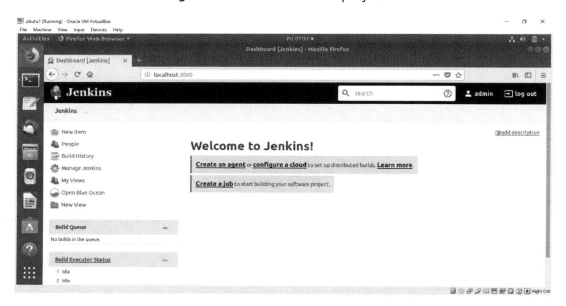

Figure 8.7: Welcome page of Jenkins

The preceding screenshot verifies that you have successfully installed Jenkins on your system.

In the next sections, we will follow the CI/CD pipeline in this chapter. The first step is uploading the code to GitHub and then integrating Jenkins with GitHub so that Jenkins can pull the code and build the image automatically. The final step will be to integrate Jenkins with the registry to push that image to the registry without any manual interference.

INTEGRATING GITHUB AND JENKINS

After installing Jenkins, we will create our first job and integrate it with GitHub. In this section, as in *Figure 8.8*, we will focus solely on GitHub and Jenkins. Docker Hub will be discussed a little later.

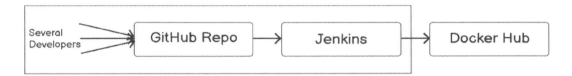

Figure 8.8: Integrating GitHub and Jenkins

We will use a simple Python application to count the number of hits on a website. Every time you refresh the page, the counter will increment, resulting in an increase in the number of hits on the website.

> **NOTE**
>
> The code files for the **Getting Started** application can be found at the following link: https://github.com/efoda/hit_counter.

The application consists of four files:

- **app.py**: This is the Python application code. It uses **Redis** to keep track of the counts of the number of hits on a website.

- **requirements.txt**: This file contains the dependencies needed for the application to work properly.

- **Dockerfile**: This builds the image with the required libraries and dependencies.

- **docker-compose.yml**: It is essential to have the YAML file when two or more containers are working together.

  In this simple application, we also have two services, **Web** and **Redis**, as shown in *Figure 8.9*:

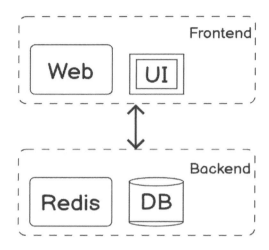

Figure 8.9: The hit_counter application architecture

If you do not know how to upload this application to your GitHub account, don't worry. The next exercise will guide you through this process.

EXERCISE 8.02: UPLOADING THE CODE TO GITHUB

You can use GitHub to save your code and projects. In this exercise, you will learn how to download and upload the code to GitHub. You can do that by forking the code on the GitHub website or pushing the code from Command Prompt. In this exercise, you will do it from Command Prompt.

Perform the following steps to upload the code to GitHub:

1. On the GitHub website, create a new empty repository with the name **hit_counter**. Open a terminal and clone the code by typing the following command:

```
$ git clone https://github.com/efoda/hit_counter
```

This results in an output similar to the following:

```
Cloning into 'hit counter'...
remote: Enumerating objects: 38, done.
remote: Counting objects: 100% (38/38), done
```

```
remote: Compressing objects: 100% (35/35), done
remote: Total 38 (delta 16), reused 0 (delta 0), pack-reused 0
Receiving object: 100% (38/38), 8.98 KiB | 2.25 MiB/s, done.
Resolving deltas: 100% (16/16), done
```

2. Verify that the code is downloaded to your local machine by listing the directories. Then, open the application directory:

```
$ cd hit_counter
~/hit_counter$ ls
```

You will find the application files downloaded to your local machine:

```
app.py docker-compose.yml Dockerfile README.md requirements.txt
```

3. Initialize and configure Git:

```
$ git init
```

You should get output similar to the following:

```
Reinitialized existing Git repository in
/home/docker/hit_counter/.git/
```

4. Enter your username and email:

```
$ git config user.email "<you@example.com>"
$ git config user.name "<Your Name>"
```

5. Specify the names of the Git accounts, **origin** and **destination**:

```
$ git remote add origin https://github.com/efoda/hit_counter.git
fatal: remote origin already exists.

$ git remote add destination https://github.com/<your Github
Username>/hit_counter.git
```

6. Add all the content in the current path:

```
$ git add .
```

You can also add a specific file instead of all the files by typing the following command:

```
$ git add <filename>.<extension>
```

7. Specify a **commit** message:

```
$ git commit -m "first commit"
```

This results in an output similar to the following:

```
On branch master
Your branch is up to date with 'origin/master'.

nothing to commit, working tree clean
```

8. Push the code to your GitHub account:

```
$ git push -u destination master
```

It will ask you for your username and password. Once you've logged in, the files will be uploaded to your GitHub repository:

```
docker@docker-VirtualBox:~/hit_counter$ git push -u destination master
Username for 'https://github.com': yourusergithubname
Password for 'https://yourusergithubname@github.com':
Counting objects: 38, done.
Compressing objects: 100% (35/35), done.
Writing objects: 100% (38/38), 8.98 KiB | 158.00 KiB/s, done.
Total 38 (delta 16), reused 0 (delta 0)
remote: Resolving deltas: 100% (16/16), done.
To https://github.com/yourusergithubname/hit_counter.git
 * [new branch]      master -> master
Branch 'master' set up to track remote branch 'master' from 'destination'.
```

Figure 8.10: Pushing the code to GitHub

9. Check your GitHub account. You will find the files are uploaded there.

Now that we have finished the first step in the CI/CD pipeline and have uploaded the code to GitHub, we will integrate GitHub with Jenkins.

> **NOTE**
>
> Starting from this point and going forward, replace the GitHub username, **efoda**, with your username.

EXERCISE 8.03: INTEGRATING GITHUB AND JENKINS

You installed Jenkins as a container in *Exercise 8.01, Installing Jenkins as a Container*. In this exercise, you will create a job in Jenkins and configure it with GitHub. You will check Jenkins' **Output Console** to verify that it has built the image successfully. You will then modify the **Dockerfile** on GitHub and ensure that Jenkins has detected the change in the **Dockerfile** and rebuilt the image automatically:

1. Go back to Jenkins in the browser. Click on **Create a job**:

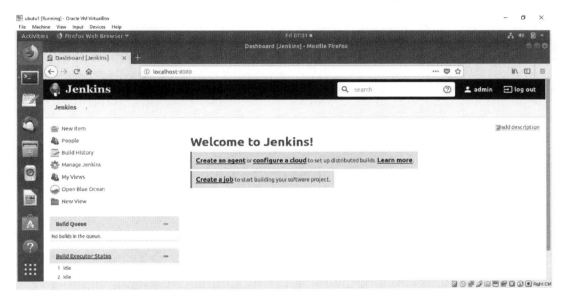

Figure 8.11: Creating a job in Jenkins

2. Fill in the **Enter an item name** textbox by providing the name of the project. Click **Freestyle project** and then click **OK**:

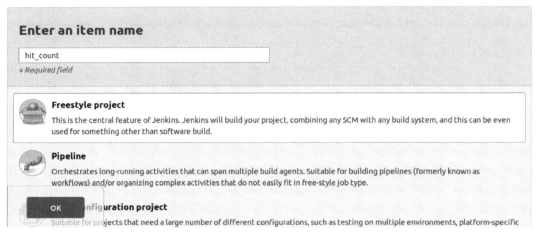

Figure 8.12: Selecting Freestyle project

You will see six tabs: **General**, **Source Code Management**, **Build Triggers**, **Build Environment**, **Build**, and **Post-build Actions**, as in *Figure 8.13*.

3. In the **General** tab, select the **Discard old builds** option so that the old builds do not eat up your disk space. Jenkins will do the housekeeping for you as well:

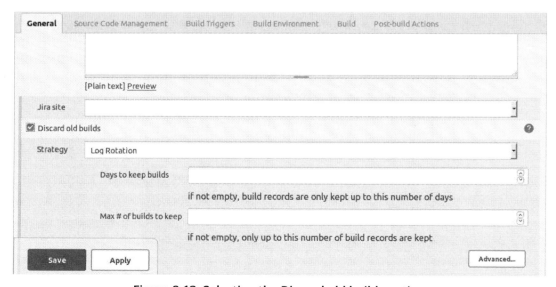

Figure 8.13: Selecting the Discard old builds option

4. In the **Source Code Management** tab, select **Git**. In **Repository URL**, enter **https://github.com/<your GitHub username>/hit_ counter**, as in *Figure 8.14*. If you do not have Git, check your plugins and download the Git plugin. We will talk about managing plugins in *Exercise 8.04, Integrating Jenkins and Docker Hub*:

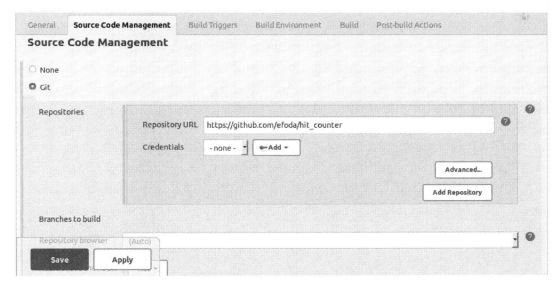

Figure 8.14: Entering the GitHub repository URL

5. In the **Build Triggers** tab, select **Poll SCM**. This is where you specify how often you want Jenkins to perform the tests. If you enter **H/5** with four asterisks and spaces in between each asterisk, this means that you want Jenkins to perform the test every minute, as in *Figure 8.16*. If you enter it as **H * * * ***, this means the polling will be done every hour. If you do it as **H/15 * * * ***, the polling will be done every 15 minutes. Click your mouse outside the textbox. If you entered the code correctly, Jenkins will show the message stating when it will execute the next job. Otherwise, it will display an error in red.

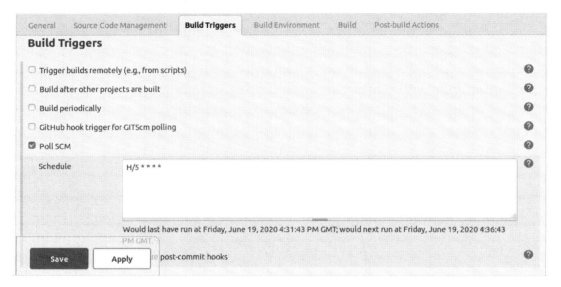

Figure 8.15: Building triggers

6. Click the **Build** tab. Click **Add build step**. Select **Execute shell**, as in *Figure 8.17*:

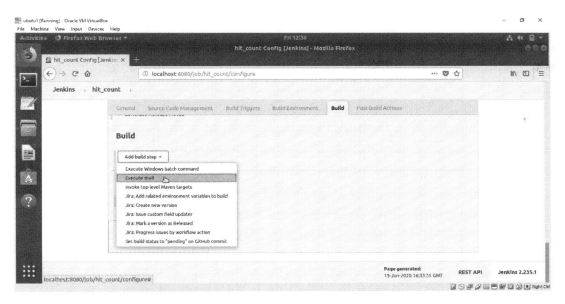

Figure 8.16: Selecting Execute shell

7. A textbox will be displayed. Write the following command:

```
docker build -t hit_counter .
```

Then click **Save**, as in *Figure 8.17*:

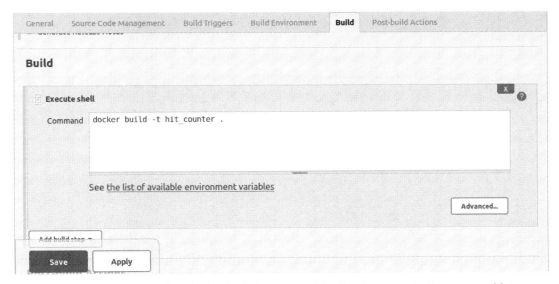

Figure 8.17: Entering the docker build command in the Execute shell command box

A screen similar to the following screenshot should appear:

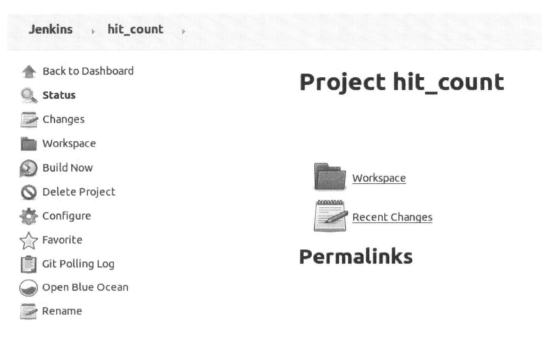

Figure 8.18: Successful creation of the hit_count project

8. Before doing anything further in Jenkins, check the images that you currently have in your host. In a terminal, run the **docker images** command to list the images:

```
$docker images
```

If you cleaned your lab before this chapter, you will have only the **jenkinsci/blueocean** image:

```
REPOSITORY            TAG      IMAGE ID      CREATED
      SIZE
jenkinsci/blueocean   latest   e287a467e019  Less than a second ago
      562MB
```

9. Go back to Jenkins. Click on **Build Now** from the menu on the left.

> **NOTE**
>
> In case you get the Permission Denied error while connecting to the Docker daemon, perform the following steps:
>
> 1. If not already exists, add a Jenkins user to the docker host:
>
> ```
> $ sudo useradd jenkins
> ```
>
> 2. Add the Jenkins user to the docker group:
>
> ```
> $ sudo usermod -aG docker jenkins
> ```
>
> 3. Obtain the docker group ID from **/etc/group** that is, **998**:
>
> ```
> $ sudo cat /etc/group | grep docker
> ```
>
> 4. Use **docker exec** command to create a bash shell in the running Jenkins container:
>
> ```
> $ docker container ls
> $ docker exec -it -u root <CONTAINER NAME |
> CONTAINER ID> /bin/bash
> ```
>
> 5. Edit the **/etc/group** file inside the Jenkins container:
>
> ```
> # vi /etc/group
> ```
>
> 6. Replace the docker group ID with the ID obtained from the host, and add the Jenkins user to the docker group:
>
> ```
> docker:x:998:jenkins
> ```
>
> 7. Save the **/etc/group** file and close the editor:
>
> ```
> :wq
> ```
>
> 8. Exit from the Jenkins container:
>
> ```
> # exit
> ```
>
> 9. Stop the Jenkins container:
>
> ```
> $ docker container ls
> $ docker container stop <CONTAINER NAME | CONTAINER
> ID>
> ```

> **NOTE**
>
> 10. Restart the Jenkins container:
>
> ```
> $ docker container ls
> $ docker container start <CONTAINER NAME |
> CONTAINER ID>
> ```
>
> Now, the job will build successfully.

10. Click on **Back to Dashboard**. The following screen will appear. In the bottom-left corner, you will see the **Build Queue** and **Build Executor Status** fields. You can see that one build has started with **#1** beside it, as in *Figure 8.19*:

Figure 8.19: Checking the Build Queue

There is no success or failure of the build yet. When the build is done, its status will be displayed on the screen. After some time, you will observe that two builds have been done.

11. Click on the small arrow beside **#2** under the **Last Success** field. A drop-down menu will appear, as shown in the following figure. Select **Console Output** to check what Jenkins did automatically for us, as in *Figure 8.20*:

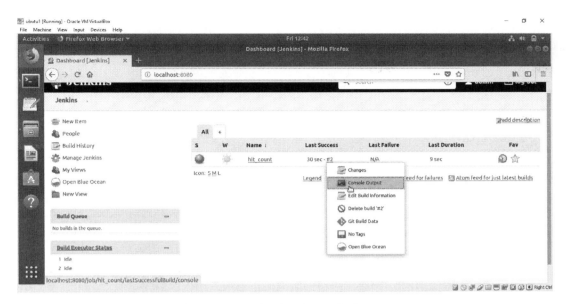

Figure 8.20: Selecting Console Output

In **Console Output**, you will find that Jenkins executed the **docker build** command you entered in the **Build** step during project configuration:

Scroll down to the bottom of **Console Output** to see the result of the execution. You will see that the image has been built successfully. You will also find the image ID and tag:

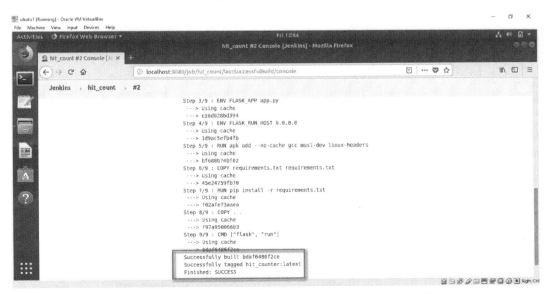

Figure 8.21: Verifying that the image is built successfully

12. Verify the image ID and tag from the terminal. Re-run the **docker images** command.

```
$docker images
```

You will find that the **hit_counter** image has been created for you. You will also find the **python:3.7-alpine** image as this is the base image in the **Dockerfile** and Jenkins has pulled it automatically:

```
REPOSITORY              TAG            IMAGE ID
  CREATED                            SIZE
jenkinsci/blueocean    latest          e287a467e019
  Less than a second ago          562MB
hit_counter            latest          bdaf6486f2ce
  3 minutes ago                   227MB
python                 3.7-alpine      6a5ca85ed89b
  2 weeks ago                     72.5MB
```

With this step, you can confirm that Jenkins was able to pull the files from your GitHub successfully.

13. Now, you will make the desired changes in the GitHub code. But first, verify that you did not commit any changes to the code yet. Return to Jenkins, scroll up and click **Back to Project** in the left-hand menu at the top. Then click on **Recent Changes**, as in *Figure 8.22*:

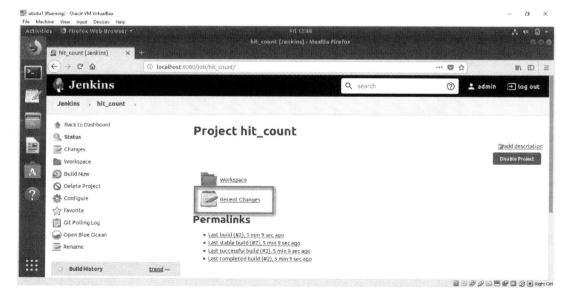

Figure 8.22: Selecting Recent Changes

Jenkins will display that there are no changes in any of the builds, as you can see in the following figure:

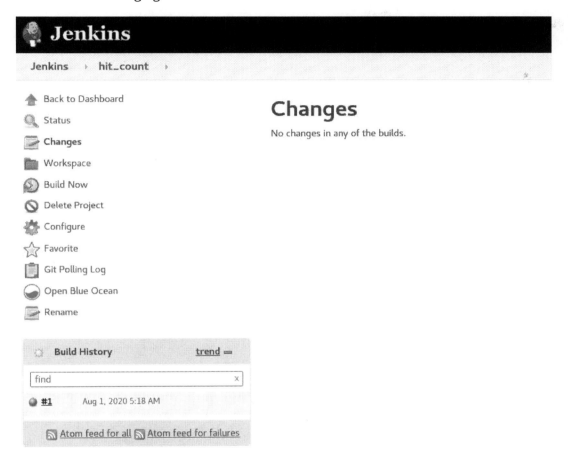

Figure 8.23: Verifying changes in the code

14. Go to GitHub and edit the **Dockerfile** by changing the base image's tag from **3.7-alpine** to **alpine** only.

    You can also do the same from the terminal as before by editing the file using any text editor. Then run the **git add** and **git push** commands:

```
$ git add Dockerfile
$ git commit -m "editing the Dockerfile"
$ git push -u destination master
```

15. Scroll down and commit your changes to GitHub.

16. Return to Jenkins. Remove the **hit_counter** and **python:3.7-alpine** images to make sure that Jenkins is not using previous local images:

```
$ docker rmi hit_counter python:3.7-alpine
```

17. Click **Build Now** again to start building the job instantly. Refresh the **Recent Changes** page. It will display a message stating that a change has occurred.

   If you click on the change that has occurred, it will forward you to GitHub, showing you the differences between the old code and the new code.

18. Click back into the browser to return to Jenkins. Check **Console Output** again to see the base image that Jenkins has used:

   At the bottom, you will find that Jenkins built the image successfully.

19. Go to the terminal and check the images again:

```
$ docker images
```

   You will find that **hit_counter** and **python:alpine** are on the list:

```
REPOSITORY            TAG            IMAGE ID
  CREATED                      SIZE
jenkinsci/blueocean   latest         e287a467e019
  Less than a second ago       562MB
hit_counter           latest         6288f76c1f15
  3 minutes ago                234MB
<none>                <none>         786bdbef6ea2
  10 minutes ago               934MB
python                alpine         8ecf5a48c789
  2 weeks ago                  78.9MB
```

20. Clean your lab for the next exercise by removing all the images listed except **jenkinsci/blueocean**:

```
$ docker image rm hit_counter python:alpine 786
```

In this exercise, you learned how to integrate Jenkins with GitHub. Jenkins was able to pull the code from GitHub automatically and build the image.

In the next section, you will learn how to push this image to your registry without manual interference to complete your CI/CD pipeline.

INTEGRATING JENKINS AND DOCKER HUB

In this section, as in *Figure 8.31*, we will focus on the last step of our CI/CD pipeline, which is integrating Jenkins with Docker Hub. As we mentioned before, there are plenty of registries out there. We will use Docker Hub because it is free and easy to use. At your workplace, your company will probably have a private local registry. You will need to ask the operations or IT admins to create an account for you and grant you some privileges so that you are able to access the registry and push your images to it.

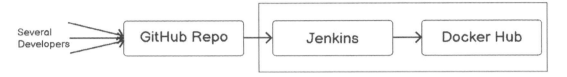

Figure 8.24: Integrating Jenkins and Docker Hub

In the following exercise, you will learn how to integrate Jenkins with Docker Hub and how to push the image that Jenkins built in the previous exercise.

EXERCISE 8.04: INTEGRATING JENKINS AND DOCKER HUB

In this exercise, you will integrate Jenkins with Docker Hub and push that image to your repository. First, you will install the **Docker**, **docker-build-step**, and **Cloudbees Docker Build and Publish** plugins so that Jenkins can connect to Docker Hub. Then, you will learn how to enter your Docker Hub credentials in Jenkins so that Jenkins can access your Docker Hub account automatically and push your images to it. Finally, you will check your images in Docker Hub to verify that the pipeline was executed correctly. At the end of this exercise, you will verify that the image is successfully pushed to the repository by checking your Docker Hub account:

1. Click on **Manage Jenkins** in the left-hand menu to install the plugins:

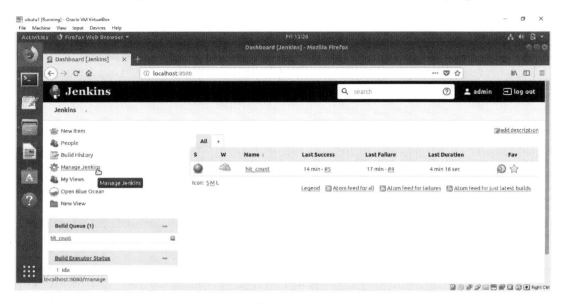

Figure 8.25: Clicking on Manage Jenkins

2. Click on **Plugin Manager**. Four tabs will appear. Click on the **Available** tab and select the **Docker**, **docker-build-step**, and **Cloudbees Docker Build and Publish** plugins:

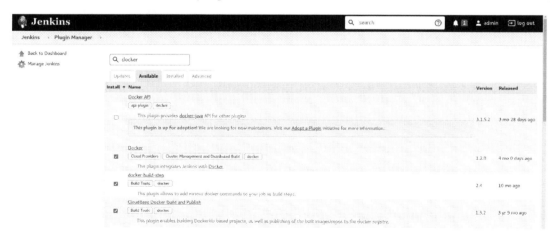

Figure 8.26: Installing the Docker, docker-build-step, and Cloudbees
Docker Build and Publish plugins

3. Click **Install without restart**. After installation, check **Restart Jenkins when installation is complete and no jobs are running**.

4. Jenkins will take an extended period of time to restart, depending upon your disk space, memory, and internet connectivity speed. Wait until it is done, and the dashboard is shown. Click on the project's name, that is, **hit_count**:

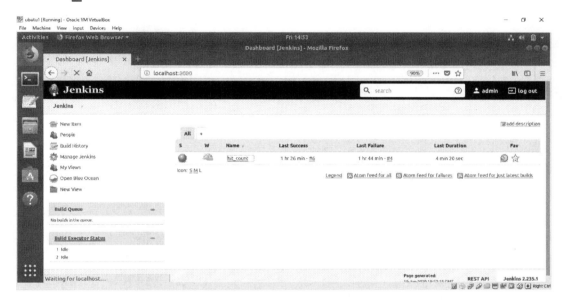

Figure 8.27: Jenkins Dashboard showing the hit_count project

5. Click **Configure** in the left-hand menu to modify the project configurations:

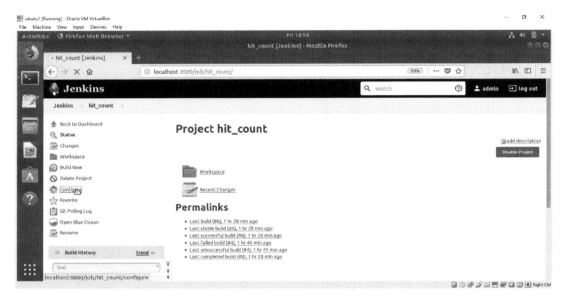

Figure 8.28: The Configure option in the left-hand menu

6. Modify the details in the **Build** tab only. Click on it and select **Add build step**. A larger menu than the one you saw before will show up. If you see **Docker Build and Publish** in that menu, it verifies that your plugins were installed successfully. Click **Docker Build and Publish**:

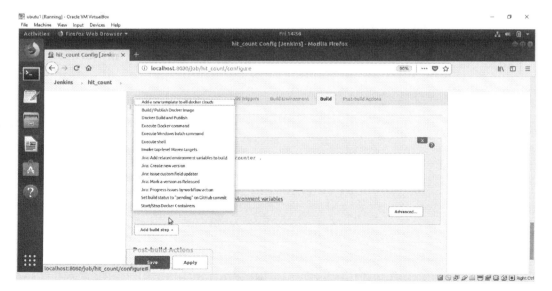

Figure 8.29: Selecting Docker Build and Publish from the menu

7. In **Registry Credentials**, click **Add**. Then select **Jenkins** from the drop-down menu.

8. A pop-up box will appear. Enter your Docker Hub username and password. Then, click **Add**:

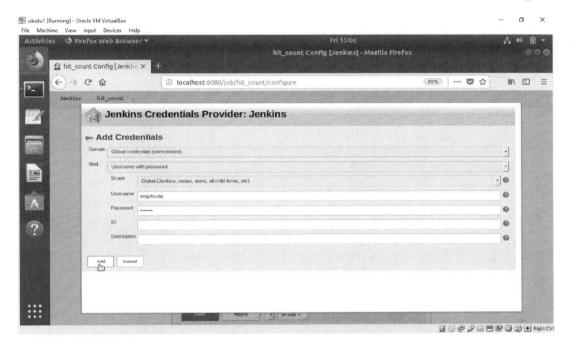

Figure 8.30: Adding Jenkins credentials

9. Now, in **Registry Credentials**, click the first drop-down menu and select the credentials that you entered in the previous step. Then, enter **<your Docker Hub username>/<image name>** in the **Repository Name** field. Remove the **Execute Shell** option that you entered in *Exercise 8.02, Uploading the Code to GitHub*, by clicking the Red **X** at the top right. Now, you will have only one build step, which is the **Docker Build and Publish** step. Click **Save** to save the new configuration:

Figure 8.31: The Docker Build and Publish step

10. Click **Build Now** again in the left-hand menu and in the **Build History** option, follow the progress of the image build. It will have the same name that you specified in **Repository Name** in the previous step. Jenkins will add the **docker build** step by itself because you chose it from the plugins. If the image passed the build successfully, Jenkins will use your Docker credentials and automatically connect to Docker Hub or any registry you specify in **Repository Name**. Finally, Jenkins will push the new image automatically to your registry, which is your Docker Hub registry in this exercise.

11. As a further check, while the image is being built and before it is done, go to the terminal and list the images you have using the **docker images** command:

```
$ docker images
```

Because you cleaned your lab at the end of the last exercise, you should find the **jenkinsci/blueocean** image only:

```
REPOSITORY               TAG        IMAGE ID
  CREATED                          SIZE
jenkinsci/blueocean      latest     e287a467e019
  Less than a second ago          562MB
```

Also, check your Docker Hub account to verify whether the **hit_counter** image is built. You will not find the **hit_counter** image:

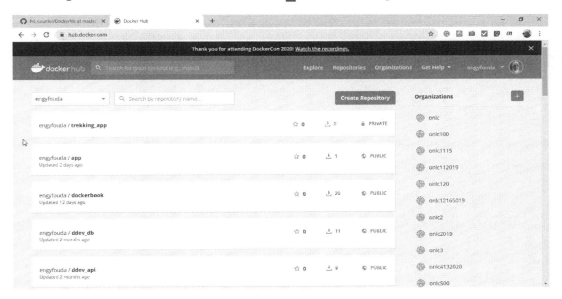

Figure 8.32: Checking your Docker Hub

12. If the job is successfully built, you will find a blue ball beside the image name. If it is a red ball, this means that there was an error. Now, click on the arrow beside the image name and select **Console Output**:

Figure 8.33: Selecting Console Output

As shown in the following image, you will find that Jenkins built the image successfully and pushed it to your Docker Hub:

Figure 8.34: In Console Output, verify that Jenkins has built and pushed the image

13. Go back to the terminal and rerun the **docker images** command to list the images:

```
$ docker images
```

You will find an image with **<your Docker Hub Username>/hit_count**:

```
REPOSITORY              TAG             IMAGE ID
  CREATED                       SIZE
jenkinsci/blueocean     latest          e287a467e019
  Less than a second ago        562MB
engyfouda/hit_count     latest          65e2179392ca
  5 minutes ago                 227MB
<none>                  <none>          cf4adcf1ac88
  10 minutes ago                1.22MB
python                  3.7alpine       6a5ca85ed89b
  2 weeks ago                   72.5MB
```

14. In the browser, refresh the Docker Hub page. You will find your image at the top; Jenkins pushed it for you automatically:

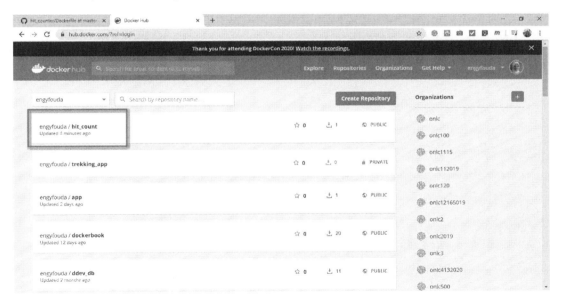

Figure 8.35: Verifying that Jenkins has pushed the image to your Docker Hub automatically

In this exercise, we finished the last phase of our CI/CD pipeline and integrated Jenkins with Docker Hub. Jenkins pushed the image it built to Docker Hub. You also verified that the image was pushed correctly by checking the Docker Hub account.

In the next activity, we will apply the same method of installing extra plugins to integrate Jenkins with SonarQube. SonarQube is another powerful tool that can analyze code and generate reports about its quality and detect bugs, code smells, and security vulnerabilities in a vast number of programming languages.

ACTIVITY 8.01: UTILIZING JENKINS AND SONARQUBE

Usually, you will be asked to evaluate the quality of your code before submitting it to testers. You can utilize Jenkins for further code inspection by generating reports about debugging bugs, code smells, and security vulnerabilities by adding the SonarQube plugin.

In this activity, we will utilize Jenkins and the SonarQube plugin for our **hit_count** Python example.

Steps:

1. Install and run SonarQube in a container, as you did in *Exercise 8.01, Installing Jenkins as a Container*. Use the default port **9000**.

2. Install the SonarQube plugin in Jenkins. Log in to SonarQube using **admin/ admin** and generate the authentication token. Do not forget to copy the token and keep it in a text file. You cannot retrieve the token after this step. If you lose your token, remove the SonarQube container, re-craft it from the SonarQube image as in *step 1*, and re-do the steps again.

3. Restart Jenkins.

4. In Jenkins, add SonarQube's authentication token to the **Global Credentials** domain as secret text.

5. Integrate Jenkins with SonarQube by adjusting the **Global System Configuration** and the **Configure System** options.

6. Modify the fields in the **Build Environment** tab by enabling the **Prepare SonarQube scanner** environment.

7. Modify the **Build** step and add the **Analysis Properties**.

8. In the browser, go to the SonarQube window, and check its report.

The output should be like the following:

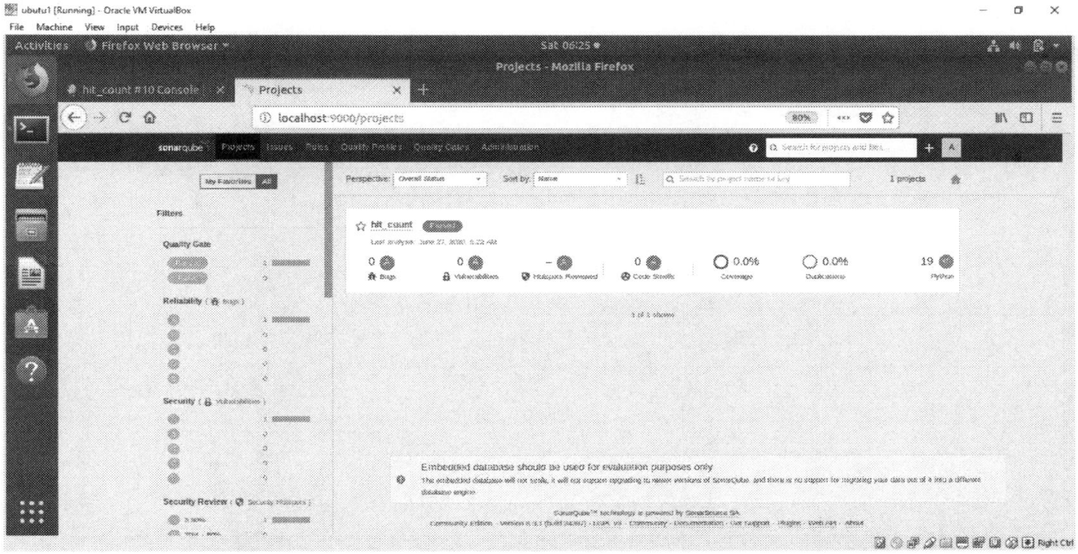

Figure 8.36: The expected SonarQube output

> **NOTE**
>
> The solution for this activity can be found on page 686.

In the next activity, you will integrate Jenkins and SonarQube with our Panoramic Trekking application.

ACTIVITY 8.02: UTILIZING JENKINS AND SONARQUBE IN THE PANORAMIC TREKKING APPLICATION

The Panoramic Trekking Application also has a frontend and backend, like the `hit_counter` application. In this activity, you will create a new project in Jenkins that is linked to the Panoramic Trekking application on GitHub. Then, you will run SonarQube to get a detailed report about its bugs and security vulnerabilities, if the trekking application has any.

Follow these steps to complete the activity:

1. Create a new item called **trekking** in Jenkins.

2. Select it as a **FREESTYLE** project.

3. In the **General** tab, select **Discard Old Builds**.

4. In **Source Code Management**, select **GIT**. Then enter the URL
    http://github.com/efoda/trekking_app.

5. In **Build Triggers**, select **Poll SCM** and set it to be analyzing and testing
    every 15 minutes.

6. In the **Build** tab, enter the **Analysis properties** code.

7. Save and click **Build Now**.

8. Check the report in the **SonarQube** tab in the browser.

The output should look like the following at SonarQube:

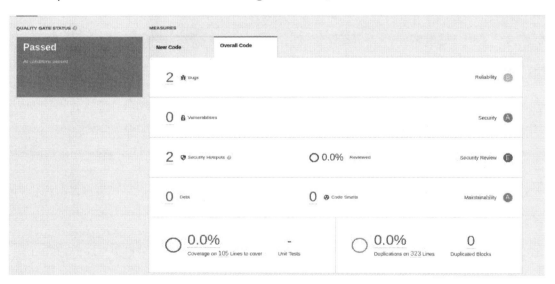

Figure 8.37: Expected output of Activity 8.02

> **NOTE**
>
> The solution for this activity can be found on page 697.

SUMMARY

This chapter has provided hands-on experience integrating your code using the CI/CD pipeline. CI helps developers to integrate code into a shared and easily accessible repository. CD helps developers to deliver the code stored in the repository to production. The CI/CD approach also helps to keep the product up to date with the latest technology and to provide the latest version to customers with a fast turnaround for new features and bug fixes.

Once this chapter's defined three phases of the CI/CD pipeline are completed successfully, you will only need to focus on editing your code on GitHub. Jenkins will then be your automated assistant, and it will automatically handle the rest of the phases for you and make the images available for production.

In the next chapter, you will learn about Docker swarm mode and how to perform service discovery, clustering, scaling, and rolling updates.

9

DOCKER SWARM

OVERVIEW

In this chapter, you will work with Docker Swarm from the command line to manage running nodes, deploy services, and perform rolling updates on your services when needed. You will learn how to troubleshoot your Swarm nodes and deploy entire stacks using your existing Docker Compose files, as well as learning how you can use Swarm to manage your service configuration and secrets. The final part of this chapter will provide you with the knowledge you need to get started using Swarmpit, which is a web-based interface for running and managing your Docker Swarm services and clusters.

INTRODUCTION

So far in this book, we've run our Docker containers and controlled the way they run from the command line using direct commands such as `docker run` to launch containers. Our next step is to automate things with the use of Docker Compose, which allows an entire environment of containers to work together. Docker Swarm is the next step in managing our Docker environments. **Docker Swarm** allows you to orchestrate how your containers can scale and work together to provide a more reliable service to your end-users.

Docker Swarm allows you to set up multiple servers running Docker Engine and organize them as a cluster. Docker Swarm can then run commands to coordinate your containers across the cluster instead of just one server. Swarm will configure your cluster to make sure your services are balanced across your cluster, ensuring higher reliability for your services. It will also decide for you which service will be assigned to which server depending on the load across your cluster. Docker Swarm is a step up in terms of managing the way you run your containers and is provided by default with Docker.

Docker Swarm allows you to configure redundancy and failover for your services while scaling the number of containers up and down depending on the load. You can perform rolling updates across your services to reduce the chances of an outage, meaning new versions of your container applications can be applied to the cluster without these changes causing an outage for your customers. It will allow you to orchestrate your container workloads through the swarm instead of manually managing containers one by one.

Swarm also introduces some new terms and concepts when it comes to managing your environment, defined in the following list:

- **Swarm**: Multiple Docker hosts run in swarm mode to act as managers and workers. Having multiple nodes and workers is not compulsory as part of Docker Swarm. You can run your services as a single node swarm, which is the way we will be working in this chapter, even though a production cluster may have multiple nodes available to make sure your services are as fault-tolerant as possible.

- **Task**: The manager distributes the tasks to run inside the nodes. A task consists of a Docker container and the commands that will run inside the container.

- **Service**: This defines the tasks to execute on the manager or worker. The difference between services and a standalone container is that you can modify a service's configuration without restarting the service.

- **Node**: An individual system running Docker Engine and participating in the swarm is a node. More than one node can run on a single physical computer at one time through the use of virtualization.

> **NOTE**
>
> We will only be using one node on our system.

- **Manager**: The manager dispatches tasks to worker nodes. The manager carries out orchestration and cluster management. It also hosts services on the cluster.
- **Leader node**: The manager node in the swarm elects a single primary leader node to conduct the orchestration tasks across the cluster.
- **Worker nodes**: Worker nodes execute the tasks assigned by the manager node.

Now that you are familiar with the key terms, let's explore how Docker Swarm works in the following section.

HOW DOCKER SWARM WORKS?

The swarm manager nodes handle cluster management, and the main objective is to maintain a consistent state of both the swarm and the services running on it. This includes ensuring that the cluster is running at all times and that services are run and scheduled when needed.

As there are multiple managers running at the same time, this means there is fault tolerance, especially in a production environment. That is, if one manager is shut down, the cluster will still have another manager to coordinate services on the cluster. The sole purpose of worker nodes is to run Docker containers. They require at least one manager to function, but worker nodes can be promoted to being a manager, if needed.

Services permit you to deploy an application image to a Docker swarm. These are the containers to run and the commands to execute inside the running container. Service options are provided when you create a service, where you can specify the ports the application can publish on, CPU and memory restrictions, the rolling update policy, and the number of replicas of an image that can run.

The desired state is set for the service, and the manager's responsibility is to monitor the service. If the service is not in the desired state, it will correct any issues. If a task fails, the orchestrator simply removes the container related to the failed task and replaces it.

Now that you know how Docker Swarm works, the next section will get you started with the basic commands and guide you through a hands-on exercise to further demonstrate its operation.

WORKING WITH DOCKER SWARM

The previous section of this chapter has shown you that Swarm uses similar concepts to what you have already learned so far in this book. You'll see that the use of Swarm takes the Docker commands you are so familiar with and expands them to allow you to create your clusters, manage services, and configure your nodes. Docker Swarm takes a lot of the hard work out of running your services, as Swarm will work out where it is best to place your services, take care of scheduling your containers, and decide which node it is best to place it on. For example, if there are already three services running on one node and only one service on your second node, Swarm will know that it should distribute the services evenly across your system.

By default, Docker Swarm is disabled, so to run Docker in swarm mode, you will need to either join an existing cluster or create a new swarm. To create a new swarm and activate it in your system, you use the **swarm init** command shown here:

```
docker swarm init
```

This will create a new single-node swarm cluster on the node you are currently working on. Your system will become the manager node for the swarm you have just created. When you run the **init** command, you'll also be provided with the details on the commands needed to allow other nodes to join your swarm.

For a node to join a swarm, it requires a secret token, and the token for a worker node is different from that of a manager node. The manager tokens need to be strongly protected so you don't allow your swarm cluster to become vulnerable. Once you have the token, IP address, and port of the swarm that your node needs to join, you run a command similar to the one shown here, using the **--token** option:

```
docker swarm join --token <swarm_token> <ip_address>:<port>
```

If for some reason you need to change the tokens (possibly for security reasons), you can run the **join-token --rotate** option to generate new tokens as shown here:

```
docker swarm join-token --rotate
```

From the swarm manager node, the following **node ls** command will allow you to see the nodes available in your swarm and provide details on the status of the node, whether it is a manager or a worker, and whether there are any issues with the node:

```
docker node ls
```

Once your swarm is available and ready to start hosting services, you can create a service with the **service create** command, providing the name of the service, the container image, and the commands needed for the service to run correctly—for example, if you need to expose ports or mount volumes:

```
docker service create --name <service> <image> <command>
```

Changes can then be made to the service configuration, or you can change the way the service is running by using the **update** command, as shown here:

```
docker service update <service> <changes>
```

Finally, if you need to remove or stop the service from running, you simply use the **service remove** command:

```
docker service remove <service>
```

We've provided a lot of theory on Docker Swarm here, and we hope it has provided you with a clear understanding of how it works and how you can use Swarm to launch your services and scale to provide a stable service when there is high demand. The following exercise will take what we have learned so far and show you how to implement it in your projects.

> **NOTE**
>
> Please use **touch** command to create files and **vim** command to work on the file using vim editor.

EXERCISE 9.01: RUNNING SERVICES WITH DOCKER SWARM

This exercise is designed to help you become familiar with using the Docker Swarm commands to manage your services and containers. In the exercise, you will activate a cluster, set up a new service, test scaling up the service, and then remove the service from the cluster using Docker Swarm:

1. Although Swarm is included by default with your Docker installation, you still need to activate it on your system. Use the **docker swarm init** command to put your local system into Docker Swarm mode:

```
docker swarm init
```

Your output might be a little different from what you see here, but as you can see, once the swarm is created, the output provides details on how you can add extra nodes to your cluster with the **docker swarm join** command:

```
Swarm initialized: current node (j2qxrpf0a1yhvcax6n2ajux69) is
now a manager.

To add a worker to this swarm, run the following command:
    docker swarm join --token SWMTKN-1-2w0fk5g2e18118zygvmvdxartd43n0
ky6cmywy0ucxj8j7net1-5v1xvrt7
1ag6ss7trl480e1k7 192.168.65.3:2377

To add a manager to this swarm, run 'docker swarm join-token
manager' and follow the instructions.
```

2. Now list the nodes you have in your cluster, using the **node ls** command:

```
docker node ls
```

You should have one node you are currently working on and its status should be **Ready**:

```
ID              HOSTNAME        STATUS    AVAILABILITY
  MANAGER STATUS
j2qx.. *        docker-desktop  Ready     Active
  Leader
```

For clarity here, we have removed the **Engine Version** column from our output.

3. From your node, check the status of your swarm using the **docker info** command, providing further details of your Swarm cluster and how the node is interacting with it. It will also give you extra information if you need to troubleshoot issues later:

```
docker info
```

As you can see from the output, you get all the specific details of your Docker Swarm cluster, including **NodeID** and **ClusterID**. If you don't have Swarm set up correctly on your system, all you will see is an output of **Swarm: inactive**:

```
...
Swarm: active
  NodeID: j2qxrpf0a1yhvcax6n2ajux69
  Is Manager: true
  ClusterID: pyejfsj9avjn595voauu9pqjv
  Managers: 1
  Nodes: 1
  Default Address Pool: 10.0.0.0/8
  SubnetSize: 24
  Data Path Port: 4789
  Orchestration:
   Task History Retention Limit: 5
  Raft:
   Snapshot Interval: 10000
   Number of Old Snapshots to Retain: 0
   Heartbeat Tick: 1
   Election Tick: 10
  Dispatcher:
   Heartbeat Period: 5 seconds
  CA Configuration:
   Expiry Duration: 3 months
   Force Rotate: 0
```

4. Start your first service on your newly created swarm. Create a service named **web** using the **docker service create** command and the **--replicas** option to set two instances of the container running:

```
docker service create --replicas 2 -p 80:80 --name web nginx
```

You will see that the two instances are successfully created:

```
uws28u6yny7ltvutq38166alf
overall progress: 2 out of 2 tasks
1/2: running   [==============================================>]
2/2: running   [==============================================>]
verify: Service converged
```

5. Similar to the **docker ps** command, you can see a listing of the services running on your cluster with the **docker service ls** command. Execute the **docker service ls** command to view the details of the **web** service created in the *step 4*:

```
docker service ls
```

The command will return the details of the **web** service:

```
ID                NAME   MODE         REPLICAS    IMAGE
   PORTS
uws28u6yny7l     web    replicated   2/2         nginx:latest
   *:80->80/tcp
```

6. To view the containers currently running on your swarm, use the **docker service ps** command with the name of your service, **web**:

```
docker service ps web
```

As you can see, you now have a list of the containers running our service:

```
ID      NAME     IMAGE     NODE             DESIRED
   CURRENT STATE
viyz    web.1    nginx     docker-desktop   Running
   Running about a minute ago
mr4u    web.2    nginx     docker-desktop   Running
   Running about a minute ago
```

7. The service will only run the default **Welcome to nginx!** page. Use the node IP address to view the page. In this instance, it will be your localhost IP, **0.0.0.0**:

Welcome to nginx!

If you see this page, the nginx web server is successfully installed and working. Further configuration is required.

For online documentation and support please refer to nginx.org. Commercial support is available at nginx.com.

Thank you for using nginx.

Figure 9.1: The nginx service from Docker Swarm

8. Scaling the number of containers running your service is easy with Docker Swarm. Simply provide the **scale** option with the number of total containers you want to have running, and the swarm will do the work for you. Perform the command shown here to scale your running web containers to **3**:

```
docker service scale web=3
```

The following output shows that the **web** service is now scaled to **3** containers:

```
web scaled to 3
overall progress: 3 out of 3 tasks
1/3: running     [============================================>]
2/3: running     [============================================>]
3/3: running     [============================================>]
verify: Service converged
```

9. As in *step 5* of this exercise, run the **service ls** command:

```
docker service ls
```

You should now see three **web** services running on your cluster:

```
ID              NAME     MODE         REPLICAS    IMAGE
    PORTS
uws28u6yny7l    web      replicated   3/3         nginx:latest
    *:80->80/tcp
```

10. The following change is more suited to a cluster with more than one node, but you can run it anyway to see what happens. Run the following **node update** command to set the availability to **drain** and use your node ID number or name. This will remove all the containers running on this node as it is no longer available on your cluster. You will be provided with the node ID as an output:

```
docker node update --availability drain j2qxrpf0a1yhvcax6n2ajux69
```

11. If you were to run the **docker service ps web** command, you would see each of your **web** services shut down while trying to start up new **web** services. As you only have one node running, the services would be sitting in a pending state with **no suitable node** error. Run the **docker service ps web** command:

```
docker service ps web
```

The output has been reduced to only show the second, third, fifth, and sixth columns, but you can see that the service is unable to start. The **CURRENT STATE** column has both **Pending** and **Shutdown** states:

```
NAME          IMAGE          CURRENT STATE
  ERROR
web.1         nginx:latest   Pending 2 minutes ago
  "no suitable node (1 node…"
\_ web.1      nginx:latest   Shutdown 2 minutes ago
web.2         nginx:latest   Pending 2 minutes ago
  "no suitable node (1 node…"
\_ web.2      nginx:latest   Shutdown 2 minutes ago
web.3         nginx:latest   Pending 2 minutes ago
  "no suitable node (1 node…"
\_ web.3      nginx:latest   Shutdown 2 minutes ago
```

12. Run the **docker node ls** command:

```
docker node ls
```

This shows that your node is ready but in an **AVAILABILITY** state of **Drain**:

```
ID            HOSTNAME         STATUS      AVAILABILITY
  MANAGER STATUS
j2qx.. *      docker-desktop   Ready       Drain
  Leader
```

13. Stop the service from running. Use the **service rm** command, followed by the service name (in this instance, **web**) to stop the service from running:

```
docker service rm web
```

The only output shown will be the name of the service you are removing:

```
web
```

14. You don't want to leave your node in a **Drain** state as you want to keep using it through the rest of the exercises. To get the node out of a **Drain** state and prepare to start managing swarm, set the availability to **active** with the following command using your node ID:

```
docker node update --availability active j2qxrpf0a1yhvcax6n2ajux69
```

The command will return the hash value of the node, which will be different for every user.

15. Run the **node ls** command:

```
docker node ls
```

It will now show the availability of our node as **Active** and ready your services to run again:

```
ID            HOSTNAME          STATUS      AVAILABILITY
   MANAGER STATUS
j2qx.. *      docker-desktop    Ready       Active
   Leader
```

16. Use the **docker node inspect** command with the **--format** option and search for the **ManagerStatus.Reachability** status to ensure that your node is reachable:

```
docker node inspect j2qxrpf0a1yhvcax6n2ajux69 --format "{{
.ManagerStatus.Reachability }}"
```

If the node is available and can be contacted, you should see a result of **reachable**:

```
reachable
```

17. Search for **Status.State** to ensure that the node is ready:

```
docker node inspect j2qxrpf0a1yhvcax6n2ajux69 --format "{{ .Status.
State }}"
```

This should produce **ready**:

```
ready
```

This exercise should have given you a good indication of how Docker Swarm is able to simplify your work, especially when you start to think about deploying your work into a production environment. We used the Docker Hub NGINX image, but we could easily use any service we have created as a Docker image that is available to our Swarm node.

The next section will take a quick sidestep to discuss some actions you need to take if you find yourself in trouble with your Swarm nodes.

TROUBLESHOOTING SWARM NODES

For the work we will be doing in this chapter, we will be using only a single-node swarm to host our services. Docker Swarm has been providing production-level environments for years now. However, this doesn't mean there will never be any issues with your environment, especially when you start hosting services in a multi-node swarm. If you need to troubleshoot any of the nodes running on your cluster, there are a number of steps you can take to make sure you are correcting any issues they may have:

- **Reboot**: Usually the easiest option is to either reboot or restart the node system to see whether this resolves the issues you may be experiencing.

- **Demote the node**: If the node is a manager on your cluster, try demoting the node using the **node demote** command:

```
docker node demote <node_id>
```

If this node is the leader, it will allow one of the other manager nodes to become the leader of the swarm and hopefully resolve any issues you may be experiencing.

- **Remove the node from the cluster**: Using the **node rm** command, you can remove the node from the cluster:

```
docker node rm <node_id>
```

This can also be an issue if the node is not communicating correctly with the rest of the swarm, and you may need to use the **--force** option to remove the node from the cluster:

```
docker node rm --force <node_id>
```

- **Join back to the cluster**: If the preceding has worked correctly, you may be able to successfully join the node back onto the cluster with the **swarm join** command. Remember to use the token that you used before when joining the swarm:

```
docker node swarm join --token <token> <swarm_ip>:<port>
```

> **NOTE**
>
> If your services are still having issues running on Docker Swarm and you have corrected all issues with the Swarm nodes, Swarm is simply using Docker to run and deploy your services onto the nodes in your environment. Any issues may come down to basic troubleshooting with the container image you are trying to run on Swarm and not the Swarm environment itself.

A cluster of managers is known as a **quorum**, and a majority of the managers need to agree on the proposed updates to the swarm, such as adding new nodes or scaling back the number of containers. As we saw in the previous section, you can monitor swarm managers' or nodes' health by running the **docker node ls** command, using the ID of the manager to then use the **docker node inspect** command as shown here:

```
docker node inspect <node_id>
```

> **NOTE**
>
> One final note on your Swarm node is to remember to deploy services to your nodes that have been created as Docker images. The container image itself needs to be available for download from a central Docker Registry, which is available for all the nodes to download from and not simply built on one of the Swarm nodes.

Although we've taken a quick detour to discuss troubleshooting your Swarm nodes, this should not be a major aspect of running services on Swarm. The next part of this chapter moves a step further by showing you how you can use new or existing **docker-compose.yml** files to automate the deployment of your services into Docker Swarm.

DEPLOYING SWARM DEPLOYMENTS FROM DOCKER COMPOSE

Deploying a complete environment is easy with Docker Swarm; you'll see that most of the work is already done if you have been running your containers using Docker Compose. This means you won't need to manually start services one by one in Swarm as we did in the previous section of this chapter.

If you already have a **docker-compose.yml** file available to bring up your services and applications, there is a good chance it will simply work without issues. Swarm will use the **stack deploy** command to deploy all your services across the Swarm nodes. All you need to do is provide the **compose** file and assign the stack a name:

```
docker stack deploy --compose-file <compose_file> <swarm_name>
```

The stack creation is quick and seamless, but a lot is happening in the background to make sure all services are running correctly—including setting up networks between all the services and starting up each of the services in the order needed. Running the **stack ps** command with the **swarm_name** you provided at creation time will show you whether all the services in your deployment are running:

```
docker stack ps <swarm_name>
```

And once you are finished using the services on your swarm or you need to clean up everything that is deployed, you simply use the **stack rm** command, providing the **swarm_name** you provided when you created the stack deployment. This will automatically stop and clean up all the services running in your swarm and ready them for you to reassign to other services:

```
docker stack rm <swarm_name>
```

Now, since we know the commands used to deploy, run, and manage our Swarm stack, we can look at how to perform rolling updates for our services.

SWARM SERVICE ROLLING UPDATES

Swarm also has the ability to perform rolling updates on the services that are running. This means if you have a new update to an application running on your Swarm, you can create a new Docker image and update your service, and Swarm will make sure the new image is up and running successfully before it brings down the old version of your container image.

Performing a rolling update on a service you have running in Swarm is simply a matter of running the **service update** command. In the following command, you can see both the new container image name and the service you want to update. Swarm will handle the rest:

```
docker service update --image <image_name:tag> <service_name>
```

You'll get the chance very shortly to use all the commands we've explained here. In the following example, you will create a small test application using Django and PostgreSQL. The web application you will be setting up is very basic, so there is no real need to have a prior understanding of the Django web framework. Simply follow along and we will explain what is happening as we move through the exercise.

EXERCISE 9.02: DEPLOYING YOUR SWARM FROM DOCKER COMPOSE

In the following exercise, you will use **docker-compose.yml** to create a basic web application using a PostgreSQL database and the Django web framework. You will then use this **compose** file to deploy your services into your swarm without the need to run your services manually:

1. First, create a directory to run your application in. Call the directory **swarm** and move into the directory using the **cd** command:

```
mkdir swarm; cd swarm
```

2. Create a **Dockerfile** for your Django application in the new directory and, using your text editor, enter the details in the following code block. The **Dockerfile** will use the default **Python3** image, set environment variables relevant for Django, install relevant applications, and copy the code into the current directory of the container image:

```
FROM python:3

ENV PYTHONUNBUFFERED 1
RUN mkdir /application
WORKDIR /application
COPY requirements.txt /application/
RUN pip install -r requirements.txt
COPY . /application/
```

3. Create the **requirements.txt** file that your **Dockerfile** uses in the previous step to install all the relevant applications needed for it to run. Add in the following two lines with your text editor to install the version of **Django** and **Psycopg2** required by the Django application to communicate with the PostgreSQL database:

```
1 Django>=2.0,<3.0
2 psycopg2>=2.7,<3.0
```

4. Create a **docker-compose.yml** file using your text editor. Add in the first service for your database, as shown in the following code. The **db** service will use the latest **postgres** image from Docker Hub, exposing port **5432**, and also set the environment variable for **POSTGRES_PASSWORD**:

```
1 version: '3.3'
2
3 services:
4   db:
5     image: postgres
6     ports:
7       - 5432:5432
8     environment:
9       - POSTGRES_PASSWORD=docker
```

5. The second half of the **docker-compose.yml** file builds and deploys your web application. Build your **Dockerfile** in *line 10*, expose port **8000** to access it from your web browser, and set the database password to match your **db** service. You will also notice a Python command in *line 13* that will start the development web server for the Django application:

```
10   web:
11     build: .
12     image: swarm_web:latest
13     command: python manage.py runserver 0.0.0.0:8000
14     volumes:
15       - .:/application
16     ports:
17       - 8000:8000
18     environment:
19       - PGPASSWORD=docker
20     depends_on:
21       - db
```

6. Run the following command to pull and build the **db** and **web** services in your **docker-compose.yml**. The command will then run **django-admin startproject**, which will create your basic Django project, named **chapter_nine**:

```
docker-compose run web django-admin startproject chapter_nine .
```

The command should return the following output, in which you see the containers being pulled and built:

```
...
Status: Downloaded newer image for postgres:latest
Creating swarm_db_1 ... done
Building web
...
Successfully built 41ff06e17fe2
Successfully tagged swarm_web:latest
```

7. The **startproject** command you ran in the previous step should have created some extra files and directories in your swarm directory. Run the **ls** command to list all the files and directories in the swarm directory:

```
ls -l
```

You previously created the **Dockerfile, docker-compose.yml** file, and **requirements.txt** file, but now the build of the container has added the **chapter_nine** Django directory and the **manage.py** file:

```
-rw-r--r--  1 user  staff  175  3 Mar 13:45 Dockerfile
drwxr-xr-x  6 user  staff  192  3 Mar 13:48 chapter_nine
-rw-r--r--  1 user  staff  304  3 Mar 13:46 docker-compose.yml
-rwxr-xr-x  1 user  staff  634  3 Mar 13:48 manage.py
-rw-r--r--  1 user  staff   36  3 Mar 13:46 requirements.txt
```

8. To get your basic application running, you need to make some minor changes to the Django project settings. Open the **chapter_nine/settings.py** file with your text editor and locate the entry that starts with **DATABASES**. This controls how Django will connect to your database, and by default, Django is set up to work with an SQLite database. The **DATABASES** entry should look like the following:

```
76 DATABASES = {
77     'default': {
78         'ENGINE': 'django.db.backends.sqlite3',
```

```
79              'NAME': os.path.join(BASE_DIR, 'db.sqlite3'),
80      }
81 }
```

You have a PostgreSQL database to deploy to Swarm as a part of our installation, so edit the **DATABASES** settings with the following eight lines so that Django will access this PostgreSQL database instead:

settings.py

```
76 DATABASES = {
77     'default': {
78         'ENGINE': 'django.db.backends.postgresql',
79         'NAME': 'postgres',
80         'USER': 'postgres',
81         'PASSWORD': 'docker',
82         'HOST': 'db',
83         'PORT': 5432,
84     }
85 }
```

The complete code for this step can be found at https://packt.live/2DWP9ov.

9. At *line 28* of our **settings.py** file, we also need to add the IP address we are going to use as the **ALLOWED_HOSTS** configuration. We will configure our application to be accessible from the IP address **0.0.0.0**. Make the relevant changes to the settings file at *line 28* so that it now looks like the code below:

```
27
28 ALLOWED_HOSTS = ["0.0.0.0"]
```

10. Now test to see whether your basic project is working as expected. From the command line, deploy your services to Swarm with the **stack deploy** command. In the following command, specify the **docker-compose.yml** file to use with the **--compose-file** option and name the stack **test_swarm**:

```
docker stack deploy --compose-file docker-compose.yml test_swarm
```

The command should set up the swarm network, the database, and the web services:

```
Creating network test_swarm_default
Creating service test_swarm_db
Creating service test_swarm_web
```

11. Run the **docker service ls** command, and you should be able to see the status for both the **test_swarm_db** and **test_swarm_web** services:

```
docker service ls
```

As you can see in the following output, they are both showing a **REPLICAS** value of **1/1**:

```
ID      NAME            MODE        REPLICAS   IMAGE
   PORTS
dsr.    test_swarm_db   replicated  1/1        postgres
kq3.    test_swarm_web  replicated  1/1        swarm_web:latest
   *:8000.
```

12. If your work has been successful, test it by opening a web browser and going to **http://0.0.0.0:8000**. If everything has worked, you should see the following Django test page displayed on your web browser:

django   View release notes for Django 2.2

The install worked successfully! Congratulations!

You are seeing this page because DEBUG=True is in
your settings file and you have not configured any
URLs.

Figure 9.2: Deploying a service to Swarm with Docker Compose file

13. To view the stacks currently running on your system, use the **stack ls** command:

```
docker stack ls
```

You should see the following output, which shows two services running under the name of **test_swarm**:

```
NAME            SERVICES        ORCHESTRATOR
test_swarm      2               Swarm
```

14. Use the **stack ps** command with the name of your swarm to view the services running and check whether there are any issues:

```
docker stack ps test_swarm
```

The **ID**, **DESIRED STATE**, and **ERROR** columns are not included in the following reduced output. Also, it can be seen that the **test_swarm_web.1** and **test_swarm_db.1** services are running:

```
NAME                    IMAGE                NODE
   CURRENT STATE
test_swarm_web.1        swarm_web:latest     docker-desktop
   Running
test_swarm_db.1         postgres:latest      docker-desktop
   Running
```

15. Just as you were able to start up all your services at once with the **deploy** command, you can stop the services all at once, as well. Use the **stack rm** command with the name of your swarm to stop all of your services from running and remove the stack:

```
docker stack rm test_swarm
```

Note that all the services are stopped in the following output:

```
Removing service test_swarm_db
Removing service test_swarm_web
Removing network test_swarm_default
```

16. You still want to perform some extra work on your swarm as part of this exercise, but first, make a minor change to the **compose** file. Open the **docker-compose.yml** file with your text editor and add the following lines to your web service to now have two replica web services created when deployed to the swarm:

```
22      deploy:
23          replicas: 2
```

The complete **docker-compose.yml** file should look like the following:

```
version: '3.3'

services:
  db:
    image: postgres
```

```
      ports:
        - 5432:5432
      environment:
        - POSTGRES_PASSWORD=docker
  web:
    build: .
    image: swarm_web:latest
    command: python manage.py runserver 0.0.0.0:8000
    volumes:
      - .:/application
    ports:
      - 8000:8000
    environment:
      - PGPASSWORD=docker
    deploy:
      replicas: 2
    depends_on:
      - db
```

17. Deploy the swarm again with the changes you have made using the same command, as you did earlier in *step 8*. Even if the **test_swarm** stack was still running, it would note and make the relevant changes to the services:

```
docker stack deploy --compose-file docker-compose.yml test_swarm
```

18. Run the **docker ps** command as follows:

```
docker ps | awk '{print $1 "\t" $2 }'
```

Only the first two columns are printed in the output shown here. You can now see that there are two **swarm_web** services running:

```
CONTAINER       ID
2f6eb92414e6    swarm_web:latest
e9241c352e12    swarm_web:latest
d5e6ece8a9bf    postgres:latest
```

19. To deploy a new version of the **swarm_web** service to your swarm without stopping the services, first, build a new Docker image of our web service. Don't make any changes to the image, but this time tag the image with the **patch1** tag to demonstrate a change while the service is running:

```
docker build . -t swarm_web:patch1
```

20. To perform a rolling update, use the **service update** command, providing details of the image you wish to update to and the service name. Run the following command, which uses the image you have just created with the **patch1** tag, on the **test_swarm_web** service:

```
docker service update --image swarm_web:patch1 test_swarm_web
```

Swarm will manage the update to make sure one of the services is always running before the update is applied to the rest of the images:

```
image swarm_web:patch1 could not be accessed on a registry
to record its digest. Each node will access
swarm_web:patch1 independently, possibly leading to different
nodes running different versions of the image.


test_swarm_web
overall progress: 2 out of 2 tasks
1/2: running    [=========================================>]
2/2: running    [=========================================>]
verify: Service converged
```

> **NOTE**
>
> You'll notice the output shows the image was not available on a repository. As we only have one node running our swarm, the update will use the image built on the node. In a real-world scenario, we would need to push this image to a central repository that all our nodes have access to so they can pull it.

21. Run the **docker ps** command given here, which pipes its output to an **awk** command to only print the first two columns of **CONTAINER** and **ID**:

```
docker ps | awk '{print $1 "\t" $2 }'
```

The command will return the output such as the following:

```
CONTAINER        ID
ef4107b35e09     swarm_web:patch1
d3b03d8219dd     swarm_web:patch1
d5e6ece8a9bf     postgres:latest
```

22. What if you wanted to control the way the rolling updates occur? Run the following command to perform a new rolling update to your **test_swarm_web** services. Revert the changes you made to deploy the image with the **latest** tag, but this time, make sure there is a **30**-second delay in performing the update as this will give your web service extra time to start up before the second update is run:

```
docker service update --update-delay 30s --image swarm_web:latest
test_swarm_web
```

23. Run the **docker ps** command again:

```
docker ps | awk '{print $1 "\t" $2 }'
```

Note that the containers are now running the **swarm_web:latest** image again after you have performed the rolling update:

```
CONTAINER       ID
414e62f6eb92    swarm_web:latest
352e12e9241c    swarm_web:latest
d5e6ece8a9bf    postgres:latest
```

By now, you should see the benefit of using a swarm, especially when we start to scale out our applications using Docker Compose. In this exercise, we have demonstrated how to easily deploy and manage a group of services onto your swarm using Docker Compose and upgrade services with rolling updates.

The next section of this chapter will expand your knowledge further to show how you can use Swarm to manage your configurations and secret values used within your environment.

MANAGING SECRETS AND CONFIGURATIONS WITH DOCKER SWARM

So far in this chapter, we have observed Docker Swarm's proficiency at orchestrating our services and applications. It also provides functionality to allow us to define configurations within our environment and then use these values. Why do we need this functionality, though?

Firstly, the way we have been storing details such as our secrets has not been very secure, especially when we are typing them in plain text in our **docker-compose.yml** file or including them as part of our built Docker image. For our secrets, Swarm allows us to store encrypted values that are then used by our services.

Secondly, by using these features, we can start to move away from setting up configurations in our **Dockerfile**. This means we can create and build our application as a container image. Then, we can run our application on any environment, be it a development system on a laptop or a test environment. We can also run the application on a production environment, where we assign it with a separate configuration or secrets value to use in that environment.

Creating a Swarm **config** is simple, especially if you already have an existing file to use. The following code shows how we can create a new **config** using the **config create** command by providing our **config_name** and the name of our **configuration_file**:

```
docker config create <config_name> <configuration_file>
```

This command creates a **config** stored as part of the swarm and is available to all the nodes in your cluster. To view the available configs on your system and the swarm, run the **ls** option with the **config** command:

```
docker config ls
```

You can also view the details in the configuration using the **config inspect** command. Make sure you are using the **--pretty** option since the output is presented as a long JSON output that would be almost unreadable without it:

```
docker config inspect --pretty <config_name>
```

Using secrets within Swarm provides a secure way to create and store sensitive information in our environments, such as usernames and passwords, in an encrypted state so it can then be used by our services.

To create a secret that is only holding a single value, such as a username or password, we can simply create the secret from the command line, where we pipe the secret value into the **secret create** command. The following sample command provides an example of how to do this. Remember to name the secret when you create it:

```
echo "<secret_password>" | docker secret create <secret_name> -
```

You can make a secret from a file. For example, say you would like to set up a certificates file as a secret. The following command shows how to do this using the **secret create** command by providing the name of the secret and the name of the file you need to create the secret from:

```
docker secret create <secret_name> <secret_file>
```

Once created, your secret will be available on all the nodes you have running on your swarm. Just as you were able to view your **config**, you can use the **secret ls** command to see a listing of all the available secrets in your swarm:

```
docker secret ls
```

We can see that Swarm provides us with flexible options to implement configurations and secrets in our orchestration, instead of needing to have it set up as part of our Docker images.

The following exercise will demonstrate how to use both configurations and secrets in your current Docker Swarm environment.

EXERCISE 9.03: IMPLEMENTING CONFIGURATIONS AND SECRETS IN YOUR SWARM

In this exercise, you will expand your Docker Swarm environment further. You will add a service to your environment that will help NGINX to route the requests through the proxy, before moving into your web service. You will set this up using traditional methods but then use the **config** and **secret** functions as part of your environment to observe their operations within Swarm and help users deploy and configure services more efficiently:

1. Currently, the web service is using the Django development web server via the **runserver** command to provide web requests. NGINX will not be able to route traffic requests through to this development server, and instead, you will need to install the **gunicorn** application onto our Django web service for traffic to be routed via NGINX. Start by opening your **requirements.txt** file with your text editor and add the application as in the highlighted third line:

```
Django>=2.0,<3.0
psycopg2>=2.7,<3.0
gunicorn==19.9.0
```

> **NOTE**
>
> Gunicorn is short for **Green Unicorn** and is used as a **Web Service Gateway Interface (WSGI)** for Python applications. Gunicorn is widely used for production environments as it is seen to be one of the most stable WSGI applications available.

2. To run Gunicorn as part of your web application, adjust your
docker-compose.yml file. Open the **docker-compose.yml** file with
your text editor and change *line 13* to run the **gunicorn** application, instead
of the Django **manage.py runserver** command. The following **gunicorn**
command runs the **chapter_nine** Django project via its WSGI service and
binds to IP address and port **0.0.0.0:8000**:

```
12      image: swarm_web:latest
13      command: gunicorn chapter_nine.wsgi:application
          --bind 0.0.0.0:8000
14      volumes:
```

3. Rebuild your web service to make sure the Gunicorn application is installed
on the container and available to run. Run the **docker-compose
build** command:

```
docker-compose build
```

4. Gunicorn can also run without the need of the NGINX proxy, so test the changes
you have made by running the **stack deploy** command again. If you already
have your services deployed, don't worry, you can still run this command again.
It will simply make the relevant changes to your swarm and match the changes
in your **docker-compose.yml**:

```
docker stack deploy --compose-file docker-compose.yml test_swarm
```

The command will return the following output:

```
Ignoring unsupported options: build
Creating network test_swarm_default
Creating service test_swarm_web
Creating service test_swarm_db
```

5. To ensure the changes have taken effect, make sure you open your web browser
and verify that the Django test page is still being provided by your web service
before moving on to the next step. As per your changes, the page should still be
displayed at **http://0.0.0.0:8000**.

6. To start your implementation of NGINX, open the **docker-compose.yml**
file again and change *lines 16 and 17* to expose port **8000** from the original
ports command:

```
10    web:
11      build: .
12      image: swarm_web:latest
```

```
13    command: gunicorn chapter_nine.wsgi:application
      --bind 0.0.0.0:8000
14    volumes:
15      - .:/application
16    ports:
17      - 8000:8000
18    environment:
19      - PGPASSWORD=docker
20    deploy:
21      replicas: 2
22    depends_on:
23      - db
```

7. Keeping the **docker-compose.yml** file open, add your **nginx** service at the end of the **compose** file. All of the information here should be familiar to you by now. *Line 25* provides the location of a new NGINX directory, the **Dockerfile** you will create shortly, and the name of the image to be used when the service is deployed. *Lines 27* and *28* expose port **1337** to port **80** and *lines 29* and *30* show that NGINX needs to depend on the **web** service to run:

```
24    nginx:
25      build: ./nginx
26      image: swarm_nginx:latest
27      ports:
28        - 1337:80
29      depends_on:
30        - web
```

8. Now, set up the NGINX **Dockerfile** and configurations for the service. Start by creating a directory called **nginx**, as in the following command:

```
mkdir nginx
```

9. Create a new **Dockerfile** in the **nginx** directory, open the file with your text editor, and add in the details shown here. The **Dockerfile** is created from the latest **nginx** image available on Docker Hub. It removes the default configuration **nginx** file in *line 3* and then adds a new configuration that you need to set up shortly:

```
FROM nginx

RUN rm /etc/nginx/conf.d/default.conf
COPY nginx.conf /etc/nginx/conf.d
```

10. Create the **nginx.conf** file that the **Dockerfile** will use to create your new image. Create a new file called **nginx.conf** in the **nginx** directory and use your text editor to add the following configuration details:

```
upstream chapter_nine {
    server web:8000;
}

server {

    listen 80;

    location / {
        proxy_pass http://chapter_nine;
        proxy_set_header X-Forwarded-For
            $proxy_add_x_forwarded_for;
        proxy_set_header Host $host;
        proxy_redirect off;
    }

}
```

If you're unfamiliar with NGINX configurations, the preceding details are simply looking for requests to the web service and will route requests through to the **chapter_nine** Django application.

11. With all the details now in place, build your new image for the NGINX service now set up in your **docker-compose.yml** file. Run the following command to build the image:

```
docker-compose build
```

12. Run the **stack deploy** command again:

```
docker stack deploy --compose-file docker-compose.yml test_swarm
```

This time, you will notice that your output shows that the **test_swarm_nginx** service has been created and should be running:

```
Creating network test_swarm_default
Creating service test_swarm_db
Creating service test_swarm_web
Creating service test_swarm_nginx
```

13. Verify that all the services are running as part of your swarm with the **stack ps** command:

```
docker stack ps test_swarm
```

The resulting output has been reduced to show only four of the eight columns. You can see that the **test_swarm_nginx** service is now running:

```
NAME                      IMAGE                NODE
   DESIRED STATE
test_swarm_nginx.1        swarm_nginx:latest   docker-desktop
   Running
test_swarm_web.1          swarm_web:latest     docker-desktop
   Running
test_swarm_db.1           postgres:latest      docker-desktop
   Running
test_swarm_web.2          swarm_web:latest     docker-desktop
   Running
```

14. To prove that requests are routing through the NGINX proxy, use port **1337** instead of port **8000**. Make sure that a web page is still being provided from your web browser by using the new URL of **http://0.0.0.0:1337**.

15. This has been a great addition to the services running on Swarm but is not using the correct configuration management features. You already have an NGINX configuration created previously in this exercise. Create a Swarm configuration by using the **config create** command with the name of the new configuration and the file you are going to create the configuration from. Run the following command to create the new configuration from your **nginx/nginx.conf** file:

```
docker config create nginx_config nginx/nginx.conf
```

The output from the command will provide you with the created configuration ID:

```
u125x6f6lhv1x6u0aemlt5w2i
```

16. Swarm also gives you a way to list all the configurations created as part of your Swarm, using the **config ls** command. Make sure the new **nginx_config** file has been created in the previous step and run the following command:

```
docker config ls
```

nginx_config has been created in the following output:

ID	NAME	CREATED	UPDATED
u125x6f6...	nginx_config	19 seconds ago	19 seconds ago

17. View the full details of the configuration you have created using the **docker config inspect** command. Run the following command with the **--pretty** option to make sure the configuration output is in a readable form:

```
docker config inspect --pretty nginx_config
```

The output should look similar to what you see here, showing details of the NGINX configuration you have just created:

```
ID:              u125x6f6lhv1x6u0aemlt5w2i
Name:            nginx_config
Created at:          2020-03-04 19:55:52.168746807 +0000 utc
Updated at:          2020-03-04 19:55:52.168746807 +0000 utc
Data:
upstream chapter_nine {
    server web:8000;
}

server {

    listen 80;

    location / {
        proxy_pass http://chapter_nine;
        proxy_set_header X-Forwarded-For
            $proxy_add_x_forwarded_for;
        proxy_set_header Host $host;
        proxy_redirect off;
    }


}
```

18. As you have now set up the configuration in Swarm, make sure the configuration is no longer built into the container image. Instead, it will be provided when the Swarm is deployed. Open the **Dockerfile** in the **nginx** directory and remove the fourth line of the **Dockerfile**. It should now look similar to the details given here:

```
FROM nginx:1.17.4-alpine


RUN rm /etc/nginx/conf.d/default.conf
```

> **NOTE**
>
> Remember that the change we are making here will make sure that we don't need to build a new NGINX image every time the configuration changes. This means we can use the same image and deploy it to a development swarm or a production swarm. All we would do is change the configuration to make the environment. We do need to create the image that can use the config we have created and stored in Swarm, though.

19. The previous step in this exercise made a change to the **nginx Dockerfile**, so now rebuild the image to make sure it is up to date:

```
docker-compose build
```

20. Open the **docker-compose.yml** file with your text editor to update the **compose** file so that our **nginx** service will now use the newly created Swarm **config**. At the bottom of the **nginx** service, add in the configuration details with the source name of the **nginx_cof** configuration you created earlier. Be sure to add it to the running **nginx** service so it can be used by the container. Then, set up a separate configuration for the file. Even though you have created it manually in the previous steps, your swarm needs to know about it when it is deployed. Add the following into your **docker-compose.yml**:

```
25    nginx:
26      build: ./nginx
27      image: swarm_nginx:latest
28      ports:
29        - 1337:80
30      depends_on:
31        - web
32      configs:
```

```
33        - source: nginx_conf
34          target: /etc/nginx/conf.d/nginx.conf
35
36 configs:
37   nginx_conf:
38     file: nginx/nginx.conf
```

21. Deploy your swarm again:

```
docker stack deploy --compose-file docker-compose.yml test_swarm
```

In the following output, you should now see an extra line showing **Creating config test_swarm_nginx_conf**:

```
Creating network test_swarm_default
Creating config test_swarm_nginx_conf
Creating service test_swarm_db
Creating service test_swarm_web
Creating service test_swarm_nginx
```

22. There is still more you can do to take advantage of Swarm, and one extra feature not used yet is the secrets function. Just as you created a configuration earlier in this exercise, you can create a **secret** with a similar command. The command shown here first uses **echo** to output the password you want as your secret value, and then, using the **secret create** command, it uses this output to create the secret named **pg_password**. Run the following command to name your new secret **pg_password**:

```
echo "docker" | docker secret create pg_password -
```

The command will output the ID of the secret created:

```
4i1cwxst1j9qoh2e6uq5fjb8c
```

23. View the secrets in your swarm using the **secret ls** command. Run this command now:

```
docker secret ls
```

You can see that your secret has been created successfully with the name of **pg_password**:

```
ID                          NAME          CREATED
  UPDATED
4i1cwxst1j9qoh2e6uq5fjb8c   pg_password   51 seconds ago
  51 seconds ago
```

24. Now, make the relevant changes to your **docker-compose.yml** file. Previously, you simply entered the password you wanted for your **postgres** user. As you can see in the following code, here, you will point the environment variable to the secret you created earlier as **/run/secrets/pg_password**. This means it will search through the available secrets in your swarm and assign the secret stored in **pg_password**. You also need to refer to the secret in the **db** service to allow it access. Open the file with your text editor and make the following changes to the file:

```
4    db:
5      image: postgres
6      ports:
7        - 5432:5432
8      environment:
9        - POSTGRES_PASSWORD=/run/secrets/pg_password
10     secrets:
11       - pg_password
```

25. The **web** service uses the same secret to access the PostgreSQL database. Move into the **web** service section of the **docker-compose.yml** and change *line 21* to resemble the following, as it will now use the secret you have created:

```
20     environment:
21         - PGPASSWORD=/run/secrets/pg_password
22     deploy:
```

26. Finally, just as you have done with your configuration, define the secret at the end of **docker-compose.yml**. Add in the following lines at the end of your **compose** file:

```
41 secrets:
42   pg_password:
43     external: true
```

27. Before deploying your changes, you have made a lot of changes to the **compose** file, so your **docker-compose.yml** file should look similar to what is shown in the following code block. You have three services running with the **db**, **web**, and **nginx** services set up, and we now have one **config** instance and one **secret** instance:

docker-compose.yml

```
version: '3.3'

services:
  db:
    image: postgres
    ports:
      - 5432:5432
    environment:
      - POSTGRES_PASSWORD=/run/secrets/pg_password
    secrets:
      - pg_password
  web:
    build: .
    image: swarm_web:latest
    command: gunicorn chapter_nine.wsgi:application --bind
      0.0.0.0:8000
    volumes:
      - .:/application
    ports:
      - 8000:8000
```

The complete code for this step can be found at https://packt.live/3miUJD8.

> **NOTE**
>
> There are a few changes to our service, and if there are any issues in deploying the changes to Swarm, it may be worth deleting the services and then re-deploying to make sure all the changes take effect correctly.

This is the final run of your Swarm deployment for this exercise:

```
docker stack deploy --compose-file docker-compose.yml test_swarm
```

28. Run the deployment and make sure the services are running and deployed successfully:

```
Creating network test_swarm_default
Creating config test_swarm_nginx_conf
Creating service test_swarm_db
Creating service test_swarm_web
Creating service test_swarm_nginx
```

In this exercise, you have practiced using Swarm to deploy a complete set of services using your **docker-compose.yml** file and have them running in a matter of minutes. This part of the chapter has also demonstrated some extra functionality of Swarm using **config** and **secret** instances to help us reduce the amount of work needed to move services to different environments. Now that you know how to manage Swarm from the command line, you can further explore Swarm cluster management in the following section using a web interface with Swarmpit.

MANAGING SWARM WITH SWARMPIT

The command line provides an efficient and useful way for users to control their Swarm. This can get a little confusing for some users if your services and nodes multiply as need increases. One way to help with managing and monitoring your Swarm is by using a web interface such as the one provided by Swarmpit to help you administer your different environments.

As you'll see shortly, Swarmpit provides an easy-to-use web interface that allows you to manage most aspects of your Docker Swarm instances, including the stacks, secrets, services, volumes networks, and configurations.

> **NOTE**
>
> This chapter will only touch on the use of Swarmpit, but if you would like more information on the application, the following site should provide you with further details: https://swarmpit.io.

Swarmpit is a simple-to-use installation Docker image that, when run on your system, creates its swarm of services deployed in your environment to run the management and web interface. Once installed, the web interface is accessible from **http://0.0.0.0:888**.

To run the installer on your system to get Swarm running, execute the following **docker run** command. With this, you name the container **swampit-installer** and mount the container volume on **/var/run/docker.sock** so it can manage other containers on our system, using the **swarmpit/install:1.8** image:

```
docker run -it --rm   --name swarmpit-installer   --volume /var/run/
docker.sock:/var/run/docker.sock   swarmpit/install:1.8
```

The installer will set up a swarm with a database, an agent, a web application, and the network to link it all together. It will also guide you through setting up an administrative user to log on to the interface for the first time. Once you log in to the web application, the interface is intuitive and easy to navigate.

The following exercise will show you how to install and run Swarmpit on your running system and start to manage your installed services.

EXERCISE 9.04: INSTALLING SWARMPIT AND MANAGING YOUR STACKS

In this exercise, you will install and run Swarmpit, briefly explore the web interface, and begin managing your services from your web browser:

1. It's not completely necessary to do so, but if you have stopped your **test_swarm** stack from running, start it up again. This will provide you with some extra services to monitor from Swarmpit:

```
docker stack deploy --compose-file docker-compose.yml test_swarm
```

> **NOTE**
>
> If you are worried that there will be too many services running on your system at once, feel free to skip this **test_swarm** stack restart. The exercise can be performed as follows on the Swarmpit stack that is created as part of the installation process.

2. Run the following **docker run** command:

```
docker run -it --rm   --name swarmpit-installer   --volume /var/run/
docker.sock:/var/run/docker.sock   swarmpit/install:1.8
```

It pulls the **install:1.8** image from the **swarmpit** repository and then runs through the process of setting up your environment details, allowing the user to make changes to the stack name, ports, administrator username, and password. It then creates the relevant services needed to run the applications:

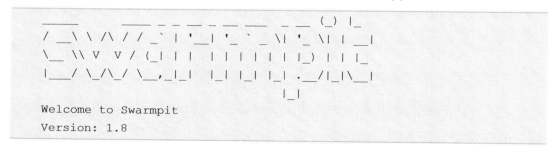

```
Welcome to Swarmpit
Version: 1.8
```

```
Branch: 1.8
...
Application setup
Enter stack name [swarmpit]:
Enter application port [888]:
Enter database volume driver [local]:
Enter admin username [admin]:
Enter admin password (min 8 characters long): ******
DONE.


Application deployment
Creating network swarmpit_net
Creating service swarmpit_influxdb
Creating service swarmpit_agent
Creating service swarmpit_app
Creating service swarmpit_db
DONE.
```

3. On the command line, run the **stack ls** command to ensure that you have the Swarmpit swarm deployed to your node:

```
docker stack ls
```

The following output confirms that Swarmpit is deployed to our node:

```
NAME              SERVICES        ORCHESTRATOR
swarmpit          4               Swarm
test_swarm        3               Swarm
```

4. Use the **service ls** command to verify that the services needed by Swarmpit are running:

```
docker service ls | grep swarmpit
```

For clarity, the output shown here only displays the first four columns. The output also shows that the **REPLICAS** value for each service is **1/1**:

```
ID               NAME                MODE          REPLICAS
vi2qbwq5y9c6     swarmpit_agent      global        1/1
4tpomyfw93wy     swarmpit_app        replicated    1/1
nuxi5egfa3my     swarmpit_db         replicated    1/1
do77ey8wz49a     swarmpit_influxdb   replicated    1/1
```

It's time to log in to the Swarmpit web interface. Open your web browser and use **http://0.0.0.0:888** to open the Swarmpit login page and enter the admin username and password you set during the installation process:

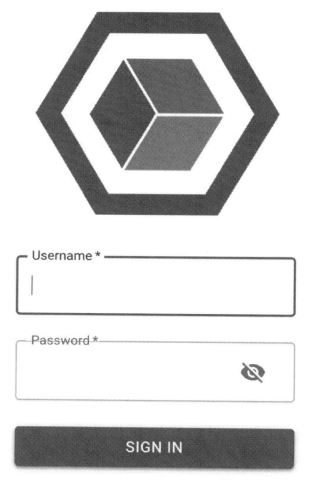

Figure 9.3: The Swarmpit login screen

5. Once you log in, you're presented with the Swarmpit welcome screen, showing your dashboard of all your services running on the node, as well as details of the resources being used on the node. The left of the screen provides a menu of all the different aspects of the Swarm stack you can monitor and manage, including the stacks themselves, **Services**, **Tasks**, **Networks**, **Nodes**, **Volumes**, **Secrets**, **Configs**, and **Users**. Click on the **Stacks** option in the left-hand menu and select the **test_swarm** stack:

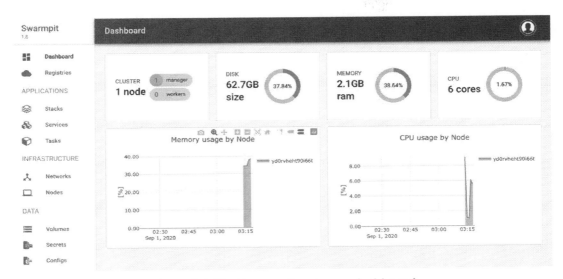

Figure 9.4: The Swarmpit welcome dashboard

6. You should be presented with a screen similar to the following. The size of the screen has been reduced for clarity, but as you can see, it provides all the details of the interacting components of the stack—including the services available and the secrets and configs being used. If you click on the menu next to the stack name, as shown here, you can edit the stack. Click **Edit Stack** now:

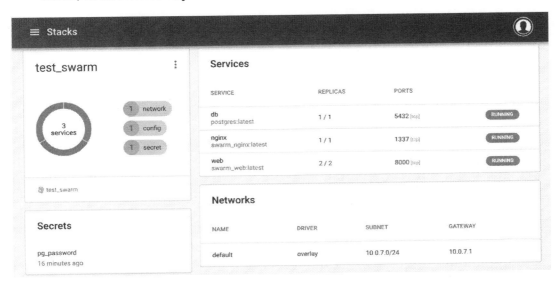

Figure 9.5: Managing your swarm with Swarmpit

7. Editing the stack brings up a page where you can make changes directly to the stack as if you were making changes to **docker-compose.yml**. Move down to the file, find the replicas entry for the web service, and change it to **3** from **2**:

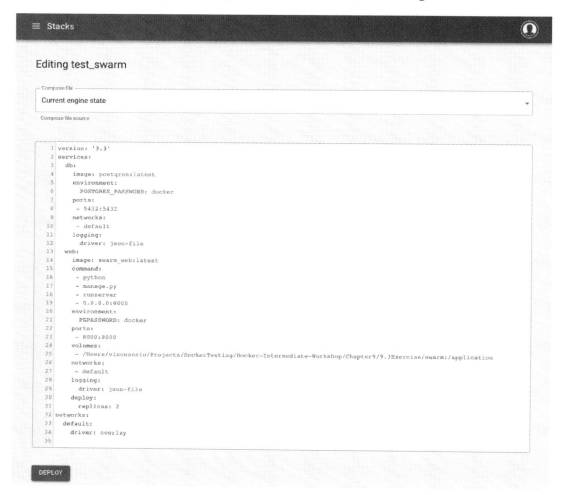

Figure 9.6: Editing your swarm with Swarmpit

8. Click on the **Deploy** button at the bottom of the screen. This will deploy the changes to your **test_swarm** stack into the environment and return you to the **test_swarm** stack screen, where you should now see **3/3** replicas of the web service running:

Services

SERVICE	REPLICAS	PORTS	
db postgres:latest	1 / 1	5432 [tcp]	RUNNING
nginx swarm_nginx:latest	1 / 1	1337 [tcp]	RUNNING
web swarm_web:latest	3 / 3	8000 [tcp]	RUNNING

Figure 9.7: Increased number of web services in Swarmpit

9. Notice that most of the options in Swarmpit are linked. On the **test_swarm** stack page, if you click on the web service from the **services** panel, you will open the **Service** page for the **test_swarm_web** service. If you click the menu, you should see the following page:

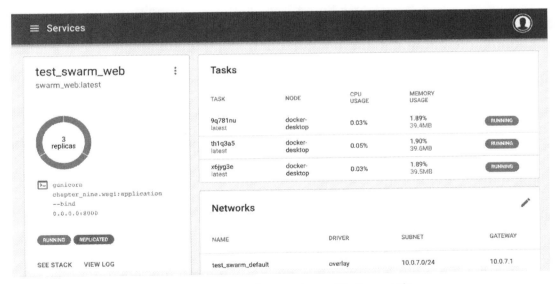

Figure 9.8: Managing services with Swarmpit

10. Select **Rollback Service** from the menu, and you will see the number of replicas of the **test_swarm_web** service roll back to two replicas.

11. Finally, return to the **Stacks** menu and select the **test_swarm** again. With the **test_swarm** stack open, you have the option to delete the stack by clicking on the trash can icon toward the top of the screen. Confirm that you would like to delete the stack, and this will bring **test_swarm** down again and it will no longer be running on your node:

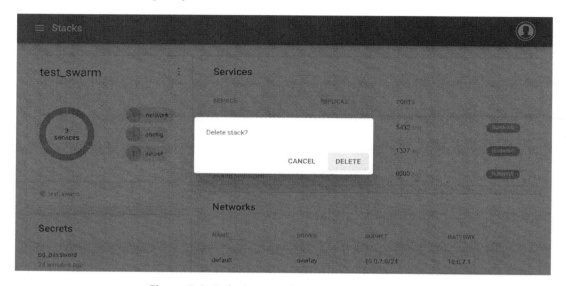

Figure 9.9: Deleting a web service in Swarmpit

> **NOTE**
>
> Note that Swarmpit will allow you to delete the **swarmpit** stack. You will see an error, but when you try to reload the page, it will simply not come up again as all the services will have been stopped from running.

Although this has been only a quick introduction to Swarmpit, using your prior knowledge from this chapter, the interface will allow you to intuitively deploy and make changes to your services and stacks. Almost anything that you can do from the command line, you can also do from the Swarmpit web interface. This brings us to the end of this exercise and the end of the chapter. The activities in the next section of this chapter are designed to help expand your knowledge further.

ACTIVITY 9.01: DEPLOYING THE PANORAMIC TREKKING APP TO A SINGLE-NODE DOCKER SWARM

You are required to use Docker Swarm to deploy web and database services in the Panoramic Trekking App. You will gather configurations to create a compose file for the application and deploy them to a single node Swarm using a **docker-compose.yml** file.

The steps you will need to take to complete this activity are as follows:

1. Gather all the applications and build the Docker images needed for the services of your swarm.

2. Create a **docker-compose.yml** file that will allow the services to be deployed to Docker Swarm.

3. Create any supporting images needed for the services to use once deployed.

4. Deploy your services onto Swarm and verify that all services are able to run successfully.

Your running services should look similar to the output shown here:

```
ID          NAME             MODE         REPLICAS
   IMAGE
k6kh...      activity_swarm_db   replicated   1/1
   postgres:latest
copa...      activity_swarm_web  replicated   1/1
   activity_web:latest
```

> **NOTE**
>
> The solution for this activity can be found on page 702.

Continue with the next activity as this will work to solidify some of the information you have already learned in this chapter.

ACTIVITY 9.02: PERFORMING AN UPDATE TO THE APP WHILE THE SWARM IS RUNNING

In this activity, you need to make a minor change to the Panoramic Trekking App that will allow you to build a new image and deploy the image to the running Swarm. In this activity, you will perform a rolling update to deploy these changes to your Swarm cluster.

The steps you'll need to complete this activity are as follows:

1. If you do not have the Swarm from *Activity 9.01, Deploying the Panoramic Trekking App to a Single Node Docker Swarm* still running, deploy the swarm again.

2. Make a minor change to the code in the Panoramic Trekking App—something small that can be tested to verify that you have made a change in your environment. The change you are making is not important, so it can be something as basic as a configuration change. The main focus of this activity is on performing the rolling update to the service.

3. Build a new image to be deployed into the running environment.

4. Perform an update to the environment and verify that the changes were successful.

> **NOTE**
>
> The solution for this activity can be found on page 705.

SUMMARY

This chapter has done a lot of work in moving our Docker environments from manually starting single-image services to a more production-ready and complete environment with Docker Swarm. We started this chapter with an in-depth discussion of Docker Swarm and how you can manage your services and nodes from the command line, providing a list of commands and their use, and later implementing them as part of a new environment running a test Django web application.

We then expanded this application further with an NGINX proxy and utilized Swarm functionality to store configuration and secrets data so they no longer need to be included as part of our Docker image and can instead be included in the Swarm we are deploying. We then showed you how to manage your swarm using your web browser with Swarmpit, providing a rundown of the work we previously did on the command line and making a lot of these changes from a web browser. Swarm is not the only way you can orchestrate your environments when using Docker.

In the next chapter, we will introduce Kubernetes, which is another orchestration tool used to manage Docker environments and applications. Here, you will see how you can use Kubernetes as part of your projects to help reduce the time you are managing services and improve the updating of your applications.

10

KUBERNETES

OVERVIEW

In this chapter, we will learn about Kubernetes, the most popular container management system in the market. Starting with the basics, architecture, and resources, you will create Kubernetes clusters and deploy real-life applications in them.

By the end of the chapter, you will be able to identify the basics of Kubernetes design and its relationship with Docker. You will create and configure a local Kubernetes cluster, work with the Kubernetes API using client tools, and use fundamental Kubernetes resources to run containerized applications.

INTRODUCTION

In the previous chapters, you ran multiple Docker containers with **Docker Compose** and **Docker Swarm**. Microservices running in various containers help developers to create scalable and reliable applications.

However, when multiple applications are spread over multiple servers across a data center, or even across multiple data centers around the world, it becomes more complex to manage the applications. There are many open-ended problems related to the complexity of distributed applications, including, but not limited to, networking, storage, and container management.

For instance, the networking of containers running on the same nodes, as well as different nodes, should be configured. Similarly, the volumes of the containers that contain the applications (which can be scaled up or down) should be managed with a central controller. Fortunately, the management of the distributed containers has a well-accepted and adopted solution: Kubernetes.

Kubernetes is an open-source container orchestration system for running scalable, reliable, and robust containerized applications. It is possible to run Kubernetes on a wide range of platforms, from a **Raspberry Pi** to a data center. Kubernetes makes it possible to run containers with mounting volumes, inserting secrets, and configuring the network interfaces. Also, it focuses on the life cycle of containers to provide high-availability and scalability. With its inclusive approach, Kubernetes is the leading container management system currently available on the market.

Kubernetes translates to the **captain of the ship** in Greek. With the Docker's analogy to boats and containers, Kubernetes positions itself as the sailing master. The idea of Kubernetes has roots in managing containers for Google Services such as Gmail or Google Drive for over a decade. From 2014 to the present, Kubernetes has been an open-source project, managed by **Cloud Native Computing Foundation** (**CNCF**).

One of the main advantages of Kubernetes comes from its community and maintainers. It is one of the most active repositories on GitHub, with nearly 88,000 commits from more than 2,400 contributors. In addition, the repository has over 62,000 stars, which means more than 62,000 people have faith in the repository:

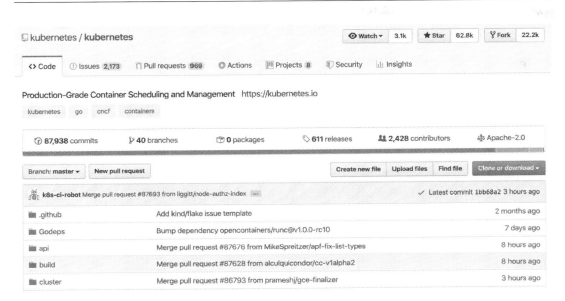

Figure 10.1: Kubernetes GitHub repository

In this chapter, you will explore Kubernetes' design and architecture, followed by its API and access, and use the Kubernetes resources to create containerized applications. Since Kubernetes is the leading container orchestration tool, getting hands-on experience of it will help you get into the world of containerized applications.

KUBERNETES DESIGN

Kubernetes focuses on the life cycle of containers, including configuration, scheduling, health checks, and scaling. With Kubernetes, it is possible to install various types of applications, including databases, content management systems, queue managers, load balancers, and web servers.

For instance, imagine you are working at a new online food delivery chain, named **InstantPizza**. You can deploy the backend of your mobile application in Kubernetes and make it scalable to customer demand and usage. Similarly, you can implement a message queue to communicate between the restaurants and customers, again in Kubernetes. To store past orders and receipts, you can deploy a database in Kubernetes with storage. Furthermore, you can use load balancers to implement **Blue/Green** or **A/B Deployment** for your application.

In this section, the design and architecture of Kubernetes are discussed to illustrate how it achieves scalability and reliability.

> **NOTE**
>
> Blue/green deployments focus on installing two identical versions (called blue and green, respectively) of the same application and instantly moving from blue to green to reduce downtime and risk.
>
> A/B deployments focus on installing two versions of the application (namely, A and B), and the user traffic is divided between the versions for testing and experiments.

The design of Kubernetes concentrates on running on one or multiple servers—namely, clusters. On the other hand, Kubernetes consists of numerous components that should be distributed over a single cluster in order to have reliable and scalable applications.

There are two groups of Kubernetes components—namely, the **control plane** and the **node**. Although there are different naming conventions for the elements that make up the Kubernetes landscape, such as master components instead of the control plane, the main idea of grouping has not changed at all. Control plane components are responsible for running the Kubernetes API, including the database, controllers, and schedulers. There are four main components in the Kubernetes control plane:

- **kube-apiserver**: This is the central API server that connects all the components in the cluster.

- **etcd**: This is the database for Kubernetes resources, and the **kube-apiserver** stores the state of the cluster on **etcd**.

- **kube-scheduler**: This is the scheduler that assigns containerized applications to the nodes.

- **kube-controller-manager**: This is the controller that creates and manages the Kubernetes resources in the cluster.

In servers with the role node, there are two Kubernetes components:

- **`kubelet`**: This is the Kubernetes client that lives on the nodes to create a bridge between the Kubernetes API and container runtime, such as Docker.

- **`kube-proxy`**: This is a network proxy that runs on every node to allow network communication regarding the workloads across the cluster.

The control plane and node components, along with their interactions, are illustrated in the following diagram:

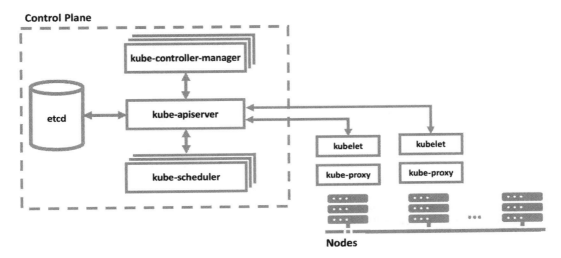

Figure 10.2: Kubernetes architecture

Kubernetes is designed to run on scalable cloud systems. However, there are many tools to run Kubernetes clusters locally. **`minikube`** is the officially supported CLI tool to create and manage local Kubernetes clusters. Its commands focus on life cycle events and the troubleshooting of clusters, as follows:

- **`minikube start`**: Starts a local Kubernetes cluster

- **`minikube stop`**: Stops a running local Kubernetes cluster

- **`minikube delete`**: Deletes a local Kubernetes cluster

- **`minikube service`**: Fetches the URL(s) for the specified service in the local cluster

- **`minikube ssh`**: Logs in or runs a command on a machine with SSH

In the following exercise, you will create a local Kubernetes cluster to check the components discussed in this chapter. To create a local cluster, you will use **minikube** as the official local Kubernetes solution and run its commands to explore Kubernetes components.

> **NOTE**
>
> **minikube** runs the cluster on hypervisors, and you need to install a hypervisor such as KVM, VirtualBox, VMware Fusion, Hyperkit, or Hyper-V based on your operating system. You can check the official documentation for more information at https://kubernetes.io/docs/tasks/tools/install-minikube/#install-a-hypervisor.

> **NOTE**
>
> Please use **touch** command to create files and **vim** command to work on the file using vim editor.

EXERCISE 10.01: STARTING A LOCAL KUBERNETES CLUSTER

Kubernetes was initially designed to run on clusters with multiple servers. This is an expected characteristic for a container orchestrator that runs scalable applications in the cloud. However, there are many times that you need to run a Kubernetes cluster locally, such as for development or testing. In this exercise, you will install a local Kubernetes provider and then create a Kubernetes cluster. In the cluster, you will check for the components discussed in this section.

To complete this exercise, perform the following steps:

1. Download the latest version of the **minikube** executable for your operating system and set the binary as executable for your local system by running the following command in your terminal:

```
# Linux
curl -Lo minikube https://storage.googleapis.com/minikube/releases/
latest/minikube-linux-amd64
# MacOS
```

```
curl -Lo minikube https://storage.googleapis.com/minikube/releases/
latest/minikube-darwin-amd64
chmod +x minikube
sudo mv minikube /usr/local/bin
```

These preceding commands download the binary for Linux or Mac and make it ready to use in the terminal:

```
/docker-ws $
/docker-ws $ curl -Lo minikube https://storage.googleapis.com/minikube/releases/latest/mi
nikube-darwin-amd64
  % Total    % Received % Xferd  Average Speed   Time    Time     Time  Current
                                 Dload  Upload   Total   Spent    Left  Speed
100 43.8M  100 43.8M     0      0  6313k       0  0:00:07  0:00:07 --:--:-- 6616k
/docker-ws $ chmod +x minikube
/docker-ws $ sudo mv minikube /usr/local/bin
/docker-ws $
```

Figure 10.3: Installation of minikube

2. Start a Kubernetes cluster with the following command in your terminal:

```
minikube start
```

The single preceding command executes multiple steps to create a cluster successfully. You can check each stage and its output as follows:

```
/docker-ws $
/docker-ws $ minikube start
😄  minikube v1.6.2 on Darwin 10.15.2
✨  Automatically selected the 'hyperkit' driver (alternates: [virtualbox])
🔥  Creating hyperkit VM (CPUs=2, Memory=9000MB, Disk=20000MB) ...
🐳  Preparing Kubernetes v1.17.0 on Docker '19.03.5' ...
🚜  Pulling images ...
🚀  Launching Kubernetes ...
⌛  Waiting for cluster to come online ...
🏄  Done! kubectl is now configured to use "minikube"
/docker-ws $
```

Figure 10.4: Starting a new Kubernetes cluster

The output starts with printing out the version and the environment. Then, the images for Kubernetes components are pulled and started. Finally, you have a locally running Kubernetes cluster after a couple of minutes.

3. Connect to the cluster node started by **minikube** with the following command:

```
minikube ssh
```

With the **ssh** command, you can continue working on the node running in the cluster:

```
/docker-ws $ minikube ssh
```

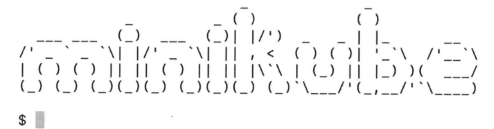

```
$
```

Figure 10.5: Cluster node

4. Check for each control plane component with the following commands:

```
docker ps --filter „name=kube-apiserver" --filter „name=etcd" --filter
„name=kube-scheduler" --filter „name=kube-controller-manager" | grep
-v „pause"
```

This command checks for the Docker containers and filters with the control plane component names. The following output does not contain the pause container, which is responsible for the networking setup of the container groups in Kubernetes, so as to make analysis easier:

```
$ docker ps --filter "name=kube-apiserver" --filter "name=etcd" --filter "name=kube
-scheduler" --filter "name=kube-controller-manager" | grep -v "pause"
CONTAINER ID        IMAGE              COMMAND            CREATED
     STATUS             PORTS              NAMES
1fbc9f8b14fd        78c190f736b1       "kube-scheduler --au…"   18 minutes ago
     Up 18 minutes             k8s_kube-scheduler_kube-scheduler-mini
kube_kube-system_ff67867321338ffd885039e188f6b424_1
7e1caeda6a49        303ce5db0e90       "etcd --advertise-cl…"   18 minutes ago
     Up 18 minutes             k8s_etcd_etcd-minikube_kube-system_3e2
cde1eca0c3b2644c8b8d16ac844c4_1
a75df7602f2e        5eb3b7486872       "kube-controller-man…"   18 minutes ago
     Up 18 minutes             k8s_kube-controller-manager_kube-contr
oller-manager-minikube_kube-system_e7ce3a6ee9fa0ec547ac7b4b17af0dcb_1
3c6fccab6823        0cae8d5cc64c       "kube-apiserver --ad…"   18 minutes ago
     Up 18 minutes             k8s_kube-apiserver_kube-apiserver-mini
kube_kube-system_878bd804e10160fa8b4c33c7c681e40b_1
$
```

Figure 10.6: Control plane components

The output shows that four control plane components are running in Docker containers in the **minikube** node.

5. Check for the first node component, **kube-proxy**, with the following command:

```
docker ps --filter "name=kube-proxy" | grep -v "pause"
```

Similar to *Step 4*, this command lists a **kube-proxy** component, which is running in a Docker container:

```
$ docker ps --filter "name=kube-proxy" | grep -v "pause"
CONTAINER ID        IMAGE                   COMMAND                      CREATED
     STATUS              PORTS              NAMES
7b32218709e8        7d54289267dc            "/usr/local/bin/kube…"   21 minutes ago
     Up 21 minutes                         k8s_kube-proxy_kube-proxy-hjp4j_kube-s
ystem_8a6763ec-8272-45bf-83a0-2160f78bb738_1
$ 
```

Figure 10.7: kube-proxy in minikube

It can be seen that the **kube-proxy** component running in the Docker container has been up for 21 minutes.

6. Check for the second node component, **kubelet**, with the following command:

```
pgrep -l kubelet
```

This command lists the process with its ID running in **minikube**:

```
2554 kubelet
```

Since **kubelet** communicates between the container runtime and API server, it is configured to run directly on the machine instead of inside a Docker container.

7. Disconnect from the **minikube** node connected in *Step 3* with the following command:

```
exit
```

You should have returned to your terminal and get output similar to the following:

```
logout
```

In this exercise, you have installed a Kubernetes cluster and checked the architectural components. In the next section, the Kubernetes API and access methods will be presented to connect and consume the cluster created in this section.

THE KUBERNETES API AND ACCESS

The **Kubernetes API** is the fundamental building block of the Kubernetes system. It is the home for all communication between the components in the cluster. External communication, such as user commands, is also executed against the Kubernetes API as REST API calls. The Kubernetes API is a resource-based interface over HTTP. In other words, the API server is oriented to work with resources to create and manage Kubernetes resources. In this section, you will connect to the API, and in the following section, you will start working with Kubernetes resources, including, but not limited to, Pods, Deployments, Statefulsets, and Services.

Kubernetes has an official command-line tool for client access, named **kubectl**. If you want to access a Kubernetes cluster, you need to install the **kubectl** tool and configure it to connect to your cluster. Then you can securely use the tool to manage the life cycle of applications running the cluster. **kubectl** is capable of essential create, read, update, and delete operations, as well as troubleshooting and log retrieval.

For instance, you can install a containerized application with **kubectl**, scale it to more replicas, check the logs, and finally delete it if you do not need it further. Furthermore, **kubectl** has cluster management commands to check the status of the cluster and servers. Therefore, **kubectl** is a vital command-line tool for accessing Kubernetes clusters and managing the applications.

kubectl is the key to controlling Kubernetes clusters with its rich set of commands. The essential basic and deployment-related commands can be listed as follows:

- **kubectl create**: This command creates a resource from a filename with the **-f** flag or standard terminal input. It is helpful when creating resources for the first time.

- **kubectl apply**: This command creates or updates the configuration to a Kubernetes resource, similar to the **create** command. It is an essential command if you are changing the resource configuration after the first creation.

- **kubectl get**: This command displays one or multiple resources from the cluster with its name, labels, and further information.

- **kubectl edit**: This command edits a Kubernetes resource directly in the terminal with an editor such as **vi**.

- **kubectl delete**: This command deletes Kubernetes resources and passes filenames, resource names, and label flags.

- **kubectl scale**: This command changes the number of resources of a Kubernetes cluster.

Similarly, the cluster management and configuration commands required are listed as follows:

- **kubectl cluster-info**: This command displays a summary of the cluster with its API and DNS services.

- **kubectl api-resources**: This command lists the supported API resources on the server. It is especially helpful if you work with different installations of Kubernetes that support different sets of API resources.

- **kubectl version**: This command prints the client and server version information. If you are working with multiple Kubernetes clusters with different versions, it is a helpful command to catch version mismatches.

- **kubectl config**: This command configures **kubectl** to connect different clusters to each other. **kubectl** is a CLI tool designed to work with multiple clusters by changing its configuration.

In the following exercise, you will install and configure **kubectl** to connect to the local Kubernetes cluster and start exploring the Kubernetes API with the help of its rich set of commands.

EXERCISE 10.02: ACCESSING KUBERNETES CLUSTERS WITH KUBECTL

Kubernetes clusters are installed in cloud systems and can be accessed from various locations. To access the clusters securely and reliably, you need a reliable client tool, which is the official client tool of Kubernetes—namely, **kubectl**. In this exercise, you will install, configure, and use **kubectl** to explore its capabilities along with the Kubernetes API.

To complete this exercise, perform the following steps:

1. Download the latest version of the **kubectl** executable for your operating system and set this as the executable for your local system by running the following command in your terminal:

```
# Linux
curl -LO https://storage.googleapis.com/kubernetes-release/
release/'curl -s https://storage.googleapis.com/kubernetes-release/
release/stable.txt'/bin/linux/amd64/kubectl

# MacOS
curl -LO "https://storage.googleapis.com/kubernetes-release/
release/$(curl -s https://storage.googleapis.com/kubernetes-release/
release/stable.txt)/bin/darwin/amd64/kubectl"

chmod +x kubectl

sudo mv kubectl /usr/local/bin
```

These preceding commands download the binary for Linux or Mac and make it ready to use in the terminal:

```
/docker-ws $ curl -LO "https://storage.googleapis.com/kubernetes-release/release/$
(curl -s https://storage.googleapis.com/kubernetes-release/release/stable.txt)/bin/
darwin/amd64/kubectl"
  % Total    % Received % Xferd  Average Speed   Time    Time     Time  Current
                                 Dload  Upload   Total   Spent    Left  Speed
100 47.2M  100 47.2M    0     0  6261k      0  0:00:07  0:00:07 --:--:-- 6551k
/docker-ws $ chmod +x ./kubectl
/docker-ws $ sudo mv ./kubectl /usr/local/bin/kubectl
/docker-ws $ ▓
```

Figure 10.8: Installation of minikube

2. In your terminal, run the following command to configure **kubectl** to connect to the **minikube** cluster and use it for further access:

```
kubectl config use-context minikube
```

The **use-context** command configures the **kubectl** context to use the **minikube** cluster. For the following steps, all commands will communicate with the Kubernetes cluster running inside **minikube**:

```
Switched to context "minikube".
```

3. Check for the cluster and client version with the following command:

```
kubectl version --short
```

This command returns the human-readable client and server version information:

```
Client Version: v1.17.2
Server Version: v1.17.0
```

4. Check for further information about the cluster with the following command:

```
kubectl cluster-info
```

This command shows a summary of Kubernetes components, including the master and DNS:

```
Kubernetes master is running at https://192.168.64.5:8443
KubeDNS is running at https://192.168.64.5:8445/api/v1/
namespaces/kube-system/Services/kube-dns:dns/proxy

To further debug and diagnose cluster problems, use
'kubectl cluster-info dump'.
```

5. Get a list of the nodes in the cluster with the following command:

```
kubectl get nodes
```

Since the cluster is a **minikube** local cluster, there is only one node named **minikube** with the **master** role:

NAME	STATUS	ROLES	AGE	VERSION
Minikube	Ready	master	41h	v1.17.0

6. List the supported resources in the Kubernetes API with the following command:

```
kubectl api-resources --output="name"
```

This command lists the **name** field of the **api-resources** supported in the Kubernetes API server. The long list shows how Kubernetes creates different abstractions to run containerized applications:

```
 /docker-ws $ kubectl api-resources --output="name"
bindings
componentstatuses
configmaps
endpoints
events
limitranges
namespaces
nodes
persistentvolumeclaims
persistentvolumes
pods
podtemplates
replicationcontrollers
resourcequotas
secrets
serviceaccounts
services
mutatingwebhookconfigurations.admissionregistration.k8s.io
validatingwebhookconfigurations.admissionregistration.k8s.io
customresourcedefinitions.apiextensions.k8s.io
apiservices.apiregistration.k8s.io
controllerrevisions.apps
daemonsets.apps
deployments.apps
replicasets.apps
statefulsets.apps
tokenreviews.authentication.k8s.io
localsubjectaccessreviews.authorization.k8s.io
selfsubjectaccessreviews.authorization.k8s.io
selfsubjectrulesreviews.authorization.k8s.io
subjectaccessreviews.authorization.k8s.io
horizontalpodautoscalers.autoscaling
cronjobs.batch
jobs.batch
certificatesigningrequests.certificates.k8s.io
leases.coordination.k8s.io
endpointslices.discovery.k8s.io
events.events.k8s.io
ingresses.extensions
nodes.metrics.k8s.io
pods.metrics.k8s.io
ingresses.networking.k8s.io
networkpolicies.networking.k8s.io
runtimeclasses.node.k8s.io
poddisruptionbudgets.policy
podsecuritypolicies.policy
clusterrolebindings.rbac.authorization.k8s.io
clusterroles.rbac.authorization.k8s.io
rolebindings.rbac.authorization.k8s.io
roles.rbac.authorization.k8s.io
priorityclasses.scheduling.k8s.io
csidrivers.storage.k8s.io
csinodes.storage.k8s.io
storageclasses.storage.k8s.io
volumeattachments.storage.k8s.io
 /docker-ws $
```

Figure 10.9: Kubernetes resource listing

The output lists the API resources available in the Kubernetes cluster we have connected to. As you can see, there are tens of resources you can use and each of them helps you to create cloud-native, scalable, and reliable applications.

In this exercise, you have connected to the Kubernetes cluster and checked the functionalities of the client tool. **kubectl** is the most critical tool for accessing and managing applications running in Kubernetes. By the end of this exercise, you will have learned how to install, configure, and connect to a Kubernetes cluster. In addition, you will have checked its version, the statuses of its nodes, and the available API resources. Using **kubectl** effectively is an essential task in daily life for developers interacting with Kubernetes.

In the following section, the primary Kubernetes resources (seen in part of the last step in the previous exercise) will be presented.

KUBERNETES RESOURCES

Kubernetes provides a rich set of abstractions over containers to define cloud-native applications. All these abstractions are designed as resources in the Kubernetes API and are managed by the control plane. In other words, the applications are defined as a set of resources in the control plane. At the same time, node components try to achieve the state specified in the resources. If a Kubernetes resource is assigned to a node, the node components focus on attaching the required volumes and network interfaces to keep the application up and running.

Let's assume you will deploy the backend of the InstantPizza reservation system on Kubernetes. The backend consists of a database and a web server for handling REST operations. You will need to define a couple of resources in Kubernetes:

- A **StatefulSet** resource for the database

- A **Service** resource to connect to the database from other components such as the web server

- A **Deployment** resource to deploy the web server in a scalable way

- A **Service** resource to enable outside connections to the web server

When these resources are defined in the control plane via **kubectl**, the node components will create the required containers, networks, and storage in the cluster.

Each resource has distinctive characteristics and schema in the Kubernetes API. In this section, you will learn about the fundamental Kubernetes resources, including **Pods**, **Deployments**, **StatefulSet**, and **Services**. In addition, you will learn about more complex Kubernetes resources such as **Ingresses**, **Horizontal Pod Autoscaling**, and **RBAC Authorization** in Kubernetes.

PODS

The Pod is the fundamental building block of containerized applications in Kubernetes. It consists of one or more containers that could share the network, storage, and memory. Kubernetes schedules all the containers in a Pod into the same node. Also, the containers in the Pod are scaled up or down together. The relationship between containers, Pods, and nodes can be outlined as follows:

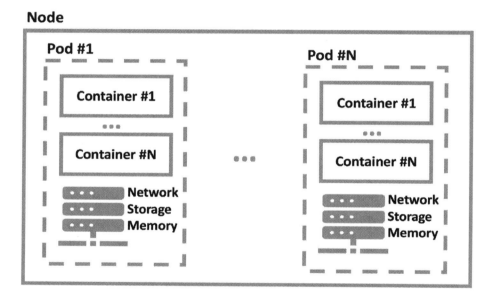

Figure 10.10: Containers, Pods, and nodes

It can be seen from the preceding diagram that a Pod can contain multiple containers. All these containers share a common network, storage, and memory resources.

The Pod definition is straightforward, with four main sections:

```
apiVersion: v1
kind: Pod
metadata:
  name: server
spec:
```

```
  containers:
  - name: main
    image: nginx
```

These four sections are required for all Kubernetes resources:

- **apiVersion** defines the versioned schema of this resource of an object.

- **kind** represents the REST resource name.

- **metadata** holds the information of the resource, such as names, labels, and annotations.

- **spec** is the resource-specific part where resource-specific information is kept.

When the preceding server Pod is created in the Kubernetes API, the API will first check whether the definition is correct according to the **apiVersion=v1** and **kind=Pod** schema. Then, the scheduler will assign the Pod to a node. Following that, the **kubelet** in the node will create the **nginx** container for the **main** container.

Pods are the first abstraction of Kubernetes over containers, and they are the building blocks of more complex resources. In the following section, we will use resources such as Deployments and Statefulsets to encapsulate Pods to create more sophisticated applications.

DEPLOYMENTS

Deployments are a Kubernetes resource that focuses on scalability and high availability. Deployments encapsulate Pods to scale up, down, and roll out new versions. In other words, you can define a three-replica web server Pod as a Deployment. Deployment controllers in the control plane will guarantee the number of replicas. Besides, when you update the Deployment to a newer version, the controllers will gradually update the application instances.

The definitions of Deployments and Pods are similar, although labels and replicas are added to the schema of Deployments:

```
apiVersion: apps/v1
kind: Deployment
metadata:
  name: server
spec:
  replicas: 10
  selector:
    matchLabels:
```

```
        app: server
  template:
    metadata:
      labels:
          app: server
    spec:
      containers:
      - name: main
        image: nginx
        ports:
        - containerPort: 80
```

The Deployment **server** has 10 replicas of the Pod specification with the label **app:server**. In addition, port **80** of the container is published for each main container of the server instance. The Deployment controller will create or delete the instances to match the 10 replicas of the defined Pod. In other words, if a node with two running instances of the server Deployment goes offline, the controller will create two additional Pods on the remaining nodes. This automation of Kubernetes allows us to create scalable and highly available applications out of the box.

In the following section, Kubernetes resources for stateful applications, such as databases and message queues, will be presented.

STATEFULSETS

Kubernetes supports running stateful applications that store their states on the disk volumes with **StatefulSet** resources. StatefulSets make it possible to run database applications or data analysis tools in Kubernetes with the same reliability and high availability of temporary applications.

The definition of StatefulSets resembles the definition of **Deployments**, with **volume mount** and **claim additions**:

```
apiVersion: apps/v1
kind: StatefulSet
metadata:
  name: database
spec:
  selector:
    matchLabels:
        app: mysql
  serviceName: mysql
  replicas: 1
```

```
template:
  metadata:
    labels:
      app: mysql
  spec:
    containers:
    - name: mysql
      image: mysql:5.7
      env:
        - name: MYSQL_ROOT_PASSWORD
          value: "root"
      ports:
        - name: mysql
          containerPort: 3306
      volumeMounts:
        - name: data
          mountPath: /var/lib/mysql
          subPath: mysql
volumeClaimTemplates:
- metadata:
    name: data
  spec:
    accessModes: ["ReadWriteOnce"]
    resources:
      requests:
        storage: 2Gi
```

The database resource defines a **MySQL** database with a disk volume of **2 GB**. When the server **StatefulSet** resource is created in the Kubernetes API, **cloud-controller-manager** will create a volume and make it ready on the scheduled node. While creating the volume, it uses the specification under **volumeClaimTemplates**. Then, the node will mount the volume in the container according to the **volumeMounts** section in **spec**.

In this resource definition, there is also an example of setting an environment variable for **MYSQL_ROOT_PASSWORD**. Statefulsets are vital resources in Kubernetes since they enable running stateful applications in the same cluster with ephemeral workloads.

In the following resource, the Kubernetes solution for the connection between Pods will be presented.

SERVICES

Kubernetes clusters host multiple applications running in various nodes, and most of the time, these applications need to communicate with each other. Assume you have a three-instance Deployment of your backend and a two-instance Deployment of your frontend application. Five Pods run, spread over the cluster with their IP addresses. Since the frontend instances need to connect to the backend, the frontend instances need to know the IP addresses of backend instances, as shown in *Figure 10.11*:

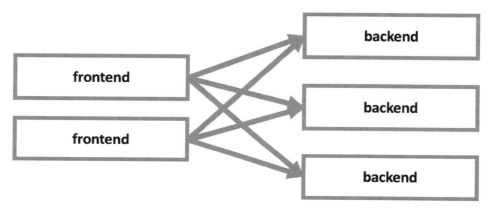

Figure 10.11: Frontend and backend instances

However, this is not a sustainable approach, with scaling up or down and the prospect of numerous potential failures in the cluster. Kubernetes proposes **Service** resources to define a set of Pods with labels and access them using the name of the Service. For instance, the frontend applications can connect to a backend instance by just using the address of **backend-service**, as illustrated in *Figure 10.12*:

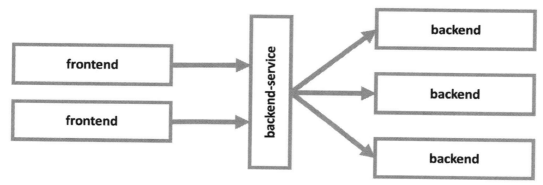

Figure 10.12: Frontend and backend instances connected via backend-service

The definition of the Service resource is reasonably straightforward, as shown here:

```
apiVersion: v1
kind: Service
metadata:
  name: my-db
spec:
  selector:
    app: mysql
  ports:
    - protocol: TCP
      port: 3306
      targetPort: 3306
```

When the **my-db** Service is created, all other Pods in the cluster will be able to connect to the Pods with the label **app:mysql** at port **3306** via the address, **my-db**. In the following resource, external access to the Services in the cluster by using the Kubernetes Ingress resources will be presented.

INGRESS

Kubernetes clusters are designed to serve applications in and outside the cluster. Ingress resources are defined to expose Services to the outside world with additional features such as external URLs and load balancing. Although the Ingress resources are native Kubernetes objects, they require an Ingress controller up and running in the cluster. In other words, Ingress controllers are not part of the **kube-controller-manager**, and you need to install one in your cluster. There are multiple implementations available on the market. However, Kubernetes currently supports and maintains **GCE** and **nginx** controllers officially.

> **NOTE**
>
> A list of additional Ingress controllers is available in the official documentation at the following link: https://kubernetes.io/docs/concepts/Services-networking/Ingress-controllers.

An Ingress resource with a host URL of **my-db.docker-workshop.io** to connect to port **3306** on the **my-db** Service looks like the following:

```
apiVersion: networking.k8s.io/v1beta1
kind: Ingress
metadata:
  name: my-db
spec:
  rules:
  - host: my-db.docker-workshop.io
    http:
      paths:
      - path: /
        backend:
          serviceName: my-db
          servicePort: 3306
```

Ingress resources are essential to open the Services to the outside world. However, their configuration can be more complicated than it seems. The Ingress resources could require individual annotations based on the Ingress controller running in your cluster.

In the following resource, automatic scaling of the Pods with the help of the Horizontal Pod Autoscaler will be covered.

HORIZONTAL POD AUTOSCALING

Kubernetes clusters provide a scalable and reliable containerized application environment. However, it is cumbersome and unfeasible to manually track the usage of applications and scale up or down when needed. Therefore, Kubernetes provides the Horizontal Pod Autoscaler to scale the number of Pods according to CPU utilization automatically.

Horizontal Pod Autoscalers are a Kubernetes resource with a target resource for scaling and target metrics:

```
apiVersion: Autoscaling/v1
kind: HorizontalPodAutoscaler
metadata:
  name: server-scaler
spec:
  scaleTargetRef:
    apiVersion: apps/v1
```

```
   kind: Deployment
   name: server
 minReplicas: 1
 maxReplicas: 10
 targetCPUUtilizationPercentage: 50
```

When the **server-scaler** resource is created, the Kubernetes control plane will try to achieve the target CPU utilization of **50%** by scaling up or down the Deployment named as the **server**. In addition, the minimum and maximum numbers of replicas are set to **1** and **10**. This ensures that the Deployment is not scaled to **0** when it is not used, nor scaled too high so that it consumes all the resources in the cluster. Horizontal Pod Autoscaler resources are essential parts of Kubernetes for creating scalable and reliable applications that are automatically managed.

In the following section, you will learn about authorization in Kubernetes.

RBAC AUTHORIZATION

Kubernetes clusters are designed to connect and make changes to resources securely. However, when the applications are running in a production environment, it is critical to limit the scope of actions of the users.

Let's assume that you have conferred extensive powers on everyone in your project group. In such circumstances, it will not be possible to protect your application running in the cluster from deletion or misconfiguration. Kubernetes provides **Role-Based Access Control** (**RBAC**) to manage users' access and abilities based on the roles given to them. In other words, Kubernetes can limit the ability of users to perform specific tasks on specific Kubernetes resources.

Let's start with the **Role** resource to define the capabilities:

```
kind: Role
apiVersion: rbac.authorization.k8s.io/v1
metadata:
  namespace: critical-project
  name: Pod-reader
rules:
  - apiGroups: [""]
    resources: ["Pods"]
    verbs: ["get", "watch", "list"]
```

The **Pod-reader** role defined in the preceding snippet is only allowed to **get**, **watch**, and **list** the Pod resources in the **critical-project** namespace. When the user only has the role **Pod-reader**, they will not be able to delete or modify the resources in the **critical-project** namespace. Let's see how roles are assigned to users using the **RoleBinding** resource:

```
kind: RoleBinding
apiVersion: rbac.authorization.k8s.io/v1
metadata:
  name: read-Pods
  namespace: critical-project
subjects:
  - kind: User
    name: new-intern
roleRef:
  kind: Role
  name: Pod-reader
  apiGroup: rbac.authorization.k8s.io
```

The **RoleBinding** resource combines the **Role** resource with the subjects. In **read-Pods RoleBinding**, the user **new-intern** is assigned to the **Pod-reader Role**. When the **read-Pods** resource is created in the Kubernetes API, it will not be possible for the **new-intern** user to modify or delete the Pods in the **critical-project** namespace.

In the following exercise, you will see the Kubernetes resources in action using **kubectl** and the local Kubernetes cluster.

EXERCISE 10.03: KUBERNETES RESOURCES IN ACTION

Cloud-native containerized applications require multiple Kubernetes resources due to their complex nature. In this exercise, you will create an instance of the popular WordPress application on Kubernetes by using one **Statefulset**, one **Deployment**, and two **Service** resources. In addition, you will check the status of the Pods and connect to the Service using **kubectl** and **minikube**.

To complete this exercise, perform the following steps:

1. Create a **StatefulSet** definition in a file, named **database.yaml**, with the following content:

```
apiVersion: apps/v1
kind: StatefulSet
```

```
metadata:
  name: database
spec:
  selector:
    matchLabels:
      app: mysql
  serviceName: mysql
  replicas: 1
  template:
    metadata:
      labels:
        app: mysql
    spec:
      containers:
      - name: mysql
        image: mysql:5.7
        env:
        - name: MYSQL_ROOT_PASSWORD
          value: "root"
        ports:
        - name: mysql
          containerPort: 3306
        volumeMounts:
        - name: data
          mountPath: /var/lib/mysql
          subPath: mysql
  volumeClaimTemplates:
  - metadata:
      name: data
    spec:
      accessModes: ["ReadWriteOnce"]
      resources:
        requests:
          storage: 2Gi
```

This **StatefulSet** resource defines a database to be used by WordPress in the following steps. There is only one container named **mysql** with the Docker image of **mysql:5.7**. There is one environment variable for the root password and one port defined in the container specification. In addition, one volume is claimed and attached to **/var/lib/mysql** in the preceding definition.

2. Deploy the **StatefulSet** to the cluster by running the following command in your terminal:

```
kubectl apply -f database.yaml
```

This command will apply the definition in the **database.yaml** file since it is passed with the **-f** flag:

```
StatefulSet.apps/database created
```

3. Create a **database-service.yaml** file in your local computer with the following content:

```
apiVersion: v1
kind: Service
metadata:
  name: database-service
spec:
  selector:
    app: mysql
  ports:
    - protocol: TCP
      port: 3306
      targetPort: 3306
```

This Service resource defines a Service abstraction over database instances. WordPress instances will connect to the database by using the specified Service.

4. Deploy the Service resource with the following command:

```
kubectl apply -f database-service.yaml
```

This command deploys the resource defined in the **database-service.yaml** file:

```
Service/database-service created
```

5. Create a file with the name **wordpress.yaml** and the following content:

```
apiVersion: apps/v1
kind: Deployment
metadata:
  name: wordpress
  labels:
    app: wordpress
spec:
```

```
replicas: 3
selector:
  matchLabels:
    app: wordpress
template:
  metadata:
    labels:
      app: wordpress
  spec:
    containers:
    - image: wordpress:4.8-apache
      name: wordpress
      env:
      - name: WORDPRESS_DB_HOST
        value: database-Service
      - name: WORDPRESS_DB_PASSWORD
        value: root
      ports:
      - containerPort: 80
        name: wordpress
```

This **Deployment** resource defines a three-replica WordPress installation. There is one container defined with the **wordpress:4.8-apache** image and **database-service** is passed to the application as an environment variable. With the help of this environment variable, WordPress connects to the database deployed in *Step 3*. In addition, a container port is defined on port **80** so that we can reach the application from the browser in the following steps.

6. Deploy the WordPress Deployment with the following command:

```
kubectl apply -f wordpress.yaml
```

This command deploys the resource defined in the **wordpress.yaml** file:

```
Deployment.apps/wordpress created
```

7. Create a **wordpress-service.yaml** file on your local computer with the following content:

```
apiVersion: v1
kind: Service
metadata:
  name: wordpress-service
spec:
```

```
type: LoadBalancer
selector:
  app: wordpress
ports:
  - protocol: TCP
    port: 80
    targetPort: 80
```

This Service resource defines a Service abstraction over the WordPress instances. The Service will be used to connect to WordPress from the outside world via port **80**.

8. Deploy the **Service** resource with the following command:

```
kubectl apply -f wordpress-service.yaml
```

This command deploys the resource defined in the **wordpress-service. yaml** file:

```
Service/wordpress-service created
```

9. Check the status of all running Pods with the following command:

```
kubectl get pods
```

This command lists all the Pods with their statuses, and there are one database and three WordPress Pods with the **Running** status:

```
/docker-ws $ kubectl get pods
NAME                          READY   STATUS    RESTARTS   AGE
database-0                    1/1     Running   0          117s
wordpress-6c59fbbb8d-gcht4    1/1     Running   0          53s
wordpress-6c59fbbb8d-rmzqv    1/1     Running   0          53s
wordpress-6c59fbbb8d-x6gmb    1/1     Running   0          53s
/docker-ws $
```

Figure 10.13: Pod listing

10. Get the URL of **wordpress-service** by running the following command:

```
minikube service wordpress-service --url
```

This command lists the URL of the Service, accessible from the host machine:

```
http://192.168.64.5:32765
```

Open the URL in your browser to access the setup screen of WordPress:

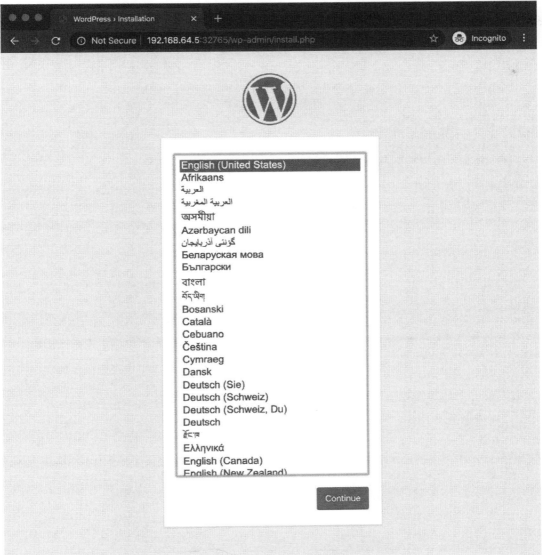

Figure 10.14: WordPress setup screen

The setup screen indicates that the WordPress instances are running and accessible via their Service. Furthermore, it shows that the **StatefulSet** database is also running and accessible via its Service by the WordPress instances.

In this exercise, you have used different Kubernetes resources to define and install a complex application in Kubernetes. First, you deployed a **Statefulset** resource for installing MySQL in the cluster. Then, you deployed a **Service** resource to reach the database inside the cluster. Following that, you deployed a **Deployment** resource to install the WordPress application. Similarly, you created another **Service** to reach the WordPress application outside the cluster. You have created independently scalable and reliable microservices using different Kubernetes resources and connected them. Furthermore, you have learned how to check the status of **Pods**. In the following section, you will learn about the Kubernetes package manager: Helm.

KUBERNETES PACKAGE MANAGER: HELM

Kubernetes applications consist of multiple containers, volumes, and networking resources due to the nature of cloud-native microservices architecture. The microservice architecture divides large applications into smaller chunks and thus results in numerous Kubernetes resources and a vast amount of configuration values.

Helm is the official Kubernetes package manager that collects the resources of applications as templates and fills them with the values provided. The essential advantage here is the accumulated community knowledge of installing the applications with the best practices. You can install an app with the most popular methods, even if you are working with it for the first time. Besides, working with Helm charts augments the developer experience.

For instance, installing and managing complex applications in Kubernetes becomes similar to downloading apps in Apple Store or Google Play Store, with fewer commands and configurations. In Helm terminology, a collection of resources for a single application is a **chart**. Charts can be used to deploy anything from a simple pod to a full web app stack with HTTP servers, databases, caches, and such when you work with the Helm package manager. The encapsulation of applications as charts makes it easier to deploy complicated applications.

In addition, Helm has a chart repository with popular and stable applications that are packaged as charts and maintained by the Helm community. The stable Helm chart repository has a high variety of applications, including databases such as MySQL, PostgreSQL, CouchDB, and InfluxDB; CI/CD tools such as Jenkins, Concourse, and Drone; or monitoring tools such as Grafana, Prometheus, Datadog, and Fluentd. The chart repository not only makes it easier to install apps but also ensures that you are deploying the application with the latest, well-accepted methods in the Kubernetes community.

Helm is a client tool, with its latest version being Helm 3. You only need to install it on your local system, configure it for the chart repository, and then you can start deploying applications. Helm is a powerful package manager with its exhaustive set of commands, including the following:

- **`helm repo`**: This command adds, lists, removes, updates, and indexes chart repositories to the local Helm installation.

- **`helm search`**: This command searches for Helm charts in various repositories using user-provided keywords or chart names.

- **`helm install`**: This command installs a Helm chart on the Kubernetes cluster. It is also possible to set variables with a value file or command-line parameters.

- **`helm list`** or **`helm ls`**: These commands list the installed charts from the cluster.

- **`helm uninstall`**: This command removes an installed chart from Kubernetes.

- **`helm upgrade`**: This command upgrades an installed chart with new values or new chart versions on the cluster.

In the following exercise, you will install Helm, connect to a chart repository, and install applications on the cluster.

EXERCISE 10.04: INSTALLING THE MYSQL HELM CHART

Helm charts are installed and managed by the official client tool, **helm**. You need to install the **helm** client tool locally to retrieve the charts from the chart repository and then install applications on the clusters. In this exercise, you will start working with Helm and install **MySQL** from its stable Helm chart.

To complete this exercise, perform the following steps:

1. Run the following command in your terminal to download the latest version of the **helm** executable with the installation script:

```
curl https://raw.githubusercontent.com/helm/helm/master/scripts/
get-helm-3 | bash
```

The script downloads the appropriate binary of **helm** for your operating system and makes it ready to use in the Terminal:

```
/docker-ws $ curl https://raw.githubusercontent.com/helm/helm/master/scripts/get-helm-3 | bash
  % Total    % Received % Xferd  Average Speed   Time    Time     Time  Current
                                 Dload  Upload   Total   Spent    Left  Speed
100  6617  100  6617    0     0  62424      0 --:--:-- --:--:-- --:--:-- 62424
Downloading https://get.helm.sh/helm-v3.0.3-darwin-amd64.tar.gz
Preparing to install helm into /usr/local/bin
helm installed into /usr/local/bin/helm
 /docker-ws $
```

Figure 10.15: Installation of Helm

2. Add the chart repository to **helm** by running the following command in your terminal:

```
helm repo add stable https://kubernetes-charts.storage.googleapis.
com/
```

This command adds the URL of the chart repository to the locally installed **helm** instance:

```
"stable" has been added to your repositories
```

3. List the charts in the **stable** repository from *Step 2* with the following command:

```
helm search repo stable
```

This command will list all the available charts in the repository:

```
 /docker-ws $ helm search repo stable
NAME                              CHART VERSION   APP VERSION         DESCRIPTION
stable/acs-engine-autoscaler      2.2.2           2.1.1               DEPRECATED Scales worker nodes within agent pools
stable/aerospike                  0.3.2           v4.5.0.5            A Helm chart for Aerospike in Kubernetes
stable/airflow                    6.0.0           1.10.4              Airflow is a platform to programmatically autho...
stable/ambassador                 5.3.1           0.86.1              A Helm chart for Datawire Ambassador
stable/anchore-engine             1.4.2           0.6.1               Anchore container analysis and policy evaluatio...
stable/apm-server                 2.1.5           7.0.0               The server receives data from the Elastic APM a...
stable/ark                        4.2.2           0.10.2              DEPRECATED A Helm chart for ark
stable/artifactory                7.3.1           6.1.0               DEPRECATED Universal Repository Manager support...
stable/artifactory-ha             0.4.1           6.2.0               DEPRECATED Universal Repository Manager support...
stable/atlantis                   3.11.0          v0.11.1             A Helm chart for Atlantis https://www.runatlant...
stable/auditbeat                  1.1.0           6.7.0               A lightweight shipper to audit the activities o...
stable/aws-cluster-autoscaler     0.3.3                               Scales worker nodes within autoscaling groups.
stable/aws-iam-authenticator      0.1.2           1.0                 A Helm chart for aws-iam-authenticator
stable/bitcoind                   1.0.0           0.17.1              Bitcoin is an innovative payment network and a ...
stable/bookstack                  1.2.0           0.27.5              BookStack is a simple, self-hosted, easy-to-use...
stable/buildkite                  0.2.4           3                   DEPRECATED Agent for Buildkite
stable/burrow                     1.5.2           0.29.0              Burrow is a permissionless smart contract machine
stable/centrifugo                 3.1.1           2.1.0               Centrifugo is a real-time messaging server.
stable/cerebro                    1.3.1           0.8.5               A Helm chart for Cerebro - a web admin tool tha...
stable/cert-manager               v0.6.7          v0.6.2              A Helm chart for cert-manager
stable/chaoskube                  3.1.3           0.14.0              Chaoskube periodically kills random pods in you...
stable/chartmuseum                2.7.1           0.11.0              Host your own Helm Chart Repository
stable/chronograf                 1.1.0           1.7.12              Open-source web application written in Go and R...
stable/clamav                     1.0.5           1.6                 An Open-Source antivirus engine for detecting t...
stable/cloudserver                1.0.4           8.1.5               An open-source Node.js implementation of the Am...
stable/cluster-autoscaler         6.4.0           1.14.6              Scales worker nodes within autoscaling groups.
stable/cluster-overprovisioner    0.2.6           1.0                 Installs a deployment that overprovisions t...
stable/cockroachdb                3.0.5           19.2.3              CockroachDB is a scalable, survivable, strongly...
stable/collabora-code             1.0.6           4.0.3.1             A Helm chart for Collabora Office - CODE-Edition
stable/concourse                  8.3.7           5.6.0               DEPRECATED Concourse is a simple and scalable C...
stable/consul                     3.9.4           1.5.3               Highly available and distributed service discov...
stable/contour                    0.2.0           v0.15.0             Contour Ingress controller for Kubernetes
stable/coredns                    1.9.2           1.6.7               CoreDNS is a DNS server that chains plugins and...
stable/cosbench                   1.0.1           0.0.6               A benchmark tool for cloud object storage services
stable/coscale                    1.0.0           3.16.0              CoScale Agent
stable/couchbase-operator         1.0.2           1.2.2               A Helm chart to deploy the Couchbase Autonomous...
stable/couchdb                    2.3.0           2.3.1               DEPRECATED A database featuring seamless multi-...
stable/dask                       3.1.1           1.1.5               DEPRECATED Distributed computation in Python wi...
stable/dask-distributed           2.0.2                               DEPRECATED: Distributed computation in Python
stable/datadog                    1.39.8          7                   DataDog Agent
stable/dex                        2.8.0           2.21.0              CoreOS Dex
stable/distributed-jmeter         1.0.1           3.3                 A Distributed JMeter Helm chart
stable/distributed-tensorflow     0.1.3           1.6.0               A Helm chart for running distributed TensorFlow...
stable/distribution               0.4.2           1.1.0               DEPRECATED A Helm chart for JFrog Distribution
stable/dmarc2logstash             1.2.0           1.0.3               Provides a POP3-polled DMARC XML report injecto...
stable/docker-registry            1.9.1           2.7.1               A Helm chart for Docker Registry
stable/dokuwiki                   6.0.6           0.20180422.201901061035  DokuWiki is a standards-compliant, simple to us...
stable/drone                      2.6.1           1.6.1               Drone is a Continuous Delivery system built on ...
stable/drupal                     6.2.4           8.8.2               One of the most versatile open source content m...
stable/efs-provisioner            0.11.0          v2.4.0              A Helm chart for the AWS EFS external storage p...
stable/elastabot                  1.2.0           1.1.0               A Helm chart for Elastabot - a Slack bot compan...
stable/elastalert                 1.2.3           0.2.1               ElastAlert is a simple framework for alerting o...
stable/elastic-stack              1.8.0           6                   A Helm chart for ELK
stable/elasticsearch              1.32.2          6.8.2               Flexible and powerful open source, distributed ...
stable/elasticsearch-curator      2.1.3           5.7.6               A Helm chart for Elasticsearch Curator
stable/elasticsearch-exporter     2.3.0           1.1.0               Elasticsearch stats exporter for Prometheus
stable/envoy                      1.9.0           1.11.2              Envoy is an open source edge and service proxy,...
stable/etcd-operator              0.10.2          0.9.4               CoreOS etcd-operator Helm chart for Kubernetes
stable/ethereum                   1.0.0           v1.7.3              private Ethereum network Helm chart for Kubernetes
stable/eventrouter                0.2.3           0.2                 A Helm chart for eventruter (https://github.com...
stable/express-gateway            1.6.3           1.16.9              Express Gateway is an API Gateway that sits at ...
stable/external-dns               2.16.1          0.5.18              ExternalDNS is a Kubernetes addon that configur...
stable/factorio                   1.0.0           0.15.39             Factorio dedicated server.
stable/falco                      1.1.1           0.19.0              Falco
stable/filebeat                   4.0.0           7.4.0               A Helm chart to collect Kubernetes logs with fi...
stable/fluent-bit                 2.8.7           1.3.5               Fast and Lightweight Log/Data Forwarder for Lin...
stable/fluentd                    2.3.2           v2.4.0              A Fluentd Elasticsearch Helm chart for Kubernetes.
stable/fluentd-elasticsearch      2.0.7           2.3.2               DEPRECATED! - A Fluentd Helm chart for Kubernet...
stable/g2                         0.3.3           0.5.0               DEPRECATED G2 by AppsCode - Gearman in Golang
stable/gangway                    0.4.0           3.3.0               An application that can be used to easily enabl...
stable/gce-ingress                1.2.0           1.4.0               A GCE Ingress Controller
```

Figure 10.16: Chart repository listing

4. Install the MySQL chart with the following command:

```
helm install database stable/mysql
```

This command will install the MySQL Helm chart from the **stable** repository under the name **database** and print information on how to connect to the database:

```
/docker-ws $ helm install database stable/mysql
NAME: database
LAST DEPLOYED: Tue Feb 11 17:09:17 2020
NAMESPACE: default
STATUS: deployed
REVISION: 1
NOTES:
MySQL can be accessed via port 3306 on the following DNS name from within your cluster:
database-mysql.default.svc.cluster.local

To get your root password run:

    MYSQL_ROOT_PASSWORD=$(kubectl get secret --namespace default database-mysql -o jsonpath="{.data.mysql-root-password}" | base64 --decode; echo)

To connect to your database:

1. Run an Ubuntu pod that you can use as a client:

    kubectl run -i --tty ubuntu --image=ubuntu:16.04 --restart=Never -- bash -il

2. Install the mysql client:

    $ apt-get update && apt-get install mysql-client -y

3. Connect using the mysql cli, then provide your password:
    $ mysql -h database-mysql -p

To connect to your database directly from outside the K8s cluster:
    MYSQL_HOST=127.0.0.1
    MYSQL_PORT=3306

    # Execute the following command to route the connection:
    kubectl port-forward svc/database-mysql 3306

    mysql -h ${MYSQL_HOST} -P${MYSQL_PORT} -u root -p${MYSQL_ROOT_PASSWORD}
/docker-ws $
```

Figure 10.17: MySQL installation

The information in the output is valuable if you want to connect to the MySQL installation using the **mysql** client inside or outside the cluster.

5. Check the status of the installation with the following command:

```
helm ls
```

We can see that there is an installation of **mysql-chart-1.6.2** with the status **deployed**:

```
/docker-ws $ helm ls
NAME        NAMESPACE   REVISION   UPDATED                            STATUS     CHART         APP VERSION
database    default     1          2020-02-11 17:09:17.130815 +0100 CET   deployed   mysql-1.6.2   5.7.28
/docker-ws $
```

Figure 10.18: Helm installation status

You can also use the **helm ls** command to check the application and chart versions, such as **5.7.28** and **mysql-1.6.2**.

6. Check for the Kubernetes resources related to the installation from *Step 4* with the following command:

```
kubectl get all -l release=database
```

This command lists all the resources with the label **release = database**:

```
/docker-ws $ kubectl get all -l release=database
NAME                                      READY   STATUS    RESTARTS   AGE
pod/database-mysql-758d95c48d-8lxfv       1/1     Running   0          98s

NAME                      TYPE        CLUSTER-IP      EXTERNAL-IP   PORT(S)    AGE
service/database-mysql    ClusterIP   10.96.170.179   <none>        3306/TCP   98s

NAME                             READY   UP-TO-DATE   AVAILABLE   AGE
deployment.apps/database-mysql   1/1     1            1           98s

NAME                                        DESIRED   CURRENT   READY   AGE
replicaset.apps/database-mysql-758d95c48d   1         1         1       98s
/docker-ws $
```

Figure 10.19: Kubernetes resource listing

There are various resources listed since the installation of a production-grade MySQL instance is not straightforward and consists of multiple resources. Thanks to Helm, we do not need to configure each of these resources and connect them. In addition, listing with the label **release = database** is helpful to provide a troubleshooting overview when some parts of your Helm installation fail.

In this exercise, you have installed and configured the Kubernetes package manager, Helm, and installed applications using it. Helm is an essential tool if you are planning to use Kubernetes for production and need to manage complex applications.

In the following activity, you will configure and deploy the Panoramic Trekking App to the Kubernetes cluster.

ACTIVITY 10.01: INSTALLING THE PANORAMIC TREKKING APP ON KUBERNETES

You have been assigned to create a Deployment of the Panoramic Trekking App on Kubernetes. You will take advantage of the three-tier architecture of the Panoramic Trekking App with state-of-the-art Kubernetes resources. You will install the database using Helm, and the backend with **nginx** using a Statefulset. Therefore, you will design it as a Kubernetes application and manage it with **kubectl** and **helm**.

Perform the following steps to complete the exercise:

1. Install the database using the PostgreSQL Helm chart. Ensure that the **POSTGRES_PASSWORD** environment variable is set to **kubernetes**.

2. Create a Statefulset with two containers for the Panoramic Trekking App backend and **nginx**. Ensure that you are using the Docker images, **packtworkshops/ the-docker-workshop:chapter10-pta-web** and **packtworkshops/ the-docker-workshop:chapter10-pta-nginx**, for the containers. In order to store the static files, you need to create a **volumeClaimTemplate** section and mount it to the **/Service/static/** paths of both containers. Finally, do not forget to publish port **80** of the **nginx** container.

3. Create a Kubernetes Service for the Panoramic Trekking App to connect to the Statefulset created in *Step 2*. Ensure that the **type** of Service is **LoadBalancer**.

4. With a successful deployment, obtain the IP of the Kubernetes Service created in *Step 3* and connect to the **$SERVICE_IP/admin** address in the browser:

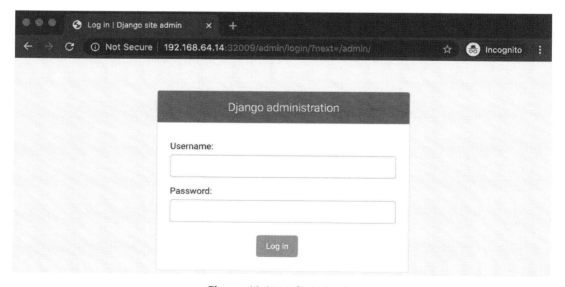

Figure 10.20: Admin login

5. Log in with the username **admin** and the password **changeme** and add new photos and countries:

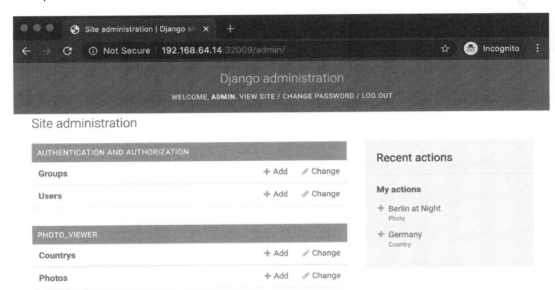

Figure 10.21: Admin setup

6. The Panoramic Trekking App will be available at the address **$SERVICE_IP/photo_viewer** in the browser:

Figure 10.22: Application view

> **NOTE**
>
> The solution for this activity can be found on page 707.

SUMMARY

This chapter focused on using Kubernetes to design, create, and manage containerized applications. Kubernetes is the up-and-coming container orchestrator in the market, with a high adoption rate and an active community. In this chapter, you have learned about its architecture and design, followed by the Kubernetes API and its access methods, and dove into the vital Kubernetes resources to create complex cloud-native applications.

Every exercise in this chapter aimed to illustrate the Kubernetes design approach and its capabilities. With the Kubernetes resources and its official client tool, `kubectl`, it is possible to configure, deploy, and manage containerized applications.

In the following chapter, you will learn about security in the Docker world. You will learn the security concepts for container runtimes, container images, and Linux environments, and how to securely run containers in Docker.

11

DOCKER SECURITY

OVERVIEW

In this chapter, we will give you the information you need to make sure your containers are secure and do not pose a security risk to the people using the applications running on them. You will work with privileged and non-privileged containers and learn why you should not be running your containers under the root user. This chapter will help you verify whether images are from a trusted source, using a signing key. You will also set up a security scan for your Docker images, ensuring your images are safe for use and distribution. You will work with AppArmor to further secure your containers by using them and Security Computing Mode (`seccomp`) for Linux to create and use `seccomp` profiles with your Docker images.

INTRODUCTION

This chapter tries to tackle a subject that could have an entire book dedicated to it. We attempt to go part of the way in educating you on how to approach security with Docker. Previous chapters have given you a solid foundation in using Docker to build your applications, and this chapter hopes to use that information to also provide secure and stable containers for them to run on.

Docker and the microservices architecture allow us to start with a more secure and robust environment to manage our services, but that doesn't mean we need to completely forget about security. This chapter provides details on some of the aspects we need to consider when we are creating and maintaining services across our environments, as well as the ways in which you can start to implement these procedures in your working systems.

Docker security should not be separated from your regular IT security process, as the concepts will be the same. Docker has a different approach to handle these concepts, but in general, a great place to start with Docker security is the following:

- **Access control**: Make sure that running containers cannot be accessed by an attacker and that privileges are also limited.

- **Updated and patched OS**: We need to make sure we are using trusted sources for our images. We also need to be able to scan our images to make sure any introduced applications are not also introducing extra vulnerabilities.

- **Data sensitivity**: All sensitive information should remain inaccessible. This could be passwords, personal information, or any other data you don't want to be made available to anyone.

In this chapter, we will cover a lot of information that will encompass the preceding points and more. We will start by considering the different access your Docker containers might have when running and how you can start to limit what can be performed by them. We will then look more closely at securing images, using signing keys, and how we can verify that they are from a trusted source. We will also practice scanning your images against known vulnerabilities to ensure that they are safe for use. The last two sections of this chapter will focus on using both the AppArmor and `seccomp` security profiles to further limit the capabilities and access your running containers can have.

> **NOTE**
>
> When using secrets and passwords in your Docker images, orchestration methods such as Swarm and Kubernetes offer secure ways to store your secrets without needing to store them as plaintext configurations for everyone to access. If you are not using one of these orchestration methods, we will also provide some ideas on how to use secrets in your images in the next chapter.

PRIVILEGED AND ROOT USER ACCESS IN CONTAINERS

One important way to improve the security of your containers is to reduce what an attacker can do if they manage to gain access. The types of command the attacker can run on the container are limited to the level of access the user who is running the processes on the container has. So, if there are no root or elevated privileges on the running container, this limits what the attacker can do. Another thing to remember is that if a container is compromised and is running as the root user, this may also allow the attacker to escape the container and access the host system running Docker.

Most processes running on the container are applications that don't need root access, and this is the same as running processes on a server, where you would not run them as root either. The applications running on the container should only have access to what they need. The reason why root access is provided, especially in base images, is because applications need to be installed on the container, but this should only be a temporary measure, with your complete image running as another user.

To do this, when creating our image, we can set up a Dockerfile and create a user that will run the processes on the container. The following line is the same as setting up a user on a Linux command line, where we set up the group first and then assign the user to this group:

```
RUN addgroup --gid <GID> <UID> && adduser <UID> -h <home_directory>
--disabled-password --uid <UID> --ingroup <UID> <user_name>
```

In the preceding command, we are also using the **adduser** option to set the **home** directory and disable a login password.

> **NOTE**
>
> **addgroup** and **adduser** are specific to Alpine-based images, which are Linux-based images but use different packages and utilities to Debian-based images. The reason why Alpine-based images use these packages is that they opt for more lightweight utilities and applications. If you are using Ubuntu-/Debian- or Red Hat-based images, you would need to instead use the **useradd** and **groupadd** commands, with the relevant options for those commands.

As you'll see in the upcoming exercise, we will then switch to the user we have specifically created to create the processes we are going to run. It is optional what you name the groups and users, but a lot of users prefer to use a four- or five-digit number as this will not highlight any further privileges of this user to a potential attacker and is usually standard practice for creating users and groups. In our Dockerfile, before we create our processes, we include the **USER** directive and include the user ID of the user we previously created:

```
USER <UID>
```

In this part of the chapter, we will introduce a new image and show the issues that can arise if the processes on the container are being run by the root user. We'll also show you how the root user in a container is the same as the root user on the underlying host. We'll then change our image to show the benefit of removing root access to the processes running on the container.

> **NOTE**
>
> Please use **touch** command to create files and **vim** command to work on the file using vim editor.

EXERCISE 11.01: RUNNING CONTAINERS AS THE ROOT USER

Many issues can arise when we are running container processes with the root user. This exercise will demonstrate specific security issues, such as changing the access rights, killing processes, making changes to DNS, and how your images and underlying operating system can be made vulnerable. You will observe that as the root user, an attacker would also be able to use tools such as **nmap** to scan the network for open ports and network targets.

You will also correct these issues, therefore limiting what an attacker can do on the running container:

1. Create a new Dockerfile named **Dockerfile_original** with your favorite text editor and enter the following code into the file. All of the commands are currently being run as the root user in this step:

```
1 FROM alpine
2
3 RUN apk update
4 RUN apk add wget curl nmap libcap
5
6 RUN echo "#!/sh\n" > test_memory.sh
7 RUN echo "cat /proc/meminfo; mpstat; pmap -x 1"
     >> test_memory.sh
8 RUN chmod 755 test_memory.sh
9
10 CMD ["sh", "test_memory.sh"]
```

This will create a basic application that will run a small script called **test_memory.sh**, which uses the **meminfo**, **mpstat**, and **pmap** commands to provide details on the container's memory status. You'll also notice that on *line 4*, we are installing some extra applications to view the network processes with **nmap** and to allow us to view the user container capabilities with the **libcap** library.

2. Build the **security-app** image and run the image in the same step:

```
docker build -t security-app . ; docker run -rm security-app
```

The output has been drastically reduced, and you should see the image build and then the memory report run:

```
MemTotal:        2036900 kB
MemFree:         1243248 kB
MemAvailable:    1576432 kB
Buffers:         73240 kB
...
```

3. Use the **whoami** command to view the running user on the container:

```
docker run --rm security-app whoami
```

It should not be any surprise that the running user is the root user:

```
root
```

4. Use the **capsh -print** command to see the processes that the user is able to run on the container. As the root user, you should have a large number of capabilities available:

```
docker run --rm -it security-app capsh -print
```

You'll notice that the user has access to changing the ownership of files (**cap_chown**), killing processes (**cap_kill**), and making changes to DNS (**cap_net_bind_service**), among other things. These are all high-level processes that can cause a lot of issues in a running environment and should not be available to the container:

```
Current: = cap_chown,cap_dac_override,cap_fowner,cap_fsetid,
cap_kill,cap_setgid,cap_setuid,cap_setpcap,cap_net_bind_service,
cap_net_raw,cap_sys_chroot,cap_mknod,cap_audit_write,
cap_setfcap+eip


groups=0(root),1(bin),2(daemon),3(sys),4(adm),6(disk),10(wheel),
11(floppy),20(dialout),26(tape),27(video)
```

5. As the root user, an attacker would also be able to use tools such as **nmap**, which we installed earlier, to scan the network for open ports and network targets. Run your container images again by passing the **nmap** command, looking for the opened **443** port under **localhost**:

```
docker run --rm -it security-app sh -c 'nmap -sS -p 443 localhost'
```

The output of the command is as follows:

```
Starting Nmap 7.70 ( https://nmap.org ) at 2019-11-13 02:40 UTC
Nmap scan report for localhost (127.0.0.1)
Host is up (0.000062s latency).
Other addresses for localhost (not scanned): ::1
PORT    STATE  SERVICE
443/tcp closed https
Nmap done: 1 IP address (1 host up) scanned in 0.27 seconds
```

> **NOTE**
>
> The preceding **nmap** scan doesn't find any open networks, but it is an elevated command that shouldn't be able to be run by any users. We will demonstrate later in this exercise that a non-root user is not able to run this command.

6. As previously mentioned, being the root user on your container is the same as being the root user on the underlying host. This can be demonstrated by mounting a file owned by the root onto the container. To do that, create a secret file. Echo your secret password into the **/tmp/secret.txt** file:

```
echo "secret password" > /tmp/secret.txt
```

Change the ownership to make sure the root user owns it:

```
sudo chown root /tmp/secret.txt
```

7. Use the **docker run** command to mount the file on the running container and check whether you are able to access it and view the data in the file. The user on the container can access the file that the root user on the host system should only have access to:

```
docker run -v /tmp/secret.txt:/tmp/secret.txt security-app sh -c 'cat /tmp/secret.txt'
```

The output from the docker run command will be the words **"secret password"**

```
secret password
```

However, the Docker container should not be able to expose this information.

8. To start making some simple changes to your container to stop this access from happening again, open the Dockerfile again and add the highlighted code (*lines 6*, *7*, *8*, and *9*), keeping the previous lines of code as they are. These lines of code will create a group, **10001**, and a user, **20002**. The user will be set up with a **home** directory, which you will then move into and start working with the **USER** directive in *line 9*:

```
1 FROM alpine
2
3 RUN apk update
4 RUN apk add wget curl nmap libcap
5
6 RUN addgroup --gid 10001 20002 && adduser 20002 -h
    /home/security_apps --disabled-password --uid 20002
    --ingroup 20002
7 WORKDIR /home/security_apps
8
9 USER 20002
```

9. Make a change to *line 15* to make sure the script is being run from the new
   security_app directory, and then save the Dockerfile:

```
11 RUN echo "#!/sh\n" > test_memory.sh
12 RUN echo "cat /proc/meminfo; mpstat; pmap -x 1" >>
   test_memory.sh
13 RUN chmod 755 test_memory.sh
14
15 CMD ["sh", "/home/security_apps/test_memory.sh"]
```

The complete Dockerfile should look like the following:

```
FROM alpine

RUN apk update
RUN apk add wget curl nmap libcap

RUN addgroup --gid 10001 20002 && adduser 20002 -h
  /home/security_apps --disabled-password --uid 20002
    --ingroup 20002
WORKDIR /home/security_apps

USER 20002

RUN echo "#!/sh\n" > test_memory.sh
RUN echo "cat /proc/meminfo; mpstat; pmap -x 1" >>
  test_memory.sh
RUN chmod 755 test_memory.sh

CMD ["sh", "/home/security_apps/test_memory.sh"]
```

10. Build the image again and run it with the **whoami** command:

```
docker build -t security-app . ; docker run --rm security-app whoami
```

You will see a new user as **20002** and not the root user:

```
20002
```

11. Previously, you were able to run **nmap** from the container. Verify whether
    the new user is stopped from accessing the **nmap** command now to scan for
    network vulnerabilities:

```
docker run --rm -it security-app sh -c 'nmap -sS -p 443 localhost'
```

By running your image again with the **nmap -sS** command, you should now be stopped from running the command since the **20002** user that the container is running as does not have sufficient privileges to run the command:

```
You requested a scan type which requires root privileges.
QUITTING!
```

12. You have now drastically limited what can be done with the running container, but are files that are owned by the host root user still accessible by the **security-app** running container? Mount the file again and see whether you can output the information on the file:

```
docker run -v /tmp/secret.txt:/tmp/secret.txt security-app sh -c 'cat
/tmp/secret.txt'
```

You should see **Permission denied** in your results, ensuring the container no longer has access to the **secret.txt** file:

```
cat: can't open '/tmp/secret.txt': Permission denied
```

As we've been able to demonstrate in this exercise, removing your running containers' access to the root user is a good first step in reducing what an attacker can achieve if they manage to gain access to your running images. The next section will take a quick look at the privileges and capabilities of running containers and how they can be manipulated with **docker run** commands.

RUNTIME PRIVILEGES AND LINUX CAPABILITIES

When running your containers, Docker provides a flag that overrides all the security and user options. This is done by running your container with the **--privileged** option. Though you have seen what the user can achieve when the container is run as the root user, we are running the container in an unprivileged state. Although the **--privileged** option is provided, it should be used sparingly, and we should be cautious if anyone is requesting to run your containers in this mode. There are some specific circumstances—for example, if you needed to run Docker on Raspberry Pi and needed to access the underlying architecture—in which you may want to add capabilities to your user.

If you need to provide extra privileges to your container to run specific commands and functions, Docker provides an easier way to do this, using the **--cap-add** and **--cap-drop** options. This means that instead of providing complete control with the **--privileged** option, you can use **--cap-add** and **--cap-drop** to limit what can be achieved by the user.

Both **--cap-add** and **--cap-drop** can be used simultaneously when running your containers. For example, you may want to include **--cap-add=all** and **--cap-drop=chown**.

Here's a short list of some of the capabilities available to both **--cap-add** and **--cap-drop**:

- **setcap**: Modify the process capabilities of your running system.
- **mknod**: Create special files on your running system using the **mknod** command.
- **chown**: Perform file ownership changes to a file's UID and GID values.
- **kill**: Bypass permissions for sending signals to stop processes.
- **setgid/setuid**: Change the process' UID and GID values.
- **net_bind_service**: Bind a socket to a domain port.
- **sys_chroot**: Change the **root** directory on the running system.
- **setfcap**: Set the capabilities of a file.
- **sys_module**: Load and unload kernel modules on the running system.
- **sys_admin**: Perform a range of administration operations.
- **sys_time**: Make changes and set the time to the system clock.
- **net_admin**: Perform a range of administration operations related to networking.
- **sys_boot**: Reboot the system and load a new kernel on the system for later execution.

To add extra capabilities, you simply need to include the capability, and if you are adding or dropping the capabilities while performing your **docker run** command, your command will be as follows:

```
docker run --cap-add|--cap-drop <capability_name> <image_name>
```

As you can see, the syntax uses **--cap-add** to add a capability and **--cap-drop** to remove the capability.

> **NOTE**
>
> If you're interested in seeing the entire list of capabilities that you can add and drop when running your containers, go to http://man7.org/linux/man-pages/man7/capabilities.7.html.

We've taken a brief look at using privileges and capabilities. Later in this chapter, we will get a chance to use the functionality when testing our security profiles. For now, though, we are going to look at using digital signatures with our Docker images to verify their authenticity.

SIGNING AND VERIFYING DOCKER IMAGES

Just as we can make sure that the applications we purchase and install on our systems are from a trusted source, we can do the same with the Docker images we use. Running an untrusted Docker image could become a huge risk and could cause major issues in our system. This is why we should look to have specific proof of the images we are using. An untrusted source could potentially add code to the running image, which could expose your entire network to the attacker.

Fortunately, Docker has a way of digitally signing our images to ensure we're using images from a verified vendor or provider. This will also ensure the image has not been changed or corrupted since it was originally signed, ensuring some authenticity. It shouldn't be the only way we trust our images. As you'll see later in this chapter, once we have our image, we can then scan it to ensure we avoid installing an image that may have security issues.

The way that Docker allows us to sign and verify images is by using **Docker Content Trust (DCT)**. DCT is provided as part of Docker Hub and allows you to use digital signatures for all the data sent and received from your registries. The DCT is associated with the image tag, so not all images need to be tagged, and as a result, not all images will have a DCT associated with it. This will mean that anyone wanting to publish an image can do so but is able to ensure the image is working correctly before needing to sign it.

DCT doesn't only stop with Docker Hub. If a user has enabled DCT on their environment, they will only be able to pull, run, or build with images that are trusted, as DCT ensures that a user will only be able to see signed images. DCT trust is managed through the use of signing keys, which are created the first time you run DCT. When a key set is created, it consists of three different types of keys:

- **Offline keys**: These are used to create tagging keys. They should be stored carefully and are owned by the user creating the images. If these keys are lost or compromised, it could cause a lot of issues for the publisher.

- **Repository or tagging keys**: These reside with the publisher and are associated with the image repository. They are used when you are signing your trusted images ready to be pushed to your repository.

- **Server managed keys**: These are also associated with the image repository and are stored on the server.

> **NOTE**
>
> Make sure you keep your offline keys safe because if you lose your offline key, it will cause a lot of problems as Docker Support will most likely need to be involved to reset the repository state. It also requires manual intervention from all consumers that have used signed images from the repository.

Just as we've seen in previous sections, Docker provides easy-to-use command-line options to generate, load, and work with signing keys. If you have DCT enabled, Docker will set up your keys and sign your images directly with them. If you'd like to control things a little further, you can use the **docker trust key generate** command to create your offline keys with the name you assign to them:

```
docker trust key generate <name>
```

Your keys will be stored in your **home** directory in the **.docker/trust** directory. If you have a set of offline keys, you can use the **docker trust key load** command with the keys and the name you created them with, as follows:

```
docker trust key load <pem_key_file> -name <name>
```

Once you have your key, or you load in your original keys, you can then start to sign your images. You need to include the full registry name and the tag of the image using the **docker trust sign** command:

```
docker trust sign <registry>/<repo>:<tag>
```

Once you sign your images, or you have an image that you need to verify is signed, you can use the **docker trust inspect** command to show the details of the signing keys and the issuer:

```
docker trust inspect -pretty <registry>/<repo>:<tag>
```

Using DCT as part of your development process prevents users from using container images from untrusted and unknown sources. We'll use the security app we've been working on in the previous sections of this chapter to create and implement a DCT signing key.

EXERCISE 11.02: SIGNING DOCKER IMAGES AND UTILIZING DCT ON YOUR SYSTEM

In the following exercise, you will learn about using DCT and implementing processes using signed images in your environment. You will begin by exporting the **DOCKER_CONTENT_TRUST** environment variable to enable DCT on your system. Moving on, you will learn how to sign the images and verify signed images:

1. Export the **DOCKER_CONTENT_TRUST** environment variable to your system to enable DCT on your system. Also, make sure the variable is set to **1**:

```
export DOCKER_CONTENT_TRUST=1
```

2. Now that DCT is enabled, you won't be able to pull or work with any Docker images that do not have a signed key associated with them. We can test this by pulling the **security-app** image from our Docker Hub repository:

```
docker pull vincesestodocker/security-app
```

As you can see from the error message, we weren't able to pull our latest image, and that's good news because we hadn't pushed it originally using a signing key:

```
Using default tag: latest
Error: remote trust data does not exist for docker.io/
vincesestodocker/security-app: notary.docker.io does
not have trust data for docker.io/vincesestodocker/security-app
```

3. Push the image to your image repository:

```
docker push vincesestodocker/security-app
```

You should not be able to do this as there are no signing keys associated with this local image either:

```
The push refers to repository
[docker.io/vincesestodocker/security-app]
No tag specified, skipping trust metadata push
```

4. Tag your new image ready to be pushed to Docker Hub as **trust1**:

```
docker tag security-app:latest vincesestodocker/security-app:trust1
```

5. As mentioned earlier, a signing key will be associated automatically with the image when we push it to our repository for the first time. Make sure to tag your image, as this will stop DCT from recognizing that it needs to be signed. Push the image to the repository again:

```
docker push vincesestodocker/security-app:trust1
```

The following lines will be printed after running the preceding command:

```
The push refers to repository
[docker.io/vincesestodocker/security-app]
eff6491f0d45: Layer already exists
307b7a157b2e: Layer already exists
03901b4a2ea8: Layer already exists
ver2: digest: sha256:7fab55c47c91d7e56f093314ff463b7f97968e
e0f80f5ee927430fc39f525f66 size: 949
Signing and pushing trust metadata
You are about to create a new root signing key passphrase.
This passphrase will be used to protect the most sensitive key
in your signing system. Please choose a long, complex passphrase
and be careful to keep the password and the key file itself
secure and backed up. It is highly recommended that you use a
password manager to generate the passphrase and keep it safe.
There will be no way to recover this key. You can find the key
in your config directory.
Enter passphrase for new root key with ID 66347fd:
Repeat passphrase for new root key with ID 66347fd:
Enter passphrase for new repository key with ID cf2042d:
Repeat passphrase for new repository key with ID cf2042d:
Finished initializing "docker.io/vincesestodocker/security-app"
Successfully signed docker.io/vincesestodocker/security-app:
trust1
```

The following output shows that as the image is being pushed to the registry, a new signing key is created as part of the process, requesting the user to create a new root key and repository key in the process.

6. It's a lot more secure now. What about running the image on your system, though? With DCT now enabled on our system, will there be any issues running on our container image? Use the **docker run** command to run the **security-app** image on your system:

```
docker run -it vincesestodocker/security-app sh
```

The command should return the following output:

```
docker: No valid trust data for latest.
See 'docker run --help'.
```

In the preceding output, we have deliberately not used the **trust1** tag. As in earlier chapters, Docker will try to run the image with the **latest** tag. As this also doesn't have a signing key associated with it, you are not able to run it.

7. You can sign the image directly from your working system, and you can use the keys created previously to sign subsequent tagged images. Tag your image with the **trust2** tag:

```
docker tag vincesestodocker/security-app:trust1 vincesestodocker/
security-app:trust2
```

8. Sign the newly tagged image with the signing key created earlier in this exercise. Use the **docker trust sign** command with the image name and tag to sign the image and layers of the image:

```
docker trust sign vincesestodocker/security-app:trust2
```

The command will automatically push the signed image to our Docker Hub repository as well:

```
Signing and pushing trust data for local image
vincesestodocker/security-app:trust2, may overwrite remote
trust data
The push refers to repository
[docker.io/vincesestodocker/security-app]
015825f3a965: Layer already exists
2c32d3f8446b: Layer already exists
1bbb374ec935: Layer already exists
bcc0069f86e9: Layer already exists
e239574b2855: Layer already exists
f5e66f43d583: Layer already exists
77cae8ab23bf: Layer already exists
trust2: digest: sha256:a61f528324d8b63643f94465511132a38ff945083c
```

```
3a2302fa5a9774ea366c49 size: 1779
Signing and pushing trust metadataEnter passphrase for
vincesestodocker key with ID f4b834e:
Successfully signed docker.io/vincesestodocker/security-app:
trust2
```

9. View the signing information using the **docker trust** command with the **inspect** option:

```
docker trust inspect --pretty vincesestodocker/security-app:trust2
```

The output will give you details of the signer, the tagged image that is signed, and other information on the image:

```
Signatures for vincesestodocker/security-app:trust2
SIGNED TAG        DIGEST                    SIGNERS
trust2            d848a63170f405ad3...      vincesestodocker
List of signers and their keys for vincesestodocker/security-app:
trust2
SIGNER            KEYS
vincesestodocker  f4b834e54c71
Administrative keys for vincesestodocker/security-app:trust2
  Repository Key:
    26866c7eba348164f7c9c4f4e53f04d7072fefa9b52d254c573e8b082
    f77c966
  Root Key:
    69bef52a24226ad6f5505fd3159f778d6761ac9ad37483f6bc88b1cb4
    7dda334
```

10. Use the **docker trust revoke** command to remove the signature of the associated key:

```
docker trust revoke vincesestodocker/security-app:trust2
Enter passphrase for vincesestodocker key with ID f4b834e:
Successfully deleted signature for vincesestodocker/security-app:
trust2
```

> **NOTE**
>
> If you're using your own Docker registry, you may need to set up a Notary server to allow DCT to work with your Docker registry. Products such as Amazon's Elastic Container Registry and Docker Trusted Registry have Notary built into their products.

As you can see, signing and verifying your Docker images using DCT makes it easy to control the images you are using as part of your applications. Using signed images from trusted sources is only part of the equation. In the next section, we'll use Anchore and Snyk to start scanning our images for vulnerabilities.

DOCKER IMAGE SECURITY SCANS

Security scans play an important part in not only ensuring the uptime of your applications but also making sure you are not running outdated, unpatched, or vulnerable container images. Security scans should be performed on all images used by your team and in your environment. It doesn't matter if you have created them from scratch and you trust them; it's still an important step in reducing the potential risk within your environment. This section of the chapter will go through two options for scanning images that can easily be adopted by your development teams.

By implementing a security scan of our Docker images, we hope to achieve the following:

- We need to keep a database of known and up-to-date vulnerabilities or use an application that will keep this database on our behalf.

- We scan our Docker images against this database of vulnerabilities, not only verifying that the underlying operating system is safe and patched but also that the open-source applications used by the container and the languages used by our software implementation are safe.

- Once the security scan is complete, we need to be provided with a full report of what has been scanned on our image, as well as report and alert any issues that may have been highlighted during the scan.

- Finally, a security scan can then provide remediation of any issues found and alerted on by updating the base image used in the Dockerfile or supporting the applications used.

There are a lot of products on the market that can perform security scans for you, both paid and open source. We are limited with our space in this chapter, so we've chosen two services that we found to be both easy to use and that provide good functionality. The first is Anchore, which is an open-source container analysis tool that we'll install onto our system and run as a local tool to test our images. We will then look at Snyk, which is an online SaaS product. There is a free version of Snyk available, which is the version we will be using in this chapter to demonstrate how it works. It provides decent functionality without needing to pay a monthly fee.

SCANNING IMAGES LOCALLY USING ANCHORE SECURITY SCAN

Anchore Container Analysis is an open-source static analysis tool that allows you to scan your Docker images and provide a pass or fail result against a policy defined by the user. The Anchore Engine allows the user to pull an image and without running it, analyze the image's content, and evaluate whether the image is suitable for use. Anchore uses a PostgreSQL database to store details of known vulnerabilities. You can then use the command-line interface to scan images against the database. Anchore also makes it very easy to get started, as we will see in the following exercise, as it provides an easy-to-use **docker-compose** file to automate installation and get you started as quickly as possible.

> **NOTE**
>
> If you're interested in learning more about Anchore, there is a large body of documentation and information at https://docs.anchore.com/current/.

In the upcoming exercise, once our environment is up and running, you will interface with Anchore using its API. The **anchore-cli** command comes with a number of easy-to-use commands to check the system status and start to assess the vulnerability of our images.

Once our system is up and running, we can use the **system status** command to provide a list of all our services and ensure they are up and running:

```
anchore-cli system status
```

One of the first things you'll need to do once your system is up and running is to verify that the feeds list is up to date. This will ensure that your database has been populated with vulnerability feeds. This is achieved with the following **system feeds list** command:

```
anchore-cli system feeds list
```

By default, **anchore-cli** will use Docker Hub as your image registry. If your image is residing on a different registry, you will need to add the registry with the **anchore-cli registry add** command and specify the registry name, as well as include a username and password that Anchore can use:

```
anchore-cli registry add <registry> <user> <password>
```

To add an image to Anchore, you can use the **image add** command-line option, including the Docker Hub location and the image name:

```
anchore-cli image add <repository_name>/<image_name>
```

If you then wish to scan the image for vulnerabilities, you can do so using the **image vuln** option, including the image name you scanned in originally. We could also use the **os** option for operating system-specific vulnerabilities and **non-os** for language-related vulnerabilities. In the following example, we have used **all** to include both the **os** and **non-os** options:

```
anchore-cli image vuln <repository_name>/<image_name> all
```

Then, to view the completed evaluation of the image and be provided with a pass or fail on whether the image is safe for use, you use the **evaluate check** option of the **anchore-cli** command:

```
anchore-cli evaluate check <repository_name>/<image_name>
```

With all that in mind, Anchore does provide a supported and paid version with an easy-to-use web interface, but as you'll see in the following exercise, there is not a lot of hard work required to get the Anchore application running and scanning on your system.

> **NOTE**
>
> The previous exercise used DCT as part of the creation and signing of containers. In the following exercise, the Anchore image needed for the exercise uses the **latest** tag, so if you are still running DCT, you will need to stop it before proceeding with the next exercise:
>
> **export DOCKER_CONTENT_TRUST=0**

EXERCISE 11.03: GETTING STARTED WITH ANCHORE IMAGE SCANNING

In the following exercise, you will install Anchore onto your local system using **docker-compose** and start to analyze the images you have been using as part of this chapter:

1. Create and tag a new version of the **security-app** image that you have been working on. Tag the image with the **scan1** tag:

```
docker tag security-app:latest vincesestodocker/security-app:scan1 ;
```

Push it to the Docker Hub repository:

```
docker push vincesestodocker/security-app:scan1
```

2. Create a new directory called **aevolume** and move into that directory using the following command. This is where we will perform our work:

```
mkdir aevolume; cd aevolume
```

3. Anchore provides you with everything you need to get started in an easy-to-use **docker-compose.yaml** file to set up and run the Anchore API. Pull the latest **anchore-engine** Docker Compose file using the following command:

```
curl -O https://docs.anchore.com/current/docs/engine/quickstart/
docker-compose.yaml
```

4. Look through the **docker-compose.yml** file. Although it contains over 130 lines, there is nothing too complex in the file. The **Compose** file is setting up the functionality for Anchore, including the PostgreSQL database, catalog, and analyzer to query against; a simple queue and policy engine; and an API to run commands and queries.

5. Pull the images needed by the **docker-compose.yml** file using the **docker-compose pull** command, making sure you are in the same directory as the **Compose** file:

```
docker-compose pull
```

The command will start pulling the database, catalog, analyzer, simple queue, policy engine, and API:

```
Pulling anchore-db          ... done
Pulling engine-catalog      ... done
Pulling engine-analyzer     ... done
Pulling engine-policy-engine ... done
```

```
Pulling engine-simpleq       ... done
Pulling engine-api          ... done
```

6. If all our images are now available, as seen in the preceding output, there is nothing left to do other than running the **Compose** file using the **docker-compose up** command. Use the **-d** option to have all of the containers running in the background as daemons:

```
docker-compose up -d
```

The command should output the following:

```
Creating network "aevolume_default" with the default driver
Creating volume "aevolume_anchore-db-volume" with default driver
Creating volume "aevolume_anchore-scratch" with default driver
Creating aevolume_anchore-db_1 ... done
Creating aevolume_engine-catalog_1 ... done
Creating aevolume_engine-analyzer_1       ... done
Creating aevolume_engine-simpleq_1        ... done
Creating aevolume_engine-api_1            ... done
Creating aevolume_engine-policy-engine_1 ... done
```

7. Run the **docker ps** command to have the running containers on your system that make up Anchore ready to start scanning our images. The **IMAGE**, **COMMAND**, and **CREATED** columns are removed from the table for convenience:

```
docker-compose ps
```

All values in the output should show **healthy** for each of the Anchore Engine containers:

```
CONTAINER ID        STATUS          PORTS
    NAMES
d48658f6aa77        (healthy)        8228/tcp
    aevolume_engine-analyzer_1
e4aec4e0b463    (healthy)        8228/tcp
    aevolume_engine-policy-engine_1
afb59721d890    (healthy)        8228->8228/tcp
    aevolume_engine-api_1
d61ff12e2376    (healthy)        8228/tcp
    aevolume_engine-simpleq_1
f5c29716aa40    (healthy)        8228/tcp
    aevolume_engine-catalog_1
```

```
398fef820252      (healthy)              5432/tcp
   aevolume_anchore-db_1
```

8. Now that the environment is deployed onto your system, use the
    docker-compose exec command to run the **anchor-cli** commands
    mentioned earlier. Use the **pip3** command to install the **anchorecli**
    package onto your running system. The **--version** command has been
    used to verify whether **anchore-cli** has installed successfully:

```
pip3 install anchorecli; anchore-cli --version
```

The command returns the version of **anchor-cli**:

```
anchore-cli, version 0.5.0
```

> **NOTE**
>
> The version may vary depending on your system.

9. You could now run your **anchore-cli** command, but you would need to
    specify the URL (using **--url**) to your API and the username and password
    (using **--u** and **--p**). Instead, export the values to your environment
    with the following commands so that you don't need to use the extra
    command-line options:

```
export ANCHORE_CLI_URL=http://localhost:8228/v1
export ANCHORE_CLI_USER=admin
export ANCHORE_CLI_PASS=foobar
```

> **NOTE**
>
> The preceding variables are the default values for the **Compose** file
> provided by Anchore. If you decide to set up the environment running inside
> your deployment environment, you will most likely change these to be
> more secure.

10. With **anchore-cli** now installed and configured, use the **anchore-cli**
    system status command to verify that the analyzer, queue, policy engine,
    catalog, and API are all up and running:

```
anchore-cli system status
```

There may be instances where one or two of the services may be down, which will mean you will most likely need to restart the container:

```
Service analyzer (anchore-quickstart, http://engine-analyzer:
8228): up
Service simplequeue (anchore-quickstart, http://engine-simpleq:
8228): up
Service policy_engine (anchore-quickstart, http://engine-policy-
engine:8228): up
Service catalog (anchore-quickstart, http://engine-catalog:
8228): up
Service apiext (anchore-quickstart, http://engine-api:8228):
up
Engine DB Version: 0.0.11
Engine Code Version: 0.5.1
```

NOTE

Engine DB Version and **Engine Code Version** may vary depending on the system.

11. Use the **anchore-cli system feeds list** command to see all of the vulnerabilities in your database:

```
anchore-cli system feeds list
```

The following output has been reduced as there is, as you can imagine, a large number of vulnerabilities provided to the database:

Feed	Group	LastSync
RecordCount		
nvdv2	nvdv2:cves	None
0		
vulnerabilities	alpine:3.	2019-10-24T03:47:28.504381
1485		
vulnerabilities	alpine:3.3	2019-10-24T03:47:36.658242
457		
vulnerabilities	alpine:3.4	2019-10-24T03:47:51.594635
681		
vulnerabilities	alpine:3.5	2019-10-24T03:48:03.442695
875		
vulnerabilities	alpine:3.6	2019-10-24T03:48:19.384824

```
      1051
vulnerabilities     alpine:3.7      2019-10-24T03:48:36.626534
      1253
vulnerabilities     alpine:3.8      None
      0
vulnerabilities     alpine:3.9      None
      0
vulnerabilities     amzn:2          None
      0
```

In the preceding output, you will notice that some of the vulnerability feeds are showing **None**. This is because the database was only recently set up and has not updated all of the vulnerabilities. Continue to display the feeds list as you did in the previous step, and once all of the entries are showing a date in the **LastSync** column, you will then be ready to start scanning images.

12. Once the feed has fully updated, add an image with the **anchore-cli image add** command. Remember to use the full path, including the image repository tags, as Anchore will use the image located on Docker Hub:

```
anchore-cli image add vincesestodocker/security-app:scan1
```

The command adds the image to the Anchore database, ready for it to be scanned:

```
Image Digest: sha256:7fab55c47c91d7e56f093314ff463b7f97968ee0
f80f5ee927430
fc39f525f66
Parent Digest: sha256:7fab55c47c91d7e56f093314ff463b7f97968ee
0f80f5ee927430fc39f525f66
Analysis Status: not_analyzed
Image Type: docker
Analyzed At: None
Image ID: 8718859775e5d5057dd7a15d8236a1e983a9748b16443c99f8a
40a39a1e7e7e5
Dockerfile Mode: None
Distro: None
Distro Version: None
Size: None
Architecture: None
Layer Count: None
Full Tag: docker.io/vincesestodocker/security-app:scan1
Tag Detected At: 2019-10-24T03:51:18Z
```

When you add the image, you will notice that we have highlighted that the output is showing **not_analyzed**. This will be queued for analysis and for smaller images, which will be a quick process.

13. Monitor your image to see whether it has been analyzed using the **anchore-cli image list** command:

```
anchore-cli image list
```

This will provide a list of all the images we have currently added and will give you a status on whether they have been analyzed:

```
Full Tag                 Image Digest           Analysis Status
security-app:scan1       sha256:a1bd1f6fec31…   analyzed
```

14. Now that the image is added and analyzed, you can start to look through the image and see what is included as part of the base image and what applications are installed, including the version and license number. Use the **image content os** command for **anchore-cli**. You can also use other content types, including **file** for all the files on the image, **npm** for all the Node.js modules, **gem** for the Ruby gems, **java** for the Java archives, and **python** for the Python artifacts:

```
anchore-cli image content vincesestodocker/security-app:scan1 os
```

The command will return an output like the following:

```
Package                  Version        License
alpine-baselayout        3.1.2          GPL-2.0-only
alpine-keys              2.1            MIT
apk-tools                2.10.4         GPL2
busybox                  1.30.1         GPL-2.0
ca-certificates          20190108       MPL-2.0 GPL-2.0-or-later
ca-certificates-cacert   20190108       MPL-2.0 GPL-2.0-or-later
curl                     7.66.0         MIT
libc-utils               0.7.1          BSD
libcrypto1.1             1.1.1c         OpenSSL
libcurl                  7.66.0         MIT
libssl1.1                1.1.1c         OpenSSL
libtls-standalone        2.9.1          ISC
musl                     1.1.22         MIT
musl-utils               1.1.22         MIT BSD GPL2+
nghttp2-libs             1.39.2         MIT
scanelf                  1.2.3          GPL-2.0
```

```
ssl_client              1.30.1          GPL-2.0
wget                    1.20.3          GPL-3.0-or-later
zlib                    1.2.11          zlib
```

15. Use the **anchore-cli image vuln** command and include the image you want to scan to check for vulnerabilities. If there are no vulnerabilities present, you should not see any output. We have used **all** in the following command line to provide a report on both OS and non-OS vulnerabilities. We could also have used **os** for operating system-specific vulnerabilities and **non-os** for language-related vulnerabilities:

```
anchore-cli image vuln vincesestodocker/security-app:scan1 all
```

16. Perform an evaluation check of the image to provide us with a **pass** or **fail** result for our image scan. Use the **anchore-cli evaluate check** command to see whether the image is safe to use:

```
anchore-cli evaluate check vincesestodocker/security-app:scan1
From the output of the above command, it looks like our image
is safe with a pass result.Image Digest:
sha256:7fab55c47c91d7e56f093314ff463b7f97968ee0f80f5ee927430fc
39f525f66
Full Tag: docker.io/vincesestodocker/security-app:scan1
Status: pass
Last Eval: 2019-10-24T03:54:40Z
Policy ID: 2c53a13c-1765-11e8-82ef-23527761d060
```

All of the preceding exercises have gone a long way to establish whether or not our image has any vulnerabilities and is safe to use. The following section will show you an alternative to Anchore, which although it has a paid component, does still provide a large amount of functionality by only accessing the free version.

UTILIZING SAAS SECURITY SCANS WITH SNYK

Snyk is an online SaaS application that provides an easy-to-use interface that allows you to scan your Docker images for vulnerabilities. Although Snyk is a paid application, it does provide a free tier with a large amount of functionality to the user. It provides unlimited tests to open source projects and allows GitHub and GitLab integration, with remediation to open source projects and continuous monitoring. You are limited to the amount of container vulnerability testing that is allowed.

The following exercise will run through using the web interface providing a guide on how to register for an account and then add your container to be scanned for security vulnerabilities.

EXERCISE 11.04: SETTING UP A SNYK SECURITY SCAN

In this exercise, you will use your web browser to work with Snyk to start implementing security scans on our `security-app` image:

1. Create an account with Snyk if you have not used Snyk before or do not have an account. You are not required to give any credit card details unless you want to upgrade your account to the paid version, but in this exercise, you will only need the free option. So, log in to Snyk or create an account at https://app.snyk.io/signup.

2. You will be presented with a web page as in the following screenshot. Choose the method by which you wish to create your account and follow the prompts to continue:

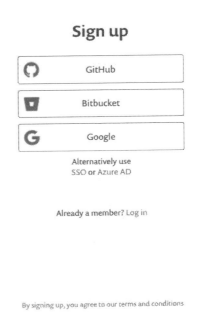

Figure 11.1: Creating an account with Snyk

3. Once logged in, you will be presented with a page similar to the one in *Figure 11.2*, asking **Where is the code you want to test?**. Snyk not only scans Docker images but also scans your code for vulnerabilities. You already have your **security-app** image in Docker Hub, so click on the **Docker Hub** button to start the process:

Figure 11.2: Starting security scans with Snyk

> **NOTE**
>
> If you are not presented with the preceding web page, you can go to the following URL to add a new repository. Remember to change **<your_account_name>** in the following URL to the account you were assigned when you created your Snyk account:
>
> `https://app.snyk.io/org/<your_account_name>/add`.

4. Authenticate with Docker Hub to allow it to view your available repositories. When presented with the following page, enter your Docker Hub details and click on **Continue**:

Figure 11.3: Authenticating with Docker Hub in Snyk

5. Once authenticated, you will then be presented with a list of all your repositories on Docker Hub, including the tags that are stored for each repository. In this exercise, you only need to select one of your images and use the **scan1** tag created in this section. Select the **security-app** image with the **scan1** tag. Once you are happy with your selection, click on the **Add selected repositories** button in the top-right corner of the screen:

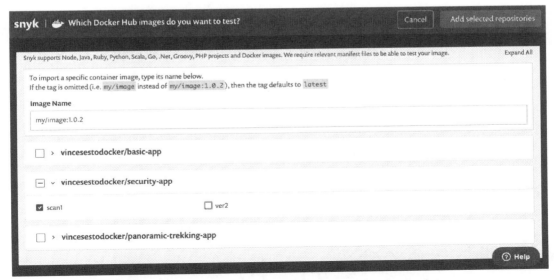

Figure 11.4: Selecting your Docker Hub repositories for Snyk to scan

6. Snyk will run a scan over your image as soon as you have added it, and depending on the size of the image, this should complete in a matter of seconds. Click on the **Projects** tab at the top of the screen to see the results of your scan, and click and select the repository and tag you would like to view:

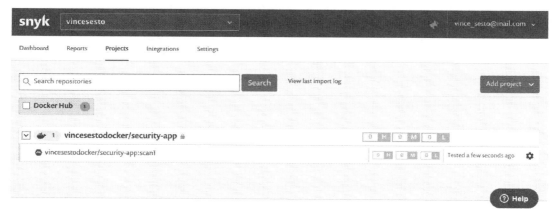

Figure 11.5: Viewing your project reports in Snyk

After clicking on the repository name, you will be presented with a report of your image scan, outlining details about the image, what base images are being used, and whether there were any high, medium, or low issues found during the scan:

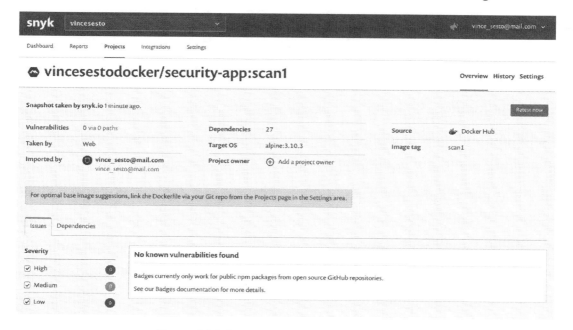

Figure 11.6: Image scan report page in Snyk

Snyk will scan your image daily and will alert you if it finds any issues. A weekly report will be emailed to you unless there are any vulnerabilities found. If there are, you will be notified as soon as possible.

With Snyk, you can scan your images for vulnerabilities with an easy-to-follow interface. As an SaaS web-based application, it also means there is no need to administer your applications and servers for security scanning. This is the end of the section on security scanning our images, and we will now move on to using security profiles with our images to help stop attackers from taking advantage of any images that they may be able to access.

USING CONTAINER SECURITY PROFILES

Security profiles allow you to leverage existing security tools in Linux and implement them across your Docker images. In the following sections, we will cover both AppArmor and **seccomp**. These are the ways by which you can reduce the amount of access that processes can gain when running on your Docker environments. They are both simple to use and you'll find you will most likely be using them already in your images. We will look at both of them separately but note that AppArmor and Security Computing for Linux do overlap with their functionality. For the time being, all you need to remember is that AppArmor stops applications from accessing files that they shouldn't be accessing, while Security Computing for Linux will help stop any Linux kernel vulnerabilities from being exploited.

By default, and especially if you have an up-to-date version of Docker running, you may already have both running. You can verify this by running the **docker info** command and looking for **Security Options**. The following is the output from a system showing both features are available:

```
docker info

Security Options:
  apparmor
  seccomp
   Profile: default
```

The following sections will cover both AppArmor and Security Computing for Linux and give you a clear view of how to implement and work with both on your system.

IMPLEMENTING APPARMOR SECURITY PROFILES ON YOUR IMAGES

AppArmor stands for Application Armor and is a Linux Security module. The goal of AppArmor is to protect the operating system from security threats, and it was implemented as part of Docker version 1.13.0. It allows the user to load a security profile to their running container and can be created to lock down the processes available to the services on the container. The default included by Docker provides moderate protection, while still allowing access to a large number of applications.

To help a user write a security profile, AppArmor provides a **complain mode**, which allows almost any task to be run without it being restricted, but any breaches will be logged to the audit log as an event. It also has an **unconfined mode**, which is the same as complain mode but will not log any events.

> **NOTE**
>
> For more details on AppArmor, including documentation, use the following link, which will take you to the AppArmor home page on GitLab:
>
> https://gitlab.com/apparmor/apparmor/wikis/home.

AppArmor also comes with a set of commands to help users administer the application, including compiling and loading policies into the kernel. The default profile can be a little confusing for new users. The main rules you need to remember are that a deny rule has precedence over allow and owner rules, which means that allow rules will be overridden by a subsequent deny rule if they are both on the same application. File operations are clearer with **'r'** as read, **'w'** as write, **'k'** as lock, **'l'** as link, and **'x'** as execute.

We can start working with AppArmor as it provides some easy-to-use command-line tools. The first one you will utilize is the **aa-status** command, which provides the status of all the profiles running on your system. These are located in the **/etc/apparmor.d** directory of your system:

```
aa-status
```

If we have profiles installed on our system, we should at least have the **docker-default** profile; it can be applied to our Docker containers with the **--security-opt** option of the **docker run** command. In the following example, you can see that we are setting the **--security-opt** value to the **apparmor** profile, or you could use the **unconfined** profile, which means there is no profile running with the image:

```
docker run --security-opt apparmor=<profile> <image_name>
```

To generate our profiles, we can use the **aa-genprof** command to gain further insight into what needs to be set up as the profile. AppArmor will scan through the logs when you perform some sample commands to then create a profile for you on your system and place it in the default profiles directory:

```
aa-genprof <application>
```

Once you're happy with your profiles, they need to be loaded onto your system before you can start to use them with your images. You use the **apparmor_parser** command with the **-r** (replace, if already set up) and **-W** (write to cache) options. The profiles can then be used with your running containers:

```
apparmor_parser -r -W <path_to_profile>
```

Lastly, if you wish to then remove a profile from AppArmor, you can use the **apparmor_parser** command with the **-R** option to do so:

```
apparmor_parser -R <path_to_profile>
```

AppArmor seems complicated, but hopefully, with the following exercises, you should become comfortable with the application and gain extra confidence in generating your custom profiles.

EXERCISE 11.05: GETTING STARTED WITH APPARMOR SECURITY PROFILES

The following exercise will introduce you to AppAmor security profiles and help you implement new rules in your running Docker containers:

1. If you're running Docker Engine version 19 or greater, AppArmor should already be set up as part of the application. Run the **docker info** command to verify that it is running:

```
docker info
…
Security Options:
  apparmor
…
```

2. Previously in this chapter, we changed the user the container was running as by creating the user **20002**. We will stop this for the time being to demonstrate how AppArmor works in this situation. Open the **Dockerfile** with your text editor and this time, comment *line 9* out as we have in the code below:

```
 8
 9 #USER 20002
```

3. Build the **Dockerfile** again and verify the user the image is once running as the root user again:

```
docker build -t security-app . ; docker run --rm security-app whoami
```

The above commands will build **Dockerfile** and then return the output like the following:

```
root
```

4. Use the AppArmor **status** command by running **aa-status** in the command line:

```
aa-status
```

> **NOTE**
>
> If you are refused to run the **aa-status** command, use **sudo**.

This will show a similar output to the following and will provide the profiles loaded and the types of profiles loaded. You'll notice that the output includes all the AppArmor profiles running on the Linux system:

```
apparmor module is loaded.
15 profiles are loaded.
15 profiles are in enforce mode.
    /home/vinces/DockerWork/example.sh
    /sbin/dhclient
    /usr/bin/lxc-start
    /usr/lib/NetworkManager/nm-dhcp-client.action
    /usr/lib/NetworkManager/nm-dhcp-helper
    /usr/lib/connman/scripts/dhclient-script
    /usr/lib/lxd/lxd-bridge-proxy
    /usr/lib/snapd/snap-confine
    /usr/lib/snapd/snap-confine//mount-namespace-capture-helper
    /usr/sbin/tcpdump
    docker-default
    lxc-container-default
    lxc-container-default-cgns
    lxc-container-default-with-mounting
    lxc-container-default-with-nesting
0 profiles are in complain mode.
1 processes have profiles defined.
1 processes are in enforce mode.
    /sbin/dhclient (920)
0 processes are in complain mode.
0 processes are unconfined but have a profile defined.
```

5. Run the **security-app** container in the background to help us test AppArmor:

```
docker run -dit security-app sh
```

6. As we didn't specify a profile to use, AppArmor uses the **docker-default** profile. Verify this by running **aa-status** again:

```
aa-status
```

You will see, toward the bottom of the output, that it now shows that two processes are in **enforce mode**, one showing **docker-default**:

```
apparmor module is loaded.
...
2 processes are in enforce mode.
```

```
    /sbin/dhclient (920)
    docker-default (9768)
0 processes are in complain mode.
0 processes are unconfined but have a profile defined.
```

7. Remove the current containers we have running so that you don't get confused later in this exercise:

```
docker kill $(docker ps -a -q)
```

8. Start your container without using an AppArmor profile using the **--security-opt** Docker option, specifying **apparmor=unconfined**. Also, use the **--cap-add SYS_ADMIN** capability to make sure you have full access to the running container:

```
docker run -dit --security-opt apparmor=unconfined --cap-add SYS_ADMIN
security-app sh
```

9. Access the container and see what type of commands you can run. Use the **docker exec** command with **CONTAINER ID** to access the container, but please note that your **CONTAINER ID** value will be different from the following:

```
docker exec -it db04693ddf1f sh
```

10. Test out the permissions you have by creating two directories and mounting them as a bind mount with the following command:

```
mkdir 1; mkdir 2; mount --bind 1 2
ls -l
```

Being able to mount directories on the container is an elevated privilege, so if you are able to do this, it will be clear that there is no profile stopping us, and we have access to mount the filesystem like this:

```
total 8
drwxr-xr-x    2 root      root        4096 Nov   4 04:08 1
drwxr-xr-x    2 root      root        4096 Nov   4 04:08 2
```

11. Exit the container using the **docker kill** command. You should see whether the default AppArmor profile will restrict access to these commands:

```
docker kill $(docker ps -a -q)
```

12. Create a new instance of the **security-app** image. In this instance, use the **--cap-add SYS_ADMIN** capability, as well, to allow the default AppArmor profile to be loaded:

```
docker run -dit --cap-add SYS_ADMIN security-app sh
```

The command will return the random hash provided to the user when a new container is created.

13. Test the changes by accessing the new running container using **exec** command, and see whether you can perform a bind mount, as in the earlier step:

```
docker exec -it <new_container_ID> sh
mkdir 1; mkdir 2; mount --bind 1 2
```

You should hopefully see **Permission denied**:

```
mount: mounting 1 on 2 failed: Permission denied
```

14. Exit the container again. Delete the original container using the **docker kill** command:

```
docker kill $(docker ps -a -q)
```

In the next part of this exercise, you will look to see whether you can implement our custom profile for our Docker container.

15. Use AppArmor tools to gather information about the resource needed to be tracked. Use the **aa-genprof** command to track details of the **nmap** command:

```
aa-genprof nmap
```

> **NOTE**
>
> If you don't have **aa-genprof** command installed, install it with the following command and then again run the **aa-genprof nmap** command:
>
> **sudo apt install apparmor - utils**

We have reduced the output of the command, but if it's successful, you should see an output showing it is profiling the **/usr/bin/nmap** command:

```
...
Profiling: /usr/bin/nmap
[(S)can system log for AppArmor events] / (F)inish
```

> **NOTE**
>
> If **nmap** is not installed in your system, run the following commands:
>
> `sudo apt-get update`
>
> `sudo apt-get install nmap`

16. Run the **nmap** command in a separate terminal window to provide **aa-genprof** with the details of the application. Use the **-u root** option as part of the **docker run** command to run the **security-app** container as the root user so that it will be able to run the **nmap** command:

```
docker run -it -u root security-app sh -c 'nmap -sS -p 443 localhost'
```

17. Move back to the terminal you have been running the **aa-genprof** command from. Press *S* to scan the system logs for events. Once the scan finishes, press *F* to finish the generation:

```
Reading log entries from /var/log/syslog.
Updating AppArmor profiles in /etc/apparmor.d.
```

All profiles are placed in the **/etc/apparmor.d/** directory. If everything has worked correctly, you should now see a file with a similar output to the following in the **/etc/apparmor.d/usr.bin.nmap** file:

```
1 # Last Modified: Mon Nov 18 01:03:31 2019
2 #include <tunables/global>
3
4 /usr/bin/nmap {
5   #include <abstractions/base>
6
7   /usr/bin/nmap mr,
8
9 }
```

18. Use the **apparmor_parser** command to load the new file onto the system. Use the **-r** option to replace the profile if it already exists and the **-W** option to write it to the cache:

```
apparmor_parser -r -W /etc/apparmor.d/usr.bin.nmap
```

19. Run the **aa-status** command to verify that the profile is now available and to see whether there is a new profile that is specifying **nmap**:

```
aa-status | grep nmap
```

Note that the profile is listed as the same name as the application, **/usr/bin/nmap**, which is what you will need to use when running it with our container:

```
/usr/bin/nmap
```

20. Now, test your changes. Run the container with the **-u root** user. Also, use the **--security-opt apparmor=/usr/bin/nmap** option to run the container with the newly created profile:

```
docker run -it -u root --security-opt apparmor=/usr/bin/nmap
security-app sh -c 'nmap -sS -p 443 localhost'
```

You should also see a result of **Permission denied** to show that the AppArmor profile we have created is restricting the usage as we would hope:

```
sh: nmap: Permission denied
```

In this exercise, we demonstrated how you can start to work with AppArmor on your system and also showed you how you can create your profiles. In the next section, we will move on to a similar application, *seccomp for Linux*.

SECCOMP FOR LINUX CONTAINERS

seccomp for Linux was added to the Linux kernel from version 3.17, and it provides a way to restrict the system calls that Linux processes can issue. This feature can also be used within our running Docker images to help reduce the processes available to running containers, ensuring that if a container is ever accessed by an attacker or infected with malicious code, the commands and processes available to the attacker will be limited.

seccomp uses profiles to establish a whitelist of system calls that can be performed, with the default profile providing a long list of system calls that can be performed, and also disables approximately 44 system calls from running on your Docker containers. You've most likely been using the default **seccomp** profile as you have been working through the chapters in this book.

Docker will be using the **seccomp** configurations from your host system, which can be located by searching for the **/boot/config** file and checking that the **CONFIG_SECCOMP** option is set to **y**:

```
cat /boot/config-'uname -r' | grep CONFIG_SECCOMP=
```

When running our containers, if we ever need to run the container with no **seccomp** profile, we can use the **--security-opt** option, followed by specifying that the **seccomp** profile is unconfirmed. The following example provides the syntax for this:

```
docker run --security-opt seccomp=unconfined <image_name>
```

We can also create our custom profiles. In these instances, we specify the custom profile file location as the value of **seccomp**, as you can see here:

```
docker run --security-opt seccomp=new_default.json <image_name>
```

EXERCISE 11.06: GETTING STARTED WITH SECCOMP

In this exercise, you will use **seccomp** profiles in your current environment. You will also create a custom profile to stop your Docker image from performing the change ownership command against files:

1. Check whether your running Linux system has **seccomp** enabled. This will then allow you to ensure that it is running for Docker as well:

```
cat /boot/config-'uname -r' | grep CONFIG_SECCOMP=
```

If you search for **CONFIG_SECCOMP** in your boot config directory, it should have a value of **y**:

```
CONFIG_SECCOMP=y
```

2. Use the **docker info** command to ensure that Docker is using a profile:

```
docker info
```

In most instances, you will note that it is running the default profile:

```
...
Security Options:
  seccomp
   Profile: default

...
```

We have reduced the output of the **docker info** command, but if you look for the **Security Options** heading, you should see **seccomp** on your system. You would need to change the value for **CONFIG_SECCOMP** to **n** if you ever wished to turn this off.

3. Run **security-app** to see whether it has also been running with a **seccomp** profile. Also, search for the word **Seccomp** in the **/proc/1/status** file:

```
docker run -it security-app grep Seccomp /proc/1/status
```

A value of **2** will show that the container has been running with a **Seccomp** profile all this time:

```
Seccomp:      2
```

4. There may be some situations where you want to run a container without a **seccomp** profile. You may need to debug a container or the application running on it. To run the container without using any **seccomp** profile, use the **--security-opt** option of the **docker run** command and specify that **seccomp** will be unconfined. Do this now with your **security-app** container to see the result:

```
docker run -it --security-opt seccomp=unconfined security-app grep
Seccomp /proc/1/status
```

A value of **0** will show that we have successfully switched off **Seccomp**:

```
Seccomp:      0
```

5. Creating custom profiles is also not very difficult, but it may require some additional troubleshooting to fully understand the syntax. First, test the **security-app** container to see whether we can use the **chown** command in the command line. Your custom profile will then look to stop this command from being available:

```
docker run -it security-app sh
```

6. The current **seccomp** profile running as the default should allow us to run the **chown** command, so while you have access to the running container, test to see whether you can create a new file and change the ownership using the **chown** command. Run the long listing of the directory at the end to verify that the change has taken place:

```
/# touch test.txt
/# chown 1001 test.txt
/# ls -l test.txt
```

The commands should provide an output like the following:

```
-rw-r--r--    1 1001      users        0 Oct 22 02:44 test.txt
```

7. Create your custom profile by modifying the default profile. Use the **wget** command to download the custom profile from this book's official GitHub account onto your system. Use the following command to rename the downloaded custom profile **new_default.json**:

```
wget https://raw.githubusercontent.com/docker/docker/v1.12.3/profiles/
seccomp/default.json -O new_default.json
```

8. Open the **new_default.json** file with your text editor and, although there will be a large list of configurations, search for the specific configurations that control **chown**. At the time of writing, this was located on *line 59* of the default **seccomp** profile:

```
59                    {
60                            "name": "chown",
61                            "action": "SCMP_ACT_ALLOW",
62                            "args": []
63                    },
```

The **SCMP_ACT_ALLOW** action allows the command to be run, but if you remove *lines 59* to *63* from the **new_default.json** file, this should now stop our profile from allowing this command to be run. Delete the lines and save the file ready for us to use.

9. As in *step 4* of this exercise, use the **--security-opt** option and specify the image to now run using our edited **new_default.json** file:

```
docker run -it --security-opt seccomp=new_default.json security-app
sh
```

10. Perform the same test as in *step 6* of this exercise, and if our changes have worked, the **seccomp** profile should now stop us from running the **chown** command:

```
/# touch test.txt
/# chown 1001 test.txt
chown: test.txt: Operation not permitted
```

With only a minimal amount of work, we've managed to create a policy to stop malicious code or an attacker from changing the ownership of files in our container. Although this is a very basic example, it gives you an idea of how you can start to configure **seccomp** profiles to fine-tune them specifically for your needs.

ACTIVITY 11.01: SETTING UP A SECCOMP PROFILE FOR THE PANORAMIC TREKKING APP

The Panoramic Trekking app is coming along nicely, but this chapter has shown that you need to make sure that the actions a user can make on the container are limited. If there is a way in which the container can be accessed by an attacker, you need to set up some safeguard against that possible attacker. In this activity, you will create a **seccomp** profile that you can use with the services in the app that will stop a user from being able to make new directories, kill processes running on the container, and lastly, find out more details about the running container by running the **uname** command.

The steps required to complete this activity are as follows:

1. Obtain a copy of the default **seccomp** profile.

2. Locate the specific controls on the profile that will disable the **mkdir**, **kill**, and **uname** commands.

3. Run the services of the Panoramic Trekking app and ensure that the new profile is applied to the containers.

4. Access the container and verify that you are no longer able to perform the **mkdir**, **kill**, and **uname** commands that have been blocked in the **seccomp** profile. For example, if we perform the **mkdir** command on our new image with the new profile added, we should see a similar output to the following:

```
$ mkdir test

mkdir: can't create directory 'test': Operation not permitted
```

> **NOTE**
> The solution for this activity can be found on page 713.

ACTIVITY 11.02: SCANNING YOUR PANORAMIC TREKKING APP IMAGES FOR VULNERABILITIES

We have been using base images for the Panoramic Trekking app that were provided by other users or developers. In this activity, you will need to scan the images for vulnerabilities and see whether they are safe for use.

The steps you'll need to take to complete this activity are as follows:

1. Decide on a service to use to scan your images.

2. Load your images into the service ready for scanning.

3. Scan the images and see whether any vulnerabilities are present on the images.

4. Verify whether the image is safe for use. You should be able to perform an evaluation check in Anchore and see a pass status similar to the following output:

```
Image Digest: sha256:57d8817bac132c2fded9127673dd5bc7c3a976546
36ce35d8f7a05cad37d37b7
Full Tag: docker.io/dockerrepo/postgres-app:sample_tag
Status: pass
Last Eval: 2019-11-23T06:15:32Z
Policy ID: 2c53a13c-1765-11e8-82ef-23527761d060
```

> **NOTE**
>
> The solution for this activity can be found on page 715.

SUMMARY

This chapter has been all about security, limiting risk when we're working with Docker and our container images, and how can we take our first steps with Docker security. We looked at the potential risks of running container processes as the root user and saw how we can make some minor changes to prevent these issues from arising if attackers were to access the running container. We then looked closer at how we can trust the images we are working with by using signing certificates for images and then implementing security scans on our Docker images.

At the end of this chapter, we started working with security profiles. We used two of the most common security profiles – AppArmor and **seccomp** – implementing both on our Docker images and looking at the result of reducing specific access to the containers. The next chapter will look at implementing best practices when running and creating our Docker images.

12

BEST PRACTICES

OVERVIEW

In this chapter, you will learn some of the best practices to use when working with Docker and your container images. This will enable you to monitor and manage the resources used by your container and limit their effect on your host system. You will analyze Docker's best practices and learn why it's important to only be running one service per container, ensuring that your containers are scalable and immutable and making sure that your underlying applications start in a short amount of time. This chapter will help you to enforce these best practices by linting your **Dockerfiles** and **docker-compose.yml** files before your applications and containers are running with the help of **hadolint's FROM:latest** command and **dcvalidator**.

INTRODUCTION

The previous chapter on security covered some best practices for Docker images and services that have adhered to these best practices. We made sure that our images and services were secure and that they limited what could be achieved if an attacker was able to access the image. This chapter will not only take you through the best practices in creating and running our Docker images, but will also focus on container performance, configuring our services, and ensuring that the services running on them are running as efficiently as possible.

We will start this chapter with an in-depth look at how you can both monitor and configure the resources being used by your services, such as memory and CPU usage. We will then take you through some important practices that you can implement in your projects, looking at how you create your Docker images and the applications that are running on them. Lastly, this chapter will give you some practical tools to use to test your **Dockerfiles** and **docker-compose.yml** files, which will serve as a way to ensure that you are following the mentioned practices.

This chapter shows how you can ensure that you optimize your services and containers as much as possible to make sure that they run without issues from your development environment through to production. The goal of this chapter is to make sure that your services are starting up as quickly as possible and are processing as efficiently as they can. The practices mentioned in this chapter also ensure reusability (that is, they make sure that anyone who wants to reuse your images or code can do so and can understand specifically what is happening at all times). To begin with, the following section discusses how to work with container resources.

WORKING WITH CONTAINER RESOURCES

One of the main benefits of moving to Docker from a traditional server environment is that it enables us to heavily reduce the footprint of our services and applications, even when moving to production. This doesn't mean we can simply run anything on our container, expecting all the processes to simply complete their execution, however. Just as we would need resources with a service running on a standalone server, we need to ensure that the resources (such as CPU, memory, and disk input and output) that are being used by our containers do not cause our production environments or any other containers to crash. By monitoring the resources used in our development system, we can help optimize processes and ensure that the end-user is experiencing seamless operation when we move it into production.

By testing our services and monitoring resource usage, we will be able to understand the resources required by the running applications and ensure that the hosts running our Docker images have adequate resources to run our service. Lastly, as you will see in the upcoming sections, we can also limit the amount of CPU and memory resources the container can have access to. When developing our services running on Docker, we need to be testing these services on our development system to know exactly what will happen when they are moved into test and production environments.

When we bring a number of different services (such as a database, web server, and API gateway) together to create an application, some services are more important than others, and in some circumstances, these services may need to have more resources allocated to them. However, in Docker, the running container does not have a real limit on the resources it can use by default.

In previous chapters, we learned about orchestration using Swarm and Kubernetes, which helps in distributing resources across your system, but this part of the chapter will teach you about some basic tools to test and monitor your resources with. We will also look at the ways in which you can configure your containers to no longer use the default resources available.

To help us in this part of the chapter, we are going to create a new image that will only serve the purpose of demonstrating resource usage in our system. In the first part of this section, we will create an image that will add an application called stress. The main function of the stress application is to impose a heavy load on our system. The image will allow us to view the resources being used on our host system and then allow us to use different options when running the Docker image to limit the resources being used.

> **NOTE**
>
> This section of the chapter will give you some brief guidelines on monitoring the resources of our running Docker containers. This chapter will only cover some simple concepts as we are going to be dedicating an entire chapter of this book to providing in-depth details on monitoring your container metrics.

To help us view the resources being consumed by our running containers, Docker provides the **stats** command as a live stream of resources being consumed by our running containers. If you wish to limit the data presented by the stream, especially if you have a large number of containers running, you can specify to only provide certain containers by specifying the name of the container or its ID:

```
docker stats <container_name|container_id>
```

The default output of the **docker stats** command will provide you with the name and ID of the container, the percentage of host CPU and memory that the container is using, the data that the container is sending and receiving, and the amount of data both read and written from the host's storage:

```
NAME                  CONTAINER           CPU %
docker-stress         c8cf5ad9b6eb         400.43%
```

The following section will highlight how we can use the **docker stats** command to monitor our resources. We will also provide format controls to the **stats** command to provide only the information we need.

MANAGING CONTAINER CPU RESOURCES

This section of the chapter will show you how to set limits on the amount of CPU being used by the container, as a container running without limits can use up all the available CPU resources on a host server. We will be looking at optimizing our running Docker container, but the actual issue with a large amount of CPU being used usually lies with the underlying infrastructure or the applications running on the container.

When we discuss CPU resources, we usually refer to a single physical computer chip. These days, a CPU will most likely have more than one core, with more cores meaning more processes. But this doesn't mean we have unlimited resources. When we display the CPU percentage being used, unless you have a system that only has one CPU with one core, you will most likely see more than 100% of the CPU being used. For example, if you have four cores in the CPU of your system, and your container is utilizing all of the CPU, you will see a value of 400%

We can modify the **docker stats** command running on our system to only provide the CPU usage details by providing the **--format** option. This option allows us to specify the output format we require, as we may only require one or two of the metrics provided by the **stats** command. The following example configures the output of the **stats** command to be displayed in a **table** format, only presenting the container's name, its ID, and the percentage of CPU being used:

```
docker stats --format "table {{.Name}}\t{{.Container}}\t{{.CPUPerc}}"
```

This command, if we have no Docker images running, will provide a table with the following three columns:

```
NAME                    CONTAINER           CPU %
```

To control the number of cores being used on the CPU by our running container, we can use the **--cpus** option with our **docker run** command. The following syntax shows us running the image, but limiting the number of cores the image will have access to by using the **--cpus** option:

```
docker run --cpus 2 <docker-image>
```

A better option is not to set the number of cores a container can use, but instead how much of the total it can share. Docker provides the **--cpushares**, or **-c**, option to set a priority to how much of the processing power a container can use. By using this option, it means we don't need to know how many cores the host machine has before running the container. It also means that we can transfer the running container to different host systems without needing to change the command the image is run with.

By default, Docker will allocate 1,024 shares to every running container. If you set the **--cpushares** value to **256**, it would have a quarter of the processing shares of other running containers:

```
docker run --cpushares 256 <docker-image>
```

> **NOTE**
>
> If no other containers are running on your system, even if you have set the **--cpushares** value to **256**, the container will then be allowed to use up the remaining processing power.

Even though your application may be running fine, it's always good practice to see how it will work when you reduce the amount of CPU it has available to it, as well as seeing how much it will consume while it is running normally.

In the next exercise, we will use the **stress** application to monitor the resource usage on the system.

> **NOTE**
>
> Please use **touch** command to create files and **vim** command to work on the file using vim editor.

EXERCISE 12.01: UNDERSTANDING CPU RESOURCES ON YOUR DOCKER IMAGE

In this exercise, you will first create a new Docker image that will help you generate some resources on your system. We will demonstrate how to use the **stress** application installed on the image. The application will allow you to start monitoring resource usage on your system, as well as allowing you to change the number of CPU resources being used by the image:

1. Create a new **Dockerfile** and open your favorite text editor to enter the following details. You will be creating the image using Ubuntu as a base because the **stress** application is not yet provided as a package to be easily installed on an Alpine base image:

```
FROM ubuntu
RUN apt-get update && apt-get install stress
CMD stress $var
```

2. Build the new image and tag it as **docker-stress** using the **-t** option of the **docker build** command:

```
docker build -t docker-stress .
```

3. Stop and remove all the other containers first before running the new **docker-stress** image to make sure that the results are not confused by other containers running on our system:

```
docker rm -f $(docker -a -q)
```

4. On *line 3* of the **Dockerfile**, you'll notice that the **CMD** instruction is running the stress application following the **$var** variable. This will allow you to add command-line options directly to the stress application running on the container via environment variables, without having to build a new image every time you want to change the functionality. Test this out by running your image and using the **-e** option to add environment variables. Add **var="--cpu 4 --timeout 20"** as a command-line option to the **stress** command:

```
docker run --rm -it -e var="--cpu 4 --timeout 20" docker-stress
```

The **docker run** command has added the **var="--cpu 4 --timeout 20"** variable, which will specifically run the **stress** command with these command-line options. The **--cpu** option is stating that four CPUs or cores of the system will be used, and the **--timeout** option will allow the stress test to run for the designated number of seconds specified – in this case, **20**:

```
stress: info: [6] dispatching hogs: 4 cpu, 0 io, 0 vm, 0 hdd
stress: info: [6] successful run completed in 20s
```

> **NOTE**
>
> If we need to run the **stress** command continuously without stopping, we will simply not include the **--timeout** option. Our examples all include the **timeout** option as we don't want to forget and continuously use resources on a running host system.

5. Run the **docker stats** command to see what effect this has on your host system. Limit the output provided to only give CPU usage by using the **--format** option:

```
docker stats --format "table {{.Name}}\t{{.Container}}\t{{.CPUPerc}}"
```

Unless you have a container running on your system, you should only see the table headings, similar to the output provided here:

```
NAME                CONTAINER           CPU %
```

6. While the **stats** command is running, move into a new terminal window and run the **docker-stress** container again, as in *step 4* of this exercise. Use the **--name** option to make sure you are viewing the correct image when using the **docker stress** command:

```
docker run --rm -it -e var="--cpu 4 --timeout 20" --name docker-stress docker-stress
```

7. Move back to the terminal running **docker stats**. You should now see some output presented on your table. Your output will be different from the following as you may have a different number of cores running on your system. The following output is showing that 400% of our CPU percentage is being used. The system on which the command is run has six cores. It shows that the stress application is using 100% of four of the cores available:

NAME	CONTAINER	CPU %
docker-stress	c8cf5ad9b6eb	400.43%

8. Once again, run the **docker-stress** container, this time with **8** set for the **--cpu** option:

```
docker run --rm -it -e var="--cpu 8 --timeout 20" --name docker-
stress docker-stress
```

As you can see in the following stats output, we have hit the limit where your Docker container is using almost 100% of all six cores on our system, leaving a small amount for processing power for minor processes on our system:

NAME	CONTAINER	CPU %
docker-stress	8946da6ffa90	599.44%

9. Manage the number of cores that your **docker-stress** image can have access to by using the **--cpus** option and specifying the number of cores you want to allow the image to use. In the following command, **2** is set as the number of cores our container is allowed to use:

```
docker run --rm -it -e var="--cpu 8 --timeout 20" --cpus 2 --name
docker-stress docker-stress
```

10. Move back to the terminal running **docker stats**. You will see that the CPU percentage being used does not exceed much more than 200%, showing that Docker is restricting resource usage to only two of the cores available on our system:

NAME	CONTAINER	CPU %
docker-stress	79b32c67cbe3	208.91%

So far, you have only been running one container on our system at a time. The next section of this exercise will allow you to run two containers in detached mode. Here, you will test using the **--cpu-shares** option on one of your running containers to limit the number of cores it can use.

11. If you don't have **docker stats** running in a terminal window, do so by starting it up as you have done previously to allow us to monitor the processes that are running:

```
docker stats --format "table {{.Name}}\t{{.Container}}\t{{.CPUPerc}}"
```

12. Access another terminal window and start up two **docker-stress** containers – **docker-stress1** and **docker-stress2**. The first will use a **--timeout** value of **60** to have the stress application running for 60 seconds, but here, limit the **--cpu-shares** value to **512**:

```
docker run --rm -dit -e var="--cpu 8 --timeout 60" --cpu-shares 512
--name docker-stress1 docker-stress
```

The container's ID will be returned as follows:

```
5f617e5abebabcbc4250380b2591c692a30b3daf481b6c8d7ab8a0d1840d395f
```

The second container will not be limited but will have a **--timeout** value of only **30**, so it should complete first:

```
docker run --rm -dit -e var="--cpu 8 --timeout 30" --name docker-
stress2 docker-stress2
```

The container's ID will be returned as follows:

```
83712c28866dd289937a9c5fe4ea6c48a6863a7930ff663f3c251145e2fbb97a
```

13. Move back to our terminal running **docker stats**. You'll see two containers running. In the following output, we can see the containers named **docker-stress1** and **docker-stress2**. The **docker-stress1** container has been set to have only **512** CPU shares while other containers are running. It can also be observed that it is only using half the amount of CPU resources as our second container named **docker-stress2**:

NAME	CONTAINER	CPU %
docker-stress1	5f617e5abeba	190.25%
docker-stress2	83712c28866d	401.49%

14. When your second container completes the CPU percentage for the **docker-stress1** container, it is then allowed to move up to using almost all six cores available on the running system:

NAME	CONTAINER	CPU %
stoic_keldysh	5f617e5abeba	598.66%

CPU resources play an important part in making sure that your applications are running at their best. This exercise has shown you how easy it is to monitor and configure your container's processing power while it is still on your system before deploying it into a production environment. The next section will move on to performing similar monitoring and configuration changes on our container's memory.

MANAGING CONTAINER MEMORY RESOURCES

Just as we can monitor and control the CPU resources our container is using on our system, we can also do the same with the memory being used. As with CPU, the running container is able to use all of the host's memory with the default settings provided by Docker, and in some cases can cause the system to become unstable if it is not limited. If the host systems kernel detects that there is not enough memory available, it will show an **out-of-memory exception** and start to kill off the processes on the system to help free up memory.

The good news is that the Docker daemon has a high priority on your system, so the kernel will first kill off running containers before it stops the Docker daemon from running. This means that your system should be able to recover if the high memory usage is being caused by a container application.

> **NOTE**
>
> If your running containers are being shut down, you will also need to make sure you have tested your application to ensure that you are limiting the impact it is having on your running processes.

Once again, the **docker stats** command gives us quite a bit of information on memory usage. It will output the percentage of the memory the container is using as well as the current memory being used compared with the total amount of memory it is able to use. As we did previously, we can restrict the output presented with the **--format** option. In the following command, we are reducing the output provided by only displaying the container name and ID, as well as the memory percentage and memory usage, via the **.Name**, **.Container**, **.MemPerc**, and **.MemUsage** attributes, respectively:

```
docker stats --format "table {{.Name}}\t{{.Container}}\t{{.MemPerc}}\t{{.MemUsage}}"
```

With no containers running, the preceding command will show the following output:

```
NAME          CONTAINER          MEM %          MEM USAGE / LIMIT
```

If we want to limit or control the amount of memory being used by our running container, there are a few options available to us. One of the options available is the **--memory**, or **-m**, option, which will set a limit for the amount of memory a running container can use. In the following example, we have used a syntax of **--memory 512MB** to limit the amount of memory available to the image to **512MB**:

```
docker run --memory 512MB <docker-image>
```

If the host system that the container is running on is also using swap space as part of its available memory, you can also assign memory from that container to be run as swap. This is simply done by using the **--memory-swap** option. This can only be used in conjunction with the **--memory** option, as we have demonstrated in the following example. We have set the **--memory-swap** option as **1024MB**, which is the total amount of memory available to the container of both memory and swap memory. So, in our example, there will be a further **512MB** available in the swap:

```
docker run --memory 512MB --memory-swap 1024MB <docker-image>
```

You need to remember, though, that swap memory will be assigned to disk, so as a consequence, it will be slower and less responsive than RAM.

> **NOTE**
>
> The **--memory-swap** option needs to be set to a number higher than the **--memory** option. If it is set to the same number, you will not be able to assign any memory from that running container to swap.

Another option available, and only to be used if you need to ensure the availability of the running container at all times, is the **--oom-kill-disable** option. This option stops the kernel from killing the running container if the host system runs too low on memory. This should only be used together with the **--memory** option to ensure that you set a limit to the memory available to the container. Without a limit, the **--oom-kill-disable** option could easily use all the memory on the host system:

```
docker run --memory 512MB --oom-kill-disable <docker-image>
```

Even though your applications will be well designed, the preceding configurations give you some options to control the amount of memory being used by your running containers.

The next section will provide you with hands-on experience in analyzing the memory resources on your Docker image.

EXERCISE 12.02: ANALYZING MEMORY RESOURCES ON YOUR DOCKER IMAGE

This exercise will help you analyze how memory is used by your active containers while running on your host system. Once again, you will be using the **docker-stress** image created earlier, but this time with options to only use memory on the running container. This command will allow us to implement some of the memory-limiting options available to ensure our running containers do not bring down our running host system:

1. Run the **docker stats** command to display the relevant information you need for the percentage memory and memory usage values:

```
docker stats --format "table {{.Name}}\t{{.Container}}\t{{.
MemPerc}}\t{{.MemUsage}}"
```

This command will provide an output like the following:

```
NAME            CONTAINER        MEM %        MEM USAGE / LIMIT
```

2. Open a new terminal window to run the **stress** command again. Your **docker-stress** image will only utilize CPU when you use the **--cpu** option. Use the **--vm** option in the following command to start up the number of workers you wish to spawn to consume memory. By default, each of them will consume **256MB**:

```
docker run --rm -it -e var="--vm 2 --timeout 20" --name docker-stress
docker-stress
```

When you move back to monitor the running container, the memory used only reached about 20% of the limit. This may be different for different systems. As only two workers are running to consume 256 MB each, you should only see it reach around 500 MB of memory usage:

```
NAME            CONTAINER        MEM %        MEM USAGE / LIMIT
docker-stress   b8af08e4d79d     20.89%       415.4MiB / 1.943GiB
```

3. The stress application also has the **--vm-bytes** option to control the number of bytes that each worker being spawned up will consume. Enter the following command, which has set each worker to **128MB**. It should show a lower usage when you monitor it:

```
docker run --rm -it -e var="--vm 2 --vm-bytes 128MB --timeout 20"
--name stocker-stress docker-stress
```

As you can see, the stress application struggles to push the memory usage up very far at all. If you wanted to use all 8 GB of RAM you have available on your system, you could use **--vm 8 --vm-bytes** of 1,024 MB:

```
NAME            CONTAINER       MEM %    MEM USAGE / LIMIT
docker-stress   ad7630ed97b0    0.04%    904KiB / 1.943GiB
```

4. Reduce the amount of memory available to the **docker-stress** image with the **--memory** option. In the following command, you will see that we have set the available memory of the running container to be limited to **512MB**:

```
docker run --rm -it -e var="--vm 2 --timeout 20" --memory 512MB
--name docker-stress docker-stress
```

5. Move back to the terminal running **docker stats**, and you will see that the percentage of memory used spikes to almost 100%. This isn't a bad thing as it is only a small percentage of the memory allocated to your running container. In this instance, it is 512 MB, which is only a quarter of what it was previously:

```
NAME            CONTAINER       MEM %     MEM USAGE / LIMIT
docker-stress   bd84cf27e480    88.11%    451.1MiB / 512MiB
```

6. Run more than one container at a time and see how our **stats** command responds. Use the **-d** option as part of the **docker run** commands to run the container as a daemon in the background of your host system. Both of the **docker-stress** containers are now going to use six workers each, but our first image, which we will name **docker-stress1**, is limited to **512MB** of memory, while our second image, named **docker-stress2**, which is only running for 20 seconds, will have an unlimited amount of memory:

```
docker run --rm -dit -e var="--vm 6 --timeout 60" --memory 512MB
--name docker-stress1 docker-stress

ca05e244d03009531a6a67045a5b1edbef09778737cab2aec7fa92eeaaa0c487
```

```
docker run --rm -dit -e var="--vm 6 --timeout 20" --name docker-
stress2 docker-stress

6d9cbb966b776bb162a47f5e5ff3d88daee9b0304daa668fca5ff7ae1ee887ea
```

7. Move back to the terminal running **docker stats**. You can see that only one
    container, the **docker-stress1** container, is limited to 512 MB, while the
    docker-stress2 image is allowed to run on a lot more memory:

```
NAME              CONTAINER       MEM %     MEM USAGE / LIMIT
docker-stress1    ca05e244d030    37.10%    190MiB / 512MiB
docker-stress2    6d9cbb966b77    31.03%    617.3MiB / 1.943GiB
```

If you wait a few moments, the **docker-stress1** image will be left to run on
its own:

```
NAME              CONTAINER       MEM %     MEM USAGE / LIMIT
docker-stress1    ca05e244d030    16.17%    82.77MiB / 512MiB
```

> **NOTE**
>
> One option we haven't covered here is the **--memory-reservation**
> option. This is also used with the **--memory** option and needs to be set
> lower than the memory option. It is a soft limit that is activated when the
> memory on the host system is running low, but it is not guaranteed that the
> limit will be enforced.

This part of the chapter has helped to identify how you can run your containers and
monitor usage so that when they are moved into production, they are not stopping
the host system by using up all the available memory. You should now be able to
identify how much memory your image is using and also limit the amount available
if there are issues with long-running or memory-intensive processes. In the next
section, we will look at how our container consumes the device's read and write
resources on our host system disks.

MANAGING THE CONTAINER DISK'S READ AND WRITE RESOURCES

The CPU and memory consumed by a running container are usually the biggest culprits for an environment running poorly, but there could also be an issue with your running containers trying to read or write too much to the host's disk drive. This would most likely have less impact than CPU or memory issues, but if there was a large amount of data being transferred to the host system's drives, it could still cause contention and slow your services down.

Fortunately, Docker also provides us with a way to control the amount of reading and writing that our running containers can perform. Just as we've seen previously, we can use a number of options with our **docker run** command to limit the amount of data we are either reading or writing to our device disks.

The **docker stats** command also allows us to see the data being transferred to and from our running container. It has a dedicated column that can be added to our table using the **BlockIO** value in our **docker stats** command, which represents the read and writes to our host disk drive or directories:

```
docker stats --format "table {{.Name}}\t{{.Container}}\t{{.BlockIO}}"
```

If we don't have any running containers on our system, the preceding command should provide us with the following output:

```
NAME                    CONTAINER           BLOCK I/O
```

If we ever need to limit the amount of data that a running container can move to our host system's disk storage, we can start by using the **--blkio-weight** option with our **docker run** command. This option stands for **Block Input Output Weight** and allows us to set a relative weight for the container to be between **10** and **1000** and is relative to all the other containers running on your system. All containers will be set with the same proportion of bandwidth, which is 500. If a value of 0 is provided to any container, this option will be switched off:

```
docker run --blkio-weight <value> <docker-image>
```

The next option we have available to use is **--device-write-bps**, which will limit the specific write bandwidth available to the device specified with a bytes-per-second value. The specific device is relative to the device the container is using on the host system. This option also has an **iops (Input/Output) per seconds** option that can also be used. The following syntax provides the basic usage of the option where the limit value is a numeric value set as MB:

```
docker run --device-write-bps <device>:<limit> <docker-image>
```

Just as there is a way to limit write processes to the host system's disk, there is also an option to limit the read throughput available. Once again, it also has an **iops (Input/Output) per seconds** option that can be used and will limit the amount of data that can be read from your running container. The following example uses the **--device-read-bps** option as part of the **docker run** command:

```
docker run --device-read-bps <device>:<limit> <docker-image>
```

If you're adhering to container best practices, overconsumption of disk input or output should not be too much of an issue. There is no reason to assume that this will not cause you any problems, though. Just as you have worked with both CPU and memory, your disk input and output should be tested on your running containers before your services are implemented in production.

EXERCISE 12.03: UNDERSTANDING DISK READ AND WRITE

This exercise will allow you to become familiar with viewing the disk read and write of your running container. It will allow you to start running your containers by configuring limits for the disk usage speeds with the options available at runtime:

1. Open a new terminal window and run the following command:

```
docker stats --format "table {{.Name}}\t{{.Container}}\t{{.BlockIO}}"
```

The **docker stats** command with the **BlockIO** option helps us monitor the levels of input and output moving from our container to the host system's disk.

2. Start the container to access it from the bash command line. Perform some tests directly on a running **docker-stress** image. The stress application does give you some options to manipulate the disk utilization on your container and the host system, but it is limited to the only disk writes:

```
docker run -it --rm --name docker-stress docker-stress /bin/bash
```

3. Unlike the CPU and memory usage, the block input and output show the total amount used by the container, so it will not be dynamic and change as the running container performs more changes. Move back to your terminal running **docker stats**. You should see **0B** for both input and output:

```
NAME                CONTAINER           BLOCK I/O
docker-stress       0b52a034f814        0B / 0B
```

4. You will be using the bash shell in this instance as it gives access to the **time** command to see how long each of these processes take. Use the **dd** command, which is a Unix command used to make copies of filesystems and backups. In the following option, create a copy of our **/dev/zero** directory, using the **if** (input file) option, and output it to the **disk.out** file with the **of** (output file) option. The **bs** option is the block size or the amount of data it should read at a time and **count** is the total amount of blocks to read. Finally, set the **oflag** value to **direct**, which means the copy will avoid the buffer cache, so you are seeing a true value of disk reads and writes:

```
time dd if=/dev/zero of=disk.out bs=1M count=10 oflag=direct


10+0 records in
10+0 records out
10485760 bytes (10 MB, 10 MiB) copied, 0.0087094 s, 1.2 GB/s


real    0m0.010s
user    0m0.000s
sys     0m0.007s
```

5. Move back into the terminal running your **docker stats** command. You will see just over 10 MB of data sent to the host system's disk. Unlike CPU and memory, you do not see this data value go down after the transfer has occurred:

```
NAME                CONTAINER           BLOCK I/O
docker-stress       0b52a034f814        0B / 10.5MB
```

You'll also notice that the command in *step 4* was almost instantly completed, with the **time** command showing it took only **0.01s** in real-time to complete. You will see what happens if you restrict the amount of data that can be written to disk, but first, exit out of the running container so that it no longer exists on our system.

6. To start our **docker-stress** container up again, set the **--device-write-bps** option to **1MB** per second on the **/dev/sda** device drive:

```
docker run -it --rm --device-write-bps /dev/sda:1mb --name docker-
stress docker-stress /bin/bash
```

7. Run the **dd** command again, preceded by the **time** command, to test how long it takes. You should see that the command takes a lot longer than what it did in *step 4*. The **dd** command is once again set to copy **1MB** blocks, **10** times:

```
time dd if=/dev/zero of=test.out bs=1M count=10 oflag=direct
```

Because the container is limited to only write 1 MB per second, this command takes 10 seconds, as displayed in the following output:

```
10+0 records in
10+0 records out
10485760 bytes (10 MB, 10 MiB) copied, 10.0043 s, 1.0 MB/s


real    0m10.006s
user    0m0.000s
sys     0m0.004s
```

We've been able to easily see how our running container can affect the underlying host system, specifically when using disk read and write. We have also been able to see how we can easily limit the amount of data that can be written to our device, so there is less contention between running containers. In the next section, we are going to quickly answer the question of what you need to do if you are using **docker-compose** and look at limiting the number of resources being used by your containers.

CONTAINER RESOURCES AND DOCKER COMPOSE

Orchestrators such as Kubernetes and Swarm go a long way in controlling and running your resources and spinning up new hosts if there are extra resources needed. But what do you do if you are running **docker-compose** in your system or a test environment? Fortunately, the previously mentioned resource configurations work nicely with **docker-compose** as well.

Within our **docker-compose.yml** file, under our service, we can use the **resources** option under the **deploy** configurations and specify our resource limits for our service. Just as we have been using options such as **--cpus**, **--cpu_shares**, and **--memory**, we would use the same options in our **docker-compose.yml** file as **cpus**, **cpu_shares**, and **memory**.

The example **compose** file in the following code block is deploying the **docker-stress** image we have been using in this chapter. If we look at *line 8*, we can see the **deploy** statement, followed by the **resources** statement. This is where we can set our limits for our container. Just as we have in the previous section, we have set **cpus** to **2** on *line 11* and **memory** to **256MB** on *line 12*:

```
1 version: '3'
2 services:
3   app:
4     container_name: docker-stress
5     build: .
6     environment:
7       var: "--cpu 2 --vm 6 --timeout 20"
8     deploy:
9       resources:
10        limits:
11          cpus: '2'
12          memory: 256M
```

Even though we have only just touched on this subject, the previous sections covering resource usage should guide you on how you should be allocating resources in your **docker-compose.yml** files. This brings us to the end of this section on resource usage of our Docker containers. From here, we will move on to look at the best practices for creating our **Dockerfiles** and how we can start to use different applications to ensure that we are adhering to these best practices.

BEST PRACTICES IN DOCKER

As our containers and services grow in size and complexity, it is important to make sure we are keeping true to the best practices when creating our Docker images. This is also true for the applications we run on our Docker images. Later in this chapter, we will look to lint our **Dockerfiles** and **docker-compose.yml** files, which will analyze our files for errors and best practices, and this will give you a clearer understanding. In the meantime, let's look into some of the more important best practices to keep in mind when you are creating your Docker images and how your applications should be working with them.

> **NOTE**
>
> This chapter may cover some points from previous chapters, but we will be able to give you more information and clarity on why we are using these practices.

In the following section, we will run through some of the more common best practices you should be following when creating your services and containers.

RUNNING ONE SERVICE PER CONTAINER

In modern microservice architecture, we need to remember that only one service should be installed in each container. The container's main process is set by the **ENTRYPOINT** or **CMD** instruction at the end of the `Dockerfile`.

The service you have installed in your container could quite easily run multiple processes of itself, but to get the full benefit of Docker and microservices, you should only be running one service per container. To break this down further, your container should only have a single responsibility, and if it is responsible for doing more than one thing, then it should be broken out into different services.

By limiting what each container can do, we effectively reduce the resources being used by the image and potentially reduce the size of the image. As we saw in the previous chapter, this will also reduce the chances of an attacker being able to perform anything they shouldn't if they gain access to a running container. It also means that if the container stops working for some reason, there is a limited effect on the rest of the applications running on the environment and the service will have an easier time recovering.

BASE IMAGES

When we start with a base image for our container, one of the first things we need to do is to make sure we are starting with an up-to-date image. Do a little research as well to make sure you are not using an image that has a lot of extra applications installed that are not needed. You may find that a base image supported by a specific language that your application uses or a specific focus will limit the size of the image needed, limiting what you need to install when you are creating your image.

This is why we are using a PostgreSQL-supported Docker image instead of installing the application on the image during build time. The PostgreSQL-supported image ensures that it is secure and running at the latest version and makes sure we are not running applications on the image that are not needed.

When specifying our base image for our **Dockerfile**, we need to make sure we are also specifying a specific version and not letting Docker simply use the **latest** image. Also, make sure you are not pulling an image from a repository or registry that is not from a reputable or trusted provider.

If you've been working with Docker for a little while, you may have come across the **MAINTAINER** instruction where you specify the author of the generated image. This has now been deprecated, but you can still provide these details using a **LABEL** directive instead, as we have in the following syntax:

```
LABEL maintainer="myemailaddress@emaildomain.com"
```

INSTALLING APPLICATIONS AND LANGUAGES

When you are installing applications on your images, always remember that there is no need to be performing **apt-get update** or **dist-upgrade**. You should be looking at a different image if you need to be upgrading the image version this way. If you are installing applications using **apt-get** or **apk**, make sure you are specifying the specific version you need as you don't want to install a version that is new or untested.

When you are installing packages, make sure you are using the **-y** switch to make sure the build does not stop and ask for a user prompt. Alternatively, you should also use **--no-install-recommends** as you don't want to install a large group of applications that your package manager has recommended and that you won't need. Also, if you using a Debian-based container, make sure that you are using **apt-get** or **apt-cache**, as the **apt** command has been specifically made for user interaction and not for a scripted installation.

If you are installing applications from other forms, such as building the application from code, make sure you are cleaning up the installation files to once again reduce the size of the image you are creating. Again, if you are using **apt-get**, you should also remove the lists in **/var/lib/apt/lists/** to clean up installation files and reduce the size of your container image.

RUNNING COMMANDS AND PERFORMING TASKS

As our image is being created, we usually need to perform some tasks within our **Dockerfile** to set up the environment ready for our services to be run. Always make sure you are not using the **sudo** command as this could cause some unexpected results. If you need to be running commands as root, your base image will most likely be running as the root user; just make sure you create a separate user to run your application and services and that the container has changed to the required user before it has completed building.

Make sure you are moving to different directories using **WORKDIR**, instead of running instructions that specify a long path, as this could be hard for users to read. Use **JSON** notation for the **CMD** and **ENTRYPOINT** arguments and always make sure you only have one **CMD** or **ENTRYPOINT** instruction.

CONTAINERS NEED TO BE IMMUTABLE AND STATELESS

We need to ensure that our containers and the services running on them are immutable. We must not treat containers like traditional servers, especially a server where you would update applications on a running container. You should be able to update your container from code and deploy it without needing to access it at all.

When we say immutable, we mean the container will not be modified at all during its life, with no updates, patches, or config changes being made. Any changes to your code or updates should be implemented by building the new image and then deploying it into your environment. This makes deployments safer as if you have any issues with your upgrade, you simply redeploy the old version of the image. It also means you have the same image running across all of your environments, making sure your environments are as identical as possible.

When we talk about a container needing to be stateless, this means that any data needed to run the container should be running outside of the container. File stores should also be outside the container, possibly on cloud storage or using a mounted volume. Removing data from the container means the container can be cleanly shut down and destroyed at any time, without fearing data loss. When a new container is created to replace the old one, it simply connects to the original data store.

DESIGNING APPLICATIONS TO BE HIGHLY AVAILABLE AND SCALABLE

Using containers in a microservices architecture is designed to allow your application to scale to multiple instances. So, when developing your applications on your Docker container, you should expect that there could be situations where many instances of your application could be deployed concurrently, scaling both up and down when needed. There should also be no issue with your services running and completing when there is a heavier-than-normal load on the container.

When your services need to scale due to increased requests, how much time your applications need to start becomes an important issue. Before deploying your services into a production environment, you need to make sure the startup time is quick to make sure the system will be able to scale more efficiently without causing any delay in service to your users. To ensure that your services adhere to the industry's best practices, your services should be starting in less than 10 seconds, but less than 20 seconds is also acceptable.

As we saw in the previous section, improving the application startup time is not simply a matter of providing more CPU and memory resources. We need to make sure that the applications on our containers run efficiently and, once again, if they are taking too long to start and run specific processes, you may be performing too many tasks in one application.

IMAGES AND CONTAINERS NEED TO BE TAGGED APPROPRIATELY

We covered this topic in detail in *Chapter 3, Managing Your Docker Images*, and made it clear that we need to think about how we name and tag our images, especially when we start working with larger development teams. To allow all users the ability to understand what the image does and gain an understanding of what version is deployed into an environment, a relevant tagging and naming strategy needs to be decided and agreed upon before the bulk of the work is started by your team.

Image and container names need to be relevant to the applications they are running, as ambiguous names can cause confusion. An agreed standard for versioning must also be put in place to make sure any user can identify what version is running in a certain environment and what version is the most recent and stable release. As we mentioned in *Chapter 3, Managing Your Docker Images*, try not to use `latest`, and instead opt for either a semantic versioning system or Git repository `commit` hash, where users can then refer to either documentation or a build environment to ensure that they have the most up-to-date version of their image.

CONFIGURATIONS AND SECRETS

Environment variables and secrets should never be built into your Docker image. By doing this, you are going against the rule of reusable images. Building images with your secret credentials is also a security risk because they will be stored in one of the image layers, and so anyone able to pull the image will be able to see the credentials.

When setting up the configuration for your application, it may need to change from environment to environment, so it is important to remember that you will need to be able to dynamically change these configurations when needed. This could include specific configurations for the language your application is written in or even the database that the application needs to connect to. We mentioned earlier that if you are configuring your application as part of your **Dockerfile**, this will then make it difficult to change and you may need to create a specific **Dockerfile** for each environment you wish to deploy your image to.

One way to configure your images, as we have seen with the **docker-stress** image, is to use an environment variable that is set on the command line when we run the image. The entry point or command should contain default values if variables have not been provided. This will mean the container will still start up and run even if the extra variables have not been provided:

```
docker run -e var="<variable_name>" <image_name>
```

By doing this, we have made our configuration more dynamic, but this could limit your configuration when you have a larger or more complex configuration. The environment variables can easily be transferred from your **docker run** command to **docker-compose** to then be used in Swarm or Kubernetes.

For larger configurations, you may want to mount a configuration file via a Docker volume. This can mean you will be able to set up a configuration file and run it on your system to test easily, and then if you need to move to an orchestration system such as Kubernetes or Swarm, or an external configuration management solution, you will be able to easily convert this into a configuration map.

If we wanted to implement this with the **docker-stress** image we have been using in this chapter, it could be modified to use a configuration file to mount the values we would like to run. In the following example, we have modified the **Dockerfile** to set up *line 3* to run a script that will instead run the **stress** command for us:

```
1 FROM ubuntu
2 RUN apt-get update && apt-get install stress
3 CMD ["sh","/tmp/stress_test.sh"]
```

This means we can build the Docker image and have it ready and available for us to use whenever we need it. We would just need a script that we would mount in the **/tmp** directory to be run. We could use the following example:

```
1 #!/bin/bash
2
3 /usr/bin/stress --cpu 8 --timeout 20 --vm 6 --timeout 60
```

This illustrates the idea of moving our values from environment variables to a file. To run both the container and the stress application, we would then perform the following, knowing that if we wanted to change the variables being used by the **stress** command, we would only need to make a minor change to the file we are mounting:

```
docker run --rm -it -v ${PWD}/stress_test.sh:/tmp/stress_test.sh docker-stress
```

> **NOTE**
>
> The first thing you are going to think when you read through this list of best practices is that we have gone against a lot of this, but please remember that we have done this in a lot of instances to demonstrate a process or idea.

MAKING YOUR IMAGES MINIMAL AND SMALL

Chapter 3, Managing Your Docker Images, also saw us do some work on making our images as small as we possibly could. We saw that by reducing the size of our images, the images can be built faster. They can also then be pulled faster and run on our systems. Any unnecessary software or applications installed on our containers can take up extra space and resources on our host system and could slow our services down as a result.

Using an application such as Anchore Engine as we did in *Chapter 11, Docker Security,* showed that we can audit our images to view their contents, as well as the applications installed on them. This is an easy way to make sure we are reducing the sizes of our images and making them as minimal as possible.

You now have an idea of the best practices you should be using in your container images and services. The following section of this chapter will help you enforce some of these best practices by using applications to verify that your **Dockerfiles** and **docker-compose.yml** are created as they should be.

ENFORCING DOCKER BEST PRACTICES IN YOUR CODE

Just as we look to make our coding easier when we are developing applications, we can use external service and tests to make sure our Docker images are adhering to the best practices. In the following sections of this chapter, we are going to use three tools to make sure that our **Dockerfiles** and **docker-compose.yml** files are adhering to the best practices, as well as making sure we are not introducing potential issues when our Docker images are built.

The tools included will be straightforward to use and provide powerful functionality. We will start by using **hadolint** to lint our **Dockerfiles** directly on our system, which will run as a separate Docker image that we feed our **Dockerfiles** into. We then take a look at **FROM:latest**, which is an online service that provides some basic functionality in helping us pinpoint issues with our **Dockerfiles**. Lastly, we then look at **Docker Compose Validator** (**DCValidator**), which will perform a similar function, but in this case, we will lint our **docker-compose.yml** files to help pinpoint potential issues.

By using these tools before we build and deploy our images, we hope to reduce our build times for our Docker images, reduce the number of errors we introduce, potentially reduce the size of our Docker images, and help us learn more about and enforce Docker best practices.

USING DOCKER LINTER FOR YOUR IMAGES

The GitHub repository containing all the code for this book also includes tests that will compare against the built Docker image. A linter, on the other hand, will analyze your code and look for potential errors before the image is built. In this section of the chapter, we are looking for potential issues with our **Dockerfiles**, specifically using an application called **hadolint**.

The name **hadolint** is short for **Haskell Dockerfile Linter** and comes with its own Docker image that allows you to pull the image and then send your **Dockerfile** to the running image for it to be tested. Even if your **Dockerfile** is relatively small and builds and runs without any issues, **hadolint** will usually offer a lot of suggestions and point out flaws in your **Dockerfile**, as well as potential issues that might break in the future.

To run **hadolint** over your **Dockerfiles**, you need to have the **hadolint** Docker image on your system. As you know by now, this is simply a matter of running the **docker pull** command with the name and repository of the required image. In this instance, both the repository and image are called **hadolint**:

```
docker pull hadolint/hadolint
```

To then use the application, you simply run the **hadolint** image and point your **Dockerfile** to it using the less than (**<**) symbol, as we've done in the following example:

```
docker run hadolint/hadolint < Dockerfile
```

If you are lucky enough to not have any issues with your **Dockerfile**, you should not see any output from the preceding command. If there is ever a situation where you need to ignore a specific warning, you can do so by using the **--ignore** option, followed by the specific rule ID that has been triggering the warning:

```
docker run hadolint/hadolint hadolint --ignore <hadolint_rule_id> - < Dockerfile
```

If you need to have a few warnings ignored, it may get a little complicated trying to implement this in the command line, so **hadolint** also has the option to set up a configuration file. The **hadolint** configuration file is limited to ignoring warnings and providing a list of trusted repositories. You can also set up a configuration file with a list of your ignored warnings listed in the YAML format. **hadolint** will then need to have this file mounted on the running image for it to be used by the application as it will look for a **.hadolint.yml** configuration file location in the application's home directory:

```
docker run --rm -i -v ${PWD}/.hadolint.yml:/.hadolint.yaml hadolint/hadolint < Dockerfile
```

hadolint is one of the better applications for linting your **Dockerfiles** and can easily be automated as part of a build and deployment pipelines. As an alternative, we are also going to look at an online application called **FROM:latest**. This application is a web-based service that does not provide the same functionality as **hadolint** but does allow you to easily copy and paste your **Dockerfile** code into the online editor and receive feedback on whether the **Dockerfile** adheres to the best practices.

EXERCISE 12.04: LINTING YOUR DOCKERFILES

This exercise will help you understand how to access and run **hadolint** on your system to help you enforce best practices on your **Dockerfiles**. We will also use an online **Dockerfile** linter called **FROM:latest** to compare the warnings we receive:

1. Pull the image from the **hadolint** repository with the following **docker pull** command:

```
docker pull hadolint/hadolint
```

2. You have a **Dockerfile** ready to go with the **docker-stress** image you used to test and manage your resources earlier in this chapter. Run the **hadolint** image to lint this **Dockerfile**, or any other **Dockerfile**, and send it to the **Dockerfile** using the less than (**<**) symbol, as in the following command:

```
docker run --rm -i hadolint/hadolint < Dockerfile
```

As you can see from the following output, even though our **docker-stress** image was relatively small, **hadolint** has given quite a few different ways where we can improve the performance and help our image adhere to the best practices:

```
/dev/stdin:1 DL3006 Always tag the version of an image explicitly
/dev/stdin:2 DL3008 Pin versions in apt get install. Instead of
'apt-get install <package>' use 'apt-get install
<package>=<version>'
/dev/stdin:2 DL3009 Delete the apt-get lists after installing
something
/dev/stdin:2 DL3015 Avoid additional packages by specifying
'--no-install-recommends'
/dev/stdin:2 DL3014 Use the '-y' switch to avoid manual input
'apt-get -y install <package>'
/dev/stdin:3 DL3025 Use arguments JSON notation for CMD
and ENTRYPOINT arguments
```

NOTE

If your **Dockerfile** runs successfully through **hadolint** and there are no issues found, there will be no output presented to the user on the command line.

3. `hadolint` also gives you the option to suppress different checks with the `--ignore` option. In the following command, we have chosen to ignore the **DL3008** warning, where it is suggesting that you pin the applications you are installing to a specific version number. Execute the **docker run** command to suppress the **DL3008** warning. Note that you need to provide the full `hadolint` command after specifying the image name you are running, as well as an extra dash (**-**) before you provide the **Dockerfile**:

```
docker run --rm -i hadolint/hadolint hadolint --ignore DL3008 - <
Dockerfile
```

You should get output like the following:

```
/dev/stdin:1 DL3006 Always tag the version of an image explicitly
/dev/stdin:2 DL3009 Delete the apt-get lists after installing
something
/dev/stdin:2 DL3015 Avoid additional packages by specifying
'--no-install-recommends'
/dev/stdin:2 DL3014 Use the '-y' switch to avoid manual input
'apt-get -y install <package>'
/dev/stdin:3 DL3025 Use arguments JSON notation for CMD and
ENTRYPOINT arguments
```

4. `hadolint` also allows you to create a configuration file to add any warnings to be ignored, as well as specifying them on the command line. Create a file named `.hadolint.yml` using the **touch** command:

```
touch .hadolint.yml
```

5. Open the configuration file with your text editor and enter in and any of the warnings you wish to ignore that you have received under the **ignored** field. As you can see, you can also add in a **trustedRegistries** field, where you can list all the registries you will be pulling images from. Note that **hadolint** will provide an extra warning if your image is not from one of the registries listed in the configuration file:

```
ignored:
    - DL3006
    - DL3008
    - DL3009
    - DL3015
```

```
   - DL3014
trustedRegistries:
  - docker.io
```

6. **hadolint** will look for your configuration file in the user's home directory. As you are running **hadolint** as a Docker image, mount the file from the current location onto the home directory on the running image when we execute the **docker run** command with the **-v** option:

```
docker run --rm -i -v ${PWD}/.hadolint.yml:/.hadolint.yaml hadolint/
hadolint < Dockerfile
```

The command will give an output as follows:

```
/dev/stdin:3 DL3025 Use arguments JSON notation for CMD and
ENTRYPOINT arguments
```

> **NOTE**
>
> The source code repository for **hadolint** provides a list of all the warnings as well as details on how to resolve them in your **Dockerfile**. If you have not done so already, feel free to look through the Hadolint wiki page at https://github.com/hadolint/hadolint/wiki.

7. Finally, **hadolint** also allows you the option to output the results of your check in JSON format. Once again, we need to add some extra values to the command line. In the command line, add the extra command-line options of **hadolint -f json** just before you have added and parsed your **Dockerfile** across to **hadolint**. In the following command, you will also need to have the **jq** package installed:

```
docker run --rm -i -v ${PWD}/.hadolint.yml:/.hadolint.yaml hadolint/
hadolint hadolint -f json - < Dockerfile | jq
```

You should get output like the following:

```
[
  {
    "line": 3,
    "code": "DL3025",
    "message": "Use arguments JSON notation for CMD and ENTRYPOINT
arguments",
    "column": 1,
    "file": "/dev/stdin",
```

```
      "level": "warning"
    }
  ]
```

> **NOTE**
>
> **hadolint** can easily be integrated into your build pipelines to have your **Dockerfiles** linted before they are built. If you are interested in installing the **hadolint** application directly onto your system instead of using the Docker image, you can do so by cloning the following GitHub repository https://github.com/hadolint/hadolint.

hadolint is not the only application that you can use to ensure your **Dockerfiles** are adhering to best practices. The next steps in this exercise will look at an online service named **FROM:latest** to also help enforce best practices on your **Dockerfiles**.

8. To use **FROM:latest**, open your favorite web browser and enter the following URL:

```
https://www.fromlatest.io
```

When the web page loads, you should see a page similar to the one in the following screenshot. On the left-hand side of the web page, you should see a sample **Dockerfile** entered, and on the right-hand side of the web page, you should see a list of potential issues or ways to optimize your **Dockerfile**. Each of the items listed on the right-hand side has a dropdown to provide more details to the user:

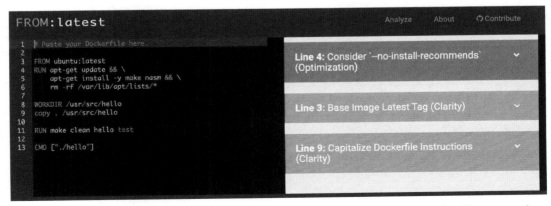

Figure 12.1: A screenshot of the FROM:latest website with a sample Dockerfile entered

9. As in the previous part of this exercise, we will use the **Dockerfile** from our **docker-stress** image. To use this with **FROM: latest**, copy the following lines of code into the left-hand side of the web page over the sample **Dockerfile** provided by the site:

```
FROM ubuntu
RUN apt-get update && apt-get install stress
CMD stress $var
```

As soon as you post the **Dockerfile** code into the web page, the page will start to analyze the commands. As you can see from the following screenshot, it will provide details on how to resolve potential issues and optimize the **Dockerfile** to have the image build quicker:

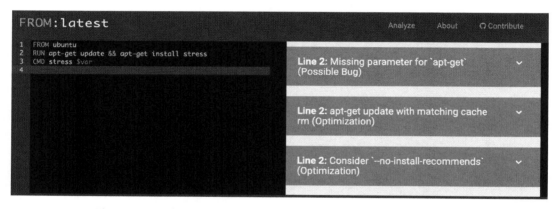

Figure 12.2: The Dockerfile entered for our docker-stress image

Both **hadolint** and **FROM latest** provide easy-to-use options to help you make sure your **Dockerfiles** are adhering to best practices. The next exercise will look at a similar way to check your **docker-compose.yml** files to make sure that they will also run without issues and are not introducing any bad practices.

EXERCISE 12.05: VALIDATING YOUR DOCKER-COMPOSE.YML FILE

Docker already has a tool to validate your **docker-compose.yml** files, but the built-in validator does not pick up all issues in your **docker-compose** files, including typos, the same ports being assigned to different services, or duplicate keys. We can use **dcvalidator** to look for issues such as typos, duplicate keys, and ports assigned to numbers services.

To perform the following exercise, you will need to have both Git and a recent version of Python 3 installed on your system. You won't be walked through how to perform the installation, but these items are required before starting:

1. To get started with the **dcvalidator**, clone the GitHub repository for the project. If you have not done so already, you will need to run the following command to clone the repository:

```
git clone https://github.com/serviceprototypinglab/dcvalidator.git
```

2. The command-line application only needs Python 3 to run, but you will need to make sure all the dependencies are installed first, so change to the **dcvalidator** directory of the repository you have just cloned:

```
cd dcvalidator
```

3. Installing the dependencies for the **dcvalidator** is easy, and your system will most likely have most of them installed on it already. To install the dependencies, run the **pip3 install** command from the **dcvalidator** directory using the **-r** option to use the **requirments.txt** file in the server directory:

```
pip3 install -r server/requirments.txt
```

4. Create a **docker-compose** file from scratch that will use some of the images you have already created in this chapter. Create a **docker-compose.yml** file by using the **touch** command:

```
touch docker-compose.yml
```

5. Open your favorite text editor to edit the **docker-compose** file. Make sure you also include the mistakes we have purposely added to the file to make sure the **dcvalidator** picks up these errors, and we will use the **docker-stress** image we created earlier in this chapter. Make sure you copy this file word for word as we are trying to make sure we force some errors in our **docker-compose.yml** file:

```
version: '3'
services:
  app:
    container_name: docker-stress-20
    build: .
    environment:
      var: "--cpu 2 --vm 6 --timeout 20"
    ports:
      - 80:8080
```

```
      - 80:8080
    dns: 8.8.8
    deploy:
      resources:
        limits:
          cpus: '0.50'
          memory: 50M


  app2:
    container_name: docker-stress-30
    build: .
    environment:
      var: "--cpu 2 --vm 6 --timeout 30"
    dxeploy:
      resources:
        limits:
          cpus: '0.50'
          memory: 50M
```

6. Run the **validator-cli.py** script with the **-f** option to parse the specific file we want to validate – in the following command line, the **docker-compose. yml** file. The **-fi** option then allows you to specify the filters available to validate over our **compose** file. In the following code, we are using all the filters available at this point for **validator-cli**:

```
python3 validator-cli.py -f docker-compose.yml -fi 'Duplicate
Keys,Duplicate ports,Typing mistakes,DNS,Duplicate expose'
```

You should get output like the following:

```
Warning: no kafka support
loading compose files....
checking consistency...
syntax is ok
= type: docker-compose
- service:app
Duplicate ports in service app port 80
=================== ERROR ====================
Under service: app
The DNS is not appropriate!
=============================================
- service:app2
```

```
==================== ERROR ====================
I can not find 'dxeploy' tag under 'app2' service.
Maybe you can use:
deploy


===============================================
services: 2
labels:
time: 0.0s
```

As expected, there are quite a few errors that **validator-cli.py** has been able to find. It has shown that you have duplicate ports assigned in your app service, and the DNS you have set up is also incorrect. **App2** is showing some spelling mistakes and suggesting we could use a different value instead.

> **NOTE**
>
> At this point, you need to specify the filters you would like your **docker-compose.yml** file to be validated against, but this will change with the coming releases.

7. You'll remember that we used a **docker-compose** file to install the Anchore image scanner. When you have the URL location of the **compose** file, use the **-u** option to pass the URL for the file to be validated. In this instance, it is on the Packt GitHub account:

```
python3 validator-cli.py -u https://github.com/PacktWorkshops/
The-Docker-Workshop/blob/master/Chapter11/Exercise11.03/
docker-compose.yaml -fi 'Duplicate Keys,Duplicate ports,Typing
mistakes,DNS,Duplicate expose'
```

As you can see in the following code block, **dcvalidator** does not pick up any errors in the **docker-compose.yml** file:

```
Warning: no kafka support
discard cache...
loading compose files....
checking consistency...
syntax is ok
= type: docker-compose=
- service:engine-api
- service:engine-catalog
- service:engine-simpleq
```

```
    - service:engine-policy-engine
    - service:engine-analyzer
    - service:anchore-db
    services: 6
    labels:
    time: 0.6s
```

As you can see, the Docker Compose validator is fairly basic, but it can pick up a few errors in our **docker-compose.yml** file that we may have missed. This could especially be the case if we have a larger file; there is a possibility that we could have missed a few minor errors before trying to deploy our environment. This has brought us to the end of this part of the chapter where we have been using some automated processes and applications to validate and lint our **Dockerfiles** and **docker-compose.yml** file.

Now, let's move on to the activities, which will help you test your understanding of the chapter. In the following activity, you will view the resources used by one of the services running on the Panoramic Trekking App.

ACTIVITY 12.01: VIEWING THE RESOURCES USED BY THE PANORAMIC TREKKING APP

Earlier in this chapter, we looked at how our running container consumed resources on our host system. In this activity, you will choose one of the services running on the Panoramic Trekking App, run the container with its default configurations, and see what CPU and memory resources it uses. Then, run the container again with changes to the CPU and memory configurations to see how this affects the resource usage:

The general set of steps you'll need to complete this activity runs as follows:

1. Decide on a service in the Panoramic Trekking App that you would like to test.

2. Create a set of tests that you can use to then measure the resource usage of the service.

3. Start your service and monitor the resource usage using the tests you created in the previous step.

4. Stop your service from running and run it again, this time with changes to the CPU and memory configurations.

5. Monitor the resource usage again using the tests you created in *step 2* and compare the changes in resource usage.

> **NOTE**
>
> The solution for this activity can be found on page 718.

The next activity will help you use **hadolint** on your **Dockerfiles** to improve the best practices.

ACTIVITY 12.02: USING HADOLINT TO IMPROVE THE BEST PRACTICES ON DOCKERFILES

hadolint provides a great way to enforce best practices when you are creating your Docker images. In this activity, you will once again use the **Dockerfile** from the **docker-stress** image to see whether you can use the recommendations from **hadolint** to improve the **Dockerfile** so that it adheres to best practices as much as possible.

The steps you'll need to complete this activity are as follows:

1. Ensure you have the **hadolint** image available and running on your system.

2. Run the **hadolint** image over the **Dockerfile** for the **docker-stress** image and record the results.

3. Make the recommended changes to the **Dockerfile** from the previous step.

4. Test the **Dockerfile** again.

You should get the following output on the successful completion of the activity:

Figure 12.3: Expected output of Activity 12.02

> **NOTE**
>
> The solution for this activity can be found on page 722.

SUMMARY

This chapter has seen us go through a lot of theory as well as some in-depth work on exercises. We started the chapter by looking at how our running Docker containers utilize the host system's CPU, memory, and disk resources. We looked at the ways in which we can monitor how these resources are consumed by our containers and configure our running containers to reduce the number of resources used.

We then looked at the Docker best practices, working through a number of different topics, including utilizing base images, installing programs and cleanup, developing your underlying application for scalability, and configuring your applications and images. We then introduced some tools to help you enforce these best practices, including **hadolint** and **FROM:latest** to help you lint your **Dockerfiles**, and **dcvalidator** to check over your **docker-compose.yml** files.

The next chapter takes our monitoring skills up another level as we introduce using Prometheus to monitor our container metrics and resources.

13

MONITORING DOCKER METRICS

OVERVIEW

This chapter will provide you with the skills needed to set up a monitoring environment for your system to start collecting container and resource metrics. By the end of this chapter, you will be able to devise a monitoring strategy for your metrics and determine what you need to think about before you start development on your project. You will also implement a basic Prometheus configuration on your system. The chapter will extend your knowledge of Prometheus by exploring the user interface, the PromQL query language, configuration options, and the collection of your Docker and application metrics. It will also enhance your visualizations and dashboarding with the inclusion of Grafana as part of your Prometheus installation.

INTRODUCTION

In the previous chapter of this book, we spent some time investigating how our containers use resources on their host system. We did this to ensure our applications and containers were running as efficiently as possible, but when we start to move our applications and containers into a larger production environment, using command-line tools such as **docker stats** will start to become cumbersome. You'll notice that as the number of your containers increases, it becomes difficult to understand the metrics by only using the **stats** command. As you'll see in the following pages, with a little bit of planning and configuration, setting up monitoring for our container environment will allow us to easily keep track of how our containers and system are functioning and ensure uptime for our production services.

As we move into more agile development processes, the development of applications needs to incorporate the monitoring of our applications. Having a clear plan to monitor our applications at the start of the project will allow developers to incorporate monitoring tools as part of their development process. This means that it is important to have a clear understanding of how we're planning to collect and monitor our applications even before we create them.

In addition to applications and services, it is also important to monitor the infrastructure, orchestration, and containers that run in our environments so that we have a complete view of everything that is happening in our environment.

Some things you will need to consider when you establish your metrics monitoring policy are as follows:

- **Applications and Services**: This includes third-party applications on which your code may be relying that don't reside on your hardware. It would also include the orchestration services your applications are running on.

- **Hardware**: It is sometimes good to step back and make sure you take note of all the hardware your services rely on as well, including databases, API gateways, and servers.

- **Services to Monitor and Alert**: As your applications grow, you may not only want to monitor a specific service or web page; you may also want to ensure that users are able to perform all the transactions. This could increase the complexity of your alerting and monitoring system.

- **Dashboarding and Reporting**: Dashboards and reports can provide a lot of useful information to non-technical users.

- **What Application Fits Your Needs**: If you are working for a larger company, they will most likely have a list of applications you can choose from. It should not be one size fits all though. The application you decide to use to monitor your environment should be fit for purpose and agreed upon by everyone involved in the project.

This is where **Prometheus** comes in. In this chapter, we will use Prometheus as a monitoring solution as it is widely adopted, open-source, and free to use. There are a number of other free and enterprise applications available in the market that provide similar monitoring, including self-hosted applications such as Nagios and SCOM, through to newer subscription-based services, including New Relic, Sumo Logic, and Datadog. Prometheus was built from a specific need to monitor services on the cloud. It provides class-leading functionality that is ahead of the other major players in the market.

Some of the other applications also provide log collection and aggregation, but we have assigned this to a separate application and will be dedicating our next chapter to log management for our Docker environment. Prometheus is only focused on metrics collection and monitoring, and as there are suitable free and open-source alternatives in log management, it has not moved to incorporate log management as part of its focus.

MONITORING ENVIRONMENT METRICS WITH PROMETHEUS

Prometheus was originally created and developed by SoundCloud as they needed a way to monitor their highly dynamic container environments and were not satisfied with the current tooling at the time because they felt it didn't fit their needs. Prometheus was developed as a way for SoundCloud to monitor not only their containers but also the underlying hosting hardware and orchestration running their services.

Its initial creation was back in 2012, and since then, the project has been free and open source and part of the Cloud Native Computing Foundation. It has also been widely adopted by companies across the globe needing to gain more insight into how their cloud environments are performing.

Prometheus works by gathering metrics of interest from our system and stores these in its local on-disk, time-series database. It does this by scraping an HTTP endpoint provided by the service or application you are collecting data from.

The endpoint can either be written into the application to provide a basic web interface providing metrics related to the application or service, or it can be provided by an exporter that will take data from the service or application and then expose it in a form that is understandable to Prometheus.

> **NOTE**
>
> This chapter mentions the HTTP endpoint on a number of occasions, and this may lead to confusion. You will see later in this chapter that the HTTP endpoint is a very basic HTTP web page provided by the service or an application. As you'll see shortly, this HTTP web page provides a list of all the metrics the service exposes to Prometheus and also provides a metrics value that is stored in the Prometheus time-series database.

Prometheus includes a number of components:

- **Prometheus**: The Prometheus application performs the scraping and collecting of metrics and stores them in its time-series database.

- **Grafana**: The Prometheus binary also includes a basic web interface to help you start to query the database. In most cases, Grafana will also be added to the environment to allow a more visually appealing interface. It will allow dashboards to be created and stored to allow metric monitoring in a much easier manner.

- **Exporters**: Exporters provide Prometheus with the metrics endpoints needed to collect data from the different applications and services. In this chapter, we will enable the Docker daemon to export data and install `cAdvisor` to provide metrics on the specific containers running on our system.

- **AlertManager**: Although not covered in this chapter, `AlertManager` will usually be installed with Prometheus to trigger an alert when services are down or other alerts that are triggered in your environment.

Prometheus also provides a web-based expression browser to allow you to then view and aggregate the time-series metrics you have collected using the functional PromQL query language. This means you are able to view your data as you collect it. The expression browser is a little limited but can be integrated with Grafana to allow you to create dashboards, monitoring services, and `AlertManager` to allow you to trigger alerts and be notified when needed.

Prometheus is easy to install and configure (as you'll see shortly) and collects data on itself to allow you to start testing your application.

Due to the rate of adoption and popularity of Prometheus, many companies have created exporters for their applications and services. We will be giving you some examples of the exporters available throughout this chapter.

It's now time to get your hands dirty. In the following exercise, you will download and run the Prometheus binary on your own system to start monitoring the services.

> **NOTE**
>
> Please use **touch** command to create files and **vim** command to work on the file using vim editor.

EXERCISE 13.01: INSTALLING AND RUNNING PROMETHEUS

In this exercise, you will download and unpack the Prometheus binary, start the application, and explore the web interface and some basic configurations of Prometheus. You will also practice monitoring metrics, such as the total HTTP requests made to the Prometheus interface.

> **NOTE**
>
> As of the time of writing this book, the latest version of Prometheus is version 2.15.1. The latest version of the application can be found at the following URL: https://prometheus.io/download/.

1. Locate the latest version of Prometheus to install. Use the **wget** command to bring the compressed archive onto your system. The URL you use in your command may differ from the one here, depending on your operating system and the version of Prometheus you are using:

```
wget https://github.com/prometheus/prometheus/releases/download/
v2.15.1/prometheus-2.15.1.<operating-system>-amd64.tar.gz
```

2. Uncompress the Prometheus archive you downloaded in the previous step using the **tar** command. The following command uses the **zxvf** options to unzip the file, and then extract the archive and files, with verbose output:

```
tar zxvf prometheus-2.15.1.<operating-system>-amd64.tar.gz
```

3. The archive provides a fully created Prometheus binary application ready to be started up. Move into the application directory to look through some of the import files included in the directory:

```
cd prometheus-2.15.1.<operating-system>-amd64
```

4. List the files in the application directory using the **ls** command to look into the important files in our application:

```
ls
```

Make note of the output as it should look similar to the following, with the **prometheus.yml** file being our configuration file. The **prometheus** file is the application binary and the **tsdb** and data directories are where our time-series database data is stored:

```
LICENSE       console_libraries     data       prometheus.yml     tsdb
NOTICE        consoles       prometheus     promtool
```

In the preceding directory listing, take note that the **console_libraries** and **consoles** directories include the binaries provided to view the Prometheus web interface we will work in shortly. The **promtool** directory includes tools you can use to work with Prometheus, including a configuration check tool to make sure your **prometheus.yml** file is valid.

5. If there is no issue with your binary and the application is ready to run, you should be able to verify the version of Prometheus. Run the application from the command line using the **--version** option:

```
./prometheus --version
```

The output should look like the following:

```
prometheus, version 2.15.1 (branch: HEAD, revision:
8744510c6391d3ef46d8294a7e1f46e57407ab13)
  build user:      root@4b1e33c71b9d
  build date:      20191225-01:12:19
  go version:      go1.13.5
```

6. You won't be making any changes to your configuration file, but before you get started, make sure it has valid information for Prometheus. Run the **cat** command to view the content of the file:

```
cat prometheus.yml
```

The number of lines in the output has been reduced here. As you can see from the following output, your global **scrap_interval** parameter and **evaluation_interval** parameter is set to **15** seconds:

```
# my global config
global:
  scrape_interval:     15s # Set the scrape interval to every
15 seconds. Default is every 1 minute.
  evaluation_interval: 15s # Evaluate rules every 15 seconds.
The default is every 1 minute.
  # scrape_timeout is set to the global default (10s).
...
```

If you have a moment to look over the **prometheus.yml** configuration file, you will notice that it is separated into four main sections:

global: This controls the server's global configurations. The configurations include **scrape_interval**, to know how often it will scrape the target, and **evaluation_interval**, to control how often it will evaluate rules to create time-series data and generate rules.

alerting: By default, the configuration file will also have alerting set up via AlertManager.

rule_files: This is where Prometheus will locate additional rules to load as part of its metric gathering. **rule_files** points to a location where the rules are stored.

scrape_configs: These are the resources Prometheus will monitor. Any additional targets we wish to monitor will be added to this section of the configuration file.

7. Starting Prometheus is simply a matter of running the binary and specifying the configuration file you would like it to use with the **--config.file** command-line option. Run the following command to start Prometheus:

```
./prometheus --config.file=prometheus.yml
```

After a few seconds, you should hopefully see the message that the **"Server is ready to receive web requests."**:

```
...
msg="Server is ready to receive web requests."
```

8. Enter the URL **http://localhost:9090**. Prometheus provides an easy-to-use web interface. If the application has started up correctly, you should now be able to open a web browser on your system. You should have the expression browser presented to you, similar to the following screenshot.
    Although the expression browser doesn't look very impressive, it does have some good functionality out of the box. It is set up in three distinct sections.

    The Main Menu: The main menu across the top of the screen, with a black background, allows you to view extra configuration details via the **Status** drop-down menu, shows you the alert history with the **Alerts** option, and brings you back to the main expression browser screen with the **Prometheus** and **Graph** options.

    The Expression Editor: This is the top textbox where we can enter our PromQL queries or select a metric from the drop-down list. You then click on the **Execute** button to start displaying data.

    The Graph and Console Display: Once you decide what data you wish to query, it will be displayed in both the **Console** tab in a table format and in a time-series graph format in the **Graph** tab, with the option to add more graphs down the web page using the **Add Graph** button:

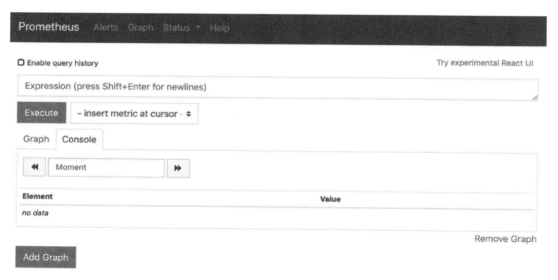

Figure 13.1: Loading the expression browser for the first time

9. Click the **Status** drop-down menu. You'll get to see the following image with useful information, including **Runtime & Build Information** to display details of the version running, **Command-Line Flags** to run the application with, **Configuration**, which displays the current **config** file running, and **Rules** for alerting rules. The final two options in the drop-down menu show **Targets**, which you are currently scraping data from, and **Service Discovery**, which is showing automatic services that are being monitored:

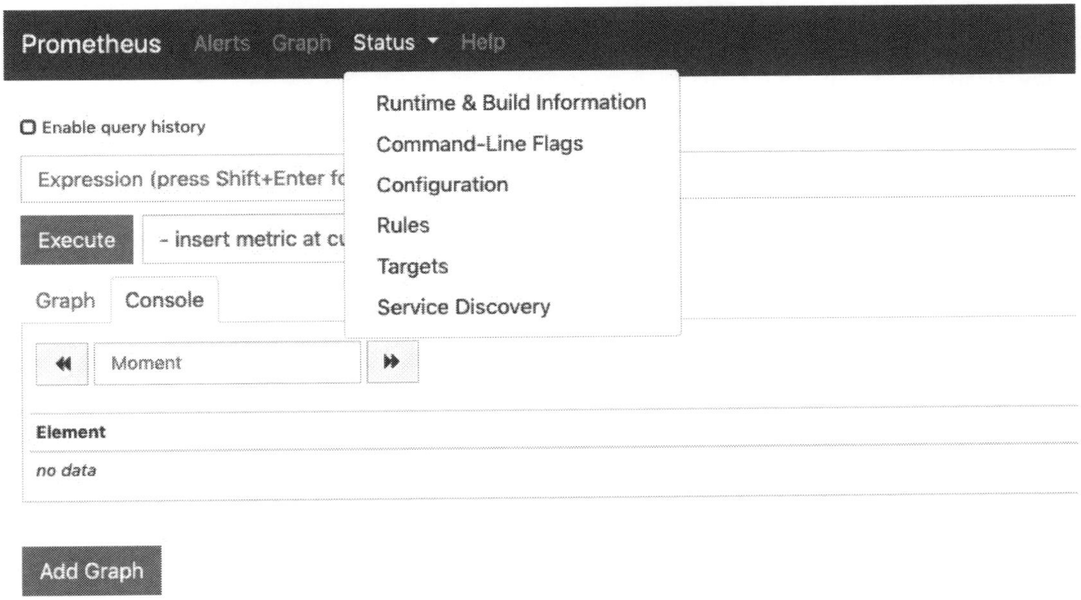

Figure 13.2: Status drop-down menu

10. From the **Status** menu, select the **Targets** option and you will be able to see what Prometheus is scraping data from. You can also get the same result by going to the URL **HTTP:localhost:9090/targets**. You should see a screenshot similar to the following, as Prometheus is currently only monitoring itself:

Figure 13.3: The Prometheus Targets page

11. Click the target endpoint. You will be able to see the metrics exposed by the target. You can now see how Prometheus makes use of its pull architecture to scrape data from its targets. Click the link or open a browser and enter the URL **http://localhost:9090/metrics** to see the Prometheus metrics endpoint. You should see something similar to the following, showing all the metrics points Prometheus is exposing to then be scraped by itself:

```
# HELP go_gc_duration_seconds A summary of the GC invocation
durations.
# TYPE go_gc_duration_seconds summary
go_gc_duration_seconds{quantile="0"} 9.268e-06
go_gc_duration_seconds{quantile="0.25"} 1.1883e-05
go_gc_duration_seconds{quantile="0.5"} 1.5802e-05
go_gc_duration_seconds{quantile="0.75"} 2.6047e-05
go_gc_duration_seconds{quantile="1"} 0.000478339
go_gc_duration_seconds_sum 0.002706392
...
```

12. Return to the expression browser by either clicking the back button or by entering the URL **http://localhost:9090/graph**. Click the drop-down list next to the **Execute** button to see all the metric points available:

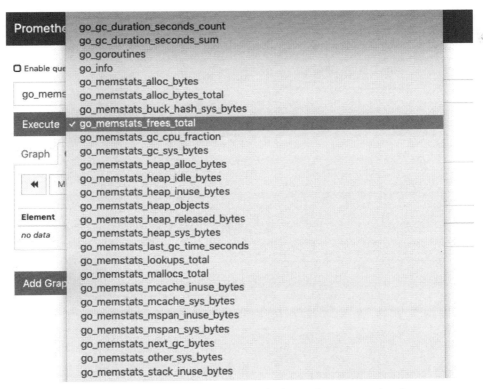

Figure 13.4: Prometheus metrics available from the expression browser

13. From the drop-down list or in the query editor, add the **prometheus_ http_requests_total** metrics to view all the HTTP requests made to the Prometheus application. Your output may differ from the following. Click the **Execute** button and click the **Graphs** tab to see a visual view of our data:

Figure 13.5: Prometheus HTTP requests graph displayed from the expression browser

Don't worry if you are still a little confused about what we have achieved so far. In a short period, we've set up Prometheus and started collecting data on it. Even though we have only been collecting data on Prometheus itself, we have been able to demonstrate how we can now quickly and easily visualize the HTTP requests being performed by the application. The next section will show you how to start to capture data from Docker and your running containers by making small changes to your Prometheus configurations.

MONITORING DOCKER CONTAINERS WITH PROMETHEUS

Prometheus monitoring is a great way to understand what the application is capable of, but it doesn't do much more to help us with monitoring Docker and the containers that we have running on our system. Fortunately, there are two ways we can collect data to give us greater insights into our running containers. We can expose metrics using the Docker daemon to Prometheus and can also install some extra applications, such as **cAdvisor**, to collect further metrics on the containers running on our system.

With some minor changes to the Docker configurations, we are able to expose metrics to Prometheus to allow it to collect specific data of the Docker daemon running on our system. This will go part of the way to collecting the metrics but will not give us the metrics of the actual running containers. This is where we will then need to install **cAdvisor**, which was created by Google specifically to collect our running container metrics.

> **NOTE**
>
> If we needed to gather more metrics on the underlying hardware, Docker and our containers are running on, we could also gather further metrics using **node_exporter**. We will not be covering **node_exporter** in this chapter but supporting documentation can be found at the following URL:
>
> https://github.com/prometheus/node_exporter.

With Docker already running on your host system, setting it up to allow Prometheus to connect metrics from it is a matter of adding a configuration change to the **/etc/docker/daemon.json** file. In most instances, the file will most likely be blank. If you already have details in the file, you will simply add *lines 2* and *3* from the following example to your configuration file. *Line 2* enables this **experimental** feature to expose metrics for Prometheus to collect, and *line 3* sets up the IP address and port for these data points to be exposed to:

```
1 {
2         "experimental": true,
3         "metrics-addr": "0.0.0.0:9191"
4 }
```

Due to a change in configuration, the Docker daemon on your system will need to be restarted for it to take effect. But once that occurs, you should then have metrics available at the specified IP address and port you added to the **daemon.json** file. In our instance above, this will be at **http://0.0.0.0:9191**.

To install **cAdvisor**, Google has provided an easy-to-use Docker image that can be pulled from Google's Cloud Registry and run on your environment.

To run **cAdvisor**, you will run the image mounting all the directories that are relevant to the Docker daemon and running containers. You also need to make sure that you expose the port the metrics will be available on. By default, **cAdvisor** is configured to expose metrics on port **8080**, which you will not be able to change unless you make changes to the underlying image of **cAdvisor**.

The following **docker run** command mounts the volumes on the container, such as **/var/lib/docker** and **/var/run**, exposes port **8080** to the host system, and finally uses the latest **cadvisor** image available from Google:

```
docker run \
  --volume=<host_directory>:<container_directory> \
  --publish=8080:8080 \
  --detach=true \
  --name=cadvisor \
  gcr.io/google-containers/cadvisor:latest
```

> **NOTE**
>
> Making changes to the underlying image of **cAdvisor** is not something we will cover in this chapter, but you will need to refer to the **cAdvisor** documentation and make specific changes to the **cAdvisor** code.

The **cAdvisor** image will also provide a useful web interface to view these metrics. **cAdvisor** does not hold any historical data, so you need to collect the data with Prometheus.

Once the Docker daemon and **cAdvisor** have data available for Prometheus to collect, we need to ensure we have a scheduled configuration to have the data added to the time-series database. The **prometheus.yml** configuration file in the application directory allows us to do this. You simply add a configuration to the **scrape_configs** section of the file. As you can see from the following example, you need to add a **job_name** parameter and provide details of where the metrics are being provided as a **targets** entry:

```
  - job_name: '<scrap_job_name>'
    static_configs:
    - targets: ['<ip_address>:<port>']
```

Once the targets are available to Prometheus, you can then start searching for data. Now that we've provided a breakdown of how you can start to collect Docker metrics using Prometheus, the following exercise will show you how to perform this on your running system.

EXERCISE 13.02: COLLECTING DOCKER METRICS WITH PROMETHEUS

In this exercise, you will configure Prometheus to start collecting data from our Docker daemon. This will allow you to see what resources are specifically being used by the Docker daemon itself. You will also run the **cAdvisor** Docker image to start collecting specific metrics on your running containers:

1. To start collecting data from the Docker daemon, you first need to enable this functionality on your system. Start by opening the **/etc/docker/daemon. json** file with your text editor and add in the following details:

```
1 {
2        "experimental": true,
3        "metrics-addr": "0.0.0.0:9191"
4 }
```

The changes you've made to the configuration file will expose the Docker daemon metrics to allow Prometheus to scrape and store these values. To enable this change, save the Docker configuration file and restart the Docker daemon.

2. Verify this has worked by opening your web browser and using the URL and port number you have set up in your configuration. Enter the URL `http://0.0.0.0:9191/metrics`, and you should see a list of metrics being exposed to allow Prometheus to scrape:

```
# HELP builder_builds_failed_total Number of failed image builds
# TYPE builder_builds_failed_total counter
builder_builds_failed_total{reason="build_canceled"} 0
builder_builds_failed_total{reason="build_target_not_reachable
_error"} 0
builder_builds_failed_total{reason="command_not_supported_
error"} 0
builder_builds_failed_total{reason="dockerfile_empty_error"} 0
builder_builds_failed_total{reason="dockerfile_syntax_error"} 0
builder_builds_failed_total{reason="error_processing_commands_
error"} 0
builder_builds_failed_total{reason="missing_onbuild_arguments_
error"} 0
builder_builds_failed_total{reason="unknown_instruction_error"} 0
...
```

3. You now need to let Prometheus know where it can find the metrics Docker is exposing to it. You do this through the **prometheus.yml** file in the application directory. Before you do this though, you will need to stop the Prometheus service from running, so the additions to the configuration file will take effect. Open the terminal Prometheus is running on and press *Ctrl + C*. You should see an output similar to the following when you do this successfully:

```
level=info ts=2020-04-28T04:49:39.435Z caller=main.go:718
msg="Notifier manager stopped"
level=info ts=2020-04-28T04:49:39.436Z caller=main.go:730
msg="See you next time!"
```

4. Open the **prometheus.yml** configuration file in the application directory with your text editor. Move to the end of the file in the **scrape_configs** section and add *lines 21* to *34*. The additional lines will tell Prometheus that it can now obtain metrics from the Docker daemon that has been exposed on IP address **0.0.0.0** and port **9191**:

prometheus.yml

```
21  scrape_configs:
22    # The job name is added as a label 'job=<job_name>' to any
         timeseries scraped from this config.
23    - job_name: 'prometheus'
24
25      # metrics_path defaults to '/metrics'
26      # scheme defaults to 'http'.
27
28      static_configs:
29      - targets: ['localhost:9090']
30
31    - job_name: 'docker_daemon'
32      static_configs:
33      - targets: ['0.0.0.0:9191']
34
```

The complete code for this step can be found at https://packt.live/33satLe.

5. Save the changes you have made to the **prometheus.yml** file and start the Prometheus application again from the command line as shown here:

```
./prometheus --config.file=prometheus.yml
```

6. If you move back to the expression browser for Prometheus, you can once again verify it is now configured to collect data from the Docker daemon. Either select **Targets** from the **Status** menu or use the URL **http://localhost:9090/targets**, which should now include the **docker_daemon** job we specified in our configuration file:

Figure 13.6: Prometheus Targets now with docker_daemon

7. Verify that you are collecting data by searching **engine_daemon_engine_ cpus_cpus**. This value should be the same as the number of CPUs or cores available on your host system. Enter this into the Prometheus expression browser and click the **Execute** button:

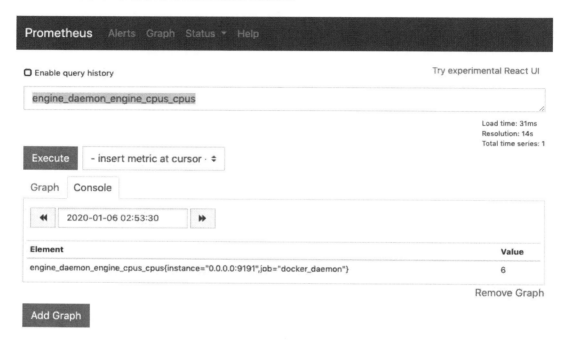

Figure 13.7: docker_daemon CPUs available on the host system

8. The Docker daemon is limited to the amount of data it can expose to Prometheus. Set up the **cAdvisor** image to collect details about your running containers. Run this as a container made available by Google with the following **docker run** command on the command line. The **docker run** command uses the **cadvisor:latest** image stored in the Google Container Registry, similar to Docker Hub. There is no need to log in to this registry; the image will automatically be pulled to your system:

```
docker run \
  --volume=/:/rootfs:ro \
  --volume=/var/run:/var/run:ro \
  --volume=/sys:/sys:ro \
  --volume=/var/lib/docker/:/var/lib/docker:ro \
  --volume=/dev/disk/:/dev/disk:ro \
  --publish=8080:8080 \
  --detach=true \
```

```
--name=cadvisor \
gcr.io/google-containers/cadvisor:latest
```

9. **cAdvisor** comes with a web interface that will give you some basic functionality, but as it does not store historical data, you will be collecting the data and storing it on Prometheus. For now, open another web browser session and enter the URL **http://0.0.0.0:8080** and you should see a web page similar to the following:

Figure 13.8: The cAdvisor welcome page

10. Enter the URL **http://0.0.0.0:8080/metrics** to view all the data that **cAdvisor** is displaying on the web interface.

> **NOTE**
>
> When changes are being made to the Prometheus configuration file, the application will need to be restarted for the changes to take effect. In the exercises we have been performing, we have been achieving this by stopping the service instead to achieve the same result.

11. As you did with the Docker daemon, configure Prometheus to periodically scrape data from the metrics endpoint. Stop the Prometheus application running and, once again, open the **prometheus.yml** configuration file with your text editor. At the bottom of the configuration, add in another configuration for **cAdvisor** with the following details:

prometheus.yml

```
35    - job_name: 'cadvisor'
36      scrape_interval: 5s
37      static_configs:
38      - targets: ['0.0.0.0:8080']
```

The complete code for this step can be found at https://packt.live/33BuFub.

12. Save your configuration changes once again and run the Prometheus application from the command line, as shown here:

```
./prometheus --config.file=prometheus.yml
```

If you now view the **Targets** available on the Prometheus web interface, you should see something similar to the following, showing **cAdvisor** also available on our interface:

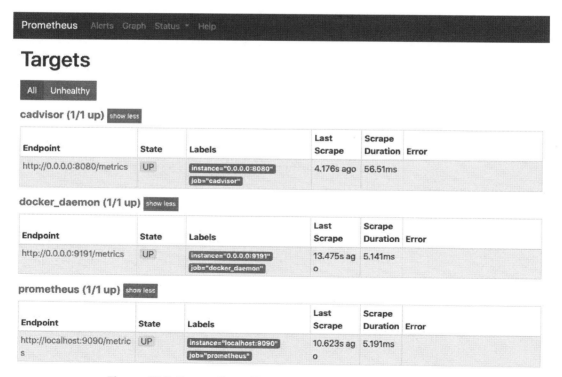

Figure 13.9: Prometheus Targets page with cAdvisor added

13. With the **Targets** page of Prometheus showing that **cAdvisor** is now available and connected, it verifies that Prometheus is now collecting metrics data from **cAdvisor**. You can also test this from the expression browser to verify it is working as it should. Move into the expression browser by selecting **Graphs** or **Prometheus** from the top menu. When the page loads, add the following PromQL query to the query editor and click the **Execute** button:

```
(time() - process_start_time_
seconds{instance="0.0.0.0:8080",job="cadvisor"})
```

> **NOTE**
>
> We are starting to use some more advanced PromQL queries, and it may look a little confusing. The next part of this chapter is dedicated to providing you with a better understanding of the PromQL query language.

The query is using the **process_start_time_seconds** metric, specifically for the **cAdvisor** application and the **time()** function to add the total seconds. You should see a result similar to the following on the expression browser:

Figure 13.10: cAdvisor uptime from the expression browser

With this exercise, we now have a running instance of Prometheus and are collecting data from the Docker daemon. We have also set up **cAdvisor** to give us some further information on the running container instances. The next part of this chapter will discuss the PromQL query language in greater depth to help you become more comfortable querying the metrics available from Prometheus.

UNDERSTANDING THE PROMETHEUS QUERY LANGUAGE

As we've seen in the previous parts of this chapter, Prometheus provides its own query language called PromQL. It allows you to search, view, and aggregate the time-series data stored in the Prometheus database. This section helps you understand the query language further. There are four core metric types in Prometheus, and we will start by describing each.

COUNTER

A counter counts elements over time; for example, this could be the number of visits to your website. The count will only go up or it will reset when a service or application is restarted. They are suited to counting the number of certain events at a point in time. Each time the counter changes, the number will also be reflected in the data you collect.

Counters usually end with the **_total** suffix. But due to the nature of counters, each time a service is restarted, the counter will be set back to 0. Using the **rate()** or **irate()** functions in our query, we will be able to view our metric rate over time and disregard any time the counter is reset to 0. The **rate()** and **irate()** functions both take in a range of values using the square brackets **[ ]** where you specify a time value, such as **[1m]**.

If you are interested in examples of counters in the data we are collecting, open the metrics page for the data being collected for **cAdvisor** at the URL **http://0.0.0.0:8080/metrics**. One of the first metrics provided is **container_cpu_system_seconds_total**. If we look through the metrics page, we will see the information provided on the metric value and the type as listed here:

```
# HELP container_cpu_system_seconds_total Cumulative system cpu time
consumed in seconds.
# TYPE container_cpu_system_seconds_total counter
container_cpu_system_seconds_total{id="/",image="",name=""}
195.86 1579481501131
...
```

Now, we will look into the second metric type available in Prometheus, in other words, gauges.

GAUGES

Gauges are designed to handle values that may decrease over time and are designed for any metric exposing the current state of something. Just like a thermometer or fuel gauge, you would be able to see the current state value. Gauges are restricted in their functionality because not all the data will be collected as there may be missing values between time points. Therefore, they are less reliable than a counter, and so counters are still used for time-series representations of data.

If we once again move to the metrics page for **cAdvisor**, you can see some of our metrics being displayed as a gauge. One of the first metrics we see is **container_cpu_load_average_10s**, which is provided as a gauge, similar to the following values:

```
# HELP container_cpu_load_average_10s Value of container cpu load
average over the last 10 seconds.
# TYPE container_cpu_load_average_10s gauge
container_cpu_load_average_10s{id="/",image="",name=""} 0
1579481501131
...
```

The next section will take you through histograms, the third type of metric available in Prometheus.

HISTOGRAMS

Histograms are a lot more complex than gauges and counters and provide additional information, like the sum of an observation. They are used to provide a distribution of a set of data. Histograms use sampling and can be used to estimate quantiles on the Prometheus server.

Histograms are less common than gauges and counters and do not seem to be set up for **cAdvisor**, but we can see some available in our Docker daemon metrics. Move to the URL **http://0.0.0.0:9191/metrics** and you'll be able to see that one of the first histogram metrics listed is **engine_daemon_container_actions_seconds**. This is the number of seconds the Docker daemon takes to process each action:

```
# HELP engine_daemon_container_actions_seconds The number of seconds
it takes to process each container action
```

```
# TYPE engine_daemon_container_actions_seconds histogram
engine_daemon_container_actions_seconds_bucket{action="changes",
le="0.005"} 1
...
```

The next section will now cover the fourth metric type available, in other words, summaries.

SUMMARIES

Summaries are an extension of histograms and are calculated on the client-side. They have the advantage of being more accurate, but they can be expensive for the client, too. We can see an example of a summary in the Docker daemon metrics where **http_request_duration_microseconds** is listed here:

```
# HELP http_request_duration_microseconds The HTTP request latencies in
microseconds.
# TYPE http_request_duration_microseconds summary
http_request_duration_microseconds{handler="prometheus",quantile=
"0.5"} 3861.5
...
```

Now, since we've explained the type of metrics available in PromQL, we can take a further look at how these metrics can be implemented as a part of our queries.

PERFORMING PROMQL QUERIES

Running queries on the expression browser is easy, but you may not always get the information you need. By simply adding the metric name, such as **countainer_cpu_system_seconds_total**, we can get quite a few responses. Though, the amount depends on the number of containers we have on our system along with the returning values for each of the filesystems that are running on our host system. To limit the number of responses provided in our result, we can search for specific text using curly braces **{ }**.

Consider the following examples. The following command provides the full name of the **"cadvisor"** container we wish to view:

```
container_cpu_system_seconds_total{ name="cadvisor"}
```

The following example uses a regular expression compatible with GO. The command looks for any names that start with **ca** and have further characters afterward:

```
container_cpu_system_seconds_total{ name=~"ca.+"}
```

The following code snippet is searching for any containers that do not have the name value as blank by using the not equal to (`!=`) value:

```
container_cpu_system_seconds_total{ name!=""}
```

If we placed any of these metrics searches in the expression browser and created a graph, what you would notice is that the graph would simply climb in a linear fashion over time. As we mentioned earlier, this is because the metric **container_cpu_system_seconds_total** is a counter and will only ever increase over time or be set back to zero. With the use of functions, we can calculate more useful time-series data. The following example uses the **rate()** function to calculate the per-second rate for the matching time-series data. We have used **[1m]**, which represents 1 minute. The higher the number, the smoother the graph will be:

```
rate(container_cpu_system_seconds_total{name="cadvisor"}[1m])
```

The **rate** function can only be used for a counter metric. If we had more than one container running, we could then use the **sum()** function to add all the values together and provide a graph by container name using the **(name)** function as we have here:

```
sum(rate(container_cpu_system_seconds_total[1m])) by (name)
```

> **NOTE**
>
> If you would like to see a list of all the functions available in PromQL, go to the following link provided by the official Prometheus documentation:
>
> https://prometheus.io/docs/prometheus/latest/querying/functions/.

PromQL also lets us perform arithmetic from our queries. In the following example, we are using the **process_start_time_seconds** metric and searching for the Prometheus instance. We can subtract this time from the **time()** function, which gives us the current date and time in epoch time:

```
(time() - process_start_time_
seconds{instance="localhost:9090",job="prometheus"})
```

> **NOTE**
>
> Epoch time is the number of seconds from January 1, 1970, and is represented by a number; for example, 1578897429 is converted to 6:37 a.m. (GMT) on January 13, 2020.

We're hoping this primer in PromQL has given you some more insight into using the query language within your projects. The following exercise will help enforce what we have learned by specifically working further with monitoring our running Docker containers.

EXERCISE 13.03: WORKING WITH THE PROMQL QUERY LANGUAGE

In the following exercise, we will introduce a new Docker image onto your system to help you demonstrate some of the available metrics specific to Docker while using Prometheus. The exercise will reinforce what you have learned so far about the PromQL query language with a tangible use case of gathering and displaying metrics data for a basic website:

1. Open a new terminal and create a new directory, calling it **web-nginx**:

```
mkdir web-nginx; cd web-nginx
```

2. Create a new file in the **web-nginx** directory and call it **index.html**. Open the new file with your text editor and add the following HTML code:

```
<!DOCTYPE html>
<html lang="en">
<head>
</head>
<body>
    <h1>
        Hello Prometheus
    </h1>
</body>
</html>
```

3. Run a new Docker container with the following command. By now, you should be familiar with the syntax, but the following command will pull the latest **nginx** image, name it **web-nginx**, and expose port **80** so that you can then view the mounted **index.html** file you created in the previous step:

```
docker run --name web-nginx --rm -v ${PWD}/index.html:/usr/share/
nginx/html/index.html -p 80:80 -d nginx
```

4. Open a web browser and access `http://0.0.0.0`. The only thing you should see is the greeting **Hello Prometheus**:

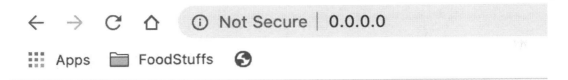

Hello Prometheus

Figure 13.11: Sample web page

5. If Prometheus is not running on your system, open a new terminal and, from the Prometheus application directory, start the application from the command line:

```
./prometheus --config.file=prometheus.yml
```

> **NOTE**
>
> We will not show screenshots of all the PromQL queries that we perform in this part of the chapter as we don't want to waste too much space. But the queries should all be valid for the running containers and system we have set up.

6. The bulk of the **cAdvisor** metrics now available in Prometheus will start with the word **container**. Use the **count()** function with the metric **container_memory_usage_bytes** to see the count of the current memory usage in bytes:

```
count(container_memory_usage_bytes)
```

The preceding query provides the 28 results on the system on which it is running.

7. To limit the information you are looking for, either use the curly brackets to search or, as in the following command, use not search (**!=**) for specific image names. Currently, you only have two containers running with image names, **cAdvisor** and **web-nginx**. By using the **scalar()** function, you can count the number of containers you have running on your system over time. Click the **Execute** button after entering the following query:

```
scalar(count(container_memory_usage_bytes{image!=""}) > 0)
```

8. Click the **Graphs** tab, and you should now have a plotted graph of the preceding query. The graph should be like the following image in which you started up a third image **web-nginx** container to show how the Prometheus expression browser displays this type of data. Remember that you are only seeing one line in the graph as this is the memory used by the two containers on our system and there is not a separate memory usage value for both:

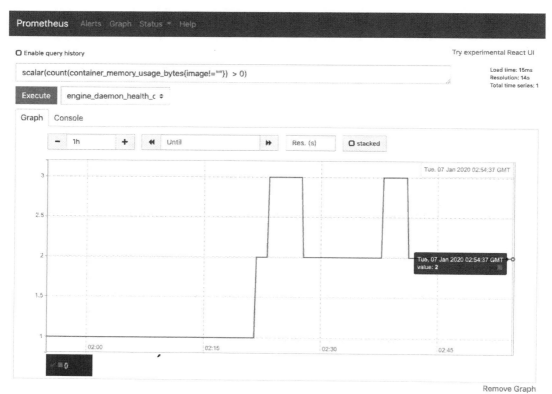

Figure 13.12: cAdvisor metrics from the expression browser

9. Use the **container_start_time_seconds** metric to get the Unix timestamp of when the container started up:

```
container_start_time_seconds{name="web-nginx"}
```

You will see something like 1578364679, which is the number of seconds past epoch time, which is 1 January 1970.

10. Use the **time()** function to get the current time and then subtract **container_start_time_seconds** from this value to show how many seconds the container has been running for:

```
(time() - container_start_time_seconds{name="web-nginx"})
```

11. Monitor HTTP requests on your application via Prometheus' **prometheus_http_request_duration_seconds_count** metric. Use the **rate()** function to plot a graph of the duration of each HTTP request to Prometheus:

```
rate(prometheus_http_request_duration_seconds_count[1m])
```

> **NOTE**
>
> It would be great to be using the **web-nginx** container to view its HTTP request time and latency, but the container has not been set up to provide this information to Prometheus yet. We will address this shortly in the chapter.

12. Use an arithmetic operator to divide **prometheus_http_request_duration_seconds_sum** by **prometheus_http_request_duration_seconds_count**, which will then provide the HTTP latency of the requests made:

```
rate(prometheus_http_request_duration_seconds_sum[1m]) /
rate(prometheus_http_request_duration_seconds_count[1m])
```

13. Run the following command using the **container_memory_usage_bytes** metric to see the memory being used by each of the running containers on your system. In this query, we are using the **sum by (name)** command to add the values per container name:

```
sum by (name) (container_memory_usage_bytes{name!=""})
```

If you execute the preceding query, you'll see the graph in the expression browser showing the memory used by the **web-nginx** and **cAdvisor** containers:

Figure 13.13: Memory of both the containers running on our system

This section has helped you gain a little more familiarity with the **PromQL** query language and put together your queries to start viewing your metrics from the expression browser. The following section will provide details on how you can start to collect metrics from the apps and services you have created in Docker using exporters to expose data in a Prometheus-friendly way.

USING PROMETHEUS EXPORTERS

In this chapter, we have configured application metrics to provide data for Prometheus to scrape and collect, so why do we need to worry about exporters? As you have seen, Docker and **cAdvisor** have nicely exposed data endpoints from which Prometheus can gather metrics. But these have limited functionality. As we have seen from our new **web-nginx** site, there is no relevant data exposed by the web page running on our image. We can use exporters to help gather metrics from the application or service, and then provide data in a way that Prometheus can understand and gather.

Although this may seem to be a major flaw in how Prometheus works, due to the increase in the use of Prometheus and the fact that it is open-source, vendors and third-party providers are now providing exporters to help you get your metrics from the application.

This means that, by installing a specific library or using a prebuilt Docker image to run your application, you can expose your metrics data for collection. As an example, the **web-nginx** application we created earlier in this chapter is running on NGINK. To get metrics on our web application, we could simply install the **ngx_stub_status_prometheus** library onto our NGINX instance that is running our web application. Or better still, we can find a Docker image that someone has already built to run our web application.

> **NOTE**
>
> This section of the chapter has focused on NGINX Exporter, but exporters for a large number of applications can be found in their supporting documentation or with the Prometheus documentation.

In the following exercise, we will use our **nginx** container as an example and use an exporter with our **web-nginx** container to expose metrics available to Prometheus to collect.

EXERCISE 13.04: USING METRICS EXPORTERS WITH YOUR APPLICATIONS

So far, we've used an **nginx** container to provide a basic web page, but we do not have specific metrics available for our web page. In this exercise, you will use a different NGINX image, built with a metrics exporter that can be exposed to Prometheus:

1. If the **web-nginx** container is still running, stop the container with the following command:

```
docker kill web-nginx
```

2. Within Docker Hub, you have an image called **mhowlett/ngx-stud-status-prometheus**, which already has the **ngx_stub_status_prometheus** library installed. The library will allow you to set up an HTTP endpoint to provide metrics to Prometheus from your **nginx** container. Pull this image down onto your working environment:

```
docker pull mhowlett/ngx-stub-status-prometheus
```

3. In the previous exercise, you used the default NGINX configuration on the container to run your web application. To expose the metrics to Prometheus, you will need to create your configuration to override the default configuration and provide your metrics as an available HTTP endpoint. Create a file named **nginx.conf** in your working directory and add the following configuration details:

```
daemon off;

events {
}

http {
  server {
    listen 80;

    location / {
      index  index.html;
    }

    location /metrics {
      stub_status_prometheus;
    }
```

```
        }
    }
```

The preceding configuration will ensure that your server is still available on port 80 in *line 8*. *Line 11* will ensure that your current **index.html** page is provided, and *line 14* will then set up a subdomain of **/metrics** to provide the details available from the **ngx_stub_status_prometheus** library.

4. Provide the mount point for the **index.html** file to start up the **web-nginx** container and mount the **nginx.conf** configuration you created in the previous step using the following command:

```
docker run --name web-nginx --rm -v ${PWD}/index.html:/usr/html/
index.html -v ${PWD}/nginx.conf:/etc/nginx/nginx.conf -p 80:80 -d
mhowlett/ngx-stub-status-prometheus
```

5. Your **web-nginx** application should be running again, and you should be able to see it from your web browser. Enter the URL **http://0.0.0.0/metrics** to see the metrics endpoint. The results in your web browser window should look similar to the following information:

```
# HELP nginx_active_connections_current Current number of
active connections
# TYPE nginx_active_connections_current gauge
nginx_active_connections_current 2
# HELP nginx_connections_current Number of connections currently
being processed by nginx
# TYPE nginx_connections_current gauge
nginx_connections_current{state="reading"} 0
nginx_connections_current{state="writing"} 1
nginx_connections_current{state="waiting"} 1
...
```

6. You still need to let Prometheus know that it needs to collect the data from the new endpoint. So, stop Prometheus from running. Move into the application directory again, and with your text editor, add the following target to the end of the **prometheus.yml** configuration file:

prometheus.yml

```
40    - job_name: 'web-nginx'
41      scrape_interval: 5s
42      static_configs:
43        - targets: ['0.0.0.0:80']
```

The complete code for this step can be found at https://packt.live/3hzbQgj.

7. Save the changes to the configuration and start Prometheus running again:

```
./prometheus --config.file=prometheus.yml
```

8. Confirm whether Prometheus is configured to collect data from the new metrics endpoint you have just created. Open your web browser and enter the URL **http://0.0.0.0:9090/targets**:

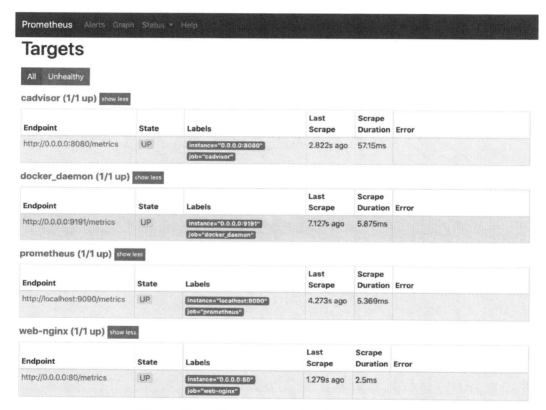

Figure 13.14: Targets page showing web-nginx

In this exercise, you learned to add an exporter to an application running on your environment. We first expanded on our previous **web-nginx** application to allow it to display more than one HTTP endpoint. We then used a Docker image that included the **ngx_stub_status_prometheus** library to allow us to display our **web-nginx** statistics. We then configured Prometheus to gather these details from the endpoint provided.

In the following section, we will set up Grafana to allow us to view our data a lot more closely and provide user-friendly dashboards for the data we are collecting.

EXTENDING PROMETHEUS WITH GRAFANA

The Prometheus web interface provides a functional expression browser that allows us to search and view the data in our time-series database with limited installation. It provides a graphical interface but doesn't allow us to save any of our searches or visualizations. The Prometheus web interface is also limited as it cannot group queries in dashboards. Also, there are not many visualizations that are provided by the interface. This is where we can expand our collected data further with the use of an application such as Grafana.

Grafana allows us to connect directly with the Prometheus time-series database and perform queries and create visually appealing dashboards. Grafana can run as a standalone application on a server. We can preconfigure the Grafana Docker image to deploy onto our system, configured with a connection to our Prometheus database, and with a basic dashboard already set up to monitor our running containers.

The following screen, Grafana Home Dashboard, is presented when you first log in to Grafana. You can always return to this page by clicking on the Grafana icon at the top left of the screen. This is the main work area where you can start to build dashboards, configure your environment, and add users' plugins:

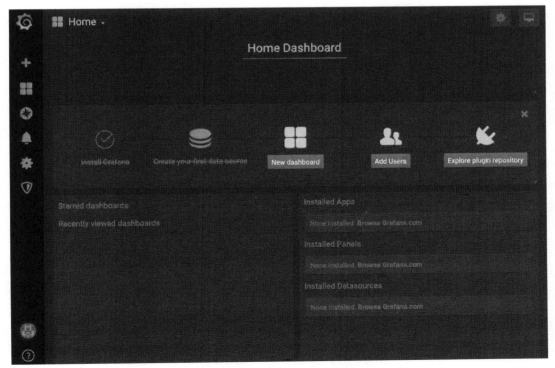

Figure 13.15: Grafana Home Dashboard

The left side of the screen is a handy menu that will help you configure Grafana further. The plus symbol will allow you to add new dashboards and data sources to your installation, while the dashboard icon (four squares) organizes all your dashboards into one area to search and view. Underneath the dashboard icon is the explore button, which provides an expression browser just like Prometheus has in order to run PromQL queries, while the alerts icon (bell) takes you to the window where you can configure alerts to trigger after different events occur. The configuration icon takes you to the screen where you can configure how Grafana operates, while the server admin icon allows you to manage who can access your Grafana web interface and what privileges they can have.

Feel free to explore the interface further when you install Grafana in the next exercise, but we will be working to automate the process as much as possible to avoid making any changes to your working environment.

EXERCISE 13.05: INSTALLING AND RUNNING GRAFANA ON YOUR SYSTEM

In this exercise, you will set up Grafana on your system and allow the application to start using the data you have stored in your Prometheus database. You will install Grafana using its Docker image, provide a brief explanation of the interface, and begin to set up basic dashboards:

1. If Prometheus is not running, start it up again. Also, make sure that your containers, **cAdvisor**, and the test NGINX server (**web-nginx**) are running:

```
./prometheus --config.file=prometheus.yml
```

2. Open the **/etc/hosts** file of your system and add a domain name to the host IP of **127.0.0.1**. Unfortunately, you will not be able to use the localhost IP address you have been using to access Prometheus to automatically provision a data source for Grafana. IP addresses such as **127.0.0.1**, **0.0.0.0**, or using localhost will not be recognized as a data source for Grafana. Depending on your system, you may have a number of different entries already added to the **hosts** file. You will usually have the IP address of **127.0.0.1** listed as one of the first IP addresses that will reference the domain of **localhost** and amend **prometheus** to this line, as we have in the following output:

```
1 127.0.0.1          localhost prometheus
```

3. Save the **hosts** file. Open your web browser and enter the URL **http://prometheus:9090**. The Prometheus expression browser should now be displayed. You no longer need to provide the system IP address.

4. To automatically provision your Grafana image, you will need to mount a **provisioning** directory from your host system. Create a provisioning directory and ensure this directory includes extra directories for **dashboards**, **datasources**, **plugins** and **notifiers**, as in the following command:

```
mkdir -p provisioning/dashboards provisioning/datasources
provisioning/plugins provisioning/notifiers
```

5. Create a file called **automatic_data.yml** in the **provisioning/datasources** directory. Open the file with your text editor and enter the following details to tell Grafana what data it will use to provide dashboards and visualizations. The following details simply name the data source, provide the type of data, and where to find the data. In this instance, this is your new Prometheus domain name:

```
apiVersion: 1

datasources:
- name: Prometheus
  type: prometheus
  url: http://prometheus:9090
  access: direct
```

6. Now, create a file, **automatic_dashboard.yml**, in the **provisioning/dashboards** directory. Open the file with your text editor and add the following details. This simply provides the location of where future dashboards can be stored on startup:

```
apiVersion: 1

providers:
- name: 'Prometheus'
  orgId: 1
  folder: ''
  type: file
  disableDeletion: false
  editable: true
  options:
    path: /etc/grafana/provisioning/dashboards
```

You've done enough to start up our Grafana Docker image. You are using the supported Grafana image provided as **grafana/grafana**.

> **NOTE**
>
> We don't have any code to add as a dashboard as yet, but in the following steps, you will create a basic dashboard that will be automatically provisioned later in this exercise. If you wanted to, you could also search the internet for existing dashboards that Grafana users have created and provision them instead.

7. Run the following command to pull and start up the Grafana image. It mounts your provisioning directory to the **/etc/grafana/provisioning** directory on your Docker image using the **-v** option. It also uses the **-e** option to set the administration password to **secret** using the **GF_SECURITY_ADMIN_PASSWORD** environment variable, which will mean you won't need to reset the administration password each time you log in to a newly started container. Finally, you also use **-p** to expose port **3000** of your image to port **3000** of our system:

```
docker run --rm -d --name grafana -p 3000:3000 -e "GF_SECURITY_ADMIN_
PASSWORD=secret" -v ${PWD}/provisioning:/etc/grafana/provisioning
grafana/grafana
```

> **NOTE**
>
> Although using a Grafana Docker image is convenient, you will lose all your changes and dashboards each time the image restarts. That is why we will provision the installation while demonstrating how to use Grafana at the same time.

8. You have started up the image on port **3000**, so you should now be able to open a web browser. Enter the URL `http://0.0.0.0:3000` in your web browser. It should display the welcome page for Grafana. To log in to the application, use the default administrator account that has a username of **admin** and the password we specified as the **GF_SECURITY_ADMIN_PASSWORD** environment variable:

Figure 13.16: The Grafana login screen

9. When you log in, you'll be presented with the Grafana Home Dashboard. Click the plus symbol on the left of the screen and select **Dashboard** to add a new dashboard:

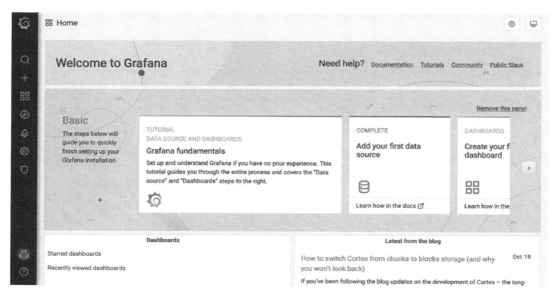

Figure 13.17: The Grafana welcome screen

> **NOTE**
>
> Your Grafana interface will most likely be displayed in the dark default theme. We have changed ours to the light theme to make it easier to read. To change this preference on your own Grafana application, you can click the user icon at the bottom left of the screen, select **Preferences**, and then search for **UI Theme**.

10. Click on the **Add new panel** button.

11. To add a new query using **Prometheus** data, select **Prometheus** as the data source from the drop-down list:

Figure 13.18: Creating our first dashboard in Grafana

12. In the metrics section, add the PromQL query **sum (rate (container_ cpu_usage_seconds_total{image!=""}[1m])) by (name)**. The query will provide the details of all the containers running on your system. It will also provide the CPU usage of each overtime. Depending on the amount of data you have, you may want to set **Relative time** to **15m** in the **Query options** drop down menu.

This example uses **15m** to make sure you have enough data for the graph, but this time range could be set to whatever you wish:

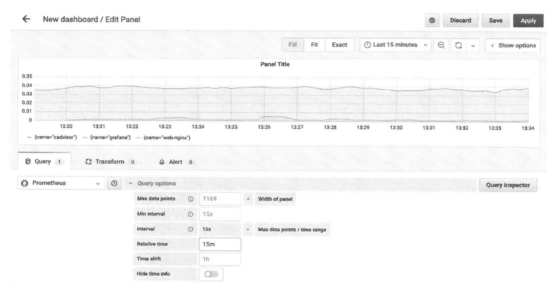

Figure 13.19: Adding dashboard metrics

13. Select the **Show options** button to add a title to your dashboard panel. In the following image, the title of your panel is set as **CPU Container Usage**:

Figure 13.20: Adding a dashboard title

14. Click the save icon at the top of the screen. This will give you the option to name the dashboard— **Container Monitoring** in this instance. When you click **Save**, you will then be taken to your completed dashboard screen, similar to the one here:

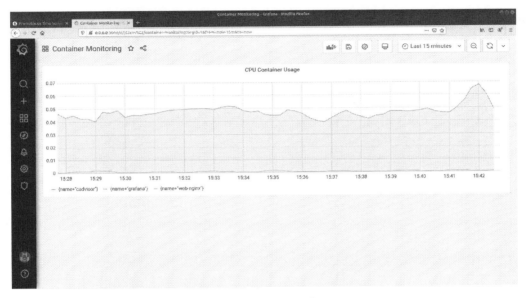

Figure 13.21: Dashboard screen

15. At the top of the dashboard screen, to the left of the save icon, you will have the option to export your dashboard in **JSON** format. If you do this, you can use this **JSON** file to add to your provisioning directory. It will help you install the dashboard into your Grafana image when you run it. Select **Export** and save the file to the **/tmp** directory where the name of the file will default to something similar to the name of the dashboard and the timestamp data. In this example, it saved the **JSON** file as **Container Monitoring-1579130313205.json**. Also make sure the **Export for sharing externally** option is not turned on, as shown in the image below:

Figure 13.22: Exporting your dashboard as JSON

16. To add the dashboard to your provisioning file, you need to first stop the Grafana image from running. Do this with the following **docker kill** command:

```
docker kill grafana
```

17. Add the dashboard file you saved in *Step 15* to the **provisioning/ dashboards** directory and name the file **ContainerMonitoring.json** as a part of the copy, shown in the following command:

```
cp /tmp/ContainerMonitoring-1579130313205.json provisioning/
dashboards/ContainerMonitoring.json
```

18. Start the Grafana image again and log in to the application using the default administration password:

```
docker run --rm -d --name grafana -p 3000:3000 -e "GF_SECURITY_ADMIN_
PASSWORD=secret" -v ${PWD}/provisioning:/etc/grafana/provisioning
grafana/grafana
```

> **NOTE**
>
> By provisioning the dashboard and data sources in this manner, this means you will no longer be able to create dashboards from the Grafana web interface. When you create a dashboard from now on, you will be presented with an option to save the dashboard as a JSON file, as we did during the exporting of our dashboard.

19. Log in to the home dashboard now. You should see the **Container Monitoring** dashboard available as a recently accessed dashboard, but if you click the home icon at the top of the screen, it will also show it available in the **General** folder of your Grafana installation:

Figure 13.23: Container monitoring dashboard available and provisioned

We have now set up a fully functional dashboard that loads automatically when we run our Grafana Docker image. As you can see, Grafana provides a professional user interface to help us monitor the resource usage of our running containers.

This has brought us to the end of this section, where we've shown you how you can collect your metrics using Prometheus to help monitor how your container applications are running. The following activities will use the knowledge you have learned in the previous sections to expand your installation and monitoring further.

ACTIVITY 13.01: CREATING A GRAFANA DASHBOARD TO MONITOR SYSTEM MEMORY

In previous exercises, you've set up a quick dashboard to monitor the system CPU being used by our Docker containers. As you saw in the previous chapter, it's also important to monitor the system memory being used by our running containers as well. In this activity, you are asked to create a Grafana dashboard that will monitor the system memory being used by our running containers and add it to our `Container Monitoring` dashboard, ensuring it can be provisioned when our Grafana image is started up:

The steps you'll need to complete this activity are as follows:

1. Ensure your environment is being monitored by Prometheus and that Grafana is installed on your system. Make sure you use Grafana to search over the time-series data stored on Prometheus.

2. Create a PromQL query to monitor the container memory being used by your running Docker containers.

3. Save the new dashboard panel on your **Container Monitoring** dashboard.

4. Ensure that the new and improved **Container Monitoring** dashboard is now available and provisioned when you start up your Grafana container.

Expected Output:

You should see the newly created **Memory Container usage** panel on the top of the dashboard when you start the Grafana container:

Figure 13.24: New dashboard panel displaying memory usage

> **NOTE**
>
> The solution for this activity can be found on page 725.

The next activity will make sure you are comfortable using exporters and adding new targets to Prometheus to start tracking extra metrics in your panoramic trekking app.

ACTIVITY 13.02: CONFIGURING THE PANORAMIC TREKKING APP TO EXPOSE METRICS TO PROMETHEUS

Your metrics monitoring environment is starting to look pretty good, but there are some applications in your panoramic trekking app that could be providing extra details and metrics to monitor—for example, the PostgreSQL application running on your database. Choose one of the applications in the panoramic trekking app to expose metrics to your Prometheus environment:

The steps you'll have to take in order to complete this activity are as follows:

1. Ensure Prometheus is running on your system and collecting metrics.

2. Choose a service or application running as part of the panoramic trekking app and research how you can expose metrics for Prometheus to collect.

3. Implement your changes to your application or service.

4. Test your changes and verify that the metrics are available to be collected.

5. Configure a new target on Prometheus to collect the new panoramic trekking app metrics.

6. Verify that you are able to query your new metrics on Prometheus.

Upon successful completion of the activity, you should see the `postgres-web` target displayed on the Prometheus **Targets** page:

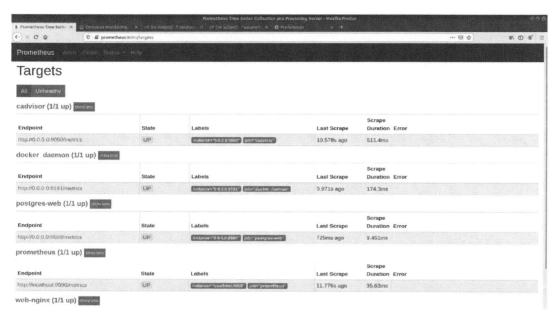

Figure 13.25: New postgres-web Targets page displayed on Prometheus

> **NOTE**
>
> The solution for this activity can be found on page 729.

SUMMARY

In this chapter, we took a long look at metrics and monitoring our container applications and services. We started with a discussion on why you need to have a clear strategy on your metric monitoring and why you need to make a lot of decisions before your project even starts development. We then introduced Prometheus and gave an overview of its history, how it works, and why it has grown in popularity over a very short period. It was then time to get back working again and we installed Prometheus onto our system, became familiar with using the web interface, started to gather metrics from Docker (with some minor changes), and by using **cAdvisor**, collected metrics on the running containers.

The query language used by Prometheus can sometimes be a little confusing, so we took some time to explore PromQL before looking at using exporters to collect even more metrics. We finished up this chapter by integrating Grafana into our environment, displaying our times-series data from Prometheus, and creating useful dashboards and visualizations on the data we are collecting.

Our next chapter is going to continue the monitoring theme with the collection and monitoring of log data from our running containers.

14

COLLECTING CONTAINER LOGS

OVERVIEW

In the previous chapter, we made sure we were collecting metrics data for our running Docker containers and services. This chapter builds on this and dedicates itself to collecting and monitoring the logs for Docker containers and the applications running on them. It will start with a discussion of why we need to have a clear log monitoring strategy for our development projects and discuss some of the things we need to remember. We will then introduce the main player in our log monitoring strategy – that is, Splunk – to collect, visualize, and monitor our logs. We'll install Splunk, forward log data from our system and running containers, and use the Splunk query language to set up monitoring dashboards that work with the log data we've collected. By the end of this chapter, you will have the skills to set up a centralized log monitoring service for your Docker container project.

INTRODUCTION

Whenever something goes wrong with our running applications or service, the first thing we usually look for in our application logs is a clue as to what is causing the issue. So, it becomes important to understand how you'll be collecting logs and monitoring log events for your project.

As we implement a microservice architecture with Docker, it becomes more important to ensure we are able to see the logs our applications and containers are generating. As the number of containers and services grows, trying to access each running container individually becomes increasingly unwieldy as a means of troubleshooting any issues that arise. For scalable applications, where they scale up and down depending on demand, it may become increasingly difficult to track log errors across multiple containers.

Ensuring we have a proper log monitoring strategy in place will help us troubleshoot our applications and ensure our services are running at their optimum efficiency. It will also help us to lessen the amount of time we spend searching through our logs.

There are a few things you will need to consider when building a log monitoring strategy for your project:

- Your application will be using a framework to handle logs. Sometimes, this can cause an overhead on the container, so make sure you are testing your containers to ensure they are able to run without any issues with this logging framework.

- Containers are transient, so the logs will be lost each time the container is shut down. You must either forward the logs to a logging service or store the logs in a data volume to make sure you can troubleshoot any issues that may arise.

- Docker contains a logging driver that's used to forward log events to a Syslog instance running on the host. Unless you are using the Enterprise version of Docker, the **log** command will not work (though it will for JSON) if you are using a specific logging driver.

- Log aggregation applications will usually charge you for the amount of data they are ingesting in their service. And, if you have a service deployed on your environment, you will also need to think about storage requirements – especially how long you plan to keep your logs.

- You will need to consider how your development environment will operate compared to your production environment. For example, there is no need to keep logs in your development environment for a long period, but production may have a requirement for you to keep them for a while.

- You may not just need application data. You may need to collect logs for your application, the container the application is running on, and the underlying host and operating system on which both the application and the container are running.

There are many applications we could use as part of our log monitoring strategy, including Splunk, Sumo Logic, Nagios Logs, Data Dog, and Elasticsearch. In this chapter, we have decided to use Splunk as our log monitoring application. It is one of the oldest applications and has a large community of support and documentation. It is also the best when it comes to working with data and creating visualizations.

You'll see in the following sections how easy it is to get the application up, running, and configured so that you can start monitoring your system logs and our container applications.

INTRODUCING SPLUNK

Long before Docker's rise in popularity, Splunk was established in 2003 to help companies discover some patterns and information from the bulk of data provided by the growing number of applications and services in their environments. Splunk is a software application that allows you to gather your logs and data from your applications and hardware systems. It then lets you analyze and visualize the data you have collected, usually in one central location.

Splunk allows you to enter your data in different formats, and in a lot of situations, Splunk will be able to recognize the data format it is in. You can then use this data to help troubleshoot your applications, create monitoring dashboards, and create alerts on specific events when they occur.

> **NOTE**
>
> In this chapter, we'll only be touching the surface of what Splunk can do, but if you're interested, there are a lot of valuable resources that will show you how to gain operational intelligence from your data, and even use Splunk to create machine learning and predictive intelligence models.

Splunk provides a number of different products to suit your needs, including Splunk Cloud for users and companies wanting to opt for a cloud log monitoring solution.

For our log monitoring strategy, we will be using Splunk Enterprise. It is easy to install and comes with a large number of features. When using Splunk, you might already know that license costs are charged by the amount of log data you send to Splunk, which is then indexed. Splunk Enterprise allows you to index up to 500 MB of data per day for free on a trial basis. After 60 days, you can either upgrade your license or continue to work on a free license, which will continue to allow you to log 500 MB of data per day. There is a developer license available to users, which can be applied for and allows users to log 10 GB of data per day.

To get started with Splunk, we first need to understand its basic architecture. This will be discussed in the following section.

BASIC ARCHITECTURE OF SPLUNK INSTALLATION

By discussing the architecture of Splunk, you will get an idea of how each part works and familiarize yourself with some of the terms that we will be using in this chapter:

- **Indexers**: For larger Splunk installations, it is recommended that you have dedicated and replicated indexers set up as part of your environment. The role of the indexer is to index your date – that is, organize the log data you have sent to Splunk. It also adds metadata and extra information to help speed up the searching process. The indexers will then store your log data, which is ready to be used and queried upon by the search head.

- **Search head**: This is the main web interface where you perform search queries and administer your Splunk installation. The search head will connect with the indexers to query data that has been collected and stored on them. In larger installations, you may even have numerous search heads to allow a larger number of queries and reporting to take place.

- **Data forwarders**: These are usually installed on a system you would like to collect logs on. It is a small application that is configured to collect logs on your system and then push the data to your Splunk indexer.

In the following section, we will be using the official Splunk Docker image, where we will be running both the search head and indexer on the active container. We will continue to use Docker for our Splunk environment as it also provides indexers and data forwarders as supported Docker images. These allow you to test and sandbox an installation before you move forward with an installation.

> **NOTE**
>
> Please note that we are using the Splunk Docker image for simplicity. It will allow us to remove the application, if needed. It is easy and straightforward to install the application and run it on your system if you prefer this option.

Another important feature of Splunk is that it includes a large app ecosystem provided by both Splunk and other third-party providers. These apps are usually created to help users monitor services where logs are forwarded to Splunk and then a third-party app will be installed on the search head. This will provide dashboards and monitoring tools specifically for these logs. For example, you can forward your logs from a Cisco device and then install a Cisco-provided Splunk app to start monitoring your Cisco devices as soon as you start indexing data. You can create your own Splunk app, but to have it listed as an officially provided app, it needs to be certified by Splunk.

> **NOTE**
>
> For a complete list of both the free and paid Splunk apps that are available, Splunk has set up their SplunkBase to allow users to search for and download the available apps from the following URL: https://splunkbase.splunk.com/apps/.

This has been a quick introduction to Splunk and should have helped you understand some of the work we are going to be doing in the following sections. The best way to get you familiar with Splunk, though, is to get the container running on your system so that you can start to work with it.

INSTALLING AND RUNNING SPLUNK ON DOCKER

As part of this chapter, we'll use the official Splunk Docker image to install it on our system. Even though installing Splunk directly on your host system is not a difficult process, installing Splunk as a container image will help extend our knowledge of Docker and push our skills further.

Our Splunk installation will run both a search head and indexer on the same container since the amount of data we'll be monitoring will be minimal. However, if you were to use Splunk in a production environment with multiple users accessing the data, you may need to look at installing dedicated indexers, as well as one or more dedicated search heads.

> **NOTE**
>
> We will be using Splunk Enterprise Version 8.0.2 in this chapter. The majority of the work that will be performed in this chapter will not be too advanced and, as a result, should be compatible with the subsequent version of Splunk in the future.

Before we start to work with Splunk, let's run through the three main directories used by the Splunk application. Although we'll only be performing basic configurations and changes, the following details will be beneficial in understanding how the directories in the application are organized and, as you'll see, will help you with your Docker container setup.

In the main Splunk application directory, usually installed as `/opt/splunk/`, you will see three main directories, as explained here:

- **etc directory**: This is where all the configuration information is held for our Splunk installation. We will create a directory and mount the etc directory as part of our running container to make sure any changes we make to the configuration is kept and not destroyed when we turn off our application. This will include user access, software settings and saved searches, dashboards, and the Splunk app.

- **bin directory**: This is where all of Splunk's application and binary files are stored. You won't need to access this directory or make changes to files in this directory at this point, but it is something you may need to investigate further.

- **var directory**: Splunk's indexed data and application logs are stored in this directory. When we first start working with Splunk, we won't bother keeping the data we are storing in the var directory. But when we have ironed out all the bugs with our deployment, we will mount the var directory to keep our indexed data and make sure we can continue to search against it, even if our Splunk container stops running.

> **NOTE**
>
> To download some of the applications and content used in this chapter, you will need to sign up for an account on splunk.com to gain access to it. There is no obligation to purchase anything or provide credit card details when you sign up as it is just a means Splunk uses to track who is using their application.

To run our Splunk container, we will pull the official image from Docker Hub and then run a command similar to the following:

```
docker run --rm -d -p <port:port> -e "SPLUNK_START_ARGS=--accept-license"
-e "SPLUNK_PASSWORD=<admin-password>" splunk/splunk:latest
```

As you can see from the preceding command, we need to expose the relevant ports needed for accessing different parts of our installation. You'll also note that there are two environment variables we need to specify as part of our running container. The first is **SPLUNK_START_ARGS**, which we have set to **--accept-license**, which you'd normally accept when you install Splunk on a running server. Secondly, we need to provide a value for the **SPLUNK_PASSWORD** environment variable. This is the password used by the Administrator account, and it is the account you will use when you first log in to Splunk.

We've provided a large amount of theory to get you ready for the next part of this chapter. It's time to put this theory into practice and get our Splunk installation running so that we can start collecting logs from our host system. In the following exercise, we will install a Splunk data forwarder on our running host system to collect logs to be forwarded to our Splunk indexer.

> **NOTE**
>
> Please use **touch** command to create files and **vim** command to work on the file using vim editor.

EXERCISE 14.01: RUNNING THE SPLUNK CONTAINER AND STARTING TO COLLECT DATA

In this exercise, you will get Splunk running using the official Splunk Docker image available on Docker Hub. You will make some basic configuration changes to help administer user access to the application on the image, and then you will install a forwarder on your system so that you can start to consume logs in your Splunk installation:

1. Create a new directory called **chapter14**:

```
mkdir chapter14; cd chapter14/
```

2. Pull the latest supported image from Docker Hub that has been created by Splunk using the **docker pull** command. The repository is simply listed as **splunk/splunk**:

```
docker pull splunk/splunk:latest
```

3. Run the Splunk image on your system with the **docker run** command. Use the **--rm** option to make sure the container is removed fully when it is killed, the **-d** option to have the container running as a daemon in the background of your system, and the **-p** option to expose port **8000** on your host machine so that you can view the applications on our web browser. Lastly, use the **-e** option to provide environment variables to the system when you start up the container:

```
docker run --rm -d -p 8000:8000 -e "SPLUNK_START_ARGS=--accept-
license" -e "SPLUNK_PASSWORD=changeme" --name splunk splunk/
splunk:latest
```

In the preceding command, you are exposing port **8000** for the web interface, accepting the Splunk license with one environment variable, and also setting an administration password as **changeme**. The command is also running in the background as a daemon with **-d**.

4. Splunk will take 1 or 2 minutes to start up. Use the **docker logs** command to view the progress of the application:

```
docker logs splunk
```

When you see a similar line to the following showing **Ansible playbook complete**, you should be ready to log in:

```
...
Ansible playbook complete, will begin streaming
```

5. Enter the URL **http://0.0.0.0:8000** to access the web interface of our Splunk installation. You should see something similar to the following. To log in, use **admin** as the username and the password we set with the **SPLUNK_PASSWORD** environment variable while running the image. In this case, you will use **changeme**:

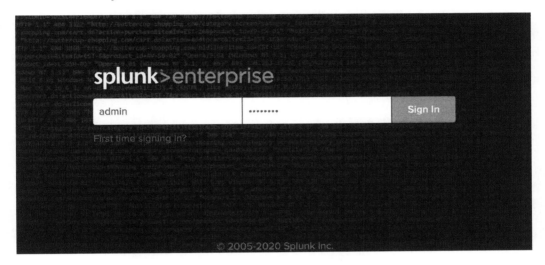

Figure 14.1: The Splunk web login page

Once you've logged in, you will be presented with the Splunk home screen, which should look similar to the following. The home screen is divided into separate sections, as outlined here:

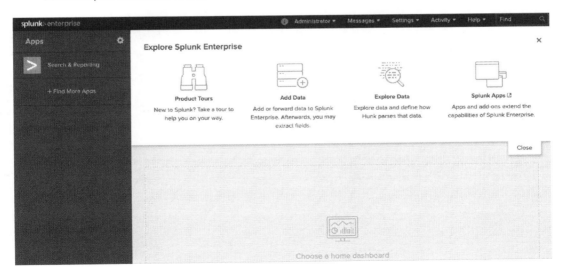

Figure 14.2: The Splunk welcome screen

The home screen can be broken down into the following sections:

- **Splunk>**: This is the icon at the top-left of the screen. It will bring you back to your home screen at any time if you simply click on the icon.

- **Apps Menu**: This runs along the left-hand side of the screen and allows you to install and configure Splunk apps.

- **Menu Bar**: This runs along the top of the screen and contains different options, depending on the level of privileges you have with your account. As you have logged in as the Administrator account, you get the full range of options. This allows us to configure and manage how Splunk is run and how it is administered. The main configuration option in the menu bar is `Settings`. It provides a large drop-down list that lets you control the majority of the aspects of how Splunk is run.

- **Main Workspace**: The main workspace fills the rest of the page and is where you can start to search your data, set up dashboards, and start to visualize your data. You can set a home dashboard so that each time you log in or click on the `Splunk>` icon, you will also be presented with this dashboard. We will set the home dashboard later in this chapter to show you how it is done.

6. You can start to make changes to our Splunk configurations, but if the container stops running for some reason, all our changes will be lost. Instead, create a directory where you can store all the relevant configuration information needed for your Splunk environment. Stop the Splunk server you currently have running with the following command:

```
docker kill splunk
```

7. Create a directory that can be mounted on the Splunk host. Call it **testSplunk** for this purpose:

```
mkdir -p ${PWD}/testsplunk
```

8. Run the Splunk container again, this time using the **-v** option to mount the directory you created in the previous step to the **/opt/splunk/etc** directory on your container. Expose the extra port of **9997** in order to forward data to our Splunk installation later in this exercise:

```
docker run --rm -d -p 8000:8000 -p 9997:9997 -e 'SPLUNK_START_ARGS=--
accept-license' -e 'SPLUNK_PASSWORD=changeme' -v ${PWD}/testsplunk:/
opt/splunk/etc/ --name splunk splunk/splunk
```

9. Once Splunk has started up again, log back into your Splunk web interface as the Administrator account.

10. Add a new user to your system to make sure you are saving the relevant configuration details in your mounted directory through the **Settings** menu at the top of the screen. Click on the **Settings** menu:

Figure 14.3: The Splunk settings menu

11. With the **Settings** menu open, move to the bottom section and click on **Users** in the **Users and Authentication** section. You should see a list of all the users that have been created on your installation of Splunk. Only the admin account will be listed in there so far. To create a new user, click on the **New User** button at the top of the screen.

12. You'll be presented with a web form where you can add your new user account details. Fill in the details for the new user. Once you're happy with the details you've added, click on the **Save** button at the bottom of the screen:

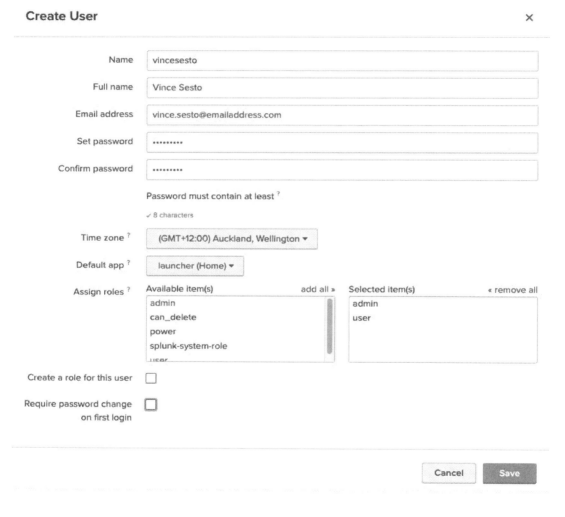

Figure 14.4: Creating new users on Splunk

13. To make sure you are now keeping this data on your mounted directory, move back to your terminal to see whether the new user is stored in your mounted directory. Simply list the directories in the **testsplunk/users** directory using the following command:

```
ls testsplunk/users/
```

You should see that a directory has been set up for the new account you created in the previous step; in this case, **vincesesto**:

```
admin          splunk-system-user          users.ini
users.ini.default          vincesesto
```

14. It's time to start sending data to the Splunk instance running on your system. Before you start collecting data from your running Docker containers, install a forwarder on your running system, and start forwarding logs from there. To access the forwarder specific to your system, go to the following URL and download the forwarder specific to your operating system: https://www.splunk.com/en_us/download/universal-forwarder.html.

15. Follow the prompts to accept the license so that you can use the application. Also, accept the default options presented in the installation program:

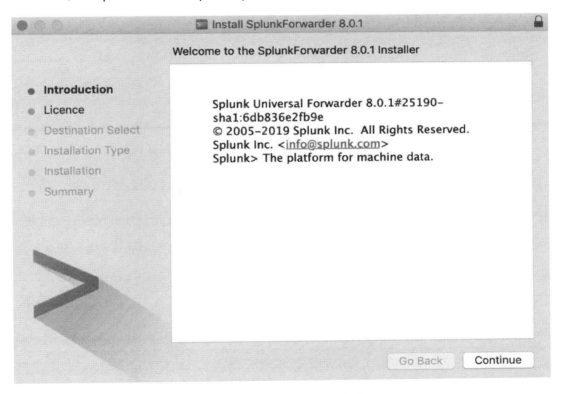

Figure 14.5: Splunk forwarder installation program

16. The forwarder will usually start automatically. Verify that the forwarder is running by accessing your terminal and changing to the installation directory on your system using the **cd** command. For the Splunk forwarder, the binary and application files will be located in the **/opt/splunkforwarder/bin/** directory:

```
cd /opt/Splunkforwarder/bin/
```

17. In the **bin** directory, check the status of the forwarder by running the **./splunk status** command, as follows:

```
./splunk status
```

If it is running, you should see something similar to the following output:

```
splunkd is running (PID: 2076).
splunk helpers are running (PIDs: 2078).
```

18. If the forwarder did not start when the installation took place, run it from the **bin** directory with the **start** option using the following command:

```
./splunk start
```

The output provided will show the Splunk daemon and services starting up. It will also show the Process ID (PID) of the services that are running on the system:

```
splunkd is running (PID: 2076).
splunk helpers are running (PIDs: 2078).

Splunk> Be an IT superhero. Go home early.
...
Starting splunk server daemon (splunkd)...Done
```

19. You need to let the Splunk forwarder know where it needs to send its data. In *step 8* of this exercise, we made sure we ran our Splunk container with port **9997** exposed for this specific reason. Use the **./splunk** command to tell the forwarder to send the data to our Splunk container running on IP address **0.0.0.0** on port **9997** using the Administrator username and password for our Splunk instance:

```
./splunk add forward-server 0.0.0.0:9997 -auth admin:changeme
```

The command should return an output similar to the following:

```
Added forwarding to: 0.0.0.0:9997.
```

20. Finally, to complete the setup of your Splunk forwarder, nominate some log files to forward to our Splunk container. Use the **./splunk** command on the forwarder to monitor the files in the **/var/log** directory of our system and send them to the Splunk container to be indexed so that we can start viewing them:

```
./splunk add monitor /var/log/
```

21. After a few minutes, if everything has worked as it should, you should have some log events ready to be viewed on your Splunk container. Move back to your web browser and enter the following URL to open a Splunk search page: **http://0.0.0.0:8000/en-US/app/search/search**.

> **NOTE**
>
> The following step uses a very basic Splunk search query to search over all the data on your installation. If you have not worked with the Splunk query language previously, don't worry; we'll spend an entire section, *Working with the Splunk Query Language*, explaining the query language in more depth.

22. Perform a basic search by simply adding an asterisk (*****) as a search query, as shown in the following screenshot. If everything has worked as it should, you should start to see log events in the results area of the search page:

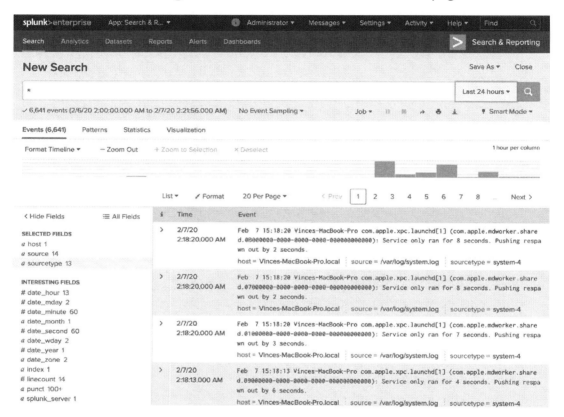

Figure 14.6: Splunk search window with data displayed from our forwarder

23. For the final part of this exercise, you will practice the easiest way to upload data to Splunk, which is by simply uploading the file directly to your running system. Download the sample data file named **weblog.csv** from https://packt. live/3hFbh4C and place it in your **/tmp** directory.

24. Move back to your Splunk web interface and click on the **Settings** menu option. Select **Add Data** from the right-hand side of the menu options, as shown in the following screenshot:

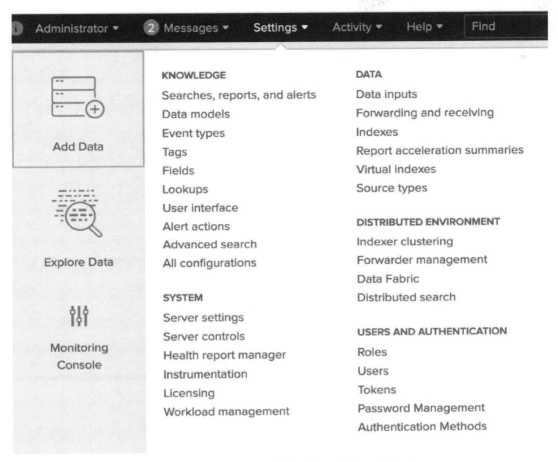

Figure 14.7: Importing files directly into Splunk

25. Click **Upload files from my computer** toward the bottom of the screen:

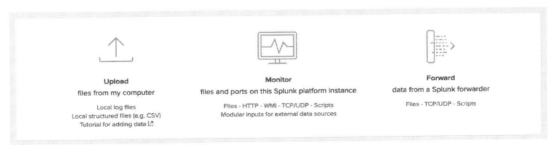

Figure 14.8: Uploading files on Splunk

26. The next screen will allow you to select the source file from your machine. Select the **weblog.csv** file you downloaded earlier in this exercise. Click the **Next** button at the top of the screen when you have selected the file.

27. Set **Source Type** to choose or accept in what format Splunk has viewed your data. In this instance, it should have recognized your data as a **.csv** file. Click the **Next** button.

28. The **Input Settings** page lets you set the name of your host but leave the index as the default. Click the **Review** button:

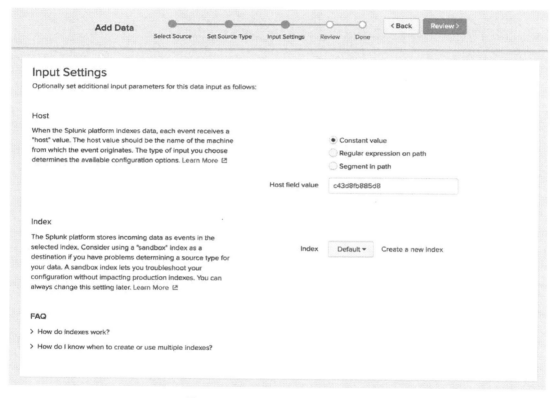

Figure 14.9: Input settings page

29. Click the **Submit** button if all the entries look correct. Then, click **Start Searching**, where you should see your search screen, along with the sample web log data available and ready to be searched. It should look similar to the following:

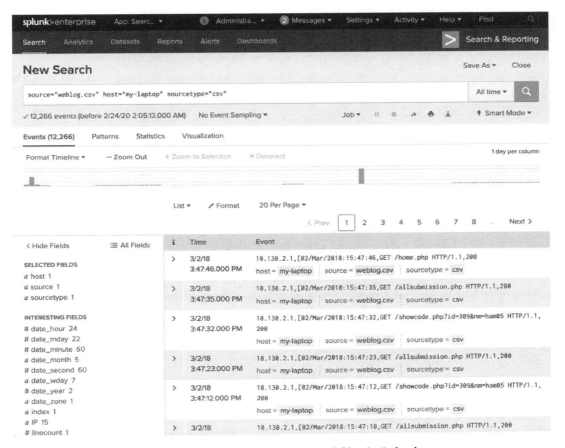

Figure 14.10: Searching imported files in Splunk

In a short amount of time, we have set up a Splunk search head and indexer on our system and installed a Splunk forwarder to send logs into the indexer and search head. We also manually added log data to our index so that we could view it.

The next part of this chapter will focus on getting your Docker container logs into the new Splunk container we have running.

GETTING CONTAINER LOGS INTO SPLUNK

Our log monitoring environment is starting to take shape, but we need to get our Docker container logs into the application to make it worth the work. We have set up our Splunk forwarder to send logs from our system to the **/var/log** directory. Up until now, we have learned that we can simply mount the log file of our container and use the Splunk forwarder to send logs to the Splunk indexer. This is one way to do this, but Docker provides an easier option for sending logs to Splunk.

Docker provides a log driver specific to Splunk that will send our container logs via our network to an HTTP Event Collector on our Splunk installation. We'll need to open a new port to expose the Event Collector as Splunk uses port **8088** to collect data in this method. So far, we've exposed ports **8000** and **9997** on our Splunk installation. Before we proceed with the rest of this chapter, let's look at all the available ports and how they function on Splunk:

- **8000**: You've been using this port for the web application, and this is the dedicated default web port used to access Splunk in your browser.

- **9997**: This port is the default port used by Splunk forwarders to forward data to the indexer. We exposed this port in the previous section of this chapter to make sure we're able to collect logs from our running system.

- **8089**: Splunk comes with an API that runs by default as part of the search head. Port **8089** is where the API manager sits to interface with the API running on your instance.

- **8088**: Port **8088** needs to be exposed to allow information to be forwarded to the Event Collector that's been set up on your system. In the upcoming exercise, we'll use this port to start sending Docker container logs to an HTTP Event Collector.

- **8080**: If we had a larger Splunk installation with dedicated indexers, port **8080** is used for indexers to communicate among themselves and allow replication among these indexers.

> **NOTE**
>
> The web interface for Splunk runs by default on port **8000**, but this may clash with our Panoramic Trekking App if you are hosting the application on the same port. If this does cause any issues, feel free to expose the port on the Splunk container to something different, such as port **8080**, as you will still be able to access the web interface and it will not cause any issues with our services using that port.

Once an **HTTP Event Collector** has been set up on Splunk, forwarding logs to Splunk is simply a matter of adding the correct options to our **docker run** command. The following sample command uses **--log-driver=splunk** to signal to the running container to use the Splunk log driver.

It then needs to include further **--log-opt** options to make sure the logs are forwarded correctly. The first is **splunk-url**, which is the URL your system is currently being hosted on. As we don't have DNS set up, we can simply use the IP address we are using to host our Splunk instance, along with the port of **8088**. The second is **splunk-token**. This is the token that's assigned by Splunk when you create the HTTP Event Collector:

```
docker run --log-driver=splunk \
--log-opt splunk-url=<splunk-url>:8088 \
--log-opt splunk-token=<event-collector-token> \
<docker-image>
```

There is the option to add Splunk logging driver details to your Docker configuration file. Here, you will need to add the following details to your **daemon.json** file in the **/etc/docker** configuration file. This will only work if you have Splunk as a separate application and not a Docker instance on your system. As we have set up our Splunk instance as a Docker container, this option will not work. This is because the Docker daemon will need to restart and connect to **splunk-url** listed in the configuration. Of course, without the Docker daemon running, **splunk-url** will never be available:

```
{
  "log-driver": "splunk",
  "log-opts": {
    "splunk-token": "<splunk-token>",
    "splunk-url": "<splunk-url>::8088"
  }
}
```

In the following exercise, we are going to extend our Splunk installation to open ports specific for our **HTTP Event Collector**, which we'll also create. We will then start to send logs from our containers into Splunk, ready for us to start viewing them.

EXERCISE 14.02: CREATING AN HTTP EVENT COLLECTOR AND STARTING TO COLLECT DOCKER LOGS

In this exercise, you will create an **HTTP Event Collector** for your Splunk installation and use the Docker **log** driver to forward your logs to your Event Collector. You will use the **random-logger** Docker image, which is provided by the **chentex** repository and available for use on Docker Hub, to generate some logs in your system and demonstrate the use of Splunk further:

1. Start the Splunk image again, this time with port **8088** exposed to all our Docker containers to push their logs to it:

```
docker run --rm -d -p 8000:8000 -p 9997:9997 -p 8088:8088 \
 -e 'SPLUNK_START_ARGS=--accept-license' \
 -e 'SPLUNK_PASSWORD=changeme' \
 -v ${PWD}/testsplunk:/opt/splunk/etc/ \
 --name splunk splunk/splunk:latest
```

2. Wait for Splunk to start up again and log back into the web interface with the Administrator account.

3. Go to the **Settings** menu and select **Data Inputs** to create a new **HTTP Event Collector**. Select **HTTP Event Collector** from the options list.

4. Click on the **Global Settings** button on the **HTTP Event Collector** page. You will be presented with a page similar to the following. On this page, click on the **Enabled** button, next to **All Tokens**, and make sure **Enable SLL** is not selected as you will not be using SSL in this exercise. This will make things a little easier for you. When you're happy with the details on the screen, click the **Save** button to save your configurations:

Edit Global Settings   ✕

All Tokens	Enabled	Disabled

Default Source Type	Select Source Type ▾

Default Index	Default ▾

Default Output Group	None ▾

Use Deployment Server ☐

Enable SSL ☐

HTTP Port Number ?	8088

Cancel   Save

Figure 14.11: Enabling HTTP Event Collector on your system

5. When you return to the **HTTP Event Collector** page, click the **New Token** button at the top-right of the screen. You'll be presented with a screen similar to the following. This is where you'll set up your new Event Collector so that you can collect your Docker container logs:

Figure 14.12: Naming your HTTP Event Collector on Splunk

The preceding screen is where you set the name of your new Event Collector. Enter the name **Docker Logs** and, for the rest of the entries, accept the defaults by leaving them blank. Click the **Next** button at the top of the screen.

6. Accept the default values for the **Input Settings** and **Review** pages until you see a page similar to the following, in which a new **HTTP Event Collector** has been created with a token available. The token is displayed as **5c051cdb-b1c6-482f-973f-2a8de0d92ed8**. Yours will be different as Splunk provides a unique token to allow for the secure transfer of data from sources that are trusted by the user. Use this token to allow your Docker containers to start logging data in your Splunk installation:

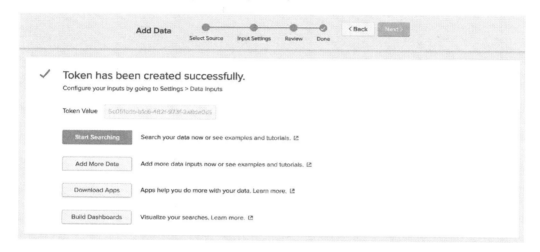

Figure 14.13: Completed HTTP Event Collector on Splunk

7. Use the **hello-world** Docker image to make sure you can send data to Splunk. In this instance, add four extra command-line options as part of your **docker run** command. Specify **--log-driver** as **splunk**. Provide the log options as the **splunk-url** of our system, including port **8088**, **splunk-token**, which you created in the previous step, and, finally, state **splunk-=insecureipverify** as **true**. This final option will limit the work required in setting up your Splunk installation so that you won't need to organize the SSL certificates that will be used with our Splunk server:

```
docker run --log-driver=splunk \
--log-opt splunk-url=http://127.0.0.1:8088 \
--log-opt splunk-token=5c051cdb-b1c6-482f-973f-2a8de0d92ed8 \
--log-opt splunk-insecureskipverify=true \
hello-world
```

The commands should return an output similar to the following:

```
Hello from Docker!
This message shows that your installation appears to be
```

```
working correctly.
...
```

8. Return to the Splunk web interface and click the **Start Searching** button. If you have already moved on from the previous screen, go to the Splunk search page at **http://0.0.0.0:8000/en-US/app/search/search**. In the search query box, enter **source="http:Docker Logs"**, as shown in the following screenshot. If everything has worked well, you should also see data entries being provided by the **hello-world** image:

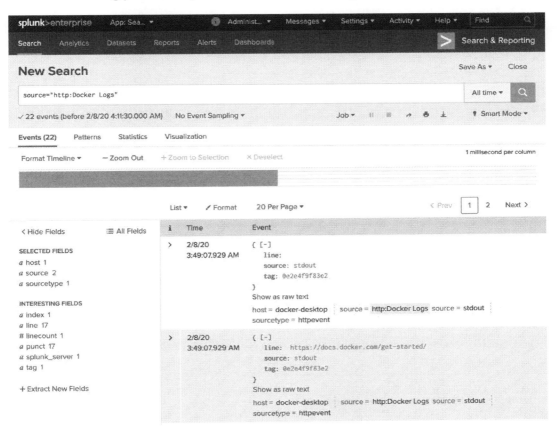

Figure 14.14: Starting to collect docker logs with Splunk

9. The previous step has shown that the Splunk installation is now able to collect Docker log data, but you will need to create a new volume to store your index data so that it is not destroyed every time you stop Splunk from running. Move back into your terminal and kill the running **splunk** container:

```
docker kill splunk
```

10. In the same directory where you created the original **testsplunk** directory, create a new directory so that we can mount our Splunk index data. In this instance, name it **testsplunkindex**:

```
mkdir testsplunkindex
```

11. From your working directory, start the Splunk image again. Mount the new directory you just created in order to store your index data:

```
docker run --rm -d -p 8000:8000 -p 9997:9997 -p 8088:8088 \
 -e 'SPLUNK_START_ARGS=--accept-license' \
 -e 'SPLUNK_PASSWORD=changeme' \
 -v ${PWD}/testsplunk:/opt/splunk/etc/ \
 -v ${PWD}/testsplunkindex:/opt/splunk/var/ \
 --name splunk splunk/splunk:latest
```

12. Use the **random-logger** Docker image to generate some logs in your system. In the following command, there's an added **tag** log option. This will mean that each log event that's generated and sent to Splunk will also include this tag as metadata, which can help you search for data when you are searching in Splunk. By using the **{{.Name}}** and **{{.FullID}}** options, these details will be automatically added, just like the container name and ID number will be added as your tag when the container is created:

```
docker run --rm -d --log-driver=splunk \
--log-opt splunk-url=http://127.0.0.1:8088 \
--log-opt splunk-token=5c051cdb-b1c6-482f-973f-2a8de0d92ed8 \
--log-opt splunk-insecureskipverify=true \
--log-opt tag="{{.Name}}/{{.FullID}}" \
--name log-generator chentex/random-logger:latest
```

> **NOTE**
>
> If your Splunk instance is not running correctly or you have not configured something correctly, the **log-generator** container will fail to connect or run. You will see an error similar to the following:
>
> **docker: Error response from daemon: failed to initialize logging driver:**

13. Once this is running, move back to the Splunk search page on the web interface and in this instance, include the tag you created in the previous step. The following query will ensure that only new data that has been provided by the **log-generator** image will display in our Splunk output:

```
source="http:docker logs" AND "log-generator/"
```

Your Splunk search should result in something similar to the following. Here, you can see the logs that have been generated by the **log-generator** image. You can see that it is logging at random times and that each entry is now tagged with the name and instance ID of your container:

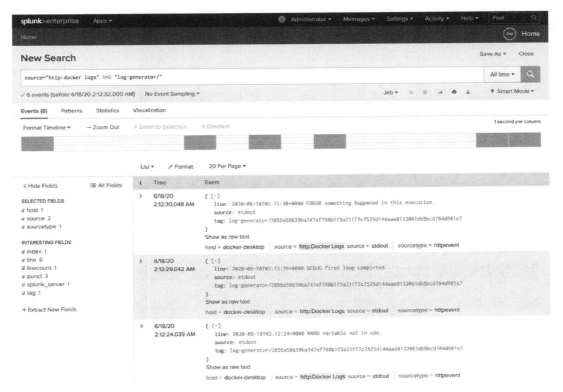

Figure 14.15: Splunk search result

Our Splunk installation is coming along nicely as we've now been able to configure the application to include an **HTTP Event Collector** and have started collecting logs from the **log-generator** Docker image. Even if we stop our Splunk instance, they should still be available for us to search and extract useful information.

The following section will provide a more in-depth demonstration of how to use the Splunk query language.

WORKING WITH THE SPLUNK QUERY LANGUAGE

The Splunk query language can be a little difficult to pick up, but once you do, you'll find it helpful to interpret, analyze, and present your data from your Splunk environment. The best way to get comfortable with the query language is to simply dive in.

The following list describes a few things to take into account when working with the query language:

- **Narrow your search**: The larger the amount of data you want to search over, the longer your query will take to return a result. If you know the time frame or a source, such as the one we created for **docker logs**, the query will return the result faster.

- **Use simple search terms**: If you have an idea of what will be included in your log (for example, **ERROR** or **DEBUG**), this is a great place to start with your search terms as it will also help limit the amount of data you are receiving. This is another reason why we used a tag in the previous section when adding logs to our Splunk instance.

- **Chain search terms**: We can use **AND** to group search terms. We can also use **OR** to search for logs with more than one search term use.

- **Add wildcards to search multiple terms**: The query language also has the option to use wildcards, such as an asterisk. If you used the **ERR*** query, for example, it would search for not only **ERROR** but also **ERR** and **ERRORS**.

- **Extracted fields provide more details**: Splunk will do its best to find and locate fields in the log events, especially if your logs are in a known log format such as Apache log file format or a recognizable format such as CSV or JSON logs. If you are creating logs for your application, Splunk will do an amazing job of extracting fields if you present your data as key-value pairs.

- **Add functions to a group and visualize data**: Adding functions to your search terms can help you transform and present your data. They are usually added to your search term with a pipe (|) character. The following exercise will use the **stats**, **chart**, and **timechart** functions to help aggregate search results and calculate statistics such as **average**, **count**, and **sum**. As an example, if we are using a search term such as **ERR***, we can then pipe this to the **stats** command to count the number of times we see an error event:

```
ERR* | stats count
```

Splunk also provides handy tips when you are entering your query. Once you have the basics down, it will help you provide additional functionality to your data.

In the following exercise, you will find that, even when Splunk cannot find your extracted fields, you can create your own so that you can analyze your data.

EXERCISE 14.03: GETTING FAMILIAR WITH THE SPLUNK QUERY LANGUAGE

In this exercise, you will run through a series of tasks that demonstrate the basic functionality of the query language and help you become more familiar with using it. This will help you examine and visualize your own data:

1. Make sure your Splunk container is running and that the **log-generator** container is sending data to Splunk.

2. When you log in to Splunk, from the home page, click **Search & Reporting app** from the left-hand side menu or go to the URL **http://0.0.0.0:8000/ en-US/app/search/search** to bring up the search page.

3. When you get to the search page, you will see a textbox that says **enter search here**. Start with a simple term such as the word **ERROR**, as shown in the following screenshot, and press *Enter* to have Splunk run the query:

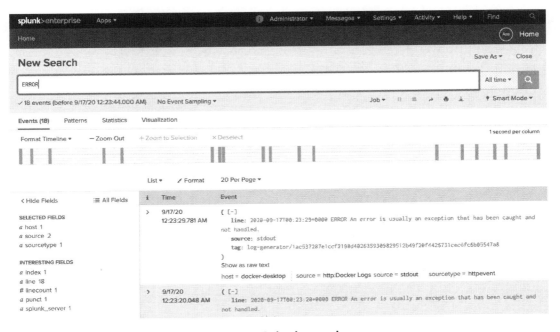

Figure 14.16: Splunk search page

If you were to only enter the term **ERR*** with an asterisk (*****) at the end of the term, this should also give results similar to the ones shown in the preceding screenshot.

4. Chain search terms together using **AND** to make sure our log events include multiple values. Enter a search similar to **sourcetype=htt* AND ERR*** to search for all **HTTP** Event Collector logs that are also showing **ERR** values in their logs:

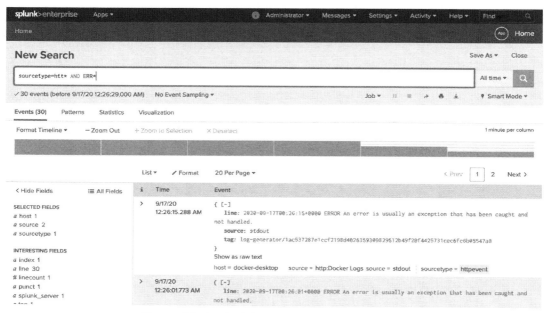

Figure 14.17: Chaining search terms together

5. The searches you enter will most likely default to searching through all the data since your installation. Looking through all your data could result in a very time-consuming search. Narrow this down by entering a time range to search over. Click the drop-down menu to the right of the query textbox to limit the data your search is run over. Limit the search to **Last 24 hours**:

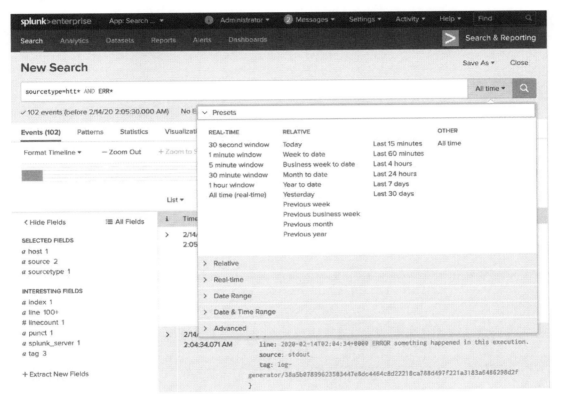

Figure 14.18: Limiting searches with time ranges

6. Look through the extracted fields on the left-hand side of the results page. You'll notice that there are two sections. The first is **SELECTED FIELDS**, which includes data specific to your search. The second is **INTERESTING FIELDS**. This data is still relevant and part of your data but not specifically related to your search query:

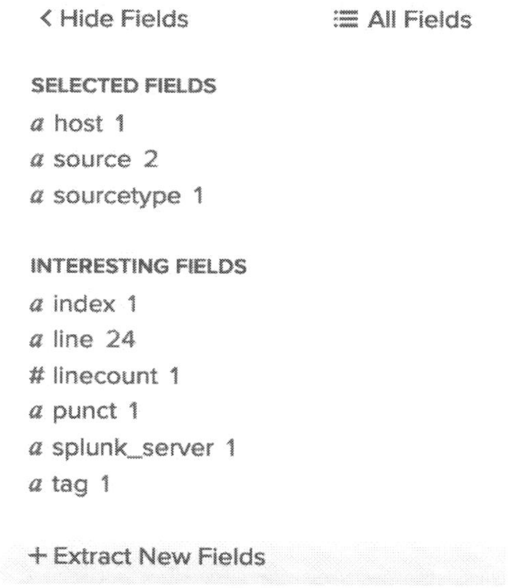

< Hide Fields   ☰ All Fields

SELECTED FIELDS
a host 1
a source 2
a sourcetype 1

INTERESTING FIELDS
a index 1
a line 24
linecount 1
a punct 1
a splunk_server 1
a tag 1

+ Extract New Fields

Figure 14.19: Extracted fields

7. To create the fields to be listed, click the **Extract Your Own Fields** link. The following steps will walk through the process of creating new fields relevant to the data the **log-generator** container is providing.

8. You'll be taken to a new page where you'll be presented with sample data from the **httpevent** source type you have recently been searching on. First, you'll need to select a sample event. Select the first line that is similar to the one listed here. Click the **Next** button at the top of the screen to move on to the next step:

```
{"line":"2020-02-19T03:58:12+0000 ERROR something happened in this
execution.","source":"stdout","tag":"log-generator/3eae26b23d667bb122
95aaccbdf919c9370ffa50da9e401d0940365db6605e3"}
```

9. You'll then be asked to choose the method you want to use in order to extract fields. If you are working with files that have a clear delimiter, such as a **.SSV** file, use the **Delimiters** method. In this instance, though, you are going to use the **Regular Expression** method. Click **Regular Expression** and then click the **Next** button:

Regular Expression

Splunk Enterprise will extract fields using
a Regular Expression.

Delimiters

Splunk Enterprise will extract fields using
a delimiter (such as commas, spaces, or
characters). Use this method for delimited
data like comma separated values (CSV
files).

Figure 14.20: Field extraction method

10. You should now have one line of data where you can start to select fields to extract. All the log data provided by the **log-generator** container is the same, so this line will serve as a template for all the events Splunk receives. As shown in the following screenshot, click **ERROR**, and when you're provided with the opportunity to enter a field name, enter **level**, and then select the **Add Extraction** button. Select the line of text after **ERROR**. In this example, it is **something happened in this execution**. Add a field name of **message**. Click the **Add Extraction** button. Then, click the **Next** button when you have selected all the relevant fields:

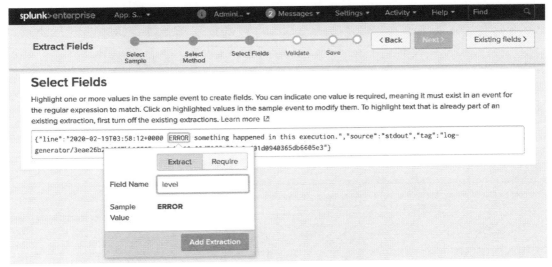

Figure 14.21: Field extraction in Splunk

11. You should now be able to see all the events with the new fields you have highlighted. Click the **Next** button:

Figure 14.22: Events with the new fields

12. Finally, you'll be presented with a screen similar to the following. In the **Permissions** section, click the **All apps** button to allow this field extraction to occur across your entire Splunk installation, not limiting it to one app or the owner. If you're happy with the extractions name and other options, click the **Finish** button at the top of the screen:

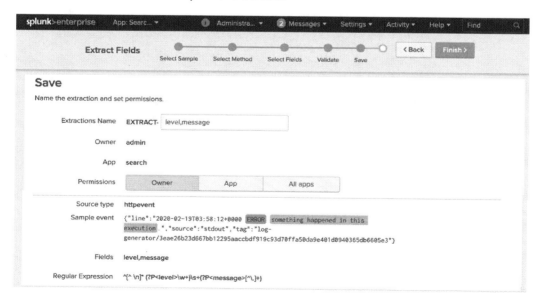

Figure 14.23: Field extraction in Splunk completed

13. Move back into your search page and add **sourcetype=httpevent** to the search query. Once it loads, look through the extracted fields. You should now have the **level** and **message** fields you added as **INTERESTING FIELDS**. If you click on the **level** field, you will get a breakdown of the number of events received, similar to what's shown in the following screenshot:

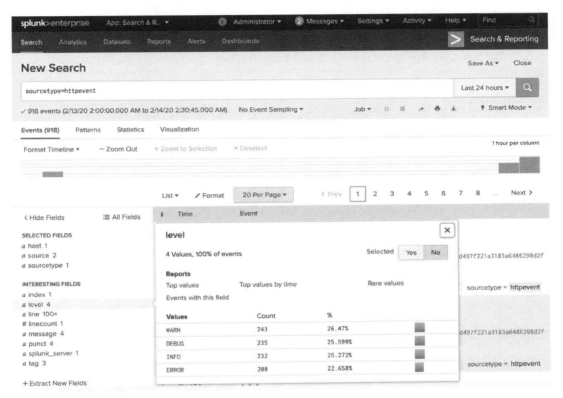

Figure 14.24: Displaying field breakdown in the search results

14. Use the **stats** function to count the number of events for each error level in your logs. Do this by using the **sourcetype=httpevent | stats count by level** search query for the results of your search from the previous step and pipe the values of the **stats** function to **count by level**:

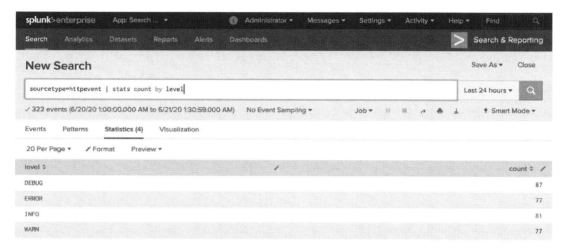

Figure 14.25: Using the stats function

15. The **stats** function gives you some nice information, but if you want to see the data presented over a period of time, use the **timechart** function. Run the **sourcetype=httpevent | timechart span=1m count by level** query to give the result over a range of time. If you perform your search over the past 15 minutes, the preceding query should give you a breakdown of data by each minute. Click the **Visualization** tab under the search query textbox. You will be presented with a graph representing the results of our search:

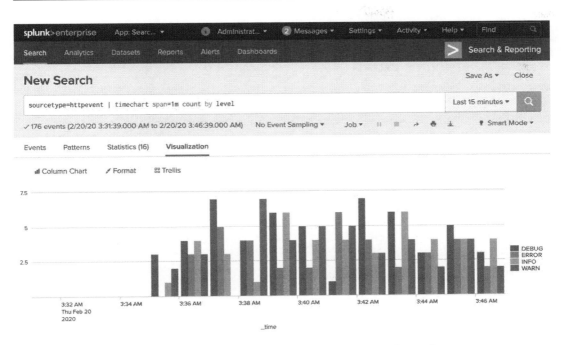

Figure 14.26: Creating visualizations from search results

You can use the span option in your query to group your data by minute (1m), hour (5), day (1d), and so on.

16. In the preceding screenshot, where it mentions the chart type (`Column Chart`), you can change the type you currently have displayed. Click the `Column Chart` text. It will let you select from a few different types of charts. In this instance, use the line chart:

Figure 14.27: Selecting the chart type

NOTE

In the following steps, you are going to create a dashboard for your data visualization. Dashboards are a way to display your data to users without them needing to know anything specific about Splunk or the data involved. It is perfect for non-technical users as you simply provide a URL to the dashboard so that the user will simply load the dashboard to see the information they need. Dashboards are also perfect for searches you need to perform on a regular basis so as to limit the amount of work you need to do.

17. When you are happy with the chart, click the **Save As** button at the top of the screen and select the **Dashboard Panel**. You'll be presented with a form similar to the one shown in the following screenshot. Create a new dashboard called **Log Container Dashboard** that is **Shared in App** (the current search app) with the specific panel you have just created, named **Error Level**:

Figure 14.28: Creating dashboards from search results

18. Click the **Save** button to create the new dashboard. You'll be given the opportunity to view your dashboard when you click save. But if you need to view the dashboard at a later stage, go to the app you've created the dashboard in (in this case, the **Search & Reporting** app) and click the **Dashboards** menu at the top of the screen. You will be presented with the available dashboards. This is where you can click the relevant one. You'll notice you have two other dashboards available that have been provided by default as part of your Splunk installation:

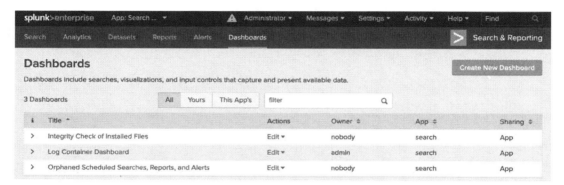

Figure 14.29: Dashboards in Splunk

19. Open the **Log Container** dashboard you just created and click the **Edit** button at the top of the screen. This will let you add a new panel to your dashboard without you needing to move back to the search window.

20. When you click on the **Edit** button, you'll be given extra options to make changes to the look and feel of your dashboard. Click the **Add Panel** button now.

21. When you select **Add Panel**, you'll be presented with some extra selections on the right-hand side of the screen. Click the **New** menu option and then select **Single Value**.

22. Name the panel **Total Errors** and add **sourcetype=httpevent AND ERROR | stats count** as the search string. The screen where you can add the new dashboard panel should look similar to the following. It should provide details regarding the **Content Title** and **Search String**:

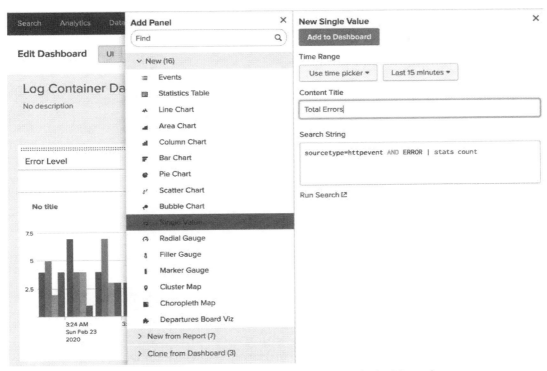

Figure 14.30: Adding panels to your Splunk dashboard

23. Click the **Add to Dashboard** button to add the new panel to the bottom of the dashboard as a single value panel.

24. While the dashboard is in edit mode, you can move and resize the panels if needed and add extra headings or details. When you are happy with your new panel, click the **Save** button at the top-right of the screen.

Your dashboard should hopefully look similar to the following:

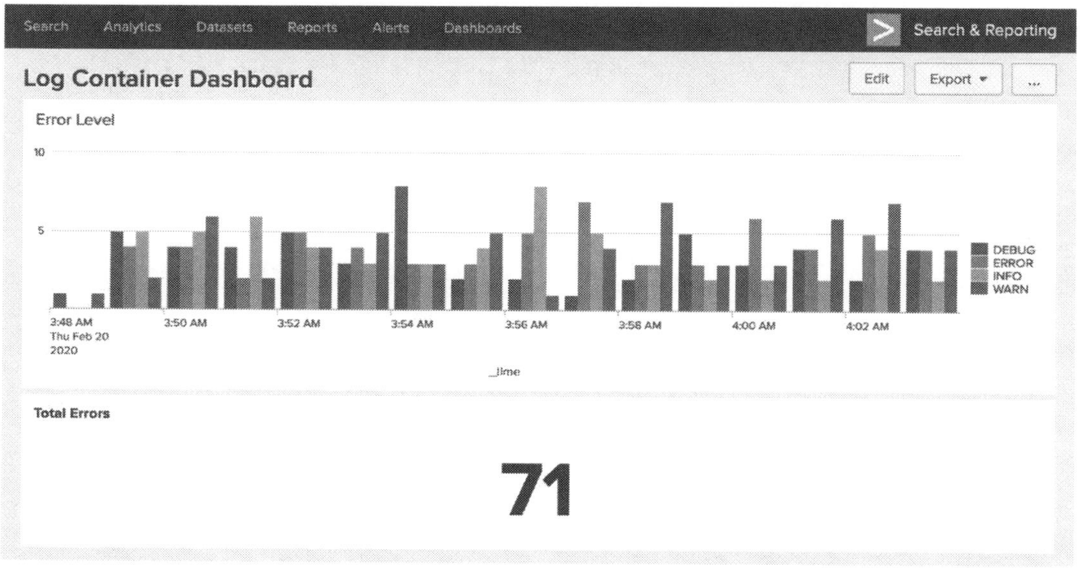

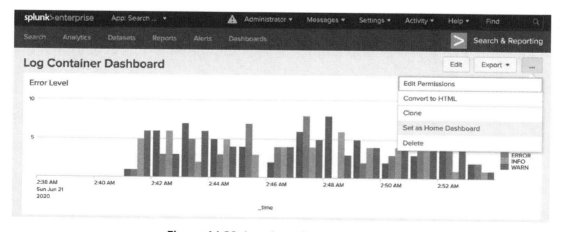

Figure 14.31: Adding new panels to your dashboards

Finally, your dashboard panel has some extra functions, which you can find by clicking on the ellipses button at the top-right of the screen. If you are unhappy with your dashboard, you can delete it from here.

25. Click the `Set as Home Dashboard Panel` option, which is available under the ellipses button. This will take you back to the Splunk home screen, where your `Log Container Dashboard` is now available and will be the first thing you see when you log in to Splunk:

Figure 14.32: Log Container Dashboard

This exercise has shown you how to perform basic queries, chain them together with functions, and start to create visualizations, dashboards, and panels. Although we've only spent a brief amount of time on this subject, it should give you a lot more confidence to work further with your Splunk queries.

In the next section, we will look at what Splunk apps are and how they can help to separate your data, searches, reports, and dashboards into different areas.

SPLUNK APP AND SAVED SEARCHES

Splunk apps are a way for you to separate your data, searches, reports, and dashboards into separate areas where you can then configure who can access what. Splunk provides a large ecosystem to help third-party developers and companies provide these apps to the general public.

We mentioned earlier in this chapter that Splunk also provides "SplunkBase" for approved apps that have been certified for users by Splunk, such as apps for Cisco Network Devices. It doesn't need to be an approved app for it to be available for use on your system. Splunk allows you to create apps of your own, and if you need to, you can distribute them in a packaged file across to users who wish to use them. The whole point of Splunk apps, dashboards, and saved searches is to reduce the amount of work that is duplicated, as well as providing information to non-technical users when needed.

The following exercise will provide you with some hands-on experience in terms of working with Splunk apps.

EXERCISE 14.04: GETTING FAMILIAR WITH SPLUNK APPS AND SAVED SEARCHES

In this exercise, you will install new apps from SplunkBase and modify them to suit your needs. This exercise will also show you how to save your searches for future use:

1. Make sure your Splunk container is running and that the **log-generator** container is sending data to Splunk.

2. When you are logged back in to Splunk, click the cog icon next to the word **Apps** in the **Apps** menu. When you are taken to the **Apps** page, you should see something similar to the following. The page contains a list of all Splunk apps currently installed on your system. You'll notice that some are enabled, while some are disabled.

You also have the option to browse more apps from the Splunk app base, install an app from a file, or create your own Splunk app:

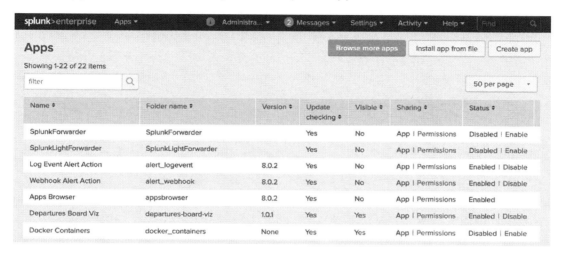

Figure 14.33: Working with the Apps page in Splunk

3. Click the **Browse more apps** button at the top of the screen.

4. You'll be taken to a page that provides a list of all the Splunk apps available to your system. Some of them are paid, but the majority of them are free to use and install. You can also search by name, category, and support level. Enter **Departures Board Viz** in the search box at the top of the screen and click *Enter*:

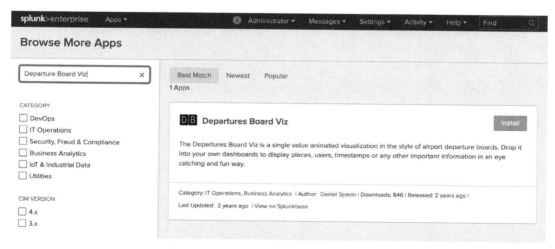

Figure 14.34: Departures Board Viz app

> **NOTE**
>
> This section uses the **Departures Board Viz** app as an example because it is easy to use and install, with minimal changes needed. Each app should give you some details on the type of information it uses and how to start working with the data needed. You'll notice there are hundreds of apps to choose from, so you're sure to find something that suits your needs.

5. You need to have registered with Splunk to be able to install and use the apps available. Click the **Install** button for the **Departures Board Viz** app and follow the prompts to sign in, if needed:

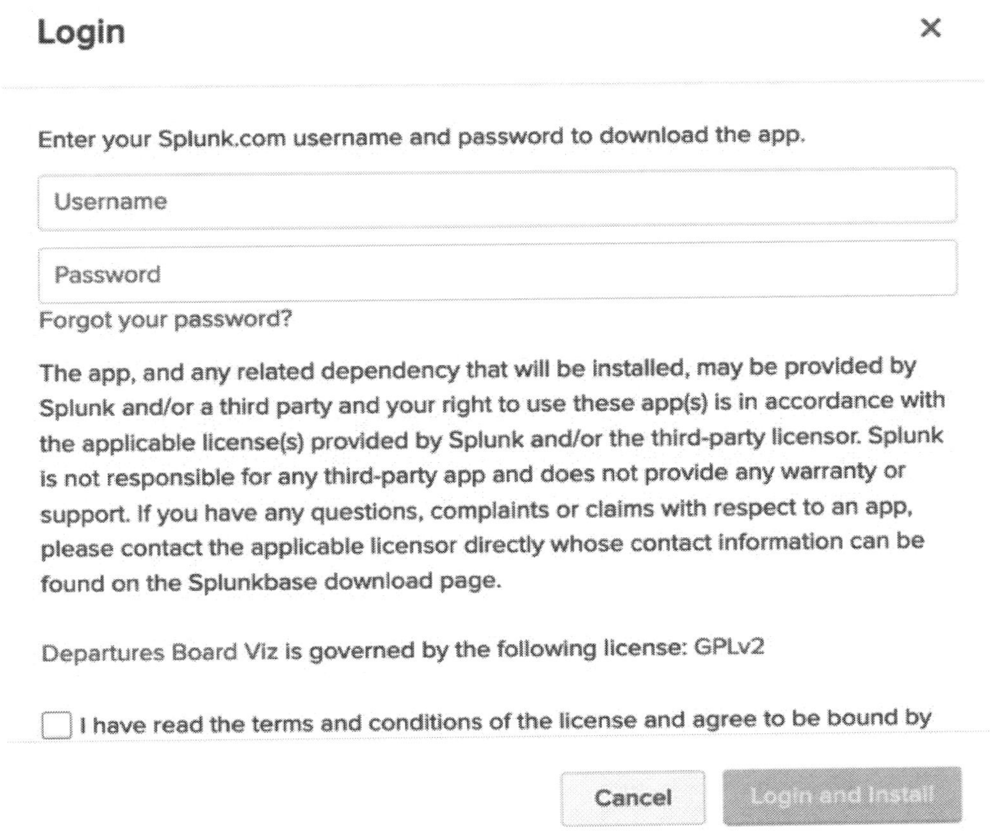

Login   ✕

Enter your Splunk.com username and password to download the app.

| Username |
| Password |

Forgot your password?

The app, and any related dependency that will be installed, may be provided by Splunk and/or a third party and your right to use these app(s) is in accordance with the applicable license(s) provided by Splunk and/or the third-party licensor. Splunk is not responsible for any third-party app and does not provide any warranty or support. If you have any questions, complaints or claims with respect to an app, please contact the applicable licensor directly whose contact information can be found on the Splunkbase download page.

Departures Board Viz is governed by the following license: GPLv2

☐ I have read the terms and conditions of the license and agree to be bound by

Cancel   Login and Install

Figure 14.35: Installing the Departures Board Viz app

6. If the installation was successful, you should be given the prompt to either open the app you have just installed or return to the Splunk home page. Return to the home page to see the changes you have made.

7. From the home page, you should now see that the new app, called **Departures Board Viz**, has been installed. This is simply a visualization extension. Click the **Departures Board Vis** button on the home screen to open the app:

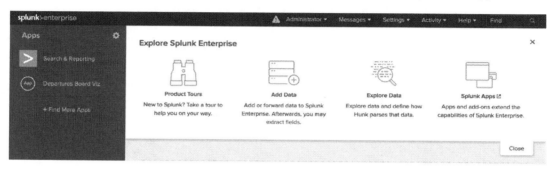

Figure 14.36: Opening the Departures Board Viz app

8. When you open the app, it will take you to the **About** page. This is simply a dashboard that provides details of the app and how to use it with your data. Click the **Edit** button at the top of the screen to continue:

Figure 14.37: The About page of the Departures Board Viz app

9. Click **Edit Search** to add a new search that displays data specific to you.

10. Remove the default search string and place the **sourcetype=httpevent | stats count by level | sort - count | head 1 | fields level** search query in the textbox. The query will look through your **log-generator** data and provide a count of each level. Then, sort the results from the highest to lowest order (**sort - count**) and provide the level with the top value (**head 1 | fields level**):

Figure 14.38: Adding a new search query

11. Click the **Save** button to save the changes you've made to the visualization. Instead of a city name that is provided by default by **Departures Board Viz**, you should see the top error level provided in our data. As shown in the following screenshot, the top error being reported in our logs is **INFO**:

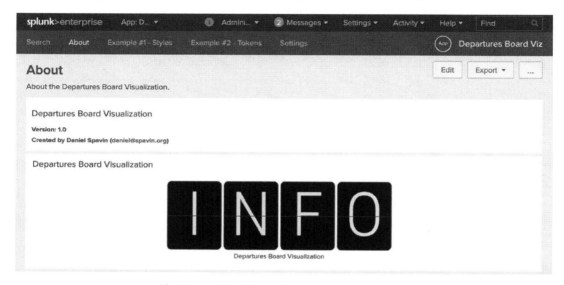

Figure 14.39: Editing Splunk apps in Splunk

12. Now that you've added a Splunk app, you will create a very basic app of your own to modify your environment further. Move back to the home screen and, once again, click on the cog next to the **Apps** menu.

13. On the **Apps** page, click on the **Create app** button on the right-hand side of the screen:

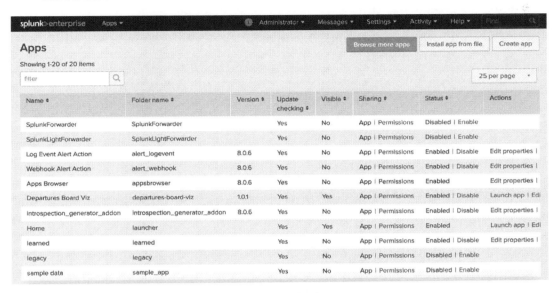

Figure 14.40: Splunk apps

14. When you create an app of your own, you'll be presented with a form similar to the one shown here. You are going to create a test app for your Splunk install. Fill in the form using the information provided in the following screenshot, but make sure you add values for **Name** and **Folder Name**. The version is also a required field and needs to be in the form of **major_version.minor_version. patch_version**. Add the version number as **1.0.0**. The following example has also selected the **sample_app** option instead of the **barebones** template. This means the app will be filled with sample dashboards and reports that you can modify for the data you are working on. You won't be working with any of these sample dashboards and reports, so you can choose either. The **Upload asset** option is only needed if you have a pre-created Splunk app available, but in our instance, it can be left blank:

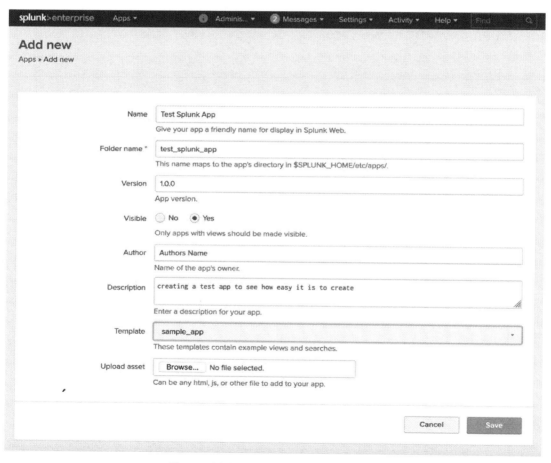

Figure 14.41: Creating a Splunk app

15. Click the **Save** button to create your new app and then move back to the home screen of your installation. You'll notice that you now have an app listed on your home screen called **Test Splunk App**. Click on your new app to open it up:

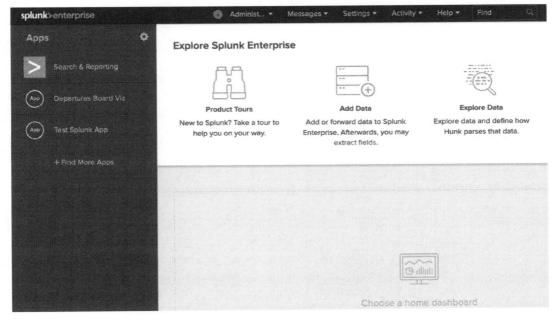

Figure 14.42: Test Splunk app on the home screen

16. The app won't look any different to the **Search & Reporting** app, but if you click the **Reports or Dashboards** tab at the top of the screen, you will notice that there will be some sample reports and dashboards in place. For the time being, though, create a report you can refer to at a later date. Start by making sure you are in the **Search** tab of your app.

17. Enter **sourcetype=httpevent earliest=-7d | timechart span=1d count by level** into the query bar. You'll notice we have set the value to **earliest=-7d**, which automatically selects the previous 7 days of data so that you do not need to specify the time range for your search. It will then create a time chart of your data, totaling the values by each day.

18. Click the **Save As** button at the top of the screen and select **Report** from the drop-down menu. You'll be presented with the following form so that you can save your report. Simply name the report and provide a description before clicking on the **Save** button at the bottom of the screen:

Figure 14.43: Creating saved reports in your Splunk app

19. When you click **Save**, you'll be given the option to view your new report. It should look similar to the following:

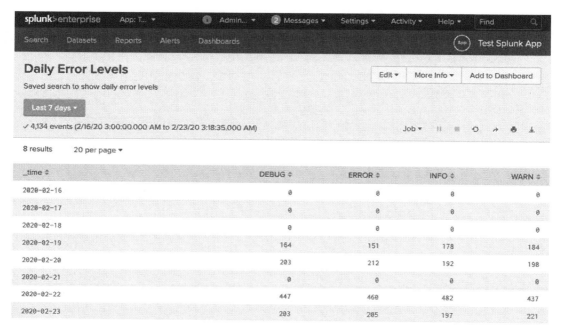

Figure 14.44: Daily Error Levels report in Splunk

If you ever need to refer to this report again, you can click on the **Reports** tab of your new Splunk app, and it will be listed with the sample reports that were provided when the app was first created. The following screenshot shows the **Reports** tab of your app with the sample reports listed, but you also have the **Daily Errors** report you just created, which has been added to the top of the list:

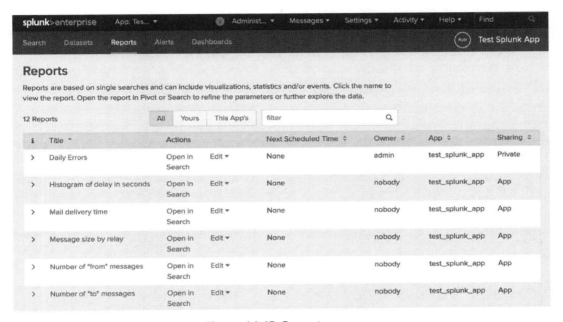

Figure 14.45: Reports page

This brings us to the end of this exercise, in which we have installed third-party Splunk apps and created our own. This also brings us to the end of this chapter. However, before you move on to the next chapter, make sure you work through the activities provided next to reaffirm everything you've learned in this chapter.

ACTIVITY 14.01: CREATING A DOCKER-COMPOSE.YML FILE FOR YOUR SPLUNK INSTALLATION

So far, you have been running Splunk on a Docker container by simply using the **docker run** command. It's time to use the knowledge you have gained in the previous sections of this book to create a **docker-compose.yml** file so that you can install and run our Splunk environment on your system when needed. As part of this activity, add one of the containers being run as a part of the Panoramic Trekking App. Also, ensure that you can view logs from the selected service.

Perform the following steps to complete this activity:

1. Decide how you would like your Splunk installation to look once it is running as part of your Docker Compose file. This will include mounting directories and ports that need to be exposed as part of the installation.

2. Create your **docker-compose.yml** file and run **Docker Compose**. Make sure it starts up your Splunk installation as per your requirements in the previous step.

3. Once the Splunk installation is up and running, start up a service from the Panoramic Trekking App and make sure you can send log data to your Splunk setup.

Expected Output:

This should result in a screen similar to the following:

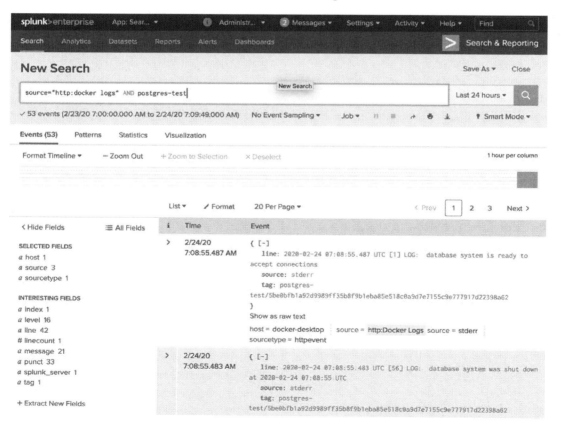

Figure 14.46: Expected output for Activity 14.01

> **NOTE**
>
> The solution for this activity can be found on page 733.

The next activity will allow you to create a Splunk app and dashboard for the new data being logged in Splunk.

ACTIVITY 14.02: CREATING A SPLUNK APP TO MONITOR THE PANORAMIC TREKKING APP

In the previous activity, you made sure one of the services that had been set up as part of the Panoramic Trekking App was logging data with your Splunk environment. In this activity, you are required to create a new Splunk app within your installation to specifically monitor your services and create a dashboard relevant to the service logging data into Splunk.

The steps you'll need to follow in order to complete this activity are as follows:

1. Ensure your Splunk installation is running and that at least one service from the Panoramic Trekking App is logging data into Splunk.

2. Create a new Splunk app and name it something relevant to monitoring the Panoramic Trekking App. Make sure you can view it from the Splunk home screen.

3. Create a dashboard relevant to the services you're monitoring and add some visualizations to help you monitor your service.

Expected Output:

A dashboard similar to the following should be displayed upon successful completion of this activity:

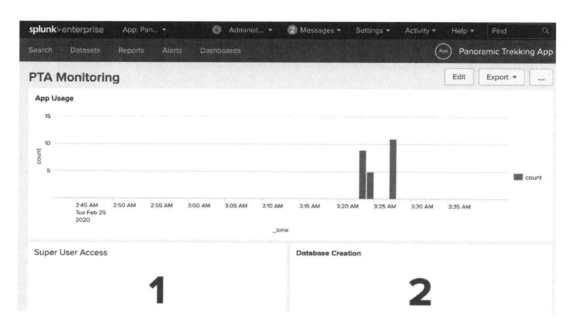

Figure 14.47: Expected solution for Activity 14.02

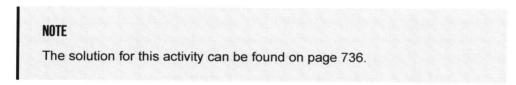

NOTE

The solution for this activity can be found on page 736.

SUMMARY

This chapter taught you how applications such as Splunk can help you monitor and troubleshoot your applications by aggregating your container logs into one central area. We started this chapter with a discussion on the importance of a log management strategy when working with Docker, and then introduced Splunk by discussing its architecture, as well as some of the finer points on how to run the application.

We worked directly with Splunk, running the Docker container image, and started to forward logs from our running system. We then used the Splunk log driver to send our container logs directly to our Splunk container, mounting important directories to make sure our data was saved and available even after we stopped our container from running. Finally, we took a closer look at the Splunk query language, with which we created dashboards and saved searches and considered the advantages of the Splunk app ecosystem.

The next chapter will introduce Docker plugins and teach you how to utilize them to help extend your containers and the services running on them.

15

EXTENDING DOCKER WITH PLUGINS

OVERVIEW

In this chapter, you will learn how to extend the capabilities of Docker Engine by creating and installing plugins. You will see how to implement your advanced and custom requirements while using Docker containers. By the end of the chapter, you will be able to identify the basics of extending Docker. You will also be able to install and configure different Docker plugins. Moving ahead, you will work with the Docker plugin API to develop custom plugins and use various Docker plugins to extend the capabilities of volumes, networking, and authorization in Docker.

INTRODUCTION

In previous chapters, you ran multiple Docker containers with **Docker Compose** and **Docker Swarm**. In addition, you monitored the metrics from containers and collected the logs. Docker allows you to manage the complete life cycle of containers, including networking, volumes, and process isolations. If you want to customize the operations of Docker to work with your custom storage, network provider, or authentication server, you need to extend the capabilities of Docker.

For instance, if you have a custom cloud-based storage system and you want to mount it to your Docker containers, you can implement a storage plugin. Similarly, you can authenticate your users from your enterprise user management system using authorization plugins and allow them to work with Docker containers.

In this chapter, you will learn how to extend Docker with its plugins. You will start with plugin management and APIs, followed by the most advanced and requested plugin types: authorization, network, and volume. The next section will cover the installation and operation of plugins in Docker.

PLUGIN MANAGEMENT

Plugins in Docker are external processes that run independently of Docker Engine. This means that Docker Engine does not rely on plugins and vice versa. We just need to inform Docker Engine about the plugin location and its capabilities. Docker provides the following CLI commands to manage the life cycle of plugins:

- **docker plugin create**: This command creates a new plugin and its configuration.

- **docker plugin enable/disable**: These commands enable or disable a plugin.

- **docker plugin install**: This command installs a plugin.

- **docker plugin upgrade**: This command upgrades an existing plugin to a newer version.

- **docker plugin rm**: This command removes plugins by removing their information from Docker Engine.

- **docker plugin ls**: This command lists the installed plugins.

- **docker plugin inspect**: This command displays detailed information on plugins.

In the following section, you will learn how plugins are implemented in Docker with the plugin API.

PLUGIN API

Docker maintains a plugin API to help the community write their plugins. This means that anyone can develop new plugins as long as they implement it in accordance with the plugin API. This approach makes Docker an open and extensible platform. The plugin API is a **Remote Procedure Call** (**RPC**)-style JSON API that works over HTTP. Docker Engine sends HTTP POST requests to the plugin and uses the responses to continue its operations.

Docker also provides an official open-source SDK for creating new plugins and **helper packages** to extend Docker Engine. The helper packages are boilerplate templates if you want to easily create and run new plugins. Currently, there are only helper packages in Go since Go is the main implementation language of Docker Engine itself. It is located at https://github.com/docker/go-plugins-helpers and provides helpers for every kind of plugin supported by Docker:

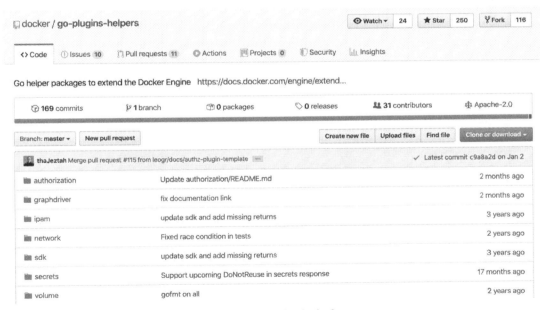

Figure 15.1: Go plugin helpers

You can check each folder listed in the repository to create and run different types of plugins easily. In this chapter, you will explore the supported plugin types—namely, authorization, network, and volume plugins—through several practical exercises. The plugins enable Docker Engine to implement custom business requirements by providing additional functionalities along with the default Docker functionalities.

AUTHORIZATION PLUGINS

Docker authorization is based on two modes: **all kinds of actions are enabled** or **all kinds of actions are disabled**. In other words, if a user can access the Docker daemon, they can run any command and consume the API or Docker client commands. If you need more granular access control methods, you need to use authorization plugins in Docker. Authorization plugins enhance authentication and permission for Docker Engine operations. They enable more granular access to control who can take specific actions on Docker Engine.

Authorization plugins approve or deny the requests forwarded by Docker daemons using the request context. Therefore, the plugins should implement the following two methods:

- **AuthZReq**: This method is called before the Docker daemon processes the request.

- **AuthZRes**: This method is called before the response is returned from the Docker daemon to the client.

In the following exercise, you will learn how to configure and install an authorization plugin. You will install the **policy-based authorization** plugin created and maintained by Open Policy Agent (https://www.openpolicyagent.org/). **Policy-based access** is based on the idea of granting access to the users based on some rules, namely **policies**. The source code of the plugin is available on GitHub at https://github.com/open-policy-agent/opa-docker-authz, and it works with policy files similar to the following:

```
package docker.authz

allow {
    input.Method = "GET"
}
```

The policy files are stored in the host system where the Docker daemon can read. For instance, the policy file shown here only allows **GET** as the method of the request. It actually makes the Docker daemon read-only by disallowing any other methods, such as **POST**, **DELETE**, or **UPDATE**. In the following exercise, you will use a policy file and configure the Docker daemon to communicate with the authorization plugin and limit some requests.

> **NOTE**
>
> Plugins and the commands in the following exercises work best in Linux environments, considering the installation and the configuration of the Docker daemon. If you are using a custom or toolbox Docker installation, you may want to complete the exercises in this chapter using a virtual machine.

> **NOTE**
>
> Please use **touch** command to create files and **vim** command to work on the file using vim editor.

EXERCISE 15.01: READ-ONLY DOCKER DAEMON WITH AUTHORIZATION PLUGINS

In this exercise, you are required to create a read-only Docker daemon. This is a common approach if you want to limit the access and changes to your production environment. To achieve this, you will install and configure the plugin with a policy file.

To complete the exercise, perform the following steps:

1. Create a file located at **/etc/docker/policies/authz.rego** by running the following commands:

```
mkdir -p /etc/docker/policies
touch /etc/docker/policies/authz.rego
ls /etc/docker/policies
```

These commands create a file located at **/etc/docker/policies**:

```
authz.rego
```

2. Open the file with an editor and insert the following data:

```
package docker.authz

allow {
    input.Method = "GET"
}
```

You can write the content into the file with the following commands:

```
cat > /etc/docker/policies/authz.rego << EOF
package docker.authz

allow {
    input.Method = "GET"
}
EOF
cat /etc/docker/policies/authz.rego
```

> **NOTE**
>
> The `cat` command is used to make the file content editable in the terminal. Unless you are running Ubuntu in headless mode, you may skip using CLI-based commands to edit the content of files.

The policy file only allows **GET** methods in the Docker daemon; in other words, it makes the Docker daemon read-only.

3. Install the plugin by running the following command in your terminal and enter *y* when it prompts for permissions:

```
docker plugin install --alias opa-docker-authz:readonly \
openpolicyagent/opa-docker-authz-v2:0.5 \
opa-args="-policy-file /opa/policies/authz.rego"
```

This command installs the plugin located at **openpolicyagent/opa-docker-authz-v2:0.5** with the alias **opa-docker-authz:readonly**. In addition, the policy file from *Step 1* is passed as **opa-args**:

```
/docker-ws $ docker plugin install --alias opa-docker-authz:readonly \
> openpolicyagent/opa-docker-authz-v2:0.5 \
> opa-args="-policy-file /opa/policies/authz.rego"
Plugin "openpolicyagent/opa-docker-authz-v2:0.5" is requesting the following privileges:
 - mount: [/etc/docker]
Do you grant the above permissions? [y/N] y
0.5: Pulling from openpolicyagent/opa-docker-authz-v2
ded550c20980: Download complete
Digest: sha256:39b8a559a8e7cbf72a9efef6202f1cc35d4a382794b978466c58f00e498a33d9
Status: Downloaded newer image for openpolicyagent/opa-docker-authz-v2:0.5
Installed plugin openpolicyagent/opa-docker-authz-v2:0.5
/docker-ws $
```

Figure 15.2: Plugin installation

4. Check for the installed plugins using the following command:

```
docker plugin ls
```

This command lists the plugins:

```
/docker-ws $ docker plugin ls
ID                  NAME                        DESCRIPTION                                       ENABLED
2d3cf7d02b97        opa-docker-authz:readonly   A policy-enabled authorization plugin for Do...   true
/docker-ws $
```

Figure 15.3: Plugin listing

5. Edit the Docker daemon configuration at **/etc/docker/daemon.json** with the following edition:

```
{
    "authorization-plugins": ["opa-docker-authz:readonly"]
}
```

You can check the contents of the file with the **cat /etc/docker/daemon. json** command.

6. Reload the Docker daemon with the following command:

```
sudo kill -HUP $(pidof dockerd)
```

This command kills the process of **dockerd** by getting its process ID with the **pidof** command. In addition, it sends the **HUP** signal, which is the signal sent to Linux processes to update their configuration. In short, you are reloading the Docker daemon with the new authorization plugin configuration. Run the following listing command to check whether the listing action is allowed:

```
docker ps
```

This command lists the running containers, and it shows that the listing action is allowed:

```
CONTAINER ID   IMAGE   COMMAND   CREATED   STATUS   PORTS   NAMES
```

7. Run the following command to check whether creating new containers is permitted:

```
docker run ubuntu
```

This command creates and runs a container; however, since the action is not read-only, it is not allowed:

```
Error response from daemon: authorization denied by plugin
opa-docker-authz:readonly: request rejected by administrative policy.
See 'docker run --help'.
```

8. Check for the logs of the Docker daemon for any plugin-related lines:

```
journalctl -u docker | grep plugin | grep "OPA policy decision"
```

> **NOTE**
>
> `journalctl` is a command-line tool for displaying logs from `systemd` processes. `systemd` processes store the logs in binary format. `journalctl` is required to read the log texts.

The following output shows that the tested actions in *Step 7* and *Step 8* passed through the authorization plugin with the **"Returning OPA policy decision: true"** and **"Returning OPA policy decision: false"** lines. It shows that our plugin has allowed the first action and declined the second one:

```
/docker-ws $ journalctl -u docker | grep plugin | grep "OPA policy decision"
Feb 29 21:19:14 test2 dockerd[16515]: time="2020-02-29T21:19:14Z" level=error msg="2020/02/29
21:19:14 Returning OPA policy decision: true" plugin=2d3cf7d02b97fe99e9f142f707e020946b21da59d
f39dee619ba26ece70dcf8f
Feb 29 21:19:14 test2 dockerd[16515]: time="2020-02-29T21:19:14Z" level=error msg="2020/02/29
21:19:14 Returning OPA policy decision: false" plugin=2d3cf7d02b97fe99e9f142f707e020946b21da59
df39dee619ba26ece70dcf8f
```

Figure 15.4: Plugin logs

9. Stop using the plugin by removing the **authorization-plugins** part from **/etc/docker/daemon.json** and reload the Docker daemon similar to what was done in *Step 6*:

```
cat > /etc/docker/daemon.json << EOF
{}
EOF
cat /etc/docker/daemon.json
sudo kill -HUP $(pidof dockerd)
```

10. Disable and remove the plugin with the following commands:

```
docker plugin disable opa-docker-authz:readonly
docker plugin rm opa-docker-authz:readonly
```

These commands disable and remove the plugin from Docker by returning the names of the plugins.

In this exercise, you have configured and installed an authorization plugin into Docker. In the next section, you will learn more about networking plugins in Docker.

NETWORK PLUGINS

Docker supports a wide range of networking technologies with the help of Docker networking plugins. Although it supports container-to-container and host-to-container networking with full functionality, the plugins enable us to extend networking to further technologies. The networking plugins implement a remote driver as a part of different network topologies, such as virtual extensible LAN (**vxlan**) and MAC virtual LAN (**macvlan**). You can install and enable networking plugins with the Docker plugin commands. Also, you need to specify the name of the network driver with **--driver** flags. For instance, if you have installed an enabled **my-new-network-technology** driver and want your new network to be a part of it, you need to set a **driver** flag:

```
docker network create --driver my-new-network-technology mynet
```

This command creates a network named **mynet**, and the **my-new-network-technology** plugin manages all networking operations.

The community and third-party companies develop networking plugins. However, there are currently only two certified networking plugins in Docker Hub – Weave Net and Infoblox IPAM Plugin:

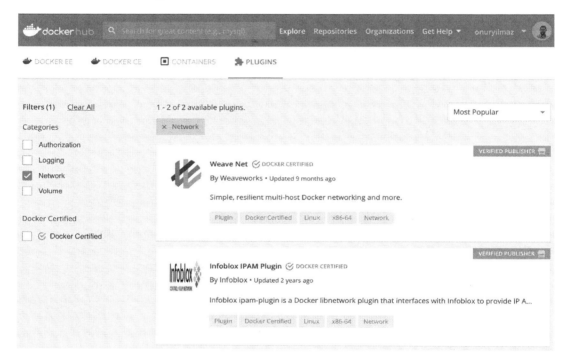

Figure 15.5: Networking plugins in Docker Hub

Infoblox IPAM Plugin focuses on providing IP address management services, such as writing DNS records and configuring DHCP settings. **Weave Net** focuses on creating resilient networking for Docker containers with encryption, service discovery, and multicast networking.

The official SDK provided in **go-plugin-helpers** has Go handlers to create network extensions for Docker. The **Driver** interface is defined as follows:

```go
// Driver represent the interface a driver must fulfill.
type Driver interface {
    GetCapabilities() (*CapabilitiesResponse, error)
    CreateNetwork(*CreateNetworkRequest) error
    AllocateNetwork(*AllocateNetworkRequest)
        (*AllocateNetworkResponse, error)
    DeleteNetwork(*DeleteNetworkRequest) error
    FreeNetwork(*FreeNetworkRequest) error
    CreateEndpoint(*CreateEndpointRequest)
        (*CreateEndpointResponse, error)
    DeleteEndpoint(*DeleteEndpointRequest) error
    EndpointInfo(*InfoRequest) (*InfoResponse, error)
    Join(*JoinRequest) (*JoinResponse, error)
    Leave(*LeaveRequest) error
    DiscoverNew(*DiscoveryNotification) error
    DiscoverDelete(*DiscoveryNotification) error
    ProgramExternalConnectivity(*ProgramExternalConnectivityRequest)
        error
    RevokeExternalConnectivity(*RevokeExternalConnectivityRequest)
        error
}
```

> **NOTE**
>
> The complete code is available at https://github.com/docker/go-plugins-helpers/blob/master/network/api.go.

When you check the interface functions, the networking plugins should provide operations for networking, endpoints, and external connectivity. For instance, a network plugin should implement a network life cycle with the **CreateNetwork**, **AllocateneNetwork**, **DeleteNetwork**, and **FreeNetwork** functions.

Similarly, the endpoint life cycle should be implemented by the **CreateEndpoint**, **DeleteEndpoint**, and **EndpointInfo** functions. In addition, there are some extension integration and management functions to implement, including **GetCapabilities**, **Leave**, and **Join**. The services also need their specific request and response types to work in a managed plugin environment.

In the following exercise, you will create a new network using the Weave Net plugin and let containers connect using the new network.

EXERCISE 15.02: DOCKER NETWORK PLUGINS IN ACTION

Docker network plugins take over the network operations for specific network instances and implement custom technologies. In this exercise, you will install and configure a network plugin to create a Docker network. You will then create a three-replica application of a Docker image and use the plugin to connect these three instances. You can use the Weave Net plugin to achieve this goal.

To complete the exercise, perform the following steps:

1. Initialize a Docker swarm (if you have not enabled one before) by running the following command in the terminal:

```
docker swarm init
```

This command creates a Docker swarm to deploy multiple instances of the application:

```
 /docker-ws $ docker swarm init
Swarm initialized: current node (uxrc2qeyt64e98nyengxfcz9s) is now a manage
r.

To add a worker to this swarm, run the following command:

    docker swarm join --token SWMTKN-1-0e4kmftwq1rninem93eckueaw4kq2wry1zp4
t3jrtkd7iv3jfe-034am4mf8ehm7cpgtn7pwc7tv 10.180.89.6:2377

To add a manager to this swarm, run 'docker swarm join-token manager' and f
ollow the instructions.

 /docker-ws $ ▌
```

Figure 15.6: Swarm initialization

2. Install the **Weave Net** plugin by running the following command:

```
docker plugin install --grant-all-permissions \
store/weaveworks/net-plugin:2.5.2
```

This command installs the plugin from the store and grants all permissions:

```
/docker-ws $ docker plugin install --grant-all-permissions \
> store/weaveworks/net-plugin:2.5.2
2.5.2: Pulling from store/weaveworks/net-plugin
808b21b1a419: Download complete
Digest: sha256:b968d45872d72ef5f1e674baa61d384db17ef7d6be85338fa24b1d5d4651
eb04
Status: Downloaded newer image for store/weaveworks/net-plugin:2.5.2
Installed plugin store/weaveworks/net-plugin:2.5.2
 /docker-ws $
```

Figure 15.7: Plugin installation

3. Create a new network using the driver with the following command:

```
docker network create  \
--driver=store/weaveworks/net-plugin:2.5.2  \
weave-custom-net
```

This command creates a new network named **weave-custom-net** using the driver provided with the plugin:

```
 /docker-ws $  docker network create  \
> --driver=store/weaveworks/net-plugin:2.5.2  \
> weave-custom-net
twcdyoe7lmbjeinnwai9ell1y
 /docker-ws $
```

Figure 15.8: Creating the network

Following the successful creation of the network, a randomly generated network name will be printed as shown in the preceding code.

4. Create a three-replica application with the following command:

```
docker service create --network=weave-custom-net \
--replicas=3 \
--name=workshop \
-p 80:80 \
onuryilmaz/hello-plain-text
```

This command creates three replicas of the **onuryilmaz/hello-plain-text** image and uses **the weave-custom-net** network to connect the instances. In addition, it uses the name **workshop** and publishes to the port **80**:

```
/docker-ws $ docker service create --network=weave-custom-net \
> --replicas=3 \
> --name=workshop \
> -p 80:80 \
> onuryilmaz/hello-plain-text
9phoeb164w6cwoq2zbee6pmxm
overall progress: 3 out of 3 tasks
1/3: running
2/3: running
3/3: running
verify: Service converged
/docker-ws $
```

Figure 15.9: Application creation

5. Get the names of the containers by running the following commands:

```
FIRST_CONTAINER=$(docker ps --format "{{.Names}}" |grep "workshop.1")
echo $FIRST_CONTAINER
SECOND_CONTAINER=$(docker ps --format "{{.Names}}" |grep
"workshop.2")
echo $SECOND_CONTAINER
THIRD_CONTAINER=$(docker ps --format "{{.Names}}" |grep "workshop.3")
echo $THIRD_CONTAINER
```

These commands list the running Docker container names and filter by **workshop** instances. You will need the name of the containers to test the connection between them:

```
/docker-ws $ FIRST_CONTAINER=$(docker ps --format "{{.Names}}" |grep "workshop.1")
/docker-ws $ echo $FIRST_CONTAINER
workshop.1.cayn722qh3jmeovzhjytu513e
/docker-ws $ SECOND_CONTAINER=$(docker ps --format "{{.Names}}" |grep "workshop.2")
/docker-ws $ echo $SECOND_CONTAINER
workshop.2.ycqtjlnrgnts3dszhfjeysxev
/docker-ws $ THIRD_CONTAINER=$(docker ps --format "{{.Names}}" |grep "workshop.3")
/docker-ws $ echo $THIRD_CONTAINER
workshop.3.11j38e23o3309g956thnaosxo
/docker-ws $
```

Figure 15.10: Container names

6. Run the following command to connect the first container to the second one:

```
docker exec -it $FIRST_CONTAINER sh -c "curl $SECOND_CONTAINER"
```

This command connects the first and second containers using the **curl** command:

```
/docker-ws $ docker exec -it $FIRST_CONTAINER sh -c "curl $SECOND_CONTAINER"
Server address: 10.0.0.4:80
Server name: 759604ff3e8d
Date: 01/Mar/2020:01:29:03 +0000
URI: /
Request ID: 625c00f2d394a25b8130e87de5f4216d
 /docker-ws $
```

Figure 15.11: Connection between containers

The preceding command is running inside the first container and the **curl** command reaches the second container. The output shows the server and the request information.

7. Similar to *Step 6*, connect the first container to the third one:

```
docker exec -it $FIRST_CONTAINER sh -c "curl $THIRD_CONTAINER"
```

As expected, different server names and addresses are retrieved in *Step 6* and *Step 7*:

```
/docker-ws $ docker exec -it $FIRST_CONTAINER sh -c "curl $THIRD_CONTAINER"
Server address: 10.0.0.5:80
Server name: 74eb20c4b92a
Date: 01/Mar/2020:01:29:15 +0000
URI: /
Request ID: 2f62d441355416b365d7fa5fed8f69c7
 /docker-ws $
```

Figure 15.12: Connection between containers

This shows that the containers created using the custom Weave Net network are working as expected.

8. You can delete the application and network with the following commands:

```
docker service rm workshop
docker network rm weave-custom-net
```

In this exercise, you have installed and used a networking plugin in Docker. Besides that, you have created a containerized application that connects using a custom network driver. In the next section, you will learn more about the volume plugins in Docker.

VOLUME PLUGINS

Docker volumes are mounted to containers to allow stateful applications to run in containers. By default, volumes are created in the filesystem of the host machine and managed by Docker. In addition, while creating a volume, it is possible to specify a volume driver. For instance, you can mount volumes over network or storage providers such as **Google**, **Azure**, or **AWS**. You can also run your database locally in Docker containers while the data volumes are persistent in AWS storage services. This way, your data volumes can be reused in the future with other database instances running in any other location. To use different volume drivers, you need to enhance Docker with volume plugins.

Docker volume plugins control the life cycle of volumes, including the `Create`, `Mount`, `Unmount`, `Path`, and `Remove` functions. In the plugin SDK, the volume driver interface is defined as follows:

```
// Driver represent the interface a driver must fulfill.
type Driver interface {
    Create(*CreateRequest) error
    List() (*ListResponse, error)
    Get(*GetRequest) (*GetResponse, error)
    Remove(*RemoveRequest) error
    Path(*PathRequest) (*PathResponse, error)
    Mount(*MountRequest) (*MountResponse, error)
    Unmount(*UnmountRequest) error
    Capabilities() *CapabilitiesResponse
}
```

> **NOTE**
>
> The complete driver code is available at https://github.com/docker/go-plugins-helpers/blob/master/volume/api.go.

The functions of the driver interface show that volume drivers focus on basic operations, such as **Create**, **List**, **Get**, and **Remove** operations, of the volumes. The plugins are responsible for mounting and unmounting volumes to and from containers. If you want to create a new volume driver, you need to implement this interface with the corresponding request and response types.

There are numerous volume plugins already available from Docker Hub and the open-source community. For instance, there are currently 18 volume plugins categorized and verified on Docker Hub:

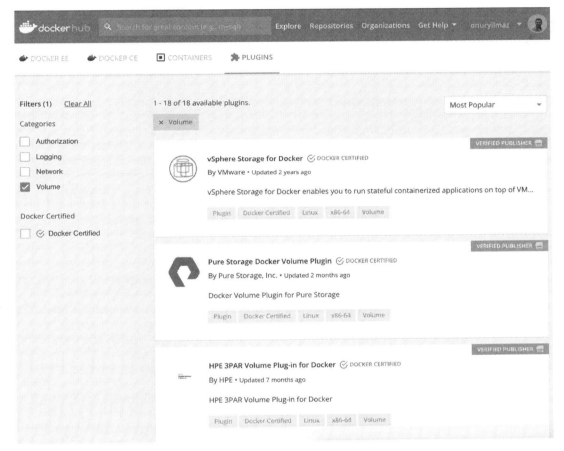

Figure 15.13: Volume plugins in Docker Hub

Most of the plugins focus on providing storage from different sources, such as cloud providers and storage technologies. Based on your business requirements and technology stack, you may consider volume plugins in your Docker setup.

In the following exercise, you will create volumes in remote systems using SSH connections and volumes in containers. For the volumes created and used over SSH connections, you will use the **open-source docker-volume-sshfs** plugin available at https://github.com/vieux/docker-volume-sshfs.

EXERCISE 15.03: VOLUME PLUGINS IN ACTION

Docker volume plugins manage the life cycle of volumes by providing storage from different providers and technologies. In this exercise, you will install and configure a volume plugin to create volumes over an SSH connection. Following the successful creation of the volumes, you will use them in containers and ensure that the files are persisted. You can use the **docker-volume-sshfs** plugin to achieve this goal.

To complete the exercise, perform the following steps:

1. Install the **docker-volume-sshfs** plugin by running the following command in your terminal:

```
docker plugin install --grant-all-permissions vieux/sshfs
```

This command installs the plugin by granting all the permissions:

```
/docker-ws $ docker plugin install --grant-all-permissions vieux/sshfs
latest: Pulling from vieux/sshfs
52d435ada6a4: Download complete
Digest: sha256:1d3c3e42c12138da5ef7873b97f7f32cf99fb6edde75fa4f0bcf9ed277855811
Status: Downloaded newer image for vieux/sshfs:latest
Installed plugin vieux/sshfs
 /docker-ws $
```

Figure 15.14: Plugin installation

2. Create a Docker container with an SSH connection to provide volumes to other containers with the following command:

```
docker run -d -p 2222:22 \
--name volume_provider \
rastasheep/ubuntu-sshd:14.04
```

This command creates and runs an **sshd** container named **volume_provider**. Port **2222** is published and will be used to connect to this container in the following steps.

You should get an output like the following:

```
87eecaca6a1ea41e682e300d077548a4f902fdda21acc218a51253a883f725d
```

3. Create a new volume, named **volume-over-ssh**, by running the following command:

```
docker volume create -d vieux/sshfs \
--name volume-over-ssh \
-o sshcmd=root@localhost:/tmp \
-o password=root \
-o port=2222
```

This command creates a new volume using the **vieux/sshfs** driver and the **ssh** connection specified with **sshcmd** and the **password** and **port** parameters:

```
volume-over-ssh
```

4. Create a new file and save it in the volume created in *Step 3* by running the following command:

```
docker run --rm -v volume-over-ssh:/data busybox \
sh -c "touch /data/test.txt && echo 'Hello from Docker Workshop' >> /
data/test.txt"
```

This command runs a container by mounting **volume-over-ssh**. It then creates a file and writes into it.

5. Check the contents of the file created in *Step 4* by running the following command:

```
docker run --rm -v volume-over-ssh:/data busybox \
cat /data/test.txt
```

This command runs a container by mounting the same volume and reads the file from it:

```
Hello from Docker Workshop
```

6. (Optional) Delete the volume by running the following command:

```
docker volume rm volume-over-ssh
```

In this exercise, you have installed and used a volume plugin in Docker. Furthermore, you have created a volume and used it from multiple containers for writing and reading.

In the next activity, you will install WordPress in Docker using networking and volume plugins.

ACTIVITY 15.01: INSTALLING WORDPRESS WITH NETWORK AND VOLUME PLUGINS

You are tasked with designing and deploying a blog and its database as microservices in Docker using networking and volume plugins. You will be using **WordPress** since it is the most popular **Content Management System** (**CMS**), being used by more than one-third of all websites on the internet. The storage team requires you to use volumes over **SSH** for the WordPress content. In addition, the network team wants you to use **Weave Net** for networking between the containers. With these tools, you will create networks and volumes using Docker plugins and use them for WordPress and its database:

1. Create a Docker network (namely, **wp-network**) using the **Weave Net** plugin.

2. Create a volume with the name **wp-content**, using the **vieux/sshfs** driver.

3. Create a container with the name **mysql** to run the **mysql:5.7** image. Ensure that the **MYSQL_ROOT_PASSWORD**, **MYSQL_DATABASE**, **MYSQL_USER**, and **MYSQL_PASSWORD** environment variables are set. In addition, the container should use **wp-network** from *Step 1*.

4. Create a container with the name **wordpress** and use the volume from *Step 2* mounted at **/var/www/html/wp-content**. For the configuration of WordPress, do not forget to set the **WORDPRESS_DB_HOST**, **WORDPRESS_DB_USER**, **WORDPRESS_DB_PASSWORD**, and **WORDPRESS_DB_NAME** environment variables in accordance with *Step 3*. In addition, you need to publish port **80** to port **8080**, reachable from the browser.

   You should have the **wordpress** and **mysql** containers running:

```
/docker-ws $ docker ps
CONTAINER ID    IMAGE                         COMMAND               CREATED          STATUS          PORTS                      NAMES
06b0baed3d13    wordpress                     "docker-entrypoint.s…" 11 seconds ago   Up 9 seconds    0.0.0.0:8080->80/tcp       wordpress
7aabc7d8dfad    mysql:5.7                     "docker-entrypoint.s…" 22 seconds ago   Up 20 seconds   3306/tcp, 33060/tcp        mysql
87eecaca6a1e    rastasheep/ubuntu-sshd:14.04  "/usr/sbin/sshd -D"   4 hours ago      Up 4 hours      0.0.0.0:2222->22/tcp       volume_provider
/docker-ws $
```

Figure 15.15: The WordPress and database containers

In addition, you should be able to reach the WordPress setup screen in the browser:

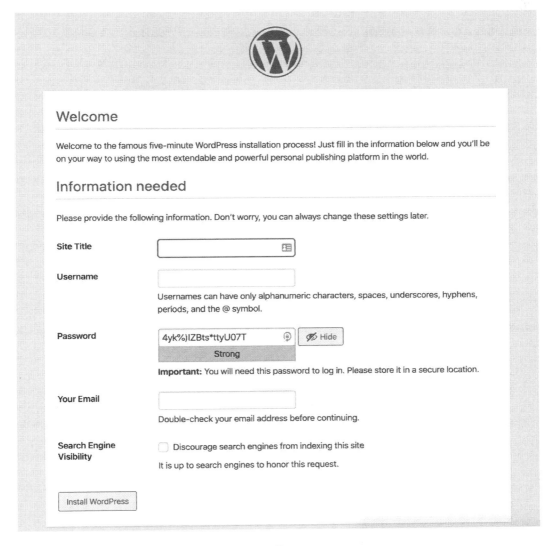

Figure 15.16: WordPress setup screen

NOTE

The solution for this activity can be found on page 742.

SUMMARY

This chapter focused on extending Docker with plugins. Docker operations can be enhanced by custom storage, network, or authorization methods by installing and using the Docker plugins. You first considered plugin management in Docker and the plugin API. With the plugin API, you are free to extend Docker by writing new plugins and make Docker work for you.

The chapter then covered authorization plugins and how the Docker daemon is configured to work with the plugins. If you are using Docker in production or enterprise environments, authorization plugins are essential tools to control who can access your containers. You then explored network plugins and how they extend communication between containers.

Although basic networking is already covered by Docker, we looked at how networking plugins are the gateway to new networking capabilities. This led to the final section, in which volume plugins were presented to show how custom storage options are enabled in Docker. If your business environment or technology stack requires you to extend Docker's capabilities, it is essential to learn the plugins and how to use them.

The end of this chapter also brings us to the end of this book. You began this journey all the way back in the first chapter learning the basics of Docker and running your very first containers on your system and look at how far you have come. Just in the course of this book, you have worked with Dockerfiles to create your images and learned how to publish these images using a public repository such as Docker Hub or to store your images on a repository running on your system. You have learned to use multi-stage Dockerfiles and implement your services using docker-compose. You have even mastered the finer details of networking and container storage, as well as the implementation of CI/CD pipelines as part of your projects and testing as part of your Docker image builds.

You practiced orchestrating your Docker environments using applications such as Docker Swarm and Kubernetes, before taking a closer look at Docker security and container best practices. Your journey then continued with real-world monitoring of your service metrics and container logs, before finishing up with Docker plugins to help extend your container service functionality. We've covered a lot of work to improve your skills and knowledge of Docker. Hopefully, it has taken your experience with the application to the next level. Please refer to the interactive version to learn how to troubleshoot and report issues when things do go wrong. You will also get to know about the current state of Docker Enterprise and the next big moves that will be made when it comes to the usage and development of Docker.

APPENDIX

CHAPTER 1: RUNNING MY FIRST DOCKER CONTAINER

ACTIVITY 1.01: PULLING AND RUNNING THE POSTGRESQL CONTAINER IMAGE FROM DOCKER HUB

Solution:

1. To start the Postgres Docker container, first determine what environment variables are required to set the default username and password credentials for the database. Reading through the official Docker Hub page, you can see that you have configuration options for the **POSTGRES_USER** and **POSTGRES_PASSWORD** environment variables. Pass the environment variables using the **-e** flag. The final command to start our Postgres Docker container will be as follows:

```
docker run -itd -e "POSTGRES_USER=panoramic" -e "POSTGRES_
PASSWORD=trekking" postgres:12
```

Running this command will start the container.

2. Execute the **docker ps** command to verify that it is running and healthy:

```
$ docker ps
```

The command should return output like the following:

```
CONTAINER ID   IMAGE         COMMAND                CREATED
   STATUS                PORTS              NAMES
29f115af8cdd   postgres:12   "docker-entrypoint.s…"  4 seconds ago
   Up 2 seconds         5432/tcp          blissful_kapitsa
```

It can be seen from the preceding output that the container with the ID **29f115af8cdd** is up and running.

In this activity, you have successfully started a PostgreSQL version 12 container that is part of the Panoramic Trekking App, which will be built over the course of this book.

ACTIVITY 1.02: ACCESSING THE PANORAMIC TREKKING APP DATABASE

Solution:

1. Log in to the database instance using **docker exec** to start the PSQL shell inside the container, passing in the **--username** flag and leaving the **--password** flag empty:

```
$ docker exec -it <containerID> psql --username panoramic --password
```

This should prompt you for the password and start a PSQL shell.

2. Use the **\l** command to list all the databases:

```
psql (12.2 (Debian 12.2-2.pgdg100+1))
Type "help" for help.


panoramic=# \l
```

A list of databases running in the container will be returned:

```
           Name          |  Owner   | Encoding |  Collate   |   Ctype    |   Access privileges
-------------------------+----------+----------+------------+------------+-----------------------
 panoramic_trekking      | postgres | UTF8     | en_US.utf8 | en_US.utf8 |
 postgres                | postgres | UTF8     | en_US.utf8 | en_US.utf8 |
 template0               | postgres | UTF8     | en_US.utf8 | en_US.utf8 | =c/postgres          +
                         |          |          |            |            | postgres=CTc/postgres
 template1               | postgres | UTF8     | en_US.utf8 | en_US.utf8 | =c/postgres          +
                         |          |          |            |            | postgres=CTc/postgres
(4 rows)
```

Figure 1.4: List of databases

3. Finally, use the **\q** shortcut to exit from the shell.

4. Use the **docker stop** and **docker rm** commands to stop and clean up the container instance.

In this activity, you accessed the database running in the container by logging in using the credentials that were set up in *Activity 1.01, Pulling and Running the PostgreSQL Container Image from Docker Hub*. You also listed the databases running in the container. The activity gave you hands-on experience of how to access the database running in any container using a PSQL shell.

CHAPTER 2: GETTING STARTED WITH DOCKERFILES

ACTIVITY 2.01: RUNNING A PHP APPLICATION ON A DOCKER CONTAINER

Solution:

1. Create a new directory named **activity-02-01** for this activity:

```
mkdir activity-02-01
```

2. Navigate to the newly created **activity-02-01** directory:

```
cd activity-02-01
```

3. Within the **activity-02-01** directory, create a file named **welcome.php**:

```
touch welcome.php
```

4. Now, open **welcome.php** using your favorite text editor:

```
vim welcome.php
```

5. Create the **welcome.php** file with the content provided at the beginning of the activity, and then save and exit from the **welcome.php** file:

```php
<?php

$hourOfDay = date('H');

if($hourOfDay < 12) {
    $message = «Good Morning»;
} elseif($hourOfDay > 11 && $hourOfDay < 18) {
    $message = «Good Afternoon»;
} elseif($hourOfDay > 17){
    $message = «Good Evening»;
}

echo $message;

?>
```

6. Within the **activity-02-01** directory, create a file named **Dockerfile**:

```
touch Dockerfile
```

7. Now, open the **Dockerfile** using your favorite text editor:

```
vim Dockerfile
```

8. Add the following content to the **Dockerfile**, and then save and exit from the **Dockerfile**:

```
# Start with Ubuntu base image
FROM ubuntu:18.04

# Set labels
LABEL maintainer=sathsara
LABEL version=1.0

# Set environment variables
ENV DEBIAN_FRONTEND=noninteractive

# Install Apache, PHP, and other packages
RUN apt-get update && \
    apt-get -y install apache2 \
    php \
    curl

# Copy all php files to the Docker image
COPY *.php /var/www/html

# Set working directory
WORKDIR /var/www/html

# Create health check
HEALTHCHECK --interval=5s --timeout=3s --retries=3 CMD curl -f
  http://localhost || exit 1

# Expose Apache
EXPOSE 80

# Start Apache
ENTRYPOINT ["apache2ctl", "-D", "FOREGROUND"]
```

We are starting this **Dockerfile** using the **ubuntu** base image followed by setting a couple of labels. Next, the **DEBIAN_FRONTEND** environment variable is set to **noninteractive** to make the package installations non-interactive. Then, the **apache2**, **php**, and **curl** packages are installed, and PHP files are copied to the **/var/www/html** directory. Next, the health check is configured and port **80** is exposed. Finally, the **apache2ctl** command is used to start the Apache web server.

9. Now, build the Docker image:

```
$ docker image build -t activity-02-01 .
```

You should get the following output after running the **build** command:

```
Enabling module php7.2.
invoke-rc.d: could not determine current runlevel
invoke-rc.d: policy-rc.d denied execution of start.
Setting up curl (7.58.0-2ubuntu3.10) ...
Setting up php7.2 (7.2.24-0ubuntu0.18.04.6) ...
Setting up php (1:7.2+60ubuntu1) ...
Processing triggers for libc-bin (2.27-3ubuntu1.2) ...
Processing triggers for ca-certificates (20190110~18.04.1) ...
Updating certificates in /etc/ssl/certs...
0 added, 0 removed; done.
Running hooks in /etc/ca-certificates/update.d...
done.
Removing intermediate container c3617d7683bd
 ---> e4d5b07f9679
Step 6/10 : COPY *.php /var/www/html
 ---> 71230d82cfde
Step 7/10 : WORKDIR /var/www/html
 ---> Running in 5b4894c0e0c3
Removing intermediate container 5b4894c0e0c3
 ---> a97b4eb3f8e0
Step 8/10 : HEALTHCHECK --interval=5s --timeout=3s --retries=3 CMD curl -f http://localhost || exit 1
 ---> Running in e881e2cccaca
Removing intermediate container e881e2cccaca
 ---> 7aa4143c321a
Step 9/10 : EXPOSE 80
 ---> Running in f96e35f62f3b
Removing intermediate container f96e35f62f3b
 ---> 6b8b9b6b8fcb
Step 10/10 : ENTRYPOINT ["apache2ctl", "-D", "FOREGROUND"]
 ---> Running in b432c96fbd0c
Removing intermediate container b432c96fbd0c
 ---> 71684e4f6bc1
Successfully built 71684e4f6bc1
Successfully tagged activity-02-01:latest
/docker $ 
```

Figure 2.22: Building the activity-02-01 Docker image

10. Execute the **docker container run** command to start a new container from the Docker image that you built in the previous step:

```
$ docker container run -p 80:80 --name activity-02-01-container -d
activity-02-01
```

Since you are starting the Docker container in detached mode (with the **-d** flag), the preceding command will output the ID of the resulting Docker container.

11. Now, you should be able to view the Apache home page. Go to the **http://127.0.0.1/welcome.php** endpoint from your favorite web browser:

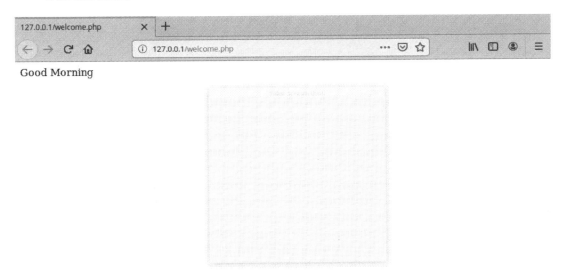

Figure 2.23: PHP application page

Note that the default Apache home page is visible. In the preceding output, you received the output as **Good Morning**. This output may differ, appearing as either **Good Afternoon** or **Good Evening** based on the time you run this container.

12. Now, clean up the container. First, stop the Docker container with the docker container stop command:

```
$ docker container stop activity-02-01-container
```

13. Finally, remove the Docker container with the **docker container rm** command:

```
$ docker container rm activity-02-01-container
```

In this activity, we learned how to use the **Dockerfile** directives that we have learned so far in this chapter to dockerize a sample PHP application. We used multiple **Dockerfile** directives, including **FROM, LABEL, ENV, RUN, COPY, WORKDIR, HEALTHCHECK, EXPOSE,** and **ENTRYPOINT**.

CHAPTER 3: MANAGING YOUR DOCKER IMAGES

ACTIVITY 3.01: BUILD SCRIPTS USING GIT HASH VERSIONING

Solution:

There are a variety of ways you could complete this activity. Here is one example:

1. Create a new build script. The first line, showing the set **−ex** command, prints each step to the screen and will fail the script if any of the steps fail. *Lines 3* and *4* set the variables for your registry and service names:

```
1 set -ex
2
3 REGISTRY=dev.docker.local:5000
4 SERVICENAME=postgresql
```

2. In *line 6*, set the **GIT_VERSION** variable to point to your short Git commit hash. The build script then prints this value to the screen in *line 7*:

```
6 GIT_VERSION=`git log -1 --format=%h`
7 echo "version: $GIT_VERSION "
```

3. Use the **docker build** command in *line 9* to create your new image and add the **docker push** command in *line 11* to push the image to your local Docker registry:

```
9 docker build -t $REGISTRY/$SERVICENAME:$GIT_VERSION .
10
11 docker push $REGISTRY/$SERVICENAME:$GIT_VERSION
```

The script file will look like the following:

```
1 set -ex
2
3 REGISTRY=dev.docker.local:5000
4 SERVICENAME= postgresql
5
6 GIT_VERSION=`git log -1 --format=%h`
```

```
7 echo "version: $GIT_VERSION "
8
9 docker build -t $REGISTRY/$SERVICENAME:$GIT_VERSION .
10
11 docker push $REGISTRY/$SERVICENAME:$GIT_VERSION
```

4. Run the following command to ensure that the script has been built and runs successfully:

```
./build.sh
```

You should get output like the following:

```
./BuildScript.sh
++ REGISTRY=dev.docker.local:5000
++ SERVICENAME=basic-app
+++ git log -1 --format=%h
++ GIT_VERSION=49d3a10
++ echo 'version: 49d3a10 '
version: 49d3a10
++ docker build -t dev.docker.local:5000/basic-app:49d3a10 .
Sending build context to Docker daemon  3.072kB
Step 1/1 : FROM postgres
 ---> 873ed24f782e
Successfully built 873ed24f782e
Successfully tagged dev.docker.local:5000/basic-app:49d3a10
++ docker push dev.docker.local:5000/basic-app:49d3a10
The push refers to repository [dev.docker.local:5000/basic-app]
```

ACTIVITY 3.02: CONFIGURING YOUR LOCAL DOCKER REGISTRY STORAGE

Solution:

The following steps describe one of the ways of achieving the goal of the activity:

1. Create the **test_registry** directory in your home directory:

```
mkdir /home/vincesesto/test_registry/
```

2. Run the local registry, but in this instance, include the **-v** option, which connects the directory you created in the preceding step to the container directory of **/var/lib/registry**. Also, use the **:rw** option to make sure you can both read and write to the directory:

```
docker run -d -p 5000:5000 --restart=always --name registry -v /home/
vincesesto/test_registry/registry:/var/lib/registry:rw registry
```

3. Now, push the image to your newly mounted registry as you normally would:

```
docker push dev.docker.local:5000/basic-app:ver1
```

4. To verify that the images are now being stored in your newly mounted directory, list the files in the **registry/docker/registry/v2/repositories/** directory.

```
ls ~/test_registry/registry/docker/registry/v2/repositories/
```

You should see the new images you have just pushed in the previous step:

```
basic-app
```

This activity has allowed us to start working with some more advanced Docker options. Don't worry, there will be further chapters dedicated to helping you understand volume mounts and storage when running your containers.

CHAPTER 4: MULTI-STAGE DOCKERFILES

ACTIVITY 4.01: DEPLOYING A GOLANG HTTP SERVER WITH A MULTI-STAGE DOCKER BUILD

Solution:

1. Create a new directory named **activity-04-01** for this activity:

```
mkdir activity-04-01
```

2. Navigate to the newly created **activity-04-01** directory:

```
cd activity-04-01
```

3. Within the **activity-04-01** directory, create a file named **main.go**:

```
$ touch main.go
```

4. Now, open the **main.go** file using your favorite text editor:

```
$ vim main.go
```

5. Add the following content to the **main.go** file, and then save and exit this file:

```
package main

import (
    "net/http"
    "fmt"
    "log"
    "os"
)

func main() {

    http.HandleFunc("/", defaultHandler)
    http.HandleFunc("/contact", contactHandler)
    http.HandleFunc("/login", loginHandler)

    port := os.Getenv("PORT")
    if port == "" {
        port = "8080"
    }
```

```
        log.Println("Service started on port " + port)


        err := http.ListenAndServe(":"+port, nil)
        if err != nil {
            log.Fatal("ListenAndServe: ", err)
            return
        }


}


func defaultHandler(w http.ResponseWriter, r *http.Request) {
    fmt.Fprintf(w, "<h1>Home Page</h1>")
}


func contactHandler(w http.ResponseWriter, r *http.Request) {
    fmt.Fprintf(w, "<h1>Contact Us</h1>")
}


func loginHandler(w http.ResponseWriter, r *http.Request) {
    fmt.Fprintf(w, "<h1>Login Page</h1>")
}
```

6. Within the **activity-04-01** directory, create a file named **Dockerfile**. This file will be the multi-stage **Dockerfile**:

```
touch Dockerfile
```

7. Now, open the **Dockerfile** using your favorite text editor:

```
vim Dockerfile
```

8. Add the following content to the **Dockerfile** and save the file:

```
FROM golang:1.14.2-alpine AS builder
WORKDIR /myapp
COPY main.go .
RUN go build -o main .

FROM alpine:latest AS runtime
WORKDIR /myapp
COPY --from=builder /myapp/main .
ENTRYPOINT ["./main"]
EXPOSE 8080
```

This **Dockerfile** has two stages, named **builder** and **runtime**. The builder stage uses the Golang Docker image as the parent and is responsible for creating the executable from the Golang source file. The runtime stage uses the **alpine** Docker image as the parent image and executes the executable file copied from the **builder** stage.

9. Now, build the Docker image with the **docker build** command:

```
docker build -t activity-04-01:v1 .
```

You should get the following output:

```
Status: Downloaded newer image for golang:1.14.2-alpine
 ---> dda4232b2bd5
Step 2/9 : WORKDIR /myapp
 ---> Running in 056d45fe3cd5
Removing intermediate container 056d45fe3cd5
 ---> 56ef45d0039a
Step 3/9 : COPY main.go .
 ---> ecb57021edb3
Step 4/9 : RUN go build -o main .
 ---> Running in 34357126abc2
Removing intermediate container 34357126abc2
 ---> aa57d4a6507b
Step 5/9 : FROM alpine:latest
latest: Pulling from library/alpine
df20fa9351a1: Pull complete
Digest: sha256:185518070891758909c9f839cf4ca393ee977ac378609f700f60a771a2dfe321
Status: Downloaded newer image for alpine:latest
 ---> a24bb4013296
Step 6/9 : WORKDIR /myapp
 ---> Running in a95a9fd1dd35
Removing intermediate container a95a9fd1dd35
 ---> 5bd7541ba4c0
Step 7/9 : COPY --from=builder /myapp/main .
 ---> 601b5d727725
Step 8/9 : ENTRYPOINT ["./main"]
 ---> Running in c5a3ea5ec05d
Removing intermediate container c5a3ea5ec05d
 ---> 991eb7796f1e
Step 9/9 : EXPOSE 8080
 ---> Running in b6df5321f124
Removing intermediate container b6df5321f124
 ---> 6c77502772ad
Successfully built 6c77502772ad
Successfully tagged activity-04-01:v1
/docker $ ▮
```

Figure 4.14: Building the Docker image

10. Use the **docker image** ls command to list all the Docker images available on your computer. Verify the size of the image:

```
docker images
```

The command will return the list of all available Docker images:

```
/docker $ docker images
REPOSITORY          TAG             IMAGE ID        CREATED             SIZE
activity-04-01      v1              6c77502772ad    About a minute ago  13.1MB
<none>              <none>          aa57d4a6507b    About a minute ago  377MB
welcome-optimized   v1              04cf352dfc37    7 minutes ago       2.03MB
welcome-runtime     v1              be3b3f630159    10 minutes ago      2.03MB
welcome-builder     v1              cc0804e7c390    15 minutes ago      841MB
welcome             v1              cc0804e7c390    15 minutes ago      841MB
golang              latest          75605a415539    2 weeks ago         839MB
alpine              latest          a24bb4013296    3 months ago        5.57MB
golang              1.14.2-alpine   dda4232b2bd5    4 months ago        370MB
/docker $ █
```

Figure 4.15: Listing all Docker images

In the preceding output, you can see that the size of the optimized Docker image named **activity-04-01** is 13.1 MB, while the parent image used at the builder stage (the Golang image) was 370 MB in size.

11. Execute the **docker container run** command to start a new container from the Docker image that you built in the previous step:

```
$ docker container run -p 8080:8080 --name activity-04-01-container
activity-04-01:v1
```

You should get an output similar to the following:

```
2020/08/30 05:14:10 Service started on port 8080
```

12. View the application at the following URL in your favorite web browser:

```
http://127.0.0.1:8080/
```

The following image shows the home page when we navigate to the URL **http://127.0.0.1:8080/**:

Home Page

Figure 4.16: Golang application – Home Page

13. Now, browse to the following URL on your favorite web browser:

```
http://127.0.0.1:8080/contact
```

The following image shows the contact page when we navigate to the URL **http://127.0.0.1:8080/contact**:

Figure 4.17: Golang application – Contact Us page

14. Now, enter the following URL in your favorite web browser:

```
http://127.0.0.1:8080/login
```

The following image shows the login page when we navigate to the URL **http://127.0.0.1:8080/login**:

Figure 4.18: Golang application – Login Page

In this activity, we learned how to deploy a Golang HTTP server that can return different responses based on the invoke URL. We used the multi-stage Docker builds in this activity to create a minimal-sized Docker image.

CHAPTER 5: COMPOSING ENVIRONMENTS WITH DOCKER COMPOSE

ACTIVITY 5.01: INSTALLING WORDPRESS USING DOCKER COMPOSE

Solution:

It is possible to create a database and install WordPress with the following steps:

1. Create the required directory and navigate into it using **cd** command:

```
mkdir wordpress
cd wordpress
```

2. Create a **docker-compose.yaml** file with the following content:

```
version: "3"
services:
  database:
    image: mysql:5.7
    volumes:
      - data:/var/lib/mysql
    restart: always
    environment:
      MYSQL_ROOT_PASSWORD: root
      MYSQL_DATABASE: db
      MYSQL_USER: user
      MYSQL_PASSWORD: password
  wordpress:
    depends_on:
      - database
    image: wordpress:latest
    ports:
      - "8080:80"
    restart: always
```

```
        environment:
          WORDPRESS_DB_HOST: database:3306
          WORDPRESS_DB_USER: user
          WORDPRESS_DB_PASSWORD: password
          WORDPRESS_DB_NAME: db
    volumes:
        data: {}
```

3. Start the application with the **docker-compose up --detach** command:

```
/docker-ws $ docker-compose up --detach
WARNING: The Docker Engine you're using is running in swarm mode.

Compose does not use swarm mode to deploy services to multiple nodes in a swarm. All containe
rs will be scheduled on the current node.

To deploy your application across the swarm, use `docker stack deploy`.

Creating network "wordpress_default" with the default driver
Creating volume "wordpress_data" with default driver
Creating wordpress_database_1 ... done
Creating wordpress_wordpress_1 ... done
/docker-ws $
```

Figure 5.22: Start of the application

4. Check for the running containers with the **docker-compose ps** command. You should get the following output:

```
/docker-ws $ docker-compose ps
         Name                      Command            State            Ports
----------------------------------------------------------------------------------------
wordpress_database_1     docker-entrypoint.sh mysqld    Up     3306/tcp, 33060/tcp
wordpress_wordpress_1    docker-entrypoint.sh apach ...  Up     0.0.0.0:8080->80/tcp
/docker-ws $
```

Figure 5.23: WordPress and database containers

5. Open **http://localhost:8080** in your browser to check the WordPress setup screen:

Figure 5.24: WordPress setup screen

In this activity, you have created a deployment for a real-life application using Docker Compose. The application consists of a database container and a WordPress container. Both container services are configured using environment variables, connected via Docker Compose networking and volumes.

ACTIVITY 5.02: INSTALLING THE PANORAMIC TREKKING APP USING DOCKER COMPOSE

Solution:

It is possible to create the database and Panoramic Trekking App with the following steps:

1. Create the required directory and change into it:

```
mkdir pta-compose
cd pta-compose
```

2. Create a **docker-compose.yaml** file with the following content:

```
version: "3"

services:

  db:
    image: postgres
    volumes:
      - db_data:/var/lib/postgresql/data/
    environment:
      - POSTGRES_PASSWORD=docker

  web:
    image: packtworkshops/the-docker-workshop:chapter5-pta-web
    volumes:
      - static_data:/service/static
    depends_on:
      - db

  nginx:
    image: packtworkshops/the-docker-workshop:chapter5-pta-nginx
    volumes:
      - static_data:/service/static
    ports:
      - 8000:80
    depends_on:
```

```
        - web

    volumes:
      db_data:
      static_data:
```

3. Start the application with the **docker-compose up --detach** command. You should get output similar to the following:

```
/docker-ws $ docker-compose up --detach
Creating network "pta-compose_default" with the default driver
Creating volume "pta-compose_db_data" with default driver
Creating volume "pta-compose_static_data" with default driver
Creating pta-compose_db_1 ... done
Creating pta-compose_web_1 ... done
Creating pta-compose_nginx_1 ... done
 /docker-ws $
```

Figure 5.25: Start of the application

> **NOTE**
>
> You can also use **docker-compose up -d** command to start the application.

4. Check for the running containers with the **docker-compose ps** command. You should get output similar to the following:

```
/docker-ws $ docker-compose ps
         Name                    Command              State         Ports
-----------------------------------------------------------------------------------
pta-compose_db_1        docker-entrypoint.sh postgres   Up      5432/tcp
pta-compose_nginx_1     nginx -g daemon off;            Up      0.0.0.0:8000->80/tcp
pta-compose_web_1       ./entrypoint.sh gunicorn p ...  Up
 /docker-ws $
```

Figure 5.26 Application, database, and nginx containers

5. Open the administration section of the Panoramic Trekking App in the browser with the address of **http://0.0.0.0:8000/admin**:

Figure 5.27: Admin setup logon

Log in with the username **admin** and password **changeme** and add new photos and countries. The following screen will appear:

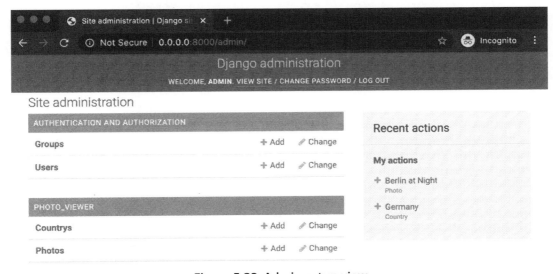

Figure 5.28: Admin setup view

6. Open the Panoramic Trekking App at the address **http://0.0.0.0:8000/ photo_viewer** in the browser:

Figure 5.29: Application view

In this activity, you have created a three-tier application using Docker Compose, with tiers for a PostgreSQL database, a backend, and a proxy service. All services are configured and connected using Docker Compose with its networking and storage capabilities.

CHAPTER 6: INTRODUCTION TO DOCKER NETWORKING

ACTIVITY 6.01: LEVERAGING DOCKER NETWORK DRIVERS

Solution:

The following is the most common way to complete this activity according to best practices:

1. Use the **docker network create** command to create a network for the NGINX web server. Call it **webservernet** and give it a subnet of **192.168.1.0/24** and a gateway of **192.168.1.1**:

```
$ docker network create webservernet --subnet=192.168.1.0/24
--gateway=192.168.1.1
```

This should create the **bridge** network, **webservernet**.

2. Use the **docker run** command to create an NGINX web server. Use the **-p** flag to forward port **8080** on the host to port **80** on the container instance:

```
$ docker run -itd -p 8080:80 --name webserver1 --network webservernet
nginx:latest
```

This will start the **webserver1** container in the **webservernet** network.

3. Use the **docker run** command to start an Alpine Linux container named **monitor** in **host** networking mode. This way, you will know that the container has access to the host ports of the main system as well as access to the **bridge** network IP address:

```
$ docker run -itd --name monitor --network host alpine:latest
```

This will start an Alpine Linux container instance in **host** networking mode.

4. Use **docker inspect** to find the IP address of the **webserver1** container:

```
$ docker inspect webserver1
```

The verbose details of the container will be displayed in JSON format; get the IP address from the **IPAddress** parameter:

```
"Networks": {
        "bridge": {
            "IPAMConfig": null,
            "Links": null,
            "Aliases": null,
            "NetworkID": "f48815e41374d0d87f90d0b96462be24503ee01bedf8347f9d844de34bc6191c",
            "EndpointID": "b9bfcc3e9378110e41296f83f8b28cda920243aee36ac341246437bfb2377f40",
            "Gateway": "192.168.1.1",
            "IPAddress": "192.168.1.2",
            "IPPrefixLen": 24,
            "IPv6Gateway": "",
            "GlobalIPv6Address": "",
            "GlobalIPv6PrefixLen": 0,
            "MacAddress": "02:42:ac:11:00:02",
            "DriverOpts": null
        }
    }
}
```

Figure 6.27: Inspecting the webserver1 container instance

5. Access an **sh** shell inside the monitoring container using the **docker exec** command:

```
$ docker exec -it monitor /bin/sh
```

This should drop you into a root shell.

6. Use the **apk install** command to install the **curl** command inside this container:

```
/ # apk add curl
```

This should install the **curl** utility:

```
fetch http://dl-cdn.alpinelinux.org/alpine/v3.11/main
/x86_64/APKINDEX.tar.gz
fetch http://dl-cdn.alpinelinux.org/alpine/v3.11/community
/x86_64/APKINDEX.tar.gz
(1/4) Installing ca-certificates (20191127-r1)
(2/4) Installing nghttp2-libs (1.40.0-r0)
(3/4) Installing libcurl (7.67.0-r0)
(4/4) Installing curl (7.67.0-r0)
Executing busybox-1.31.1-r9.trigger
Executing ca-certificates-20191127-r1.trigger
OK: 7 MiB in 18 packages
```

7. Use the **curl** command to validate connectivity works at the host level, by calling port **8080** on the host machine:

```
/ # curl -v http://localhost:8080
```

You should receive a **200 OK** response from NGINX, indicating successful connectivity at the host level:

```
*   Trying 127.0.0.1:8080...
* TCP_NODELAY set
* Connected to localhost (127.0.0.1) port 8080 (#0)
> GET / HTTP/1.1
> Host: localhost:8080
> User-Agent: curl/7.67.0
> Accept: */*
>
* Mark bundle as not supporting multiuse
< HTTP/1.1 200 OK
< Server: nginx/1.17.10
< Date: Thu, 21 May 2020 01:37:46 GMT
< Content-Type: text/html
< Content-Length: 612
< Last-Modified: Tue, 14 Apr 2020 14:19:26 GMT
< Connection: keep-alive
< ETag: "5e95c66e-264"
< Accept-Ranges: bytes
<
<!DOCTYPE html>
<html>
<head>
<title>Welcome to nginx!</title>
```

Figure 6.28: Accessing the webserver1 container from the exposed ports on the host

8. Likewise, use the **curl** command to access the IP address of the container in the Docker **bridge** network directly over port **80**:

```
/ # curl -v 192.168.1.2:80
```

You should similarly receive another **200 OK** response, indicating a successful connection:

```
Press ENTER or type command to continue
*   Trying 192.168.1.2:80...
* TCP_NODELAY set
* Connected to 192.168.1.2 (192.168.1.2) port 80 (#0)
> GET / HTTP/1.1
> Host: 192.168.1.2
> User-Agent: curl/7.67.0
> Accept: */*
>
* Mark bundle as not supporting multiuse
< HTTP/1.1 200 OK
< Server: nginx/1.19.0
< Date: Fri, 03 Jul 2020 13:41:31 GMT
< Content-Type: text/html
< Content-Length: 612
< Last-Modified: Tue, 26 May 2020 15:00:20 GMT
< Connection: keep-alive
< ETag: "5ecd2f04-264"
< Accept-Ranges: bytes
<
<!DOCTYPE html>
<html>
<head>
<title>Welcome to nginx!</title>
```

Figure 6.29: Accessing the NGINX web server from the IP
address of the container instance

In this activity, we were able to illustrate the connectivity between containers using different Docker networking drivers. This scenario applies to real-world production infrastructure because, when deploying a containerized solution, engineers will strive to deploy an infrastructure that is as immutable as possible. With the ability to deploy containers in Docker that exactly mimic the networking at the host level, infrastructure can be designed that requires very minimal configuration on the host OS. This makes it very easy to deploy and scale the host that Docker is deployed on. Packages such as **curl** and other monitoring tools can be deployed into containers that run on the Docker hosts instead of being installed on the hosts themselves. This guarantees ease of deployment and maintenance, as well as increasing the speed at which additional hosts can be deployed to meet increasing demand.

ACTIVITY 6.02: OVERLAY NETWORKING IN ACTION

Solution:

1. Create a Docker **overlay** network called **panoramic-net** on **Machine1** in the Docker swarm cluster, using the **docker network create** command, by passing the custom **subnet**, **gateway**, and **overlay** network driver:

```
$ docker network create panoramic-net --subnet=10.2.0.0/16
--gateway=10.2.0.1 --driver overlay
```

2. Use the **docker service create** command on **Machine1** to create a service named **trekking-app** in the **panoramic-net** network:

```
$ docker service create -t --name trekking-app --replicas=1 --network
panoramic-net alpine:latest
```

    This will start a service called **trekking-app** in the **panoramic-net overlay** network.

3. Use the **docker service create** command on **Machine1** to create a service named **database-app** in the **panoramic-net** network. Set default credentials and specify the **postgres:12** version of the Docker image:

```
$ docker service create -t --name database-app --replicas=1
--network panoramic-net -e "POSTGRES_USER=panoramic" -e "POSTGRES_
PASSWORD=trekking" postgres:12
```

4. Use **docker exec** to access an **sh** shell inside the **trekking-app** service container:

```
$ docker exec -it trekking-app.1.qhpwxol00geedkfa9p6qswmyv /bin/sh
```

    This should drop you into a root shell inside the **trekking-app** container instance.

5. Use the **ping** command to validate network connectivity to the **database-app** service:

```
/ # ping database-app
```

    The ICMP replies should indicate the connectivity is successful:

```
PING database-app (10.2.0.5): 56 data bytes
64 bytes from 10.2.0.5: seq=0 ttl=64 time=0.261 ms
64 bytes from 10.2.0.5: seq=1 ttl=64 time=0.352 ms
64 bytes from 10.2.0.5: seq=2 ttl=64 time=0.198 ms
```

In this activity, we leveraged a custom Docker **overlay** network across a Docker swarm cluster to illustrate connectivity between two Docker swarm services using Docker DNS. In a real-world multi-tier application, many microservices can be deployed in large Docker swarm clusters that use an **overlay** network mesh to directly talk to each other. Understanding how **overlay** networking works in tandem with Docker DNS is vital to achieving efficient scalability as your containerized infrastructure continues to grow.

CHAPTER 7: DOCKER STORAGE

ACTIVITY 7.01: STORING CONTAINER EVENT (STATE) DATA ON A POSTGRESQL DATABASE

Solution:

1. Run the following commands to remove all the objects in your host:

```
$ docker container rm -fv $(docker container ls -aq)
$docker image rm $(docker image ls -q)
```

2. Get the volume names, and then remove all the volumes using the following commands:

```
$docker volume ls
$docker volume rm <volume names separated by spaces>
```

3. Get the network names and then remove all the networks using the following commands:

```
$docker network ls
$docker network rm <network names separated by spaces>
```

4. Open two terminals, one dedicated to seeing **docker events --format '{{json .}}'** in effect. The other one should be opened to execute the previously mentioned high-level steps.

5. In the first terminal, run the following command:

```
docker events --format '{{json .}}'.
```

You should get an output like the following:

Figure 7.11: Output of the docker events command

6. Run the following command to start the **ubuntu** container in the second terminal:

```
$docker run -d ubuntu:14.04
```

You should get an output like the following:

```
docker@docker-VirtualBox:~$ docker run -d ubuntu:14.04
Unable to find image 'ubuntu:14.04' locally
14.04: Pulling from library/ubuntu
2e6e20c8e2e6: Pull complete
30bb187ac3fc: Pull complete
b7a5bcc4a58a: Pull complete
Digest: sha256:ffc76f71dd8be8c9e222d420dc96901a07b61616689a44c7b3ef6
a10b7213de4
Status: Downloaded newer image for ubuntu:14.04
43903b966123a7c491b50116b40827daa03da5d350f8fef2a690fc4024547ce2
```

Figure 7.12: Output of the docker run command

7. Create a volume named **vol1** using the following command in the second terminal:

```
$docker volume create vol1
```

8. Create a network named **net1** using the following command in the second terminal:

```
$docker network create net1
```

9. Remove the container using the following command:

```
$docker container rm -fv <container ID>
```

10. Remove the volume and the network using the following commands:

```
$docker volume rm vol1
$docker network rm net1
```

11. Click *Ctrl + C* in the **docker events** terminal to terminate it.

12. Check the following two examples to understand the JSON output:

Example 1:

```
{"status":"create","id":"43903b966123a7c491b50116b40827daa03
da5d350f8fef2a690fc4024547ce2","from":"ubuntu:14.04","Type":
"container","Action":"create","Actor":{"ID":"43903b966123a7c
491b50116b40827daa03da5d350f8fef2a690fc4024547ce2","Attributes":
{"image":"ubuntu:14.04","name":"upbeat_johnson"}},"scope":"local",
"time":1592516703,"timeNano":1592516703507582404}
```

Example 2:

```
{"Type":"network","Action":"connect","Actor":{"ID":"52855e1561
8e37b7ecc0bb26bc42847af07cae65ddd3b68a029e40006364a9bd",
"Attributes":{"container":"43903b966123a7c491b50116b40827daa03d
a5d350f8fef2a690fc4024547ce2","name":"bridge","type":"bridge"}},
"scope":"local","time":1592516703,"timeNano":1592516703911851347}
```

You will find that there are different attributes and structures depending on the object.

13. Run a PostgreSQL container with a volume. Name the container **db1**:

```
$docker container run --name db1 -v db:/var/lib/postgresql/data -e
POSTGRES_PASSWORD=password -d postgres
```

14. Run the **exec** command so that bash is replaced with the command to be executed. The shell will change to **posgres=#** to indicate that you are inside the container:

```
$ docker container exec -it db1 psql -U postgres
```

15. Create a table with two columns: **ID** of the **serial** type and **info** of the **json** type:

```
CREATE TABLE events (ID serial NOT NULL PRIMARY KEY, info json NOT
NULL);
```

16. Insert the first row of the **JSON** output from the first example into the table:

```
INSERT INTO events (info) VALUES
('{"status":"create","id":"43903b966123a7c491b50116b40827daa03da
5d350f8fef2a690fc4024547ce2","from":"ubuntu:14.04","Type":
"container","Action":"create","Actor":{"ID":"43903b966123a7c49
1b50116b40827daa03da5d350f8fef2a690fc4024547ce2","Attributes":
{"image":"ubuntu:14.04","name":"upbeat_johnson"}},"scope":
"local","time":1592516703,"timeNano":1592516703507582404}');
```

17. Verify that the row is saved in the database by typing the following SQL statement:

```
select * from events;
```

You should get an output like the following:

```
postgres=# select * from events;
 id |
                         info

----+---------------------------------------------------------------------------------
------------------------------------------------------------------------------------
------------------------------------------------------------------------------------
------------------------------------------------------------------------------------
---------------------------------------------------
  1 | {"status":"create","id":"43903b966123a7c491b50116b40827daa03da5d350f8fef2a
690fc4024547ce2","from":"ubuntu:14.04","Type":"container","Action":"create","Act
or":{"ID":"43903b966123a7c491b50116b40827daa03da5d350f8fef2a690fc4024547ce2","At
tributes":{"image":"ubuntu:14.04","name":"upbeat_johnson"}},"scope":"local","tim
e":1592516703,"timeNano":1592516703507582404}
(1 row)

postgres=#
```

Figure 7.13: Verifying that the row is saved in the database

18. Insert Docker events into the **events** table using the SQL **insert** command.

> **NOTE**
>
> Please refer to the **events.txt** file at https://packt.live/2ZKfGgB to insert Docker events using the **insert** command.

You should get an output like the following:

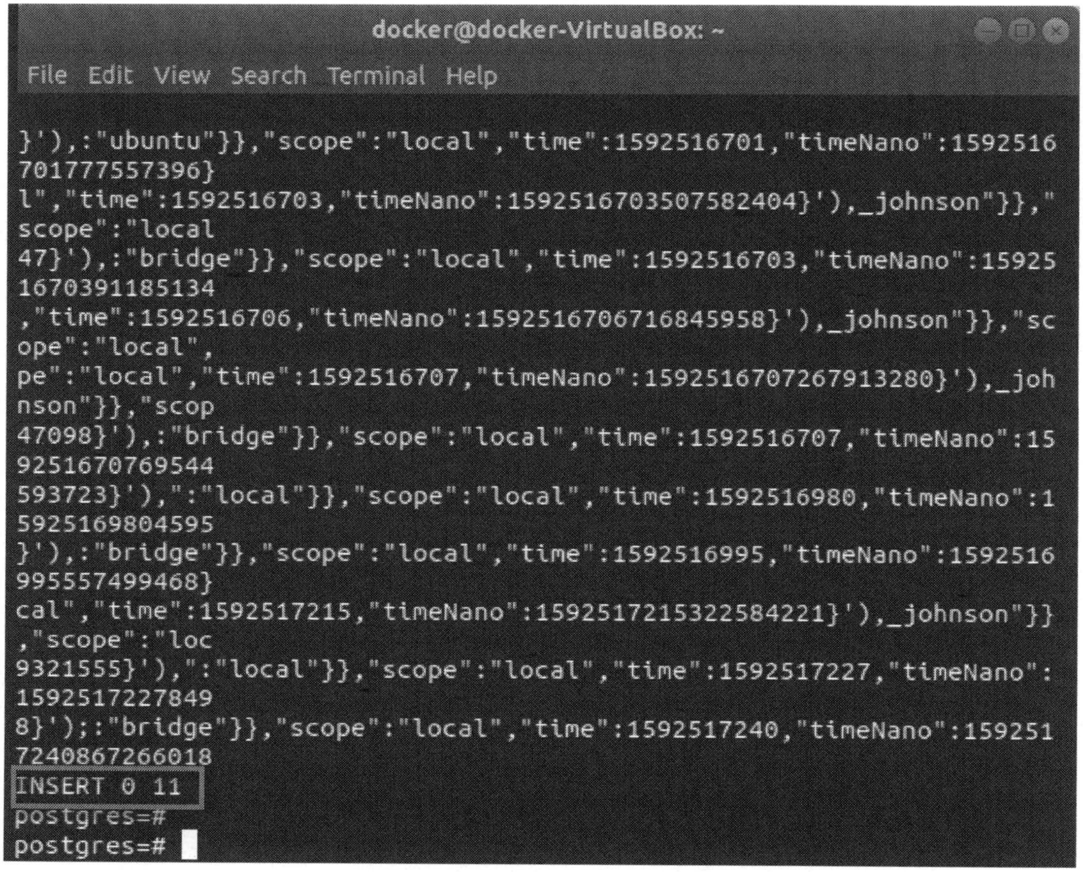

```
docker@docker-VirtualBox: ~

File  Edit  View  Search  Terminal  Help

}'),:"ubuntu"}},"scope":"local","time":1592516701,"timeNano":1592516
701777557396}
l","time":1592516703,"timeNano":1592516703507582404}'),_johnson"}},"
scope":"local
47}'),:"bridge"}},"scope":"local","time":1592516703,"timeNano":15925
1670391185134
,"time":1592516706,"timeNano":1592516706716845958}'),_johnson"}},"sc
ope":"local",
pe":"local","time":1592516707,"timeNano":1592516707267913280}'),_joh
nson"}},"scop
47098}'),:"bridge"}},"scope":"local","time":1592516707,"timeNano":15
9251670769544
593723}'),":"local"}},"scope":"local","time":1592516980,"timeNano":1
5925169804595
}'),:"bridge"}},"scope":"local","time":1592516995,"timeNano":1592516
995557499468}
cal","time":1592517215,"timeNano":1592517215322584221}'),_johnson"}}
,"scope":"loc
9321555}'),":"local"}},"scope":"local","time":1592517227,"timeNano":
1592517227849
8}');:"bridge"}},"scope":"local","time":1592517240,"timeNano":159251
7240867266018
INSERT 0 11
postgres=#
postgres=#
```

Figure 7.14: Inserting multiple rows in the database

From this output, it is clear that 11 events have been inserted successfully into the PostgreSQL database.

19. Run the following three queries one by one.

Query 1:

```
SELECT * FROM events WHERE info ->> 'status' = 'pull';
```

The output will be as in the following:

```
postgres=# SELECT * FROM events WHERE info ->> 'status' = 'pull';
 id |
                                    info
----+----------------------------------------------------------------
-----------------------------------------------------------------
---------------------------------------------------------------
  2 | {"status":"pull","id":"ubuntu:14.04","Type":"image","Action":
"pull","Actor":{"ID":"ubuntu:14.04","Attributes":{"name":"ubuntu"}},
"scope":"local","time":1592516701,"timeNano":1592516701777557396}
(1 row)
```

Figure 7.15: Output of Query 1

Query 2:

```
SELECT * FROM events WHERE info ->> 'status' = 'destroy';
```

The output will be as in the following:

```
postgres=# SELECT * FROM events WHERE info ->> 'status' = 'destroy';

 id |



                                                            info

----+----------------------------------------------------------------
-----------------------------------------------------------------
----------------------------------------------------------------
-----------------------------------------------------------------
-----------------------------------------------------------
 10 | {"status":"destroy","id":"43903b966123a7c491b50116b40827daa03d
a5d350f8fef2a690fc4024547ce2","from":"ubuntu:14.04","Type":"containe
r","Action":"destroy","Actor":{"ID":"43903b966123a7c491b50116b40827d
aa03da5d350f8fef2a690fc4024547ce2","Attributes":{"image":"ubuntu:14.
04","name":"upbeat_johnson"}},"scope":"local","time":1592517215,"tim
eNano":1592517215322584221}
(1 row)
```

Figure 7.16: Output of Query 2

Query 3:

```
SELECT info ->> 'id' as id FROM events WHERE info ->> 'status'=
    'destroy';
```

The output will be as in the following:

```
postgres=# SELECT info ->> 'id' as id FROM events WHERE info ->> 'st
atus' = 'destroy';
                                  id
---------------------------------------------------------------------
 43903b966123a7c491b50116b40827daa03da5d350f8fef2a690fc4024547ce2
(1 row)
```

Figure 7.17: Output of Query 3

In this activity, you learned how to log and monitor a container and query the container's events using SQL statements, as well as how to get a JSON output of the events and save in a PostgreSQL database. You also studied the JSON output structure and learned how to query it.

ACTIVITY 7.02: SHARING NGINX LOG FILES WITH THE HOST

Solution:

1. Verify that you do not have the **/var/mylogs** folder on your host by running the following command:

```
$cd /var/mylogs
```

You should get an output like the following:

```
Bash: cd: /var/mylogs: No such file or directory
```

2. Run a container based on the NGINX image. Specify the path of the shared volumes on the host and inside the container in the **run** command. Inside the container, NGINX uses the **/var/log/nginx** path for the log files. Specify the path on the host as **/var/mylogs**:

```
$docker container run -d -v /var/mylogs:/var/log/nginx nginx
```

The Docker Engine will pull the image automatically if you do not have it locally:

```
docker@docker-VirtualBox:~$ docker container run -d -v /var/mylogs:/var/log/nginx nginx
Unable to find image 'nginx:latest' locally
latest: Pulling from library/nginx
8559a31e96f4: Already exists
8d69e59170f7: Pull complete
3f9f1ec1d262: Pull complete
d1f5ff4f210d: Pull complete
1e22bfa8652e: Pull complete
Digest: sha256:21f32f6c08406306d822a0e6e8b7dc81f53f336570e852e25fbe1e3e3d0d0133
Status: Downloaded newer image for nginx:latest
fdbc872a6f9efc05145df7d927197107b8c66e9c21879817f76fa5539700c1db
```

Figure 7.18: Output of the docker run command

3. Go to the path of **/var/mylogs**. List all the files in that directory:

```
$cd /var/mylogs
$ls
```

You should find two files there:

```
access.log          error.log
```

4. (Optional) If no errors were generated, the two files will be empty. You check the contents by using the **cat** Linux command or by using the **tail** Linux command. As we used the **cat** command before, let's use the **tail** command for this example:

```
$tail -f *.log
```

You should get an output like the following:

```
==>  access.log  <==
==>  error.log   <==
```

As this NGINX server did not generate any errors or was not accessed, the files are currently empty. However, if NGINX crashes at any instant, the errors generated will be saved in **error.log**.

In this activity, you learned how to share the log files of a container to the host. You used the NGINX server, so if it crashes, you can trackback what happened from its log files.

CHAPTER 8: SERVICE DISCOVERY

ACTIVITY 8.01: UTILIZING JENKINS AND SONARQUBE

Solution:

1. Install SonarQube and run it as a container using the following command:

```
docker run -d --name sonarqube -p 9000:9000 -p 9092:9092 sonarqube
```

You should get the container ID as the output:

```
4346a99b506b1bec8000e429471dabac57e3f565b154ee921284ec685497bfae
```

2. Log in to SonarQube by using **admin/admin** credentials:

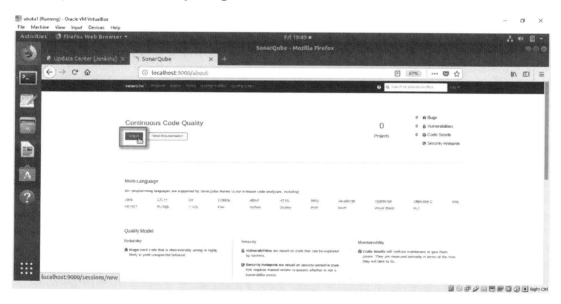

Figure 8.38: Log in to SonarQube

After the successful login, a screen similar to the following should appear:

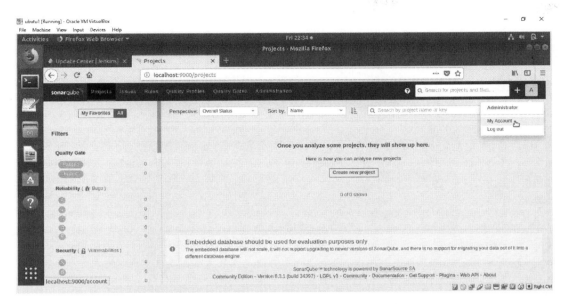

Figure 8.39: The SonarQube dashboard

3.   At the top right, click on the user. A drop-down menu will appear.
     Click on **My Account**:

4.   Scroll down and click on **Generate** under **Security** to generate a token.
     You must copy it now because you will not be able to access it later:

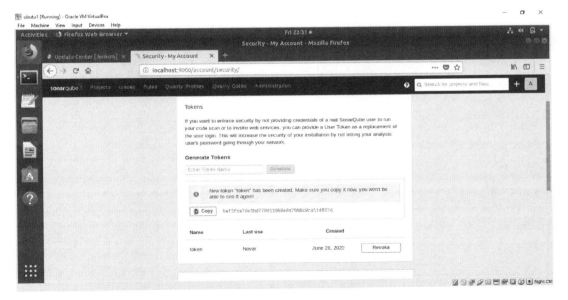

Figure 8.40: Generating the token

5. In Jenkins, click on **Manage Jenkins** > **Plugin Manager**. Search for **Sonar** in the **Available** list. Install the **SonarQube Scanner** plugin.

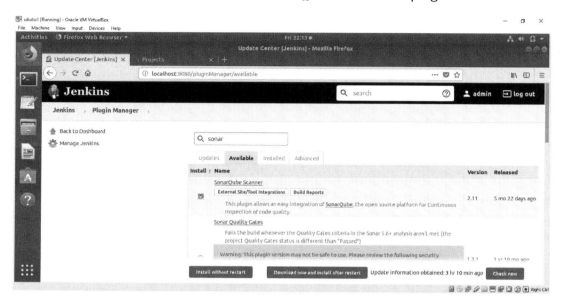

Figure 8.41: Installing the SonarQube Scanner plugin

6. Verify that the installation is correct by clicking on the **hit_count** project and then clicking the **Configure** option. Click on **Add build step** and then **Execute SonarQube Scanner** on the **Build** tab, as in *Figure 8.43*:

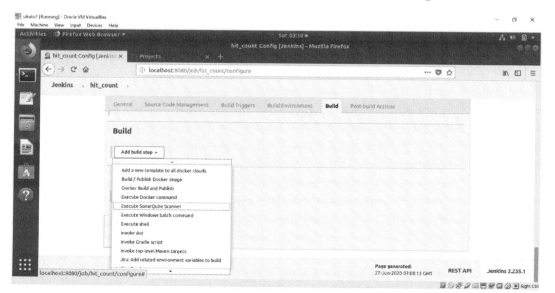

Figure 8.42: Selecting Execute SonarQube Scanner

7. However, the new box will generate errors, like the one shown in the following screenshot. To rectify that, integrate SonarQube and Jenkins through the **system configuration** and **global tool configuration** options:

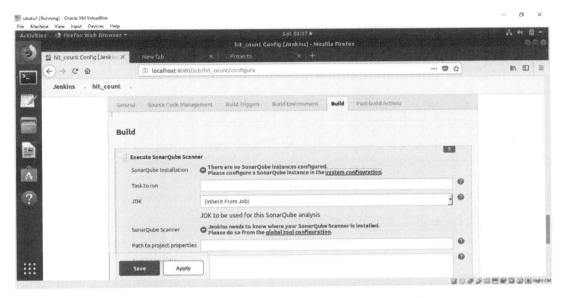

Figure 8.43: Errors generated since SonarQube is not configured yet

8. In Jenkins, click on **Manage Jenkins**. Click the **Global Tool Configuration** option and then click **Add SonarQube Scanner**:

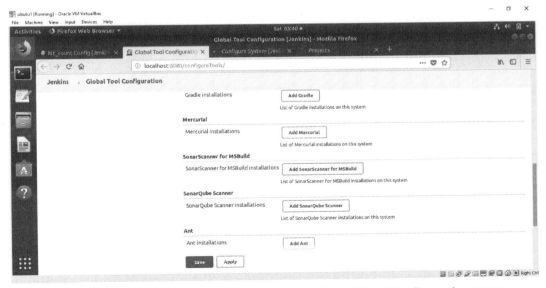

Figure 8.44: Adding SonarQube Scanner on the Global Tool Configuration page

9. Enter the name **SonarQube Scanner**. Check **Install automatically**. Under **Install from Maven Central**, in **Version**, select **SonarQube Scanner 3.2.0.1227**. Click on **Add Installer**. In the **Label** field, enter **SonarQube**. In the **Download URL for binary archive** field, enter the link **https://binaries.sonarsource.com/Distribution/sonar-scanner-cli/sonar-scanner-cli-3.2.0.1227-linux.zip**.

Click on **Save**.

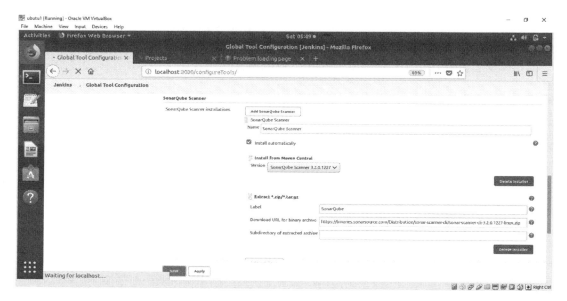

Figure 8.45: Adding details for SonarQube Scanner

You are now done with the **Global Tool Configuration** option, so it is time to go to the **Configure System** option.

10. In **Manage Jenkins**, click **Configure System**:

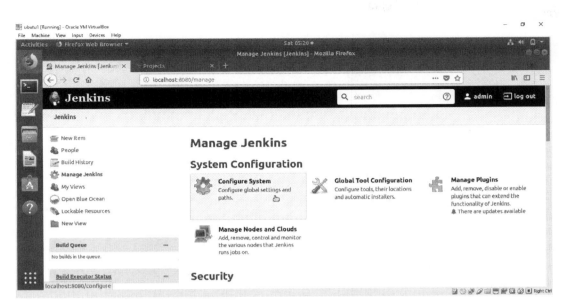

Figure 8.46: Click on Configure System on the Manage Jenkins page

11. You cannot enter the system configuration right now as it asks for **Server Authentication Token**. When you click the **Add** button, it will do nothing. Enter the token as secret text in the following steps, and then return to **Manage Jenkins**:

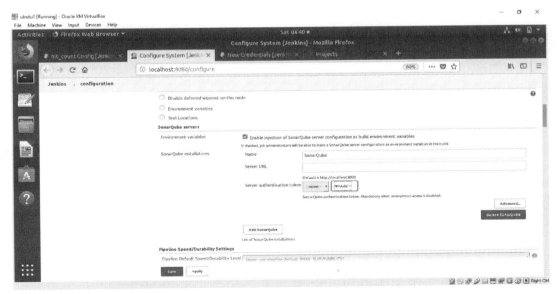

Figure 8.47: Inserting the SonarQube token in Jenkins configuration

12. Click on **Manage Credentials**:

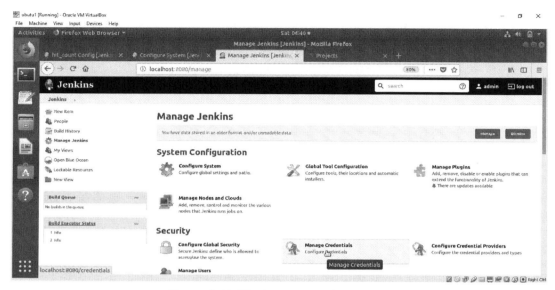

Figure 8.48: The Manage Jenkins page

13. Click on **Jenkins**:

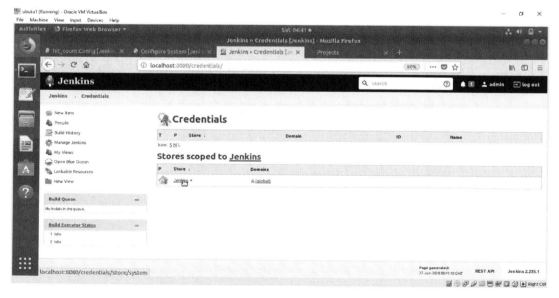

Figure 8.49: The Jenkins Credentials page

14. Click on **Global credentials (unrestricted)**:

Figure 8.50: The Global credentials (unrestricted) domain

15. Click on **adding some credentials**:

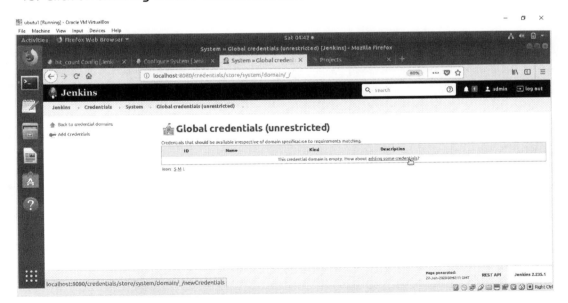

Figure 8.51: Adding some credentials

16. In the **Kind** drop-down menu, click on **Secret text**:

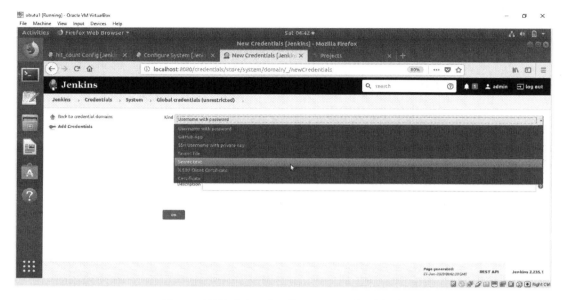

Figure 8.52: Selecting Secret text for Kind

17. In the **Secret** textbox, paste the token that you copied in *Step 5* in this activity. In the **ID** field, enter **SonarQubeToken**. Click **OK**:

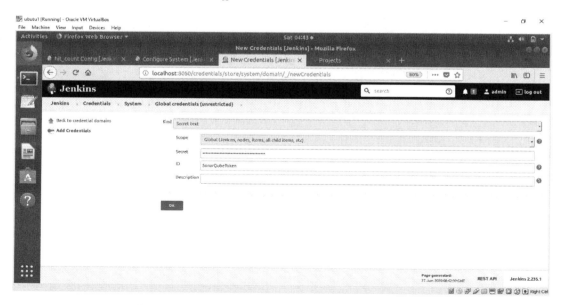

Figure 8.53: Adding the token to the Secret textbox

SonarQubeToken will be saved in the **Global credentials** option. You will see a screen similar to the following:

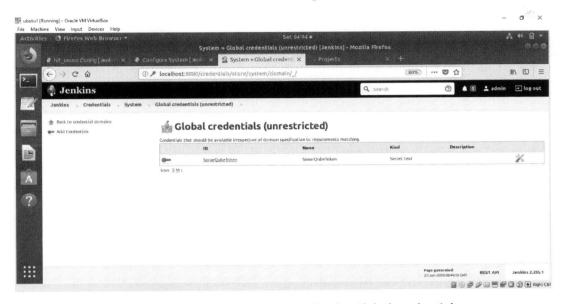

Figure 8.54: SonarQubeToken saved in the Global credentials

18. Return to **Manage Jenkins**. Click **Configuration System** and then **Refresh**. Now, in the **Server Authentication Token** drop-down menu, you will find **SonarQubeToken**. Check **Enable injection of SonarQube server configuration as build environment variables**. Enter **SonarQube** in the **Name** field. Enter **http://<your IP>:9000** in the **Server URL** field. Then click **Save**:

    You can run the **ifconfig** command to fetch your IP. You will find the IP in the **en0** section of the output:

    ```
    $ ifconfig
    ```

    This is the last step in integrating Jenkins with SonarQube. Let's return to the project.

19. In **Build Environment**, check **Prepare SonarQube Scanner environment**. Set **Server authentication token** to **SonarQubeToken**:

20. Now, click on the project name and then **Configure**. In the **Build** step, enter the following code in the **Analysis Properties** field:

```
sonar.projectKey=hit_count
sonar.projectName=hit_count
sonar.projectVersion=1.0
sonar.sources=.
sonar.language=py
sonar.sourceEncoding=UTF-8
# Test Results
sonar.python.xunit.reportPath=nosetests.xml
# Coverage
sonar.python.coverage.reportPath=coverage.xml
# Linter (https://docs.sonarqube.org/display/PLUG/Pylint+Report)
#sonar.python.pylint=/usr/local/bin/pylint
#sonar.python.pylint_config=.pylintrc
#sonar.python.pylint.reportPath=pylint-report.txt
```

Click **Save**.

21. After saving, you will find the SonarQube logo showing on the project page, as in *Figure 8.55*. Click on **Build Now**:

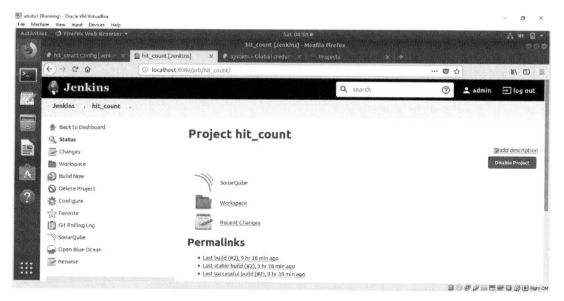

Figure 8.55: The SonarQube option showing on our project's dashboard

22. In **Build History**, click on **Console Output**. You should get the screen similar to the following:

Figure 8.56: Console Output

23. Check the report on **SonarQube**. In the browser, type **http://<ip>:9000** or **http://localhost:9000**. You will find that Jenkins added your **hit_count** project automatically to SonarQube:

24. Click **hit_count**. You will find a detailed report. Whenever Jenkins builds the project, SonarQube will analyze the code automatically

In this activity, you learned how to integrate Jenkins with SonarQube and install the required plugins, which you verified by checking SonarQube in the browser. You also applied SonarQube to your simple web application, **hit_counter**.

ACTIVITY 8.02: UTILIZING JENKINS AND SONARQUBE IN THE PANORAMIC TREKKING APPLICATION

Solution:

1. Create a new item named **trekking** in Jenkins. Select it as a **FREESTYLE** project. Click **OK**.

2. In the **General** tab, select **Discard old builds**.

3. In the **Source Code Management** tab, select **GIT**. Then enter the URL `http://github.com/efoda/trekking_app`:

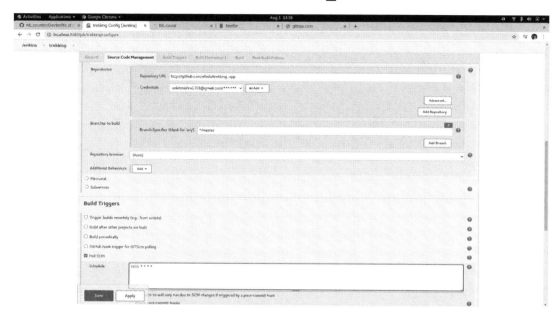

Figure 8.57: Inserting the GitHub URL

4. In **Build Triggers**, select **Poll SCM** and enter **H/15 * * * ***:

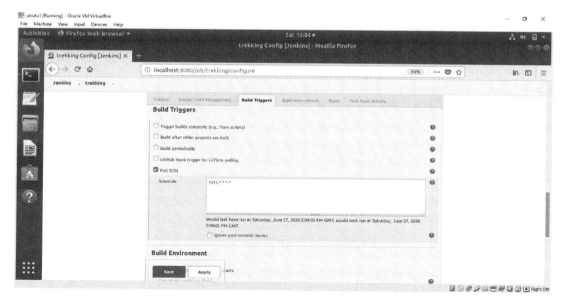

Figure 8.58: Inserting the scheduling code

5. In the **Build Environment** tab, select **Prepare SonarQube Scanner environment**. Select the **Server authentication token** from the drop-down menu:

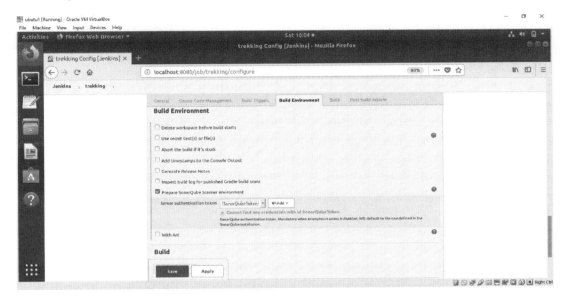

Figure 8.59: Selecting SonarQubeToken as the Server authentication token

6. In the **Build** tab, enter the following code in **Analysis properties**:

```
sonar.projectKey=trekking
sonar.projectName=trekking
sonar.projectVersion=1.0
sonar.sources=.
sonar.language=py
sonar.sourceEncoding=UTF-8
# Test Results
sonar.python.xunit.reportPath=nosetests.xml
# Coverage
sonar.python.coverage.reportPath=coverage.xml
# Linter (https://docs.sonarqube.org/display/PLUG/Pylint+Report)
#sonar.python.pylint=/usr/local/bin/pylint
#sonar.python.pylint_config=.pylintrc
#sonar.python.pylint.reportPath=pylint-report.txt
```

Click **Save**.

7. Select **Build Now**. When the build is done successfully, select **Console Output**. The following output will indicate that it finished successfully:

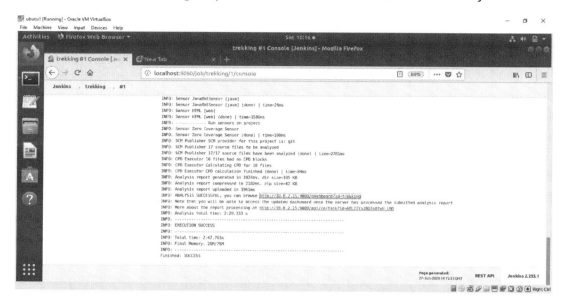

Figure 8.60: Verifying Jenkins has built the image successfully

8. Switch to the **SonarQube** tab in the browser and check the output. The following report indicates that the trekking app has two bugs and zero security vulnerabilities:

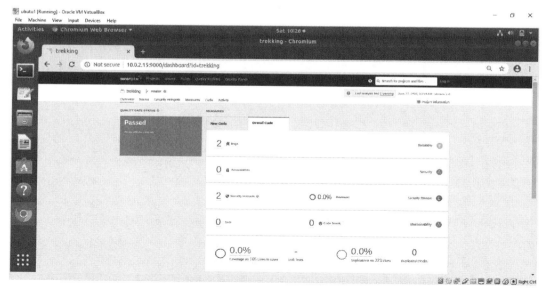

Figure 8.61: Report shown in the SonarQube browser tab

If you click on **New Code**, it will be blank as you built the project only once. When Jenkins builds it another time, you will find a comparison between the two builds.

9. If you want to edit the project's code, fork the GitHub code to your account and edit the code to fix the bugs and the vulnerabilities. Edit the project's configuration to have your GitHub code instead of the code provided in the **Source Code** tab.

In this activity, you integrated Jenkins with SonarQube and applied it to the Panoramic Trekking application. At the end of the activity, you inspected the reports that SonarQube generated showing the bugs and the vulnerabilities in the code.

CHAPTER 9: DOCKER SWARM

ACTIVITY 9.01: DEPLOYING THE PANORAMIC TREKKING APP TO A SINGLE-NODE DOCKER SWARM

Solution:

There are a number of ways in which you can perform this activity. These steps are one way to do it:

1. Create a directory for the application. In this instance, you will create a directory called **Activity1** and move into the new directory using the **cd** command:

```
mkdir Activity1; cd Activity1
```

2. Clone the application from its GitHub repository to ensure that you will have all the relevant information and applications needed for the Panoramic Trekking App services you want to deploy to your swarm:

```
git clone https://github.com/vincesesto/trekking_app.git
```

3. You won't need any of the supporting directories for NGINX, but ensure that your web service and database running are listed here, including the **panoramic_trekking_app** and **photo_viewer** directories and the **Dockerfile**, **entrypoint.sh**, **manage.py**, and **requirements.txt** scripts and files:

```
ls -l
```

The command should return output similar to the following:

```
-rw-r--r--    1 vinces   staff     533 12 Mar 15:02 Dockerfile
-rwxr-xr-x    1 vinces   staff    1077 12 Mar 15:02 entrypoint.sh
-rwxr-xr-x    1 vinces   staff     642 12 Mar 15:02 manage.py
drwxr-xr-x    9 vinces   staff     288 12 Mar 15:02
panoramic_trekking_app
drwxr-xr-x   12 vinces   staff     384 12 Mar 15:02 photo_viewer
-rw-r--r--    1 vinces   staff     105 12 Mar 15:02 requirements.txt
```

4. Create the **.env.dev** file in the directory and add in the following details for **panoramic_trekking_app** to use in its **settings.py** file. These environment variables will set up the database name, user, password, and other database settings:

```
SQL_ENGINE=django.db.backends.postgresql
SQL_DATABASE=pta_database
SQL_USER=pta_user
SQL_PASSWORD=pta_password
SQL_HOST=db
SQL_PORT=5432
PGPASSWORD=docker
```

5. Create a new **docker-compose.yml** file and open it with your text editor and add in the following details:

```
version: '3.3'

services:
  web:
    build: .
    image: activity_web:latest
    command: python manage.py runserver 0.0.0.0:8000
    volumes:
      - static_volume:/service/static
    ports:
      - 8000:8000
    environment:
      - PGPASSWORD=docker
    env_file:
      - ./.env.dev
    depends_on:
      - db

  db:
    image: postgres
    volumes:
      - postgres_data:/var/lib/postgresql/data/
    environment:
      - POSTGRES_PASSWORD=docker
    ports:
```

```
        - 5432:5432

volumes:
  postgres_data:
  static_volume:
```

As you can see from the highlighted line in the **docker-compose.yml** file, the **web** service relies on the **activity_web:latest** Docker image.

6. Run the following **docker build** command to build the image and tag it appropriately:

```
docker build -t activity_web:latest .
```

7. It's now time to deploy the stack to Swarm. Run the following **stack deploy** command using **the docker-compose.yml** file you have created:

```
docker stack deploy --compose-file docker-compose.yml activity_swarm
```

Once the network has been created, you should see the **activity_swarm_web** and **activity_swarm_db** services made available:

```
Creating network activity_swarm_default
Creating service activity_swarm_web
Creating service activity_swarm_db
```

8. Run the **service ls** command:

```
docker service ls
```

Verify that all the services have started successfully and are showing **1/1** replicas, as we have here:

```
ID        NAME               MODE        REPLICAS
   IMAGE
k6kh...   activity_swarm_db  replicated  1/1
   postgres:latest
copa...   activity_swarm_web replicated  1/1
   activity_web:latest
```

9. Finally, open your web browser and verify that you are able to access the site from **http://localhost:8000/admin/** and **http://localhost:8000/photo_viewer/**.

The Panoramic Trekking App is created and set up in a similar way to some of the other services you have already completed in this chapter.

ACTIVITY 9.02: PERFORMING AN UPDATE TO THE APP WHILE THE SWARM IS RUNNING

Solution:

There are a number of ways in which we can perform this activity. The following steps detail one way to do this:

1. If you do not have a Swarm running, deploy the **docker-compose.yml** file you created in *Activity 9.01*, *Deploying the Panoramic Trekking App to a Single-Node Docker Swarm*:

```
docker stack deploy --compose-file docker-compose.yml activity_swarm
```

As you can see, all three services are now running:

```
Creating network activity_swarm_default
Creating service activity_swarm_web
Creating service activity_swarm_db
```

2. In the same directory where you have performed the **stack deploy** command, open the **photo_viewer/templates/photo_index.html** file with your text editor and change line four to match the following details, basically adding the word **Patch** to the main heading:

photo_index.html

```
1 {% extends "base.html" %}
2 {% load static %}
3 {% block page_content %}
4 <h1>Patch Panoramic Trekking App - Photo Viewer</h1>
```

You can find the complete code here https://packt.live/3ceYnta.

3. Build a new image, this time tagging the image as **patch_1** with the following command:

```
docker build -t activity_web:patch_1 .
```

4. Deploy the patch to your Swarm web service using the **service update** command. Provide the image name and the service the update is going to be applied to as well:

```
docker service update --image activity_web:patch_1 activity_swarm_web
```

The output should look like the following:

```
…
activity_swarm_web
overall progress: 1 out of 1 tasks
1/1: running   [==========================================>]
verify: Service converged
```

5. List the services running and verify that the new image is running as part of the **activity_swarm_web** service:

```
docker service ls
```

As you can see from the output, the web service is no longer tagged with the **latest** tag. It is now displaying the **patch_1** image tag:

```
ID              NAME                 MODE          REPLICAS
    IMAGE
k6kh…           activity_swarm_db    replicated    1/1
    postgres:latest
cu5p…           activity_swarm_web   replicated    1/1
    activity_web:patch_1
```

6. Verify that the changes have been applied to the image by accessing **http://localhost:8000/photo_viewer/** and seeing that the heading now shows **Patch Panoramic Trekking App**:

Patch Panoramic Trekking App - Photo Viewer

Figure 9.10: Patch version of the Panoramic Trekking App

In this activity, you made a minor change to the Panoramic Trekking App so that a rolling update can be made to the service. You then deployed the image into the running environment and performed a rolling update to verify that the changes were successful. The change in the heading showed that the rolling update was performed successfully.

CHAPTER 10: KUBERNETES

ACTIVITY 10.01: INSTALLING THE PANORAMIC TREKKING APP ON KUBERNETES

Solution:

It is possible to create the database and Panoramic Trekking App with the following steps:

1. Install the database with the following **helm** command:

```
helm install database stable/postgresql --set
postgresqlPassword=kubernetes
```

This will install multiple Kubernetes resources for PostgreSQL and show a summary as follows:

```
/docker-ws $ helm install database stable/postgresql --set postgresqlPassword=kubernetes
NAME: database
LAST DEPLOYED: Tue May 12 07:46:33 2020
NAMESPACE: default
STATUS: deployed
REVISION: 1
TEST SUITE: None
NOTES:
** Please be patient while the chart is being deployed **

PostgreSQL can be accessed via port 5432 on the following DNS name from within your cluster:

    database-postgresql.default.svc.cluster.local - Read/Write connection

To get the password for "postgres" run:

    export POSTGRES_PASSWORD=$(kubectl get secret --namespace default database-postgresql -o
jsonpath="{.data.postgresql-password}" | base64 --decode)

To connect to your database run the following command:

    kubectl run database-postgresql-client --rm --tty -i --restart='Never' --namespace defau
lt --image docker.io/bitnami/postgresql:11.7.0-debian-10-r9 --env="PGPASSWORD=$POSTGRES_PASS
WORD" --command -- psql --host database-postgresql -U postgres -d postgres -p 5432



To connect to your database from outside the cluster execute the following commands:

    kubectl port-forward --namespace default svc/database-postgresql 5432:5432 &
    PGPASSWORD="$POSTGRES_PASSWORD" psql --host 127.0.0.1 -U postgres -d postgres -p 5432
 /docker-ws $
```

Figure 10.23: Database installation

This output first lists Helm chart-related information such as name, deployment time, status, and revision, followed by information related to the PostgreSQL instance and how to access it. This is a widely accepted method in Helm charts to give such information following the installation of a chart. Otherwise, it would be difficult to learn how to connect to the applications installed by Helm.

2. Create a **statefulset.yaml** file with the following content:

```
apiVersion: apps/v1
kind: StatefulSet
metadata:
  name: panoramic-trekking-app
spec:
  serviceName: panoramic-trekking-app
  replicas: 1
  selector:
    matchLabels:
      app: panoramic-trekking-app
  template:
    metadata:
      labels:
        app: panoramic-trekking-app
    spec:
      containers:
      - name: nginx
        image: packtworkshops/the-docker-workshop:
          chapter10-pta-nginx
        ports:
        - containerPort: 80
          name: web
        volumeMounts:
        - name: static
          mountPath: /service/static
      - name: pta
        image: packtworkshops/the-docker-workshop:
          chapter10-pta-web
        volumeMounts:
        - name: static
          mountPath: /service/static
  volumeClaimTemplates:
  - metadata:
      name: static
```

```
spec:
  accessModes: [ "ReadWriteOnce" ]
  resources:
    requests:
      storage: 1Gi
```

This file creates a Statefulset with the name **panoramic-trekking-app**. There are two containers defined in the **spec** section with the names **nginx** and **pta**. In addition, a volume claim is defined with the name **static** and is mounted to both the containers.

3. Deploy the **panoramic-trekking-app** StatefulSet with the following command:

```
kubectl apply -f statefulset.yaml
```

This will create a StatefulSet for our application:

```
StatefulSet.apps/panoramic-trekking-app created
```

4. Create a **service.yaml** file with the following content:

```
apiVersion: v1
kind: Service
metadata:
  name: panoramic-trekking-app
  labels:
    app: panoramic-trekking-app
spec:
  ports:
  - port: 80
    name: web
  type: LoadBalancer
  selector:
    app: panoramic-trekking-app
```

This Service definition has a **LoadBalancer** type to access the Pods with the label **app: panoramic-trekking-app**. Port **80** will be made available to access the **web** port of the Pods.

5. Deploy the **panoramic-trekking-app** Service with the following command:

```
kubectl apply -f service.yaml
```

This will create a Service resource as follows:

```
Service/panoramic-trekking-app created
```

6. Get the IP of the Service with the following command:

```
minikube service panoramic-trekking-app --url
http://192.168.64.14:32009
```

Store the IP to access the Panoramic Trekking App in the following steps.

7. Open the administration section of the Panoramic Trekking App in the browser with **http://$SERVICE_IP/admin**:

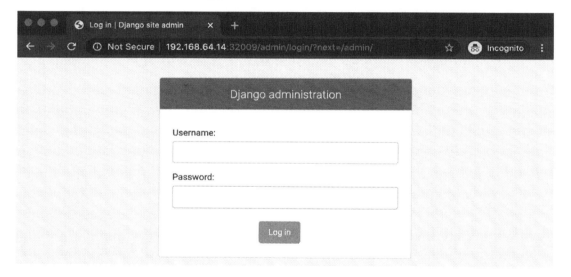

Figure 10.24: Admin login view

8. Log in with the username **admin** and the password **changeme** and add new photos and countries:

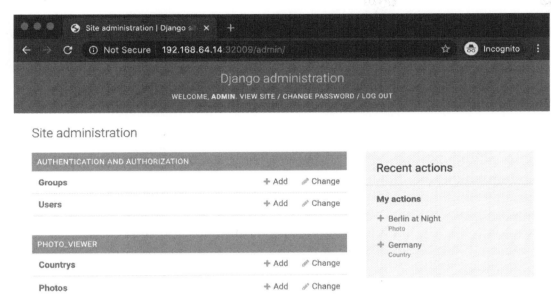

Figure 10.25: Admin setup view

9. Open the Panoramic Trekking App at `http://$SERVICE_IP/photo_viewer` in the browser:

Berlin at Night

Oberbaum Bridge...

May 12, 2020 | Country: Germany

Read More

Figure 10.26: Application view

The Photo Viewer application shows that the photos and countries have been retrieved from the database. It also indicates that the application is set up correctly and is running flawlessly.

In this activity, you have deployed the Panoramic Trekking App to a Kubernetes cluster. You started with a database using its Helm chart and then created Kubernetes resources for the application. Finally, you accessed the app from the browser and tested it with the addition of new photos. By the end of this activity, you have discovered how to deploy a database by using its official Helm chart, created a series of Kubernetes resources to connect to the database and deploy your application, and gathered information from the cluster to access the application. The steps in the activity covered the life cycle of a containerized application being deployed in a Kubernetes cluster.

CHAPTER 11: DOCKER SECURITY

ACTIVITY 11.01: SETTING UP A SECCOMP PROFILE FOR THE PANORAMIC TREKKING APP

Solution:

There are a number of ways in which you can create a **seccomp** profile that will stop users from performing the **mkdir**, **kill**, and **uname** commands. These steps show one way that this can be done:

1. If you don't already have **postgres** image locally, execute the following command:

```
docker pull postgres
```

2. Use the **wget** command on your system to obtain a copy of the default **seccomp** profile. Name the file you are downloading as **activity1.json**:

```
wget https://raw.githubusercontent.com/docker/docker/v1.12.3/profiles/
seccomp/default.json - O activity1.json
```

3. Remove the following three commands from the profile to allow us to further lock down our image. Open the **activity1.json** file with your favorite text editor and remove the following lines from the file. You should look to remove *lines 1500* to *1504* to remove the **uname** command, *669* to *673* to remove the **mkdir** command, and *lines 579* to *583* to remove the **kill** command from being available:

```
1500                    {
1501                            "name": "uname",
1502                            "action": "SCMP_ACT_ALLOW",
1503                            "args": []
1504                    },

669                     {
670                             "name": "mkdir",
671                             "action": "SCMP_ACT_ALLOW",
672                             "args": []
673                     },

579                     {
580                             "name": "kill",
581                             "action": "SCMP_ACT_ALLOW",
```

```
582                              "args": []
583                    },
```

You can find the modified **activity1.json** file at the following link: https://packt.live/32BI3PK.

4. Test the new profile with the **postgres** image by assigning a new profile as it is running, using the **--security-opt seccomp=activity1.json** option when we are running the image:

```
docker run --rm -it --security-opt seccomp=activity1.json postgres sh
```

5. As you are now logged on to the running container, test the new permissions of the profile you have now assigned to the container. Perform a **mkdir** command to create a new directory on the system:

```
~ $ mkdir test
```

The command should show an **Operation not permitted** output:

```
mkdir: can't create directory 'test': Operation not permitted
```

6. To test that you are no longer able to kill the running processes, you need to start something up. Start the **top** process and run it in the background. Do this by typing **top** into the command line and then adding **&**, before pressing *Enter* to run the process in the background. The following command then provides the process command (**ps**) to see what processes are running on the container:

```
~ $ top & ps
```

As you can see from the following output, the **top** process is running as **PID 8**:

```
PID    USER         TIME    COMMAND
 1     20002        0:00    sh
 8     20002        0:00    top
10     20002        0:00    ps
[1]+  Stopped   (tty output)        top
```

> **NOTE**
>
> The **ps** and **top** commands aren't available in a container based on **postgres** image. However, this doesn't cause any issues, as running **kill** command with any random pid number is sufficient to demonstrate that the command is not permitted to run.

7. Kill the top process by using the `kill -9` command followed by the PID number of the process you want to kill. The `kill -9` command will try to force the command to stop:

```
~ $ kill -9 8
```

You should see **Operation not permitted**:

```
sh: can't kill pid 8: Operation not permitted
```

8. Test the **uname** command. This is a little different from the other commands:

```
~ $ uname
```

You will get an **Operation not permitted** output:

```
Operation not permitted
```

This has been a good activity to show that there is still a lot we can do to limit what can be done to our images if they are accessed by an attacker.

ACTIVITY 11.02: SCANNING YOUR PANORAMIC TREKKING APP IMAGES FOR VULNERABILITIES

Solution:

There are a number of ways in which we can scan our images for vulnerabilities. The following steps are one way to do this, using Anchore to verify whether the **postgres-app** image is safe for use by our application:

1. Tag the image and push it to your Docker Hub repository. In this case, tag the **postgres-app** image with our repository name and tag it as **activity2**. We are also pushing it to our Docker Hub repository:

```
docker tag postgres <your repository namespace>/postgres-
app:activity2 ; docker push <your repository name>/postgres-
app:activity2
```

2. You should still have the **docker-compose.yaml** file you were using originally in this chapter. If you don't have Anchore running already, run the **docker-compose** command and export the **ANCHORE_CLI_URL, ANCHORE_CLI_URL,** and **ANCHORE_CLI_URL** variables, as you did previously, to allow us to run the **anchore-cli** commands:

```
docker-compose up -d
```

3. Check the status of the Anchore application by running the **anchore-cli system status** command:

```
anchore-cli system status
```

4. Use the **feeds list** command to check whether the feeds lists are all updated:

```
anchore-cli system feeds list
```

5. Once all the feeds have been updated, add the **postgres-app** image that we've pushed to Docker Hub. Use the **image add** command provided by **anchore-cli**, and provide the repository, image, and tag of the image we want to scan. This will add the image to our Anchore database, ready for it to be scanned:

```
anchore-cli image add <your repository namespace>/postgres-
app:activity2
```

6. Use the **image list** command to allow us to verify that our image has been analyzed. Once it is complete, you should see the word **analyzed** displayed in the **Analysis Status** column:

```
anchore-cli image list
```

7. Use the **image vuln** command with our image name to see a list of all the vulnerabilities found on our **postgres-app** image. This image is a lot larger and a lot more complex than the images we have tested previously, so there is a long list of vulnerabilities found when we use the **all** option. Fortunately, most of the vulnerabilities present either **Negligible** or **Unknown**. Run the **image vuln** command and pipe out the results to the **wc -l** command:

```
anchore-cli image vuln <your repository namespace>/postgres-
app:activity2 all | wc -l
```

This will give us a count of the numbers of vulnerabilities found. There are over 100 values in this case:

```
108
```

8. Finally, use the **evaluate check** command to see whether the vulnerabilities found will give us a pass or fail:

```
anchore-cli evaluate check <your repository namespace>/postgres-
app:activity2
```

Fortunately, as you can see from the following output, we have a pass:

```
Image Digest: sha256:57d8817bac132c2fded9127673dd5bc7c3a97654
636ce35d8f7a05cad37d37b7
Full Tag: docker.io/vincesestodocker/postgres-app:activity2
Status: pass
Last Eval: 2019-11-23T06:15:32Z
Policy ID: 2c53a13c-1765-11e8-82ef-23527761d060
```

As the image is provided by a large organization, it is in their best interests to make sure it is safe for you to use, but as it is so easy to scan the images, we should be still scanning them to verify that they are 100% safe for use.

CHAPTER 12: BEST PRACTICES

ACTIVITY 12.01: VIEWING THE RESOURCES USED BY THE PANORAMIC TREKKING APP

Solution:

There are a number of ways in which we perform the first activity in this chapter. The following steps are one way to do this by using the **docker stats** command to view the resources being used by a service in the Panoramic Trekking App. For this example, we are going to use the **postgresql-app** service, which is running as part of the Panoramic Trekking App:

1. Create a script that will create a new table and fill it with random values. The following script does exactly what we want in this situation as we want to create a long processing query and see how it affects the resources on our container. Add in the following details and save the file as **resource_test.sql** using your favorite editor:

```
1 CREATE TABLE test_data
2 (
3      random_value NUMERIC NOT NULL,
4      row1         NUMERIC NOT NULL,
5      row2         NUMERIC NOT NULL
6 );
7
8 INSERT INTO test_data
9      SELECT random_value.*,
10      gen.* ,
11      CEIL(RANDOM()*100)
12      FROM GENERATE_SERIES(1, 300) random_value,
13      GENERATE_SERIES(1, 900000) gen
14      WHERE gen <= random_value * 300;
```

Lines 1 to *6* create the new table and set up the three different rows it includes, while *lines 8 to 14* run through a new table, populating it with random values.

2. If you have not got a copy of the PostgreSQL Docker image already, pull the image from the supported PostgreSQL Docker Hub repository using the following command:

```
docker pull postgres
```

3. Move into a new terminal window and run the **docker stats** command to view the **CPU** percentage being used, as well as the memory and memory percentage being used:

```
docker stats --format "table {{.Name}}\t{{.CPUPerc}}\t{{.
MemPerc}}\t{{.MemUsage}}"
```

In the following command, we are not displaying the container ID as we wanted to limit the amount of data showing on our output:

```
NAME          CPU %          MEM %          MEM USAGE / LIMIT
```

4. To simply test this image, you don't need to have the running container mounted on a specific volume to use the data you have previously used for this image. Move into a different terminal to the one monitoring your CPU and memory. Start the container and name it **postgres-test** and ensure that the database is accessible from your host system by exposing the ports needed to run a **psql** command. We have also specified a temporary password of **docker** in this instance using the environment variable (**-e**) option:

```
docker run --rm --name postgres-test -v ${PWD}/resource_test.sql:/
resource_test.sql -e POSTGRES_PASSWORD=docker -d -p 5432:5432
postgres
```

5. Before you run your test script, move to the terminal where you are monitoring the CPU and memory usage. You can see that our container is already using some of the resources without even really doing anything:

```
NAME          CPU %          MEM %          MEM USAGE / LIMIT
postgres-test    0.09%          0.47%          9.273MiB / 1.943GiB
```

6. Enter the terminal inside your container using the following command:

```
docker exec -it postgres-test /bin/bash
```

7. Use the **psql** command to send the **postgres-test** container command to create a new database called **resource_test**:

```
psql -h localhost -U postgres -d postgres -c 'create database
resource_test;'

Password for user postgres:
CREATE DATABASE
```

8. Run the script you created earlier. Make sure you include the **time** command before you run the script as this will allow you to see the time it takes to complete:

```
time psql -h localhost -U postgres -d resource_test -a -f resource_
test.sql
```

We have reduced the output of the command in the following code block. It took 50 seconds to fill up the **resource_database** tables with data:

```
Password for user postgres:
...
INSERT 0 13545000


real    0m50.446s
user    0m0.003s
sys     0m0.008s
```

9. Move to the terminal where your **docker stats** command is running. You will see an output depending on the number of cores your system is running and the memory it has available. The script being run doesn't seem to be very memory-intensive, but it is pushing up the CPU available to the container to 100%:

```
NAME            CPU %     MEM %     MEM USAGE / LIMIT
postgres-test   100.66%   2.73%     54.36MiB / 1.943GiB
```

10. Before you can run the container with the changes to the CPU and memory configuration, delete the running container to make sure you have a fresh database running by using the following command:

```
docker kill postgres-test
```

11. Run the container again. In this instance, you will limit the CPU available to only half of one core on the host system, and as the test was not too memory-intensive, set the memory limit to **256MB**:

```
docker run --rm --name postgres-test -e POSTGRES_PASSWORD=docker -d
-p 5432:5432 --cpus 0.5 --memory 256MB postgres
```

12. Enter the container using the **exec** command:

```
docker exec -it postgres-test /bin/bash
```

13. Again, before running your tests, create the **resource_test** database:

```
psql -h localhost -U postgres -d postgres -c 'create database
resource_test;'

Password for user postgres:
CREATE DATABASE
```

14. Now, to see what changes have been made to our resources, limit what can be used by the container. Run the **resource_test.sql** script again and by limiting the resources, specifically the CPU, we can see that it now takes more than 1 minute to complete:

```
time psql -h localhost -U postgres -d resource_test -a -f resource_
test.sql

Password for user postgres:
...
INSERT 0 13545000


real    1m54.484s
user    0m0.003s
sys     0m0.005s
```

15. Move to the terminal where your **docker stats** command is running. It should also look different as the percentage of CPU available to be used will be halved. The change you have made to the CPU slows the running of the script and, as a result, seems to reduce the memory being used as well:

```
NAME            CPU %     MEM %     MEM USAGE / LIMIT
postgres-test   48.52%    13.38%    34.25MiB / 256MiB
```

This activity gave you a good indication of the balancing act you sometimes need to perform when you are monitoring and configuring your container resources. It does clarify that you need to be aware of the tasks your services are performing, as well as how changes to configurations will then affect how your services will operate.

ACTIVITY 12.02: USING HADOLINT TO IMPROVE THE BEST PRACTICES ON DOCKERFILES

Solution

There are a number of ways in which we can perform this activity. The following steps show one way to do this:

1. Pull the image from the **hadolint** repository with the following **docker pull** command:

```
docker pull hadolint/hadolint
```

2. Use **hadolint** to lint the **docker-stress Dockerfile** we have been using throughout this chapter and document the warnings presented:

```
docker run --rm -i hadolint/hadolint < Dockerfile
```

You will get warnings such as the following:

```
/dev/stdin:1 DL3006 Always tag the version of an image explicitly
/dev/stdin:2 DL3008 Pin versions in apt get install. Instead of
'apt-get install <package>' use 'apt-get install
<package>=<version>'
/dev/stdin:2 DL3009 Delete the apt-get lists after installing
something
/dev/stdin:2 DL3015 Avoid additional packages by specifying
'--no-install-recommends'
/dev/stdin:2 DL3014 Use the '-y' switch to avoid manual input
'apt-get -y install <package>'
/dev/stdin:3 DL3025 Use arguments JSON notation for CMD
and ENTRYPOINT arguments
```

There are no real changes from when you originally tested the image. However, there are only three lines of code in the **Dockerfile**, so see whether you can reduce the number of warnings being presented by **hadolint**.

3. As mentioned earlier in this chapter, the **hadolint** wiki page will provide you with details on how to resolve each of the warnings presented. However, if you move through each line, you should be able to resolve all these warnings. The first one presented, **DL3006**, asks to tag the version of the Docker image you are using, which is a new version of the Ubuntu image. Change *line 1* of your **Dockerfile** to now include the **18.08** image version, as shown:

```
1 FROM ubuntu:18.08
```

4. The next four warnings are all related to the second line of our **Dockerfile**. **DL3008** asks to pin the version of the application being installed. In the following case, pin the stress application to version 1.0.3. **DL3009** states that you should delete any lists. This is where we have added *lines 4* and *5* in the following code. **DL3015** states that you should also use **--no-install-recommends**, making sure you don't install applications you don't need. Lastly, **DL3014** is suggesting you include the **-y** option to make sure you are not prompted to verify the installation of your application. Edit the **Dockerfile** to look as follows:

```
2 RUN apt-get update \
3 && apt-get install -y stress=1.0.4 --no-install-recommends \
4 && apt-get clean \
5 && rm -rf /var/lib/apt/lists/*
```

5. **DL3025** is your last warning and states that you need to have your **CMD** instruction in JSON format. This could cause issues as you are trying to use environment variables with your stress application. To clear up this warning, run the **stress** command with the **sh -c** option. This should still allow you to run the command with environment variables:

```
6 CMD ["sh", "-c", "stress ${var}"]
```

Your complete **Dockerfile**, now adhering to the best practices, should look as follows:

```
FROM ubuntu:18.04
RUN apt-get update \
  && apt-get install -y stress=1.0.4 --no-install-recommends \
  && apt-get clean \
  && rm -rf /var/lib/apt/lists/*
CMD ["sh", "-c", "stress ${var}"]
```

6. Now, lint the **Dockerfile** again using **hadolint**, with no more warnings presented:

```
docker run --rm -i hadolint/hadolint < Dockerfile
```

7. If you want to be 100% sure that the **Dockerfile** is looking as good as it can be, perform one final test. Open **FROM:latest** in your browser and you will see the **Dockerfile** with the latest changes showing **No problems or suggestions found!**:

Figure 12.4: The docker-stress Dockerfile now adhering to the best practices

Your **Dockerfiles** may be a lot larger than the ones presented in this chapter, but as you can see, a systematic line-by-line approach will help you correct any issues that your **Dockerfiles** may have. Using applications such as **hadolint** and **FROM latest**, with their suggestions on how to resolve warnings, will familiarize you with the best practices as you go along. This brings us to the end of our activities and this chapter, but there is still more interesting content to go, so don't stop now.

CHAPTER 13: MONITORING DOCKER METRICS

ACTIVITY 13.01: CREATING A GRAFANA DASHBOARD TO MONITOR SYSTEM MEMORY

Solution:

There are a number of ways in which you can perform this activity. The following steps are one such method:

1. Make sure that Prometheus is running and collecting data, Docker and **cAdvisor** are configured to expose metrics, and Grafana is running and configured with Prometheus as a data source.

2. Open the Grafana web interface and the **Container Monitoring** dashboard you created in *Exercise 13.05: Installing and Running Grafana on Your System*

3. There is an **Add panel** option at the top of the dashboard and to the right of the dashboard name. Click the **Add panel** icon to add in your new dashboard panel:

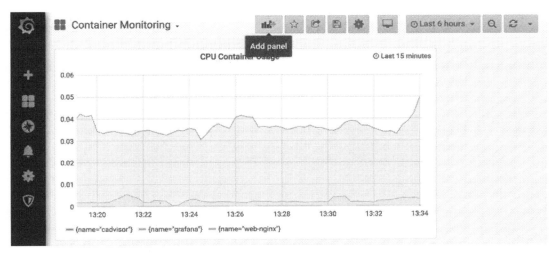

Figure 13.26: Adding a new panel to the container monitoring dashboard

4. Select **Prometheus** from the drop-down list as the data source we will be using to produce the new dashboard panel.

5. In the **metrics** section, add the following PromQL query, **container_ memory_usage_bytes**, searching only for entries that have a name value. Then, sum by each name to provide a line graph for each container:

```
sum by (name) (container_memory_usage_bytes{name!=""})
```

6. Depending on the amount of data you have available in your time-series database, adjust the relative time if needed. Perhaps set the relative time to **15m**. The previous three steps are captured in the following diagram:

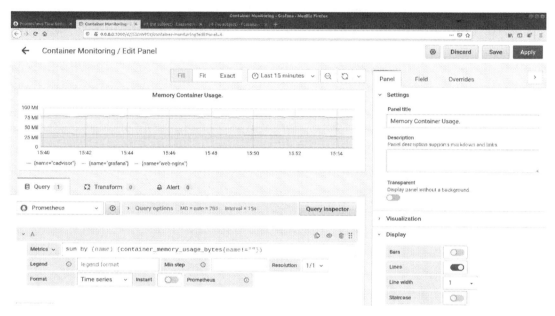

Figure 13.27: Adding a new panel to the Container Monitoring dashboard

7. Select **Show options** and add the title of **Memory Container Usage**.

8. If you click on **Save**, you will notice that you cannot save the panel as the dashboard has been provisioned on startup. You can export the JSON, which you can then add to your provisioning directory. Click the **Share Dashboard** button and export the JSON. Select **Save JSON to file** and store the dashboard file in the **/tmp directory**:

Figure 13.28: Warning that we cannot save the new dashboard

9. Stop your Grafana container from running so that you can add to the provisioning file in your environment. Do this with the following **docker kill** command:

```
docker kill grafana
```

10. You already have a file named **ContainerMonitoring.json** in the **provisioning/dashboards** directory. Copy the JSON file you have just created from your **tmp** directory and replace the original file in the **provisioning/dashboards** directory:

```
cp /tmp/ContainerMonitoring-1579130313205.json provisioning/
dashboards/ContainerMonitoring.json
```

11. Start the Grafana image again and log in to the application using the default administration password:

```
docker run --rm -d --name grafana -p 3000:3000 -e "GF_SECURITY_ADMIN_
PASSWORD=secret" -v ${PWD}/provisioning:/etc/grafana/provisioning
grafana/Grafana
```

12. Log in to Grafana one more time and move to the **Container Monitoring** dashboard you have been provisioning. You should now see the newly created **Memory Container usage** panel at the top of our dashboard, similar to the following screenshot:

Figure 13.29: New dashboard panel displaying memory usage

This should now make it a lot easier to monitor the memory and CPU usage of containers running on your system. The dashboard provides an easier interface than looking through the **docker stats** command, especially when you start to run a few more containers on your system.

ACTIVITY 13.02: CONFIGURING THE PANORAMIC TREKKING APP TO EXPOSE METRICS TO PROMETHEUS

Solution:

There are a number of ways in which we can perform this activity. Here, we have chosen to add an exporter to the PostgreSQL container we have running as part of the panoramic trekking app:

1. If you don't have the panoramic trekking app running, make sure that at least the PostgreSQL container is running so that you can complete this activity. You won't need to have Prometheus running yet as you will need to make some changes to the configuration file first. Run the following command to verify that the PostgreSQL database is running:

```
docker run --rm -d --name postgres-test -e POSTGRES_PASSWORD=docker
-p 5432:5432 postgres
```

    To gather further metrics from your PostgreSQL container, you can locate an exporter already created by the user **albertodonato** on GitHub. Using one that someone has already created makes it a lot easier than having to create your own. Documentation and details can be found at the following URL: https://github.com/albertodonato/query-exporter.

2. The aforementioned GitHub account has a good breakdown of how to set up the configuration and metrics. Set up a basic configuration file to get started. Find the IP address that the PostgreSQL container is running on by running the following **docker inspect** command. This gives you the internal IP address your container is running on. You'll also need to substitute the container name you have running for **<container_name>**:

```
docker inspect --format '{{ .NetworkSettings.IPAddress }}'
<container_name>
```

    Your IP address might be different to the one here:

```
172.17.0.3
```

3. For this exporter, you need to set up some extra configurations to feed into the exporter. To start with, create a configuration file named **psql_exporter_config.yml** in your working directory and open the file with your text editor.

4. Enter the first four lines into your configuration file below. This is how the exporter connects to the database. You will need to provide the password with which the database can be accessed and the IP address that you obtained in the previous step or if a domain is assigned to the database:

```
1 databases:
2   pg:
3     dsn: postgresql+psycopg2://postgres:<password>@<ip|domain>/
      postgres
4
```

5. Add your first metric to the configuration file. Enter the following lines to add your metric name, type of gauge, description, and a label:

```
5 metrics:
6   pg_process:
7     type: gauge
8     description: Number of PostgreSQL processes with their
      states
9     labels: [state]
10
```

6. Set up a database query to gather the metric details you want for the **pg_process** gauge. *Line 13* shows that you want to create a database query with *lines 14* and *15,* assigning the results to the metric you created earlier. *Lines 16* to *23* are the query we want to run on our database in order to create a gauge for the number of processes running on the database:

psql_exporter_config.yml

```
11 queries:
12   process_stats:
13     databases: [pg]
14     metrics:
15       - pg_process
16     sql: >
17       SELECT
18         state,
19         COUNT(*) AS pg_process
20       FROM pg_stat_activity
21       WHERE state IS NOT NULL
22       GROUP BY state
23       FROM pg_stat_database
```

You can find the complete code here https://packt.live/32C47K3.

7. Save the configuration file and run the exporter from the command line. The exporter will expose its metrics on port **9560**. Mount the configuration file you created earlier in this activity. You are also getting the latest version of the **adonato/query-exporter** image:

```
docker run -p 9560:9560/tcp -v --name postgres-exporter ${PWD}/psql_
exporter_config.yml:/psql_exporter_config.yml --rm -itd adonato/query-
exporter:latest -- /psql_exporter_config.yml
```

8. Open a web browser and use the URL **http://0.0.0.0:9560/metrics** to view the new metrics you have set up for the PostgreSQL container running as part of the panoramic trekking app:

```
# HELP database_errors_total Number of database errors
# TYPE database_errors_total counter
# HELP queries_total Number of database queries
# TYPE queries_total counter
queries_total{database="pg",status="success"} 10.0
queries_total{database="pg",status="error"} 1.0
# TYPE queries_created gauge
queries_created{database="pg",status="success"}
1.5795789188074727e+09
queries_created{database="pg",status="error"}
1.57957891880902e+09
# HELP pg_process Number of PostgreSQL processes with their states
# TYPE pg_process gauge
pg_process{database="pg",state="active"} 1.0
```

9. Move into the directory where you have Prometheus installed, open the **prometheus.yml** file with your text editor, and add in the exporter details to allow Prometheus to start collecting the data:

```
45     - job_name: 'postgres-web'
46       scrape_interval: 5s
47       static_configs:
48       - targets: ['0.0.0.0:9560']
```

10. Save the changes you've made to the **prometheus.yml** file and start the Prometheus application again from the command line, as shown here:

```
./prometheus --config.file=prometheus.yml
```

11. If everything has worked as it should, you should now see the **postgres-web** target displayed on the Prometheus **Targets** page, as demonstrated here:

Figure 13.30: New postgres-web Targets page displayed on Prometheus

That brings us to the end of the activities and the end of this chapter. The activities should have helped to solidify the knowledge learned earlier on and provided you with experience in gathering metrics for your applications and running systems and displaying them in a more user-friendly fashion.

CHAPTER 14: COLLECTING CONTAINER LOGS

ACTIVITY 14.01: CREATING A DOCKER-COMPOSE.YML FILE FOR YOUR SPLUNK INSTALLATION

Solution:

There are a number of ways in which we can perform this activity. The following steps outline one possible method.

Here, you will set up a **docker-compose.yml** file that will at least run your Splunk container the same way it has been running throughout this chapter. You will set up two volumes in order to mount the **/opt/splunk/etc** directory, as well as the **/opt/splunk/var** directory. You need to expose ports **8000**, **9997**, and **8088** to allow access to your web interface and allow data to be forwarded to the Splunk instance. Finally, you will need to set up some environment variables that will accept the Splunk license and add the Administrator password. Let's get started:

1. Create a new file called **docker-compose.yml** and open it with your favorite text editor.

2. Start with the version of **Docker Compose** you prefer and create the volumes you are going to use in order to mount the **var** and **ext** directories:

```
1 version: '3'
2
3 volumes:
4   testsplunk:
5   testsplunkindex:
6
```

3. Set up the service for the Splunk installation, using **splunk** as the hostname and **splunk/splunk** as the image you have been using as your installation. Also, set up the environment variables for **SPLUNK_START_ARGS** and **SPLUNK_PASSWORD**, as shown here:

```
7 services:
8   splunk:
9     hostname: splunk
10     image: splunk/splunk
11     environment:
12       SPLUNK_START_ARGS: --accept-license
13       SPLUNK_PASSWORD: changeme
```

4. Finally, mount the volumes and expose the ports your installation will need to access the web interface and forward data from a forwarder and the containers:

```
14      volumes:
15        - ./testsplunk:/opt/splunk/etc
16        - ./testsplunkindex:/opt/splunk/var
17      ports:
18        - "8000:8000"
19        - "9997:9997"
20        - "8088:8088"
```

5. Run the **docker-compose up** command to make sure it is all working correctly. Use the **-d** option to make sure it is running as a daemon in the background of our system:

```
docker-compose up -d
```

The command should return an output similar to the following:

```
Creating network "chapter14_default" with the default driver
Creating chapter14_splunk_1 ... done
```

6. Once your Splunk installation is running again, it's time to get one of your services from the Panoramic Trekking App running so that you can forward logs to Splunk to be indexed. When using the **docker run** command, add the log driver details, as you did previously in this chapter, and make sure you include the correct token for your **HTTP Event Collector**:

```
docker run --rm -d --name postgres-test \
-e POSTGRES_PASSWORD=docker -p 5432:5432 \
--log-driver=splunk \
--log-opt splunk-url=http://127.0.0.1:8088 \
--log-opt splunk-token=5c051cdb-b1c6-482f-973f-2a8de0d92ed8 \
--log-opt splunk-insecureskipverify=true \
--log-opt tag="{{.Name}}/{{.FullID}}" \
postgres -c log_statement=all
```

> **NOTE**
>
> Observe that we are using **-c log_statement=all** in the **docker run** command as this will make sure all of our PostgreSQL queries will be logged and sent to Splunk.

7. Log in to the Splunk web interface and access the **Search & Reporting** app. Enter the **source="http:docker logs" AND postgres-test** query into the interface and press *Enter*. Since you have tagged our container, you should see your containers tagged with the name and full ID, so adding **postgres-test** to your search will make sure only your PostgreSQL logs are visible:

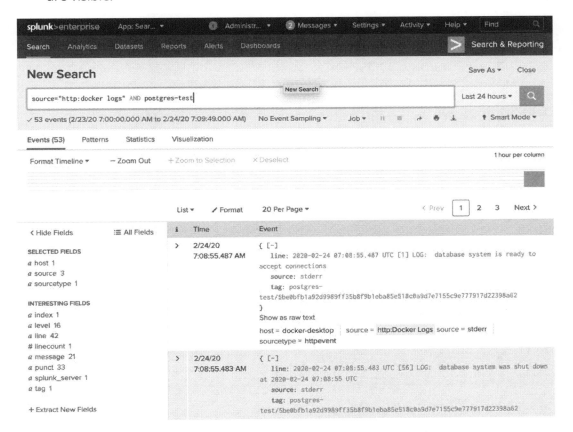

Figure 14.48: PostgreSQL logs displaying in Splunk

As you can see from the preceding screenshot, our logs are flowing through Splunk successfully. Make note of the tag that was added to the log entries, as shown in the preceding screenshot.

This activity taught us how to implement the logging procedures in our development projects using Docker Compose.

ACTIVITY 14.02: CREATING A SPLUNK APP TO MONITOR THE PANORAMIC TREKKING APP

Solution:

There are a number of ways in which you can perform this activity. The following steps are one way to do this. Here, you will add an exporter to the `PostgreSQL` container you have running as part of the Panoramic Trekking App:

1. Make sure Splunk is running and that the service you have been monitoring has been running for a little while to make sure you are collecting some logs for this activity.

2. Log in to the Splunk web interface. From the Splunk home screen, click on the cog icon next to the **Apps** menu; you will be presented with the **Apps** page for your Splunk environment:

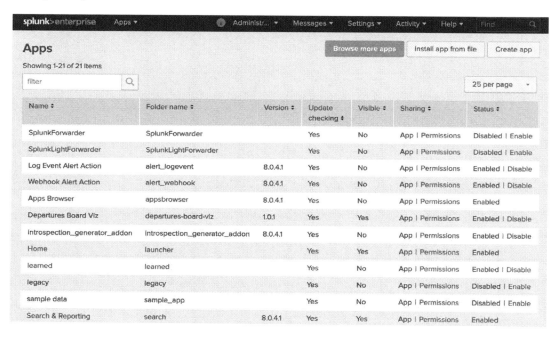

Figure 14.49: Apps page of the Splunk environment

3. Click the **Create** app button and fill in the form. It will be similar to the following, in which **Name** is set to **Panoramic Trekking App**, **Folder name** is set to **panoramic_trekking_app**, and **Version** is set to **1.0.0**. Click **Save** to create the new app:

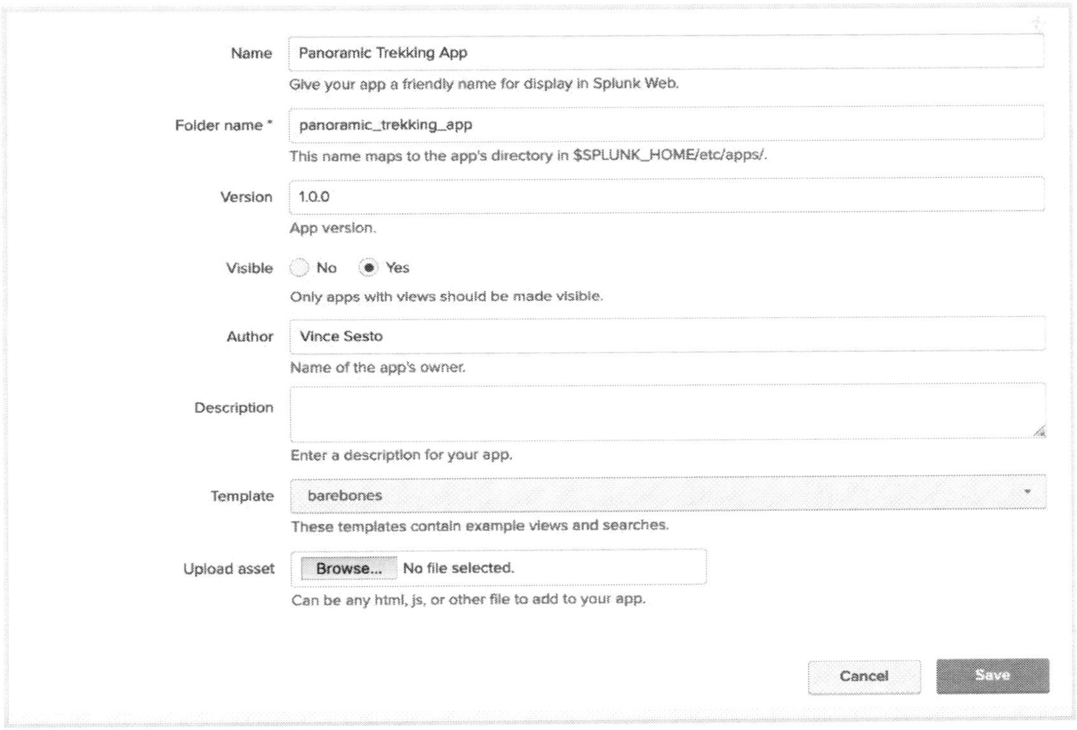

Figure 14.50: Creating your new app in Splunk

4. Return to the Splunk home page and make sure your **Panoramic Trekking App** is visible from the **Apps** menu. Click **Panoramic Trekking App** to bring up the **Search & Reporting** page so that you can start querying your data:

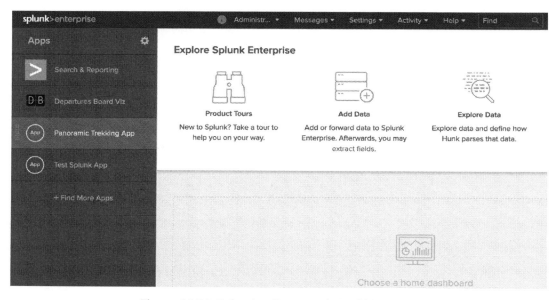

Figure 14.51: Selecting Panoramic Trekking App

5. Type **source="http:docker logs" AND postgres-test AND INSERT AND is_superuser | stats count** into the query bar and press *Enter*. The search will look for any **Super Users** that were created as part of the application. When your data comes up, click the **Visualization** tab and change it to display a single-value visualization:

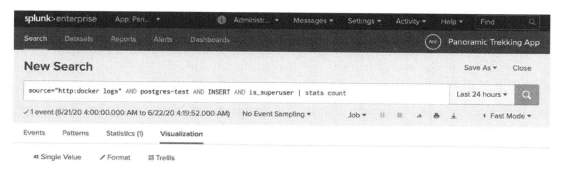

Figure 14.52: Entering a query in the query bar

6. Click the **Save As** button at the top of the screen and select the **Dashboards** panel. When you are presented with this screen, select the panel to be added to a new dashboard and give it the name **PTA Monitoring**. Also, give the panel the title **Super User Access** and click **Save**:

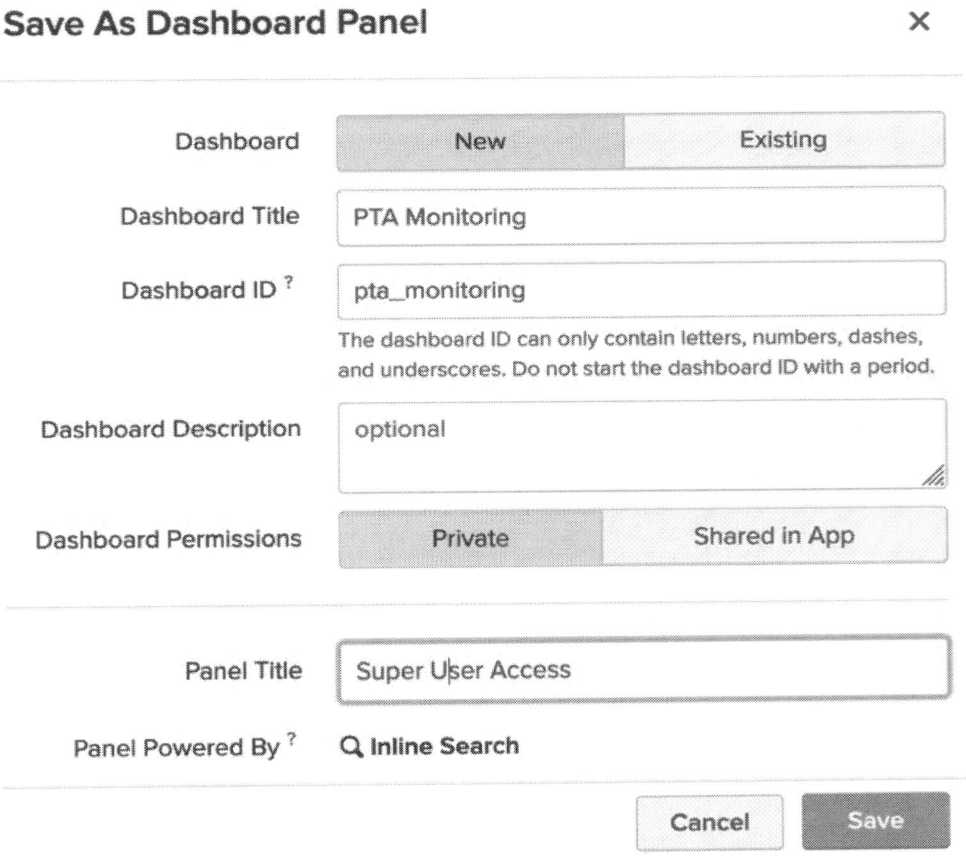

Save As Dashboard Panel   ✕

Dashboard	New	Existing

Dashboard Title   PTA Monitoring

Dashboard ID ?   pta_monitoring

The dashboard ID can only contain letters, numbers, dashes, and underscores. Do not start the dashboard ID with a period.

Dashboard Description   optional

Dashboard Permissions	Private	Shared in App

Panel Title   Super User Access

Panel Powered By ?   🔍 **Inline Search**

Cancel   Save

Figure 14.53: Adding details to the dashboard panel

7. When you are presented with your new dashboard, click the **Edit** and **Add** panel buttons. Select **New** and then `Single Value` as the visualization type. Set `Content Title` to `Database Creation`. Add the `source="http:docker logs" AND postgres-test AND CREATE DATABASE | stats count` source string and click **Save**. This will search through your logs to show if anyone has created any databases on the PostgreSQL database, which should only happen when the app is set up and created:

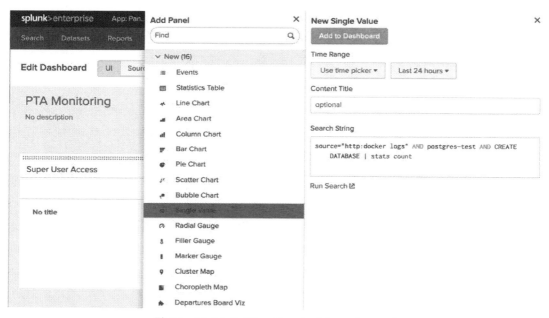

Figure 14.54: Editing the dashboard panel

8. Again, click the **New Panel** button and select **New** and then `Column Chart` from the visualizations. Add a `Content Title` of `App Usage`, add the `source="http:docker logs" AND postgres-test AND SELECT AND photo_viewer_photo earliest=-60m | timechart span=1m count` search query, and click **Save**. This search will provide you with a count over time of people who are using the app to view your photos.

9. Feel free to move the panels around the dashboard. When you are happy with the changes, click the **Save** button. Your dashboard should look similar to the following:

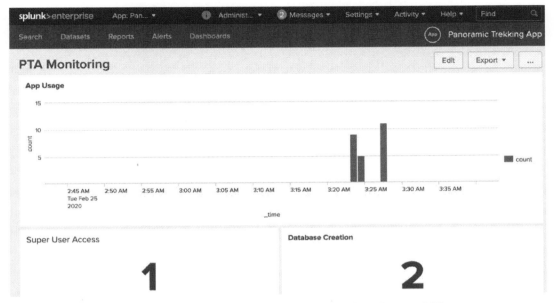

Figure 14.55: New dashboard panel used to monitor PostgreSQL usage

This activity helped you gather log data for your Panoramic Trekking App and display it in a more user-friendly fashion using Splunk.

CHAPTER 15: EXTENDING DOCKER WITH PLUGINS

ACTIVITY 15.01: INSTALLING WORDPRESS WITH NETWORK AND VOLUME PLUGINS

Solution:

It is possible to create containers for the database and the WordPress blog using volume and networking plugins with the following steps:

1. Create a network with the following command:

```
docker network create \
--driver=store/weaveworks/net-plugin:2.5.2 \
--attachable \
wp-network
```

This command creates a network using the Weave Net plugin, specified with the **driver** flag. In addition, the volume is specified as **attachable**, which means you can connect to Docker containers in the future. Finally, the name of the container will be **wp-network**. You should get output like the following:

```
mk0pmhpb2gx3f6s00o57j2vd
```

2. Create a volume with the following command:

```
docker volume create -d vieux/sshfs \
--name wp-content \
-o sshcmd=root@localhost:/tmp \
-o password=root \
-o port=2222
```

This command creates a volume over SSH using the **vieux/sshfs** plugin. The name of the volume is **wp-content** and additional options are passed for the **ssh** command, port, and password:

```
wp-content
```

3. Create the **mysql** container with the following command:

```
docker run --name mysql -d \
-e MYSQL_ROOT_PASSWORD=wordpress \
-e MYSQL_DATABASE=wordpress \
-e MYSQL_USER=wordpress \
-e MYSQL_PASSWORD=wordpress \
--network=wp-network \
mysql:5.7
```

This command runs the **mysql** container in detached mode, with the environment variables and the **wp-network** connection.

4. Create the **wordpress** container with the following command:

```
docker run --name wordpress -d \
-v wp-content:/var/www/html/wp-content \
-e WORDPRESS_DB_HOST=mysql:3306 \
-e WORDPRESS_DB_USER=wordpress \
-e WORDPRESS_DB_PASSWORD=wordpress \
-e WORDPRESS_DB_NAME=wordpress \
--network=wp-network \
-p 8080:80 \
wordpress
```

This command runs the **wordpress** container in detached mode with the environment variables and the **wp-network** connection. In addition, port **80** of the container is available at port **8080** of the host system.

With the successful start, you will have two containers running for **mysql** and **wordpress**:

```
docker ps
```

```
/docker-ws $ docker ps
CONTAINER ID   IMAGE                           COMMAND                CREATED         STATUS          PORTS                      NAMES
06b0baed3d13   wordpress                       "docker-entrypoint.s…" 11 seconds ago  Up 9 seconds    0.0.0.0:8080->80/tcp       wordpress
7aabc7d8dfad   mysql:5.7                       "docker-entrypoint.s…" 22 seconds ago  Up 20 seconds   3306/tcp, 33060/tcp        mysql
87eecaca6a1e   rastasheep/ubuntu-sshd:14.04    "/usr/sbin/sshd -D"    4 hours ago     Up 4 hours      0.0.0.0:2222->22/tcp       volume_provider
/docker-ws $
```

Figure 15.17: The WordPress and database containers

5. Open `http://localhost:8080` in your browser to check the WordPress setup screen:

Figure 15.18: WordPress setup screen

The WordPress setup screen verifies that WordPress is installed using the network and volume plugins.

In this activity, you have created a custom network using the Weave Net plugin and a custom volume using the **sshfs** plugin. You created a database container that uses the custom network and a WordPress container that uses the custom network and the custom volume. With a successful setup, your Docker containers connect with each other over custom networking and use the volume over SSH. With this activity, you have used Docker extensions for a real-life application. You can now confidently extend Docker with your custom business requirements and technologies.

INDEX

Printed in Great Britain
by Amazon